Government and Politics in the Lone Star State

Eighth Edition

L. Tucker Gibson, Jr.
Professor Emeritus, Trinity University

Clay Robison

PEARSON

Boston Columbus Indianapolis New York San Francisco
Upper Saddle River Amsterdam Cape Town Dubai London Madrid Milan
Munich Paris Montréal Toronto Delhi Mexico City São Paulo Sydney
Hong Kong Seoul Singapore Taipei Tokyo

Editorial Director: Craig Campanella
Editor in Chief: Dickson Musslewhite
Senior Acquisitions Editor: Vikram Mukhija
Assistant Editor: Beverly Fong
Editorial Assistants: Emily Sauerhoff, Isabel Schwab
Director of Development: Sharon Geary
Senior Development Editor: Lisa Sussman
VP, Director of Marketing: Brandy Dawson
Executive Marketing Manager: Wendy Gordon
Marketing Assistant: Courtney Stewart
Senior Managing Editor: Ann Marie McCarthy
Project Manager: Heather McNally
Operations Supervisor: Mary Fischer
Operations Specialist: Mary Ann Gloriande
Art Director and Text Design: John Christiana
Cover Designer and Cover Art: Daniel Roldan of Epecho Designs, LLC
Director of Digital Media: Brian Hyland
Senior Digital Media Editor: Paul DeLuca
Digital Media Editor: Alison Lorber
Digital Media Project Manager: Joe Selby
Full-Service Project Management and Composition: Revathi Viswanathan/PreMediaGlobal
Printer/Binder: R.R. Donnelley/Willard
Cover Printer: Lehigh-Pheonix Color/Hagerstown
Text Font: Adobe Caslon Pro 10.5/13

Credits and acknowledgments borrowed from other sources and reproduced, with permission, in this textbook appear on appropriate page within text (or on page 451).

Library of Congress Cataloging-in-Publication Data
Gibson, L. Tucker.
Government and politics in the Lone Star State / L. Tucker Gibson, Clay Robison.—8th ed.
p. cm.
Includes bibliographical references and index.
ISBN-13: 978-0-205-92706-7
ISBN-10: 0-205-92706-8
1. Texas—Politics and government—1951- I. Robison, Clay. II. Title.
JK4816.G53 2013
320.4764—dc23
2012023842

10 9 8 7 6 5 4 3 2 1

PEARSON

ISBN 10: 0-205-92706-8
ISBN 13: 978-0-205-92706-7

Brief Contents

Contents

3

Texas Government and Politics in the Federal System 58

Interest Groups and Political Power in Texas 92

The Mass Media in Texas Politics 120

Preface

exas, never very far from the national spotlight, took center stage again for several months in late 2011 and early 2012, following Governor Rick Perry's plunge into the race for the Republican presidential nomination. News reporters, lobbyists, academicians, and other Texans with more than a passing knowledge of their state's politics and policies were barraged with phone calls and emails from national media, seeking quick courses on what made Texas and its governor tick.

How had the Texas economy managed to stay afloat while other states had fared much worse during the Great Recession from which the country was beginning to emerge? Would Texas and its governor continue to be able to brag about job creation following the deep cuts the legislature had made to the public schools and other state programs only a few months before the governor launched his presidential campaign? How soon would the emerging Hispanic majority have enough clout to wrest state government from Republican control? Would Hispanics remain overwhelmingly Democratic?

In Texas, questions also began to be raised about Perry's future after his presidential campaign faltered badly and limped to a close only five months after it had begun. During his record-setting tenure in Austin, he had transformed a weak constitutional office into one of the strongest Texas gubernatorial administrations of modern times. But after his national failure, would he be able to maintain his aura of political invincibility back home?

These are some of the questions we have attempted to answer in the eighth edition of *Government and Politics in the Lone Star State*...or, more precisely, we have tried to give readers sufficient information with which to develop their own questions and answers.

New to This Edition

The eighth edition of *Government and Politics in the Lone Star State* includes the same pedagogical features students currently enjoy in traditional American Government textbooks, extending their learning experience from the 2305 course seamlessly into 2306. The book has been revised and updated extensively from start to finish, beginning with 2010 census data to reflect Texas's population and economic characteristics. Other new or significantly revised material includes the following:

- Chapter introductions and features that have been updated to reflect new political and policy developments
- Coverage of border issues between Texas and Mexico, including trade and commerce, illegal immigration, border security, and violence related to the drug crisis in Mexico
- The strong Republican electoral surge in 2010 and the resulting deep budget cuts and other policy changes enacted by the legislature in 2011
- The impact and potential impact of those cuts and policy changes on the public schools, institutions of higher education, women's health care, and other important public services
- The enactment of a voter photo identification law and the political firestorm surrounding it
- An analysis of the redistricting controversies that followed the 2010 census and their potential implications for the Voting Rights Act and the future influence of Hispanics and African Americans in Texas politics
- Governor Rick Perry's short-lived presidential race
- The emergence of the tea party movement and discussion of whether it will have a lasting impact on Texas politics
- Updates on the continuing transformation of the Texas media, the Texas judiciary, criminal justice, and the issue of the death penalty, as well as other major state policy areas, including education and water conservation
- A discussion of the continued concentration of the state's population in the sixty-six counties described as the Texas Urban Triangle
- An analysis of how local governments are dealing with financial problems resulting from recessionary pressures and state and federal mandates

Features

In this book, we describe and analyze Texas government and politics from two perspectives—that of a political scientist who has taught a variety of courses in national, state, and local politics and served as a redistricting consultant to more than forty governments and that of a journalist who covered state Capitol politics for almost forty years. We incorporate general theories of the political science discipline into each chapter to provide a conceptual framework for the reader. For example, the chapter on political parties draws from research on party realignment and explains how Texas politics transformed from one-party Democratic control to the current period of Republican dominance. The chapter on the legislature draws from the concept of institutionalization, addressing changes that occurred as the legislature adapted to a more complex political environment. Although the theoretical aspects of the book's analysis are critical building blocks, we also focus on the story of how the theory plays out in current political events and policy decisions. Features and anecdotes throughout the book demonstrate the underlying concepts of each chapter and include questions that prompt the reader to think critically.

We also are committed to helping the reader move beyond learning about governments and politics to "doing politics." We believe in civic education and political participation. We also recognize that most students who read this text will not become political scientists, journalists, or elected officeholders. However, we firmly believe that informed citizenship is the only way individuals can exercise some control or influence over those who make political or policy decisions.

We are passionately committed to democracy, and although we may sound skeptical at times, we have not lost faith in Texas citizens. Democracy is predicated not only on the right but also the obligation of citizens to participate in a wide range of political activities. Our passion for democracy calls for open, transparent government; public access to information about the actions of public officials; informed and civil discourse that recognizes intense differences of political opinions; and accountability on the part of those who hold public office.

To provide greater focus and direct the reader to think about the core themes of each chapter, we have structured our analysis around learning objectives, restructured the chapter summaries and conclusions around these learning objectives, and provided test questions at the end of each chapter.

- **Learning objectives** tied to the major headings in every chapter identify the key concepts that students should know and understand with respect to Texas politics and government; these learning objectives also structure the end-of-chapter summaries and the content within MyPoliSciLab.
- **Streamlined "Talking Texas" feature boxes** provide students with an inside look at politics in Texas, including new and humorous anecdotes unique to the Lone Star State. Each of these features is accompanied by **critical thinking questions**.
- **"Review the Chapter" summaries organized around the learning objectives** highlight the most important concepts covered in each chapter.
- **Fifteen "Test Yourself" multiple-choice questions** at the end of each chapter assess students' comprehension and understanding of the most important terms, concepts, and ideas; an answer key is provided at the end of the book.
- **Annotated suggested readings** at the end of each chapter feature seminal books and articles and are accompanied by notes from the authors of this book pinpointing the significance of each of the included works.
- **A running marginal glossary** clearly defines bolded key terms for students at the points in chapters where the terms are discussed.
- **A four-color interior design,** with a fully designed art and photo program, provides a friendly and accessible reading experience whether in print or online.

What follows is a summary of the content covered in each chapter of the eighth edition:

- **Chapter 1** focuses on the political culture of Texas. It draws from the scholarship of Daniel Elazar and attempts to explain the conservative patterns in Texas politics and what some scholars refer to as "Texas exceptionalism." Additionally, drawing on the most recent U.S. census, this chapter describes the various ethnic and racial groups now living in Texas, their original settlement patterns, and subsequent changes.

We discuss the economic and social attributes of these groups to lay the basis for much of the political and policy discussions that follow in later chapters.

- Texas draws from the general American tradition of constitutionalism, and **Chapter 2** links the Constitution of 1876 to these influences, discusses the restrictions it imposes on state government, and delves into the similarities and differences among state constitutions and the U.S. Constitution.
- **Chapter 3** places the government and politics of Texas within the nation's federal framework. This chapter explores the state's changing relationship with the national government and its dependency on federal funds, as well as the unitary relationship between state and local governments. This chapter also includes a discussion of Texas's proximity and relationship to Mexico and the benefits and problems that come with that proximity and relationship.
- **Chapter 4** asks who "rules" Texas by outlining the elitist-pluralist debate and then focusing attention on the diverse interest groups that participate in the state's political system. Although the elitist-pluralist question tends to elude a definitive answer, we believe interest groups in Texas are central to the policymaking process. Public policy can be understood in terms of the roles that groups play at every stage of that process.
- The mass media in Texas, which continue to undergo major changes, receive attention in **Chapter 5**. The media link citizens to those in office. What the public knows about politics and the actions of officeholders comes, directly or indirectly, through the media. The media have traditionally played a major role in shaping public policy, although that role continues to evolve. Despite access to multiple sources of information, it is not clear how well informed most Texans are about politics and the decisions of elected officeholders.
- **Chapter 6** is structured to a large extent around theories of party realignment, detailing the transformation of the state from one-party Democratic control to Republican domination. The story is complex and parallels realignment in the national party system. The coalitions that form the bases of the two parties have changed, increasing the polarization between the two parties.
- **Chapter 7** turns our attention to elections and campaigns with the purpose of explaining differences in the ways Texans engage in the political process. We discuss changing campaign technology, increasing campaign costs, the people and interests who contribute large sums of money to political candidates, and the questions raised by their contributions.
- The Texas legislature, a part-time institution that meets regularly for only five months every two years, has the primary responsibility of enacting public policy and appropriating the billions of dollars that go into each biennial budget. **Chapter 8** describes a more complex institution than what existed forty years ago. Its members and committees now have professional staffs. More interest groups and lobbyists attempt to influence its decisions. Although many other industrialized states have developed complex party structures within their legislatures, voting alignments in the Texas legislature are based more on ideology than party affiliation. However, political parties are beginning to exercise more influence on selected issues.
- Historically, the governor of Texas has been ranked as one of the weaker institutional governors in the United States, in part because of the plural executive described in **Chapter 9**. Although the powers of the office are institutionally weak, some governors, such as Rick Perry, have developed a strong role in state policymaking, using a number of informal and personal resources.
- As noted in **Chapter 10**, some 1.3 million public employees work for state and local governments in Texas. Despite anti-bureaucracy sentiment, governments grow as the population increases and new or expanded programs are implemented. Bureaucrats do much more than shuffle paper. They are involved in every stage of the policymaking process. Texans expect that public services—roads, water treatment, trash collection, and education, to name a few—will be provided effectively and efficiently.
- **Chapter 11** notes the five levels of courts in Texas. This decentralized court structure with overlapping jurisdictions has been at the center of a long-standing discussion of needed court reforms. With the exception of municipal judges, Texas judges are elected in partisan elections. Most other states rely on appointments, nonpartisan elections, or judicial appointments with retention elections. Many Texans, including some judges, dislike the high costs of judicial campaigns and the implication that

campaign contributions influence judicial decisions. However, the legislature has refused to change the partisan election system.

- **Chapter 12** focuses on local governments, including counties, cities, towns, and special districts. The state creates local governments, and most of the functions or powers of local governments are defined by the state. In many respects, local governments have developed without a statewide or comprehensive perspective on how they should interact or coordinate public services in highly urbanized areas. Consequently, some have overlapping or possibly competing jurisdictions. In other instances, special districts have been created to serve narrowly defined objectives when no other government was available.
- **Chapter 13** provides theoretical perspectives on the policymaking process and then applies these concepts to state finances, the budgeting process, educational policies, the criminal justice system, health and human services, and environmental policies.

MyPoliSciLab® for *Government and Politics in the Lone Star State*

The Moment You Know

Educators know it. Students know it. It's that inspired moment when something that was difficult to understand suddenly makes perfect sense. Our MyLab™ products have been designed and refined with a single purpose in mind—to help educators create that moment of understanding with their students.

MyPoliSciLab delivers ***proven results*** in helping individual students succeed. It provides ***engaging experiences*** that personalize, stimulate, and measure learning for each student. It comes from a ***trusted partner*** with educational expertise and a deep commitment to helping students, instructors, and departments achieve their goals.

MyPoliSciLab can be used by itself or linked to any learning management system. To learn more about how MyPoliSciLab combines proven learning applications with powerful assessment, visit **www.mypoliscilab.com**.

MyPoliSciLab Delivers *Proven Results* in Helping Individual Students Succeed

- Pearson MyLabs are currently in use by millions of students each year across a variety of disciplines.
- MyPoliSciLab works, but don't take our word for it. Visit **www.pearsonhighered.com/elearning** to read white papers, case studies, and testimonials from instructors and students that consistently demonstrate the success of our MyLabs.

MyPoliSciLab Provides *Engaging Experiences* that Personalize, Stimulate, and Measure Learning for Each Student

- *Assessment.* Track progress and get instant feedback on every chapter, video, and multimedia activity. With results feeding into a powerful gradebook, the assessment program identifies learning challenges early and suggests the best resources to help.
- *Personalized Study Plan.* Follow a flexible learning path created by the assessment program and tailored to each student's unique needs. Organized by learning objectives, the study plan offers follow-up reading, video, and multimedia activities for further learning and practice.
- *Pearson eText.* Just like the printed text, highlight and add notes to the eText online or download it to a tablet. Also included are full texts of the U.S. and Texas Constitutions.
- *Flashcards.* Learn key terms by word or definition.
- *Video.* Analyze current events by watching streaming video from the *Texas Tribune.*

- *Texas Constitution Exercises.* Take a closer look at key passages that illustrate what drives the evolution of Texas government and its citizens' relationship to it.
- *Social Explorer.* Use interactive maps to think about key questions in Texas politics like a political scientist.
- *Lone Star News Review.* Join the political conversation by following headlines in *Texas Tribune* newsfeeds, reading analysis in the blog, taking weekly current events quizzes and polls, and more.
- *Class Preparation.* Engage students with class presentation resources collected in one convenient online destination.

MyPoliSciLab Comes from a *Trusted Partner* with Educational Expertise and an Eye on the Future

- Pearson supports instructors with workshops, training, and assistance from Pearson Faculty Advisors so you get the help you need to make MyPoliSciLab work for your course.
- Pearson gathers feedback from instructors and students during the development of content and the feature enhancement of each release to ensure that our products meet your needs.

To order MyPoliSciLab with the print text, use ISBN 0-205-92601-0.

Supplements

Pearson is pleased to offer several resources to qualified adoptees of the eighth edition of *Government and Politics in the Lone Star State* and their students that will make teaching and learning from this book even more effective and enjoyable. Several of the supplements for this book are available at the Instructor Resource Center (IRC), an online hub that allows instructors to quickly download book-specific supplements. Please visit the IRC welcome page at www.pearsonhighered.com/irc to register for access.

INSTRUCTOR'S MANUAL/TEST BANK This resource includes chapter summaries, teaching suggestions, multiple-choice questions, true/false questions, and essay questions for each chapter. Available exclusively on the IRC.

PEARSON MYTEST This powerful assessment-generation program includes all of the items in the Instructor's Manual/Test Bank. Questions and tests can be easily created, customized, saved online and then printed, allowing flexibility to manage assessments anytime and anywhere. To learn more, please visit www.pearsonhighered.com/mytest or contact your Pearson representative.

TEST BANK FOR BLACKBOARD This Blackboard-compatible file includes all of the items in the test bank. Available exclusively on the IRC.

POWERPOINT PRESENTATION Organized around a lecture outline, these multimedia presentations also include photos, figures, and tables from each chapter. Available exclusively on the IRC.

SAMPLE SYLLABUS This resource provides suggestions for assigning content from this book and MyPoliSciLab. Available exclusively on the IRC.

CHOICES FOR *GOVERNMENT AND POLITICS IN THE LONE STAR STATE*

Give your students choices. *Government and Politics in the Lone Star State* is available in the following formats to give you and your students more choices—and more ways to save.

- **MyPoliSciLab with eText** improves results through data-driven insights into learning and premier content that engages students at each stage of learning. Built for your Texas government course, MyPoliSciLab offers a customizable digital learning experience that supports each individual student's and educator's success. Refined after a decade of real-world use, MyPoliSciLab comes from Pearson, an experienced partner with an eye on the future of education. MyPoliSciLab with eText offers a full digital version of the printed text and is readable on iOS and Android tablets. *New MyPoliSciLab with eText access code card: 9780205928088. Instant Access: Save on purchasing a print book and buy online access now at* **www.mypoliscilab.com**.

- The **Books à la Carte edition** offers a convenient, three-hole-punched, loose-leaf version of the traditional text at a discounted price—allowing students to take only what they need to class. Books à la Carte editions are available both with and without access to MyPoliSciLab. *Books à la Carte edition:* 9780205927180. *Books à la Carte edition plus MyPoliSciLab:* 9780205927302.
- Build your own **Pearson Custom course material**. For enrollments of at least 25 students, create your own textbook by combining chapters from bestselling Pearson textbooks and/or reading selections in the sequence you want. Work with a dedicated Pearson Custom editor to create your ideal textbook and web material—publishing your own original content or mixing and matching Pearson content. *Contact your Pearson representative to get started or visit* **www.pearsoncustomlibrary.com** *to begin building your custom text.*
- The **CourseSmart eTextbook** offers the same content as the printed text in a convenient online format—with highlighting, online search, and printing capabilities. *CourseSmart eTextbook:* 9780205927203. *Instant Access: Save on purchasing a print book and buy online access now at* **www.coursesmart.com**.
- **Traditional printed text.** *Government and Politics in the Lone Star State printed text: 9780205927067. Government and Politics in the Lone Star State printed text plus MyPoliSciLab: 9780205926015.*

Acknowledgments

We run the risk of overlooking individuals who have provided assistance in our research and writing, but we want to start our acknowledgments with the twenty-five or so government teachers who participated in a series of panels at the 2012 Texas Community College Teachers Association meeting in Frisco, Texas. They provided valuable insights into the approaches they take in teaching Texas government. Consequently, we have a better sense of class sizes, reading levels of their students, topics that are difficult to teach, effective testing tools, and the problems of maintaining a current perspective on state government and politics. We extend a sincere note of thanks to these classroom teachers, who helped us understand what we were doing well and what we needed to do to improve our text.

Two research assistants—Christian Nardini and Thomas Bell—have supported us. They checked and rechecked many of the facts that are incorporated throughout the chapters. They were instrumental in helping us identify new sources, especially government documents, and they helped us think about transforming tables into more reader-friendly graphs and charts.

David Crockett (and he really is related to the historical Davy Crockett of the Alamo) assisted us in refining the chapter learning objectives and helped us construct the test questions that are located at the end of each chapter. His careful read of the manuscript helped us clarify some of our analysis.

Many other individuals are part of the editorial and production staff of Pearson. Although they remain anonymous to us, we have a keen appreciation for their craft and their abilities to transform text into a readable finished product.

Special kudos go to Vikram Mukhija and Lisa Sussman.

Vikram, Pearson's political science editor, gave us the opportunity to redevelop and expand our text. He believed our work could be expanded, reorganized, and updated to incorporate the latest online technology and meet the needs of those who teach Texas government and politics. Moreover, he effectively coordinated his editorial and production staff to help us move efficiently through the revision process.

Lisa Sussman is an efficient and encouraging development editor who kept us on task with her gentle but firm nudging. She anticipated issues early in the process, provided suggestions to resolve these issues, and worked post-haste to return manuscripts to us for further changes or editing. Several of the chapters were restructured to provide a more integrated analysis that reads much better than earlier editions. Lisa, thank you.

We have read and reread the manuscript and checked and rechecked the data. If there are errors, the fault is ours.

Listen on MyPoliSciLab

1 The Social and Economic Milieu of Texas Politics

Life is too short not to live it in Texas.

—Bumper sticker seen on a car in San Antonio

It is therefore necessary, if we would become acquainted with the legislation and the manners of a nation, to begin by the study of its social condition.

—Alexis de Tocqueville, 1835

Texas, in many respects, is a state of extreme contrasts, beginning with its geography. The rugged, desert-like landscape of far West Texas does not look like it belongs on the same planet as the lush, tall Piney Woods of deep East Texas, let alone in the same state. The semitropical Rio Grande Valley in far South Texas is home to citrus orchards, whereas, several hundred miles away in the Panhandle, Amarillo suffers through the same frigid winters as much of the Midwest. Over the years, Texas has perpetuated a frontier image of cowboys and wide-open spaces, but almost 90 percent of its population now lives in crowded cities and suburbs. Three of the nation's ten largest cities—Houston, San Antonio, and Dallas—are in Texas.

1.1 Summarize the basic challenges facing Texas as it moves through the twenty-first century, p. 5.

1.2 Explain some of the myths of Texas's political culture, p. 6.

1.3 Compare and contrast the political subcultures of Texas, p. 9.

1.4 Trace the historical origins of political subcultures and identify the subcultures that have most influenced Texas's political culture, p. 10.

1.5 Describe the basic history and characteristics of the major population groups in Texas, p. 11.

1.6 Outline the demographic and economic changes that have occurred over Texas's history, p. 16.

THE ALAMO, site of the historic 1836 siege and battle, is a popular destination for tourists and students in downtown San Antonio.

1.1
1.2
1.3
1.4
1.5
1.6

Some of the wealthiest political contributors in the United States live in Texas, and presidential candidates of both parties regularly drop in for fund-raising. But millions of Texans live below the poverty line. Some of the poorest counties, per capita, in the country are along the Texas-Mexico border. Fewer than 100 years ago, wildcatters were striking it rich in the "oil patch," and as recently as a generation ago, oil and natural gas were still kings of the Texas economy. But the state's economy has diversified, and oil and gas producers now work alongside high-tech companies, telecommunications giants, and other important business sectors.

To some outsiders, Texas may still have a rugged, bigger-than-life mystique. And, many Texans, particularly those who are native born, continue to celebrate their historic legacy. However, not unlike many other states, Texas struggles with a host of twenty-first century, growth-related problems. Roads and highways in urban and suburban areas are clogged, and air pollution is an ever-present problem for many communities. State policymakers must continually weigh the electricity needs of a growing population—and the potential for rolling blackouts during 100-degree Texas summers—with the environmental risks posed by power plants. Texas also must figure out how to assure an adequate water supply for an ever-increasing demand, a necessity stamped with a special sense of urgency during the record drought in 2011.

Although immigration policy is a federal issue, immigration from Mexico heavily impacts Texas, a border state, and that spills over into political debates over border security, education, health care, and other issues. Within a generation or so, the majority of Texas's population will be Hispanic. Texas's high incidence of poverty and the global competition the state increasingly faces for high-paying jobs make it imperative, some people believe, that state government restructure an outdated, inadequate, and regressive tax system that fails to raise enough revenue to meet public needs. Texas consistently ranks near the bottom of the states in spending on education, welfare, and health care for the poor. For the present, Texas remains a politically conservative state, electing policymakers who support a low-tax, low-regulatory climate. But that may change as the state's population, fueled by immigration, continues to change.

Texans, as are most citizens of other states, are woefully ignorant of their state and local governments and the public officials who make important decisions affecting their daily lives. Many view government as something in Austin or at the courthouse, where people do things to them, not for them. Government is often described in terms of red tape, inefficiency, and anonymous or rude bureaucrats. Political campaigns are perceived as a form of organized mud wrestling in which candidates characterize each other as despicable, immoral, incompetent, or whatever, and this perception results in large numbers of Texans tuning out politics. Many people distrust government—a traditionally strong sentiment in Texas—and hope it interferes with their lives as little as possible. Most Texans do not vote in elections, leaving the selection of public leaders to a minority of voters.

But, like most Americans, Texans assume there will be clean water flowing through their kitchen taps, streets and highways on which to drive their cars, quality public schools to which they can send their children, parks for family outings, and police officers to help protect their lives and property. Many people have come to believe they can have all this—and pay lower taxes—an attitude perpetuated by many politicians who promise more services but refuse to address their costs.

We all have a stake in what governments do because these institutions have a daily impact on our livelihoods and our quality of life. We pay taxes for a multitude of programs and services and would like to believe that the benefits we receive are worth what we pay. People generally do not get excited or concerned about government, however, until it fails to meet their demands or expectations. Such indifference and ignorance can be harmful to the people's interests, particularly today, as Texas undergoes changes that will determine what kind of state it will be for years to come and, consequently, how well or how poorly it will meet the public's needs. Our past, marked by good times as well as bad, is a prelude to our future, and decisions that we make about our politics, governments, and public policies will determine how well we can adapt to change.

regressive tax
A tax that imposes a disproportionately heavier burden on low-income people than on the more affluent.

Challenges of the Twenty-First Century

1.1 Summarize the basic challenges facing Texas as it moves through the twenty-first century.

The issues cited at the beginning of this chapter are some of the challenges of contemporary Texas politics. They reflect the fundamental conflicts between competing interests and the way Texans decide "who gets what, when, and how."[1] Government and politics are the systems that we have developed to structure conflict; develop an orderly and stable process by which competing interests can be expressed; and, finally, decide who will benefit and who will pay the bill.

As we begin our analysis of Texas government and politics, we ask why Texans and their public officials make the political choices they do. Why, for example, do expenditures for public education in Texas rank low in comparison to most other states? How do we account for Texas's **regressive tax** system, which requires low-income and middle-income citizens to pay a higher proportion of their income in state and local taxes than do the wealthy? Why are Texans so willing to fund the construction of highways, roads, and prisons while letting their state rank near the bottom of all the states in expenditures for public welfare?[2]

These policy issues are directly linked to a variety of other questions about government and the political system. Why are Texans content to live under a state constitution that most scholars regard as obsolete? Why, until recently, was Texas a one-party Democratic state? Why do Republicans now dominate state politics? And what difference, if any, does this make in public policies? Does a small group of powerful individuals determine the primary policy decisions for the state, or are there various competitive centers of power? Do Texans believe they are paying more but getting less for their tax dollars? Are Texans increasingly disenchanted with government?

Most of these issues affect Texans personally. They pay the costs, even though they may not receive the benefits of every policy decision. The actions of governmental leaders can have an immediate and direct effect on people's lives, and, from time to time, those holding positions of power have made decisions that have cost Texans dearly. For example, the implosion of Houston-based Enron Corp. in 2001 and the subsequent loss of thousands of jobs and retirement nest eggs were the result, in large part, of the failure of state and federal governments to adequately regulate the energy industry. Cuts in education, health care, and other public services—or increases in tuition at state-supported universities—often result when the Texas legislature refuses to increase taxes.

Each generation has to address fundamental questions of the role of government, the relationship of the people to that government, and what can be done to make government more responsive and responsible. When one hears or reads of many of the contemporary policy debates or policy failures, there is a real sense of *déjà vu*—we have seen these problems and issues before. Funding of public education, a major problem now, also was an issue during the Texas revolution of 1836, the Reconstruction era after the Civil War, and throughout much of the state's history. There also are new issues, such as the regulation of genetic engineering and the changing international economy. But many of today's issues are enduring issues of government and politics.

economic diversification
The development of new and varied business activities. New businesses were encouraged to relocate to or expand in Texas after the oil and gas industry, which had been the base of the state's economy, suffered a major recession in the 1980s.

political myths
Generally held views rooted in the political culture that are used to explain common historical and cultural experiences.

republic
A political system in which sovereign power resides in the citizenry and is exercised by representatives elected by and responsible to them.

The fundamental changes in the social, economic, and political structure of the state require new solutions. Funding public education in the days of the one-room schoolhouse was one thing. Funding today's educational system in a way that provides equity among the state's 1,000-plus school districts is much more complex.

The demographics, or population characteristics, of the state have changed dramatically since the 1940s, when Texas was still predominantly rural. Texas is now an urban state with urban problems. With more than 25 million residents, Texas is second only to California in population. Its ethnic and racial composition has changed, and it is now home to a large number of individuals who were born and reared in other parts of the United States or outside the country—people who have a limited sense of Texas history and politics. Although oil and natural gas are still important to the state's economy, business leaders, governmental officials, and economists promote **economic diversification** as the dominant theme. Change places heavy demands on the state's governmental institutions, and Texans will need to give increased attention to modernizing and adapting their government to new realities.

In this chapter, we introduce you to the people of Texas, the views they have of themselves, the state's political subcultures, and its economy. We refer to these factors generally as the "political environment," a concept developed by political scientist David Easton to refer to the milieu, or context, in which political institutions function.[3] Although much of our discussion focuses on broad patterns or characteristics of the political environment, individual and collective behavior of groups will determine how our governments respond to changing conditions.

The Myths of Texas's Political Culture

1.2 Explain some of the myths of Texas's political culture.

lthough most Texans have only a cursory knowledge of their state's governmental institutions, political history, and contemporary public policy, they do have views—often ill defined—of the state, its people, and its culture. Key elements of these views, shared by millions of Texans, are described by some scholars as **political myths**.

In recent years, serious scholarship has focused on myths as a way to assess the views people have of their common historical and cultural experiences. A myth can be regarded as a "mode of truth that codifies and preserves moral and spiritual values" for a particular culture or society.[4] Myths are stories or narratives that are used to describe past events, explain their significance to successive generations, and provide an interpretive overview and understanding of a society and its culture.[5] Myths provide a world picture or, in our case, a picture of the state of Texas. Myths serve, in part, to affirm the values, customs, and beliefs of Texans.[6] The relevance of a myth depends, in part, on the degree to which it approximates the events it describes and its pervasiveness in the literature, symbols, rituals, and popular culture of the state.

Texas has produced its own myth of origin, which continues to be a powerful statement about the political system and the social order on which it is based. For many Texans, the battle of the Alamo clearly serves to identify the common experiences of independence and the creation of a separate, unique political order.[7] No other state was a **republic** prior to joining the Union, and several scholars argue that independence and "going at it alone" from 1836 to 1845 resulted in a cultural experience that distinguishes the Texas political system from that of other states. The state's nickname—the Lone Star State—is a constant reminder of this unique history. A set of heroes came out of the formative period of Texas history, including many who fought and died at the Alamo or secured Texas independence on the San Jacinto battlefield. Texas schoolchildren are introduced to these heroes at a very early age with field trips, or "pilgrimages," to the Alamo in San Antonio and visits to the San Jacinto monument in Houston.

The Texas mythology also includes the Texas Ranger and the cowboy. There is considerable lore about the invincible, enduring ranger defeating overwhelming odds. Newspapers and dime novels in the nineteenth century introduced readers throughout the United States to the cowboy, who was often portrayed as an honest, hardworking individual wrestling with the harsh Texas environment (see *Talking Texas: Not Every "Cowboy" Can Be President*).

The cowboy's rugged **individualism**, with strong connotations of self-help and independence, symbolizes a political culture in Texas that does not like to look to government as a solution to many of its problems.[8] It is the kind of individualism that continues to be exploited by political candidates in campaign ads and by the state legislature in limited appropriations for welfare, health care, and other public-assistance programs. This legacy of individualism and risk taking is further reinforced by the stories of wildcatters who made and lost fortunes in the early days of oil exploration in the state.

individualism
An attitude, rooted in classical liberal theory and reinforced by the frontier tradition, that citizens are capable of taking care of themselves with minimal governmental assistance.

The frontier to which the Texas Ranger and the cowboy belong is part of a cultural myth of limited government and unlimited personal opportunity. The Texas frontier experience also perpetuates the myth of "land as wilderness and land as garden."[9] The hostile Chihuahuan Desert of the far southwestern part of the state eventually gives way to the more endemic green of the Piney Woods of East Texas.

Talking ★ TEXAS Not Every "Cowboy" Can Be President

Two back-to-back Texas governors—each with an affinity for boots and a swaggering type of "cowboy" persona—ran for president of the United States. George W. Bush was elected in 2000 and served two terms in the White House. Rick Perry, a country boy from Paint Creek who once shot a coyote while jogging, stumbled in 2012. Perry was not any less self-assured than Bush, and his outdoorsy image may have been more authentic. However, he was less prepared for the rigors of Republican primary debates, let alone the international stage.

Bush was born in Connecticut and never had lived on a ranch before he purchased one for vacation getaways—and media photo-ops—with some of the millions he received from selling a major league baseball team. But he talked tough and during his administration came to be described by some as the "cowboy president."

At least two of his predecessors, Theodore Roosevelt and Ronald Reagan, also were portrayed as cowboys, either in cartoons, photos, or prose. The cowboy mythology resonates with most Americans, and presidents can use it to symbolize their style of leadership. At the beginning of the invasion of Iraq, Bush branded former Iraqi leader Saddam Hussein an "outlaw" and declared that he wanted terrorist Osama Bin Laden "dead or alive." At a conference in Aqaba on the Red Sea, Bush said that he was going to appoint a coordinator to "ride herd" on Middle East leaders along the peace trail. Many in his audience had no idea what he was talking about.

Bush wore a stylish Stetson and a large belt buckle. He conveyed an "aw shucks" demeanor, scrambled his words in a folksy manner, cut brush on his ranch in view of camera lenses, and seemed to enjoy driving his guests around in his Jeep. Some observers, particularly his critics, thought a lot of this behavior was orchestrated by his staff and consultants, but the cowboy imagery made for good press. It also fed the perception that many non-Texans have of the frontier culture of Texas and its style of politics.

CRITICAL THINKING QUESTIONS

1. Do our presidents and governors need a certain amount of brashness to be successful? Or, do they run the risk of antagonizing potential allies? Explain your answer.
2. How do officials use their public image to shape public opinion or deflect attention from their policy decisions?

THE TEXAS RANGER

Even in the modern era, Texas Ranger Gerry Villalobos, a Hispanic American, has ridden horseback to search for criminal suspects in the rough, remote country near Fort Stockton in far West Texas. However, to many Hispanics and other minorities, the Texas Ranger represents a symbol of violent suppression.

Descriptions of space, distance, and size are pervasive in a great deal of the literature on the state. Literally thousands of books written about Texas provide varied perspectives on the geography and topography of the land. One might argue that the "wide-open spaces" of the frontier shaped Texans' views of their autonomy, independence, and vulnerability. It has clearly shaped attitudes toward land and the legal rights to use land as one sees fit.

The Texas myths, however, have been primarily the myths of the white (Anglo) population and have limited relevance to the cultural and historical experiences of many African American and Hispanic Texans. From the 1840s to the mid-1960s, these latter groups were excluded from full participation in Texas politics and the state's economic and social life. To many Hispanics, for example, the Texas Ranger is not a hero, but a symbol of ruthless suppression.

Since the 1970s, African Americans, Hispanics, and Asian Americans have made significant political and economic gains. Their share of the population has been increasing as well, and these three groups combined now constitute a majority of the state's population. As this shift occurs, Hispanic and African American historical experiences are likely to be incorporated into the mythology of the state, and some components of the contemporary mythology will be challenged and redefined. These revisions may already be underway, as demonstrated by the heated debate over what actually took place during the battle of the Alamo.[10]

Disputing years of popular Texas beliefs, some scholars recently concluded that some of the Alamo's heroes surrendered to Mexican soldiers and were executed, rather than fighting to the death. African Americans in Texas were successful, after several years, in convincing the state legislature to make Martin Luther King Jr.'s birthday a state holiday in 1991. June 19, the day slaves in Texas learned of their emancipation in 1865, also has significant meaning for the state's African Americans and is celebrated as the Juneteenth holiday. For Hispanics, the *Cinco de Mayo* and *Diez y Seis* celebrations speak to common cultural and historical experiences with Mexico.

The Political Culture of Texas

1.3 Compare and contrast the political subcultures of Texas.

political culture
A widely shared set of views, attitudes, beliefs, and customs of a people as to how their government should be organized and run.

individualistic subculture
A view that government should interfere as little as possible in the private activities of its citizens while assuring that adequate public facilities and a favorable business climate are available to permit individuals to pursue their self-interests.

moralistic subculture
A view that government's primary responsibility is to promote the public welfare and should actively use its authority and power to improve the social and economic well-being of its citizens.

Texas shares the common constitutional, institutional, and legal arrangements that have developed in all fifty states, including a commitment to personal liberties, equality, justice, the rule of law, and popular sovereignty with its limitations on government. But there are cultural differences among the states and even among regions within individual states. Texas is a highly diverse state, with racial and ethnic differences from one region to another and divergences in political attitudes and behavior that are reflected in the state's politics and public policies.

The concept of **political culture** helps us compare some of these differences. Political culture has been defined as the "set of attitudes, beliefs, and sentiments which give order and meaning to a political process and which provide the underlying assumptions and rules that govern behavior in the political system."[11] The political culture of the state includes fundamental beliefs about the proper role of government, the relationship of the government to its citizens, and who should govern.[12] These complex attitudes and behaviors are rooted in the historical experience of the nation, shaped by the groups that immigrated to the United States, and carried across the continent to Texas.

One authority on American political culture, Daniel Elazar, notes that three political subcultures have emerged over time in the United States: the individualistic, the moralistic, and the traditionalistic. All three draw from the common historical legacy of the nation, but they produced regional political differences. Sometimes they complement one another; at other times, they produce conflict.[13]

☐ The Individualistic Subculture

The political view of the **individualistic subculture** holds that politics and government function as a marketplace. Government does not have to be concerned with creating a good or moral society but exists for strictly "utilitarian reasons, to handle those functions demanded by the people it is created to serve."[14] Government should be limited, and its intervention in the private activities of its citizens should be kept to a minimum. The primary function of government is to ensure the stability of a society so that individuals can pursue their own interests.

In this view, politics is not a high calling or noble pursuit but is like any other business venture in which skill and talent prevail and the individual can expect economic and social benefits. Politics is often perceived by the general public to be a dirty business that should be left to those willing to soil their hands in the political arena. This tradition may well contribute to political corruption, and members of the electorate who share this view may not be concerned when government corruption is revealed. New policies are more likely to be initiated by interest groups or private individuals than by public officials, and it is assumed that those elected to public office will pursue their self-interests.[15]

☐ The Moralistic Subculture

The **moralistic subculture** regards politics as one of the "great activities of man in his search for the good society."[16] Politics, it maintains, is the pursuit of the common good. Unlike the attitude expressed in the individualistic subculture that governments are to be limited, the moralistic subculture considers government a positive instrument

traditionalistic subculture
A view that political power should be concentrated in the hands of a few elite citizens who belong to established families or influential social groups. Public policy basically serves the interests of this small group.

with a responsibility to promote the general welfare.[17] Politics, therefore, is not to be left to the few but is a responsibility of every individual. Politics is a duty and possibly a high calling. This cultural tradition has a strong sense of service. It requires a high standard for those holding public office, which is not to be used for personal gain. Politics may be organized around political parties, but this tradition produced nonpartisanship whereby party labels and organizations play a reduced role.[18] The moralistic subculture yields a large number of "amateur" or "nonprofessional" political activists and officeholders and has little toleration for political corruption. From the moralistic perspective, governments should actively intervene to enhance the social and economic interests of their citizens. Public policy initiatives can come from officeholders as well as from those outside the formal governmental structure.[19]

☐ The Traditionalistic Subculture

The **traditionalistic subculture** holds the view that there is a hierarchical arrangement to the political order. This hierarchy serves to limit the power and influence of the general public, while allocating authority to a few individuals who comprise self-perpetuating elites. The elites may enact policies that benefit the general public, but that is secondary to their own interests and objectives. Public policy reflects the interests of those who exercise influence and control, and the benefits of public policy go disproportionately to the elites.

Family, social, and economic relationships, not mass political participation, form the basis for maintaining this elite structure. In fact, in many regions of the country where traditionalistic patterns existed, there were systematic efforts to reduce or eliminate the participation of the general public. Although political parties may exist in such a subculture, they have only minimal importance that is often subject to manipulation or control by elites. Many of the states characterized by the traditionalistic subculture were southern states in which factionalism within the Democratic Party replaced two-party politics.[20]

Historical Origins of Political Subcultures

1.4 Trace the historical origins of political subcultures and identify the subcultures that have most influenced Texas's political culture.

The historical origins of these three subcultures can be explained, in part, by the early settlement patterns of the United States and by the cultural differences among the groups of people who initially settled the eastern seaboard. In very general terms, the New England colonists, influenced by Puritan and congregational religious groups, spawned the moralistic subculture. Settlers with entrepreneurial concerns and individualistic attitudes tended to locate in the Mid-Atlantic states, whereas traditionalistic elites who aspired, in part, to recreate a semifeudal society, dominated the initial settlement of the South.

Expansion toward the western frontiers progressed in identifiable migration patterns from the initial three settlement regions. Texas was settled primarily by people holding the individualistic and traditionalistic views of a political system. The blending of these two views, along with the historical experience of the Republic and frontier, contributed to the distinct characteristics of Texas's political culture.[21]

These two political subcultures have merged to shape Texans' general views of what government should do, who should govern, and what constitutes good public policy. Given the characteristics of these two traditions, one might well conclude, as have many scholars, that the Texas political culture is conservative. Politics in Texas tends to minimize the role of government, is hostile toward taxes—especially those that are allocated toward social services—and often is manipulated by the few for their narrow advantages at the expense of the general population. During much of its history, Texas was one of the least democratic states, with restrictions on voting rights, limited party competition, and low rates of voter participation.[22]

Some scholars, however, have reservations about the concept of political subcultures because the theory is difficult to test. Although these reservations are legitimate, we know of no other single theory that presents such a rich historical perspective on the relationship of settlement patterns in the state and the evolution of political attitudes and behavior.

The People of Texas

1.5 Describe the basic history and characteristics of the major population groups in Texas.

The politics and government of Texas can be understood, in part, from the perspective of the people living in the state. What follows is an assessment of a select number of demographic, or population, characteristics of Texans. In subsequent chapters, we examine the relationship of race, ethnicity, and other demographic characteristics to partisan behavior, public opinion, institutional power, and public policy.

Native Americans

Only three small Native American groups (Alabama-Coushatta, Tigua, and Kickapoo) live on reservations in Texas, and the Native American population is less than one-half of 1 percent of the state's total population. Unlike Native Americans in Oklahoma, New Mexico, and Arizona, those in Texas have little influence on governmental institutions, politics, or public policy.

In the early nineteenth century, at least twenty-three Native American groups resided in Texas (see *Talking Texas:* Tejas *Means Friendship*). During the period of the Republic (1836–1845), President Sam Houston attempted to follow a policy of "peace and friendship" with the Native Americans, but he was followed by President Mirabeau B. Lamar, who set out to "expel, defeat, or exterminate" them. Statehood did not improve the Native Americans' conditions, and the period between annexation in 1845 and the Civil War (1861–1865) was "one of devastation, decimation, and dislocation" for many of the state's tribes.[23] As Anglo settlers expanded to lands traditionally claimed by various Native American tribes, conflict ensued, and most of the Native American population was eventually eliminated or displaced to other states.

In recent years, Native American tribes have cooperated with officials in many states to establish gambling casinos on tribal reservations. Such casinos are allowed under federal law, but most forms of casino gambling are barred by Texas law. The Kickapoos operate a limited casino outside of Eagle Pass, but the Tiguas and Alabama-Coushattas have been denied the right to run casinos on their reservations. Some Native American leaders consider casinos a major potential source of revenue, jobs, and economic development for their people, but recent efforts to change state law have been unsuccessful.

Hispanics

In the eighteenth and nineteenth centuries, neither Spain nor Mexico was successful in convincing Hispanics to settle in the Tejas territory of Mexico. The Spanish regarded

Talking ★ TEXAS *Tejas* Means Friendship

The Native American legacy in Texas remains in the state's name. The word "Texas" is derived from *tejas*, which means "friends" or "allies" in Spanish. As Spanish explorers and missionaries moved across Texas, they confronted a Native American confederacy, the Hasinai. It was to this particular group that they applied the term, and, eventually, the Anglo form of the name became the permanent name of the region and then the state.[a]

Several years ago, the Texas Department of Transportation proposed changing the state's vehicle license plates to include the phrase "The Friendship State." But the agency quickly abandoned the idea, following a public reaction that was largely hostile. Some Texans apparently found the phrase incompatible with the state's rugged frontier image. Or, perhaps they believed that the state's increasingly clogged freeways, especially in urban and suburban areas, were anything but friendly. In any event, it is ironic that the common nomenclature for the state, which means friendship, is used almost every day by every Texan.

CRITICAL THINKING QUESTIONS

1. Do Texans take their rugged, frontier heritage too seriously? Why or why not?
2. What, if anything, do modern Texans owe to the people, including the Native Americans, who were present when the state was carved out of the wilderness?

[a]Rupert N. Richardson, Ernest Wallace, and Adrian Anderson, *Texas: The Lone Star State*, 5th ed. (Englewood Cliffs, NJ: Prentice Hall, 1988), p. 1.

it as a border province of relatively little value, except as a strategic buffer between Spanish colonies and those held by the British and the French. By the time Mexico declared its independence from Spain in 1821, the total Texas population under Spanish control was estimated to be approximately 5,000 people. With the rapid expansion of Anglo-American immigration to Texas in the 1820s and 1830s, Hispanics became a small minority of the population.[24]

Some Hispanics were part of the Texas independence movement from Mexico. After independence in 1836, men such as Jose Antonio Navarro and Juan Seguin were part of the Republic's political establishment. But the Anglo migration rapidly overwhelmed the Hispanic population and greatly reduced its political and economic power. There was even an effort at the Constitutional Convention of 1845 to strip Hispanics of the right to vote. The attempt failed, but it was an early indication of Anglo hostility toward the Hispanic population.[25]

By 1887, the Hispanic population had declined to approximately 4 percent of the state's population. In 1930, it was 12 percent and was concentrated in the border counties from Brownsville to El Paso (see Figure 1–1). Modest increases in the Hispanic population continued until it reached 18 percent of the state's population in 1970, after which it grew at a more rapid rate. By 1990, it had reached 25 percent, spurred by immigration from Mexico and other Latin American countries, as well as by higher birth rates among Hispanic women. These growth patterns continued in the next two decades, and by 2010, Hispanics comprised 37.6 percent of the state's population.[26] In addition to their traditional concentrations in the Rio Grande Valley and South-Central Texas, large Hispanic populations are found in most metropolitan areas. Except for the Asian American population, which is considerably smaller, the Hispanic population is growing at a significantly higher rate than other populations in Texas.

Hispanics will continue to increase at a higher rate than most other populations; by around 2030, Hispanics are likely to exceed 50 percent of the state's total.[27] This growth in population is steadily increasing the political power and influence of this group. Seven Hispanics have been elected to statewide office. After successful redistricting and legal challenges to city, county, school board, and state legislative districts, Hispanics held some 2,520 elected positions in Texas in 2011, the highest number of any state.[28]

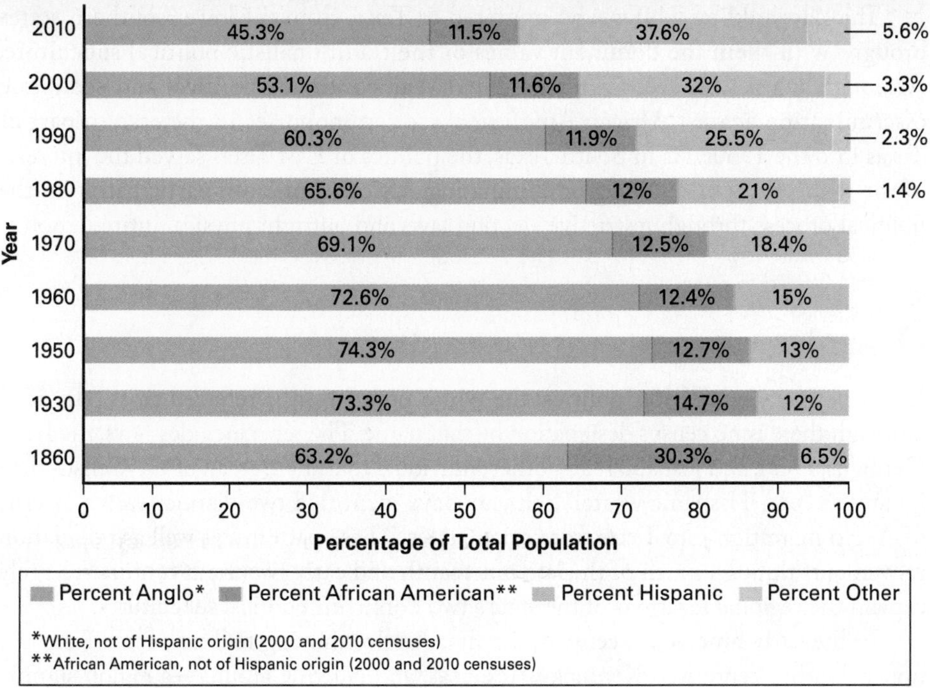

FIGURE 1–1 ETHNIC AND RACIAL COMPOSITION OF TEXAS, 1860–2010

The composition of the state's population has changed significantly since the 1960s with large increases in the Hispanic and Asian American populations.

Source: Terry G. Jordan with John L. Bean Jr. and William M. Holmes, *Texas: A Geography* (Boulder, CO: Westview Press, 1984), pp. 81–83; U.S. Census Bureau, U.S Censuses, 1860–2010.

The regions of the state where Hispanics concentrated (South Texas and along the Mexican border) before their more widespread migration to cities were areas heavily influenced by the traditionalistic subculture. Extreme poverty, low levels of education, and local economies based on agriculture contributed to the development of political systems dominated by a few Anglos, who often considered Hispanics to be second-class citizens. Hispanics' increasing political clout, however, has produced major political and governmental changes in those regions.

□ African Americans

Relatively few African Americans lived in Texas during the colonization period, and the modern story of African American settlement did not begin until after independence in 1836. When Texas was part of Mexico, Mexican law restricted slavery within the territory. During the period of the Republic and early statehood prior to the U.S. Civil War, the African American population increased significantly as Anglo-Americans settling in Texas brought cotton cultivation and the slavery system with them. At the time of the Civil War, 30 percent of the state's residents were African American, but that percentage declined after the war. By 1960, it had leveled off at 12 percent, about the same level counted in the 2010 census. African Americans are expected to represent between 11 percent and 12 percent of the state's population through the 2020 census.

Large concentrations of African Americans can be found in East Texas, where white southerners and their slaves originally settled. African Americans also settled in large numbers in the urban areas of Dallas, Fort Worth, Houston, and Austin. Relatively few African Americans live in the western counties or in the counties along the Mexican border. The increased number of African American state legislators, city council members, county commissioners, and school board trustees representing urban communities indicates the political power of the African American population in selected areas.

The slaveholding whites who migrated to Texas from the lower southern states brought with them the dominant values of the traditionalistic political subculture. Although slaves were freed after the Civil War, continued political and economic discrimination against African Americans was commonplace in the eastern part of Texas into the 1960s. As in South Texas, the politics of East Texas served the interests of the white elites by reducing or eliminating African American participation in the political process through restrictive election laws and outright physical intimidation.

☐ Anglos

In the vernacular of Texas politics, the white population is referred to as "Anglos," although there is no census designation by that name. The term includes Jews, the Irish, Germans, Poles, and just about any other individual that the Bureau of the Census designates as "non-Hispanic white." Scholars have identified two distinct early patterns of Anglo migration into Texas from other states. These patterns, as well as population movements through much of the late nineteenth and early twentieth centuries, largely explain the regional locations of the state's two dominant political subcultures.

In the early nineteenth century, the first Anglos moving to Texas came from the upper South—Tennessee, Kentucky, Arkansas, and North Carolina—a region significantly influenced by the individualistic subculture that emphasized limited government. The earliest settlements were primarily in what is now Northeast Texas, in the Red River Valley. After Mexican independence from Spain, a second wave of immigration came from the upper South and generally settled in Northeast Texas.[29] Few of these early colonists were plantation slaveholders from the lower South.

After Texas gained its independence and legalized slavery, settlers from the lower South began arriving. By the outbreak of the Civil War, Anglos who had moved to Texas from the lower South were roughly equal in number to those from the upper South. Newcomers from the slaveholding lower South initially settled in southeastern Texas, near Louisiana, but soon they began to move northward and westward.

A line drawn from Texarkana to San Antonio in effect divides Texas subcultures. Most of those Anglos who settled north and west of this line were from the upper South and heavily influenced by the individualistic subculture. Anglos who settled south and east of the line were by and large from the lower South and shaped by the traditionalistic subculture. Although the characteristics of these two subcultures were somewhat different, they merged to create a conservative political system that limited the scope of government and often served the interests of elites.

This pattern of immigration and settlement continued after the Civil War. It was primarily those populations from the upper South that pushed westward to the Panhandle and West Texas. This expansion introduced into the western part of the state the cultural experience of those who resisted the notion that government existed to solve all of society's ills. To this day, West Texas is still one of the most politically conservative areas of the state.[30]

In 1860, Anglos constituted approximately 63 percent of Texas's population. The Anglo population increased until it reached 74 percent in 1950. But by 1990, the stabilization of the African American population and the increase in the Hispanic population had reduced the Anglo share to 60 percent. Anglos accounted for only 53 percent of Texas's population by the year 2000 and 45.3 percent in 2010. Although the number of Anglos will continue to increase with Texas's projected growth, their share of the total population will continue to decrease.

The Anglo population is diverse, as exhibits in the Institute of Texan Cultures in San Antonio remind us. Towns throughout Texas are identified by immigrants of national origin other than Anglo-Saxon, and these national groups brought with them a rich heritage. Castroville, for example, is identified with the Alsatians; New Braunfels and Fredericksburg, the Germans; Panna Maria, the Poles; and West and Halletsville, the Czechs.

☐ Asian Americans

In 1980, Asian Americans accounted for 0.8 percent of Texas's population. By 2010, this group had grown to 3.8 percent and was projected to increase to 4.2 percent by 2020. This rapid increase parallels national trends. Changes in immigration policy and the dislocation of Asians because of war and political persecution have resulted in larger numbers of Asian immigrants entering the United States and Texas since the 1970s. Moreover, the Asian population is increasingly diverse and includes individuals from Vietnam, China, Iraq, Iran, Pakistan, South Korea, and a number of other countries.

The largest concentration of Asian Americans in Texas is in Houston, where several Asian Americans have been elected to major public offices. Among them, community activist Martha Wong was elected to the Houston City Council in 1993 and then to the Texas House of Representatives in 2002. Wong, who was defeated in her reelection bid in 2006, was the second Asian American to serve in the Texas House. Tom Lee of San Antonio, who served in the 1960s, was believed to be the first. Another Houstonian, Hubert Vo, a Vietnamese American, was elected to the Texas House in 2004 and was reelected to a fourth term in 2010. Angie Chen Button (R-Richardson) was elected to the house in 2008 and reelected in 2010. Asian Americans also hold local offices in several other Texas cities.

☐ Politics, Race, and Ethnicity

Today, few Texans run around the state wearing Ku Klux Klan robes, burning crosses, or marching in support of white supremacy. But there still are occasions of racial violence and cruelty, such as the murder of James Byrd Jr., an African American who was dragged to death behind a pickup truck by three white men in early 1999 near Jasper in East Texas. Despite such incidents, the state has made progress in creating a more equitable society. A state law barring African Americans from voting in party primaries was declared unconstitutional in the 1940s, and many other laws that were intended to reduce the political participation of African Americans and Hispanics have been eliminated. The federal Voting Rights Act, which was enacted in 1965 and extended to Texas in 1975, also helped open up state and local electoral systems to minorities. There is still evidence of employment and housing discrimination, but restrictive codes prohibiting a specific group of people from buying residential property have been declared unconstitutional, and federal and state laws have given minorities greater access to jobs.

Nonetheless, race and ethnicity are implicit in many contemporary political and policy issues. Throughout the ongoing debate on restructuring the school finance system, the protagonists are identified as the "rich" and the "poor" school districts of the state. In large part, these are alternative terms for "nonminority" and "minority" school systems. There have been bitter legal battles about redistricting of political districts to increase Hispanic and African American representation on city councils, school boards, special districts, the state legislature, and the U.S. Congress. Although many poor Anglos live in Texas, the disproportionately high poverty rates among minority groups often influence discussions about social services. Many minority legislators were particularly outspoken against deep cuts to health and human services programs imposed by the legislature during budget crises in 2003 and 2011.

Many state and local elections show evidence of polarized voting along ethnic lines. Race and ethnicity also emerge as factors in jury selection, employment patterns, and contracts with state and local governments. Admissions policies of Texas colleges and universities over the years have produced a series of legal challenges centering on affirmative action and reverse discrimination.

More than sixty years ago, V. O. Key, a Texan scholar of American politics, concluded that Texas politics was moving from issues of race to issues of class and economics. He argued that voters in Texas "divide along class lines in accord with their class interests as related to liberal and conservative candidates."[31] In part, he was correct that unabashed racial bigotry and public demagoguery are no longer acceptable; however, he was much too optimistic. If the state divides on economic issues, this division often puts the majority of Anglos on one side and the majority of Hispanics and African Americans on the other.[32]

Growth and Changing Demographics

1.6 Outline the demographic and economic changes that have occurred over Texas's history.

As noted earlier, Texas's population has grown at a significant rate for many years. That growth will continue, and the more the state grows, the more its population will change.

Population Growth

Over the past fifty years, the population of Texas has increased much faster than the national average. According to the 2010 census, the state's population was 25,145,561, an increase of approximately 4.3 million people in ten years. This growth rate of 20.6 percent was significantly higher than the national growth rate of 9.7 percent.[33] Texas is the second most populous state, second only to California.[34]

High birth rates explain part of the population increase; migration from other states and from Mexico also have been significant factors. In recent decades, demographers (those who study populations) have described a nationwide shift in population from the Northeast and Midwest to the South and West. For each census from 1940 to 1970, in-migration from other areas accounted for less than 10 percent of Texas's growth. But in-migration jumped to 58.5 percent of the total growth between 1970 and 1980, the period in which demographers identified massive shifts of population from the "Frostbelt" to the "Sunbelt." Between 1980 and 1990, it contributed 34.4 percent to the state's growth.[35] In-migration slowed down somewhat between 1990 and 2000; by 2010, approximately 22 percent of Texas residents reported other states as their place of birth.[36]

Although it is expected to become less significant in the future, this influx of residents from other states already has contributed to the restructuring of Texas's traditional one-party, Democratic political system into a Republican-dominated one. Many new residents came from states with strong Republican Party traditions and brought their party affiliation with them.

Texas also attracts people from other countries. Approximately 2.9 million, or 14 percent, of Texas residents were identified as foreign born in the 2000 census, and this number increased to 3.9 million, or 16.1 percent, in 2010. More than 70 percent of Texans born in other countries come from Latin America. Some 1.2 million foreign-born persons have become U.S. citizens, but approximately 11 percent (or 2.7 million) of all Texas residents are not U.S. citizens, a fact that has several implications.[37]

Citizenship is directly related to political participation; noncitizens, although counted in the census for reapportionment of congressional seats, cannot vote. The overwhelming majority of noncitizens are Hispanic, thus reducing the number of eligible Hispanic voters in relation to their population. Under current federal policy, noncitizens have been denied access to some public social services that are funded in whole or in part by the national government. Needy immigrants are especially affected by such policies; in some instances, the state has found it necessary to use its own funds to provide services.

urbanization
The process by which a predominantly rural society or area becomes urban.

Approximately one-third of Texans older than age 5 speak languages other than English at home, and 42 percent of this group, or some 3.2 million people, report that they do not speak English well.[38] Some states have adopted English as their official language, but there has not been a significant English language movement in Texas. Nonetheless, language is a policy issue for Texas in terms of bilingual education, official documents and publications, translators for court proceedings, and a host of related issues in the workplace.

The increase in population places demands on all levels of government, and many local governments throughout Texas are hard pressed to provide adequate services. Many Texas cities, for example, are running out of landfill space. Environmental laws make it difficult to obtain new licenses for garbage and waste disposal. Without additional dumpsites, new population growth cannot be served. The increased population also has raised questions about the adequacy of water supplies throughout the state with cities, regions, and industries competing intensely for the resources now available. These water battles will intensify in the future.

Streets and highways in urban and suburban areas are clogged with traffic. A survey, released in the fall of 2011 by the Texas Transportation Institute, indicated continued increases in daily commute time in metropolitan areas. Congestion also is increasing during nonpeak traffic hours as well. This means additional gasoline consumption, pollution, and costs in time.[39] Building new roads is one solution, but it is impossible to build enough new roads to keep up with the increasing population demand. Other possible solutions include managing road systems more efficiently, restructuring demand, relieving choke points, diversifying patterns for new housing developments, and increasing use of public transportation.[40]

☐ The Aging Population

According to the 2010 census, Texas ranked forty-ninth among the states in median age, largely as a result of the high birth rates of a growing Hispanic population. The percentage of senior citizens living in Texas, nevertheless, is increasing. In 2010, the median age in Texas was 33.6 years, compared to 37.2 years for the entire country.[41] Approximately 10 percent of the state's population was older than sixty-five in 2010, and that group was expected to increase to 18 percent by 2040.[42] This aging population will place unprecedented demands on the public and private sectors for goods and services, including expanded health care and long-term care. In recent years, increasing state expenditures under the Medicaid program for long-term nursing care have strained the state's budget, resulting in shifts of some funding from other public programs.

Younger Texans will be asked to pay increased taxes to support the needs of the projected aging population. These intergenerational obligations, critical to a stable political system, often are overlooked in debates over funding public services. Younger Texans need older voters to support public education through their tax dollars, and older voters need younger Texans to support health care services. If push comes to shove and civility and respect disappear, the older population has significantly more political clout than do younger voters, who are less informed about politics and who vote at rates much lower than the older population.

☐ Urban Texas

Although Texas was a rural state during the first 100 years of its history, 88 percent of the state's population in 2010 resided in areas classified by the Bureau of the Census as urban (see Figure 1–2).[43] **Urbanization** and suburban sprawl now characterize Texas's settlement patterns, and many urban corridors and suburban areas cross county boundaries, often making it difficult for local governments to address growth problems. Approximately 80 percent of Texans live in 66 counties (58,000 square miles)—the so-called Texas Urban Triangle—anchored by the metropolitan areas of

population density
Number of persons residing within a square mile.

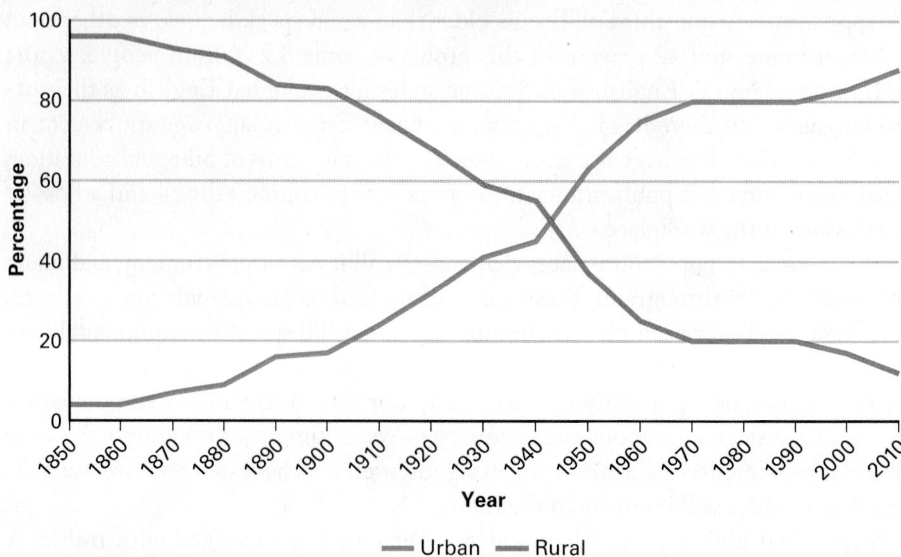

FIGURE 1–2 URBAN-RURAL POPULATION OF TEXAS, 1850–2010

Texas's population has become increasingly urban, as this graph dramatically illustrates. Almost 90 percent of Texans now live in urban areas.

Sources: U.S. Census Bureau, *U.S. Censuses, 1850–2000*; United States Department of Agriculture, Economic Research Service, "State Fact Sheets: Texas," data updated January 17, 2012.

Dallas–Fort Worth, Houston, San Antonio, and Austin. For the foreseeable future, three-fourths of the state's population growth will occur in this area.

The dramatic growth of Texas's largest cities is shown in Figure 1–3. From 1960 to 2010, the populations of Houston, San Antonio, El Paso, and Laredo more than doubled. Dallas increased by 76 percent. Arlington had a population of only 44,775 in 1960; in 2010, its population was 365,438, an increase of more than 700 percent. During this fifty-year period, Austin's population increased from 186,545 to 790,390, and the Austin–Round Rock area has been one of the fastest growing metropolitan areas in the nation.[44] (See *Talking Texas: The Texas Urban Triangle.*)

Three of the ten largest cities in the United States—Houston, San Antonio, and Dallas—are in Texas, and, like urban areas throughout the country, Texas's largest cities increasingly are home to minority and lower-income residents. This trend results from higher birth rates among minority populations, urban migration patterns, and what is often referred to as "white flight" from the cities to suburban areas. Minority groups now account for the majority of the population in eight of Texas's ten largest cities (Houston, San Antonio, Dallas, Fort Worth, El Paso, Arlington, Corpus Christi, and Laredo). These minority residents include Hispanics, African Americans, and Asian Americans—groups that do not always constitute cohesive interest blocs. As minority growth continues, there will be areas of potential conflict among these groups.

Population density refers to the number of people per square mile in a specific political jurisdiction, and it provides another measure of urbanization. As people crowd into smaller areas, living in closer proximity to one another, problems are inevitable. Noise, land use, property maintenance, traffic patterns, and numerous other issues must be addressed.

Marked differences exist in the population density of Texas's 254 counties. Loving County in West Texas has a population of about 82 living in an area of 669 square miles. The most populous county is Harris County (Houston), with more than 4.1 million people living within 1,703 square miles.[45] Clearly, the problems and issues that Loving County faces are significantly different from those that Harris County faces, but both counties have to function with the same form of government created by the state's constitution of 1876.

Texas politics often have divided along urban-rural lines, creating conflict, a trend compounded by suburban areas of the state taking on more importance. Redistricting battles and a host of other public policy issues are evidence of that. Until relatively

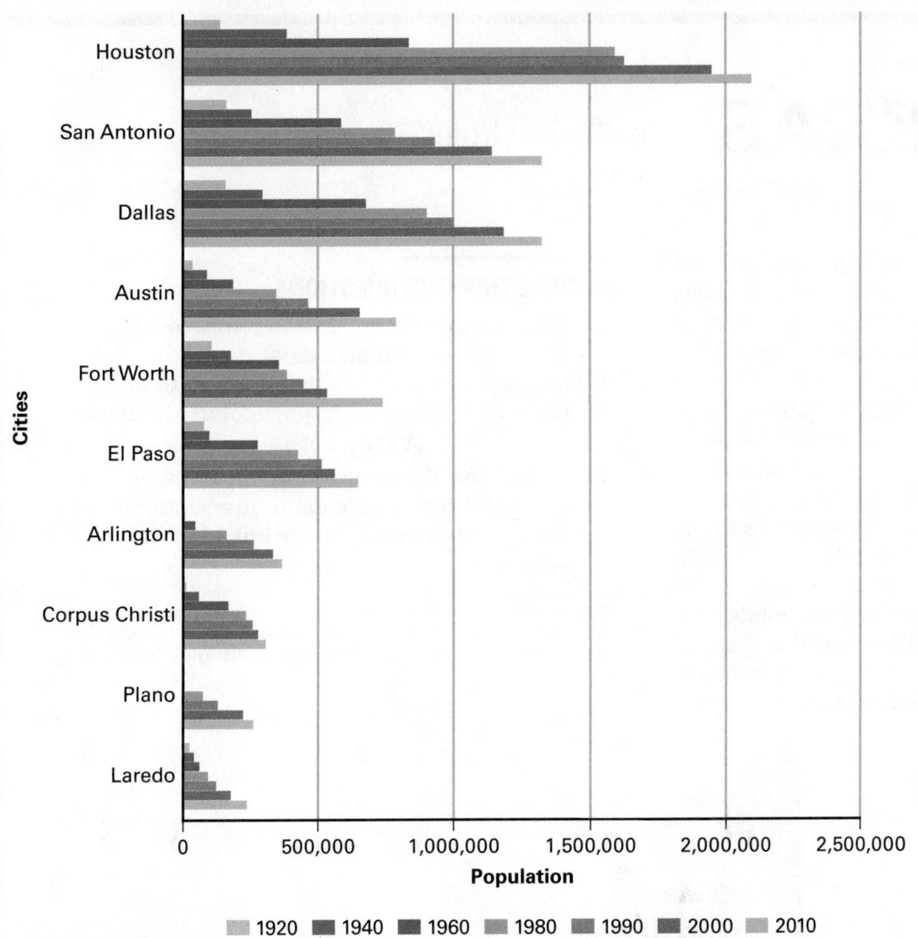

FIGURE 1–3 TEN LARGEST TEXAS CITIES, 1920–2010

A strong indication of the urbanization of Texas is the growth of its ten largest cities. Three of the ten largest cities in the United States—Houston, San Antonio, and Dallas—are in Texas.

Sources: U.S. Censuses, 1920–2010.

recently, the Texas legislature was dominated by rural lawmakers, many of whom often were insensitive to urban needs. Now, suburban legislators with a different constituency base and interests often pursue policies in conflict with both the central city and rural legislators. Moreover, many of urban Texas's problems are aggravated by constitutional restrictions written when Texas was still a rural state.

☐ Wealth and Income Distribution

There is a wide disparity in the distribution of income and wealth across the state. In 2010, the median household income was $48,615 and the median family income was $56,575, both below national income levels (see Table 1–1). Approximately 25 percent of Texas households reported incomes less than $25,000 per year. By contrast, 31.5 percent of Texas households reported incomes in excess of $75,000.

Income disparities are evident among the different regions of the state, ethnic groups, and racial minorities. The median household income for Collin County, north of Dallas, was $80,504 in 2010, and only 6.9 percent of the population fell below the poverty line. In sharp contrast, the median household income for Hidalgo County on the border with Mexico was $31,879, with 34.4 percent of the population falling below the poverty level.[46]

On all measures of income, Hispanics and African Americans fall significantly below the Anglo and Asian American populations. More than one-third of Texas's Hispanic and African American households recently reported incomes below $25,000,

1.1

1.2

1.3

1.4

1.5

1.6

Talking ★ TEXAS The Texas Urban Triangle

About 80 percent of the state's population lives within or near a triangular area of sixty-six counties (often referred to as the Texas Urban Triangle) formed by linking the metropolitan areas of Dallas–Fort Worth, Houston, and San Antonio. Population from the core cities is expected to expand into neighboring counties. Most of the state's population growth between 2000 and 2010 occurred in this area, which dominates the state's economy and is projected to play an even greater role in the future. The area has major research and educational institutions, investment capital, an ample supply of low-cost labor, available energy, a pro-business tax structure, affordable housing, medical facilities, cultural venues, and other amenities. Each of the metropolitan areas has its own distinct characteristics, but their economies will become increasingly integrated and interdependent.[a]

CRITICAL THINKING QUESTIONS

1. Will Texas ever be able to improve its highway system and meet its other infrastructure needs fast enough to keep pace with its growth, particularly in urban areas? Why or why not?
2. Would the Texas economy be on safer ground if the state's major metropolitan areas were not so closely linked? Why or why not?

[a]Federal Reserve Bank of Texas, "Houston Business—A Perspective on the Houston Economy," April 2004; and James P. Gaines, "Looming Boom: Texas Through 2030," *Tierra Grande*, January 2008 (published by the Real Estate Center at Texas A&M University).

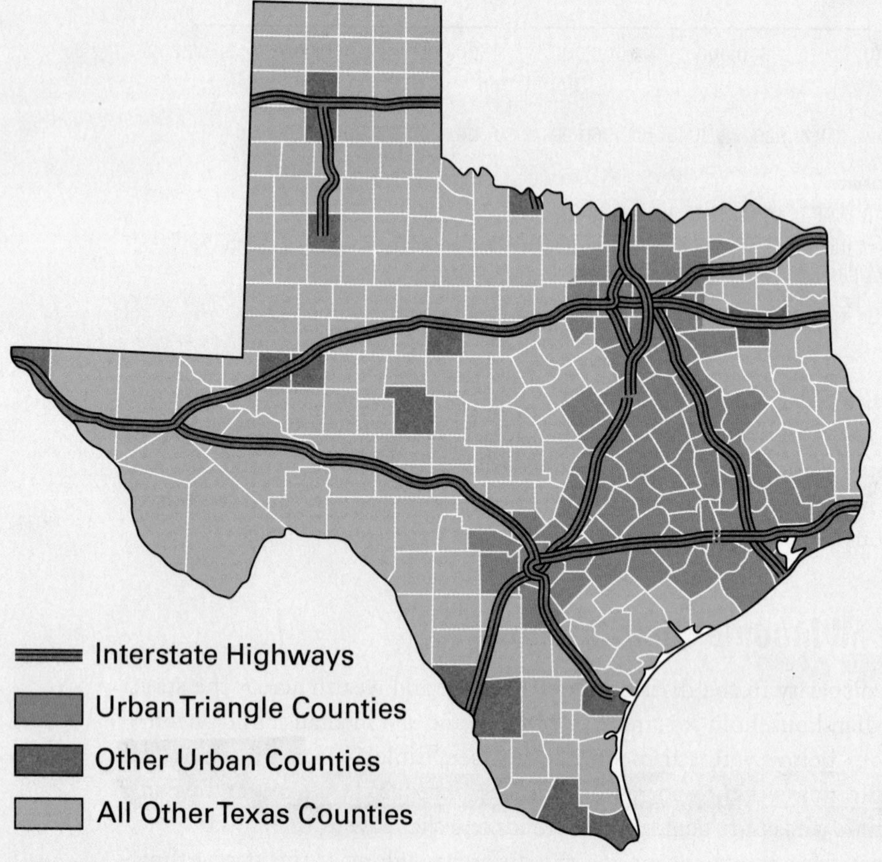

THE TEXAS URBAN TRIANGLE

Most Texans live within or near the Texas Urban Triangle, the shaded area shown here. Based on current population estimates, most of the state's future population growth will occur in this area.

Source: Connor, Karen J.; Sabato, Larry J.; Yanus, Alexandra, B.; Gibson, L. Tucker J.; Robison, Clay, American Government: Roots and Reform, 2011 Texas Edition, 6th Ed., © 2011. Reprinted and Electronically reproduced by permission of Pearson Education, Inc., Upper Saddle River, New Jersey.

TABLE 1–1 U.S. AND TEXAS INCOME FIGURES, 2010

	UNITED STATES	TEXAS				
	All Persons	All Persons	Anglos	Hispanics	African American	Asian American
Median Income						
Household	$50,046	$48,615	$59,772	$37,087	$35,640	$63,947
Families	60,609	56,575	73,873	38,712	42,387	76,126
Per Capita Income	26,059	23,863	33,544	13,910	17,902	27,549
Percentage of Persons below Poverty Level	15.3%	17.9%	9.3%	26.8%	24.8%	12.6%

SOURCE: U.S Census Bureau, *2010 American Community Survey.*

compared to 18 percent of Anglo households and a similar proportion of Asian American households. By contrast, 41 percent of Anglo households, but only 18.6 percent of Hispanic and 19.5 percent of African American households reported incomes of more than $75,000.[47]

Many Texans live in severe poverty. Some of the nation's poorest counties are in Texas. These are border counties (Cameron, Dimmit, Hidalgo, Maverick, Starr, Willacy, Zapata, and Zavala) with large Hispanic populations and unemployment rates that are more than twice the state average. The per capita income (total state income divided by the population) for Texas was $23,863 in 2010. For the Anglo population, it was significantly higher, $33,544, but for African Americans, the figure was $17,902, and for Hispanics, $13,910.

In 2010, the poverty level guidelines used in Texas to establish eligibility for many federal and state assistance programs were $22,050 for a family of four and $10,830 for one person. According to the U.S. Bureau of the Census, 17.9 percent of the state's population, or 4.4 million people, fell below the poverty level. Nationally, 15.3 percent, or 46 million persons, fell below the poverty level in 2010.[48] The impact of poverty disproportionately affects children, particularly those living in a one-parent household, and those who are Hispanic or African American. In the eight counties mentioned earlier, some 30 percent or more of the population fell below the poverty level in 2010, with 40 percent or more of all children living in families below the poverty line.[49] Many of these families do not have adequate housing or health care and depend on food stamps or charities for food. Some 25 percent of Texans do not have health insurance, including some individuals who can afford it but choose not to purchase coverage.

At the other end of the economic scale, a relatively small number of Texans are super wealthy, including those on the annual *Forbes* 400 list of the richest Americans. Forty-three Texans made the list in 2010, with a reported net worth ranging from $1.1 billion to $20.9 billion apiece.[50] The vast majority of Texans, however, have incomes or assets that are nowhere near those of this select group.

Although the state's economic growth over the past decade has reduced poverty somewhat, scholars who study demographic trends fear that poverty is likely to worsen in Texas if several policy issues are not addressed. Without significant changes in educational levels and expanded economic opportunities, it is possible that approximately 20 percent of the state's households will fall below the poverty level by 2030, and income disparity will be especially problematic for minorities.[51]

Financial resources can be translated into political power and influence through campaign contributions; funding one's own campaign for public office; access to the mass media; and active support for policy think tanks, interest groups, and lobbying activity. Wealth is not the only dimension of political power, but some Texans obviously have the potential for much greater clout than others.

THIS AIN'T LUXURY

A young boy closes the door to his family's outhouse in Los Fresnos, Texas in 2009. The boy's family lives in a home in the colonia, which does not have running water or proper sewage. There are some 1,200 colonias or settlements along the Texas-Mexico border with sub-standard housing and little or no access to running water, sewer lines, or paved roads. The state has allocated funds for improvements, but much more needs to be done.

☐ Education and Literacy

Public education has been a dominant issue in state politics for many years. Litigation has forced the legislature to struggle with changes in the funding of public schools, and education will be a primary factor in determining whether Texas can successfully compete in the global economy.

Over the next decade, a large proportion of the new jobs created in Texas will be in service industries. Most of these jobs will require increased reading, writing, and math skills, and high-school dropouts will find fewer and fewer opportunities for decent paying jobs. Across the nation, millions of low-skilled jobs have been outsourced to other countries, and most of the higher paying jobs now require a college education. Texas faces a crisis in public education, largely because it has not been adequately and equitably funded, and the state's ability to resolve it will directly affect the financial well-being of many Texans.

According to the *2010 American Community Survey,* 80.7 percent of Texans age 25 and older had completed high school, and 25.9 percent had completed college (see Table 1–2). Educational attainment has improved since 1990 with positive changes reported for all racial or ethnic groups in the state.[52] However, wide disparities in the educational levels of the three major ethnic-racial groups still exist, and some of these differences are directly linked to the number of residents born in other countries.

In 2010, some 92 percent of the Anglo population reported that they had completed high school, and more than one-third had college degrees. By contrast, 59.6 percent of the Hispanic population had high school diplomas, and only 11.6 percent reported having college degrees. Some 86 percent of African Americans graduated from high school, with 19.6 percent indicating they had college degrees. Particularly noteworthy is the Asian population, which reported that 51.8 percent of those age 25 and older had college degrees. Education not only helps determine a person's employment and income potential, but it also affects his or her participation in politics. Individuals with high educational levels are much more likely to believe they can be informed about politics, participate in the political process, and influence the actions of policymakers.

TABLE 1–2 EDUCATIONAL ATTAINMENT BY RACE AND ETHNICITY, 2010

	UNITED STATES		TEXAS	
	High School Diploma	College Degree	High School Diploma	College Degree
Anglo*	90.7%	31.4%	92.0%	34.1%
Hispanic	62.2	13.0	59.6	11.6
African American	81.9	17.9	86.1	19.6
Asian	85.4	49.9	85.8	51.8
All Persons	85.6	28.2	80.7	25.9

*White, not of Hispanic origin.

SOURCE: U.S. Census Bureau, *2010 American Community Survey.*

☐ The Size and Geographic Diversity of Texas

Texas is a big state. Covering 261,231 square miles, it is second only to Alaska in landmass. Although Texans appear to have adjusted to long distances—they do not seem to mind driving fifty miles for a night out—visitors from out-of-state often are overwhelmed by Texas's size and diversity. The distance from Texarkana in Northeast Texas to El Paso in far West Texas is about 800 miles, which makes a person living in Texarkana closer to Chicago than to El Paso. Brownsville in South Texas is closer to Mexico City than it is to Texline in the Texas Panhandle.[53]

Many would argue that perceptions of the state's size have helped shape political attitudes and concepts, and size obviously has affected state policy. Roads and highways, for example, historically have received a significant—and, some would argue, a disproportionate—share of the state's budget. Economic development in such a large and diverse state required a commitment to highway construction because roads were regarded as essential to the development of an integrated economy. Size also contributes to the economic diversity of the state. Some parts of the state experience economic growth, whereas other areas may experience economic downturns.

One scholar argued that the great distances in Texas were politically important because they made it difficult for a politician to develop a statewide following, such as could be cultivated in many southern states. Size works against the organizational strategies and continued negotiations necessary to sustain a statewide political machine similar to those that developed in Virginia and Louisiana in the 1920s and 1930s. Although there have been regional or local political machines, such as the now-defunct Parr machine, which controlled politics for many years in parts of South Texas, none of these was extended statewide.[54]

Size also contributes to the high costs of political campaigns. Candidates in statewide campaigns spend millions of dollars to communicate with and mobilize Texas voters. The candidates in the 2002 gubernatorial race alone spent more than $100 million, and the figure for all gubernatorial candidates in 2010 exceeded $82 million. Texas has more than twenty separate media markets, and the cost of communicating with the voters on a statewide basis continues to increase despite new technologies.

If Texas were still an independent nation, it would be the thirty-seventh largest in geographic area. The state has one-twelfth of the total coastline of the United States. It has 23 million acres of forest and more than 4,790 square miles of lakes and streams. A traveler driving across Texas is struck by the diversity in topography, climate, and vegetation. The state's "landforms range from offshore bars and barrier beaches to formidable mountains, from rugged canyons, gorges, and badlands to totally flat plains."[55] The western part of the state is dry and semiarid, whereas the east is humid and covered with vegetation. South Texas often enjoys a semitropical winter, whereas North Texas experiences cold winters with snowfall.[56] The growing seasons in the south are virtually year-round; those in the north are approximately 180 days.

Geography shaped historical migration and land use in Texas. Although we can partially compensate for climate and geography through modern technology, geography continues to shape the economy and population patterns of the state.

☐ The Economy of Texas

Politics, government, and economics are inextricably linked. An economy that is robust and expanding provides far more options to government policymakers than an economy in recession. A healthy tax base is dependent on an expanding economy. When the economy goes through periods of recession, state and local governments confront the harsh reality of increasing taxes or cutting back on public services, usually at a time when more people are in need of governmental assistance.

Historically, the health of the Texas economy had been linked to oil and natural gas, but by the last decade of the twentieth century, the state's economy experienced significant diversification. In 1981, for example, 27 percent of the state's economy was tied to energy-related industries. The decade started with rapid increases in the world price of oil, and an economic boom occurred throughout the financial, construction, and manufacturing sectors of the state's economy.[57] Changes in international fuel markets, particularly a big drop in oil prices in the 1980s, staggered the Texas petroleum industry. Natural gas prices also fell. Thousands of energy-related jobs were lost, and many exploration and drilling companies went out of business. Cheaper foreign oil replaced the demand for Texas oil, and a decline in recoverable reserves further reduced the importance of fossil fuels to the state's commerce. Within two decades, oil- and gas-related industries were contributing only 10 percent to the Texas economy; in 2009, the figure was slightly higher than 11 percent.[58]

The drop in oil prices was not the only factor that put the Texas economy into a tailspin in the 1980s. Mexico's peso also experienced a precipitous decline, which had a negative impact on the economies of border cities and counties. In 1983, a harsh freeze in South Texas and a severe drought in West Texas had serious adverse effects on the agricultural sector. There also was a worldwide slump in the electronics industry. These events hurt the construction and real estate sectors of the economy and, in turn, manufacturing and retail trade. For sixteen straight months in 1986 and 1987, the state's employment rate dropped, with a loss of an estimated 233,000 jobs.[59]

These reversals had disastrous effects on Texas's banks and savings and loan institutions. "In 1987 and 1988, more Texas financial institutions failed than at any other time since the Great Depression," the state comptroller's office reported. And the pattern of bank failures continued through 1990. The federal government developed a plan to bail out institutions that were covered by the federal deposit insurance program, and the state's banking system ultimately was restructured. But as the magnitude of the problem became clearer, there was a bitter debate over its causes, including the deregulation of the savings and loan and banking industries, inadequate government scrutiny of banking practices, a frenzy of speculation with questionable or unsecured loans, and outright fraud and malfeasance.[60]

State and local governments consequently suffered declines in revenues. With falling property values, local governments that depended on property taxes were particularly vulnerable. The legislature convened a special session in 1986 to pass an $875 million tax bill and cut the state budget by about $580 million in an attempt to "patch up" the widening holes in projected state revenues. In 1987, the legislature, mandated by the constitution to a "pay as you go" system of government and denied the option of deficit financing, enacted a $5.6 billion tax bill, including an increase in the sales tax, a regressive tax that most adversely affects low-income people.[61]

As a result of these changes, except for a few years, the Texas economy outpaced the overall national economy from 1990 through 2010. One significant downturn during that period was the recession of 2001, which lasted in Texas until the summer of 2003. Unlike previous recessions linked to energy production, this recession reflected structural changes in the Texas economy, including the growth of jobs in the high-tech industry. A "bust" in the high-tech industry nationwide cost the Texas economy an estimated 100,000 lost jobs. In addition, the recessionary pressures were compounded by the terrorist attacks of September 11, 2001, which adversely affected the state's transportation industry.[62]

Several good years followed, but the "Great Recession" that broke across the nation in the summer of 2008 arrived in Texas by the late winter of 2009.[63] The worldwide crisis in financial and credit markets was linked to subprime lending, accounting scandals, overextended credit to consumers, dramatic declines in manufacturing and trade, and a loss of confidence on the part of the consumer. With massive federal intervention, a concerted effort was made to stop the slide, and by early 2012, the Texas economy had begun recovering. The recession was partly to blame for billions of dollars in state budget cuts in 2011, but state revenue soon began rebounding. The state's unemployment rate, which had fared better than the national unemployment rate, fell.

In 2010, Texas had a gross state product of $1.2 trillion in current dollars, or $1.1 trillion "chained" to the value of 2005 dollars to control for the effects of inflation. By comparison, the gross domestic product of the United States in 2010 was $13.1 trillion in 2005 dollars or $14.5 trillion in current dollars.[64] The Texas economy was the second largest among the states, following California. If Texas were a nation, its economy would rank fifteenth in the world.[65]

Several lessons can be drawn from the state's recent economic history. The health of the state's economy for much of the twentieth century was directly tied to the price of oil. Even during national recessions, high oil prices served to insulate Texas from their effects. In effect, the Texas economy grew or contracted in relationship to the price of oil.

Initiatives to diversify the state's economy, which began some fifty years ago, have transformed the economy's basic structure. With economic diversification paralleling the structure of the national economy, Texas is in a much stronger position to minimize the impact of economic downturns. One or more core sectors of the economy may be in recession whereas other sectors experience growth. These core economic sectors are not distributed uniformly across the state, and growth and recession are not experienced in the state's varied economic regions in the same way. Only certain areas of the state, for example, will suffer the brunt of low beef or other agricultural commodity prices.

Economic diversification has been directly tied to high-tech industries, including companies that produce semiconductors, microprocessors, computer hardware, software, telecommunications devices, fiber optics, aerospace guidance systems, and medical instruments.[66] High tech also includes biotechnology industries that produce new medicines, vaccines, and genetic engineering of plants and animals. State and local governments developed aggressive recruitment programs, including tax breaks, for high-tech companies.

Texas's restructured economy is heavily oriented to exports with approximately 35 percent of the state's employment "in industries that can be classified as basic, or exportable."[67] Approximately 26,650 companies exported goods from their Texas locations in 2009.[68] Just as we can speak of the **globalization of the economy** nationally, a similar pattern has developed in Texas. In 1999, Texas exported some $83 billion in merchandise to other countries. By 2011, exports totaled $281 billion with approximately 31 percent ($87 billion) going to Mexico.[69] The North American Free Trade Agreement (NAFTA) among the United States, Mexico, and Canada has produced changes in the economic relationships among these countries with more economic interdependence anticipated. It also is critical to recognize the relationship of the Texas economy to the Mexican economy. In earlier periods, economic declines in Mexico were felt primarily in the counties along the Mexican border. But NAFTA and the *maquiladora* program, a cooperative manufacturing program between the United States and Mexico, have linked most areas of the state to the Mexican economy.

globalization of the economy
Increased interdependence in trade, manufacturing, and commerce between the United States and other countries.

□ Economic Regions of Texas

The economic diversity of Texas can be described in terms of twelve distinct economic regions (see Figure 1–4).[70] One region may be undergoing rapid economic growth, whereas another may be experiencing stagnation. Regions vary in population, economic infrastructure, economic performance, and rates of growth. One region's economy may be heavily dependent on only two or three industries. If one or two of those industries suffer an economic downturn, that region may have a more severe recession than the state overall. There also are marked differences in personal income, poverty levels, and geography among the areas. All regions, though, share in one economic sector—significant levels of government employment.

The economic factors at play in a region help shape the priorities of local governments and the priorities of state legislators elected from that area. The following descriptions of three of the twelve regions offer a sampling of the economic differences encountered throughout Texas.

The *High Plains Region* is made up of forty-one counties and includes Amarillo, Lubbock, the XIT Ranch, and Palo Duro Canyon. Agricultural production, whose major source of water is the Ogallala Aquifer, is a dominant industry. Related businesses include agricultural services; food processing; and the manufacturing of feed, fertilizers, and farm machinery and equipment. Oil and gas production is still an important component of the region's economy, but employment in the energy industry has declined from earlier periods.[71]

The *South Texas Border Region* encompasses twenty-eight counties, including the cities of Corpus Christi, Brownsville, Laredo, Del Rio, McAllen, Eagle Pass, and Harlingen. Eight of its counties share their borders with Mexico, and a significant amount of commerce ($125 billion in 2007) flows through border crossings within these counties. The region has five seaports, including the Port of Corpus Christi, one of the nation's largest ports in total cargo tonnage. This area is identified with agriculture, including cattle, cotton, sugarcane, citrus, table produce, and food processing. Oil and gas extraction and processing also are key parts of the area's economy. In recent years, this area has received a significant boost from the construction of manufacturing

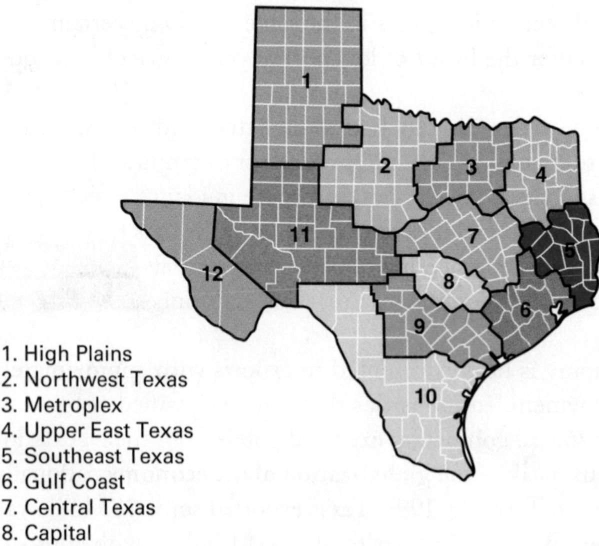

FIGURE 1–4 ECONOMIC REGIONS OF TEXAS, 2012

This map shows the twelve economic regions of Texas, which vary markedly in terms of population, economic infrastructure, economic performance, and rates of growth.

Source: Texas Comptroller of Public Accounts.

plants in Mexico and increased trading prompted by NAFTA. Health care also has been a growth industry in this area. More than 80 percent of the population of this region is Hispanic. The region has been growing at a faster rate than the state as a whole, but its residents' educational attainment and income are below the state average.[72]

The *Upper East Texas Region*, which includes twenty-one counties, is located in the northeast corner of the state. It includes the cities of Longview, Texarkana, and Tyler (the "City of Roses"). Since 2000, its growth rate has been significantly lower than the statewide average. The average population of this region is older than the state's average and is predominately Anglo. Agriculture—including horticulture, timber, and the dairy industry—is a key component of the region's economy, as are food processing and food distribution. Transportation-related industries—including the manufacture of railroad rolling stock and motor vehicle bodies—have a strong presence. So do distribution, warehousing, and storage. Oil and gas production also can be found in this region.[73]

Review the Chapter

Challenges of the Twenty-First Century

1.1 Summarize the basic challenges facing Texas as it moves through the twenty-first century, p. 5.

With an ever-increasing population that is now highly urban, Texas confronts a range of economic, social, and political issues that directly shape the state's political system and political leadership. Some of these major issues include transportation and other infrastructure, air and water pollution, education, health care, and an outdated and regressive tax system.

The Myths of Texas's Political Culture

1.2 Explain some of the myths of Texas's political culture, p. 6.

Political myths are common views that people have of their historical experiences, and Texans have a distinguishable myth tradition rooted in their state's period of independence, its large landmass, and its rugged frontier experience. Some of these myths, including the cowboy and the Texas Ranger, continue to be popular reminders of the state's independence and rugged individualism. The prevailing Texas myths were rooted in the earlier Anglo history of the state, however, and some critics argue they neglect the contributions of Native Americans, African Americans, and Hispanics. Only time will tell if these myths are redefined in terms of the increasing minority populations of the state.

The Political Culture of Texas

1.3 Compare and contrast the political subcultures of Texas, p. 9.

The conservative politics of Texas are rooted in its individualistic and traditionalistic subcultures stemming from the historical migration and settlement patterns of the state. The moralistic subculture has had limited impact on Texans' value system. The beliefs Texans hold about the role of governments, what they should do or not do, who should govern, expectations of leaders, and what constitutes good public policy are rooted in these cultural patterns that vary across the state.

Historical Origins of Political Subcultures

1.4 Trace the historical origins of political subcultures and identify the subcultures that have most influenced Texas's political culture, p. 10.

Texas was a vast, mostly unpopulated land prior to independence and statehood. The distinct settlement patterns of different populations provide insight into the development of the regional patterns of the state's political culture. Anglo immigrants who arrived from the United States brought with them the individualistic and traditionalistic subcultures, and the Spanish subculture was traditionalistic. As settlers spread out over the state, they carried with them the core values of their political cultures, producing a mosaic of local variations that have blended into a dominant conservative political culture.

The People of Texas

1.5 Describe the basic history and characteristics of the major population groups in Texas, p. 11.

Demographic patterns serve to provide an understanding of the development of the state's contemporary political culture. Native Americans, who now comprise a very small part of the state's population, were the prevailing population prior to the period of European conquest of Texas, but their influence on Texas contemporary politics is negligible. African Americans arrived in Texas as slaves; although slavery ended with the Civil War, they experienced a long history of political and economic discrimination. In the post–Civil Rights era, African Americans have played a significant role in state politics and in regions of the state where they reside in greatest numbers. Hispanics were part of Texas's population at independence but were marginalized through most of the nineteenth and twentieth centuries. With the dramatic increase of the Hispanic population, however, they have played an ever-increasing role in the state's politics over the past four decades. Throughout the formative period and through the modern era, Texas was dominated by highly diverse Anglo national origin groups. With expanded immigration from the other states and European countries, distinguishable patterns of settlements spread across the state. Politics and public policy were shaped primarily by these conservative populations. Asian Americans, another highly diverse group, arrived late as a significant component of the state's population. They tend to locate in urban areas, where they are showing some evidence of political influence.

Growth and Changing Demographics

1.6 Outline the demographic and economic changes that have occurred over Texas's history, p. 16.

The dominant demographic themes that run through the state's modern history center on population growth, urbanization, inequities in wealth and income, disparities in education and literacy, and geographical diversity. The state's population now exceeds 25 million and is projected to continue to increase at a fast clip during the next decades. The state is now 88 percent urban with most of the state's population concentrated in the sixty-six counties designated as the Texas Urban Triangle.

Despite the size of the state's economy and the impressive gains in personal income and wealth for many, there are significant disparities among ethnic and racial groups. African Americans and Hispanics are more likely to have lower incomes than Anglos or Asian Americans. And, Asian Americans are among the most educated of the state's residents. The disparities in education have spawned an extensive debate about the state's educational system and its ability to sustain future economic growth that is dependent on a highly educated population.

The gross domestic product of Texas exceeds one trillion dollars. With some exceptions during recessionary periods, the state's economy has outstripped the national economy and the economies of most other states in its rate of growth. No longer heavily reliant on oil and gas, the state's economy is highly diversified, and a substantial part of its growth is based on exports to other countries.

Learn the Terms

Study and **Review** the Flashcards

regressive tax, p. 5
economic diversification, p. 6
political myths, p. 6
republic, p. 6
individualism, p. 7
political culture, p. 9
individualistic subculture, p. 9
moralistic subculture, p. 9
traditionalistic subculture, p. 10
urbanization, p. 17
population density, p. 18
globalization of the economy, p. 25

Test Yourself

Study and **Review** the Practice Tests

1. A regressive tax system means that

a. everyone pays the same percentage of his or her income in taxes.
b. low-income and middle-income citizens pay a higher proportion of their income in taxes than the wealthy.
c. wealthy citizens pay a higher proportion of their income in taxes than low-income and middle-income citizens.
d. the tax system exempts low-income citizens from paying any taxes.
e. the state has an income tax but not a sales tax.

2. What is central to the cowboy myth in Texas?

a. the Battle of the Alamo
b. strong community values
c. strong government
d. multiethnic cooperation
e. the notion of rugged individualism

3. What is one of the alternative non-Anglo experiences being incorporated into Texas culture?

a. Stephen F. Austin's birthday
b. the massacre at Goliad
c. secession from the Union
d. Juneteenth
e. Martin Luther King Jr.'s assassination

4. What is one of the features of the individualistic subculture?

a. Politics promotes the general welfare.
b. Elites tend to run politics for their own interests.
c. Government intervention in private activities should be kept to a minimum.
d. Nonpartisanship is strong.
e. Politics is the responsibility of every individual.

5. One of the features of the moralistic subculture is that

a. politics is a high calling.
b. political parties have only minimal importance.
c. politics is perceived as a dirty business.
d. government should be limited.
e. citizens tolerate political corruption as part of human nature.

6. One of the features of the traditionalistic subculture is that

a. political parties are controlled by elites.
b. the primary goal of political elites is to serve the general public.
c. politics is the responsibility of every individual.
d. politics is seen as a dirty business.
e. politics is seen as a high calling.

7. Which of the following subculture combinations has most influenced Texas history and politics?

a. individualistic and moralistic
b. individualistic and Puritan
c. moralistic and traditionalistic
d. individualistic and traditionalistic
e. entrepreneurial and congregational

8. It is projected that by 2030 a majority of the state's population will be

a. Native American.
b. Hispanic.
c. African American.
d. Anglo.
e. Asian American.

9. Which of the following statements concerning the population groups in Texas is true?

a. Texas is home to more than twenty different Native American groups.
b. During the period of the Republic, Hispanics comprised a majority of the population.
c. At the time of the Civil War, African Americans outnumbered Hispanics in the state.
d. In the 2010 census, Anglos still comprised a majority of the state population.
e. The largest concentration of Asian Americans in Texas is in the state capital.

10. One of the explanations for the conservative political culture in Texas is the

a. merging of Hispanic traditions and Puritan moralism.
b. expansion of Hispanics from South Texas across the entire state.
c. geographic dispersal of the African American population.
d. impact of German, Polish, and Czech influences in the state.
e. merging of upper South and lower South Anglo subcultures.

11. Which of the following is true about population growth in Texas?

a. Texas is the most populous state in the nation.
b. As much as one-fourth of the state's population is foreign born.
c. In-migration from other states helped transform Texas into a Republican-dominated state.
d. Increased population has not yet had a significant effect on water supplies.
e. National population shifts have moved from the Sunbelt to the Frostbelt.

12. The Texas Urban Triangle is composed of the area anchored by

a. Dallas, Fort Worth, and Austin.
b. Dallas–Fort Worth, El Paso, and Houston.
c. El Paso, San Antonio, and Houston.
d. Houston, San Antonio, and Austin.
e. Dallas–Fort Worth, Houston, and San Antonio.

13. Which of the following statements concerning wealth and income distribution is true?

a. The poorest counties in the state are in East Texas.
b. The poverty rate in Texas is higher than the national average.
c. Hispanics earn a higher per capita income than African Americans.
d. There is no correlation between ethnicity and poverty.
e. Texas is home to only four billionaires.

14. All of the following are true about Texas's geography EXCEPT that

a. Texas is second only to California in landmass.
b. Texarkana is closer to Chicago than to El Paso.
c. The state's size has given transportation disproportionate weight in the state budget.
d. The state's size makes it difficult to win statewide races.
e. The state's size contributes to expensive campaigns.

15. What was one of the factors that sent Texas's economy into recession in the 1980s?

a. a large rise in oil prices
b. a "bust" in the high-tech industry
c. increasing diversity of the state's economy
d. a large decline in the Mexican peso
e. overdrilling in the Gulf of Mexico

Explore Further

Buenger, Walter L., and Robert A. Calvert, eds., *Texas Through Time: Evolving Interpretations.* College Station: Texas A&M University Press, 1991. Analyzes Texas myths with an emphasis on potential distortions of the state's history and the need to use critical historical analysis in providing a more accurate assessment of Texans and their historical experiences.

Elazar, Daniel, *The American Mosaic: The Impact of Space, Time, and Culture on American Politics.* Boulder, CO: Westview, 1994. Supplies a geographical and historical perspective on the development of the political cultures of the United States.

Erickson, Robert S., Gerald Wright, and John P. McIver, *Statehouse Democracy: Public Opinion and Policy in the American States.* New York: Cambridge University Press, 1993. Uses ideology to establish the relationship between public opinion and politics across the fifty states; the authors demonstrate the utility of political subcultures to explain the conservative politics of Texas.

Fehrenbach, T. R., *Lone Star: A History of Texas and the Texans.* New York: Collier, 1968. Provides one of the most comprehensive histories of Texas; a must read for the serious student of Texas history and politics.

Hill, Kim Quaile, *Democracy in the Fifty States.* Lincoln: University of Nebraska Press, 1994. A provocative "comprehensive, empirical theory-based analysis of the extent in which the governments of the fifty states can be judged to be democratic," emphasizing the policy consequences of the states' political cultures.

Jillson, Cal, *Lone Star Tarnished: A Critical Look at Texas Politics and Public Policy.* New York: Routledge, 2012. Takes a critical view of Texas politics, raising questions regarding public policy decisions.

Jordan, Terry G., with John L. Bean Jr. and William M. Homes, *Texas: A Geography.* Boulder, CO: Westview, 1984. Introduces the physical, demographic, economic, and cultural geography of Texas.

Murdock, Steve H., Steve White, Md. Nazrul, Beverly Pecotte, Xuihong You, and Jennifer Balkan, *The New Texas Challenge: Population Change and the Future of Texas.* College Station: Texas A&M University Press, 2003. Uses extensive demographics data to point to future problems for Texas if significant educational and economic disparities among racial, ethnic, and economic groups are not addressed; written by a former state demographer and his colleagues.

O'Conner, Robert F., ed., *Texas Myths.* College Station: Texas A&M University Press, 1986. Uses the general concept of myth to address various aspects of the state's history and political culture through fourteen essays.

Richardson, Rupert, Ernest Wallace, and Adrian N. Anderson, *Texas: The Lone Star State*, 9th ed. Upper Saddle River, NJ: Prentice Hall, 2005. Provides a comprehensive history of Texas.

Listen on MyPoliSciLab

2 The Texas Constitution

Humbly invoking the blessings of Almighty God, the people of the State of Texas do ordain and establish this Constitution.

—**Preamble to the Constitution of Texas 1876**

If men were angels, no government would be necessary. If angels were to govern men, neither external nor internal controls on government would be necessary. In framing a government which is to be administered by men over men, the great difficulty lies in this: you must first enable the government to control the governed; and in the next place oblige it to control itself.

—**James Madison,** *Federalist No. 51*

The year was 1874, and unusual events marked the end of the darkest chapter in Texas history—the Reconstruction era and the military occupation that followed the Civil War. Texans, still smarting from some of the most oppressive laws ever imposed on U.S. citizens, had overwhelmingly voted their governor out of office, but he refused to leave the Capitol and hand over his duties to his elected successor. For several tense days, the city of Austin was divided into two armed camps—those supporting the deposed governor, Edmund J. Davis, and those supporting the man who defeated him at the polls, Richard Coke. Davis finally gave up only after the Texas militia turned against him and marched on the Capitol.

That long-ago period bears little resemblance to modern Texas, but the experience still casts a long shadow over state government. The state constitution, written by Texans at the close of Reconstruction, was designed to put strong restraints on government to guard against future abuses, and most of those restraints remain in place today. The Texas Constitution, adopted in

2.1 Identify the functions of a constitution and place the Texas Constitution in a national comparative context, p. 35.

2.2 Describe the historical influences, similarities, and differences of each of Texas's seven constitutions, p. 36.

2.3 Explain the major features and general principles of the current Texas Constitution, p. 42.

2.4 Outline the weaknesses and criticisms of the current Texas Constitution, particularly as they pertain to how the framers failed to anticipate economic and social changes in the state, p. 44.

2.5 Contrast the ease and frequency of the constitutional amendment process with the difficulty of enacting more fundamental change through the constitutional convention process, p. 47.

THE TEXAS DECLARATION OF INDEPENDENCE, adopted in 1836, is reproduced, in part, on the building of the Texas State Library and Archives Commission in Austin.

1876 and amended many times since, is so restrictive that many scholars and politicians believe it is counterproductive to effective, modern governance. They believe the document, which is bogged down with statutory detail, is a textbook example of what a constitution should not be. State government functions despite its constitutional shackles: an institutionally weak chief executive; an outdated, part-time legislature; a poorly organized judiciary; and dedicated funds that limit the state's budgetary options. But a total rewrite of the constitution has been elusive, thanks to numerous special interests that find security in the present document and from those who hold obsolete public offices in Texas and those who benefit from dedicated funds. Public ignorance and indifference to the problems created by the restrictive constitutional provisions also thwart an overhaul of the document.

It is our position, shared by others who study state governments, that one cannot develop a clear understanding of Texas government or its politics without some familiarity with the Texas Constitution.[1] Constitutions are more than the formal frameworks that define the structure, authority, and responsibilities of governmental institutions. They also reflect fundamental political, economic, and power relationships as determined by the culture, values, and interests of the people who create them and the events of the period in which they were written.[2]

The constitution of Texas is not easy to read, and many of its details may make little sense to casual readers. But a careful study of the document can provide insight into the distribution of power among competing groups and regions within the state. The constitution outlines the powers of and defines the limits imposed on state and local governments. From the perspective of political economy, the constitution also speaks to "the relation of the state to economic activity, including both the extent of direct governmental support for enterprise and the appropriate balance between promotion and regulation of economic development."[3]

Texas has had seven constitutions, and understanding that legacy is critical to understanding contemporary Texas politics and public policy (see Table 2–1). The first constitution was adopted in 1827, when the state was still part of Mexico. The second was drafted when Texas declared its independence from Mexico in 1836 and became a republic. The third was adopted in 1845 when the state joined the Union. The fourth constitution was written when Texas joined the Confederacy in 1861, and the fifth was adopted when the state rejoined the Union in 1866. The sixth constitution was adopted in 1869 to satisfy the Radical Reconstructionists' opposition to the 1866 constitution, and the seventh constitution was adopted in 1876 after the termination of Reconstruction policies.

TABLE 2–1 THE SEVEN TEXAS CONSTITUTIONS

1827: Constitution of Coahuila y Tejas
Adopted in 1827 while Texas was still part of Mexico, this constitution recognized Texas as a Mexican state with Coahuila.
1836: Constitution of the Republic
The constitution of March 16, 1836, declared independence from Mexico and constituted Texas as an independent republic.
1845: Constitution of 1845
Texas was admitted to the Union under this constitution.
1861: Civil War Constitution
After the state seceded from the Union and joined the Confederacy in 1861, Texans adopted this constitution.
1866: Constitution of 1866
This was a short-lived constitution under which Texas sought to be readmitted to the Union after the Civil War and before the Radical Reconstructionists took control of the U.S. Congress.
1869: Reconstruction Constitution
Power was centralized in the state government, and local governments were significantly weakened under this constitution, which reflected the sentiments of Radical Reconstructionists, not of most Texans.
1876: Texas Constitution
Adopted at the end of Reconstruction and amended 474 times since, this is the constitution under which Texas currently functions. Highly restrictive and antigovernment, this constitution places strict limitations on the powers of the governor, the legislature, and other state officials.

Constitutionalism

2.1 Identify the functions of a constitution and place the Texas Constitution in a national comparative context.

constitution
A document that provides for the legal and institutional structure of a political system. It establishes government bodies and defines their powers.

statutory law
A law enacted by a legislative body. Unlike constitutional law, it doesn't require voter approval.

A **constitution** defines the principles of a society and states or suggests the political objectives that society is attempting to achieve. It outlines the specific institutions that the people will use to achieve their objectives, and it defines who can participate in collective decisions and who can hold public office. It also defines the relationship between those people who govern and those who are governed and sets limits on what each group can and cannot do. Because of the stability of the American political system and a general commitment to the rule of law, we often overlook the fact that a constitution also reflects the way a society structures conflict through its institutional arrangements.[4]

Constitutions do not lend themselves to easy reading. The formal, legal language often obscures the general objectives of the document and its relevance to contemporary issues of political power and public policy. Scholars believe, first, that constitutions should be brief and should include general principles rather than specific legislative provisions. In other words, constitutions should provide a basic framework for government and leave the details to be defined in **statutory law**. Second, experts say, constitutions should grant authority to specific institutions, so as to increase the responsiveness and the accountability of individuals elected or appointed to public office. Scholars also believe that constitutions should provide for orderly change but should not be written in such a restrictive fashion that they require continual modifications to meet contemporary needs.[5]

Amended only twenty-seven times since its adoption in 1789, the U.S. Constitution is a concise, 7,000-word document that outlines broad, basic principles of authority and governance. No one would argue that the government of the twenty-first century is comparable to that of the 1790s, yet the flexibility of the U.S. Constitution makes it as relevant now as it was in the eighteenth century. It is often spoken of as "a living constitution" that does not have to be continually amended to meet society's ever-changing needs and conditions. Its reinterpretations by the courts, the Congress, and the president have produced an expansion of powers and responsibilities within the framework of the original language of the document.

By contrast, the Texas Constitution—like those of many other states—is an unwieldy, restrictive document. With more than 87,000 words, it has been on a life-support system—the piecemeal amendment process—for most of its lifetime (see Figure 2–1). It is less a set of basic governmental principles than a compilation of detailed statutory language, often referred to as "constitutional legislation," reflecting the distrust of government that was widespread in Texas when it was written and the fact that the national Constitution says so very little about state government.[6] In effect, it attempts to diffuse political power among many different institutions. As drafted in 1875, it also included restrictions on elections and civil rights that were later invalidated by the U.S. Supreme Court. Those early provisions were efforts to limit the power of minority groups to fully participate in state government.[7]

The historical constitutional experiences of Texas parallel those of many southern states that have had multiple constitutions in the post–Civil War era. The former Confederate states, Texas included, are the only states whose constitutions formally acknowledge the supremacy of the U.S. Constitution, a provision required for readmission to the Union.

unicameral
A single-body legislature.

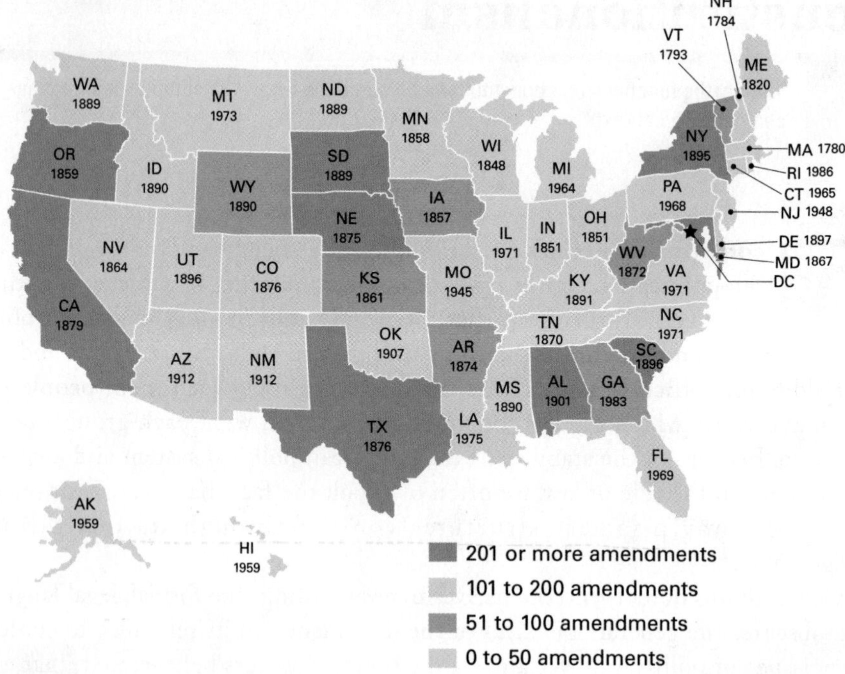

FIGURE 2–1 FREQUENCY OF AMENDMENTS: TEXAS CONSTITUTION COMPARED WITH OTHER STATE CONSTITUTIONS, JANUARY 2011

This map shows the date that each state's current constitution was ratified and also the number of amendments that have been added to the constitution since it was ratified. Texas is one of only nine states that have added more than 200 amendments to its state constitution.

Source: Based on data found in *The Book of the States*, 2011 Edition, vol. 43, Table 1.1 (Lexington, KY: The Council of State Governments, 2011).

The Constitutional Legacy

2.2 Describe the historical influences, similarities, and differences of each of Texas's seven constitutions.

Each of Texas's seven constitutions was written in a distinct historical setting. There are significant differences—as well as similarities—among these documents, and each contributed to the state and local governments that we know today.

☐ The Constitution of Coahuila y Tejas (1827)

Texas was part of Mexico when Mexico secured its independence from Spain in 1821, about the time that Stephen F. Austin began to bring Anglo colonists to the sparsely populated Texas region. In 1824, the new Republic of Mexico adopted a constitution for a federal system of government that recognized Texas (Tejas) as a single state with Coahuila, which adjoined Texas across the Rio Grande. Saltillo, Mexico, was the state capital.

The constitution of *Coahuila y Tejas,* completed in 1827, provided for a **unicameral** congress of twelve deputies, including two from Texas, elected by the people. Most of the members of congress were from the more populous and Spanish-speaking Coahuila, and the state's laws were published in Spanish, which few Anglo colonists in Texas understood. The executive department included a governor and a vice governor. The governor enforced the law, led the state militia, and granted pardons. Catholicism was the state religion, but that provision was not enforced among Texas's Anglo settlers. Anglo Texans also were not subject to military service, taxes, or custom duties. Texas primarily served as a buffer between Mexico and various Native American tribes—and the United States.

But as Anglo immigration increased, Mexico began to fear the possibility of U.S. expansion and soon started trying to exercise more control over Texas. This development reinforced cultural differences and soon led to revolution by Anglo Texans.[8]

This formative period, nevertheless, produced contributions to the Texas constitutional tradition that still exist, including some property and land laws, water laws and water rights, and community property laws. One justification for the Texas revolution of 1836 was the Mexican government's failure to sufficiently fund public education. But even though there were expectations of funding by the central government, a "concept of local control over school development was firmly established" during that era.[9] Issues of local control and adequate funding of public schools persist today.

☐ The Constitution of the Republic of Texas (1836)

During the late 1820s and the early 1830s, increased immigration into Texas from the United States heightened tensions between the Anglo settlers and the Mexican government. Mexico's efforts to enforce its laws within Texas produced conflicts between cultures, legal traditions, and economic interests that sparked open rebellion by the colonists.

At the same time, Mexico was embroiled in its own internal dissension, which resulted in the seizure of power by the popular general Antonio Lopez de Santa Anna Perez de Lebron. Santa Anna began to suspend the powers of the Mexican Congress and local governments, and, in October 1835, the national Constitution of 1824 was voided. Mexico adopted a new constitution providing for a **unitary system** with power centralized in the national congress and the presidency. It repealed the principle of **federalism**, which had divided power between the national government and the Mexican states. This major change intensified conflict between the national government and the states; although Texas was eventually successful in establishing its autonomy, several other Mexican states were subjected to harsh military retaliation.

As the new Mexican government tried to enforce control over Texas, colonists who initially supported the national government and others who were ambivalent began to support the independence movement. Stephen Austin had initially supported the position that Texas was a Mexican state, and he represented a large part of the Texas Anglo population. But when Mexican troops marched into Texas in the fall of 1835, he called for resistance.

Fifty-nine male colonists convened in the small Texas settlement of Washington-on-the-Brazos to declare Texas's independence from Mexico on March 2, 1836, and to adopt a constitution for the new republic two weeks later. They had two overriding interests: the preservation of their fledgling nation and the preservation of their own lives. By the time they had finished their work, the Alamo—only 150 miles away—had fallen to a large Mexican army under Santa Anna, and a second Mexican force had crossed the Rio Grande into Texas. So, the frontier constitution writers wasted little time making speeches.

Consequently, the Constitution of the Republic, adopted on March 16, 1836, was not cluttered with the details that weaken the present Texas Constitution. It drew heavily from the U.S. Constitution and from the constitutions of several southern states, from which most of the delegates had immigrated to Texas. The new constitution created an elected **bicameral legislature** and provided for an elected president. There was no official, state-preferred religion, and members of the clergy were prohibited from serving as president or in Congress. Slavery was legal under the new document, but it prohibited the importation of slaves from any country other than the United States.

On April 21, 1836, approximately six weeks after the Texans' defeat at the Alamo, the Texas army, under the command of Sam Houston, defeated Santa Anna's army at the

unitary system
A system in which ultimate power is vested in a central or national government and local governments have only those powers granted to them by the central government. This principle describes the relationship between the state and local governments in Texas.

federalism
A system that balances the power and sovereignty of state governments with that of the national government. Both the states and the national government derive their authority directly from the people, and the states have considerable autonomy within their areas of responsibility.

bicameral legislature
A lawmaking body, such as the Texas legislature, that includes two chambers.

TEXAS DECLARATION OF INDEPENDENCE
Fifty-nine Texas colonists convened on March 2, 1836, in the small community of Washington-on-the-Brazos, declared independence from Mexico, and wrote a constitution, which they adopted on March 16, 1836.

Battle of San Jacinto. The war for independence had been relatively short and had limited casualties, but the problems of creating a stable, new political system in the sparsely populated, wilderness republic were seemingly formidable. There was no viable government in place, no money to pay for a government, and no party system.[10] In addition, although defeated, Mexico did not relinquish its claims to Texas and remained a threat to try to regain its lost territory. Nevertheless, the "transition from colony to constitutional republic was accomplished quickly and with a minimum of disorganization."[11]

The experience of national autonomy from 1836 to 1845 contributed significantly to the development of a sense of historical uniqueness among Texans. Although the effects on the state's political psyche may be difficult to measure, the "Lone Star" experience has been kept alive through school history texts, the celebration of key events, and the development of a mythology of the independence period.

□ The Constitution of 1845

During the independence movement and immediately thereafter, some Texans made overtures to the United States for annexation. That possibility initially was blocked by the slavery issue and its relationship to economic and regional influence in U.S. politics. But increased immigration to Texas in the late 1830s and early 1840s, more interest among Texans in joining the Union, and expansionist policies of the U.S. government stepped up the pressure for annexation. It was a major issue in the U.S. presidential campaign of 1844, and James K. Polk's election to the White House accelerated Texas's admission to the United States in 1845 because he campaigned for it.

The annexation bill approved by the U.S. Congress included a compromise that allowed slavery to continue in Texas.[12] Racial issues emerging from this period continue to affect politics and public policy in the state. Texas still struggles with voting rights issues, inequities in education funding, and the maldistribution of economic resources affecting the quality of life of many minority group members.

The state constitution drafted to allow Texas's annexation was about twice as long as the Constitution of 1836. It borrowed from its predecessor and from the constitutions of other southern states, particularly Louisiana.

The Constitution of 1845 created an elected legislature that included a House of Representatives and Senate, which met biennially. It provided for an elected governor and an elected lieutenant governor, and it empowered the governor to appoint a secretary of state, attorney general, and state judges, subject to Senate confirmation. The legislature appointed a comptroller, treasurer, and land commissioner. In 1850, however, Texas voters amended the constitution to make most state offices elective, following a national pattern of fragmenting the powers of the executive branch of state government. Texas still has a **plural executive** under which practically all statewide officeholders are elected independently of the governor, a system that contrasts sharply with the appointive cabinet system of executive government headed by the president of the United States.

The 1845 constitution established a permanent fund for the support of public schools, protected homesteads from foreclosure, and guaranteed separate property rights for married women—provisions still found in the present constitution. The 1845 charter also recognized slavery, prohibited state-chartered banks, and barred anyone who had ever participated in a duel from holding public office. This constitution "worked so well that after several intervening constitutions, the people of Texas recopied it almost *in toto* as the Constitution of 1876."[13]

plural executive
A fragmented system of authority under which most statewide, executive officeholders are elected independently of the governor. This arrangement, which is used in Texas, places severe limitations on the governor's power.

confederacy
A view of the constitution taken by eleven southern states, including Texas, that a state could withdraw, or secede, from the Union. Upon secession that began in 1860, the Confederate States of America was formed, leading to the Civil War.

□ The Civil War Constitution (1861)

When Texas seceded from the Union in 1861, just before the outbreak of the Civil War, the state constitution was again revised. Most of the provisions of the 1845 document were retained, but significant changes were made in line with Texas's new membership in the Confederacy. The constitution required public officials to pledge their support of the Confederate constitution, gave greater protection to slavery, and prohibited the freeing of slaves.

Slavery and secession destroyed any semblance of a two-party system in Texas. Personalities, factions, and war-related issues dominated state politics. Factionalism within the Democratic Party persisted for more than 100 years, until the emergence of a two-party system in the 1980s.

The Civil War era also contributed to a legacy of states' rights, which persisted well into the next century and sparked an extended struggle for desegregation. The southern states contended that the national government was a **confederacy**, from which a state could withdraw, or secede. Although the northern victory dispelled this interpretation, Texas and other southern states found ways to thwart national policy through the 1960s. Their efforts were based, in part, on their continued arguments for states' rights.

□ The Constitution of 1866

After the Civil War, Texas government returned to national control, first through a military government and then through a provisional government headed by A. J. Hamilton, a former U.S. congressman who had remained loyal to the Union. These were dark days for Texans. Although relatively few battles had been fought in Texas and the state had not suffered from the scorched-earth tactics used by Union generals elsewhere, the economy was in disarray. Many Texas families had lost loved ones, and many surviving Confederate veterans had been wounded physically or psychologically. New policies adopted by the federal government to assist newly freed slaves were never fully funded and were halfheartedly—and often dishonestly—carried out. The presence of an occupation army also heightened tensions and shaped subsequent political attitudes.

The Reconstruction plan initiated by President Abraham Lincoln but never fully carried out envisioned a rapid return to civilian government for the southern states and their quick reintegration as equals in the U.S. political system. Requirements were few: the abolition of slavery, the repudiation of the Secession Ordinance of 1861, and the repudiation of all debts and obligations incurred under the Confederacy.[14]

Texas voters revived the Constitution of 1845 and amended it to include the new Union requirements. The new constitution formally eliminated slavery and gave former slaves the right to own property and legal rights before a jury. But African Americans were prohibited from testifying in court against whites. And African Americans were

Radical Reconstructionists
The group of Republicans who took control of Congress in 1866 and imposed hated military governments on the former Confederate states after the Civil War.

Edmund J. Davis
Republican governor (1870–1874) whose highly unpopular policies contributed to the decisions of the Constitutional Convention of 1875 to limit and fragment the powers of the governor.

denied the right to vote.[15] The new constitution was adopted in June 1866; a new government was elected; and on August 20, 1866, President Andrew Johnson, who had become president after Lincoln's assassination, "declared the rebellion in Texas at an end."[16]

Very soon, however, **Radical Reconstructionists**, who had captured control of the U.S. Congress in 1866, replaced Johnson's mild Reconstruction policies with more severe ones. Congress invalidated the new Texas Constitution. It also passed, over the president's veto, the Reconstruction Acts, which established military governments throughout the South. The civilian government initiated by the state's Constitution of 1866 was short lived, and Texas functioned for two years under a reinstituted military government.

This period had an enduring impact on Texas constitutional law and politics. It prolonged the full reintegration of Texas into the national political system, and it transformed Texas's constitutional tradition into one of hostility and suspicion toward government.

□ The Constitution of Reconstruction (1869)

The Reconstruction Acts required a Texas Constitution that would grant African Americans the right to vote and include other provisions acceptable to Congress. A Republican Party slate of delegates to a new constitutional convention drafted a new charter in 1869. It did not reflect the majority of Texans' sentiments of the time, but it conformed to Republican wishes. Centralizing more powers in state government while weakening local government, the charter gave the governor a four-year term and the power to appoint other top state officials, including members of the judiciary. It gave African Americans the right to vote; provided for annual legislative sessions; and, for the first time in Texas, established a centralized, statewide system of public schools. Texans were unhappy with their new constitution and outraged by the widespread abuses that followed under the oppressive and corrupt administration of Radical Republican Governor **Edmund J. Davis**.

In the 1869 election, the first under the new constitution, large numbers of former slaves voted, whereas Anglos who had fought for the Confederacy were not allowed to cast ballots as retribution for taking up arms against the United States. Radical supporters of Davis, a former Union Army officer, supervised the election process. The military governor certified that Davis beat Conservative Republican A. J. Hamilton by 39,901 to 39,092 votes, despite widespread, flagrant incidents of voter fraud, which also were ignored by President Ulysses S. Grant and Congress. A Radical majority in the new Texas legislature then approved a series of authoritarian—and, in some respects, unconstitutional—laws proposed by Davis. They gave the governor the power to declare martial law and suspend the laws in any county and created a state police force under the governor's control that could deprive citizens of constitutional protections. The governor also was empowered to appoint mayors, district attorneys, and hundreds of other local officials. Another law designating newspapers as official printers of state documents in effect put much of the press under government control.

Davis exercised some of the most repressive actions ever imposed on U.S. citizens. And Texans struck back. In 1872, they elected a Democratic majority to the legislature, which abolished the state police and repealed other oppressive laws. Then, in 1873, they elected a Confederate veteran, Democrat Richard Coke, governor by more than a two-to-one margin over Davis. Like the Radical Republicans in the previous gubernatorial election, the Democrats also abused the democratic process. Voting fraud again was widespread. "Democrat politicos bluntly indicated that power would be won depending on who outfrauded whom. No practice was ignored. There was terror, intimidation, and some murders on both sides," wrote historian T. R. Fehrenbach.[17]

As noted at the start of the chapter, Davis initially refused to leave office and appealed to President Grant for federal troops to help him retain power. Grant refused, however, and the Texas militia turned against him and marched on the Capitol in January 1874. Davis eventually gave up, preventing additional bloodshed. Reconstruction was ending, and the Constitution of 1869 was doomed.

☐ The Constitution of 1876: Retrenchment and Reform

The restored Democratic majority promptly took steps to assemble a new constitutional convention, which convened in Austin on September 6, 1875. The delegates were all men. Most were products of a rural and frontier South, and still smarting from Reconstruction abuses, they considered government a necessary evil that had to be heavily restricted. Many, however, had previous governmental experience. Initially, seventy-five Democrats and fifteen Republicans were elected delegates, but one Republican resigned after only limited service and was replaced by a Democrat.[18]

The vast majority of the delegates were white, and some disagreement remains over how many African Americans served in the convention. Some historians say there were six. According to one account, however, six African Americans were elected but one resigned after only one day of service and was replaced in a special election by a white delegate. All of the African American delegates were Republicans.[19]

Only four of the delegates were native Texans. Most had immigrated to Texas from other southern states, including nineteen—the largest single group—from Tennessee. Their average age was forty-five. The oldest was sixty-eight; the youngest was twenty-three.[20] Eleven of the delegates had been members of previous constitutional conventions in Texas, but there is disagreement over whether any had participated in drafting the Reconstruction Constitution of 1869. In any event, the influences of the 1869 constitution were negative, not positive.

At least thirty delegates had served in the Texas legislature, two had served in the Tennessee and Mississippi legislatures, two had represented Texas in the U.S. Congress, and two had represented Texas in the Confederate Congress. Delegates also

MEMBERS OF THE 1875 CONVENTION

Ninety delegates, including six recently emancipated African Americans, were elected to the Constitutional Convention of 1875.

2.1

2.2

2.3

2.4

2.5

Grange
An organization formed in the late nineteenth century to improve the lot of farmers. Its influence in Texas after Reconstruction was felt in constitutional provisions limiting taxes and government spending and restricting banks, railroads, and other big businesses.

included a former Texas attorney general, a former lieutenant governor, and a former secretary of state of Texas, and at least eight delegates had been judges. Many had been high-ranking Confederate military officers. One, John H. Reagan, had been postmaster general of the Confederacy.[21] Reagan later would become a U.S. senator from Texas and the first chairman of the Texas Railroad Commission.

Another delegate who epitomized the independent, frontier spirit of the time was John S. "Rip" Ford, a native of South Carolina who had come to Texas in 1836 as a physician. He later became a lawyer, journalist, state senator, mayor of Austin, and Texas Ranger captain. In 1874, he was a leader of the militia that marched on the Capitol and forced Edmund J. Davis to relinquish the governor's office to his elected successor. Ford had been a secessionist delegate to the 1861 convention and, during the Civil War, had commanded a makeshift cavalry regiment that fought Union soldiers along the Texas-Mexico border.[22]

According to one account, delegates to the 1875 convention included thirty-three lawyers, twenty-eight farmers, three physicians, three merchants, two teachers, two editors, and one minister. At least eleven other delegates were part-time farmers who also pursued other occupations.[23] Other historians have suggested slightly different breakdowns, but all agree that agricultural interests substantially influenced the writing of the new Texas charter.

About half the delegates were members of the Society of the Patrons of Husbandry, or the **Grange**, an organization formed to improve the lot of farmers. The Grange became politically active in the wake of national scandals involving abuses by big business and government. It started organizing in Texas in 1873, and it influenced constitutional provisions that limited taxes and governmental expenditures and restricted banks, railroads, and other corporations.

The delegates did not try to produce a document that would be lauded as a model of constitutional perfection or mistaken for a literary classic. They faced the reality of addressing serious, pressing problems—an immediate crisis that did not encourage debate over the finer points of academic or political theory or produce any prophetic visions of the next century.

The Civil War and Reconstruction had ruined the state economically and driven state government deeply into debt, even though Texas citizens, particularly property owners, had been heavily taxed. Land prices had plummeted, a disaster for what was then an agricultural state. Pervasive governmental corruption and Governor Davis's oppressive administration left deep scars and resentments among Texans.

In an effort to restore economic stability and governmental control to the people, the framers of the Texas Constitution of 1876 drafted what was essentially an antigovernment charter. They replaced centralization with more local control; strictly limited taxation; and put short leashes on the legislature, the courts, and the governor.[24]

Agricultural interests, which had been called upon to finance industrial development and new public services during Reconstruction, were again protected from onerous governmental intrusion and taxation. The retrenchment and reform embodied in the new constitution would later hamper the state's commercial and economic development. But the post-Reconstruction Texans liked all the restrictions placed on government. They ratified the new constitution in February 1876 by a vote of 136,606 to 56,052.

General Principles of the Texas Constitution

2.3 Explain the major features and general principles of the current Texas Constitution.

The underlying principle of the Texas Constitution of 1876 is expressed in a relatively short preamble and the first two sections of a Bill of Rights (see Table 2–2). It is a social compact, formed by free men (no women participated in its drafting), in which "all political power is inherent in the

TABLE 2–2 COMPARISON OF THE TEXAS CONSTITUTION AND THE U.S. CONSTITUTION

	U.S. Constitution	Texas Constitution
General principles	Popular sovereignty Limited government Representative government Social contract theory Separation of powers	Popular sovereignty Limited government Representative government Social contract theory Separation of powers
Context of adoption	Reaction to weakness of Articles of Confederation—strengthened national powers significantly	Post-Reconstruction—designed to limit powers of government
Style	General principles stated in broad terms	Detailed provisions
Length	7,000 words	87,000-plus words
Date of implementation	1789	1876
Amendments	27	474
Amendment process	Difficult	Relatively easy
Adaptation to change	Moderately easy through interpretation	Difficult; often requires constitutional amendments
Bill of Rights	Amendments to the Constitution—adopted in 1791	Article 1 of the Constitution of 1876
Structure of government	Separation of powers, with a unified executive based on provisions of Articles 1, 2, 3	Separation of powers with plural executive defined by Article 2
Legislature	Bicameral	Bicameral
Judiciary	Creation of one Supreme Court and other courts to be created by the Congress	Detailed provisions creating two appellate courts and other state courts
Distribution of powers	Federal	Unitary
Public policy	Little reference to policy	Detailed policy provisions

people...founded on their authority, and instituted for their benefit."[25] These sections are based on the principles of **popular sovereignty** and **social contract** theory, both part of a legacy of constitutional law in the United States. But the declarations of a free and just society were limited in scope and application. Women and minorities were initially denied full citizenship rights. Women would not gain the right to vote until 1920, and it would take much longer for African Americans and Hispanics to receive full constitutional protections.

Another major principle of the Texas Constitution is **limited government**. The Bill of Rights and other provisions throughout the constitution place limits on governmental power and spell out traditional citizens rights, including religious freedom and procedural due process of law.

A final major principle embodied in the constitution is **separation of powers**. Unlike the U.S. Constitution, in which this principle emerges through powers defined in the three articles related to Congress, the president, and the judiciary, Article 2 of the Texas Constitution specifically provides for a separation of powers.

The Constitution of 1876 created three branches of government—legislative, executive, and judicial—and provided for a system of checks and balances to assure that no branch would dominate the others. This principle originated with the U.S. Constitution, whose drafters were concerned about the so-called mischief of factions.[26] They feared that special interest groups would be able to capture control of governmental institutions and pursue policies harmful to the national interest. To guard against that potential problem, they fragmented institutional power. In some respects, this was an issue of even greater concern to the framers of the Texas Constitution. Reacting to the highly centralized authority and abuses of the Davis administration, they took the separation of powers principle to its extreme.

Lawmaking authority in Texas is assigned to an elected legislature that includes a 150-member House of Representatives and a 31-member Senate. It meets in regular sessions in odd-numbered years and in special sessions of limited scope and duration

popular sovereignty
The constitutional principle of self-government; the belief that the people control their government and governments are subject to limitations and constraints.

social contract
The view that governments originated from the general agreement among and consent of members of the public to address common interests and needs.

limited government
The constitutional principle restricting governmental authority and spelling out personal rights.

separation of powers
The division of authority among three distinct branches of government—the legislative, the executive, and the judicial—which serve as checks and balances on one another's power.

2.1

2.2

2.3

2.4

2.5

when called by the governor. The sixty-five sections of Article 3 spell out in detail the powers granted and the restrictions imposed on the legislature.

An elected governor shares authority over the executive branch with several other independently elected, statewide officeholders. The governor can veto bills approved by the legislature, and a veto can be overridden only by a two-thirds vote of the House and the Senate.

Also elected are members of the judiciary—from justices of the peace, with limited jurisdiction at the county level, to the highest statewide appellate courts. This provision reflects the strong sentiment of post-Reconstruction Texans for an independent judiciary and is a major difference from the federal government, in which the president appoints judges to lifetime terms. Also unlike the federal system, in which the U.S. Supreme Court is the court of last resort in both civil and criminal appeals, Texas has two courts of last resort. The Texas Supreme Court has jurisdiction over civil matters, and the Texas Court of Criminal Appeals has final review of criminal cases.

Weaknesses and Criticisms of the Constitution of 1876

2.4 Outline the weaknesses and criticisms of the current Texas Constitution, particularly as they pertain to how the framers failed to anticipate economic and social changes in the state.

The Texas Constitution of 1876 has been criticized for inherent weaknesses built into the document. Experts point to the excessive fragmentation of government authority with respect to the executive, a poorly paid and part-time legislature, and a decentralized judiciary. They also have identified an inequitable public education system, budgeting and finances that cannot be easily altered to meet changing state needs, past restrictions on individual rights for African Americans and other groups, an unnecessary level of confusing statutory detail, and an amendment process that requires excessive amendments to enable the state government to adapt to changes.

Executive Branch

Many experts believe that the Texas Constitution excessively fragments governmental authority and responsibility, particularly in the executive branch. Although the public may expect the governor to establish policy priorities, the governor does not have control over other elected state executives but, instead, shares both authority and responsibility for policy with them. This restriction can create problems. Former Republican Governor Bill Clements, for example, shared executive responsibilities with Democrats who sharply disagreed with his priorities. Even when the governor and other elected officials are of the same party, differences in personality, political philosophy, and policy objectives can produce tension and sometimes deadlock. This divisiveness became particularly strident in 2006, when Comptroller Carole Keeton Strayhorn, a Republican, repeatedly questioned Republican Governor Rick Perry's policies and then became an independent candidate to unsuccessfully challenge his reelection.

The governor's power has been further diffused by the creation over the years of numerous boards and commissions that set policy for executive agencies not headed by elected officials. Although the governor appoints most of these board members, they serve staggered six-year terms that are longer than a governor's term. And a newly elected governor—who cannot fire a predecessor's appointees—usually has to wait through most of his or her first term to gain a majority of appointees to most boards.

Fragmented authority also is a characteristic of county governments, which the constitution created as administrative agents of the state. Various elected county officials often clash over public policy, producing inefficiencies or failing to meet public needs. And just as voters have to fill out a long ballot for statewide offices, they also must choose among a long, often confusing list of county officers. A long ballot discourages many people from voting, and this obstacle reduces public accountability, an end result that the framers of the Constitution of 1876 certainly never intended.

☐ Legislative Branch

The constitution created a low-paid, part-time legislature to ensure the election of citizen-lawmakers who would be sensitive to the needs of their constituents, not those of professional politicians who would live off the taxpayers. Unwittingly, however, the constitution writers also produced a lawmaking body easily influenced by special interest groups. And the strict limitations placed on the legislature's operations and powers slow its ability to meet the increasingly complex needs of a growing, modern Texas.

In 1972, voters approved a constitutional amendment to lengthen the terms of the governor and other executive officeholders from two to four years. This change gave the governor more time to develop public policies with the prospect of seeing them implemented. But voters repeatedly have rejected proposals to provide for annual legislative sessions, and legislative pay remains among the lowest in the country.

☐ Judicial Branch

The Texas Constitution also created numerous locally elected judicial offices, including justices of the peace and county and district courts. Although there are appeal procedures, these judges derive a great deal of autonomy, power, and influence through their local constituencies.

☐ Public Education

Another example of decentralization is the public school system. The centralized school system authorized under the Constitution of 1869 was abolished, and local officials were given the primary responsibility of supervising public education. The concept of "local control" over their schools is important to many Texans, but decentralization and wide disparities in local tax bases have produced an inequitable public education system.

☐ Budgeting and Finances

The Texas Constitution, including amendments adopted after 1876, requires a balanced state budget and heavily restricts the legislature's choices over spending. It also dedicates large amounts of revenue to specific purposes, making it increasingly difficult for lawmakers to address changing state needs.

☐ Individual Rights

Although declaring a general commitment to democracy and individual rights, the constitution was used for many years to slow democratic development in Texas.[27] Like many other southern states, Texas had restrictive laws on voter participation. It levied a poll tax, which reduced voting by minorities and poor whites until 1966, when an amendment to the U.S. Constitution and a U.S. Supreme Court decision outlawed poll taxes. Federal courts also struck down a Texas election system that excluded African Americans from voting in the Democratic primary, which decided elections when Texas was a one-party Democratic state. The elimination of significant numbers of people from participating in elections helped perpetuate the one-party political system for approximately 100 years.[28]

☐ Excessive Details

The Texas Constitution also is burdened with excessive detail. Although few individuals have ever read the entire 87,000-plus-word document, a person casually perusing it can find language, for example, governing the operation of hospital districts in specific counties. Another provision deals with expenditures for relocating or replacing sanitation sewer lines on private property. And, if one rural county wants to abolish an outdated constitutional office, the legislature and voters throughout the state have to approve the necessary constitutional amendment. Whereas the 7,000-word U.S. Constitution leaves the details for implementation to congressional legislation, the Texas Constitution often spells out the authority and power of a governmental agency in specific detail. Most experts would argue that many constitutional articles are of a legislative nature and have no business being in a constitution.[29] The excessive detail limits the adaptability of the constitution to changing circumstances and places undue restrictions on state and local governments.

Consequently, obsolete and contradictory provisions in the constitution create confusion in its interpretation and application. Constitutional amendments have been periodically approved to "clean up" such deadwood, but the problem persists.[30]

☐ The Amendment Process

Another important criticism of the Texas Constitution focuses on amendments and the amendment process. Alabama has had more constitutional amendments than any other state (see Figure 2–2), but Texas ranked fourth, behind Alabama, California and South Carolina with 474 amendments from 1876 through 2011. In contrast, the U.S. Constitution has been amended only twenty-seven times since 1789, and ten of those amendments were adopted as the Bill of Rights immediately after the government organized. The numerous restrictions and prohibitions in the Texas Constitution require excessive amendments to enable state government to adapt to social, economic, and political changes.

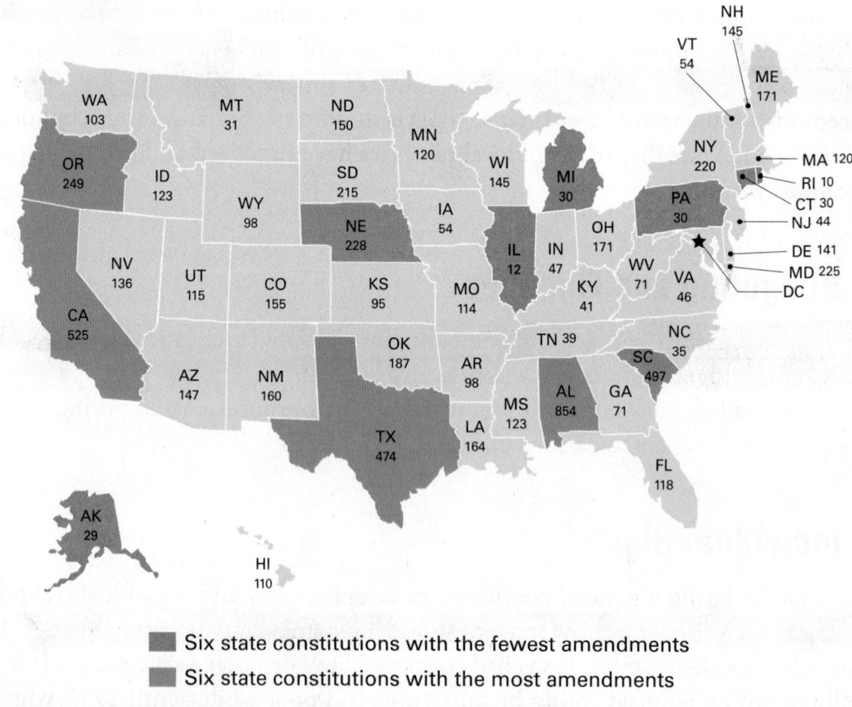

FIGURE 2–2 STATE CONSTITUTIONS WITH THE MOST AND FEWEST AMENDMENTS, 2011

This map highlights the states whose constitutions have had the most and fewest amendments adopted as of 2011. Texas ranks fourth behind Alabama, California and South Carolina.

Source: Based on information in *The Book of States*, 2011 Edition, Volume 43, (Lexington, KY: The Council of State Governments, 2011).

*The number shown in each state is the number of amendments that have been added to the state constitution as of 2011.
**The Texas Constitution was amended in November 2011 when voters approved seven of ten amendments.

Constitutional Change and Adaptation

2.5 Contrast the ease and frequency of the constitutional amendment process with the difficulty of enacting more fundamental change through the constitutional convention process.

lthough they loaded the constitution with numerous restrictive provisions, the nineteenth century drafters also provided a relatively easy method of amending it. Over the years, this piecemeal amendment process has enabled the state government to meet some changing needs, but it also has added thousands of words to the document.

Amendments

Proposed constitutional amendments can be submitted to Texas voters only by the legislature (see *Talking Texas: Should Constitutional Amendments be Submitted to the Voters in Special Elections?*). Approval by two-thirds of the House and the Senate puts them on the ballot; adoption requires a majority vote. Although voters had approved 474 amendments through 2012, they had rejected 178 others. The first amendment was adopted on September 2, 1879. Each regular legislative session normally approves several amendments for the voters to approve or reject. A record twenty-five amendments were placed on the November 3, 1987 ballot. Seventeen were adopted, and eight were defeated.

Some amendments are of major statewide importance, but many have affected only a single county or a handful of counties or have been offered simply to rid the

Talking ★ Texas — Should Constitutional Amendments Be Submitted to the Voters in Special Elections?

> ***Proposition 12,** The constitutional amendment covering civil lawsuits against doctors and health care providers, and other action, authorizing the legislature to determine limitations on noneconomic damages.* (SPECIAL CONSTITUTIONAL AMENDMENTS ELECTION, SEPTEMBER 2003)

Supporters said Proposition 12 was a cure for high medical malpractice insurance premiums that were forcing some doctors, particularly in rural areas, to close their practices. Opponents argued that medical malpractice coverage was high because state regulators were not effectively clamping down on bad doctors, and they warned that Proposition 12 was instead an effort by business and insurance interests to further restrict access to the courts for injured or aggrieved consumers.

Texas voters narrowly approved the constitutional amendment in 2003 after a multimillion-dollar advertising war. Doctors, hospitals, nursing homes, and other business interests primarily financed the campaign promoting the amendment. Plaintiffs' lawyers—who make their living suing doctors, hospitals, and businesses on behalf of injured consumers—picked up most of the tab for the media campaign against it, although numerous consumer advocacy groups also opposed the proposal.

The amendment did two things. First, it ratified a 2003 law enacted by the legislature to put new limits on noneconomic damages—money awarded for such things as pain, suffering, and disfigurement—in medical malpractice suits. Such damages, which are in addition to medical costs and other actual economic losses that could be awarded a patient who suffered from a botched medical procedure, were capped at $750,000 for each case. Of that amount, only $250,000 could be recovered from physicians or other medical personnel. The remainder would come from hospitals, nursing homes, or other health care facilities that might have been involved. Additionally—and potentially more far-reaching—Proposition 12 included language clearing the

2.1

2.2

2.3

2.4

2.5

way for future sessions of the legislature to enact new limits on damages in other civil lawsuits.

Opponents of Proposition 12 accused legislative sponsors of trying to sneak the proposal past the voters by scheduling the constitutional amendments election for September 13, rather than November 4, the general election date on which constitutional amendments were traditionally set for voter review. Supporters of the amendment said it was important to win voter approval earlier than normal to remove any legal uncertainty over the new malpractice limits. However, opponents argued that the early election, with no other issues to attract voters, was designed to avoid the higher voter turnout that would be generated by a hotly contested mayoral race in Houston on November 4. Voters in Houston, the state's largest city, usually are a major factor in determining statewide elections, and a high voter turnout there could prove to be pivotal in determining the fate of Proposition 12. According to this argument, the higher the voter turnout in Houston, the higher the likelihood that the amendment would be defeated, because Democrats and plaintiffs' lawyers still had some clout over elections in that city. Opponents of Proposition 12, as it turned out, had reason to fear the early election date. The proposal narrowly passed statewide, but 58 percent of Houston voters—turning out in far fewer numbers than would vote two months later in the mayor's race—cast ballots against it.

CRITICAL THINKING QUESTIONS

1. Does the ballot language for Proposition 12 make it clear that the amendment puts caps on monetary awards for medical malpractice? Explain your answer.
2. Did supporters of Proposition 12 "cheat" by scheduling the election on a date when they knew the voter turnout among likely opponents would be lower? Why or why not?

initiative
A petition and election process whereby voters propose laws or constitutional amendments for adoption by a popular vote.

referendum
An election, usually initiated by a petition of voters, whereby an action of a legislative body is submitted for approval or rejection by the voters.

Constitutional Convention of 1974
The last major attempt to write a new Texas Constitution. Members of the legislature served as delegates and failed to overcome political differences and the influence of special interests.

constitution of obsolete language (see *Talking Texas: Adding a Cup of Java to the Constitution*). One amendment adopted in 1993 affected only about 140 families, two church congregations, and one school district in two counties. It cleared up a property title defect.

Unlike voters in many other states, Texas citizens cannot force the placement of constitutional amendments or binding referenda on the ballot because Texas does not have an **initiative** or **referendum** system on a statewide level. Adopting that process would require still another constitutional amendment, and the legislature historically has opposed giving such a significant policy prerogative to the electorate.

Sometimes, however, the legislature has sought political cover by selectively letting voters decide particularly controversial issues, such as a binding referendum in 1987 to legalize pari-mutuel betting on horse and dog racing. In 1993, the legislature proposed a constitutional amendment, which voters overwhelmingly endorsed, to prohibit a personal income tax in Texas without voter approval.

□ Constitutional Convention

The constitution also provides for revision by constitutional convention, which the legislature can call with the approval of the voters. Delegates to such a convention have to be elected, and proposed changes adopted by a constitutional convention also must be approved by voters. Voters overwhelmingly rejected a proposal for a constitutional convention in 1919.[31] Subsequent efforts, including an attempt by Governor John Connally in 1967, to hold conventions also were defeated.[32] Connally's efforts, however, resulted in adoption of a "cleanup" amendment in 1969 that removed many obsolete provisions from the constitution, and it laid the groundwork for a constitutional convention in 1974.

□ The Constitutional Reform Efforts of 1971 to 1975

The **Constitutional Convention of 1974** has been the only one ever held under the present constitution, and it ended in failure. Its delegates were the 181 members of the legislature. The idea originated in 1971, when state Representative Nelson Wolff of San Antonio and several other first-term legislators won the leadership's backing for a full-scale revision effort, and the legislature submitted a constitutional amendment for

Talking ★ Texas Adding a Cup of Java to the Constitution

Many people may enjoy a cup of coffee with a chocolate dessert. But do such treats belong in the state constitution? Most Texas voters thought so. One of nineteen propositions approved on the 2001 ballot exempted from property taxes raw coffee beans and cocoa imported through the Port of Houston. The proposal was promoted by business people seeking to increase imports of those commodities through Houston. More imports, they hoped, would increase the need for more warehouses, create more jobs, and boost business profits. The tax exemption met a condition necessary for the New York Board of Trade to award "exchange port" status to the Port of Houston, a key requirement for import growth.

There was no organized opposition to the amendment, and the amendment also was endorsed by city and county officials in Houston who believed it offered a potential boost to the area's overall economy. But the proposal was approved by a relatively close margin—52 percent—perhaps because many non-Houstonians viewed it as a special-interest favor for the state's largest city and did not like the way it tasted.

CRITICAL THINKING QUESTIONS

1. Why was it necessary for voters in Dallas, San Antonio, Lubbock, and everywhere else in Texas to vote on the coffee and chocolate amendment that apparently applied only to Houston?
2. Do voters from one area of the state care about or give much attention to local issues that impact other areas of the state? Why or why not?

a convention to the voters. In 1972, voters approved the amendment, which provided that the delegates would be the state senators and house members elected that year.

In 1973, the legislature created a thirty-seven-member Constitutional Revision Commission to hold public hearings throughout the state and make recommendations to the convention. The constitutional convention, or "con–con," as it came to be called by legislators and members of the media, convened on January 8, 1974. House Speaker Price Daniel Jr. was elected president, and Lieutenant Governor Bill Hobby, in an address to delegates, offered a prophetic warning: "The special interests of today will be replaced by new and different special interests tomorrow, and any attempt to draft a constitution to serve such interests would be futile and also dishonorable."[33]

Hobby's plea was ignored. Special interests dominated the convention, which adjourned in failure on July 30, failing by three votes to get the two-thirds vote necessary to send a new constitution to Texas voters for ratification.

The crucial fight was over a business-backed attempt to lock the state's **right-to-work law** into the constitution. The right-to-work law prohibits union membership as a condition of employment, so organized labor bitterly fought the effort. Then as now, business was politically stronger than labor in Texas, but the two-thirds vote necessary to put a new constitution on the ballot was too great an obstacle.

right-to-work law
Law prohibiting the requirement of union membership in order to get or hold a job.

Governor Dolph Briscoe's refusal to exercise leadership for a new constitution also hurt the revision effort. Except for opposing proposals that he thought would further weaken the governor's authority, Briscoe provided little input to the convention. Louisiana voters approved a new state constitution that same year, and Governor Edwin Edwards's strong support had been considered instrumental. Gubernatorial leadership in other states also appears to have been critical to successful constitutional conventions.

Another major obstacle was the convention's makeup. The 181 members of the legislature were the delegates; soon after the convention began its work, many of them faced reelection campaigns in the party primaries, which diverted their attention and, in some cases, affected their willingness to vote for significant constitutional changes.

Additionally, a minority of legislators—dubbed "cockroaches" by President Daniel—did not want a new constitution and attempted to delay or obstruct the convention's work at every opportunity. Most legislators, even those who wanted a

FINAL DAYS OF THE 1974 CONVENTION.
After three years of preparation and deliberations, the proposed constitution of 1974 failed by three votes in the final hectic session of the constitutional convention, when the gallery was filled with interested onlookers, including many representatives of labor and other interest groups.

new constitution, were susceptible to the influence of special interests, far more susceptible than most private-citizen delegates likely would have been. And special interests were legion at the convention. In addition to various business and professional groups and organized labor, many county officeholders whose jobs—protected by the Constitution of 1876—were suddenly in jeopardy put pressure on the delegates.

During its next regular session in 1975, the legislature tried to resurrect the constitutional revision effort. Lawmakers voted to present to Texans—as eight separate constitutional amendments—the basic document that the convention had barely rejected the previous summer. The first three articles dealing with the separation of powers and the legislative and executive branches were combined into one ballot proposition. Each of the remaining seven propositions was a separate article, each to be independently approved or rejected by the voters. The most controversial issues that the 1974 convention had debated, such as right-to-work, were excluded. The streamlined amendments would have considerably shortened the constitution and provided major changes, including annual legislative sessions, a unified judicial system, and more flexibility in county government. But voters rejected all eight propositions on November 4, 1975, some by margins of more than two to one.

A stock fraud scandal in the legislature in 1971 and the Watergate scandal that forced the resignation of President Richard Nixon in 1974 had raised Texans' distrust of government, and the proposed new constitution had been drafted by state officials, not by private citizens.

Nelson Wolff, who years later would be elected mayor of San Antonio and then county judge of Bexar County, also noted a general lack of citizen interest in the work of the constitutional convention. In his book, *Challenge of Change,* he wrote:

> The constitutional revision effort in Texas had attempted to use every means known to get citizen participation in the process. A toll-free telephone had been set up for the convention. Committees of the convention met at night and on weekends to provide working people an opportunity to testify. We provided to the best of our ability optimum conditions for testimony. Yet many people avoided participation in the revision process.[34]

Most people know little about the details of constitutions and constitutional revisions, and many voters distrust governmental institutions.[35] Voter distrust and apathy played into the hands of numerous special interests, who did not want a new constitution because they did not want to give up the protections that the old constitution afforded them.

The comprehensive constitutional amendments also were thwarted, again, by Governor Dolph Briscoe. Although he had never taken an active role in the revision effort, three weeks before the 1975 election, he openly opposed the eight propositions and suggested that the existing constitution had served the state well and would continue to be adequate for the future.[36]

☐ Further Piecemeal Reforms

The legislature then returned to its pattern of piecemeal constitutional changes. Between 1975 and 2012, Texas voters approved 255 amendments, and 42 were rejected. Amendments that were adopted during this period included the creation of the state lottery in 1991, the 1993 amendment to ban a personal income tax without voter approval, and a series of propositions authorizing $3 billion in tax-backed bonds for a huge prison expansion program. In 1985, voters approved an amendment to give the governor and legislative leaders limited authority to deal with budgetary emergencies between legislative sessions, and in 1995, they approved an amendment to abolish the state treasurer's office and transfer its duties to the comptroller. In 1999, the legislature rejected another proposal to rewrite the constitution but approved an amendment, which voters also approved, to remove more obsolete language from the document. In 2003, in a major dispute between doctors and trial lawyers, voters narrowly approved Proposition 12, which ratified new limits on monetary damages in medical malpractice lawsuits. (See *Talking Texas: Should Constitutional Amendments Be Submitted to the Voters in Special Elections?*)

Tackling another controversial issue, voters overwhelmingly approved a constitutional amendment in 2005 to ban same-sex marriages in Texas (see *Talking Texas: Protecting Marriage or Promoting Discrimination?*). In 2007, voters—encouraged by Governor Rick Perry and cycling champion Lance Armstrong, a cancer survivor—approved $3 billion in bonds to boost state funding for cancer research.

☐ Constitutional Provisions, Interest Groups, and Elites

Only a small percentage of registered voters—often fewer than 10 percent—participate in elections when constitutional amendments are the only issues on the ballot (Table 2–3). Turnout is higher when the legislature submits amendments to voters in gubernatorial or presidential election years. But in many instances, a

TABLE 2–3 AVERAGE PERCENT TURNOUT FOR CONSTITUTIONAL AMENDMENT ELECTIONS, 1970–2011

Type of Election	Number of Elections	Percentage of Registered Voters	Percentage of Voting Age Population
Special*	19	12.1	8.3
General (Gubernatorial)	11	42.3	28.1
General (Presidential)	10	62.8	45.3

*Only constitutional amendments on the ballot.

SOURCE: Texas Secretary of State, Elections Division.

relative handful of Texans decides on fundamental changes in government, and often they are heavily influenced by one special interest group or another.

Interest groups, which historically have been strong in Texas, work to get provisions into the constitution that would benefit them or to keep provisions out that they fear would hurt them. Because most amendments do not involve partisan issues, a well-financed public relations campaign is likely to produce public support for an amendment.[37]

Interest groups often play defense to maintain their status quo and are able to kill many proposed constitutional changes in the legislature, where the two-thirds vote requirement works to their advantage. Only a small fraction of constitutional amendments proposed by legislators get put on the ballot. In addition, one or more interest groups usually support those amendments and finance publicity campaigns to promote the propositions to the voters. Few amendments attract organized opposition after being put on the ballot, but there have been exceptions. In 2003, doctors, insurance companies, and business interests heavily promoted Proposition 12, the ratification of new medical malpractice limits. They were successful, despite a media campaign against the amendment financed primarily by plaintiffs' lawyers.

Many recent constitutional changes have reflected a pro-industry and economic development push that contrasts sharply with the antibusiness sentiment of the original constitutional framers. However, one notable exception occurred in 2011, when voters, in a low-turnout, off-year election, rejected a proposed amendment that would have permitted counties to issue bonds for economic development. The amendment—one of ten on the ballot that year—received little publicity, and voters may have been influenced by the fact that Texas and the country were emerging from a recession that had hit hard at both household and government budgets.

Other recent amendments have helped build up a public-bonded indebtedness that the nineteenth-century constitution writers would have been unable to comprehend. Texas was rural then. It is now largely urban and the country's second most populous state. As it works to diversify and expand its economy as well as provide the infrastructure required to support continued population increases, business has

Talking ★ Texas

Protecting Marriage or Promoting Discrimination?

Texas became the eighteenth state to add a ban on same-sex marriage to its constitution when voters overwhelmingly approved Proposition 2 in 2005. The amendment had the strong support of Governor Rick Perry and many church leaders, who argued that it was necessary to guard against any legal challenges to an already existing state law that defined marriage as a union of one man and one woman. Opponents, however, contended the measure was unnecessary and, intentionally or not, promoted hostility toward homosexuals, a minority group.

"I'm not sure the right to desegregate schools, the freedom to marry another race or even access to contraception in many states would exist if those issues were put up for a vote," said Matt Foreman, executive director of the National Gay and Lesbian Task Force.[a]

But Garrett Booth, pastor of Grace Community Church in Clear Lake and a supporter of the amendment, had a different viewpoint. "It's important we do not sit idly by and let an extreme minority set aside what God has set in place. We are living in a day when the things that you and I hold precious are being redefined," Booth said. The proposition, one of nine amendments on the ballot, was approved by a three-to-one margin.[b]

CRITICAL THINKING QUESTIONS

1. **Do restrictions on marriage, such as those enacted in Proposition 2, belong in a state constitution? Why or why not?**
2. **Does a ban on same-sex marriage violate any rights provided in the U.S. Constitution? Why or why not?**

[a]Janet Elliott, "Electon 2005 – Gay Marriage Ban Put in Texas Constitution," *Houston Chronicle*, November 9, 2005, p. 1A.

[b]Kristen Mack, "Election 2005 – Prop 2 Battle to Wire – Grassroots Campaigns on Both Sides Focus on Same-sex Marriage Issue," *Houston Chronicle*, November 7, 2005, p. 1B.

repeatedly turned to the Texas state government for tax breaks and other economic incentives and has found receptive ears in the legislature and the governor's office.

It has been argued that the Texas Constitution serves the interests of a small number of elites—individuals who control businesses and other dominant institutions in the state. According to this argument, the constraints built into the constitution limit the policy options of state government and have historically thwarted efforts to restructure or improve the tax system, education, social services, health care, and other policies that would benefit low- and middle-income people. Power is so fragmented that public interest advocates have repeatedly had to turn to the courts to force change. This same argument also has been made often about the U.S. Constitution.

If this interpretation is accurate, it is ironic that the original writers of the Texas Constitution of 1876 directed much of their wrath against railroads, banks, and other institutions that are today considered elitist. The tumultuous last quarter of the nineteenth century witnessed much class and economic conflict with the emergence of the Greenback and the Populist political parties, which promoted the interests of the lower income groups. But moneyed business interests eventually used the state constitution and subsequent legislation to reestablish their dominance over Texas government. Although the elite structure of the state has changed since 1876, some scholars argue that there has been a gradual transfer of power and control to new elites, who continue to exercise enormous influence over public policy.

□ Change Through Court Interpretation

Some recent legal decisions indicate that Texas courts have become more active in interpreting the constitution in cases involving major state policies. In 1989, the Texas Supreme Court invalidated the system of funding public education and ordered the legislature to provide more equity in tax resources among the state's 1,000-plus school districts. The court ruled that wide disparities in spending on students between rich and poor districts—the result of wide disparities in local property values—violated the state constitution's requirement for an "efficient" system of public schools. The decision prompted a succession of changes to the school funding system and subsequent lawsuits.

More recently, in February 2012, the Texas Supreme Court, in a major water rights case, ruled in favor of two farmers who had challenged governmental restrictions on how much water they could pump from a well on their own land. The ruling was viewed as a major victory for landowners. But environmentalists, who feared it would curtail state water conservation efforts at a time when the state's water resources were being rapidly depleted due to continued population growth, greeted it with concern.[38]

□ Prospects for Future Change

Experts can point out the many flaws of the Texas Constitution, but attempts at wholesale revision have not been successful. Prospects for an overhaul, at least in the near future, are unlikely.

For generations, most Texans have been suspicious of government. They are more concerned about governmental abuses and excesses than they are about restrictions on government's ability to respond quickly and efficiently to public needs. In the popular vernacular, "If it ain't broke, don't fix it." And the average layperson, if he or she thinks much about the state constitution at all, does not consider it to be "broke." Besides, if something really needs fixing, adding another constitutional amendment could do it.

Also, many special interests benefit from the existing constitution, and they resist efforts to change it. Most Texans, though, know little about the document and how it can or does affect their lives. Enormous educational problems must be overcome if citizens are to be motivated to press for constitutional revision. It would take an exceptional statewide effort by reform advocates to mobilize the necessary political resources and develop a successful strategy to produce a constitutional overhaul.[39]

Review the Chapter

Listen to Chapter 2

Constitutionalism

2.1 Identify the functions of a constitution and place the Texas Constitution in a national comparative context, p. 35.

In addition to defining the formal institutional structure of governments, constitutions reflect the primary values and political objectives of a state. A constitution defines the relationships between those who govern and the general population and ultimately structures political power. A constitution limits the power and authority of government and provides basic protection for citizens from excesses and abuses of those who hold power. Whereas the U.S. Constitution is a concise, 7,000-word document that outlines broad, basic principles of authority and governance, the Texas Constitution, like those of many states, is an unwieldy and restrictive document with more than 90,000 words.

The Constitutional Legacy

2.2 Describe the historical influences, similarities, and differences of each of Texas's seven constitutions, p. 36.

Texas (similar to many other states) has functioned under a series of constitutions: the Constitution of Coahuila y Tejas (1827), the Constitution of the Republic of Texas (1836), the Constitution of 1845, the Civil War Constitution (1861), the Constitution of 1866, the Constitution of Reconstruction (1869), and the Constitution of 1876. Each is appropriately understood from the perspective of the period in which it was adopted. There are general similarities in the seven constitutions, but careful attention to each reveals a progression of changes that have occurred over the state's constitutional history. Some of these changes improved the institutions of state government; others served to constrain both state and local governmental institutions.

General Principles of the Texas Constitution

2.3 Explain the major features and general principles of the current Texas Constitution, p. 42.

Texas currently operates under a constitution that was adopted following the Civil War and the Radical Reconstruction era. Events of that period left an enduring legacy of suspicion of government, limited government, and fragmented governmental institutions. The 1876 constitution was predicated on the theory that governmental excesses could be minimized by carefully defining what governments could or could not do. The major guiding principles of the current Texas Constitution are popular sovereignty, limited government, representative government, social contract theory, and separation of powers.

Weaknesses and Criticisms of the Constitution of 1876

2.4 Outline the weaknesses and criticisms of the current Texas Constitution, particularly as they pertain to how the framers failed to anticipate economic and social changes in the state, p. 44.

What the delegates to the Constitutional Convention of 1875 regarded as the strengths of the constitution—fragmented authority, detailed limitations on the power of governmental institutions, and decentralization—have served to limit the ability of state and local governments to adapt effectively to economic and demographic changes. The perceived solutions to so many of the problems of 1875 have compounded the problems of state and local governments today. The framers failed to anticipate that the limitations they imposed on governmental institutions would ultimately allow major economic interests within the state to dominate the policymaking process, often to the detriment of the lower socioeconomic groups.

Constitutional Change and Adaptation

2.5 Contrast the ease and frequency of the constitutional amendment process with the difficulty of enacting more fundamental change through the constitutional convention process, p. 47.

Efforts to overhaul the Texas Constitution have failed. Consequently, the state has been forced to amend the document continually on a piecemeal basis. This process has produced some success in modernizing the charter, but many structural problems of state government require major institutional changes that cannot be resolved through this amendment process.

Over the years, numerous groups have attempted to protect their interests through constitutional amendments. But the same groups usually oppose any proposed changes that threaten their influence, power, or benefits. Therefore, the interests of small segments of the state's population often prevail over the interests of the majority.

In many ways, the Texas Constitution reflects the values of the state's conservative political culture, which continues to be suspicious of far-reaching constitutional changes. Moreover, constitutions and the debates that surround them are complex, and most people pay little attention to these issues. Consequently, it is much easier to mobilize public opinion against rather than for wholesale change.

Learn the Terms

 **Study** and **Review** the Flashcards

constitution, p. 35
statutory law, p. 35
unicameral, p. 36
unitary system, p. 37
federalism, p. 37
bicameral legislature, p. 37
plural executive, p. 39
confederacy, p. 39
Radical Reconstructionists, p. 40
Edmund J. Davis, p. 40
Grange, p. 42
popular sovereignty, p. 43
social contract, p. 43
limited government, p. 43
separation of powers, p. 43
initiative, p. 48
referendum, p. 48
Constitutional Convention of 1974, p. 48
right-to-work law, p. 49

Test Yourself

 **Study** and **Review** the Practice Tests

1. In contrast to the U.S. Constitution, the Texas Constitution

a. is much shorter in length.
b. has the quality of statutory law.
c. has been amended only twenty-seven times in its history.
d. was written to provide for maximum flexibility to meet new problems.
e. was drafted in 1865 in response to the Civil War.

2. What is one feature of the Constitution of Coahuila y Tejas that continues to influence Texas today?

a. existence of a unicameral legislature
b. protection of Catholicism as the state religion
c. division of the executive branch into three officials
d. local control over public education
e. publication of laws in English and Spanish

3. All of the following influenced the move for an independent republic EXCEPT the

a. enforcement of the principle of federalism by the central government in Mexico City.
b. suspension of the Mexican Constitution of 1824.
c. repudiation of the principle of federalism by Santa Anna.
d. stationing of Mexican army troops on Texas soil.
e. rising tensions between Anglo settlers and Mexican officials.

4. What did the Constitution of the Republic of Texas do?

a. It created a unicameral legislature.
b. It retained Catholicism as the official state religion.
c. It prohibited clergy from serving in the legislature or as president.
d. It abolished the institution of slavery.
e. It lasted for thirty years.

5. The one feature of the Constitution of the Republic that is not found in the current state constitution is

a. an elected governor and lieutenant governor.
b. a bicameral legislature.
c. a plural executive.
d. property rights for married women.
e. annual legislative sessions.

6. Texas drafted and ratified the Constitution of 1845 because it

a. became a state in the United States of America.
b. became a state in the Confederate States of America.
c. became a state in the Republic of Mexico.
d. became the Lone Star Republic.
e. reentered the Union after the Civil War.

7. Under the Civil War Constitution

a. the two-party system was made stronger.
b. the Southern Baptist Church became the official state church.
c. the basic structure of governmental institutions changed significantly.
d. slave owners were prohibited from freeing their slaves.
e. the Texas government was subject to national control.

8. What happened after the Civil War?

a. The Constitution of 1866 gave freed slaves the right to vote.
b. The federal government imposed a military government on the state.
c. The Constitution of Reconstruction enjoyed widespread popular support.
d. The Constitution of Reconstruction returned to biennial legislative sessions.
e. The Constitution of Reconstruction strengthened local government.

9. All of the following can be said about the drafting and ratification of the Constitution of 1876 EXCEPT that

a. most of the delegates to the constitutional convention were white.
b. the constitution was heavily influenced by agricultural interests.
c. convention delegates reacted against the abuse of power under the Reconstruction government.
d. it enjoyed widespread popular support.
e. it favored centralization of state power at the expense of local control.

10. What does the current constitution call for?

a. a bicameral legislature that appoints the governor
b. a bicameral legislature that meets annually
c. a judicial branch that is popularly elected
d. a veto power that can be overridden by a simple majority vote of the legislature
e. a very weak system of separation of powers

11. All of the following are weaknesses of the Constitution of 1876 EXCEPT that

a. the governor has little control over executive branch agencies.
b. the legislative branch is part time.
c. centralization of public schools leads to lack of accountability to local populations.
d. excessive detail makes it difficult for the government to adapt to changing circumstances.
e. amending the constitution is the only way to enable the government to adapt to changing circumstances.

12. The Constitution of 1876

a. gives the governor tremendous power over his or her cabinet.
b. gives low-paid legislators immunity from the influence of interest groups.
c. expands voter participation with the use of a poll tax.
d. has been amended more than 470 times.
e. is one of the most concise of all state constitutions.

13. Which of the following is true about an amendment to the Texas Constitution?

a. It must be proposed by the legislature.
b. It can be recommended by citizen initiative.
c. It requires a simple majority vote in both houses of the legislature.
d. It requires a two-thirds vote of the public to become effective.
e. It may address only statewide issues.

14. All of the following are reasons the Constitutional Convention of 1974 failed EXCEPT that

a. a right-to-work provision was opposed by organized labor.
b. the governor's strong leadership of the effort was resisted by the legislature.
c. the members of the convention were also members of the legislature.
d. several legislators opposed to the effort obstructed the convention's work.
e. the convention could not get two-thirds support to put the new constitution on the ballot.

15. What can be said about the modern amendment process?

a. More voters participate in constitutional amendment elections than in presidential elections.
b. Interest groups have a minor influence in the process.
c. Texas voters are typically very interested in constitutional amendments.
d. Constitutional amendments never deal with controversial social issues.
e. The process tends to serve the interests of small, organized elites.

Explore Further

Braden, George D., et al., *The Constitution of the State of Texas: An Annotated and Comparative Analysis.* 2 vols. Austin: Texas Advisory Commission on Intergovernmental Relations, 1977. Originally designed as a research tool for delegates to the 1974 Constitutional Convention, this work provides an explanation of the historical development of the Texas Constitution and a comparative perspective on other state constitutions.

Bruff, Harold H., "Separation of Powers under the Texas Constitution," *Texas Law Review* 68 (June 1990), pp. 1337–67. Summarizes leading state court cases pertaining to the separation of powers clause of the Texas Constitution and addresses issues of judicial review.

Dinan, John J., *The American State Constitutional Tradition.* Lawrence: University Press of Kansas, 2006. A study based on 114 state constitutional conventions in which the author differentiates state constitutions from the national Constitution, noting differences in constitutional principles incorporated into the state constitutions.

Gardner, James A., *Interpreting State Constitutions.* Chicago, IL: The University of Chicago Press, 2005. Provides a general theory as to the interpretation of state constitutions in the area of civil liberties jurisprudence.

Lutz, Donald S., *Principles of Constitutional Design.* New York: Cambridge University Press, 2006. The author works from a comparative perspective to introduce the theoretical foundations of constitutionalism, principles of constitutional design, and constitutionalism and democratic theory.

Lutz, Donald S., "The Purposes of American State Constitutions," *Publius: The Journal of Federalism* 12 (Winter 1982), pp. 27–44. A general introduction to state constitutions, placing the states' documents within the framework of U.S. constitutionalism.

Mauer, John Walker, "State Constitutions in a Time of Crisis: The Case of the Texas Constitution of 1876," *Texas Law Review* 68 (June 1990), pp. 1615–47. Focuses on the enactment of post-Reconstruction constitutions in Texas and the South, arguing that the constitutional framers of 1875 were reacting not only to Republican Reconstruction but also to the recently elected Democratic administration.

May, Janice C., *The Texas Constitution Revision Experience in the 70s.* Austin, TX: Sterling Swift, 1975. The author, a close observer of Texas politics, chronicles the events surrounding the Constitutional Convention of 1974.

Tarr, G. Alan, *Understanding State Constitutions.* Princeton, NJ: Princeton University Press, 1998. An introduction to state constitutional theory that addresses differences among state constitutions and differences between the federal and state constitutions.

Wolff, Nelson, *Challenge of Change.* San Antonio, TX: The Naylor Co., 1975. Written by a delegate to the 1974 Constitutional Convention, the author discusses the divisive issues that eventually led to the convention's failure and provides an abbreviated history of the convention proceedings.

Listen on MyPoliSciLab

3 Texas Government and Politics in the Federal System

In the compound republic of America, the power surrendered by the people is first divided between two distinct governments, and then the portion allotted to each sub-divided among distinct and separate departments.

—James Madison, 1788

American federalism was born in ambiguity, it institutionalizes ambiguity in our form of government, and changes in it tend to be ambiguous too.

—Martha Derthick, 2001

3.1 Explain the ways in which nations can structure the relationships among their national, regional, and local governments, p. 61.

3.2 Define federalism and explain the constitutional relationship between the states and the national government, p. 62.

3.3 Summarize the different theories of federalism using generalized views or metaphors, p. 66.

3.4 Trace the development of federalism over the course of American history, focusing primarily on changes in the relationship between the national government and the states, p. 67.

3.5 Assess the impact of federalism on state finances and the extent to which state governments depend on federal funds, p. 76.

3.6 Compare and contrast the arguments for and against the expanded role of the federal government, p. 76.

3.7 Describe the increased interdependency between the United States and Mexico and list common issues faced by both nations, p. 77.

COOPERATION, COORDINATION, AND COLLABORATION WITHIN THE FRAMEWORK OF THE FEDERAL SYSTEM
When major natural disasters occur, there are provisions in place for governments at all levels to bring their resources together to provide relief and recovery. Shown here, joint responders—including those from the Texas Air National Guard and the Texas Army National Guard—work with civilian emergency responders to help people in Galveston, Texas, affected by Hurricane Ike in 2008.

reserved powers
Powers given to state governments by the Tenth Amendment. These are powers not delegated to the national government nor otherwise prohibited to the states by the Constitution.

In a new twist on the old "states' rights" argument, conservative Texas legislators, with the support of Governor Rick Perry, tried to pass a state law in 2011 that would have prohibited "intrusive touching" by government agents of an individual at airports and other public buildings. This challenge of some federal Transportation Security Administration (TSA) airport screening procedures—those involving touching of private body parts—was prompted by widespread public unpopularity with the process. It became another rallying cry for conservatives, including Perry and Texans affiliated with the tea party movement, who advocated more independence from Washington. Basing their arguments on the Tenth Amendment to the U.S. Constitution, they contended that the federal government had been illegally extending its reach over the states for many years and it was time for the states to take a stand against federal encroachment. The Tenth Amendment, adopted by Congress in 1789 and ratified by the states in 1791, provides, "The powers not delegated to the United States by the Constitution, nor prohibited by it to the States, are reserved to the States respectively or to the people."

However, in a letter to Texas officials on behalf of the TSA, U.S. Attorney John Murphy interpreted the Tenth Amendment's **reserved powers** differently from the governor and conservative lawmakers. Murphy said the state legislation, if enacted, would "criminalize searches that are required under federal regulations" and would "conflict directly with federal law." He said Texas lacked the authority to regulate federal agents and employees in the performance of their official duties and said the federal government would seek a court order, if necessary, to ban enforcement of such a law. Moreover, he added, "TSA would likely be required to cancel any flight or series of flights for which it could not ensure the safety of the passengers and crew."

The federal government never had to carry out its implied threat to shut down Texas airports because the legislation died, even though the states' rights sentiment among some legislators did not. "This was a come and take it moment for the state of Texas," fumed state Senator Dan Patrick, a Houston Republican and chairman of the legislative Tea Party Caucus, repeating a slogan Texas colonists had made famous during their nineteenth-century war of independence from Mexico.[1]

It is not unusual for governments to fight over turf, and when they do, the disputes often are political. In this case, Republican legislators in Texas were using the airport security bill to attack a federal administration then in the hands of a Democratic president. Usually, though, jurisdictional disputes—particularly between the states and the federal government—are not resolved in a state legislature. They are resolved in federal courts, which apply constitutional principles outlined later in this chapter.

The state and federal governments, of course, are just two of many governments with authority in one fashion or another over Texas citizens. If you live in a large metropolitan area, you may be under the jurisdiction of as many as ten or more different governments or taxing authorities. A person living within the corporate limits of San Antonio is subject to the laws, regulations, and taxes of the federal government, the state of Texas, Bexar County, the city of San Antonio, the Alamo Community College District, one of sixteen independent school districts, the Edwards Aquifer Authority, the San Antonio River Authority, the Bexar County Hospital District, and a public transportation authority.

There are more than 89,000 governmental units in the United States, with approximately 500,000 persons serving on their governing bodies. According to a 2007 census of governments (see Table 3–1), Texas had 4,836 individual governments, including 254 counties, 1,209 municipalities, and 3,372 school districts and other special districts. What's more, the total number of governments in Texas increased by some 1,400 between 1967 and 2007. Most of the additional ones were special districts.

The jurisdictional structure of governments in this country is complex and confusing, and people often are frustrated when they try to identify the government that has the authority or responsibility to address one of their specific needs or concerns. Governments in the United States and in Texas share many responsibilities, and it is quite possible for individuals to find themselves enmeshed in jurisdictional disputes between agencies of different governments.

TABLE 3–1 GOVERNMENTS IN THE UNITED STATES AND TEXAS, 2007*

	U.S.	TEXAS
U.S. Government	1	—
State Government	50	1
Counties	3,033	254
Municipalities	19,492	1,209
Townships and Towns	16,519	—
School Districts	13,051	1,081
Special Districts	37,381	2,291
Total	89,527	4,836

* The U.S. Census Bureau conducts a Census of Governments of all state and local government organization units every 5 years, for years ending in 2 and 7.

SOURCE: U.S. Department of Commerce, Bureau of the Census, *2007 Census of Governments, Government Organizations*, vol. 1, Table 3.

unitary system
A system in which ultimate power is vested in a central or national government and local governments have only those powers granted to them by the central government. This principle describes the relationship between the state and local governments in Texas.

confederation
A system in which each member government is considered sovereign, and the national government is limited to powers delegated to it by its member governments.

From our country's very beginnings, Americans have been leery of highly centralized government.[2] These diverse and complex jurisdictional arrangements, therefore, were created to limit government, especially the federal government. Moreover, the enormous size of the country and the great distances between settlements during the nation's formative period made it extremely difficult for a centralized government at either the national or state level to serve and control political subdivisions. This contributed to the proliferation of smaller governmental units. Regional differences in religion, economics, and political cultures also encouraged decentralization and the development of local governments.

Structuring Regional and National Interests

3.1 Explain the ways in which nations can structure the relationships among their national, regional, and local governments.

Governments around the world have struggled to find ways to coordinate local and regional interests with national interests. Countries in the former Soviet bloc, for example, have struggled, sometimes violently, with political systems for diverse racial, cultural, and ethnic groups. Canada, which has a stable political system, still seeks political and institutional solutions for the movement for French separatism. The effort to rebuild Iraq has been compounded by debate over the geographical distribution of power among the Sunnis, Shiites, Arabs, and Kurds. Many similar issues confronted the framers of the U.S. Constitution during the formative period of the United States.

Three fundamental systems—unitary, confederal, and federal—are used in structuring the relationship of a central government to its constituent parts. Over the history of our nation, all three organizational principles have been used at one time or the other.

In some countries, democratic as well as authoritarian, ultimate power is vested in a national or central government. Under such a **unitary system**, local or regional governments are created by the national government, have only the power and authority granted to them by the national government, and serve "only to implement policies established by the national government."[3] In the United States, the unitary principle has been used only to define relationships between state and local governments.

A **confederation** is based on the principle that each component government is sovereign in its own right, and the powers of the national government are limited to those powers delegated to it by the member governments. The United States experimented with a confederal system prior to the adoption of the present Constitution

federalism
A system that balances the power and sovereignty of state governments with those of the national government. Both the states and the national government derive their authority directly from the people, and the states have considerable autonomy within their areas of responsibility.

Dillon rule
A principle holding that local governments are creations of state government and their powers and responsibilities are defined by the state.

in 1789, and the southern states used the confederal principle during the Civil War. There are inherent weaknesses in such a system, including the ability of member governments to nullify the acts of the national government and withdraw from the relationship. Citizenship in and loyalty to the component governments take precedence over citizenship in and loyalty to the central government.

Delegates to the U.S. Constitutional Convention of 1787 rejected the confederal principle in favor of **federalism**, which balances the power and sovereignty of the state governments with those of the national government. Both the states and the national government derive their authority directly from the people, and the states have considerable latitude and autonomy within their areas of defined power and responsibility. In many respects, federalism is a middle ground between a confederal system and a unitary system of government.

The unitary principle, however, is the basis for the relationship between state and local governments under the Texas Constitution and state laws. Counties, cities, and special districts have only those powers granted to them by the state. Sovereignty of local government does not exist in Texas. Local governments are primarily administrative subdivisions of the state. The prevailing constitutional theory regarding local governments in the United States, which has been incorporated into Texas law, was articulated in the **Dillon rule**, which held that if a state could create local governments, it also could destroy or eliminate them.[4] Political and practical considerations, however, usually preclude the elimination of local governments.

Defining Federalism

3.2 Define federalism and explain the constitutional relationship between the states and the national government.

lthough the U.S. Constitution outlines federalism in broad terms, it does not clearly specify the governmental relationships that should be established. For more than 200 years, scholars, politicians, judges, and bureaucrats not only have been debating the complexities of the federal system, but they also have been trying to figure out how to define federalism.[5] One scholar has identified 267 definitions and concepts relating to the term.[6] The problem is compounded by the fact that the relationships among federal, state, and local governments have changed over the past two centuries, and they continue to change.

If scholars cannot agree on a definition of federalism and the current elements of these complex governmental relationships, how can you, as the student, understand contemporary federalism? First, it is important to assess federalism over time. There were periods in our political history when the pendulum of power shifted from the states to the national government. At other points, a decentralizing tendency in federal-state relationships occurred. Our discussion attempts to provide a broad overview of these historical patterns.

An assessment of broad historical periods leads to a tendency to overgeneralize and to simplify. In any given period, the three branches of the federal government do not speak with a unified voice on federal issues. A Congress and the president may pursue policies that centralize power in Washington; the federal judiciary may pursue a different course of action through its decisions in cases involving federal issues. Moreover, different subunits within the executive and congressional branches of the national government may pursue different objectives in federal-state relationships.

Finally, the policy process relating to federalism is so complex with so many different actors that it often is difficult to measure the exact impact of the national government's actions on the states. The complex "policy networks" discussed later involve many participants, including elected officials, administrators, political parties, interest groups, and private organizations. Some policy arenas show a tendency for centralization of public goods and services. In others, participants favor decentralization.[7]

☐ Federal-State Relationships from a Constitutional Perspective

We tend to think of federalism as a division of power between the states and the national government, and we look to the U.S. Constitution to specify the powers and responsibilities of each. However, the Constitution is vague on these points, and "all efforts to define the distribution of authority among governments have been unsuccessful."[8] The structure and operation of our federal system of government confuse many individuals. It is a system of numerous shared functions and responsibilities that often make it difficult to identify a single person or institution as having the ultimate responsibility for addressing a specific issue or problem.

Ambiguous constitutional provisions have helped produce jurisdictional conflicts throughout the nation's history. We even fought a war among ourselves to determine the powers and authority of the states and national government. Although the Civil War resolved the issue that a state could not withdraw from the federal Union, many other questions continue to be debated. These ambiguities and changes in political and economic conditions make the relationships among governments subject to further change in the future. Over the past several decades, much debate at all levels of government over **devolution**, or the return of power to the states, has occurred.

The enumerated or **delegated powers** of the national government are outlined primarily in Article 1, Section 8, of the U.S. Constitution. They include the powers to tax, to borrow and coin money, to declare war, and to regulate interstate and foreign commerce. The first seventeen paragraphs of Section 8 are rather specific, in part because the framers of the Constitution, apprehensive about potential abuses, intended to limit the powers of the national government. They did not, however, close the door to unforeseen events. In paragraph 18 of Section 8, they further provided that Congress shall have the power "to make all Laws which shall be necessary and proper for carrying into Execution the foregoing Powers."[9] This provision is the **implied powers** clause, which has been used to justify the subsequent expansion of the federal government's powers.

To further compound the jurisdictional question, Article 6 states that the U.S. Constitution and the laws made in pursuance "shall be the supreme Law of the Land."[10] This **supremacy clause** suggests that when a conflict develops between the powers of the states and the national government, the federal law prevails.

Although the Constitution does not spell out the authority of the states and their subdivisions in detail, the states have assumed a formidable array of powers and responsibilities in domestic affairs. State or local governments take most actions affecting our daily lives as they relate to police, regulatory, and taxing powers, and most litigation in the country takes place in state or local courts, not in federal courts.

The absence of specific constitutional language spelling out many powers of the state concerned many state governments. The Tenth Amendment, with its reserved powers clause, described at the beginning of this chapter, was adopted to address these concerns. Today, conservatives in Texas and other states cite it to argue for more limits on federal power, although their interpretation is far from universal.

In addition to the Tenth Amendment's reserved powers for the states, there are **concurrent powers** held by the states and the national government. Both have the power to raise taxes, develop and implement public policies, spend money, borrow money, and establish their own court systems.

There also are certain constitutional guarantees to the states. Texas is assured a republican form of government, protection against invasion and domestic violence, and the power to maintain a militia. If a person is accused of a federal crime in Texas, the trial is to be held in a federal court in Texas. Texas cannot be divided into another state without its permission and is assured two members in the U.S. Senate and membership in the U.S. House of Representatives based on its population in relation to the other states. After the 2010 census, Texas had 36 members in the U.S. House. The state also has a role in ratifying amendments to the U.S. Constitution and controls many aspects of federal elections.[11]

devolution
Return of powers assumed by the federal government to the states.

delegated powers
Powers specifically assigned to the national, or federal, government by the U.S. Constitution, including powers to tax, borrow and coin money, declare war, and regulate interstate and foreign commerce.

implied powers
Although not specifically defined by the U.S. Constitution, powers assumed by the national government as necessary in carrying out its responsibilities.

supremacy clause
A provision of the U.S. Constitution that says federal law prevails in conflicts between the powers of the states and the national government.

concurrent powers
Powers shared by both the national and state governments.

denied powers
Powers that are denied to both the states and national government. The best-known restrictions are listed in the Bill of Rights.

full faith and credit clause
A provision in the U.S. Constitution (Article 4, Section 1) that requires states to recognize civil judgments and official documents rendered by the courts of other states.

Reflecting its drafters' concerns about governmental excesses, the Constitution also limits the powers of both the states and the national government. These prohibitions or **denied powers** are interspersed throughout the document and are enumerated, in particular, in the first ten amendments—the Bill of Rights. The original intent of the Bill of Rights was to limit the powers of the national government. Since the Civil War, however, the federal courts have gradually incorporated the Bill of Rights into the Fourteenth Amendment, which was intended to restrict the powers of the state governments. Some have described this expansion as the nationalization of the Bill of Rights.

The broad and often ambiguous language of the U.S. Constitution lends itself to controversy and interpretation. Over the years, Congress, the states, and the courts have attempted to resolve conflicts about powers and jurisdiction. In many instances, the Supreme Court has played an instrumental role in redefining the relationship between the states and the federal government.

□ Relationships among the States

The federal system is not limited to the relationship between the states and the national government (vertical federalism). It also includes the relationship of the states to one another (horizontal federalism). Many of these constitutional-legal obligations were included in the Articles of Confederation, which established the first system of national government in the United States. Conflict as well as cooperation among the states during that period provided the rationale for defining the obligations and responsibilities of the states to one another.

The Constitution states, "Full Faith and Credit shall be given in each State to the public Acts, Records, and judicial Proceedings of every other state."[12] To eliminate chaos and to stimulate cooperation, this **full faith and credit clause** ensures that official governmental actions of one state are accepted by other states. Business contracts in Texas are recognized as legal in other states, as are drivers' licenses and heterosexual marriages. However, the 1996 federal Defense of Marriage Act, which denies federal recognition of same-sex marriages or civil unions, has enabled states to refuse to recognize marriages or civil unions of same-sex couples performed in other states. This divisive issue continues to be fought in the courts and the political arena.

The Obama administration announced in 2011 that it considered the Defense of Marriage Act unconstitutional and would no longer defend it against legal challenges. At least two federal judges, one in Massachusetts and another in California, have declared the Defense of Marriage Act unconstitutional in cases involving same-sex spousal benefits.[13] Sooner or later, the U.S. Supreme Court likely will address the constitutionality of the federal law and its impact on same-sex marriage laws and prohibitions in the states. A number of conservatives, including Texas Governor Rick Perry, have advocated for an amendment to the U.S. Constitution that would ban same-sex marriages in any state. However, the political obstacles against such an amendment, which would require approval by a two-thirds vote in both houses of Congress and ratification by three-fourths of the states, are high.

As of 2012, Texas was one of forty-one states to prohibit same-sex marriages, either by state statute or a provision in the state constitution. Texas adopted a constitutional amendment prohibiting same-sex marriages in 2005. Nine states, including California and New York, have legalized same-sex marriages, but some of those laws have been challenged in court. A same-sex marriage law in California in effect for a few months in 2008 was struck down by Proposition 8, a citizen initiative that placed a ban on same-sex marriages in the state constitution. By early 2012, Proposition 8 had been overturned in rulings by a federal district judge and a federal appeals court on grounds that Proposition 8 violated the U.S. Constitution's equal protection clause. "Proposition 8 serves no purpose, and has no effect, other than to lessen the status and human dignity of gay men and lesbians in California," Judge Stephen R. Reinhardt

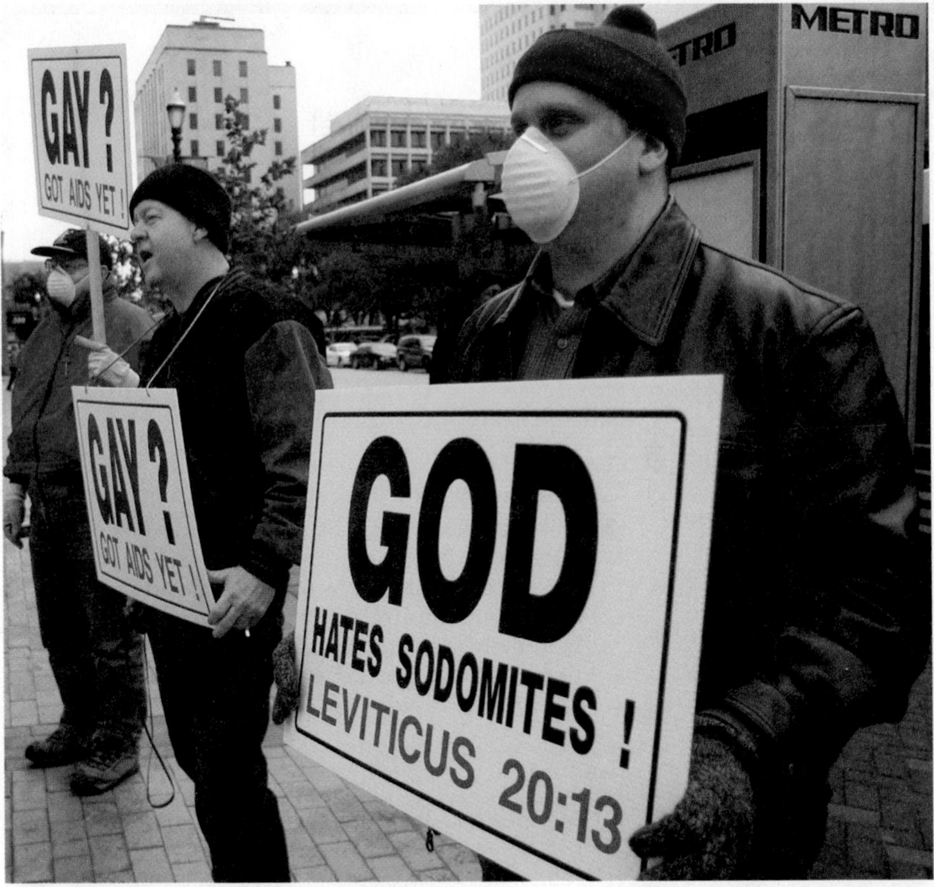

PROTESTING SAME-SEX MARRIAGE

Members of the Ku Klux Klan demonstrate against gay couples outside the Harris County Clerk's office in Houston in 2004. About 30 gay couples entered the office to request marriage licenses in protest of the federal Defense of Marriage Act, which prevents Texas from legally recognizing same-sex unions. But they were denied marriage licenses.

privileges and immunities
The right of a resident of one state to be protected by the laws and afforded the legal opportunities in any other state he or she visits. Certain exceptions, however, have been allowed by the courts, including the right of states to charge nonresidents higher college tuition or higher hunting and fishing license fees.

extradition
A process by which a person in one state can be returned to another state to face criminal charges.

interstate compacts
Formal, long-term cooperative agreements among the states dealing with common problems or issues and subject to approval of the U.S. Congress.

wrote in the appellate court decision in February 2012. An appeal to the U.S. Supreme Court, however, is considered likely.[14]

As a person travels from one state to another, the Constitution entitles that person to the **privileges and immunities** of the states where he or she goes. A person can acquire property in another state, establish residency and eventually citizenship, and be assured of access to the legal system of that state. But exceptions have been established by court interpretation. States, for example, can charge nonresidents higher college tuition or higher fees for hunting and fishing licenses.

The Constitution also provides for the return of a person accused of a crime. If a person who has been charged with a crime in Texas attempts to avoid trial by fleeing to another state, he or she can be returned to Texas by a process called **extradition**. States routinely handle hundreds of these cases each year. Once the accused has been located, the state seeking the individual will request that the second state arrest and return him or her. The governor is responsible for granting extradition requests.

Until fairly recently, governors used an 1861 court decision to maintain that they had the discretion to refuse another state's extradition request.[15] This was the prevailing view for 125 years, until Puerto Rico challenged the discretionary powers of the governor in a 1987 case.[16] The Supreme Court held that the "duty to extradite is mandatory, and the federal courts are available to enforce that duty."[17]

The U.S. Constitution also anticipated the need for structuring more formal, long-term, cooperative relationships among the states. Article 1, Section 10, allows the states, with the approval of Congress, to enter into **interstate compacts**. There are more than 100 of these, some affecting only two states, whereas others include all

Talking ★ TEXAS Get Off Our Land, You Varmints!

Sometimes around the state Capitol, one has to look for humor wherever it can be found. A few years ago that humor came in the form of news that a New Mexico legislator had filed a bill in that state's Senate to recover some 603,485 acres—a three-mile strip along the Texas–New Mexico border—that had been wrongly assigned to Texas in 1859 as a result of a surveyor's error. For whatever reason, officials in New Mexico periodically resurrect the issue.

No one in Texas expected the latest claim to go anywhere, and it did not. But as the issue churned around in the corridors of the New Mexico legislature and the newsrooms of state papers, an element of absurdity emerged. New Mexico papers began to pick up on the potential humor and demanded that Texans vacate the disputed area. An *Albuquerque Tribune* headline ordered: "Waltz off our land, you Texas varmints."[a]

About the same time, Texas Land Commissioner Jerry Patterson challenged his counterpart in New Mexico, Patrick H. Lyons, to a duel. According to one account—the information is sketchy—the alleged "duel" took place a few months later in Austin. The weapons of choice were vintage flintlocks. We do not know if shots were fired, but both officials claimed the honor of their respective states had been served.[b]

CRITICAL THINKING QUESTIONS

1. **Should a land dispute, even as minor as this one, be resolved in court? Why or why not?**
2. **It is quite likely that other surveying errors may have occurred in the nineteenth century as vast amounts of the Western frontier were divided up into territories and, later, states. Is it likely that any state would be willing to give back a portion of its land to another state? Why or why not?**

[a]Kate Nelson, "Waltz Off Our Land, You Texas Varmints," *The Albuquerque Tribune*, March 4, 2003.

[b]Patrick H. Lyons, New Mexico State Land Office, Press Release, March 14, 2003; Ray Cooklis, "Border Dispute: Texas Strip Stake," *Cincinnati Enquirer*, March 14, 2003; and Texas General Land Office, Press Release, January 7, 2004.

dual federalism
Nineteenth century concept of federalism in which the powers or functions of the national and state governments were sharply differentiated with limited overlapping responsibilities.

fifty states. Texas now belongs to several interstate compacts, including the Interstate Oil and Gas Compact, the Interstate Mining Compact, and the Low Level Radioactive Waste Compact.

Although cooperation is desired, states often find themselves involved in disagreements that only lawsuits can resolve (see *Talking Texas: Get Off Our Land, You Varmints!).* Boundary disputes, control or use of water resources, and licensing fees that affect interstate shipping are among issues that are litigated in the federal judiciary, where the Supreme Court has jurisdiction in the first instance or original jurisdiction in all "controversies between two or more states."[18]

Metaphors for Federalism

3.3 Summarize the different theories of federalism using generalized views or metaphors.

The constitutional-legal descriptions of federalism outlined earlier can leave one with the idea that the federal, state, and local levels of government are autonomous and function independently with distinct and separate spheres of responsibility, a view often linked to **dual federalism** or a "layer-cake" theory of intergovernmental relations. Morton Grodzins, an authority on federalism, has argued that this perspective is now inaccurate and suggests that intergovernmental relations can be symbolized more accurately by the metaphor of a "marble cake." Rather than possessing distinct and separate powers and responsibilities, governments have shared responsibilities. In describing federalism, Grodzins writes:

> Whenever you slice through it [marble cake] you reveal an inseparable mixture of differently colored ingredients. There is no neat horizontal stratification. Vertical and diagonal lines almost obliterate the horizontal ones, and in some places there

> are unexpected whirls and imperceptible merging of colors, so that it is difficult to tell where one ends and the other begins. So it is with federal, state, and local responsibilities in the chaotic marble cake of American Government.[19]

cooperative federalism
Policies emphasizing cooperative efforts among the federal, state, and local governments to address common problems and provide public services to the citizens.

Public functions are not neatly divided among the different levels of government. In virtually every area of public policy, governments coordinate, collaborate, and cooperate to meet shared goals and objectives. This view reflects, in large measure, governmental relationships associated with **cooperative federalism**, which we discuss later in this chapter.

Another metaphor, the "picket-fence" theory of federalism, builds on Grodzins's notions of shared powers and responsibilities but focuses on specific policy arenas that cut across each level of government. This metaphor suggests that we look at a specific policy arena (e.g., highways, education, or welfare), identify the primary participants at each level of government, and map out their patterns of interaction. Although the concept is an oversimplification, it does suggest complex institutional and political relationships that cut across all levels of government.[20]

As might be expected, the complexity of federalism has generated much discussion about how to best describe and assess the relationships among governments. The problem, of course, is compounded by the fact that governmental relationships are shaped by changes in the political parties, presidents, the composition of Congress, the courts, prevailing economic and social conditions, and the public's expectations of their governments.

Changing Patterns in Federal Relationships

3.4 Trace the development of federalism over the course of American history, focusing primarily on changes in the relationship between the national government and the states.

Federal relationships have changed over the nation's history, generating some of the confusion in reaching conclusive descriptions and definitions of federalism. We can assess broad patterns of federal-state relationships by historical periods, although relationship patterns do not start or stop in specific years but can continue over multiple eras. Various scholars have developed different classifications of federalism, but centralization and federal authority have generally increased over the years.

State-Centered and Dual Federalism

In both theory and practice, federal relationships from 1790 to the 1930s usually are defined in terms of dual federalism. During the early decades of our political history, the primary responsibility for domestic policy fell to the states and local governments with very little involvement or intervention by the federal government. Yet, there were domestic policies that generated conflict, and both the national and state governments continually engaged in legal and policy issues that attempted to define the lines of demarcation between their respective powers.[21] Conflicts usually were resolved through court cases and statutory laws, but the federal-state issues centering on slavery erupted into the Civil War. The dual federalism of this era was marked by adversarial, if not antagonistic, relationships at various levels of government.

The U.S. Supreme Court first addressed the issue of state-federal relationships in 1819 in the case of *McCulloch* v. *Maryland*.[22] The state of Maryland had levied a tax on the Baltimore branch of the Bank of the United States. McCulloch, the bank's cashier, refused to pay the tax, thus precipitating a lawsuit. The case raised a fundamental issue

categorical grants-in-aid
Grants of federal money that can be spent only for specific programs or purposes. This is the source of most federal assistance to state and local governments.

3.1

3.2

3.3

3.4

3.5

3.6

3.7

regarding federalism. Did the national government have the power to create a bank that, in fact, would compete with state banks? The Supreme Court, then headed by Chief Justice John Marshall, an advocate of central power, ruled that the implied powers clause of the Constitution, linked to the delegated or enumerated powers, gave the federal government this authority.

A second issue was whether a state could tax the branch bank, an institution of the national government. The court again ruled in favor of the U.S. government. It held that the states do not have the power to tax the national government because, if this were to be permitted, the states could destroy national institutions, and federal laws would become subordinate to those of the states, thus undermining the supremacy clause of the Constitution.

Hundreds of federal-state issues have been litigated in the federal courts since *McCulloch*, and those cases making it to the Supreme Court demonstrate the role of the court in arbitrating disputes between state and federal authority.[23] Along with political and economic changes, these cases have been central to redefining federal-state relationships over the past 200 years, although the principles outlined in *McCulloch* remain intact.

☐ Cooperative Federalism

The economic hardships produced by the Great Depression of the 1930s resulted in demands for a greater role of the federal government in domestic policy. States and cities simply were unable to provide many basic services or address the personal needs of large numbers of people who were unemployed. The states did not have the economic resources to deal with problems that extended beyond their borders, and many lacked the political or institutional will to implement new policies. Moreover, the increased economic interdependency of the states and the national scope of economic problems provided compelling arguments for federal intervention. Although there were precedents for greater federal-state cooperation prior to the 1930s, the New Deal expanded dramatically the role of the federal government in relation to the states and local governments.[24]

V. O. Key, who wrote extensively on state government, summarized the extent of these changes:

> The federal government underwent a radical transformation after . . . 1932. It had been a remote authority with a limited range of activity. It operated the postal system, improved rivers and harbors, maintained armed forces on a scale fearsome only to banana republics, and performed other functions of which the average citizen was hardly aware. Within a brief time, it became an institution that affected intimately the lives and fortunes of most, if not all, citizens.[25]

Those supporting the development of cooperative federalism rejected the notion of dual federalism, whereby each level of government had virtual or exclusive authority in select areas of domestic policy. The commerce and the supremacy clauses of the Constitution were used to support an expanded role of the federal government. Many of the new programs engaged local, state, and federal policymakers in cooperative efforts—from program development to program implementation. Cooperative federalism ensures that all three levels of government share the responsibility for domestic programs "by making the larger governments primarily responsible for raising revenues and setting standards and the smaller ones primarily responsible for administering the programs."[26]

Throughout the nation's history, the federal government has used various devices to shape and implement domestic programs, but the primary vehicle has been the provision of federal funds for public programs through **categorical grants-in-aid**. There are more than 500 grant programs with approximately 90 percent of federal funds allocated to states and local governments as categorical grants-in-aid.[27] Money allocated under a specific program can be spent only for that purpose. Federal laws also include specific standards or requirements that recipients must meet, such as prohibitions against racial or sex discrimination or prohibitions against nonunion pay scales.

There are two types of categorical grants. The first is the **project grant**, which requires a state or local government to apply for a grant to the appropriate federal agency and compete against other state or local governments for the funds. The money is awarded on the merits of an application. There are hundreds of these grant programs ranging from airport construction to youth programs. The second type of categorical grant is the **formula grant**. As the name implies, federal funds are allocated to states and local governments on the basis of a prescribed formula. These formulas vary from program to program but might include a state's population or income or the poverty level of its residents. Congress determines the formulas for specific programs such as Medicaid, highway construction, and family assistance, to name a few, and the federal dollars then are distributed on the basis of the statutory criteria. Many of these federal grants require **matching funds** from the governments that receive the money. The percentage of costs borne by the federal government varies from program to program, with the state or local governments picking up the balance. One reason for requiring such matches is to encourage state and local governments to have a strong commitment to the funded program and its policy objectives.

In 2011, the federal government spent $606.8 billion on these grants and was projected to spend $612 billion in 2012 and $633 billion in 2013. These increases, largely because of the 2009 Recovery Act, were designed to stimulate the nation's economy.[28]

project grant
A federal grant for a defined project.

formula grant
A federal grant based on specific criteria, such as income levels or population.

matching funds
Money that states or local governments have to provide to qualify for certain federal grants.

☐ Centralized Federalism

The domestic initiatives introduced by President John F. Kennedy (1961–1963) and expanded by President Lyndon B. Johnson (1963–1969) in the Great Society programs resulted in a dramatic expansion of the federal government's role to virtually every area of domestic policy. The number of federal grant programs and funding increased significantly during those years, as did the federal share of state and local budgets. Many programs targeted specific populations for assistance and were intended to redistribute resources primarily to lower income groups. Several federal programs bypassed state governments and went directly to local governments, thus eroding the legal relationship of local governments to the states.[29] Some scholars suggest that this massive extension of federal initiatives in domestic policy transformed cooperative federalism into coercive federalism or regulatory federalism, a relationship in which state power is subordinate to federal power in a wide range of policy areas.[30]

☐ The Multiple Phases of New Federalism

Conservative opposition to cooperative federalism started at its beginnings in the 1930s. This opposition became more intense against the centralized federal programs of the Kennedy and Johnson administrations, and the Republican Party began to stake out what has become a rather consistent rhetorical theme of decentralization and devolution, or return of more authority to the states.

Opposition to the increased role of the national government in domestic policy is based on many factors. Some argue that the Constitution never provided for the expanded powers claimed by the national government. The new programs, many of which were required, placed a heavy financial burden on state and local governments. Moreover, these policies often encouraged state and local governments to pursue federal dollars even when the funded programs were not their most pressing needs. The new programs also helped swell the federal bureaucracy, some programs were inefficient, and some were mismanaged. Finally, federal programs placed restrictions on how monies could be spent, and it was argued that federal requirements did not always meet local conditions or needs.

The expanded federal role also created new political issues. As grant programs evolved, various groups and individuals—that is, stakeholders—developed vested

new federalism
A term used to describe recent changes in federal-state relationships. Used primarily by conservative presidents, it suggests a devolution or return of power to the states and a decreased role of the federal government in domestic policy.

block grants
Federal grants of money to states and local governments for broad programs or services rather than narrowly defined programs. These grants give state and local governments more discretion over the use of the funds.

revenue sharing
A program begun under President Nixon and later repealed in which state and local governments received federal aid that could be used for virtually any purpose the recipient government wanted.

interests in maintaining them. Members of Congress viewed many of the programs as "pork" for the folks back home, and administrators at all levels of government justified their jobs and their agencies' existence on the basis of these programs. Many of the constituencies that benefited from federal grants traditionally supported the Democratic Party. If the Republican Party wanted to become the majority party, it would have to break up the implicit alliances built on federal funding of state and local programs.

THE NIXON YEARS (1969–1974) Republicans, beginning with President Richard Nixon (1969–1974), defined their views of federal-state relationships with the term **new federalism**. Although there have been several versions of "new federalism," reflecting the philosophical differences among Republican presidents, the general objective was to return responsibilities for many domestic policies to state and local governments. This also included efforts to reduce federal spending for many domestic programs and reduce the federal budget, a policy widely supported by Republican constituents.

Nixon said his new federalism was designed to "rationalize the intergovernmental system by restructuring the roles and responsibilities of governments at all levels."[31] Nixon wanted to reduce the role of the federal government and largely decentralize federal programs. He proposed changes to expedite the grant application process and consolidate many categorical grants into a few large **block grants**, which would give state and local governments greater discretion over how to spend federal money. He also proposed the replacement of many categorical grants with **revenue sharing** dollars, which could be used by recipient governments for virtually any purpose—with "no strings attached." Nixon also unsuccessfully proposed a plan to restructure the nation's welfare system.[32]

But after almost six years of supposedly trying to increase state and local powers, Nixon's administration produced results that appeared to be just the opposite. Many believe that Nixon actually left behind "a more centralized federal system than the one he inherited."[33] Federal expenditures for many domestic programs had increased dramatically, and the regulatory powers of the federal government had been expanded.

THE FORD (1974–1977) AND CARTER (1977–1981) YEARS Nixon was followed by Presidents Gerald Ford (1974–1977) and Jimmy Carter (1977–1981). President Ford, a Republican who took over the White House after Nixon's resignation, also called for a greater balance between the national and state governments. Initiatives enacted during his administration, including an extension of revenue sharing and two block grants—community development and workforce programs—were similar to those of his predecessor.[34]

President Carter, a Democrat who had served as governor of Georgia, attempted to expand the federal role to assist local governments. His budgets reduced revenue sharing dollars to the states, and he attempted to redirect those funds to cities with several new policy initiatives. The federal government participated in a lot of planning and consultation with mayors and other local officials during Carter's administration, but little of his urban program made its way through Congress.[35]

THE REAGAN (1981–1989) AND BUSH I (1989–1993) YEARS President Ronald Reagan (1981–1989), a Republican who often is given credit for initiating what some call the "Reagan Revolution," also expressed a commitment to reducing federal programs—especially welfare programs—and revitalizing the powers of state and local governments. In 1981, Reagan "convinced Congress to consolidate seventy-six categorical grant-in-aid programs and a block grant program into nine new or reconstituted block grants."[36] He also attempted to consolidate additional grant programs during subsequent congressional sessions but had little success because of Democratic legislative opposition.

Reagan opposed revenue sharing, the program initiated under President Nixon, and the federal government ended it in 1986. Reagan attacked the program for contributing to the federal budget deficit, funding governments that did not need the money, funding programs of questionable merit, and producing a reliance on revenue sharing dollars for the operating budgets of many state and local governments.

Despite Reagan's announced goals, little was done during his administration and that of his successor, President George H. W. Bush (1989–1993) to reduce federal power and return more authority to the states. Although some efforts were made, primarily through executive orders and administrative initiatives, to increase the discretionary powers of the states, **mandates** and **preemptions** enacted by Congress, as well as court decisions affecting federal relations during this period, had the opposite effect. Moreover, some argue that Reagan's New Federalism supported a smaller role for the national government but not a correspondingly larger role for state and local governments.[37]

Congress had begun enacting laws preempting state or local authority in 1789, but the number of these preemptions increased significantly after 1965. Many preemptions adopted with Reagan's approval appear to reflect his commitment to marketplace economics and a reduced role for all government.[38] They certainly did little to restore governmental authority to the states.

The federal government also can require states or local governments "to undertake a specific activity or provide a service meeting minimum national standards."[39] Throughout the 1980s, although decentralization and return of power to the states were major themes of the Reagan and first Bush administrations, Congress enacted numerous laws and mandates that imposed additional requirements on the states.[40] The numerous mandates and preemptions have imposed billions of dollars in costs on state and local governments and have forced them to "divert funds from many worthy projects to finance the national policies."[41] According to data from the Congressional Budget Office, federal regulations adopted between 1983 and 1990 imposed cumulative estimated costs of between $8.9 billion and $12.7 billion on states and localities, depending on how mandates were defined. These costs increased at a pace faster than overall federal aid.[42] In 1994, the Texas Legislative Budget Board reported that increases in mandates and other federal programs had accounted for $13 billion, or 65 percent, of a $20 billion increase in the Texas budget since 1990–1991.[43]

The first President Bush was perceived to be sensitive to state and local problems, but a huge federal deficit and agreements to cap federal expenditures provided no prospects for additional financial assistance to the states. Congress, with his approval, continued to impose mandates that added to the financial burdens of states and cities while preempting more and more authority over programs from the states.[44] During Bush's administration, Congress passed the Americans with Disabilities Act in 1990. The act prohibits discrimination against persons with disabilities and requires governments to make extensive and costly changes in public facilities to accommodate disabled individuals.[45] During 1990, Congress also passed three other major pieces of legislation (the Clean Air Act Amendments, the Education of the Handicapped Act Amendments, and the Fiscal 1991 Budget Reconciliation Act), which imposed additional requirements on the states and local governments.

THE CLINTON (1993–2001) YEARS Democrat Bill Clinton became president in 1993 after serving six terms as governor of Arkansas, and many expected him to be more responsive to the impact of mandates and other issues facing the states. But, like his predecessor, Clinton failed to provide a coherent theory of federalism in the wide range of proposals he initially submitted to Congress. Under the leadership of Vice President Al Gore, Clinton's emphasis on "reinventing government" led to the elimination of some 400,000 positions in the federal bureaucracy and a similar reduction in the military and a considerable increase in governmental contracting with private firms for services previously provided by government employees or the military. Clinton's policies reduced the size of the federal bureaucracy, but with the exception of welfare reforms, no significant devolution of powers to the states occurred.[46]

Committed to deficit reduction, Clinton and Congress left little leeway to provide financial relief or expand funding to states and local governments. The Motor Voter Bill (i.e., National Voter Registration Act) enacted in 1993 encouraged the registration of

mandates
Federal laws or regulations that require state or local governments to take certain actions, often at costs that the federal government does not reimburse. The state government also imposes mandates on local governments.

preemptions
Federal laws that limit the authority or powers of state and local governments.

more voters but also expanded federal authority over state elections. The Family and Medical Leave Act, enacted the same year, requires firms with fifty or more employees and state and local governments to provide up to twelve weeks of unpaid personal leave to employees under certain circumstances, such as the birth of a child. Congress passed the Goals 2000: Educate America Act in 1994, which expanded the federal role in public education through the development of national curriculum content and student performance standards.

Many of the Republicans who took control of both houses of Congress in 1994 were committed to restricting the powers of the national government. In response to state demands, Congress enacted the Unfunded Mandates Reform Act (1995). Any legislation that would impose $50 million or more in costs to state and local governments would be subject to a parliamentary procedure requiring members of Congress to go on record that they were voting to impose more costs on the state and local governments. The act did nothing to remedy mandates that were already on the books, and since its enactment, it has had very little effect on reducing costs to the other governments in the federal system.[47]

Congress enacted a welfare overhaul bill in 1996 that eliminated the entitlements under the sixty-one-year-old Aid to Families with Dependent Children program. This was replaced with a new program, Temporary Assistance for Needy Families, which is funded by block grants to the states and gives the states a wide range of options for establishing their own welfare programs.[48] Under waivers permitted by federal law, states also experimented with a variety of managed health care reforms in the Medicaid program, which serves low-income people. States, supported by new federal funds, expanded the medical insurance coverage of low-income children in 1997 and obtained relief from some of the regulations of the Environmental Protection Agency. In 1998, Congress enacted a $216 billion public works program, which was designed to help states and local governments build roads, bridges, and mass transit systems.[49] Despite the Unfunded Mandates Act of 1995, Congress enacted additional requirements and preemptions in health care, telecommunications, immigration reform, securities reform, and minimum wages in 1997.[50]

Some argued that the "devolution revolution" of 1996 transformed the federal system into a "new federal order," in which the "federal government intrudes less into the affairs of states and also offers less financial assistance."[51] Others concluded that congressional action gave states and local governments greater "flexibility" in carrying out federally funded programs because of waivers included in several pieces of legislation. But there were skeptics. John Kincaid, a specialist in federalism, argued that "devolution [was] plodding along at a turtle's pace while centralization [was] still racing ahead at a rabbit's pace."[52] Despite symbolic rhetoric about greater state and local responsibility, a closer assessment suggested minimal changes in federal relationships. There also was some evidence of the national government actually increasing its influence in select policy areas such as the National Voter Registration Act of 1993.[53]

THE BUSH II YEARS (2001–2009) In the initial months of his administration, President George W. Bush gave few clues of how his domestic policy objectives would affect state-federal relationships. He established an Interagency Working Group on Federalism in February 2001, but there is no evidence that it met.[54] Some government watchers expected him to outline and pursue policies similar to his Republican predecessors, but the September 11, 2001, terrorist attacks sidetracked the development of any initiatives that he may have been considering. Homeland security took priority.

Historically, the federal government had played a limited role in police functions or domestic security. America has never had a national police force because that responsibility was—and still is—allocated to the states and local governments. But the magnitude of the terrorist threat to domestic security prompted President Bush to call for the creation of a new national agency charged with coordinating security programs of federal, state, and local agencies. The Department of Homeland Security, created by Congress in November 2002, represented a comprehensive realignment of federal agencies with functions relating to security, including everything from commercial air travel to patrols along U.S. borders. The new department also developed collaborative programs with states and local governments. With greater emphasis on domestic security, it was argued, these initiatives tipped "the federal system—in matters of politics, police functions, and the law—towards Washington to an unprecedented degree."[55]

With President Bush's support, Congress also enacted the USA Patriot Act soon after the September 11 attacks. That measure increased government surveillance powers in investigations of espionage or terrorism. Supporters contended the legislation was essential for combating terrorists. Civil libertarians, among other critics, feared that the changes it made in federal law enforcement tactics could be abused. By the end of 2003, more than 170 cities and counties around the country had passed resolutions criticizing the law, and several state legislatures passed resolutions expressing concern about excesses in how it was enforced.[56]

As more and more of the states' National Guard troops were federalized to fight the wars in Iraq and Afghanistan, states began to resist, and the issue came to a head when Louisiana Governor Kathleen Blanco "refused to accede to the president's request that Guard troops be placed under federal command in the immediate response to Hurricane Katrina."[57] Congress passed legislation in 2006 that increased "the president's ability to federalize Guard troops without gubernatorial consent."[58] Congress also enacted the REAL ID Act in 2005 as part of the nation's security policy. This act required the Department of Homeland Security to establish federal standards for state driver's licenses, which were to be used for boarding airplanes or admission to federal facilities. The law encountered strong opposition from state officials across the country, who did not want to bear the costs of enforcement. The Obama administration has urged repeal of the law, and although it is still on the books, it remains in limbo.

Another significant piece of legislation that passed and was unrelated to the fight against terrorism was the No Child Left Behind (NCLB) Act of 2002. As governor of Texas, Bush had boasted of his record on education, which was intended to bring accountability into the public schools while expanding state support for local school districts. Education reform was a cornerstone of his presidential campaign and his legislative agenda. His education initiatives as president were significant to state-federal relationships because, historically, education had been primarily a function of state and local governments. Federal aid to public education had been limited and often targeted toward specific groups of students, such as the disabled or those from low-income families. The impact of NCLB was enormous because it included new federal mandates for reading and math proficiency. Test scores were to be used to evaluate the progress of a school or a school district. If schools failed to meet specified standards, they would suffer repercussions, including loss of funding and loss of students, who would be allowed to transfer to better performing schools.[59]

Experts across the political spectrum agreed that the power of the states was diminished during the second Bush administration. Bush said relatively little about federalism, neither did he develop an explicit federalism agenda.[60] As noted, his homeland security and education policies expanded the presence of the federal government in domestic programs. Without significant legislative approval and often asserting that laws enacted by Congress could not restrain the president, his administration compiled a record replete with attacks on the fundamental provisions of the Bill of Rights.[61] Preemptions, mandates, and other "centralizing statutes" continued at a significant rate; tax policy, especially tax cuts and the phasing out of the federal estate tax, hurt state finances; and federal rule making, with limited waivers, constrained state discretion.[62]

It is ironic that conservative Republicans, who have long decried centralization, helped lead the country in that direction. As far as we know, Bush never used the term "new federalism," but if his administration inspired a new term for federalism, it would be "big government conservatism" in which the powers of the "federal government and the executive branch were expanded" to achieve a social and economic policy agenda.[63]

As details of the Bush administration's policies became clear, states began a counteroffensive against the increased centralization and conservative economic and social objectives. Through effective lobbying and political maneuvering, states successfully secured some relief from "burdensome federal directives regarding the National Guard, homeland security, education, and welfare policy."[64] Several state legislatures passed measures vowing they would not cooperate with the federal government and demanding repeal of a variety of federal directives. Some federal officials became more cooperative with state governments, producing a number of significant waivers in federal programs. States also were at the center of debates about immigration, climate change, universal health care, election reform, property rights, social policy, capital punishment, and water allocation.[65]

THE OBAMA (2009–) YEARS The verdict is still out on President Barack Obama's policies on federalism. He came into office in the middle of an economic crisis, and much of his initial focus was on economic recovery. Obama won congressional approval in 2009 of a $787 billion stimulus package with $280 billion to be administered by states and local governments. He obtained additional stimulus legislation in 2010 with a tax cut and an unemployment extension agreement.[66] But the president failed to win congressional approval of two subsequent stimulus proposals.

Despite Governor Rick Perry's criticisms of Washington and government centralization, Texas accepted at least $14.4 billion in stimulus funds to help balance the state budget drafted by the legislature in 2009. The only money that Perry rejected was about $500 million in extra unemployment compensation funds. Some 70 percent of the money that Texas accepted was used to help fund education, transportation, and health and human services programs.[67] More recent figures estimate that Texas received as much as $17 billion in federal stimulus money in all.[68]

Aware of long-standing state complaints about federal mandates and preemptions, the White House issued a memorandum shortly after Obama took office that attempted to address this issue. The memo declared that, as a general policy, the Obama administration would preempt state laws "only with full consideration of the legitimate prerogatives of the States and with a sufficient legal basis for preemption."[69] Although not everyone agrees, the Obama administration appears to be less aggressive at preempting state laws and authority.[70]

By 2012, the most significant domestic achievement of the Obama administration was the Patient Protection and Affordable Care Act of 2010, a major reform of health insurance, which was attacked by twenty-six states, including Texas. In a lawsuit heard before the U.S. Supreme Court, the states objected to, among other things, provisions expanding Medicaid coverage and requiring virtually every American to have health insurance. To help carry out the latter provision, the law required that states create health exchanges to assist individuals in shopping for insurance coverage.[71] The states argued that the law was an onerous, unconstitutional intrusion into state authority. But the Supreme Court, in a 5-4 decision issued in June 2012, said the individual health insurance mandate and most other provisions of the law were constitutional.

☐ The Role of the U.S. Supreme Court in Defining Federalism

The federal courts have played a central role in defining power, authority, and jurisdiction in the federal system. In looking to the courts to provide the definitive theory of federalism, we might expect a conservative Supreme Court to be more concerned with states' rights and to reconsider the doctrines underlying mandates and preemptions. But this has not always been the case.

In a 1985 Texas case, *Garcia* v. *San Antonio Metropolitan Transit Authority*, the U.S. Supreme Court held 5 to 4 that states could not claim immunity from federal regulation over functions that have been defined as "integral" or "traditional."[72] This case, which involved municipal employees and their coverage by the Fair Labor Standards

Act, had far-reaching implications for federal-state relationships.[73] In the extreme, the case suggested that Congress, not the courts interpreting the Constitution, would define federalism. The case also suggested that there were no "discrete limitations on the objects of federal authority" other than those provisions of the Constitution that give the states a role in the selection of the president and members of Congress.[74]

By 1995, the court, under the leadership of Chief Justice William Rehnquist, had become much more concerned with the expansion of federal powers and reasserted itself in cases that involved federal issues. The court ruled 5 to 4 in the case of *United States* v. *Lopez* that "the Congress had overreached its constitutional power to regulate interstate commerce when it passed the Gun-Free School Zones Act of 1990."[75] In *Bush* v. *Vera,* the court struck down a Texas political redistricting plan, suggesting that it was less likely to support redistricting that was designed primarily to benefit minority groups. Other cases soon followed challenging race and ethnicity as criteria for redistricting, and the court's position was clarified somewhat in a 2001 decision (*Easley* v. *Cromartie*) in which it held that race is not an unconstitutional consideration in redistricting as long as it is not the "dominant and controlling" factor.[76] In another case, the court held that federal laws did not preempt state laws that penalized negligent manufacturers.[77]

A Texas case, *City of Boerne, Texas* v. *Flores* (1997), also demonstrated the Supreme Court's disposition to place limits on congressional powers.[78] In this case, the high court ruled that the Religious Freedom Restoration Act of 1993 was unconstitutional because it was too broad in its protection of religious freedom. The court ruled that provisions of the act infringed on state powers and also threatened "the authority of the court to determine the constitutionality of federal and state laws."[79] The ruling was handed down after a Roman Catholic parish in Boerne used the law to challenge the city's decision to deny it a permit to enlarge a church in a historic district. The court also struck down provisions of the Brady Handgun Violence Prevention Act, which required background checks on gun purchasers, in *Printz* v. *United States.*[80]

The court has not been single-minded in its efforts to restrain the powers of the national government.[81] In 1996, the court handed down several civil rights decisions that imposed limits on state powers. It also struck down a 1992 Colorado constitutional amendment that prohibited governments from defining homosexuals as a protected class. In another case, Virginia, on the basis of the Fourteenth Amendment, was required to permit women to attend Virginia Military Institute, which had been an all-male school.[82] In the *Seminole Tribe* v. *Florida* case, the Supreme Court concluded that Congress had virtually all "authority to legislate in the area of Indian affairs and states had none."[83]

Although the Rehnquist court handed down a number of notable decisions that advanced the conservatives' "New Federalism" agenda, it still is not clear how the current U.S. Supreme Court under Chief Justice Roberts will deal with the balance of state and federal power. So far, it has been "fairly quiet in this area."[84] But there have been some indications that the Roberts court is more receptive to federal powers. It has "decided more preemption cases in favor of the federal government at a higher rate" than previous courts, "separately and combined."[85] In *U.S.* v. *Comstock,* it upheld the authority of federal judges to issue civil commitment orders for sex offenders after they had completed their criminal sentences on a broad interpretation of the necessary and proper clause of the U.S. Constitution.[86]

In addition, the Roberts court upheld state sovereignty in *Sossamon* v. *Texas,* a case in which a Texas inmate sued the state for monetary damages, arguing he was denied access to the prison's chapel in violation of the Religious Land Use and Institutionalized Persons Act (RLUIPA). The court ruled that Texas, even though it accepted federal funds, did not waive its right to sovereign immunity from private suits for monetary damages.[87]

In the early spring of 2012, the U.S. Supreme Court heard a challenge by twenty-six states, including Texas, to President Obama's health care law, as discussed earlier in this chapter, and later upheld most of the law.

The Impact of Federalism on State Finances

3.5 Assess the impact of federalism on state finances and the extent to which state governments depend on federal funds.

Federal taxes paid into the national treasury from Texas in 2010 totaled approximately $189 billion, or about $7,522 per person. Only California and New York paid larger amounts. Federal expenditures in the state were $225.7 billion or $8,976 per capita. Texas ranked forty-third among the states in per capita federal government expenditures. These expenditures include federal government payroll, defense and other procurement, direct payments to residents under programs such as Social Security and Medicare, and grants to state and local governments.[88] Grants and other payments to Texas's state and local governments totaled $43.7 billion in 2010, placing Texas forty-first among the states in per capita payments.[89]

For years, state officials have complained about the disparity between federal taxes collected in Texas and the distribution of federal funds in the state. The state has long attempted through its congressional delegation and the Office of State-Federal Relations to obtain more equitable formulas as Congress amends or reauthorizes grant programs.

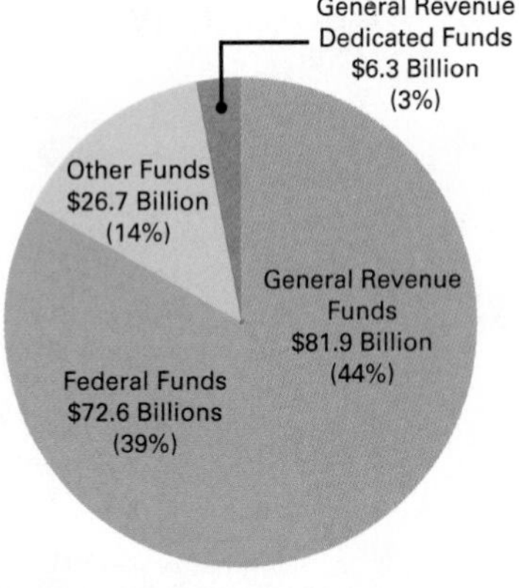

FIGURE 3–1 SOURCES OF REVENUE FOR TEXAS'S 2010–2011 BIENNIAL BUDGET

As indicated by this chart, Texas government receives a large share of its funding from the federal government.

Source: Texas Legislative Budget Board, *Legislative Budget Board Fiscal Size-Up: 2012–2013 Biennium*, January 2012.

Federal funds accounted for approximately $72.6 billion, or about 39 percent, of the $187.5 billion state budget for the 2010–2011 biennium (see Figure 3–1). Health and human services, including a wide range of social services for millions of low-income Texans, received some 58 percent of all federal funds allocated to the state for this period. Business and economic development programs received 16 percent, and education programs received 19 percent.[90]

State government, through the Office of State-Federal Relations, and many of the larger cities in Texas have full-time staffers working to obtain additional federal dollars. Like other states, Texas also lobbies the federal government for additional programs, changes in existing programs, relief from mandates and preemptions, and adjustments in funding formulas that adversely affect the state.

Many of the grants that come to Texas are formula grants, based on population, levels of poverty, or some other criteria written into the federal act. Others are competitive and must be sought out by Texas governments. Some state agencies and local governments are aggressive and often successful in obtaining competitive grants, but others are not. Governments with limited staff often find it difficult to reallocate employees' time to the complex grant application process. Available programs must be identified through publications such as the *Federal Register*, and applications must be submitted in a timely manner. Some assistance is available to local governments through their regional councils of governments, and some consultants provide grant-writing services. Some local governments may not apply for grants because of disinterest, political opposition, or other reasons.

State agencies are required to pursue relevant federal grants for their programs. The governor's office has a State Grants Team that works to increase Texas's access to available federal money. This group helps identify grant programs, informs other state and local agencies of available grants, and helps write grant applications.[91]

Reactions to the Expanded Role of the Federal Government

3.6 Compare and contrast the arguments for and against the expanded role of the federal government.

Many citizens argue that economic, environmental, and social issues are national in scope and cannot be adequately addressed at the state or local level. These problems, they believe, require a coordinated national effort with common standards and objectives. Not all governments have the

financial resources to deal with many of these problems, and without federal assistance, some significant segments of our society would suffer.

Many governments, it also has been argued, would not address such issues if they were not required to do so by federal mandates. People also note the long history of discrimination in the United States and argue that changes promoting civil rights and equality would not have occurred if the federal government had not taken the lead through legislation and public policy.

Government centralization, however, has been a dominant fear ever since our country's origins and throughout its history. In the eighteenth-century debates over ratifying the U.S. Constitution, the anti-Federalists made many of the arguments against a strong national government that still are heard today. In addition to a fear of tyranny, corruption, and abuses was a concern that people in one area of the country could impose their will on others. Was it possible for officials in Washington to understand local issues and problems facing citizens across the country?

Today, the large number of federal mandates and preemptions restrict the policy options of state and local governments and often increase their costs. Even when the federal government provides money, it usually has strings attached. State agencies and local communities sometimes resist taking federal dollars because they do not want these restrictions to force them to rearrange their own local priorities. Most public officeholders, though, find it difficult to refuse to accept available federal dollars.

Some federal grant programs have provisions that link different policy areas together. For example, the Texas legislature, after lowering the legal drinking age to 18 for a few years, restored it to 21 in 1986. Although many Texans had lobbied for the restoration of the older drinking age, another major impetus for the change came from a federal law linking a state's drinking age to federal grants for road construction. Texas could have refused to adopt the higher age, but it would have lost 10 percent of its federal highway dollars after 1988.

Many of the federal assistance programs were designed to redistribute resources from wealthier Americans to those with lower incomes, a policy that some people oppose. Moreover, this redistribution is linked in Texas to issues of race and ethnicity because minority groups constitute a disproportionate part of the state's low-income population. Some political leaders have resisted federal grant programs for fear that funding projects would enhance the political position of minority groups.

Some suggest that the increased use of fiscal federalism (federal grants linked to preemptions and mandates) has produced a mind-set that the federal government should assume more responsibility for domestic programs, in terms of both program development and funding.[92] They fear that federal dominance undermines the creative capacity of states and local governments to deal with many local and regional problems. Moreover, many would argue that the states are now much more innovative than the federal government in policy initiatives and administrative streamlining.

transnational regionalism
The expanding economic and social interdependence of South Texas and Mexico.

Transnational Regionalism

3.7 Describe the increased interdependency between the United States and Mexico and list common issues faced by both nations.

Texas shares a 1,200-mile border with Mexico, and common problems and interests that bond the two neighbors, referred to as **transnational regionalism**, have taken on increased importance since the mid-1980s. Historically, relations between the United States and Mexico often were strained. The United States fought a war against Mexico from 1846 to 1848, and on subsequent occasions, American troops entered Mexican territory, ostensibly to protect U.S. economic and national security interests. Apprehension about U.S. objectives resulted in Mexican policies on trade, commerce, and foreign ownership of property that were designed to insulate the country from excessive foreign influence

maquiladora program
Economic program initiated by Mexico to increase manufacturing and the assembly of goods.

North American Free Trade Agreement (NAFTA)
Treaty signed in 1993 to lower trade barriers among the United States, Mexico, and Canada and to create a common economic market. It is widely referred to as NAFTA.

and domination. Nevertheless, the interests of the two countries have long been bound by geopolitical factors, economics, and demographics. One Mexican author has compared the interdependence of the two countries to Siamese twins, warning that "if one becomes gangrenous, the other twin will also be afflicted."[93]

☐ Maquiladoras

Changes in the economic relationship between Mexico and the United States began with the **maquiladora program**, an initiative under Mexico's 1964 Border Industrialization Program to boost employment, foreign exchange, and industrial development. It also was designed to transfer technology to Mexico, help train workers, and develop managerial skills among Mexican nationals.[94]

The concept was to develop twin plants, one in the United States and one in Mexico, under a single management. The plant in the United States would manufacture parts, and its Mexican counterpart would assemble them into a product, which, in turn, would be sent back to the United States for further processing or for shipping to customers.[95] Parts shipped into Mexico would not be subject to the normal tariffs, and the tax imposed on the assembled product would be minimal. In 1984, Mexico changed its laws to permit the United States and other foreign countries to establish these relationships throughout Mexico, rather than just on the border, and to permit 100 percent foreign ownership of the assembly plants in Mexico. The latter step was a radical departure from previous Mexican law, which prohibited such foreign ownership.[96]

The maquiladora program has not resulted in the construction of a significant number of manufacturing plants on the Texas side of the border because American companies have used existing plants throughout the United States to produce parts to be assembled in Mexico. Nevertheless, Texas's border counties have benefited through the creation of thousands of support jobs in transportation, warehousing, and services.[97] Some 2,800 maquiladora plants were in operation in 2007, providing hundreds of thousands of jobs but also contributing to increased population density along the Mexican side of the border, where most of the Mexican assembly plants are located.[98]

The maquiladora program continues to play a major role in transnational economic development. American organized labor opposes the program, arguing that the maquiladoras drain jobs from the United States. But the program provides a source of inexpensive labor for American businesses, which have complained for years that they cannot compete against low foreign labor costs.

☐ The North American Free Trade Agreement (NAFTA)

Negotiations on a free trade agreement in 1991 marked another significant change in the relationship between Mexico and the United States. The negotiations were precipitated, in part, by world economics and the emergence of regional trading zones. But the administration of Mexican President Carlos Salinas de Gortari also reacted to the failure of Mexico's economic policies of the 1980s and a fear of economic isolation. The end of the cold war, a reduction in Central American conflicts, and internal population pressures also were factors.[99]

The convergence of interests of the United States, Mexico, and Canada produced the **North American Free Trade Agreement (NAFTA)** to reduce tariffs and increase trade among the three countries. It created the world's largest trading bloc, which had a combined population of approximately 463 million in 2012 and combined gross domestic products (GDP) of more than $18.1 trillion in 2011.[100] Other regions of the world have recognized the value of creating large trading blocs, and the European Union, now composed of twenty-seven nations, is estimated to have a combined population of 504 million and a combined GDP of $15.4 trillion.[101]

Approved by the U.S. Congress in late 1993, NAFTA has increased trade among the three countries, strengthened previous economic ties, and created new ones. Texas has experienced significant economic changes from these new relationships, but the benefits have not been uniformly distributed throughout the state.

CONCERNS ABOUT NAFTA Some people on both sides of the U.S.-Mexico border believe that NAFTA harms their respective countries. Labor unions in the United States are particularly concerned that low labor costs in Mexico are moving jobs from the United States. Some manufacturers argue that labor and capital costs in Mexico threaten their American markets.

In Mexico, there is concern that American corporations will dominate and reduce Mexico's control over its own economy because approximately 80 percent of Mexico's exports are going to the United States. Human rights advocates have expressed concerns about working conditions, workers' benefits, and the broader social impact of the plants on the lives of hundreds of thousands of Mexican citizens.

Environmentalists on both sides of the border have argued that increased manufacturing and commerce worsen the air, water, and waste pollution problems in the area. Both countries have environmental laws, and the treaty calls for collaboration on environmental issues, but allegations have surfaced that U.S. manufacturers have shipped their dirty plants to Mexico, which, as an emerging country, is less inclined or able to crack down on polluters.

Ever since NAFTA's approval, there has been strong opposition in Texas and throughout the United States to a provision of the treaty allowing Mexican trucks to deliver products between destinations in Mexico and the U.S. interior. Many residents and government officials in the United States feared that the Mexican trucks would increase safety problems on American highways, and American truckers and labor unions opposed the competition from lower-paid Mexican drivers. Despite the treaty, the Clinton administration prohibited Mexican trucks from hauling goods to U.S. destinations. Mexican trucks had to transfer their loads at the border to American trucks for final shipment. After years of negotiations failed to win access to American highways, the Mexican government in 2009 imposed retaliatory tariffs on American goods and agricultural products imported into Mexico.

The tariffs prompted more negotiations, and in 2011, the Obama administration reached a trucking agreement with the Mexican government. Mexican trucks were allowed to make deliveries to destinations in the U.S. interior. The Mexican trucks were subject to U.S. inspections, and the drivers were subject to drug screening and had to demonstrate an ability to speak English and understand American highway signs and rules. In addition, the Mexican trucks were to be electronically monitored to ensure that their operators took regular breaks from driving. The U.S. Chamber of Commerce applauded the agreement, saying it would reduce shipping costs, but it was sharply criticized by the Teamsters Union and independent truck owner-operators, who feared the loss of American trucking jobs.[102] Mexican trucks started crossing the border under the new agreement in late 2011, but it remains to be seen if the new arrangement lasts. Some members of Congress sought to halt the program by ending necessary funding, including the cost of the electronic truck monitoring.[103]

TRADE PATTERNS BETWEEN TEXAS AND MEXICO The United States and Texas do a lot of business with Mexico. U.S. exports to Mexico totaled $12.4 billion in 1986 and $198 billion in 2011 (see Figure 3–2). Imports from Mexico, now the third largest trading partner of the United States, totaled more than $263 billion in 2011. Mexico accounted for 12 percent of all goods imported into the United States in 2011 and 13 percent of U.S. exports.[104] Texas exported nearly $250 billion worth of goods worldwide and accounted for 44 percent of U.S. exports to Mexico in 2011.

The sheer volume of goods, services, and people is obvious on the highways leading into Mexico and in the long lines of people on foot and in autos and trucks at border crossings in Brownsville, Laredo, and El Paso. There were 78 million

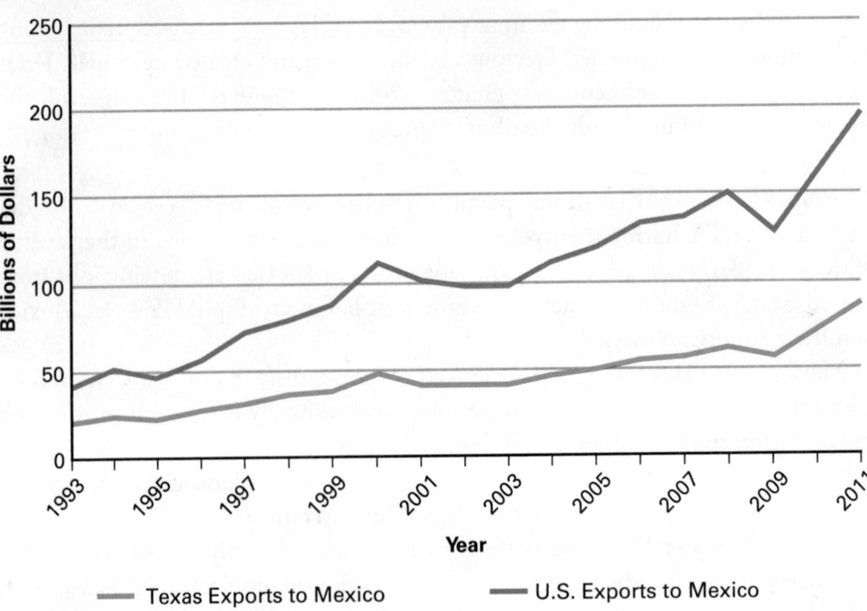

FIGURE 3–2 TEXAS AND U.S. EXPORTS TO MEXICO, 1993–2011

This chart depicts the dramatic increase in exports from Texas and the U.S to Mexcio since the creation of NAFTA in 1993.

Source: Massachusetts Institute of Social and Economic Research and the U.S. Census Bureau (based on "origin of movement to port" state-level data series); Texas Department of Economic Development, April 2000; and International Trade Administration, *Trade Stats* program, 2012.

border crossings at points of entry between Texas and Mexico in 2010, including approximately 44.3 million small vehicle crossings, 27.4 million pedestrian crossings, and 5.7 million truck crossings. More than 12,000 pedestrians crossed the border at Brownsville each day, and more than 7,900 trucks crossed the border each day at Laredo, the nation's largest inland port.[105] Billions of dollars are required to upgrade and expand the roads, highways, bridges, water and sanitation systems, and other facilities on both sides of the border. Both countries have taken some initiatives, but many of these facilities will not be completed for years, contributing to delays and gridlock in both countries at border crossings. The North American Development Bank was created to help address these needs.

□ Illegal Immigration

Population growth in Texas always has been affected by migration from other states and foreign countries. But the proximity of Texas to Mexico has put the state at the center of a long-running dispute over the illegal immigration of large numbers of Mexicans and other Latin Americans.

FEDERAL GOVERNMENT LAWS AND POLICIES The federal government, not the states, has the authority to determine immigration laws and policies.[106] Congress enacted the Nationalization Act of 1790, which limited naturalization to "free white persons" of "good moral character" and established residency requirements for citizenship. The Chinese Exclusion Act (1882) was the first major law restricting immigration into the United States. It limited Chinese immigration and denied this population naturalization rights. Quotas based on national origin were central to national immigration policy until 1965 and gave preference to immigrants from northern European countries. Piecemeal legislation dealing with immigration was consolidated in the Immigration and Nationality Act of 1952, which maintained the quota system, established preferences for skilled labor and relatives of U.S. citizens, and enhanced screening and security procedures.

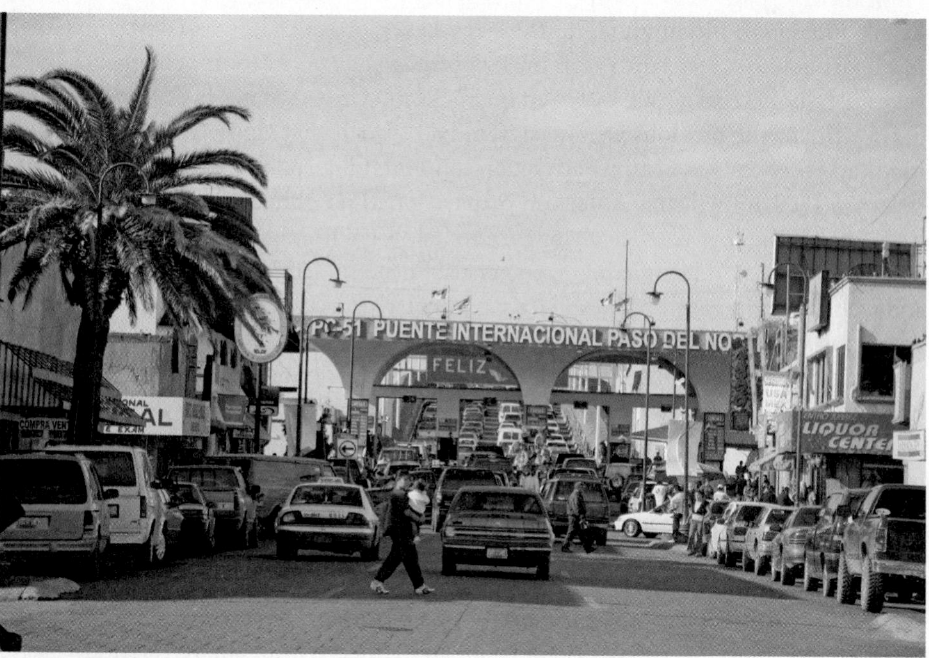

ENOUGH TO TRY ONE'S PATIENCE

Texas-Mexico border crossings are busy places, as these long lines of cars demonstrate at a crossing between El Paso and Ciudad Juarez, Mexico.

The quota system discriminated against Asians, eastern Europeans, African Americans, and Latin Americans. But during World War II, the United States faced a labor shortage and negotiated a *Bracero Program* with Mexico, which made it possible for temporary workers from Mexico to enter the United States. This program was terminated in 1964.

The Immigration and Nationality Act of 1965 eliminated national quotas but set limits on the number of immigrants from different regions of the world. The law produced a dramatic shift in immigration patterns with large numbers of Asians now entering the country. As war and political instability affected developing countries, additional immigrants began entering the United States, creating a huge backlog in applications for legal immigrant status. Consequently, a massive influx of illegal immigration began. If arrested, illegal immigrants were deported; but until 1986, it was not illegal for American employers to hire them.[107] Moreover, large portions of the Texas and American economies were built on the availability of cheap, low-skilled foreign labor, and businesses and individuals were willing to ignore the illegal status of millions of immigrants, particularly from Mexico and other Latin American countries.[108]

As the scale of the problem became more evident, the U.S. Congress enacted the Immigration Reform and Control Act in 1986. That law imposed fines on employers who hired illegal immigrants and provided jail sentences for flagrant violators. Potential employees had to provide documentation, and employers had to verify their employees' citizenship. Because there was no practical way to deport millions of illegal immigrants, the law also provided a means for giving legal status, or amnesty, to illegal immigrants who had moved to the United States before January 1, 1982. It also provided for temporary status for agricultural workers who could satisfy specific residency requirements.[109]

But illegal immigration continued, and public pressure mounted for more rigorous action. Additional legislation passed in 1996 to increase funds for border guards and inspectors, to increase penalties for smuggling people into the United States and using fraudulent documents, to construct fences along the border, and to make it easier to detain and deport illegal immigrants.[110] The U.S. Congress also passed major changes in welfare laws in 1996, cutting off most public assistance, except for emergency medical care, to both legal and illegal immigrants in the United States.

Critics of the previous welfare system had argued that the accessibility of public funds and services was a strong attraction to immigrants, many of whom were poverty stricken. They argued that American taxpayers had no obligation to support anyone who entered the country illegally or even to help legal immigrants who could not support themselves. Undocumented workers also increase demands on public health care and welfare programs.[111] Some citizens, particularly unskilled workers, view the illegal arrivals as a threat to their jobs and standard of living.

Several years after the 1996 public assistance restrictions were enacted, however, considerable evidence showed that the restrictions were not deterring illegal immigration or reducing immigrants' use of public services.[112] For one thing, children of illegal immigrants represent a heavy financial burden for many school districts and taxpayers throughout the country, but the U.S. Supreme Court, in a case from Texas, ruled years ago that public school districts were required to educate immigrant children who sought enrollment.

Immigration reform was a centerpiece of President George W. Bush's domestic program, but border security became a greater concern after the terrorist attacks of September 11, 2001. The creation of the Department of Homeland Security in 2002 combined and realigned a number of existing agencies to increase controls on the borders. Meanwhile, political debate increased over the competition for jobs between U.S. citizens and illegal immigrants and a host of other immigration-related issues.

In late 2005, the U.S. House approved a bill to improve border security and make undocumented immigrants criminals, ignoring a proposal by President Bush to provide illegal immigrants already in the country a way to become citizens. The U.S. Senate rejected the House bill and approved legislation providing a so-called "pathway" to citizenship for illegal immigrants who paid fines, learned to speak English, and met certain other requirements. The controversy also played out in peaceful, but noisy, demonstrations in many American cities, including Dallas, Houston, and San Antonio, and in numerous political campaigns. Thousands of immigrants, their descendants, and supporters took to the streets to wave American and Mexican flags for their cause.

Although immigration reform legislation failed, Congress in 2005 authorized a border wall or fence along the U.S.-Mexico border by attaching it as a rider to the REAL ID Act, a law requiring states to develop a standard driver's license for use as identification. When details of the fence became public in 2007, another round of intense political controversy on both sides of the border followed. More fuel was added to the political fire in 2008, when the Department of Homeland Security announced it would pursue construction despite potential conflicts with some thirty-four existing laws. Given the physical barrier that the Rio Grande presents to vehicles, most fences built on the Texas border are designed to prevent illegal crossings by pedestrians.[113]

President Bush also ordered several thousand National Guard troops to the border to help the Border Patrol in 2006. It was widely believed the president took this additional step to "secure" the border in order to boost support for his proposal to allow immigrants already in the country illegally to earn citizenship and to help members of his party in the 2006 congressional elections. Border security remained an issue during President Barack Obama's administration. As drug-related violence increased on the border, President Obama ordered 1,200 National Guard troops to help contain the violence.[114]

President Obama also sought comprehensive immigration changes, including a way for illegal but law-abiding immigrants who already were in the country to become citizens, but by 2012 his efforts remained unsuccessful. Obama actively lobbied for the so-called Development, Relief and Education for Alien Minors (DREAM) Act, a measure that initially had been proposed several years before he took office. It would allow children who were brought to the country illegally to eventually receive legal, permanent residency if they went to college or signed up for the military. Despite Obama's efforts, a filibuster by Senate Republicans blocked the bill in a showdown vote in late 2010. Opponents contended the bill would offer amnesty to as many as 2 million illegal immigrants and would increase the federal deficit. Although Senator Orrin Hatch, a Republican from Utah, initially offered the DREAM Act in 2001 with bipartisan support, Republicans began to abandon it as conservatives took over more control of their party.[115]

The Obama administration also deported a record number of illegal immigrants, including many who had been convicted of crimes in this country. Deportations increased to 396,906 in fiscal 2011, an increase over the previous record set in fiscal 2010.[116] With Congress still refusing to act on immigration reform, Obama in 2012 used his executive authority to offer work permits to several hundred thousand illegal immigrants younger than 30 who had come to the U.S. before they were 16. The policy didn't grant legal status to these people but allowed them to avoid deportation.

According to the U.S. Department of Homeland Security, as of January 2011, some 11.5 million people were in the United States illegally, a slight decrease from the 11.6 million estimated a year earlier. The agency attributed the small drop to unemployment problems in the United States, improved economic conditions in Mexico, and increased border enforcement. About 59 percent, or 6.8 million, of the illegal immigrants were from Mexico. About 1.8 million illegal immigrants were in Texas, second only to the 2.83 million estimated in California.[117]

It is virtually impossible to stop all illegal immigration, and divided public opinion over the issue makes enforcement even more difficult. Some immigrants violate the law for economic reasons. They are willing to take the risk they will be caught, knowing that the worst thing that can happen is that they will be deported or receive limited jail time. Others have binational families, with relatives who are U.S. citizens. In addition, many businesses and individuals in the United States are eager to hire the less expensive labor that many undocumented immigrants provide.

STATE ACTIONS The federal government's failure to address the immigration problem has prompted many states and local communities to enact their own restrictions, including those on drivers' licenses, penalties for companies that hire illegal immigrants, and restrictions on immigrants' access to higher education and public services.[118] Two of the harshest laws have been enacted in Alabama and Arizona, and the constitutionality of each likely is to be decided by the U.S. Supreme Court. The Obama administration sued to block key provisions of both, contending they conflict with federal laws and policies.

The Arizona law, among other provisions, requires state law enforcement officers to determine the immigration status of anyone they stop or arrest if they suspect the person may be an illegal immigrant. The law makes it a state crime for immigrants to fail to register and for illegal immigrants to work or seek jobs. The statute also allows police to arrest people without warrants if they have probable cause to believe the individuals are deportable under federal law.[119] The U.S. Supreme Court in 2012 upheld the requirement that police verify the legal status of people they arrest but struck down much of the rest of the law.

Many considered Alabama's law, which was enacted in 2011, to be even tougher on immigrants. It would require police officers to try to determine the immigration status of people they stop or arrest, it would require officials to check the immigration status of public school students, and it would make it a crime for illegal immigrants to enter into a "business transaction" with the state, including applying for a driver's license or a business license. The Eleventh U.S. Court of Appeals in Atlanta later that year blocked some parts of the law, including the requirement for checking a student's immigration status. But the provision making it a crime for an undocumented immigrant to apply for a driver's license remained enforceable.[120]

MOST OF THESE WEAPONS COME FROM TEXAS

From all indications, the vast majority of weapons used by Mexican drug cartels to carry out their violent activities in Mexico come from the United States. U.S. Immigration and Customs Enforcement seized these weapons in its efforts to stem the tide of weapons flowing into Mexico.

The Texas legislature has not enacted such far-reaching immigration legislation, but it did approve in 2011 a requirement that people prove U.S. citizenship or legal residence in order to obtain or renew a driver's license. A so-called "sanctuary cities" bill, which would have prohibited local governments from adopting policies that prevent police from asking about detainees' immigration status, died in 2011, despite being designated an "emergency" by Governor Rick Perry. [121]

☐ Border Drug Violence

No one knows for sure how many people have died in the war among Mexico's competing drug cartels. News media estimates ranged as high as 47,000 through January 2012, about five years after Mexican President Felipe Calderon declared "war" on the drug lords. Thousands of the killings have occurred along the border with Texas, including in the Mexican city of Ciudad Juarez, directly across the border from El Paso.

Bodies have been found dangling from freeway overpasses, and human heads have been discovered in public places, as the competing drug gangs have carried out vengeance killings and sought to intimidate rivals, local officials, and journalists. Many of the victims have been suspected drug gang members, and others have been Mexican police and security forces. Still others have been journalists, targeted by drug gangs for what they had been reporting, and innocent bystanders.

Many Texans fear that the violence could spread across the border, and it is a popular subject for political figures advocating tougher border security. Governor Perry frequently makes border security an issue, and President Obama ordered National Guard troops to the border in 2010. Obviously, there is a lot of drug trafficking across the Rio Grande, since residents of the United States are the drug dealers' biggest customer base. Residents along the Texas side of the border sometimes hear gunfire on the other side of the river, and occasionally a stray bullet flies across the international boundary (see *Talking Texas: Another Tale of Two Cities*). Although little violence has spilled over into Texas, for those people who cross the border almost every day for work or to visit relatives, the threat of violence is very real.

Common Borders, Common Problems

To anyone living on the border, the economic interdependence of the United States and Mexico is evident every day. Tens of thousands of pedestrians, cars, and trucks move across the international bridges, to and from the commercial centers on both sides of the Rio Grande. When the Mexican economy suffered a precipitous decline in 1982, the peso devaluation severely disrupted the Texas border economy, causing unemployment to skyrocket and a considerable number of U.S. businesses to fail.

Much of the effort toward improving relations between the United States and Mexico has focused on potential economic benefits, but other complex problems confronting both countries also merit attention. One is health care. On both sides of the border, many children have not been immunized against basic childhood diseases. On the Texas side are hundreds of *colonias*—rural, unincorporated slums that have substandard housing, roads, and drainage and, in many cases, lack water and sewage systems. These conditions have contributed to severe health problems, including hepatitis, dysentery, and tuberculosis. Higher than normal numbers of both Texan and Mexican children along the border also have been born with serious birth defects. Public health officials in Texas report that Mexican women come across the border to give birth to their children in American facilities. This practice, which has the effect of creating binational families, increases the burden on public hospitals—and taxpayers—in Texas. Children born in the United States are U.S. citizens and are entitled to various public services.[122]

Industrial development and population growth along the border also increase environmental problems. U.S. antipollution laws have been more stringent than those of Mexico, but air and water pollution generated in Mexico does not stop at the border. A side agreement to NAFTA on the environment provides a basic framework for addressing these problems, but some have argued that a country such

Talking ★ TEXAS Another Tale of Two Cities

Ciudad Juarez, a Mexican city of more than 1 million people, sits directly across the border from El Paso. Downtown El Paso is a stone's throw—or short rifle shot—from the crowded areas of Juarez, but in one important respect, it may as well be miles away.

Juarez has been at the center of much of the drug cartel violence afflicting Mexico. Thousands of people have been killed in the city over the past five years, and media accounts have even referred to Juarez as the "Murder Capital of the World." El Paso, by contrast, was cited in 2010, for the second year in a row, for having the lowest crime rate among American cities with populations of more than 500,000. In fact, El Paso has ranked among the top three American cities with the lowest crime rates since 1997. El Paso leaders frequently point out the city's high safety ranking when other politicians portray the border as a violent place.[a]

Occasionally however, the violence across the border can get a little too close for comfort, even in one of America's safest cities. Maria Romero, a Mexican citizen, moved legally to El Paso from Juarez to avoid the violence. But one day in 2012, as she was standing on a downtown El Paso sidewalk, a stray bullet, believed to have been fired in Juarez during a gunfight between police and suspected carjackers, struck her in the leg. El Paso officials said the .223 caliber bullet was fired more than a half mile away. "There is nobody to fault. The bullet came, and I was in its way," a recovering Romero said in a media interview. Asked if the incident had changed her perception of El Paso, she replied, "I still feel safe."[b]

CRITICAL THINKING QUESTIONS

1. Is it likely that El Paso can continue to hold on to its distinction as one of America's safest cities with its close proximity to Juarez? Why or why not?
2. How much do consumers of illegal drugs in the United States contribute to the violence over the drug trade in Mexico?

[a]Susannah Jacob, "El Paso Is Tops Again on Low-Crime Cities List," *The Texas Tribune*, December 8, 2011.

[b]Daniel Borunda, "Violence Catches up to Victim of Stray Bullet in Downtown El Paso," *El Paso Times*, February 23, 2012.

3.1

3.2

3.3

3.4

3.5

3.6

3.7

as Mexico, under enormous pressure to industrialize rapidly, is less likely to be concerned with environmental issues. In addition, U.S. efforts to impose its environmental standards on Mexico could be interpreted as another American effort to dominate the country.[123] In June 1994, several maquiladora plants in Matamoros, across the border from Brownsville, settled lawsuits alleging that pollution caused rare birth defects in children born in Texas.

Regional interdependence, though perhaps not recognized by most people on both sides of the border, has taken on greater importance in the press and in academic, business, and labor communities in the United States. Transnational public policies are emerging, creating legal issues in product liability, insurance, copyrights, and patents that still must be resolved.

Review the Chapter

Structuring Regional and National Interests

3.1 Explain the ways in which nations can structure the relationships among their national, regional, and local governments, p. 61.

Countries around the world have used three forms of government to structure relationships among national, regional (or state), and local governments. All three of these forms—federal systems, confederations, and unitary systems—have been used in the United States at different points in time. The U.S. Constitution provides for a federal system, which divides powers between the national and state governments, according to extensive constitutional provisions. In a confederation, the individual states retain extensive powers, and the authority of the central government is limited. The confederation principle was used twice in the nation's history—prior to the Constitution of 1787 and by the southern states during the Civil War. The unitary system gives central governments the authority to create local governments and impose restrictions on them. Some democratic and authoritarian governments structure national and regional powers on the unitary principle. It defines the relationship between state and local governments in Texas.

Defining Federalism

3.2 Define federalism and explain the constitutional relationship between the states and the national government, p. 62.

Scholars have advanced various definitions of federalism, in part because of the ongoing changes that occur in federal relationships. In its simplest terms, federalism is the division of power between the states and the national government. These powers are defined in the U.S. Constitution. The national government has delegated powers specifically spelled out in Article 1, as well as implied powers. States have reserved powers under the Tenth Amendment. The supremacy clause of the Constitution provides that the national government prevails when there are jurisdictional conflicts between the national government and the states. Finally, there are powers denied to both national and state governments and constitutional limits on what governments can do.

Federalism also applies to the states. States must recognize most actions taken by other states, including contracts and drivers' licenses. States also must extend the same protections to individuals from other states as they do to their own citizens. The Constitution provides for extradition, a process whereby persons fleeing prosecution for criminal offenses in one state are, if apprehended in another state, to be returned for prosecution to the state in which the offenses occurred.

Metaphors for Federalism

3.3 Summarize the different theories of federalism using generalized views or metaphors, p. 66.

To help explain the complexities of American federalism, some scholars have used metaphors to describe the relationships between the national government and the states. The constitutional language defining the powers of each level of government may lead to a layer-cake metaphor, which explains dual federalism. But difficulty in establishing sharp lines between the functions and actions of the various levels of government prompted Morton Grodzins to argue that federalism is more analogous to a marble cake or cooperative federalism. Another view, picket-fence federalism, links specific areas of public policy across the three levels of government.

Changing Patterns in Federal Relationships

3.4 Trace the development of federalism over the course of American history, focusing primarily on changes in the relationship between the national government and the states, p. 67.

In the nation's formative period, state and local governments were much more prominent and played a much greater role in the lives of Americans than did the national government. Over the nation's 225-year history because of changing economic, social, demographic, and political conditions, as well as the expanded role of the national government in foreign affairs, federalism has changed.

During the era of dual federalism from 1790 to the 1930s, state and local governments took the lead in domestic policy. But states were unable to address the economic hardships caused by the Great Depression in the 1930s, and the federal government assumed a more dominant domestic role through the enactment of New Deal policies, such as Social Security. This era of cooperative federalism dramatically expanded the role of the federal government. The national government's authority increased even more during the era of centralized federalism, which included the enactment of major welfare, education, and civil rights legislation championed by Presidents Kennedy and Johnson during the 1960s.

In more recent years, the increased role of the national government has produced a countermovement with a series of presidents arguing for new federalism. They argued that the powers of the federal government had been extended too far and much authority should be returned to the states, a process called devolution. Those efforts, although prompting much debate, have done nothing to curb Washington's power. In fact, Washington assumed even more power under President George W. Bush's administration, with the creation of the Department of Homeland Security, following the terrorist attacks of September 11, 2001, and an expanded role of the federal government in setting public education accountability requirements.

The Impact of Federalism on State Finances

3.5 Assess the impact of federalism on state finances and the extent to which state governments depend on federal funds, p. 76.

State and local governments depend on a massive infusion of federal funds to help support public health care, public housing, transportation, and other programs. Although often critical of the "strings," or policy conditions, usually attached to federal funds, state and local officials readily accept the money and often lobby for more. More than 30 percent of the Texas budget is funded by federal dollars.

Reactions to the Expanded Role of the Federal Government

3.6 Compare and contrast the arguments for and against the expanded role of the federal government, p. 76.

Federalism was a core issue at the Constitutional Convention in 1787, and it remains a core issue today. Supporters of the federal government's role note that the federal government has more resources than many states and local governments for funding important services. They also argue that many environmental and civil rights initiatives ordered by the federal government might never have been enacted if left up to state and local governments.

Other people argue that federal policies can be administered in a heavy-handed fashion. The availability of federal grants may prompt state and local governments to distort their priorities and pursue programs that their residents do not need. It also has been argued that excessive dependency on the federal government stifles innovation by state and local governments. Finally, some observers believe that the mandates and preemptions imposed by the federal government also limit the policy options of state and local governments.

Transnational Regionalism

3.7 Describe the increased interdependency between the United States and Mexico and list common issues faced by both nations, p. 77.

The politics, economy, and social system of Texas are inextricably linked to those of Mexico. Transnational regionalism can be used to explain and assess the complex interdependency that exists between the two neighbors. Mexico and Texas are major trading partners, a role that was enhanced by the ratification of the North American Free Trade Agreement in 1993. Texas, as a border state and home to an estimated 1.8 million illegal immigrants, is at the center of the prolonged political dispute over Washington's failure to enact a workable immigration policy. Immigrants, both legal and illegal, have a huge impact on education, health care and other social services in Texas. Although the war between illegal drug cartels, which has killed thousands of people in Mexico, has not yet spilled over into Texas, political figures still use the threat of drug violence to advocate for stronger security along the Texas-Mexico border. The increased industrialization along the border has worsened environmental problems affecting both countries.

Learn the Terms

Study and **Review** the Flashcards

reserved powers, p. 60
unitary system, p. 61
confederation, p. 61
federalism, p. 62
Dillon rule, p. 62
devolution, p. 63
delegated powers, p. 63
implied powers, p. 63
supremacy clause, p. 63
concurrent powers, p. 63
denied powers, p. 64
full faith and credit clause, p. 64
privileges and immunities, p. 65
extradition, p. 65
interstate compacts, p. 65
dual federalism, p. 66
cooperative federalism, p. 67
categorical grants-in-aid, p. 68
project grant, p. 69
formula grant, p. 69
matching funds, p. 69
new federalism, p. 70
block grants, p. 70
revenue sharing, p. 70
mandates, p. 71
preemptions, p. 71
transnational regionalism, p. 77
maquiladora program, p. 78
North American Free Trade Agreement (NAFTA), p. 78

Test Yourself

Study and **Review** the Practice Tests

1. Which of the following is a system of governmental relations in which both the state and the national governments derive their authority directly from the people?

a. unitary system
b. national system
c. confederation
d. federal system
e. Dillon rule

2. The basis for the relationship between state and local governments is the

a. unitary principle.
b. confederal principle.
c. state's rights principle.
d. federal principle.
e. sovereignty principle.

3. Which constitutional clause suggests that federal law prevails over the powers of the state when there is a conflict?

a. devolution
b. implied powers clause
c. supremacy clause
d. Tenth Amendment
e. full faith and credit clause

4. Which constitutional clause ensures that official governmental actions of one state are accepted by other states?

a. extradition
b. devolution
c. interstate compacts
d. supremacy clause
e. full faith and credit clause

5. The powers of the states under the U.S. Constitution are protected by which constitutional principle?

a. enumerated powers
b. reserved powers
c. concurrent powers
d. implied powers
e. denied powers

6. Which model of federalism argues that policy arenas and political relationships cut across all levels of government?

a. state-centered federalism
b. picket-fence federalism
c. coercive federalism
d. dual federalism
e. new federalism

7. The era of cooperative federalism began because of the

a. attack on the Bank of the United States.
b. Civil War.
c. Great Depression.
d. war in Vietnam.
e. September 11, 2001 terrorist attacks.

8. In which era were categorical grants-in-aid the primary vehicle for providing federal funds for public programs?

a. dual federalism
b. cooperative federalism
c. new federalism
d. devolution federalism
e. preemptive federalism

9. President Richard Nixon attempted to decentralize federal programs through the use of

a. project grants.
b. formula grants.
c. mandates.
d. block grants.
e. devolution.

10. Which of the following is an example of "big government conservatism," in which the federal government is used to achieve a social and economic agenda?

a. Paper Reduction Act of 1995
b. Unfunded Mandates Act of 1995
c. U.S. Highway Trust Fund
d. *United States* v. *Lopez*
e. No Child Left Behind

11. When analyzing the impact of federalism on state finances, we can say that Texas

a. pays more in federal taxes than it receives in federal expenditures.
b. receives more in federal expenditures than it gives in federal taxes.
c. pays more in federal taxes than any other state in the union.
d. receives more in federal expenditures per capita than any other state in the union.
e. pays as much in federal taxes as it receives in federal expenditures.

12. Which of the following has the primary responsibility to lobby the federal government for additional federal dollars?

a. Treasurer
b. Comptroller
c. Office of Federalism and Revenue Equalization
d. Office of State-Federal Relations
e. Office of Fiscal Federalism

13. Which of the following reduced tariffs among the United States, Mexico, and Canada?

a. transnational regionalism
b. the maquiladora program
c. The North American Free Trade Agreement
d. The Central American Free Trade Agreement
e. General Agreement on Tariffs and Trade

14. All of the following are major concerns about U.S.-Mexico border relations under the North American Free Trade Agreement EXCEPT

a. cheap labor in South Texas taking jobs from Mexico.
b. Mexican trucking on American highways.
c. domination of American corporations over the Mexican economy.
d. environmental problems.
e. human rights concerns about working conditions in Mexico.

15. Which program made it possible for temporary workers from Mexico to enter the United States to work?

a. Mexican Inclusion Act
b. Bracero Program
c. Nationalization Act
d. Sanctuary Cities Program
e. DREAM Act

Explore Further

Chemerinsky, Erwin, *Enhancing Federalism: Federalism for the 21st Century.* Palo Alto, CA: Stanford University Press, 2008. Challenges restrictive views of federalism that strive to limit the power of the federal government and argues for federalism as "empowerment" whereby governments at all levels take on more responsibility in dealing with social problems.

Dye, Thomas R., and Susan McManus, *Politics in States and Communities*, 14th ed. Boston, MA: Pearson, 2012. Introduces state and local governments comprehensively, covering governmental structures, federalism, state constitutions, state elections, legislative bodies, state and local executives, state courts, and special districts from the perspective of "conflict management."

Gamkhar, Shama, and J. Mitchell Pickerill, "The State of American Federalism 2010–2011: The Economy, Healthcare Reform and Midterm Elections Shape the Intergovernmental Agenda," *Publius* 41 (Summer 2011), pp. 361–94. Discusses a variety of topics including the impact of the recession on state budgets, the health care act and its impact on the states, the impact of the 2010 elections, unfunded mandates, and court decisions impacting federalism; this is a yearly article published by *Publius* on the state of American federalism.

Gerston, Larry N., *American Federalism: A Concise Introduction*. New York: M. E. Sharp, 2007. Introduces American federalism, focusing on the competing interests of the various levels of government.

Metzger, Gillian E., "Federalism Under Obama," *William and Mary Law Review* 53 (November 2011), pp. 567–619. Assesses the impact of the Obama administration's policies—affordable health care, economic recovery legislation following the recession of 2008, financial sector reforms, and administrative developments on federalism.

O'Toole, Laurence J., Jr., ed., *American Intergovernmental Relations: Foundations, Perspectives, and Issues.* Washington, DC: Congressional Quarterly Press, 2007. Covers a variety of topics on intergovernmental relationships in the United States; presents selected articles by recognized scholars.

Posner, Paul L., and Timothy J. Conlan, eds., *Intergovernmental Management for the 21st Century.* Washington, DC: Brookings Institution Press and National Academy of Public Administration, 2007. Presents articles by scholars of federalism that deal with the enormous challenges of government function within the federal framework.

Scheberle, Denise, *Federalism and Environmental Policy,* 2nd ed. Washington, DC: Georgetown University Press, 2004. Uses a policy framework for analyzing the formation and implementation of policy; the author focuses on four environmental policy programs, offering a perspective on "why environmental laws sometimes go awry."

Stephens, G. Ross, and Nelson Wikstrom, *American Intergovernmental Relations: A Fragmented Polity.* New York: Oxford University Press, 2007. Covers a range of topics—the history of federalism, cooperation and conflict in intergovernmental relations, fiscal federalism, key actors in federal relationships, regulation, and the states and local governments in the federal system; the authors place their analyses within the framework of changes that have occurred in the American political system.

Zimmerman, Joseph F., *Contemporary American Federalism: The Growth of National Power*, 2nd ed. Albany: State University of New York Press, 2008. Presents a historical perspective on American federalism and covers federal preemption authority, the courts and federalism, fiscal relationships, state-state relations, and state-local relations.

4

Listen on MyPoliSciLab

Interest Groups and Political Power in Texas

In America there is no limit to freedom of association for political ends.

—Alexis de Tocqueville, 1835

The citizens shall have the right, in a peaceable manner, to assemble together for their common good; and apply to those invested with the powers of government for redress of grievances or other purposes, by petition, address or remonstrance.

—Texas Constitution, Article 1, Section 27

Texas always has had a strong gun culture. It is a state in which many young people, even from urban areas, learn to hunt before they learn to drive. Governor Rick Perry sometimes packs a pistol while jogging and once made headlines by shooting and killing a coyote he encountered along his route through the hills in suburban Austin. Not surprisingly, Texas also is a state in which the National Rifle Association (NRA), the politically powerful pro-gun lobby, strongly impacts public policy. In 1995, the NRA successfully lobbied for a law allowing Texans age 21 and older to obtain state licenses to arm themselves with concealed handguns. More than 461,000 Texans possessed concealed handgun licenses at the end of 2010.

4.1 Define interest groups and describe what makes them distinctive from other types of organizations, p. 95.

4.2 Compare and contrast the pluralist and elitist theories of political behavior and explain how they apply to Texas, p. 97.

4.3 Summarize the factors that determine the power and influence of an interest group, p. 101.

4.4 Assess the strengths and weaknesses of the various types of interest groups that are active in Texas, p. 101.

4.5 Describe the characteristics of Texas lobbyists and their career patterns, p. 107.

4.6 Explain the different types of activities involved with indirect and direct lobbying, p. 108.

POWER OF LOBBYISTS
In addition to the gun lobby, business interests carry a lot of weight in Austin and can purchase influence with major political contributions. State officials who wish to build public support for new policy proposals often solicit the support of the business community first. Here, Lieutenant Governor David Dewhurst speaks to a group of Texas business people.

4.1

4.2

4.3

4.4

4.5

4.6

But some places in Texas, including college campuses, still prohibit handguns, and the NRA made a strong push to overturn that ban in 2011. It spent at least one-half million dollars on lobbyists that session and nearly succeeded in getting legislation passed. Its main argument was that students needed to be able to protect themselves if someone opened fire on campus. Supporters of the NRA-backed legislation frequently cited the 2007 tragedy at Virginia Tech, where a young man killed thirty-two people before shooting himself. "It's strictly a matter of self-defense," said state Senator Jeff Wentworth, a Republican from San Antonio and sponsor of the bill. He added, "I don't ever want to see repeated on a Texas college campus what happened at Virginia Tech, where some deranged, suicidal madman goes into a building and is able to pick off totally defenseless kids like sitting ducks."[1]

Initially, Wentworth was confident he had enough votes for the bill to be enacted into law. The Senate had approved a similar bill in 2009. Although the legislation had died in the House, this time more than half of the House members cosponsored the bill, mainly because of strong conservative, pro-gun, Republican gains in the 2010 elections. Despite this strong support, however, Wentworth—and the NRA—lost again, thanks to heavy opposition from students and university administrators, who were not without some political influence themselves. They argued that an emotionally overwrought student might pull a gun over a poor grade or during a drunken fraternity argument. Some students said they would be uncomfortable sitting in a classroom or taking a test next to someone who might have a gun, and university administrators said they feared that arming students could lead to campus suicides. Students rallied at the Capitol against the bill, and opponents barraged legislators with phone calls and emails. The opposition was so heavy that two Democratic senators who had told Wentworth they would vote for his bill switched their positions and lined up against it. Wentworth, therefore, was unable to advance the legislation. Despite this setback, the National Rifle Association will remain influential in Texas politics and will likely try again to pass a campus gun bill in upcoming legislative sessions.

The NRA's interest in the handgun bill was obvious, as are the interests of groups promoting or fighting other high-profile issues, such as a proposed tax increase, an effort to strengthen regulations for insurance companies, or new limits on consumer lawsuits against businesses. But much of the influence of interest groups and their lobbyists is subtle, elusive to public scrutiny, and reflects complex relationships among interest groups, elected public officials, and those who administer the law. These influences, however, do not always provoke angry public outcries, as the NRA encountered in 2011.

Political candidates often claim to be running against "the special interests" and promise to be responsive to all the people rather than to a few well-financed business, trade, or union groups. But most successful candidates freely accept campaign contributions from interest groups, and many Texans, along with other Americans, believe that governments are dominated by a few big interests looking out for themselves. National election surveys conducted by the University of Michigan for many years indicate a clear pattern of increased public distrust of government. In 1964, only 28 percent of those surveyed thought that a few big interests ran government, but during most of the years since 1974, more than 60 percent of Americans expressed this sentiment. In 2010, results from a survey conducted by the Pew Research Center indicated that only 22 percent of Americans expressed trust in the government in Washington.[2] Texans tend to have more confidence in their state and local governments than in the national government, but there are also elements of distrust or dissatisfaction. The UT-Austin Texas Politics Poll in 2008 reported that 35 percent of those surveyed thought they could trust state government to do what is right just about always or most of the time. But a larger proportion of the respondents (58 percent) indicated that state government could be trusted to do what is right only some of the time or none of the time.[3]

Two studies, conducted more than forty years apart, placed Texas among states with strong pressure-group systems.[4] Powerful pressure groups usually evolve in states with weak political parties, which always has been the case in Texas.[5] During the many years that Texas was a one-party Democratic state, the Republican Party posed no serious challenge to the Democratic monopoly, and intense factionalism marked the Democratic Party. Although the conservative Democratic wing dominated state politics through the 1970s,

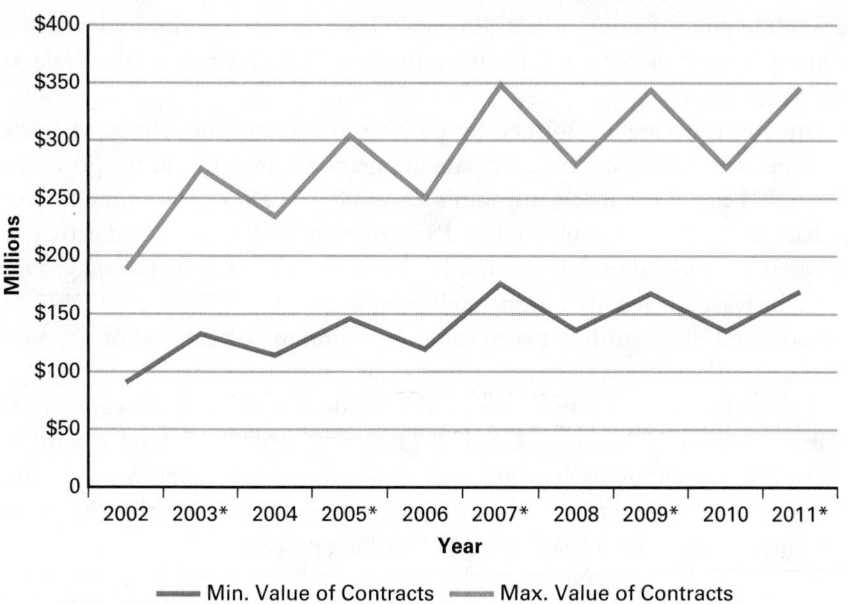

FIGURE 4–1 LOBBY CONTRACTS IN TEXAS, 2002–2011

With the expansion of the state's economy and the greater diversity of groups, organizations, and corporate interests in the state, there is an ever-increasing number of lobbyists working to advance the interests of their clients before the legislature and state agencies.

Source: Texans for Public Justice, "*Austin's Oldest Profession: Texas' Top Lobby Clients & Those Who Service Them,*" February 15, 2012.

interest group
A group of people with common goals who are organized to seek political or policy objectives they are unable to achieve by themselves.

interest groups often played a greater role in the policymaking process. Subsequent Republican growth has changed Texas's party system, but interest groups remain strong in the state and spend millions of dollars trying to elect favored candidates and influence governmental decisions (see Figure 4–1). More often than not, these interest groups still have a greater impact on the policymaking process than do the political parties.

What Are Interest Groups?

4.1 Define interest groups and describe what makes them distinctive from other types of organizations.

An **interest group** may be defined as "an organized collection of individuals who are bound together by shared attitudes or concerns and who make demands on political institutions in order to realize goals which they are unable to achieve on their own."[6] Members of an interest group share common interests or goals, organize to pursue those goals collectively because they cannot achieve them individually, and focus some of their efforts on influencing governmental decisions.[7] These characteristics, particularly the political and policy objectives, distinguish these groups from other organizations.

We do not know exactly how many groups or organizations there are in the United States or even in Texas. The *Encyclopedia of Associations* has identified approximately 25,000 associations of national scope. Across the country at the regional, state, and local levels, some 115,000 associations have been documented.[8] Comparing these totals with earlier estimates, it is clear that there has been an "explosion" of group activity since the 1950s.[9] Thousands of such groups exist in Texas. Some have long histories; others are formed to address a specific need, interest, or problem and disappear after a relatively short period. Although most organizations have the potential to

4.1 4.2 4.3 4.4 4.5 4.6

participate in the policymaking process, many will not. In our attempt to define the pressure-group system in Texas, we focus on those groups that can be identified as continuous active players.

Most organizations are not formed for political purposes. One scholar suggests that only 10 percent of the people participate in organizations active in the pressure-group system.[10] People usually do not join a chess club or a fraternal order, for example, to have an impact on public policy. Participation in church-related activities is usually based on spiritual or personal needs, although some religion-related groups have become increasingly involved in the political process.

We also should distinguish between categorical groups and interest or pressure groups. Women collectively constitute a categorical grouping of the female population; senior citizens, African Americans, and Hispanics also comprise categorical groups. Although these often are spoken of as groups of people with similar political objectives, individuals within each group hold a wide diversity of interests, concerns, and goals. By contrast, an interest group is a segment of the population that organizes for specific purposes and objectives in the policymaking process.

☐ Who Joins Groups?

Americans join a wide array of civic, sports, service, fraternal, hobby, economic, religious, and professional organizations. Surveys of American adults in the mid-1970s indicated that approximately 74 percent belonged to some type of organization while 28 percent reported they belonged to three or more organizations. Thirty years later, surveys conducted from 2000 to 2004 indicated that an estimated 62 percent of American adults belonged to some type of organization while 25 percent indicated they belonged to three or more organizations. Well over 80 percent of Americans identify with a particular religion or religious tradition, and approximately 40 to 45 percent of the adult population claims weekly attendance at religious services.[11]

At first glance, it would appear that the overwhelming majority of Americans have potential access to the policymaking process through their group memberships. Closer inspection, however, raises serious questions about the distribution of political power and resources. The argument that the policy playing field is tilted to benefit some groups or interests to the exclusion of others has some validity.[12] If part of the population has limited potential to affect the decisions of government, there are serious questions about the very nature of a democratic society and the role of groups within this political structure.

Those who study organizations generally agree that persons with higher incomes, better educations, higher status occupations, and higher standards of living are more likely than other people to belong to groups.[13] Historically, men have joined at a higher rate than have women; older people join at higher rates than do younger people; Anglos are more likely to be members than are Hispanics or African Americans; and people with established community ties are more likely to participate. Not only do these people join more groups, but they also are more likely to be active participants. These findings suggest that there is a class bias in the interest group system in Texas. People from higher socioeconomic classes are more easily organized and are more likely to maintain their support for these organizations.[14] Lower socioeconomic groups, minorities, and diffused constituencies, such as consumers, find it very difficult to compete on an equal footing with business, industrial, and professional groups, which also can better afford lobbying expenses and the financial contributions to political campaigns that usually guarantee access to officeholders.

☐ Why Do People Join Interest Groups?

Individuals join groups for a variety of reasons, which may change over time. One is the personal and material benefits that can be derived from interest groups.[15] A teacher, for example, may join the Texas State Teachers Association (TSTA) because it lobbies for higher teacher salaries, better fringe benefits and working conditions, and general educational issues. But TSTA also offers its members publications, insurance programs, potential legal assistance, discounts for travel, and valuable professional information.

People also realize social benefits from joining groups. Membership and participation provide them with a sense of personal identification with larger organizations and institutions that are likely to be more visible and potentially effective in the policymaking process than an individual would be if acting alone.[16] They may believe group membership enhances their personal status and prestige.[17]

Finally, a person can receive personal satisfaction or a sense of purpose from belonging to a group that he or she believes has a worthwhile cause or objective. Some people join groups to try to make the world a better place.[18] One motivation for joining such groups as Common Cause or the League of Women Voters, for example, may be a commitment to improving the election system in Texas. For many people, reform of the election system provides broad, but intangible, benefits that go well beyond the group or organization.

mischief of factions
Term coined by James Madison to describe the complex relationships among groups and interests within the American political system and the institutional arrangements that potentially balance the power of groups.

pluralism
Theories holding that a diversity of groups—and people—are instrumental in the policymaking process and no one group is able to dominate the decisions of government.

Interest Group Theory

4.2 Compare and contrast the pluralist and elitist theories of political behavior and explain how they apply to Texas.

The issue of interest groups and political power in American politics has been debated since the Constitutional Convention of 1787. Writing in the *Federalist Papers* at a time when there were no political parties or interest groups as we know them today, James Madison argued that it was inevitable that people would organize into groups, or "factions," and attempt to impose their will on others and use governments for their specific purposes. Madison also recognized two basic problems: there was a potential for the majority to tyrannize or impose its will on others, and a potential for the minority, in its pursuit of narrow self-interests, to harm the long-term interests of society as a whole. Most of his argument centered on the problem of majorities, in that small groups (the minority) could be outvoted.[19]

The cure for this **mischief of factions** was both institutional and socioeconomic. If the number of factions or groups increased, there would be greater competition and less likelihood that any one group could dominate the policymaking process. Competitors would have to find compromises. Also, institutional power would be fragmented among three branches of government and a federal system, in which powers would be further divided between the national government and the states. Elections for different offices are staggered in different years, and there are significant variations in electoral constituencies. The effect of the variations in national, state, and local elections is to make it even more difficult to construct large, permanent coalitions that could exercise absolute control over all institutions and subsequently dominate all policies.

Pluralism and Democratic Theory

Drawing in part on this tradition established by Madison, David Truman, an American political scientist, argued in his classic study, *The Governmental Process*, that American politics can be understood primarily in terms of the way groups interact with one another.[20] Expanding on Truman's theories, other scholars have attempted to develop a general understanding of politics organized around groups. These scholars, often referred to as pluralists and their philosophy as **pluralism**, believe that significant numbers of diverse and competing interest groups share political influence in a way that limits the power of any single group.

Although there are differences in emphasis among the pluralists, they have established the following general characteristics of a pluralistic society:

- Groups are the primary actors in the policymaking process. They provide the individual with political resources and link a person to governmental institutions.
- Politics is basically group interaction, in which groups come into conflict with one another over the limited resources of society, and public policy is ultimately the resolution of group conflict and differences.
- Because there are so many groups, no one group can dominate the political process. Although some groups have more resources than others, a group always has the potential to influence policy. If there is no group to address a particular concern or problem, one can be organized.
- Although most people do not actively participate in the policymaking process, they have access to the process through the leaders of the groups to which they belong. There are numerous leadership opportunities within groups for individuals who want active roles.
- Most group leaders are committed to democratic values, and competition makes them responsive to other members and serves to check or constrain their actions.[21]

Pluralism is appealing because it gives credence to our general views of a democratic society and offers potential solutions, or at least hope, for those people who are excluded from full political participation or benefits. One can find evidence in Texas to support the pluralist view. Thousands of groups are organized on a statewide or community level. Hundreds of lobbyists are registered in Austin to represent a wide variety of economic, social, civic, and cultural organizations. A growing state population and a diversifying economy have significantly increased the number of interest groups over the past three decades.

David Truman suggests that there are periods, or "waves," in American political history in which groups proliferate rapidly in response to economic, social, or political change.[22] To compensate for imbalances in the political system, additional groups organize in an attempt to reestablish equilibrium.

Groups form for any number of reasons. Concerns over economic changes, public school funding, environmental protection, medical care for low-income Texans, and other pressing issues have generated additional interest groups in Texas in recent years. Movements focusing on the interests of Hispanics, African Americans, women, and homosexuals led to the creation of interest groups lobbying to advance their concerns. Still other organizations emerged to protect existing interests, or the status quo, and some groups formed in response to new governmental policies and regulations.[23]

With the elimination of historic discriminatory practices, minority Texans have made significant economic, social, and political gains. In addition to having increased access to mainstream groups, minorities have formed their own professional and economic organizations. It is not uncommon to find Hispanic chambers of commerce or African American bar associations in many Texas cities.

Advocates of pluralism use the foregoing arguments and examples to support their view. Despite the earlier periods in Texas history, when large segments of the population were excluded from the political and policymaking processes, they argue that the political system is now open and accessible to new groups. They believe that those holding public office are responsive to the needs and interests of a greater diversity of Texans than ever before.

☐ The Elitist Alternative

Other political scientists, however, insist that the pluralist theories simply do not describe the realities of power and policymaking in Texas or the United States. They say the pluralists have not given enough attention to the fact that a few individuals still control enormous resources. Although there are thousands of groups, neither are they equal in political resources nor can they equally translate their interests or demands

4.1
4.2
4.3
4.4
4.5
4.6

into public policy. These scholars believe the political system in Texas can be more accurately described in terms of **elitism**.

According to this view, a few individuals who derive power from their leadership positions in large organizations or institutions, particularly those with great financial resources, monopolize the influence on most important policy decisions. From the elitist perspective, power is not an individual commodity or resource but an attribute of social organizations.[24]

People who subscribe to this theory also believe that the existence of elites within any society is inevitable. Robert Michels, a European social scientist writing during the first part of the twentieth century, argued that any organization, no matter how structured, will eventually produce an "oligarchy," or rule by a few individuals. Michels's **iron rule of oligarchy** was applicable to any organization and was a universal law applied to all social systems.[25]

Beginning with C. Wright Mills and his book *The Power Elite*, many American scholars have been proponents of the elitist theory.[26] A number of generalizations can be derived from the elitist school of thought:

- Power is held by a few individuals and is derived from their positions in large institutions. In addition to economic institutions, these include the government, the mass media, and civic organizations.
- Historically, political elites constituted a homogeneous group drawn primarily from the upper and upper-middle classes. They were older, well-educated, primarily white, Anglo-Saxon males.
- Although there is competition among elites and the institutions they represent, there is considerable consensus and cohesion among elites on primary values, interests, and the rules of the game.
- Elites are linked by a complex network of interlocking memberships on the governing bodies of corporations, financial institutions, foundations, and civic and cultural organizations.
- Policy decisions are made by a few individuals and primarily reflect the interests of the dominant institutions. The interests of the dominant elites are not necessarily opposed to those of other classes of society.
- The vast majority of people are passive spectators to the policymaking process. Voting has been the primary means by which the general population can participate in governmental decisions, but other than selecting governmental officials, elections have limited effects on policy decisions.[27]

A number of students of Texas government and politics have argued from the elitist perspective. George Norris Green, writing about the period from 1938 to 1957, concluded that Texas was "governed by conservatives, collectively dubbed the Establishment."[28] **The Establishment** was a "loosely knit plutocracy comprised mostly of Anglo businessmen, oilmen, bankers and lawyers" that emerged in the late 1930s, in part as a response to the liberal policies of the New Deal.[29] They were extremely conservative, producing a "virulent" strain of conservatism marked by "Texanism" and "super-Americanism."[30]

Texas's "traditionalistic-individualistic" political culture was especially conducive to the dominance of the conservative establishment, which had little interest in the needs of the lower socioeconomic groups within the state. The exclusion of minorities from participation in elections and the low rates of voter turnout resulted in the election of public officials who were sympathetic to the views of the conservative elites. In addition, "unprincipled public relations men" and "the rise of reactionary newspapers" manipulated public opinion.[31]

In a more recent study of Texas politics, Chandler Davidson argues that there is a group of Texans, extraordinarily wealthy or linked to large corporations, who constitute "an upper class in the precise meaning of the term: a social group whose common background and effective control of wealth bring them together politically."[32] Although warning against a hasty conclusion that an upper class is a ruling class,

elitism
The view that political power is primarily held by a few individuals who derive power from leadership positions in large business, civic, or governmental institutions.

iron rule of oligarchy
A theory developed by Robert Michels, a European sociologist, that all organizations inevitably are dominated by a few individuals.

The Establishment
In the days of one-party Democratic politics in Texas, it was a loosely knit coalition of Anglo businessmen, oilmen, bankers, and lawyers who controlled state policymaking.

hyperpluralism
The rapid expansion of interest groups that serves to disrupt and potentially deadlock the policymaking process.

iron triangles of government
Relationships among the interest groups, the administrative agencies, and the legislative committees involved in drafting the laws and regulations affecting a particular area of the economy or a specific segment of the population.

single-issue groups
Single-purpose or highly ideological groups that promote a single issue or cause with only limited regard for the views or interests of other groups. Such groups often are reluctant to compromise.

Davidson describes their shared values, group cohesiveness, and interlocking relationships.[33] The upper class has enormous political power. When united on specific policy objectives, its members usually have prevailed against "their liberal enemies concentrated in the working class."[34] Moreover, the institutional arrangements of the state's economic and political structures work to produce an upper-class unity that contributes to its successes in public policy.[35]

The sharply contrasting views of political power in Texas have produced an ongoing debate. To a large extent, the issue of who controls Texas politics has not been resolved because of insufficient data to support one position over the other. There also is evidence suggesting that power relationships have changed over time. Historically, an upper class or a conservative establishment dominated Texas government and public policy. But with the enormous social, economic, and political changes that have taken place since the 1970s, Texans may well be moving from an elitist system to some variation of pluralism.

□ Hyperpluralism, Policy Subsystems, and Single-Issue Interest Groups

Some scholars believe that the rapid expansion of interest groups in Texas and the nation has produced a system of hyperpluralism. In effect, **hyperpluralism** is the interest group system out of control.[36] Historically, competition and bargaining among interest groups achieved political stability. Public policy had some degree of coherence and reflected shared views of the general interest. But as groups proliferate, there is a potential for the policy process to degenerate into a series of subsystems. This problem has been compounded by the notion that the demands of all interest groups are legitimate and that governments should attempt to respond to as many groups as possible. This theory of interest group liberalism is developed at length by Theodore Lowi in *The End of Liberalism.*[37]

Governments respond to the demands of various groups by enacting laws and regulations or appropriating funds to address their priorities. In many cases, additional governmental agencies may be created to carry out the new laws. Legislative committees also may be given control over new programs. Eventually, the interactions among the interest groups, the administrative agencies, and the legislative committees produce permanent relationships that have been described as the **iron triangles of government**.

Lowi's concerns about the excesses of pluralism may be valid. Some state agencies are closely tied to the industries they regulate. Sometimes, interest groups even lobby for dedicated sources of funding for their programs, thus assuring they will benefit from specific taxes year after year, regardless of other state needs.

Hyperpluralism also can lead to deadlock. Lobbying, described in the next section, has become increasingly sophisticated. Often, lobbyists representing a single influential group can block policy initiatives that have widespread support but threaten the group's priorities. Considering the difficulties in addressing problems facing state and local governments in recent years, one can conclude that it is easier to block solutions than to enact policies addressing pressing needs for change.

In recent years, a number of scholars have identified another threat to the stability of the political system—the **single-issue groups**. These are highly ideological groups that attempt to push on the public agenda a single issue or cause without regard for the views or attitudes of other groups. These groups may be reluctant to compromise and often engage in tactics and strategies designed to extract concessions upon threat of policy deadlock. Their position on an issue leaves no grounds for accommodation or compromise. These groups also base their support for or opposition to a political candidate on a single issue with little regard for the candidate's other policy positions.

Resources of Interest Groups

4.3 Summarize the factors that determine the power and influence of an interest group.

Some interest groups are extremely powerful and exercise considerable influence over the formation of public policy, whereas others are ineffectual and weak. The differences can be explained by a number of factors. One is the size of a group and the number of members and voters it can potentially influence. Numerous teachers' and educational groups within the state, for example, represent a significant number of people. The promise of support or the threat of retaliation by such groups will be assessed by a legislator as he or she decides to support or oppose the groups' policy proposals. Individual educational groups do not always agree on legislation, but their numbers are difficult to ignore. Teachers who had been instrumental in the 1982 election of Governor Mark White withdrew that support in 1986 in a dispute over some of White's educational reforms; the loss of that support contributed to his defeat.

The size of a group alone, however, does not guarantee power or influence. A large group internally divided, with no clear policy focus, is less likely to be successful than a smaller group with a fixed goal. Other major factors in a group's success are its cohesiveness and the ability of its leaders to mobilize its membership in support of policy objectives.

Another key factor is the distribution of a group's membership across the state. A group concentrated in one geographic area has less potential impact on the election of a large number of legislators than does a group with members distributed across the state. Organized labor, for example, has its greatest membership strength in the Houston and Beaumont areas in Southeast Texas. On the other hand, teachers and small business owners are plentiful throughout the state and have the potential to affect more local and district elections.

A group's financial resources also determine its power. Groups that represent low-income people have difficulty raising the dollars necessary to mount effective lobbying or public relations campaigns. By contrast, organizations representing large corporations or high-income professional groups are in a much better position to raise funds for the campaign contributions and lobbying expenditures necessary to ensure access to policymakers.

In addition, a group's reputation, both within the legislature and among the general public, affects a group's influence. A major function of interest groups is to provide information to policymakers, and the reliability and accuracy of this information are critical. If a group lies, unduly distorts information, or is less than forthright in its dealings with other actors in the policymaking process, its reputation can be irreparably damaged.[38]

The leadership of a group and its hired staff also contribute to its success. As policy issues develop, a competent staff will conduct research, provide position papers, draft specific proposals, contact key decision makers and the press, maintain communication with the membership, and develop public relations strategies to mobilize the membership to bring pressure on policymakers.

Dominant Interest Groups in Texas

4.4 Assess the strengths and weaknesses of the various types of interest groups that are active in Texas.

hroughout much of our history, large corporations and banks, oil companies, and agricultural interests that backed the conservative Democratic officeholders (who had a stranglehold on the legislature, the courts, and the executive branch) dominated state government.[39] Big business still

LOBBYISTS CROWD THE AREA OUTSIDE THE TEXAS HOUSE OF REPRESENTATIVES CHAMBER

In the closing days of a legislative session, with the fate of much legislation still undecided, each lobbyist waits to talk with lawmakers about specific bills.

carries a lot of weight in Austin and can purchase a lot of influence with major political contributions and the sophisticated skills of public affairs strategists. State officials who want to build public support for new policy proposals usually solicit the support of the business community first.

Beginning in the 1970s, however, influence began to be more diffused. The number of minorities, Republicans, and liberal Democrats elected to the legislature from single-member districts increased. Consumer, environmental, and other public advocacy groups emerged. Organized labor, which had been shut out by the corporate establishment, found some common interests with the trial lawyers, who earned fees suing businesses on behalf of consumers and other plaintiffs claiming damages or injuries caused by various companies or products. The decline of oil and gas production and the emergence of high-tech service industries also helped diffuse the business lobby into more competitive factions.

☐ Business

The diverse business interests in Texas organize in several ways to influence the policymaking process. First, broad-based associations, including the Texas Association of Business (TAB) and the Texas Taxpayers and Research Association (TARA), represent business and industry in general. Their overall goal is to maintain and improve upon a favorable business climate by seeking favorable tax and regulatory policies.

The business community also organizes through trade associations that represent and seek to advance the interests of specific industries. Some of the more active associations include the Texas Bankers Association, the Texas Association of Realtors, the Wholesale Beer Distributors of Texas, the Texas Independent Producers & Royalty Owners Association, the Texas Chemical Council, the Texas Automobile Dealers Association, and the Texas Restaurant Association.

Many individual companies also retain their own lobbyists to represent them before the legislature and administrative agencies. A lobbyist may be a salaried employee of a company or a professional, freelance lobbyist—or "hired gun"—who is retained by several clients. Some wealthy individuals hire their own lobbyists to help protect their interests.

Finally, a group representing a broad range of business members can be organized to pursue a single issue. Perhaps the best-known example of this is Texans for

Lawsuit Reform, which for years has doggedly lobbied for a series of limitations on civil lawsuits and damage awards against businesses and their insurance companies.

Business groups form coalitions in opposition to organized labor, consumer advocates, and trial lawyers on major political and philosophical issues, such as limits on consumer lawsuits. But the business lobby is far from monolithic. Various companies or trade associations differ on numerous issues, including tax policy and utility regulation. During the 1999 legislative session, for example, lawmakers had to perform a delicate balancing act to put together an electric deregulation bill allowing petrochemical plants and other heavy industrial users of electricity to generate and sell power in competition with utility companies. Government frequently has been confronted in recent years with rivalries in the lucrative telecommunications industry.

For many years, the interest groups associated with oil and natural gas played a dominant role among the business and industry lobbies. At one time, oil and natural gas accounted for 30 percent of the state's economic output. But this contribution has sharply declined since the 1980s recession, which began to redefine Texas's economy. The oil and gas lobby, though still effective, now has to work with political leaders who are focused on economic diversification.

☐ Professional Groups

A number of professional groups have played dominant roles in Texas politics and the policymaking process. One of the better known is the Texas Medical Association (TMA), which in recent years has joined forces with business against trial lawyers to push for laws putting limits on malpractice suits and other damage claims against physicians and the business community. The TMA's political action committee (TEXPAC) is a major contributor of campaign dollars to candidates for the legislature, the Texas Supreme Court, and other state offices. It won a major victory in 2003, with legislative and voter approval of a constitutional amendment imposing new limits on monetary damages in medical malpractice cases.

Lawsuits over medical malpractice, product liability, and workers' compensation also raised the profile of trial lawyers, who make their living representing injured persons, or plaintiffs. Trial lawyers (sometimes called plaintiffs' lawyers) are compensated with a share of the damages awarded their clients by a court or negotiated in a settlement with the defendant or the defendant's insurance company. A defendant can be a doctor accused of malpractice in the handling of an individual's care, a manufacturer accused of making a faulty product that caused an injury, a city whose truck was involved in an auto accident, an employer whose worker suffered an injury on the job, or just about any legal entity deemed responsible for causing harm to someone. Individually and through their political action committee, trial lawyers have contributed millions of dollars to judicial, legislative, and other selected candidates since the 1970s. In the early 1980s, they succeeded in electing several Texas Supreme Court justices who shared their viewpoint, and the court issued precedent-setting opinions making it easier for plaintiffs to win large damage awards. The business and medical communities retaliated by boosting their own political contributions and lobbying efforts and, by 1990, succeeded in tipping the state Supreme Court's philosophical scale back to its traditional business-oriented viewpoint.

Although the war over tort law, as these types of damage suits are called, continued to rage—before the courts and in the legislature—trial lawyers usually were on the defensive in the era of Republican control. As noted earlier, lawmakers in recent years have enacted several laws restricting consumer lawsuits and limiting damage awards.

☐ Education

A variety of educational interests are visible in the policymaking process in Austin. The changing global economy and increased technology have enhanced the importance of

public interest groups
Groups that are primarily concerned with consumer or environmental protection, the promotion of strong ethical standards for public officials, or increased funding for health and human services programs. Since they often are poorly funded, grassroots, volunteer efforts are crucial to their success.

education in developing the state's future, and there is widespread public support for improving the public schools and expanding access to colleges and universities.

Most university regents, chancellors, and presidents are well connected politically. Universities also are capable—through the use of donations and other non-tax funds—of hiring a well-paid cadre of legislative liaisons, or lobbyists. Another effective lobbying source for universities, particularly the larger ones, are the armies of alumni, many of them politically influential, ready to make phone calls, send emails, or write letters on behalf of their alma maters when the need arises. The business community also is a strong supporter of higher education. The influence of the University of Texas System, in particular, was instrumental in the legislature's enactment of a law in 2003 giving university governing boards the authority, for the first time in Texas, to raise student tuition independently of legislative control. But university officials were unable in 2011 to head off deep budgetary cuts to higher education, when Governor Rick Perry and the legislative majority insisted on reducing spending, rather than raising taxes, to bridge a huge revenue shortfall. The public schools and other state programs also were hit with cuts.

The struggle for equity and quality in public elementary and secondary education involves a number of groups representing various—and sometimes conflicting—interests within the educational community. Four associations or unions represent teachers and other school employees, one represents school boards, and a separate lobby group represents school administrators. Still another group, the Equity Center, which represents school districts with low property wealth, has been a major player in lawsuits over school finance. Most recently, it organized several hundred school districts as plaintiffs in a suit filed against the state in late 2011, seeking additional improvements in state funding.

All of these groups lobby the legislature, and they all seek to improve public education. But, individually, they also seek to protect the specific interests of their members, which means they can line up against one another on some issues. As the legislature prepared to impose deep cuts in school budgets in 2011, for example, the teachers' groups fought the school boards and administrators over legislation making it easier for school districts to fire or furlough teachers or cut teachers' pay. The teachers argued that it was poor public policy to encourage cuts directly affecting the classroom before exhausting all other possibilities for savings, including further reductions in school administration.

☐ Public Interest Groups

Most of the **public interest groups** represented in Austin are concerned primarily with protecting consumers and the environment from big business; promoting stronger ethical standards for public officials; and increasing funding for health and human services programs for the poor, the elderly, the young, and the disabled. Many have full-time lobbyists and some staff, but nowhere near the financial resources of the business and professional groups. Grassroots volunteer efforts and the effective use of the mass media are crucial to their success. The most active include the Center for Public Policy Priorities, the Sierra Club, Texas Watch, the Gray Panthers, Americans Disabled for Attendant Programs Today (ADAPT), and Public Citizen, a Texas affiliate of the national public interest group founded by consumer advocate Ralph Nader.

Although public interest lobbyists concentrate most of their attention on the legislature, some consumer groups also are active before state regulatory agencies, particularly the Public Utility Commission, the Department of Insurance, and the Texas Commission on Environmental Quality. Among the more militant groups is ADAPT, which has staged highly visible demonstrations by wheelchair-bound Texans—including an overnight occupation of the governor's reception room—to demand more money for community-based facilities and attendant services for the disabled.[40]

Public interest advocates usually play more defense—trying to keep anticonsumer legislation from becoming law—than they do offense whenever lawmakers meet. But they scored a rare, significant victory during the 2003 regular session, when lawmakers enacted one of their priorities—a strengthened ethics law for public officials and political candidates. Among other things, the new law required officeholders to list the occupations and employers of their political contributors and imposed new financial-reporting requirements on mayors and city council members.[41]

☐ Minorities

The advent of single-member, urban legislative districts in the 1970s significantly increased the number of African American and Hispanic lawmakers and strengthened the influence of minority interest groups. These groups often have found that the courthouse can still be a shorter route to success than the statehouse, but the legislature has become increasingly attentive to their voices.

The League of United Latin American Citizens (LULAC) and the Mexican American Legal Defense and Educational Fund (MALDEF) are two of the better-known Hispanic organizations. LULAC, founded in 1929, is the oldest and largest Hispanic organization in the United States and continues to be particularly influential in causes such as education and election reform in Texas.

MALDEF, formed in San Antonio in 1968, fights in the courtroom for the civil rights of Hispanics. It has been successful in numerous battles over the drawing of political boundaries for governmental bodies in Texas and in lengthy litigation over public school finance. MALDEF represented property-poor school districts that won a unanimous landmark Texas Supreme Court order (*Edgewood* v. *Kirby*) in 1989 for a more equitable distribution of education aid between rich and poor districts. The victory eventually led to major legislative changes in the school finance system.

The National Association for the Advancement of Colored People (NAACP) is a leader in promoting and protecting the interests of African Americans. The NAACP initiated many of the early court attacks on educational inequality and has fought for voting rights for minority citizens. The organization also has worked to increase employment opportunities for African Americans in state agencies and has attacked lending practices in the mortgage industry that it found discriminatory.

In recent years, the Industrial Areas Foundation (IAF), a collection of well-organized, church-supported community groups, also has been a strong and effective voice for low-income minorities. Member groups include Valley Interfaith in South Texas, Communities Organized for Public Service (COPS) in San Antonio, The Metropolitan Organization (TMO) and the Fort Bend Interfaith Council in the Houston area, and the El Paso Interreligious Sponsoring Organization (EPISO).

The first IAF chapter in Texas, San Antonio's COPS, developed an early reputation for being confrontational and raucous in demanding better drainage facilities and other improvements for the city's impoverished neighborhoods. COPS members would surround city council members in city hall offices and hallways, yell their demands, and refuse to take "no" or "maybe" for an answer. The group began to moderate its tactics as it matured politically and developed influential friends. At the state level, it has lobbied for health care for the poor; more equity in school funding; and water and sewer service for the *colonias*, or unincorporated slums, along the Texas-Mexico border.

☐ Labor

Organized labor has traditionally taken a back seat to business in Texas, a strong "right-to-work" state in which union membership cannot be required as a condition of employment. Antilabor sentiment ran particularly high in the 1940s and 1950s, at the height of the conservative Democratic establishment's control of Texas politics. Labor-baiting campaigns in which unions were portrayed as evil communist sympathizers were not uncommon then.[42]

Today, about 534,000 Texans, or 5.2 percent of the workforce, are members of labor unions.[43] The largest unions in the state include the Communications Workers of America (CWA) and the American Federation of State, County, and Municipal Employees (AFSCME). Unions can provide grassroots support for political candidates through endorsement cards, phone banks, and other get-out-the-vote efforts, and this support has historically gone to Democratic candidates. With Republican and conservative gains in recent years, many labor-backed candidates have not fared well in Texas, especially in statewide elections.

Labor generally sides with the trial lawyers on such issues as workers' compensation, worker safety, and business liability for faulty products. It also has many common interests with public interest groups. One of labor's major victories in Texas politics was the defeat of a proposal to lock the right-to-work law into the state constitution. That dispute helped scuttle the Constitutional Convention of 1974, and labor prevailed only because of a convention rule that required proposals to receive a two-thirds vote.

□ Local Governments

State laws and budgetary decisions significantly affect local governments. The stakes are particularly high now because governments are finding revenue harder to raise—especially with the federal government passing the cost of numerous programs on to the states, and the states issuing similar mandates to local governments. As a result, lobbyists represent counties, cities, prosecutors, metropolitan transit authorities, and various special districts in Austin.

Many local governments belong to umbrella organizations, such as the Texas Municipal League, the Texas Association of Counties, and the Texas District and County Attorneys Association, which have full-time lobbyists. Several of the larger cities and counties also retain their own lobbyists, and mayors, city council members, and county judges frequently travel to Austin to visit with legislators and testify for or against bills. The city of Houston, the state's largest city, spent as much as $1 million on nineteen state lobbyist contracts in 2011. The city of Austin spent as much as $1 million on fourteen lobbyist contracts that year.[44]

□ Agricultural Groups

Although Texas is now predominantly urban, agriculture still is an important part of the state's economy, and a number of agricultural groups are represented in Austin. Their influence is obviously strongest among rural legislators. But the Texas Farm Bureau, the largest such group, was instrumental in Rick Perry's 1990 election defeat of liberal Democratic Agriculture Commissioner Jim Hightower, who had angered many agricultural producers and the chemical industry with tough stands on farm worker rights and pesticide regulation. Other producer groups include the Texas and Southwestern Cattle Raisers Association, the Texas Nurseryman's Association, and the Texas Corn Producers Board.

The United Farm Workers Union has been a strong advocate of better conditions for workers and frequently has been at odds with agricultural producers. Represented in court by the Texas Civil Liberties Union and Texas Rural Legal Aid attorneys, farm workers won major lawsuits and legislation in the 1980s on such issues as unemployment compensation, picketing rights, the right to be informed about dangerous pesticides used in fields, and a higher minimum wage.

□ Religious Groups

Influenced in part by their views of separation of church and state, many people think religious groups have little or no legitimate role in the political process. Nevertheless, religious groups have helped influence policy in Texas, and the abortion issue and other social and economic issues have increased the presence of religious groups in Austin.

A number of religious groups began emerging on the political scene in the 1940s, with an identifiable right-wing orientation. These groups, predecessors of what now is known as the "Religious Right," combined Christian rhetoric and symbols with anticommunism, antilabor, anti–civil rights, antiliberal, or anti–New Deal themes. Although these groups often were small, they were linked to the extreme right wing of the Texas establishment, and they were the precursors to many of the conservative ideological groups that have emerged in American politics since the 1970s.[45] Many of these organizations gravitated toward the Republican Party.[46] With a strong organizational effort, religious conservatives influenced the conservative takeover of leadership positions in the Texas Republican Party in 1994.

The Texas Freedom Network, founded in 1995, provides an alternative voice to the Christian right. It now claims a membership of some 30,000 people supporting religious freedom and individual liberties. The organization claims success in "defeating initiatives backed by the religious right in Texas, including private school vouchers, textbook censorship, and faith-based deregulation."[47]

Many religious denominations have boards or commissions responsible for monitoring governmental action. One well-known religious interest group is the Christian Life Commission of the Baptist General Convention of Texas, a strong advocate of human services programs and an outspoken opponent of gambling.

Churches across the state, particularly the Catholic Church, whose policies on social action have been shaped by papal encyclicals and Vatican II, have established links to community-based organizations that address the social and economic needs of the poor. In many regards, this is a redefinition of the Social Gospel, a church-based political movement of the late nineteenth and early twentieth centuries.

Who Are the Lobbyists?

4.5 Describe the characteristics of Texas lobbyists and their career patterns.

During each regular session of the Texas legislature, hundreds of individuals representing businesses, trade associations, and other interests register as lobbyists with the Texas Ethics Commission. Some 1,836 lobbyists represented 2,908 clients in 2011.[48] Lobbyists run the gamut from well-dressed corporate types with generous expense accounts to volunteer consumer and environmental advocates in blue jeans and sneakers. Most are male, although the number of female lobbyists has increased in recent years, and many women now hold major lobbying positions. The highest billing lobbyist in 2011 was a woman, Carol McGarah (see *Talking Texas: Does Money Talk? Sometimes, It Screams*). Most lobbyists came to their careers by way of other occupations and jobs, but they have, on the whole, an acute understanding of the policymaking process and the points of access and influence in that process.

Many lobbyists are former legislators (see Figure 4–2). They bring to the process their legislative skills, personal relationships with former legislative colleagues, and expertise in substantive policy areas. A number of other lobbyists are former legislative staffers. Some are former gubernatorial assistants.

Many of the trade and professional associations, labor unions, and public interest groups have full-time staffs in Austin who function as their lobbyists. Many corporations also use their own employees to lobby. Some companies have governmental affairs departments or offices staffed by employees with experience in government or public affairs. In large corporations that do business across the country, the governmental affairs staffs may be rather large because such companies will attempt to follow the actions of numerous state legislatures, city councils, and the U.S. Congress.

A number of lawyers have developed highly successful lobbying practices. Some of these professional freelancers (the previously mentioned hired guns) specialize in

Talking ★ TEXAS Does Money Talk? Sometimes, It Screams

If money does not talk when the Texas legislature is in session, it is not for a lack of trying. In fact, you could say that money screams. According to Texans for Public Justice (TPJ), which tracks money spent in Texas politics, 2,908 clients, including a wide range of public policy interests, paid somewhere between $169 million and $345 million to 1,836 lobbyists in 2011. A more exact figure is difficult to determine because lobbyist expenditures to the Texas Ethics Commission, on which the TPJ report is based, are reported by general brackets, not by exact amounts. But, regardless, lobbying is a major enterprise in Austin.

The biggest spender was AT&T Corp., the communications giant, which spent a maximum $10.5 million on 110 lobby contracts. Twenty-six other companies, law firms, or groups, including the cities of Houston and Austin, also spent as much as $1 million or more apiece.

The biggest spending industry was energy and natural resources, whose members spent as much as $64 million on lobbyists, or 19 percent of the lobby spending total. The health care industry ranked number 2, spending as much as $53 million. Ideological and single-interest clients, including local governments, the National Rifle Association and others, were third, spending as much as $44 million.

Thirty lobbyists reported maximum 2011 incomes of more than $1.5 million apiece. Collectively, they received as much as $68 million, about 20 percent of all lobby dollars. The top-billing lobbyist was Carol McGarah, who reported $4.3 million in payments from 77 clients.[a]

CRITICAL THINKING QUESTIONS

1. Can limits be placed on the amount of money companies and groups spend on lobbying in Texas? Why or why not?
2. Do you think lobbyists should be required to report the specific dollar amounts they receive for or expend on lobbying rather than a range of revenue and expenditures? Why or why not?

[a] Texans for Public Justice, "Austin's Oldest Profession: Texas' Top Lobby Clients & Those Who Service Them," February 15, 2012.

lobbying
An effort, usually organized and using a variety of strategies and techniques, to influence the making of laws or public policy.

specific policy areas, whereas others represent a wide array of clients. Some may be identified as "super lobbyists" because of their ability to exercise considerable influence in the policymaking process. Many work for the state's largest law firms, which have established permanent offices in Austin. Some of the topnotch freelancers are not attorneys, but they have a strong knowledge of the governmental process (see *Talking Texas: Long-Term Survival Assessments for Lobbyist-to-Be*).

Some public relations firms also offer their services to interest groups. These companies specialize in "image creation" or "image modification."[49] Although they may not handle direct lobbying efforts, they often are retained to assist in indirect lobbying campaigns. They are responsible for developing relationships with the press, developing media campaigns, and assisting in political campaigns.

Interest Groups and the Policymaking Process

4.6 Explain the different types of activities involved with indirect and direct lobbying.

For many people, the term **lobbying** may suggest shady characters lurking in the halls of the state Capitol, attempting to bribe legislators with money, sex, or booze. That perception was reinforced, especially before a new ethics law in 1991, by published reports of lobbyists treating legislators to trips, golf tournaments, concerts, and other diversions. Lobbyists still spend money to entertain legislators, but wining and dining now are limited by state law and are only one aspect of the complex relationships between interest groups and policymakers. Lobbying is central to a pluralistic society, and the legal foundations of lobbying activity are found in the U.S. and Texas

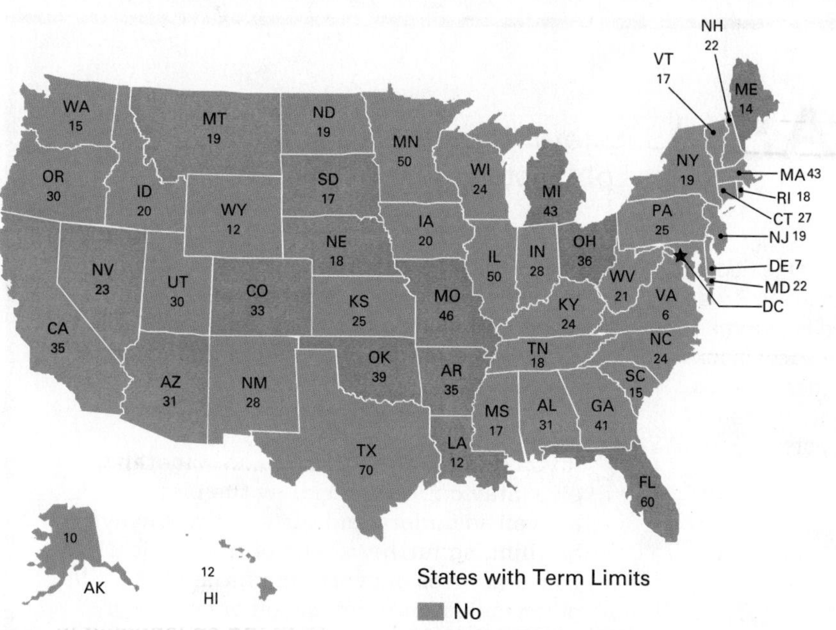

FIGURE 4–2 TEXAS COMPARED TO OTHER STATES: EX-LEGISLATORS REGISTERED TO LOBBY

Many former legislators across the fifty states pursue careers as lobbyists, and Texas, with seventy ex-legislators registered as lobbyists, led the nation.

Source: Center for Public Integrity, "Statehouse Revolvers," October 12, 2006.

Constitutions, which provide for the right to petition "the governments for a redress of grievances."[50]

In the broadest sense, lobbying is "simply the practice of attempting to influence the decisions of government."[51] Most scholars take this view. Lobbying may be both indirect and direct and includes, but is not limited to, electoral activities, public relations campaigns, protests and demonstrations, and direct contact with policymakers (see Table 4–1). According to political scientist Carol Greenwald, "Lobbying may thus

TABLE 4–1 TECHNIQUES USED BY LOBBYISTS TO INFLUENCE POLICYMAKERS

1. Conduct and maintain relevant research and information pertaining to policy issues
2. Provide reliable research results or technical information supporting a group's policy interests to decision makers, the press, and other audiences
3. Contact government officials or their key staff members directly to present the organization's point of view on policy
4. Testify at hearings of committees and subcommittees
5. Engage with and maintain informal contacts with legislators and other policymakers at conventions, over lunch, on the golf course, and so on
6. Communicate by email or newsletter with members of the organization to inform them about organizational activities on public policy issues
7. Enter into coalitions with other organizations to support or block policy initiatives
8. Establish and cultivate media contacts to advance a group's policy position
9. Consult with government officials to plan and execute legislative strategies
10. Help draft legislation
11. Work with the group's members, allies, or the general public in letter-writing, email, or telephone campaigns to influence policymakers' decisions
12. Mount grassroots lobbying efforts to encourage members and the general public to contact public officials
13. Mobilize influential constituents to contact their representatives' offices
14. Help formulate and draft administrative regulations, rules, or guidelines
15. Serve on advisory commissions and boards
16. Inform legislators of the effects of a bill on their districts
17. Make campaign contributions to political candidates
18. Endorse candidates running for office
19. File lawsuits or otherwise engage in litigation to impact policy

SOURCES: From Kay Lehman Scholzman and John T. Tierney, *Organized Interests and American Democracy*. New York: Harper & Row, 1986, and Rogan Kersh, "The Well-Informed Lobbyist: Information and Interest Groups Lobbying," in *Interest Group Politics*, 7th ed., edited by Allan J. Cigler and Burdett A. Loomis (Washington, DC: Congressional Quarterly Press, 2007), pp. 389–411.

4.1
4.2
4.3
4.4
4.5
4.6

Talking ★ TEXAS

Long-Term Survival Assessments for Lobbyist-to-Be

Jack Gullahorn, whose work in and around the Capitol began when he was a legislative aide in 1973, has a wealth of experience as a lobbyist and governmental insider. He is currently president and general counsel for the Professional Advocacy Association of Texas, the state professional association for lobbyists. Here is some advice that he offers would-be lobbyists:

JACK GULLAHORN
Veteran insider offers advice to would-be lobbyists.

Lobbying *Is* a career

It seems, however, that most people accept it as a vocational choice somewhat akin to prostitution, deciding to engage in the activity after acknowledging that selling your body for immoral purposes is the prevalent public view of the lobbyist's job description. It doesn't have to be that way. What follows is a suggested template for what could become a career type. How well suited are you to the key elements of the profession that could allow you to be successful and at the same time maintain your sense of ethical responsibility and enhance the image of a lobbyist to the public?

1. *Ego Subjugation*

   How impressed are you with yourself? Nothing wrong with that (as a matter of fact, you shouldn't be considering this as a lifestyle if you don't think that you are pretty much able to handle any situation extemporaneously). But if you want to succeed at this game, be prepared to mask that superior intellect and ability. Most policymakers actually believe that they are there as a fulfillment of a mission. Your role is to make them feel as if you are there to help them fulfill that destiny. One of the reasons that the majority of former legislators and officeholders make such lousy lobbyists is that they just aren't able to make the ego transition—from imperious to supplicant.

2. *Political Addiction*

   If you don't love politics, go do something else. Stay current and know the players as well as understand the system. Always be thinking further ahead of the political consequences of every action than the policymaker with whom you are dealing.

3. *Ethics*

   Don't leave home without it. Your personal morality in how you handle your business is what will show through to your audience. Assume that every phone conversation; every email; every tweet, text or post; every memo will be on the front page of the *New York Times*.

4. *Truth or Consequences*

   Never, never lie to a policymaker. Once you develop the reputation for bending the facts, start preparing for mediocrity. By the way, it's actually against the law to provide false information to a legislator. (Too bad the reverse isn't also a crime.)

5. *Relationships*

   It's not who you know; it's how you know them. The key maxim of lobbying is the realization that policymakers come and go, but lobbyists stay around a lot longer and, as a result, meeting and learning about those you seek to convince is a continuing art form. Relationships build trust. Trust inspires action. Action is what you get paid for.

6. *Learn to Type with Your Thumbs*

   The future is social and virtual. Lobbyists will always be essential to the process, because as issues get more complicated and vast in scope, your understanding of details will be critical. But the information flow will kill you if you aren't in tune with everything electronic, and what's being said about your issues by the people who vote.

7. *Pay Your Dues*

   Don't expect to walk into the lifestyle of a successful lobbyist without earning the right to be there. Government is a great training ground for lobbyists because it allows you to

(continued)

experience firsthand the system and the ego glorification of the process. So are [political] campaigns because the same lessons are taught: fidelity, loyalty, friendship, and the importance of relationships. Both of these are better done when young—when you can afford it, monetarily and physically, especially the wear and tear on your mind, body, and soul.

8. *Staying Fresh*

   You are only going to be as good as your last creative strategy. Tomorrow, everyone else will be doing the same thing, and you better be figuring out a new and improved way to move your message so it will stand out from the masses. Read and reserve a special time for yourself dedicated to shutting your eyes and actually thinking.

9. *Ideas Have Consequences*

   Subscribe to the belief that for every action, there will be a reaction, a consequence. It may be either positive or negative, but you should be prepared to deal with whichever consequence you are dealt, so you can make the most of every situation.

10. *Life Is Easier if You Believe Your Own BS*

    To thine own self be true. Sometimes the engagement may be tempting: the profile, the money, the players. But if you can't believe in the issue, pass on the opportunity. If your standard is to not represent issues and clients with which/whom you disagree personally, your credibility will be much easier to maintain.

CRITICAL THINKING QUESTIONS

1. What do you perceive to be the most essential personal attributes or characteristics of successful lobbyists? Why?
2. How does a lobbyist maintain his or her ethical compass when there is pressure to succeed on the client's behalf?

be defined as any form of communication, made on another's behalf, and intended to influence a governmental decision."[52]

indirect lobbying
Activities designed to mobilize public support for a policy position and bring pressure to bear on public officials through electoral activities, public relations campaigns, and sometimes protests or marches.

Indirect Lobbying

Effective lobbying starts with the election of officeholders supportive of a group's viewpoint on key issues and the building of general public support for a group and its objectives. **Indirect lobbying** takes different forms and is used in tandem with direct communications with public officials. It is designed to mobilize public support for a policy position and bring pressure to bear on public officials through electoral activities, public relations campaigns, and sometimes protests or marches. Creating a favorable climate and the ability to mobilize the actions of citizens in support of or opposition to policy proposals often are central to the success of a group in the policy process.

ELECTORAL ACTIVITIES Although the electoral activities of interest groups are similar to those of political parties, there are some significant differences. Political parties are broad coalitions of voters concerned with a wide range of issues, whereas most interest groups are focused on only a limited set of issues. Parties function not only to contest elections but also to govern once elected. Interest groups primarily are concerned with influencing and shaping only those policies that directly affect them. Most interest groups also cross party lines in supporting candidates.

Interest groups must decide which candidates they will back through campaign contributions, organizational support, and public endorsements. Most groups are not interested in political ideology or philosophy but primarily are concerned with electing their "friends" and defeating their "enemies."

Most interest groups spend their money selectively, contributing to those legislators who serve on the committees that have jurisdiction over their industry or areas of concern. The Texas legislature's highly centralized leadership encourages groups to concentrate their resources on a small number of key lawmakers.

4.1

4.2

4.3

4.4

4.5

4.6

In some cases, interest groups will use promises of financial campaign support to recruit opponents for incumbent legislators who consistently vote against them. In other instances, incumbents and potential challengers will approach interest groups for support. Although this process has become a permanent fixture of contemporary elections, it still can present an unsavory image of a mutual shakedown. Although a candidate cannot legally promise a specific vote for financial or other campaign support, an interest group will make every effort to ensure that a potential recipient of campaign contributions is "sympathetic" and will be "accessible" to the group.

Under state and federal laws, interest groups and many corporations may form political action committees (PACs) for raising and distributing campaign funds. Money is contributed to a PAC by individual members of a group or employees of a corporation and then distributed among selected candidates. In most instances, the professional staff of the interest group manages a PAC, and the campaign contributions are a key part of the organization's overall lobbying strategy.

Federal campaign finance restrictions and reporting requirements are stricter than the state's. Federal law limits individual contributions to $2,500 per candidate for each election and PAC contributions by corporations, labor unions, trade associations, and other organizations to $5,000 per candidate per election.[53] But the U.S. Supreme Court, ruling in *Citizens United* v. *Federal Election Commission* (2010) opened up a major loophole by allowing independent, super-PACS to make unlimited contributions to federal races, provided there was no coordination between the PAC and the candidate.[54] These super-PACs became major players in the 2012 presidential race.

Texas law prohibits corporations or labor unions from making direct contributions to state and local political candidates, but it sets no limits on the amount of money a PAC or an individual can give to candidates for nonjudicial offices. In many cases, PACs and wealthy individuals have given several hundred thousand dollars to a single candidate.

Interest groups sometimes provide in-kind support for political candidates. A group may make its phone banks available to a candidate, it may conduct a poll and provide the candidate with the results, or it may provide office space and equipment to a candidate's campaign. Some organizations may even "loan" the services of their staffers to a campaign or provide postage, cars for travel, printing services, and other types of assistance. State law requires such in-kind contributions to be publicly reported to the Texas Ethics Commission, just as financial donations are. Some groups, depending on how they are organized under federal tax laws, cannot make in-kind contributions directly but can do so through their political action committees.

Groups also endorse candidates and publicize their endorsements on their websites; in emails or newsletters; or through social media, news releases, press conferences, and conventions. Some groups maintain phone banks during election campaigns to inform their members of their endorsements and encourage them to get out and vote for their chosen candidates. Candidates often seek public endorsements when a group's size, prestige, and influence are considered valuable, and candidates use these endorsements in their advertising campaigns.

PUBLIC OPINION Interest groups also may try to cultivate favorable public opinion about themselves through media campaigns. One objective is to "develop a reservoir of good will in the minds of the citizenry that can be drawn upon when political battles over specific issues occur."[55] Although this practice is more pronounced at the national level, state organizations in Texas that are associated with national interest groups often participate in national campaigns.

Public relations campaigns also are used to mobilize public support for a group's position on a specific issue being debated in Austin.[56] Voters may be encouraged to write, call, fax, or send email messages to their legislators. The Texas Medical Association, for example, has sought public support for restrictions on medical malpractice awards by distributing cards to doctors' waiting rooms that attempt to explain how the high cost of malpractice insurance can affect the costs and quality of health care.

Interest groups may sponsor advertising campaigns featuring emotional language and imagery. They may use press conferences and informal media contacts to encourage favorable editorials or put their "spin," or viewpoint, on news coverage. For years, Texas legislators resisted pari-mutuel horserace betting and the lottery. But groups supporting those proposals continued to wage strong media campaigns, insisting that gambling would boost state revenue. Eventually, during economic downturns when the legislature was struggling to find new sources of revenue, they won the fight.

Public interest advocates, in their efforts to protect consumers and the environment, cannot match the financial firepower that utilities, insurance companies, and other big industries can muster. Their success depends on their ability to stir up public concern—or outrage—over pocketbook issues and the relationships between moneyed special interests and government. Quality research that focuses on political issues, such as campaign contributions or policy options, is one of the more effective resources available to public interest groups. Using this research, they avidly work the traditional news media or social networking sites, which are crucial to their ability to spread their message. They seldom can afford paid advertising campaigns, but they hold frequent news conferences, issue a stream of press releases and emails, and readily return reporters' phone calls. They also recognize strength and efficiency in numbers and sometimes issue joint statements or hold joint news conferences on issues of mutual concern.

direct lobbying
The communication of information and policy preferences directly to policymakers or their staffs.

PROTESTS AND MARCHES Staged demonstrations against governmental decisions or inaction have long been used by individuals or groups attempting to influence public policy. Although many people have mixed feelings about such tactics, protests and marches can be effective in capturing public attention. Television coverage of such events, in particular, can convey powerful and intense images. The civil rights movement capitalized on this resource, and that movement's success, in large measure, turned on the ability of minority leaders to show the nation that discriminatory policies were incompatible with the values of a democratic society.

In recent years, both antiabortion groups and abortion rights activists in Texas have marched in support of their positions. Animal rights groups have picketed stores that sell fur coats. Gay and lesbian groups have held vigils to protest incidents of "gay bashing," and a variety of other groups have used public demonstrations to dramatize their particular issues or concerns. It is not clear what effects these tactics have. But many groups that use them have limited resources and recognize their value in gaining free media attention.

☐ Direct Lobbying

Although interest groups may spend much time and money electing "friendly" candidates and building public support for their objectives, their work has only begun. The next crucial step is **direct lobbying**, or the communication of information and policy preferences directly to policymakers. Lobbying often is associated with legislatures, but it is directed to other governmental institutions as well. Public officials depend on the information provided by interest groups, and many policy initiatives, including proposed legislation, come from lobbyists. Interest groups also attempt to use the courts to advance their policy goals. They file lawsuits to challenge existing laws or regulations—and force changes—or file briefs supporting or opposing other groups' positions in pending litigation.[57]

Lobbyists engage in a wide range of activities, from drafting legislation to personally contacting legislators and other groups to testifying at hearings. Most groups understand the necessity of pursuing their legislative agendas at every conceivable opportunity, and they also realize it usually is easier to block policy initiatives than to enact new policies.

DRAFTING LEGISLATION Interest groups often will draft proposed laws for formal introduction into the legislature. In any given legislative session, hundreds of bills are drafted by the legal or technical staffs of interest groups. The groups usually work closely with legislative sponsors or their staffs in the drafting process, and they may consult staffers from the agencies that would be affected by the legislation.[58]

PLANNING AND IMPLEMENTING A LEGISLATIVE STRATEGY Interest groups supporting a bill will usually work closely with the bill's sponsor, committee chairs, and other legislative leaders at every stage of the process. Strategy will be planned to include the introduction of the legislation through committee hearings and then through final action by the House and the Senate. Potential opposition will be assessed, and ways of diffusing that opposition and building support for the bill will be mapped out.

PERSONAL CONTACTS AND COMMUNICATIONS If one were to ask most interest groups why they contribute to political candidates and what they expect in return, the overwhelming response would be "access." The interest group system revolves around communication and the exchange of ideas and information with policymakers. To have some prospects of success, a group must have access to lawmakers, something that often is no small task to achieve.

With thousands of bills considered during each regular legislative session, interest groups have to compete for the opportunity to discuss their programs with lawmakers. Lobbyists are denied direct access to legislators on the floor of the House and the Senate while legislators are in session, but there are numerous other opportunities for direct or indirect contact.

During House and Senate sessions, many lobbyists will wait outside the chambers to stop legislators who pass by. Or they will have the doorkeepers send messages asking individual lawmakers to step outside the chambers for brief meetings in the lobby—hence the term "lobbyists." It is not unusual for several dozen lobbyists to be gathered at one time outside the House or the Senate chamber on the second floor of the Capitol, particularly on days when major bills are being debated. Lobbyists also sit in the House and Senate galleries. In some instances, a lobbyist's presence in the gallery is simply a matter of minor interest or a way to kill some time before a committee meeting. But sometimes special interest groups will pack the gallery in a show of force to threaten recrimination against lawmakers who do not vote their way.

Effective lobbyists, however, do most of their work long before a bill reaches the House or the Senate floor for a vote. They will stop by legislators' offices to present information and solicit support for or against specific legislation. If they cannot meet personally with a legislator, they will meet with his or her staff. In many cases, lobbyists will provide lawmakers with written reports, summarizing the highlights of an issue and their position on it. Many interest groups will back up the personal efforts of their lobbyists with letter-writing, email, or telephone campaigns directed at legislators by the groups' members.

Much of the personal lobbying is done away from the Capitol, sometimes far away—over lunch and dinner tables, at cocktail parties, and on golf courses. Although these occasions involve a great deal of socializing, they also provide lobbyists with golden opportunities to solidify friendships with lawmakers and make pitches for or against specific legislative proposals. A five- or ten-minute business conversation reinforced with a few hours of social camaraderie can work wonders, as many interest groups and their lobbyists very well know. Such entertainment, however, is expensive, and it can be used to abuse the policymaking process. Repeated news accounts of extravagant and questionable lobby spending finally convinced the legislature in 1991 to ban many lobby-paid trips for lawmakers and to limit lobbyist expenditures on entertaining legislators. Many lobbyists and legislators were concerned that the 1991 ethics law also may have outlawed that most sacred and basic of lobby handouts—the free lunch. Their uncertainty prompted the legislature to pass a bill in 1993 to make sure that it remained legal for lawmakers to dine at lobbyists' expense.

TESTIFYING AT HEARINGS During each regular legislative session, House and Senate committees and subcommittees hold hundreds of hearings on bills that have to

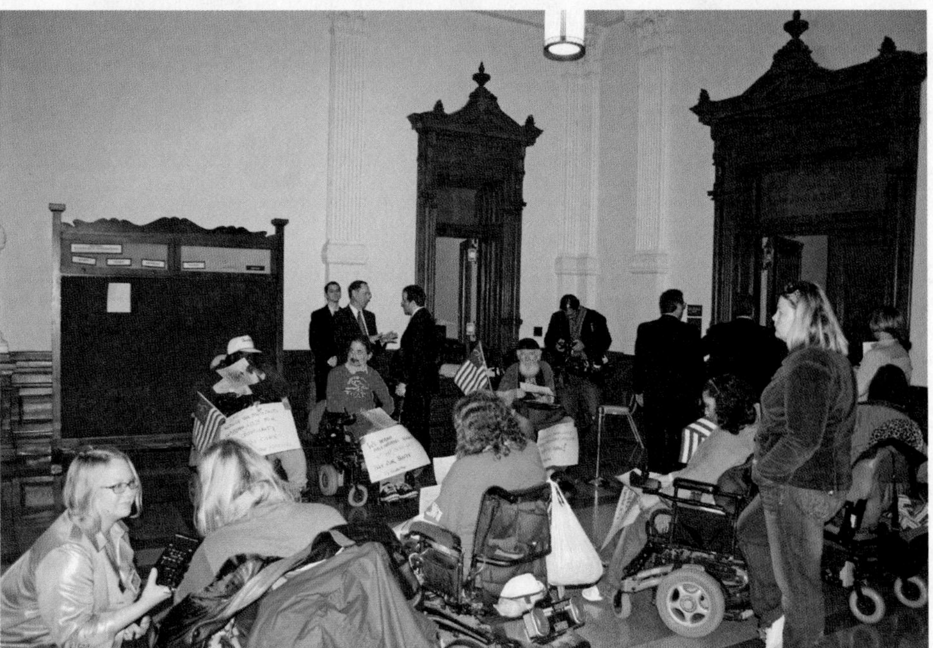

LOBBYING IS NOT LIMITED TO THE HIRED PROFESSIONALS

Citizens and visitors, who are denied access to the floor of the Senate or House while they are in session, are seen mingling in the lobby outside the House chamber waiting for the opportunity to "chat" with a legislator.

win committee approval before they can be considered by the full House and Senate. Interest groups can use committee hearings to present information formally to legislators or to help mobilize public support for or against a bill. Testifying at public hearings often is symbolic and secondary to the personal communications with legislators and their staffs.

COALITIONS OF INTEREST GROUPS Sometimes, a group will not have sufficient resources to influence the outcome of a contested issue, or a legislative or regulatory proposal may affect many groups. Groups thus sometimes find it advantageous to form coalitions to coordinate their electoral and direct lobbying activities. These coalitions are informal, tenuous, or short lived, based on current common interests or objectives and a desire to maximize resources and share costs and expenses.[59]

In 1991, some consumer advocates teamed up with the Texas Trial Lawyers Association to defeat a products-liability bill that would have made it more difficult for consumers injured by defective products to sue manufacturers and retailers. Two years later, consumers learned how tenuous that alliance was when trial lawyers and key legislators negotiated a products-liability compromise with the business community. Consumer groups, which opposed the legislation, were excluded from the negotiations.

On MyPoliSciLab

Review the Chapter

What Are Interest Groups?

4.1 Define interest groups and describe what makes them distinctive from other types of organizations, p. 95.

There are literally thousands of groups and organizations of all sizes and purposes in Texas. Only some, however, are interest groups in the political sense. Social scientists use the term "interest group" to define an organization of people who have shared attitudes or concerns and make demands on political or governmental institutions. In effect, interest groups want governments to do something for them. Political power in Texas is essentially structured around an organizations, whether they are corporations, professional associations, or interest groups. The interaction and conflict among these groups in the policymaking process help decide who gets what, when, and how.

Interest Group Theory

4.2 Compare and contrast the pluralist and elitist theories of political behavior and explain how they apply to Texas, p. 97.

For years, political scientists have debated whether politics and public policy in Texas are controlled or dominated by a small handful of people—the elitist theory—or based on a complex system of many groups or sectors of society—the pluralist theory. Pluralists recognize the inequities in political resources but argue that individual interests are adequately represented through membership in interest groups. With thousands of groups competing, no one group can dominate the policy process. New groups are constantly being formed to provide new leadership opportunities and greater access to the decision-making process for people who have been historically denied influence. Elitists emphasize the marked differences in the resources and subsequent political influence of groups and contend that relatively few corporations and other institutions with great financial resources dominate the policy process in Texas. Evidence suggests that the source of political power and influence lies somewhere between the elitist and pluralist positions. The narrow, limited interests of a few groups sometimes prevail, but public policy at other times is responsive to the needs and interests of broad segments of the population.

Resources of Interest Groups

4.3 Summarize the factors that determine the power and influence of an interest group, p. 101.

Not all groups are equal players in the state's interest group system. The effectiveness of an interest group in the policymaking process is determined by its size, the geographical distribution of its membership, its economic resources, its reputation, and its leadership and staff.

Dominant Interest Groups in Texas

4.4 Assess the strengths and weaknesses of the various types of interest groups that are active in Texas, p. 101.

Groups are classified according to their place within the state's economic and social structure. Some economic or social sectors are dominated by a small number of groups, whereas other sectors have multiple groups. Although people join groups for diverse reasons, there are common political interests among groups. Some single-interest groups are concerned with only one policy. Other groups have a range of interests. The strongest groups financially are professional groups and corporations, and they wield significant political power in Texas. Public interest groups rarely have the funds to match those of corporations or professional groups and usually rely on the mass media to mobilize support for their issues.

Who Are the Lobbyists?

4.5 Describe the characteristics of Texas lobbyists and their career patterns, p. 107.

In recent sessions of the Texas legislature, one can see a general pattern of 10 lobbyists for the legislature's 181 members. No academic training or licensing is required for one to lobby state agencies, but whatever a lobbyist's profession, he or she must know the players and the policy process. Historically, lobbying was a "man's world," although this is now changing. There are a good number of ex-legislators and former legislative staff among the lobbyists. In addition, officials of associations, significant numbers of lawyers, and public relations or media specialists have gravitated toward lobbying.

Interest Groups and the Policymaking Process

4.6 Explain the different types of activities involved with indirect and direct lobbying, p. 108.

Interest groups and other organizations engage in indirect and direct lobbying. Indirect lobbying includes campaign financing and other efforts to elect candidates who share a group's views. It also includes efforts to shape and mobilize public opinion in favor of the group's objectives. Direct lobbying involves a variety of strategies and techniques, including direct one-on-one conversations with legislators and other policymakers, testifying at legislative hearings, providing information about pending legislation, communicating with legislative staff, and building coalitions in support of legislative goals. Although lobbying has a negative connotation for many Texans, it is essential to elected and appointed policymakers, who depend on the information, coalition building, and public support of groups for their decisions and actions.

Learn the Terms

interest group, p. 95
mischief of factions, p. 97
pluralism, p. 97
elitism, p. 99
iron rule of oligarchy, p. 99
The Establishment, p. 99
hyperpluralism, p. 100
iron triangles of government, p. 100
single-issue groups, p. 100
public interest groups, p. 104
lobbying, p. 108
indirect lobbying, p. 111
direct lobbying, p. 113

Test Yourself

Study and **Review** the Practice Tests

1. An interest group

- **a.** tries to win elections and take control of governmental institutions.
- **b.** attempts to influence governmental decisions.
- **c.** is any group that opposes those who hold political power.
- **d.** is another name for a political party.
- **e.** always seeks objectives that are contrary to the common good.

2. Why do we see evidence of a class bias in the interest group system in Texas?

- **a.** Women are more likely than men to join interest groups.
- **b.** Young people are more likely than older people to join interest groups.
- **c.** Wealthier people are more likely than those from lower socioeconomic groups to join interest groups.
- **d.** Minorities are more likely than Anglos to join interest groups.
- **e.** People with lower levels of education are more likely than those with higher levels of education to join interest groups.

3. According to the pluralist theory of politics,

- **a.** there are so many groups that usually just one or two end up dominating the political process.
- **b.** elections have very little impact on public policy.
- **c.** most groups do not really compete with one another, but they enjoy considerable consensus on issues.
- **d.** groups always harm the long-term interests of society as a whole.
- **e.** most people have access to the political process through the leaders of the groups to which they belong.

4. According to the elitist theory of politics

- **a.** policy decisions are made by a few individuals.
- **b.** elections have the biggest influence on policy decisions.
- **c.** the large number of groups means no single group can dominate the political process.
- **d.** political elites are drawn from a wide variety of backgrounds.
- **e.** the interests of elites always conflict with the interests of other classes of society.

5. One argument for the pluralist theory of interest groups in Texas is the

- **a.** dominance of state politics by Anglo businessmen, oilmen, bankers, and lawyers.
- **b.** common background of those who lead large corporations.
- **c.** absence of single-issue groups.
- **d.** development of public interest and minority groups.
- **e.** decline of the conservative business establishment.

6. Which of the following is a key factor in strengthening an interest group's power and influence?

- **a.** The group is internally unified.
- **b.** The group is concentrated in one geographic area.
- **c.** The group is known as a manipulator of data.
- **d.** The group is large, with diverse and fragmented goals.
- **e.** The group does not care about public relations.

7. Which of the following statements best describes big business interests in Texas?

- **a.** Big business is monolithic and generally speaks with one voice on most policy issues.
- **b.** Big business has generally supported the policy interests of labor.
- **c.** Big business is dominated by the oil and gas industry.
- **d.** Many business interests organize to influence public policy through their trade associations.
- **e.** Trial lawyers and consumer groups are closely aligned with big business.

8. Lobbying for change in public elementary and secondary education is complicated by the fact that

- **a.** teachers' associations tend to support the same goals as school boards.
- **b.** public schools rarely face budget cuts.
- **c.** different educational associations sometimes seek conflicting interests and goals.
- **d.** university alumni are politically influential.
- **e.** the state usually raises taxes when schools need money.

9. All of the following are public interest groups EXCEPT

- **a.** the Sierra Club.
- **b.** the Texas Medical Association.
- **c.** the Gray Panthers.
- **d.** Public Citizen.
- **e.** Americans Disabled for Attendant Programs Today.

10. Which of the following is a minority interest group?

- **a.** TMA
- **b.** ADAPT
- **c.** GOP
- **d.** LULAC
- **e.** TAB

11. Organized labor

- **a.** is as strong as business in Texas because Texas is a "right-to-work" state.
- **b.** generally sides with the trial lawyers on many issues.
- **c.** comprises up to half of the workforce in Texas.
- **d.** has become even more powerful with the rise of the Republican Party.
- **e.** generally opposes public interest groups.

12. The Texas Freedom Network

- **a.** took control of the leadership of the Texas Republican Party in 1994.
- **b.** was the earliest anticommunist interest group.
- **c.** works to counter the Christian right.
- **d.** lobbies for the telecommunications industry.
- **e.** supports antiabortion legislation.

13. What can be said about political action committees in Texas?

- **a.** They have no limits on how much they can give to state and local nonjudicial candidates.
- **b.** They are limited to giving no more than $2,400 per state and local candidate.
- **c.** They are banned from making direct contributions to state and local candidates.
- **d.** They focus more on protests than elections.
- **e.** They care more about partisan success in elections than interest group victories.

14. The most important and influential phase of the direct lobbying process takes place

- **a.** after a bill has gone to the governor for signature.
- **b.** when sitting in the House and Senate galleries.
- **c.** when writing a campaign check for a candidate.
- **d.** when testifying at public hearings.
- **e.** when meeting with legislators before a bill gets to a vote.

15. Interest groups contribute money to political candidates to

- **a.** make sure one party wins the election.
- **b.** avoid having to perform political favors later.
- **c.** cultivate a more favorable reputation with voters.
- **d.** get access to policymakers.
- **e.** get news media attention.

Explore Further

Berry, Jeffrey M., and Clyde Wilcox, *The Interest Group Society*, 5th ed. New York: Longman, 2009. Provides a short but comprehensive introduction to interest groups within the American political system and insights into the new technologies used by interest groups in pursuit of their agendas.

Cigler, Allen J., and Burdett A. Loomis, eds., *Interest Group Politics*, 8th ed. Washington, DC: Congressional Quarterly Press, 2012. Presents sixteen essays by twenty-one scholars covering group organization, groups in the electoral process, and groups in policy making.

Davidson, Chandler, *Race and Class in Texas Politics*. Princeton, NJ: Princeton University Press, 1990. Adapts V. O. Key's earlier analysis to contemporary Texas politics; this work assesses the dimensions of race and class and addresses the issue of a governing elite in the state.

Elliott, Charles P., "The Texas Trial Lawyers Association: Interest Group Under Siege," in *Texas Politics*, eds. Anthony Champagne and Edward J. Harpham. New York: W. W. Norton, 1997. Examines the activities of the Texas Trial Lawyers Association, the organization's relationships with like-minded interest groups, and the problems it faces battling the dominant business interests in the state.

Green, George Norris, *The Establishment in Texas Politics, 1938–1957*. Westport, CT: Greenwood Press, 1979. Provides a historical perspective that concludes that Texas politics was controlled by corporate elites who, in their reaction to the New Deal, developed and fostered a form of reactionary conservatism permitting predatory interest groups to dominate the electoral and policy processes.

Hrebenar, Robert J., and Clive S. Thomas, eds., *Interest Group Politics in Southern States*. Tuscaloosa: University of Alabama Press, 1992. Details a twelve-state study of interest groups; the authors conclude that interest groups in Texas have moved from personalized lobbying to information-based communications.

Pittman, H. C., *Inside the Third House*. Austin, TX: Eakin, 1992. Profiles some seventy Texas leaders and "discusses some of the major interest groups that played influential roles in the enactment and administration of Texas laws." Written by a fifty-year veteran lobbyist in the Texas Capitol.

Rosenthal, Alan, *The Third House: Lobbyists and Lobbying in the States*. Washington, DC: Congressional Quarterly Press, 1993. Presents a comparative analysis of lobbying in state capitals; written by one of the foremost authorities on state legislatures.

Texas Ethics Commission, "Lobbying in Texas: A Guide to the Texas Law," September 28, 2011. http://www.ethics.state.tx.us/guides/LOBBY_guide.htm. Compiles state statutes pertaining to lobbying, including definitions of what constitutes lobbying, expenditures allowed, reporting requirements, prohibited activities, and penalties.

Texans for Public Justice, "Austin's Oldest Profession: Texas' Top Lobby Clients & Those Who Serve Them." Austin: Texans for Public Justice, February 2012. Uses data filed by lobbyists with the Texas Ethics Commission; this study approximates the amount of money involved in lobby contracts and identifies major lobbyists and lobby clients.

Listen on MyPoliSciLab

5

The Mass Media in Texas Politics

When the right of every citizen to cooperate in the government of society is acknowledged, every citizen must be presumed to possess the power of discriminating between the different opinions of his contemporaries, and of appreciating the different facts from which inferences may be drawn.

—Alexis de Tocqueville, 1835

The people, in delegating authority, do not give their public servants the right to decide what is good for the people to know and what is not good for them to know.

—Texas Legislature, 1973

In another sign of the changing media times, particularly for newspapers, the *Fort Worth Star-Telegram* announced in 2012 that it was shutting down its state Capitol bureau in Austin. This was an institution that had once covered the activities of an ambitious young Texas congressman named Lyndon B. Johnson and more recently had been home base to the late Molly Ivins, the nationally syndicated columnist who had skewered Texas politicians, big and small, with her barbed wit. For many years, its reporters chronicled the highs and lows of dozens of legislative sessions, numerous governors, and countless other political figures and decision makers. The *Fort Worth Star-Telegram* was an important source of information for generations of North and West Texas readers about state government's impact on their lives and livelihoods. Its last correspondent, the veteran reporter Dave Montgomery, had been among the best.

5.1 Explain the role of the mass media in the policy agenda process, emphasizing the strengths and weaknesses of its influence, p. 122.

5.2 Describe the various features of mass media coverage of elections and the use of the mass media by campaigns in Texas, p. 124.

5.3 Outline the mass media's role as a guardian of open government and describe the problems of combating media bias, p. 129.

5.4 Trace the development of the news media in Texas, from frontier newspapers to the Internet, p. 132.

5.5 Evaluate the consequences of the shrinking size of the Capitol press corps, p. 141.

5.6 List the ways elected officials and interest groups use public relations personnel and resources, p. 143.

5.7 Assess the consequences of an uninformed citizenry in Texas politics, p. 144.

THE DALLAS MORNING NEWS remains a major source of news about Texas government and political institutions, despite financial setbacks that have beset the industry and prompted reductions in staff.

5.1 5.2 5.3 5.4 5.5 5.6 5.7

agenda setting
A theory that the media's choice of which news events and issues to cover helps define what is important for the public to know and what issues to think about.

Only a few years earlier, the bureau reduced the number of reporters from three to one to save costs. But with newspapers still struggling to stay afloat in a rising sea of new media, and with the Texas legislature normally in session for only five months every other year, editor Jim Witt said it did not make sense financially for the newspaper to continue to maintain a full-time presence in Austin. Instead, it would occasionally send reporters from Fort Worth to Austin for major stories and rely on other reporting sources, including *The Texas Tribune*, an Austin-based, nonprofit, online paper devoted to politics that had made its debut in late 2009. "This is not the first Capitol newspaper office to close, and it probably won't be the last. But the demise of the *Star-Telegram*'s Austin bureau is another troubling milestone for the newsgathering business, and it's particularly sad for me," wrote reporter Jay Root, a former *Star-Telegram* Austin bureau chief, for his newest employer, *The Texas Tribune*.[1]

As recently as 2000, Texas news organizations assigned more than fifty newspaper reporters and broadcast correspondents to the Capitol. For many years, these reporters provided information about state government and politics for millions of Texans. By 2012, there were fewer than half that many full-time Capitol reporters, and with the media landscape continuing to undergo an overhaul, no one knew when the shakeout would end. In one form or fashion, the media will continue to be a primary source of information about state government and politics and will impact the policymaking process. However, the traditional media are finding it difficult to compete with online forms of media that continue to expand.

News consumers, particularly younger people, are increasingly getting their news online. On any given day, they are barraged with political news and views from blog postings, Twitter feeds, social media messages, emails, and YouTube videos. Some of those are from traditional news organizations—newspapers, news magazines, and television stations—which still try to be objective or to differentiate fact from opinion as they continue to adjust to the new instant communications age. Many other information conduits, however, are unabashedly partisan or opinionated. They take the news reported by a newspaper or other traditional news source and spin it to suit their own agendas.

In adopting First Amendment guarantees of press freedom more than 200 years ago, the framers of the U.S. Constitution recognized that a free press was an independent provider of information essential to making a representative democracy work. By providing a public forum for the exchange of ideas and a means of scrutinizing the actions of public officials, the press established accountability. The Internet and an influx of social media sources have turned up the volume on that public discourse. However, it remains to be seen whether audiences are actually better informed as a result.

The Mass Media and the Policy Agenda

5.1 Explain the role of the mass media in the policy agenda process, emphasizing the strengths and weaknesses of its influence.

Some scholars and experts who study the traditional media—newspapers, television, and radio—believe one of the major contributions of the media to politics is **agenda setting**. By choosing which events and issues to cover and how extensively to cover them, they say, the media help define what is important for the public and, by omission, what is not important. Maxwell McCombs and Donald Shaw, recognized authorities on the traditional mass media, argued several years ago that "the idea of agenda setting asserts that the priorities of the press to some degree become the priorities of the public. What the press emphasizes is in turn emphasized privately and publicly by the audiences of the press."[2]

To a great extent, that role is still an important function of the media, but it may be evolving in this era of instant communications. New technology has made it much easier for well-organized, tech-savvy interest groups to bypass the media's filter and take their own messages—and threats—on policy priorities directly to voters and policymakers. During the Texas budgetary crisis of 2011, for example, in news articles and editorials, many people expressed their desire for the legislature to spend a significant part of the state's emergency Rainy Day Fund to minimize spending cuts to important state programs. Late in the session, a majority of the Texas House, including many Republican members, approved an amendment to make a contingency Rainy Day appropriation of $2 billion for the public schools, if economic conditions improved. Not too many years ago, opponents of the amendment would have been quoted, expressing their disappointment or anger, in newspaper and television reports, and that likely would have been the end of the story. But not this time. Overnight, conservatives, well organized and intent on seeing the legislature make deep cuts in government spending, barraged the offices and constituents of Republican House members with calls and emails protesting the vote. The next day, the House took another vote on the same amendment, and it was defeated with many Republican legislators—fearful of retaliation by conservative voters back home—switching their votes.

The media use five basic criteria to select which events and subjects to cover. First, a story must have a significant impact on its audience, such as a legislative proposal to increase taxes or, as in the 2011 legislative debate, to make deep cuts to public education and other state programs. Second, it needs to be something that generates considerable interest. That may be an act of violence or conflict, a natural disaster, a political scandal, or legislation to ban assault rifles. A third component is familiarity—the public identifies with well-known individuals or familiar situations. A fourth requirement is that an event occurs in some proximity to readers and viewers, and, finally, a news story should be timely. [3] Some stories on governmental policy and politics, of course, include more than one of these elements, and some stories are going to attract and sustain public interest more than others.

When the public interest is aroused, some experts extend the agenda-setting role of the media to **agenda building**. The media's coverage of specific issues creates a climate for political action by shaping the atmosphere in which these issues will be debated and their solutions developed.[4] By helping to make an issue relevant, the media gives people reasons for taking sides and converting the problem into a serious political issue. From this perspective, "the public agenda is not so much set by the media as built up through a cycle of media activity that transforms an elite issue into a public controversy."[5] Issues and concerns of a few individuals now become the concerns of many, and the dynamics of the policymaking process change.[6]

agenda building
The process of groups or individuals identifying problems or issues that affect them and keeping pressure on policymakers to develop and implement public policy solutions.

Most key public officials and their staffs spend a lot of time keeping up with media coverage of public issues. Checking newspaper websites and blog postings are important parts of the routine in many state offices. However, some people familiar with the workings of Texas government believe that the policy-building role of the press is overstated. This view suggests that the media merely mirror what others think about public issues.

This passive view is supported by the argument that the Texas press was largely reactive in reporting some of the most crucial issues facing Texans in recent memory, including educational funding and criminal justice. Although newspapers prompted the legislature to make improvements in all of these areas in the years following World War II, deterioration in some important public programs set in, and the media and the legislature later took back seats to the judiciary. The media largely ignored a recurrence of substandard conditions in state prisons and, consequently, so had the legislature until after the federal courts stepped in with a landmark reform order. Disparities in property wealth and educational opportunities between rich and poor school districts had been growing wider for years, worsening a dropout problem that, in turn, helped keep the prisons crowded. But educational disparities received only occasional attention from news reporters until after the Mexican American Legal Defense and Educational Fund won a state court judgment declaring the school finance system unconstitutional. Once the courts had forced the issues, however, the media devoted

5.1
5.2
5.3
5.4
5.5
5.6
5.7

issue-attention cycle
A pattern in which public interest in an issue or problem is heightened by intensive media coverage. Media attention and public interest will wane after government takes steps to address their concerns, but most issues or problems are never permanently resolved. Another crisis, perhaps years later, will restart the cycle.

sound bite
A short, quotable phrase by a public official or political candidate that may sound good on television or radio but lacks depth and often is meaningless.

extensive coverage to them, keeping the problems, their causes, and potential solutions in the public eye.

The media's attention to public problems and officialdom's response form something of a never-ending cycle, what scholar Anthony Downs once described as an **issue-attention cycle**.[7] There is a pre-public phase in which a problem, such as poor nursing home conditions, quietly affects numerous individuals. Someone, perhaps a relative of a nursing home resident, then attempts to transform the issue into a public concern through the media. Press coverage starts slowly but rapidly intensifies, prompting more and more outraged citizens to discuss the problem. But initial enthusiasm for solutions gives way to the realization that significant progress will be costly not only in terms of money but political conflict, and many people begin to lose interest. After the enactment of policies to address some of the problems, governmental responses tend to become institutionalized, and many of the initial changes are ignored or become ineffective. Although press coverage may continue intermittently, it has limited effect in renewing public opinion or prompting further governmental action—until someone, usually several years later, restarts the cycle.

The media's degree of influence over specific governmental actions can vary considerably, and sometimes the media fail in their agenda building role, as occurred in 2011 during the legislative debate over the budget. Governor Rick Perry and the Republican legislative majority ignored viewpoints expressed in the media for a balanced approach to bridging a $27 billion revenue shortfall that would have included spending several billion dollars from the state's Rainy Day Fund and, perhaps, some modest tax increases in addition to spending reductions. Instead, the governor and the legislative majority followed the demands of conservative activists and made deep cuts in public services. As noted earlier, those demands in some cases bypassed the media and were delivered directly to legislators.

The Mass Media and the Electoral Process

5.2 Describe the various features of mass media coverage of elections and the use of the mass media by campaigns in Texas.

Candidates for public office in Texas still attend rallies in the park and salute the flag at Fourth of July parades. Some legislative and local candidates, particularly those with more shoe leather than money, still rely heavily on door-to-door campaigning. But in races for statewide offices, and many local and district offices as well, the campaign stump has long since been replaced by the **sound bite**; the press conference; the contrived pseudo-event developed by the campaign consultant; and, increasingly, Twitter feeds, emails, YouTube videos, and other online overtures. Campaigning is now constructed around the mass media, including paid television and Internet advertising, and the media, in effect, have displaced the political party as the major information link between the voters and those in government.

Journalists and political scientists repeatedly debate the effects of news coverage on elections. Unlike many political bloggers, who portray points of view and may take sides in political campaigns, most traditional journalists believe their job is to be as objective as possible in outlining the issues and reporting and evaluating the backgrounds, philosophies, activities, and policy proposals of candidates. The news media try to determine which issues should be important in a campaign, although ads, in which the candidates themselves seek to dictate what the electorate should consider important, increasingly are challenging journalists.

News media reports, paid political advertising, and political bloggers all play roles in shaping voters' decisions. Studies have indicated that party identification helps determine voters' choices in general elections—there is a lot of straight-ticket, one-party voting—but long ballots in primaries and general elections force many voters to seek other sources of information about the candidates as well.[8] These voters may rely on news reports, political blogs, and television advertising to clarify the candidates' characteristics, campaign issues, policy positions, and electoral prospects, information that is not included on ballots. Newspaper editorial endorsements of candidates also provide additional cues to many voters. Candidates, of course, welcome editorial endorsements and often feature them in political advertising, but favorable exposure on the news pages and on television screens is often more crucial to a candidate's electoral success.

☐ Covering the "Horse Race"

The media have long been criticized for covering campaigns much as they would a horse race (i.e., who is ahead and who is behind). Some critics argue that reporters often neglect candidates' positions on substantive policy issues in favor of stories about how much money candidates are raising, their stable of consultants, campaign strategies, tactics, and personalities. The criticism may not be entirely fair because most media outlets devote a lot of political coverage to substantive issues, although the "horse race" is never far from view.

During the lengthy campaign for the 2012 Republican presidential nomination, for example, a significant amount of media coverage focused on the candidates' efforts to appeal to conservative primary voters on such hot-button issues as abortion, immigration, and gay rights. There also was coverage of economic issues and how the candidates were—or were not—responding to them. But many of the stories focused on which candidate was leading the pack during one particular week or in one critical state, as measured by a seemingly endless stream of voter-preference polls. Political polls of candidate matchups at different stages of a campaign have become a staple of media coverage and may be increasing in frequency. The results of an internal campaign poll sometimes are released to reporters if the poll makes the candidate look strong or opponents appear weak. The media, partisan organizations, and independent groups conduct other polls periodically. Although some of these surveys also attempt to measure public opinion on selected issues, their primary focus is on who is winning and who is losing.

☐ Campaigning for Television

Most candidates for major offices plan their daily campaign appearances with television newscasts in mind. They participate in activities—such as visits to schools or high-tech plants—that look good in a thirty-second news segment. Unfortunately for the viewers, such superficial coverage does not even begin to shed light on the complex issues in a race or the candidate's positions on them. Neither does a candidate's paid television advertising.

During campaigns, reporters in Austin frequently are given copies of a candidate's latest television advertisement. It may be a positive, "feel good" spot, portraying the candidate in the best possible light—playing with children, visiting a hospital, or shaking hands with the president of the United States. Or it may be a negative, "attack" advertisement, charging an opponent with a weakness or an indiscretion unworthy of the public trust or deliberately misrepresenting the opponent's record or position on an issue. Reporters often write reviews of the ads, usually getting reaction from the candidate's opponent or the opponent's campaign consultant.

Some newspapers and television stations analyze paid television spots for accuracy and report their findings to their readers and viewers. But a *Texas Poll* published by Harte-Hanks Communications during the gubernatorial race between

Democrat Ann Richards and Republican George W. Bush indicated that more people believed the TV ads than the news media's "fact checks." Fifty-four percent of the survey's respondents said they trusted what they saw and heard in both Bush's and Richards's commercials, whereas only 48 percent said they trusted the media's independent analyses of them. Forty-one percent of the respondents indicated the impressions they formed of the candidates from televised images affected how they voted more than published news accounts or the candidates' stands on the issues.[9]

Before their recent staff cutbacks, major Texas newspapers devoted considerable resources to coverage of candidates and issues, attempting to provide the in-depth perspective missing from many online sources. Some newspapers, though, may not be able to continue providing that level of coverage. Even though candidates soon may find online ads to be a more efficient way of communicating with large numbers of voters, many Texas voters will continue to become acquainted with candidates through television, at least for the foreseeable future.

Over the past thirty years or so, television has allowed wealthy or well-financed candidates to, in effect, "buy" elections in Texas—or come very close. Multimillionaire Bill Clements, who had never held elective office and was a stranger to most Texans, spent millions of dollars of his own fortune on television advertisements in 1978 to become the first Republican to capture the governor's office in modern times. In 1990, Clayton Williams, another wealthy businessman and political neophyte, spent more than $21 million, including $8.4 million from his own pocket, to create an attractive public image that won him the Republican nomination for governor. Laredo businessman Tony Sanchez, a Democrat making his first statewide race, spent $56.7 million of his own fortune on a 2002 gubernatorial campaign, only to lose to Republican Rick Perry.

Political scientists, reporters, many voters, and even some candidates loudly criticize what television has done to campaigns for public office, putting style over substance and orchestrated events over thoughtful debates of the issues. But the creators of superficial television ads know they have a large audience. Since candidates are in the race to win office and not to reform the system, they spend millions of dollars perpetuating the problem.

Nationwide, more and more objective television coverage of political campaigns has given way in recent years to paid commercials, soft news, and "talking head" commentary with distinct political viewpoints, particularly on cable TV channels. Many opinion leaders fear the trend is further destroying Americans' interest in politics and have urged the major television networks to voluntarily give free airtime to presidential candidates. "Politics isn't going very well on television these days. . . . Campaigns unfold on all commercial television as a bread-and-circus blur of thirty-second attack ads and eight-second sound bites. Citizens feel cheated. They grow cynical," wrote the late *CBS News* anchor Walter Cronkite.[10] Cronkite died several years ago, but the problem about which he was writing is still with us.

An estimated $2 billion-plus was spent on paid political advertising on television during the 2008 campaign cycle, including the presidential race, with special interest contributions to candidates picking up much of the tab.[11] But most local television stations and the national networks each broadcast an average of fewer than forty seconds a night of discussion or debate by candidates, according to reports by the University of Southern California and the Annenberg Public Policy Center. "Citizens are trapped in a system controlled by big-money candidates, special-interest donors and profit-hungry broadcasters," said Paul Taylor, chairman of the Alliance for Better Campaigns, which encouraged broadcasters to offer candidates more free airtime.[12] He added, "Increasingly, political campaigns have become a transfer of income from wealthy donors to wealthy broadcasters. Meantime, substantive issue discussion is disappearing from the public square of broadcast television."[13]

☐ Media Coverage of Recent Gubernatorial Campaigns in Texas

One reason Governor Rick Perry stumbled so badly during his brief campaign for the 2012 Republican presidential nomination was that he was unprepared for the tough, high-stakes competition of a national campaign and the intense media spotlight. This is no reflection on the Texas media and its coverage of Perry's administration and gubernatorial campaigns. Texas reporters have aggressively covered the governor. With one or two notable exceptions, much of the political "dirt" dredged up on Perry by national reporters during his presidential race stemmed from stories that already had been reported and published by Texas news organizations. But Perry has lived a charmed life in Texas politics. He is a Republican governor in a state where Republicans have won all statewide elections since 1996; his conservative ideology appeals to the conservative voters who dominate Texas's Republican primary; he is a strong fundraiser; he is an aggressive campaigner (at least in Texas); and his reelection opposition has mostly wilted.

In Perry's most recent reelection race in 2010, U.S. Senator Kay Bailey Hutchison challenged him in the Republican primary. Like Perry, Hutchison had never lost a statewide election, but Perry never gave her a chance. Even before the campaign got underway, Perry repeatedly attacked the senator for being a Washington "insider"—a bad word in the Republican primary—and Hutchison never recovered. Throughout the campaign year, Texas reporters wrote about Texas's lackluster record on such critical issues as education and health care funding during Perry's administration and questioned whether some of Perry's major financial backers were getting special treatment from the governor's office. But Perry barged ahead, sending Twitter feeds to supporters; bragging about Texas's job creation record under his watch; and blaming Washington, particularly President Barack Obama, for most of the country's problems. Either out of disdain for the Texas media or else because he felt the exercise would be a waste of time, he took the unusual step of boycotting all meetings with newspaper editorial boards. Breaking with another political tradition, he refused to debate his Democratic opponent, former Houston Mayor Bill White. Perhaps it was no accident that Perry, a year later, found himself stumbling through Republican presidential debates. He was out of practice.

All of the state's major newspapers endorsed White. In its editorial, *The Dallas Morning News* rebuked Perry for his "impervious air," a "strident tea party tone" and his "strong arm style." In the editorial, the newspaper noted its long record of supporting Perry in previous elections but added, "Texas requires a different kind of leadership at this important juncture."[14] Perry defeated White by more than 12 percentage points.

Perry's toughest election campaign as governor came in 2002, and it included some of the worst aspects of contemporary political campaigning. The race between Perry and Democratic challenger Tony Sanchez, a multimillionaire businessman from Laredo who spent about $56.7 million of his own money on his unsuccessful race, was characterized by **negative television ads** and personal attacks by the candidates on each other's integrity.

negative television ads
Television commercials in which political candidates attack their opponents, sometimes over a legitimate issue, but more often over an alleged flaw in their opponent's character or ability to hold office. Many such ads are deliberately misleading or outright false.

The news media's performance in covering the 2002 campaign was mixed. Voters who followed the campaign through the state's major daily newspapers—if they periodically wiped off the mud—were given more than enough information to compare the candidates' qualifications and personalities and evaluate their proposed solutions—or lack thereof—to the state's major problems. But many voters never got past the paid TV commercials, and they became almost vicious.

In one spot, Perry even tried to link Sanchez to the murder of a federal law enforcement officer. That ad was one of a series of commercials in which the Perry campaign attacked Sanchez over his previous ownership of Tesoro Savings & Loan, a financial institution in Laredo that had failed during the recession of the 1980s. In his advertising and campaign statements, Perry repeatedly attacked Sanchez over $25 million in drug money that had been laundered through Tesoro. The deposits, made in 1983 and 1984, had been investigated by federal authorities, but no one at the

5.1

5.2

5.3

5.4

5.5

5.6

5.7

financial institution was ever charged with a crime. Sanchez and other former Tesoro officials said they had not known the money belonged to drug dealers, which was fully explained by the journalists covering the campaign. But Perry's Tesoro ads continued. They culminated in a commercial in which two former Drug Enforcement Agency (DEA) agents blamed the drug lords who had laundered the money through Tesoro for the torture and slaying of a DEA agent. Sanchez called the attack sleazy, and his supporters said it was racist.

Sanchez ran television commercials blaming Perry for high consumer electric bills, but the Democratic nominee could not counter the devastating effect of Perry's attack. Perry's Tesoro ads ensured the Republican governor's election, said University of Houston political scientist Richard Murray. He said the ads were influential because Sanchez had never held elective office and many voters already were uncertain of his abilities.[15]

The last Texas governor's race won by a Democrat, in 1990, was extremely close. Republican nominee Clayton Williams lost to Democrat Ann Richards primarily because he destroyed himself—in full view of the media. Williams had used an effective TV advertising campaign, financed mainly by his own wealth, to win the Republican nomination over three opponents. He received little critical media attention during his primary race. Almost immediately after he was nominated, he found himself thrust into the spotlight, beginning with negative news stories about a rape joke that he told several reporters in what he thought was an informal, off-the-record setting (see *Talking Texas: Telling a Bad Joke*).

Talking ★ TEXAS Telling a Bad Joke

Clayton Williams, a rancher-oilman from Midland, took full advantage of Texas's television markets to swamp three opponents and win the 1990 Republican nomination for governor. Bankrolling his own campaign to the tune of $6 million for the March primary, Williams literally galloped to the nomination across the small screen. With paid television spots of himself riding horseback in cowboy duds across his ranch, he cultivated an image as an independent, successful businessman and governmental outsider with strong traditional roots who would mount a no-nonsense attack on the problems in Austin.

After the primary, however, Williams faced more critical scrutiny. His first encounter with increased media attention occurred in spectacular fashion when he invited reporters to his West Texas ranch for spring roundup. Sharing a cup of coffee around an early morning campfire with cowhands, campaign staffers, and three male reporters, Williams saw no reason for caution. When he told an old joke comparing the morning's foggy weather to rape—"if it's inevitable, just relax and enjoy it"—he certainly had no idea it would become page one headlines in the next day's newspapers and an issue in the remainder of the campaign. But it did.

Only a few years earlier, such remarks in an informal setting, where the candidate was hosting reporters, might have been treated as "off the record." Now, however, every aspect of a public official's or candidate's life was subject to public scrutiny, as demonstrated on the national scene by the widespread reporting of sexual misconduct by President Bill Clinton around that time. Reporters were making greater efforts to present voters with a candid view of a candidate, "warts" and all, something that viewers would not see in the candidate's television commercials.

In reporting Williams's rape joke, the media also took into consideration society's increasing sensitivity to sexual abuse and harassment, the fact that a violent crime was no laughing matter, and the question of whether Williams, as governor, would be sensitive to issues of particular concern to half of Texas's population—women.

Had the rape joke incident occurred more recently, Williams's gaffe would have raged all over the blogosphere within minutes. No one would have had to wait for the next morning's headlines.

CRITICAL THINKING QUESTIONS

1. Should everything a political candidate says in the presence of journalists or bloggers be considered fair game for reporting? Why or why not?
2. How has the Internet changed the reporting of political gaffes or misstatements?

Williams's campaign operatives then tried to restrict the media's access to him and to manage his public appearances more carefully. Nevertheless, Williams saw a gradual erosion of an early lead, with costly losses among Texas women. He also committed other major gaffes late in the campaign.

Only a few days before the November election, he admitted that he had paid no federal income tax in 1986 because of business losses, an admission that angered tax-weary voters of more modest means. In the fall, the *Houston Chronicle* also reported allegations that a bank, of which Williams was a director, had illegally required high-risk auto loan customers to purchase credit life insurance.[16]

The Mass Media and Public Ethics

5.3 Outline the mass media's role as a guardian of open government and describe the problems of combating media bias.

Perhaps the greatest potential for media influence in Austin is over the ethical conduct of legislators and other public officials, simply because of the potential embarrassment and political damage that can befall an elected official caught in an impropriety. But even that influence is sporadic because memories are short, and, sooner or later, there will be another scandal. Seldom, too, is the relationship between reporters and governmental officials more adversarial than when the media are questioning the ethical behavior of officeholders or reporting on a prosecutor who is doing so.

Tension was high in 1990 and 1991 when House Speaker Gib Lewis (D-Fort Worth) fought two misdemeanor ethics charges stemming from a grand jury investigation of his relationship with a tax-collection law firm. After Lewis was indicted on December 28, 1990—twelve days before the 1991 legislative session was to convene—the speaker mailed letters to newspapers across the state, urging editors to avoid a "rush to judgment" about his case. Maintaining his innocence, Lewis said, "All I ask is basic fairness—that I be given the time and opportunity to gather the facts and present my case before you judge me." The *Houston Chronicle* ran the letter at the top of its "Viewpoints," or letters-to-the-editor, column, accompanied by the front and side view mug shots taken of Lewis when he surrendered to law enforcement officers at the Travis County jail.[17]

Another ethics furor erupted in 1993, when Ronnie Earle, the same Travis County prosecutor who had investigated Lewis, turned his attention to newly elected U.S. Senator Kay Bailey Hutchison, a Republican. The Travis County district attorney's office, located only a few blocks from the state Capitol, is responsible for prosecuting wrongdoing by state officials. Hutchison was accused of using state employees for political and personal chores while she was state treasurer, the office she had previously held. Her conduct initially had been questioned months earlier in a story in the *Houston Post,* and she was indicted by a Travis County grand jury in 1993. She was acquitted in February 1994. During the months in between, Republican leaders bombarded reporters with press releases and telephone calls accusing Earle of prosecuting the senator for political purposes.

Although the Republicans' public relations campaign did not influence Hutchison's acquittal, GOP officials said they were forced to attack Earle and try to influence public opinion in order to repair any political damage to the senator and other Republican candidates. Hutchison supporters met with newspaper editorial boards and spoke on radio talk shows. Her attorneys even sent grand jury members packets of news clippings about the case. John Todd, an associate professor of political science at the University of North Texas, told *The Dallas Morning News* that the Republicans had "surprising success in planting the idea that this has all been just a political enterprise undertaken against [Hutchison]."[18]

Open Meetings and Public Information Acts
Laws that require state and local governmental bodies to conduct most of their actions in public and maintain records for public inspection.

media bias
A perception—sometimes real, sometimes imagined—that reporters and news organizations slant their news coverage to favor one side or the other in particular issues or disputes.

Reporters also were caught in a political firefight between Travis County District Attorney Ronnie Earle and Republicans when an investigation by the Democratic prosecutor led to campaign finance charges against U.S. Representative Tom DeLay of Sugar Land and two associates over donations made to several Republican legislative candidates in 2002. DeLay and his associates were accused of laundering corporate money to the candidates through the Republican National Committee. Corporate contributions to state political candidates are illegal in Texas. DeLay, then the Republican leader of the U.S. House, and his codefendants denied any wrongdoing, while Earle and his GOP detractors battled each other in the headlines and TV newscasts. The charges prompted DeLay to resign from Congress, and in late 2010, he was convicted of money laundering and sentenced to three years in prison.

Guardians of Open Government

Because the soundness of any governmental policy or program is affected by the motives and capabilities of those officials who design and administer it, most Capitol reporters take very seriously their role as watchdogs over the behavior and performance of elected officials and bureaucrats. As a result, newspeople are persistent guardians of the public's access to governmental business through the state's **Open Meetings and Public Information Acts**. These laws, which apply to state and local governments, basically provide that the public's business is to be conducted in public and that most records produced in the conduct of the public's business are to be made available to the public on demand. Each law provides for certain exceptions. Governmental bodies, for example, are allowed to hold closed-door meetings to consider personnel matters, to discuss lawsuits in which they are involved, and to consider real estate purchases, although all formal actions are to be taken in public. The Open Meetings Act requires a governmental body to post advance notices of all its meetings, even closed-door, executive sessions, and the Public Information Act establishes a procedure whereby the state attorney general's office decides disputes over whether specific governmental records can be kept confidential. Media representatives are engaged in a constant struggle against abuses and outright violations of the laws and attempts by school boards, city councils, and other governments to expand the list of exceptions that allow them to discuss business in private.

Several media organizations monitor and promote open government issues. The Freedom of Information Foundation of Texas, a nonprofit corporation that includes journalists, educators, and attorneys among its directors, maintains a telephone hotline to advise newspeople on open meetings and open-records rights and procedures and generally promotes openness in government. The Texas Daily Newspaper Association, the Texas Press Association, and the Texas Association of Broadcasters also lobby the legislature on open government issues. It's a difficult struggle because many public officials throughout Texas prefer to conduct the public's business in private. Numerous attempts usually are made each legislative session to weaken the Open Meetings and Public Information Acts, and some have been successful.

Media organizations are obviously in the business of disseminating information, but it is important to remember that they are not the only ones with a stake in strong open government laws. Every Texan also has a right to know what his or her government is doing, to find open doors in city council chambers and school board meeting rooms, and to have ready access to public documents.

Media Bias

Most public officials are sensitive about what is written and broadcast about them, particularly if a controversial issue has thrust them into the spotlight. Therefore, they often will respond to news stories slanted against them or their viewpoints. Readers and viewers also make complaints about alleged **media bias**, and the issue has sparked considerable debate and research.[19] National studies have indicated that most reporters are more liberal than the general population in personal ideology and on many public policy issues, and conservatives have exploited these findings to support their contention of a liberal media bias.[20] But other people, including many liberals, have pointed to corporate media ownership and concluded that those who make the final decisions as to what news is covered and how it is covered reflect more conservative biases.

The newspaper, television, and radio reporters who cover events and personalities at the state Capitol in Austin normally attempt to present all sides of an issue. Most believe they are objective, dedicated to principles of fairness and balance, and report events as they happen. This view of the press as a mirror was summarized years ago by Frank Stanton, former president of CBS, when he testified before a congressional committee that "what the media do is to hold a mirror up to society and try to report it as faithfully as possible." But newspeople and the organizations they represent sometimes have strong personal or corporate opinions about the issues or individuals they cover, and bias and the perception of bias are problems the media constantly has to fight.[21] Moreover, the emergence of cable television, which encourages audience segmentation by political or partisan philosophy, and online bloggers, many of whom are obviously biased, has made that task even more difficult for traditional media outlets.

Subjective decisions—such as a reporter's own strong interest in an issue—may determine which news events are covered on a particular day or which angle is emphasized in a particular story. Unless they are personal friends, reporters seldom discuss their political preferences with one another, but their personal politics doubtlessly cover the spectrum—Democrats, Republicans, and independents; conservatives, moderates, and liberals.

More often than not, however, reporters eagerly provide a forum for the viewpoints of consumer advocates, environmentalists, and other individuals purporting to promote the public interest. One reason for this is that spokespersons for these groups are readily accessible, hold frequent news conferences, send emails, and actively cultivate media contacts. They depend on free media exposure to compensate for limited budgets in their battles against the business lobby for the tougher regulations and higher taxes that progressive programs often require. Another reason is that stories about the age-old struggle between the powerful and the powerless, the rich and the poor, attract considerable reader and viewer interest, centering as they do on controversy and conflict.

The prominence with which editors or news directors "play" stories—page one versus inside the paper or at the top of the website versus at the bottom—is usually determined by the newsperson's perception of the public's interest in a given story. But an editor's or publisher's own opinion of an issue also may be a factor. Newspapers and broadcast stations often disagree with one another—and with their own reporters—on how stories should be played. Ultimately, a relatively few individuals decide which stories will be reported, how prominently they will be presented, and how much space or time will be allotted to them. People alleging media bias will point out that fact.[22] Michael Parenti, a critic of institutional elites in the United States, concluded that "the very process of selection allows the cultural and political biases and class interests of the selector to operate as censor."[23] Other media watchers argue, however, that the media "gatekeepers"—those who decide what news to publish or broadcast—are constrained, at least in part, by their readers' or viewers' preferences, as determined through market research.

Stories about governmental scandals and political corruption often are displayed on the front pages of newspapers, at the top of evening television newscasts, or prominently on newspaper or television websites. Attempting to follow in the footsteps of the early muckrakers of American journalism, some Texas newspeople view themselves as crusaders and are determined to "clean up" government. In their eagerness, however, they can become susceptible to charges of unfair, personal bias against the public officials they are targeting. This is particularly true when haste to be the first with the latest development in an ongoing scandal produces reporting or editing mistakes.

Newspapers and radio and television stations in Texas are businesses and, as such, sometimes have their own special interests to protect. Media opposition, for example, has played a major role in killing periodic attempts by legislators to put a sales tax on advertising. An advertising tax could raise millions of dollars for education, human services, and other programs that media outlets generally support, but media owners fear it would reduce advertising volume and deprive them of critical revenue.

Media bias will grow with the continued expansion of online information sources, including bloggers and other so-called "citizen journalists" who are not bound by traditional journalistic ethics and make no pretense of objectivity. The digital environment is "more open to bias and to journalism for hire," warned Paul Starr, a professor of communications and public affairs at the Woodrow Wilson School at Princeton University. "Online there are few clear markers to distinguish blogs and other sites that are being financed to promote a viewpoint from news sites operated independently on the basis of professional rules of reporting," he wrote in the *New Republic*, adding "So the danger is not just more corruption of government and business—it is also more corruption of journalism itself."[24]

The Development of the Media in Texas

5.4 Trace the development of the news media in Texas, from frontier newspapers to the Internet.

he dissemination of news and information in Texas has come a long way from the days of the frontier to the era of smart phones and tablets, and the journey has not always been easy. But it will continue, in one form or another.

Frontier Newspapers

Frontier Texans, isolated in their farmhouses and small settlements, lacked many creature comforts, but most had the opportunity to keep informed about the political sentiment of the day. The short-lived *Graceta de Tejas,* or the *Texas Gazette,* was established in Nacogdoches in 1812 long before Texas won its independence in 1836.[25] By 1860, according to historian T. R. Fehrenbach, there were seventy-one daily and weekly newspapers in Texas, with a total circulation of about 100,000: "Ninety-five percent of the white population could read and write and some publication reached virtually every family."[26] Like other early American newspapers, these publications often were highly partisan and primarily devoted to commentary on public issues—the local, state, and national political events of that turbulent period. Social calendars and stories about floods, fires, murders, and other everyday disasters were not yet standard journalistic fare. Editorial writing, however, had already developed into a backwoods art form: "This writing was often irate, biased, and misinformed—but much of it was clear and sound. It kept the freeholders of Texas fully aware of events; many farmers could quote Senator Stephen Douglas or Sam Houston at length. Texans were already keen political animals."[27]

Newspapers and "The Establishment"

Throughout much of the twentieth century, Texas's major newspapers were active members of the conservative, big-business, big-oil establishment that ran the statehouse and the state. During the pretelevision years of the 1940s and 1950s, in particular, publishers of some of the state's major newspapers, such as Amon Carter in Fort Worth and Jesse Jones in Houston, were oilmen and financiers who helped control local and state politics for the dominant conservative wing of the Texas Democratic Party. Another strong voice for the establishment was *The Dallas Morning News,* a tireless anticommunist, antilabor, antiliberal crusader. At various times, the *News* editorialized that "the presidency of Franklin Roosevelt was actually destructive of the Republic, the Senate's censure of Joe McCarthy [was] 'a happy day for Communists,' and the Supreme Court [was] 'a threat to state sovereignty second only to Communism itself.'"[28] There was little pretense of detached, neutral reporting, as the newspapers actively participated in the political process.

The establishment's close relationship with the Texas press was convincingly demonstrated in numerous election campaigns, including the 1954 Democratic gubernatorial runoff between Governor Allan Shivers, who had led conservative Texas Democrats in supporting Republican Dwight Eisenhower in the 1952 presidential race, and liberal challenger Ralph Yarborough, a party loyalist and strong supporter of organized labor. In the closing weeks of the campaign, ninety-five of the state's one hundred daily newspapers carried editorials endorsing Shivers, who won the runoff. Yarborough would later win election to the U.S. Senate, but the establishment's opposition to him was rabid. In its editorial endorsement of Shivers in 1954, *The Dallas Morning News,* however, was kind enough to concede that some of Yarborough's Texas supporters were not "reds . . . radicals or goon squad supporters."[29]

☐ Evolution of Texas Newspapers

News coverage has changed significantly since 1970, and today's readers and viewers of the traditional media almost never will find the kind of inflammatory, racist, demagogic writing that characterized much of the earlier Texas press. The media today are much more disposed to cover issues affecting the lower income populations, minorities, and others struggling against the power structure. Texas still is largely a conservative state, and a restructured business community still is influential in the setting of state policy. But the media—particularly the large newspapers and television stations—are much more eager to challenge the political and business establishment today.

For one reason, there is a high level of distrust of government now. A turning point in Texas was the Sharpstown stock fraud scandal that broke in 1971. It revealed that the legislature had given quick passage in 1969 to two banking regulation bills sought by Houston financier Frank Sharp and that high-ranking state officials had profited from insurance stock purchases financed with loans from Sharp's bank. That was soon to be followed by the Watergate scandal, which would force the resignation of President Richard Nixon and shake public confidence in government throughout the country, much as the bitter experience of the Vietnam War already had begun to do.

Newspeople still depend on government officials for much of their information, but now they more readily question the motives of the governor, legislators, and other public officeholders and political candidates. The ethical behavior of officeholders and their relationship to the special interests that spend millions of dollars trying to influence state government came under closer scrutiny after the Sharpstown and Watergate scandals. The media also reexamined its own ethics. Most news organizations adopted policies prohibiting their reporters from accepting free airplane rides, junkets, and other "freebies" from state officials or candidates, practices that had been fairly common in Texas in the past.

Another significant factor in the evolution of the Texas press was the passing of the high-profile publishers who had been part of the conservative establishment. Many of their newspapers were subsequently sold to large national conglomerates with newspapers and broadcast holdings in many cities. Such purchases of major, once independently owned newspapers such as the *Houston Chronicle,* the *Fort Worth Star-Telegram,* and the *Austin American-Statesman* were part of a consolidation of media

5.1

5.2

5.3

5.4

5.5

5.6

5.7

editorial autonomy
The freedom of a local newspaper or television station to set its own news policies independently of absentee owners who may run a chain of media outlets throughout the country.

ownership across the country, a development regarded as unhealthy by many within and outside the industry.

Such consolidations raised concerns that national owners, who had no personal ties to the local communities, were more concerned about profits and losses than the quality of news coverage—or diversity of editorial viewpoints—in their local outlets. Those concerns have been renewed—and in some cases validated—in the wake of recent corporate mergers, downsizing of newspaper staffs, and newspaper closures.

Perhaps paradoxically, however, national ownership can offer newspapers a greater degree of independence than was true in the past. Absentee corporate owners do not have sacred cows to protect in the Texas statehouse, the local courthouse, or city hall, and do not feel compelled to defend old provincial prejudices. Texas newspapers, for the most part, have maintained considerable **editorial autonomy** under national owners.

The Dallas Morning News is the only major metropolitan newspaper in the state still owned by a Texas-based corporation, and it still presents one of the most conservative editorial viewpoints on its opinion pages. It aggressively covers governmental and political institutions on its news pages and its website, despite financial setbacks that prompted a significant reduction in staff a few years ago.

The 1970s and 1980s were turning points for many Texas newspapers. Many changed owners during this period, and the overall quality of Texas journalism began to improve noticeably. The most dramatic and most influential change occurred in Dallas, and it was brought about by the brief entry of one of the nation's media giants, the Times Mirror Company, into the Dallas newspaper market.

Times Mirror, publisher of the *Los Angeles Times,* one of the country's most respected newspapers, purchased the *Dallas Times Herald* from local owners in 1970. Within a few years, it precipitated a major newspaper war with its dominant competitor, the *Morning News.* Times Mirror brought in new editors, recruited reporters from all over the country, improved the quality and aggressiveness of its news coverage—"The Only Sacred Cow Here Is Hamburger," read a sign on the newsroom wall—and awakened the *Morning News* from what many media watchers had considered a long, provincial slumber. At one point, the *Times Herald* briefly passed the *Morning News* in Sunday circulation. But the *Morning News* responded by bringing in new editors of its own, expanding its news staff, and vastly improving its product. During this period, both newspapers became major national award winners.

Initially, Times Mirror's foray into Dallas was extremely profitable, but with the precipitous decline in the Texas economy during the 1980s, the *Times Herald* began to lose money and was still second in advertising and circulation. The paper was sold in 1986 to a Texan, who was unable to reverse its financial position. It changed hands one more time before the *Morning News* purchased the struggling property and closed it in 1991. Despite a recent financial downturn, the *Morning News* remained one of the nation's premier newspapers, thanks in large part to the swift kick administered by Times Mirror. Moreover, the higher journalistic standards that emerged in Dallas had positive effects on some of the state's other newspapers, which soon began undergoing transformations of their own. But journalistic improvements were soon to be replaced by financial decline in the newspaper industry.

☐ Modern Newspapers, Modern Problems

Today, the daily newspaper industry in Texas and the United States is fighting for its survival. Hundreds of newspapers in the United States have ceased publication since 1900, a reflection of declining circulation; corporate consolidations; the emergence of television; the proliferation of radio stations with targeted audiences; the development of specialized magazines; and, most recently, the development of the Internet as a major information and advertising source. The folding of the *Dallas Times Herald* was followed by the closing of the *San Antonio Light* in 1993, the *Houston Post* in 1995, and the *El Paso Herald-Post* in 1997, leaving all of the large cities in Texas with only one daily newspaper each. By 2012, the survivors were still taking cost-cutting steps, including staff reductions, to stay afloat in the face of declining circulation and advertising revenue for their traditional print editions.

The Hearst Corporation, the *San Antonio Light*'s longtime owner, closed the paper after purchasing the rival *San Antonio Express-News,* which had gained the circulation lead in San Antonio. The *Light* had been published in San Antonio for 112 years but lost a reported $60 million during its last six years of operation.[30] During its final years, the *Houston Post* also lost millions of dollars as it went through a succession of owners. Texas now has about ninety daily newspapers and about 450 weekly, biweekly, or monthly newspapers.

Most small-town weekly newspapers are oriented primarily to their local communities and carry little news of state government or politics, but most of the small towns served by weeklies also are in the circulation areas of daily newspapers. There are also a number of African American–oriented and Spanish-language papers in Texas, but they have limited circulations. The demise of major daily newspapers has raised the profiles of aggressive, alternative weeklies in some Texas cities. Two of the better known are the *Houston Press* and the *Dallas Observer.* Statewide, the *Texas Observer,* a favorite of Texas liberals for more than fifty years, continues to publish every other week. In November 2009, *The Texas Tribune*, a new online nonprofit newspaper based in Austin and specializing in state political coverage, made its debut (see *Talking Texas:* The Texas Tribune*: A Paperless Newspaper*).

Talking ★ TEXAS *The Texas Tribune:* A Paperless Newspaper

The Texas Tribune, a nonpartisan, nonprofit, online newspaper, opened a new chapter in Texas journalism when it made its debut on November 3, 2009. Three years later, it was going strong and gaining readership while the state's older, more traditional newspapers were still fighting to secure their futures in the new media age. Cofounded by Austin venture capitalist John Thornton and journalists Evan Smith and Ross Ramsey, *The Tribune* announced an ambitious goal—"to serve the journalism community as a source of innovation and to build the next great public media brand in the United States."

Devoting itself primarily to coverage of Texas government and politics, it publishes news articles online and supplements those with explanatory features and interactive databases, which readers can peruse for information about political contributions, government employee salaries, public education expenditures for their local school districts, and a variety of other facts and figures. It also posts videos and podcast discussions of political news and views. In a content partnership with the *New York Times, The Tribune* provides news articles and commentary that are published in expanded front sections of the Friday and Sunday print editions of the *Times* distributed in Texas. *The Tribune* also has a reporting partnership with KUT, the public radio station in Austin, and collaborates with other Texas newspapers and radio stations.[a]

The Tribune's reporting staff includes several veteran reporters from other Texas news organizations. Smith, the CEO and editor-in-chief, is a former editor of *Texas Monthly* magazine, and Ramsey, the managing editor, is a longtime Austin-based reporter. As a nonprofit organization, *The Tribune* supports itself through tax-exempt donations from individuals, foundations, and corporations; ticket sales to sponsored events; and income from advertising sales. The newspaper expected to break even by the end of 2012, its initial targeted date. *The Tribune* attracted more than 12 million visits, including more than 6 million unique visitors, to its website during its first two years of operation (including more than 58 million page views).

"You believe in our mission," CEO Smith wrote in a report to readers in late 2011, "You believe that a smarter Texas is possible, and therefore that a better Texas is possible. We can only hope."[b]

CRITICAL THINKING QUESTIONS

1. **Are nonprofit news organizations the wave of the future? Should they be?**
2. **Are you likely to read an online newspaper with interactive graphics and data of public information, such as school expenditures and political contributions to officeholders? Why or why not?**

[a] "About Us, *The Texas Tribune*: A Brief Organizational Overview," *The Texas Tribune.*

[b] Evan Smith, "T-Squared: *The Texas Tribune*'s Two-Year Stats," *The Texas Tribune,* November 3, 2011.

5.1
5.2
5.3
5.4
5.5
5.6
5.7

Newspapers can thoroughly explain a pending issue, its history, and possible options for its resolution, but they also have their limits, primarily in the amount of space they can or will devote to governmental news. Responding to the popularity of television and its drain on available advertising revenue, newspapers already had reduced the proportion of space allocated to so-called "hard news." "Newspaper editors, like TV producers, have discovered the American public's insatiable hunger for 'fluff,'" one critic wrote.[31] Then news space was reduced even more following the Internet's raid on advertising dollars.

Newspapers now have their own websites, which are updated with breaking news stories throughout the day. Some newspapers also post staff-produced audio reports, or podcasts, as well as video reports on their websites. They post blogs by staff reporters on politics, sports, and a variety of other subjects. Some also publish blogs by readers—so-called "citizen journalists"—and interactive polls and graphics to promote more online readership. The Internet makes a newspaper's stories easily accessible to a national, or even international, audience well beyond its local or regional print circulation.[32] Most newspapers initially made their online content available to readers free of charge, a business practice that many papers have come to regret. As a result, some Texas newspapers, including *The Dallas Morning News*, have started charging for access to their online content, as have newspapers in other states. Newspapers sell advertising on their websites, but that revenue has not yet begun to replace the millions of dollars in print advertising that the papers have lost to online competitors. Meanwhile, news coverage, including coverage of state government, has suffered.

☐ Electronic and Digital Media

Television and the emergence of the Internet have had major impacts on the role of the media in government and politics. An estimated 98 percent of American homes have at least one television set, and most are linked to cable television systems. Television has replaced the newspaper as the public's primary source of news, but, like newspapers, it increasingly competes with online sources for the public's attention. There have been no recent studies focusing specifically on Texas, but there have been a series of national surveys of news consumption habits. In a 2010 national survey by the Pew Research Center for the People & the Press, 46 percent of respondents said they obtained news online at least three days a week, compared to 31 percent in a similar survey in 2006. Respondents who said they had watched television news the previous day had remained stable over the four years at 57 percent to 58 percent, but newspaper readership had declined. Respondents who said they had read a newspaper the previous day had fallen from 40 percent to 31 percent (see Figure 5–1).[33]

In a 2011 survey, the Pew Research Center's Project for Excellence in Journalism tried to take a more refined look at Americans' sources for news about their local communities and concluded that most news consumers were regularly using a variety of sources, depending on the type of news or information they sought. This survey found that television remained the most frequently used medium, with 74 percent of respondents watching local newscasts or visiting a local TV station's website at least once a week. Fifty percent read a newspaper or a newspaper website, 51 percent received news from a radio station (either on the air or online), and 47 percent turned to nontraditional, web-only sources. Moreover, 64 percent said they used at least three types of media every week. Although television was the most-used news source, most Americans, according to the survey, relied on it mainly for weather reports; breaking news; and, to a lesser degree, traffic reports. Newspapers, despite declining readership, remained a primary source of information about civic affairs, such as government. The Internet (excluding traditional media websites) was a primary source of information about restaurants and other local businesses and was tied with newspapers as a top source of information about housing, jobs, and schools. The 2011 Pew survey determined that age remained a factor in news source preferences. Older people still relied

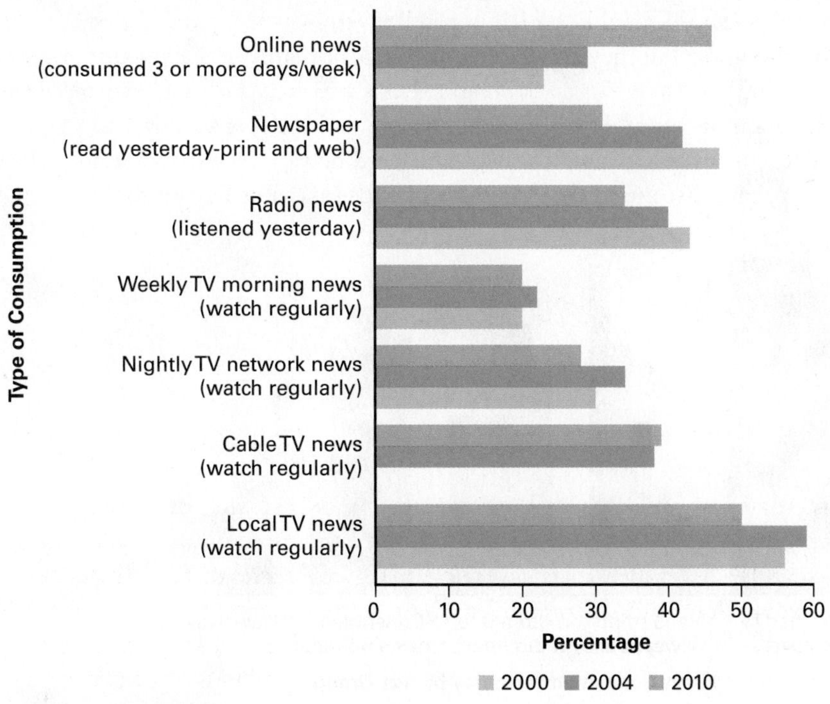

FIGURE 5–1 CHANGING NEWS CONSUMPTION PATTERNS, 2000–2010

Significant changes in news consumption patterns of Americans have occurred in recent years with a dramatic increase in the use of the Internet as a news source and a continued erosion of news consumption from newspapers.

Source: Pew Research Center for the People & the Press, *Pew Research Biennial News Consumption Survey*, August 17, 2008, and *Pew Biennial News Consumption Survey*, September 12, 2010.

more heavily on traditional media outlets, whereas younger Americans relied more on online sources (see Figure 5–2).[34]

TELEVISION There are about 160 television stations in about twenty-three markets in Texas, ranging in size from Dallas–Fort Worth and Houston, which rank among the largest markets in the country, to numerous small cities. Some cable stations now are offering full-time news coverage. The first was established in Austin in 1999 by Time Warner Cable, which holds the cable TV franchise in Austin. Political news coverage by Texas TV stations is not dominated by the partisan and political bickering and hyperbole that mark the talking-head lineups on some national cable networks, but television coverage of state government and politics in Texas has become inconsistent in recent years, even in the larger cities. Austin TV stations regularly cover events at the state Capitol, but no TV station from outside Austin has a full-time Capitol bureau. Stations sometimes send news crews to Austin for special events, such as a gubernatorial inauguration or the opening day of a legislative session, but their overall coverage is spotty.

Even at its best, television is an inadequate substitute for newspaper coverage of government and politics. Most local television news programs provide only cursory reports on governmental issues and activities, and people who rely solely on television for news have little substantive information upon which to make critical and informed judgments. Television—which, of course, is visually oriented—is good at covering a protest demonstration on the Capitol steps, getting a sound bite from the governor, or gathering interviews with citizens outraged over a tax increase. But the limited airtime given to even the most important stories makes it difficult to explain why the protesters marched on the Capitol or to explore the economic and political factors that produced the tax bill.

RADIO Most radio news also is of the headline variety, a quick summary of the day's news highlights. A handful of exceptions include public radio stations, such as KUT

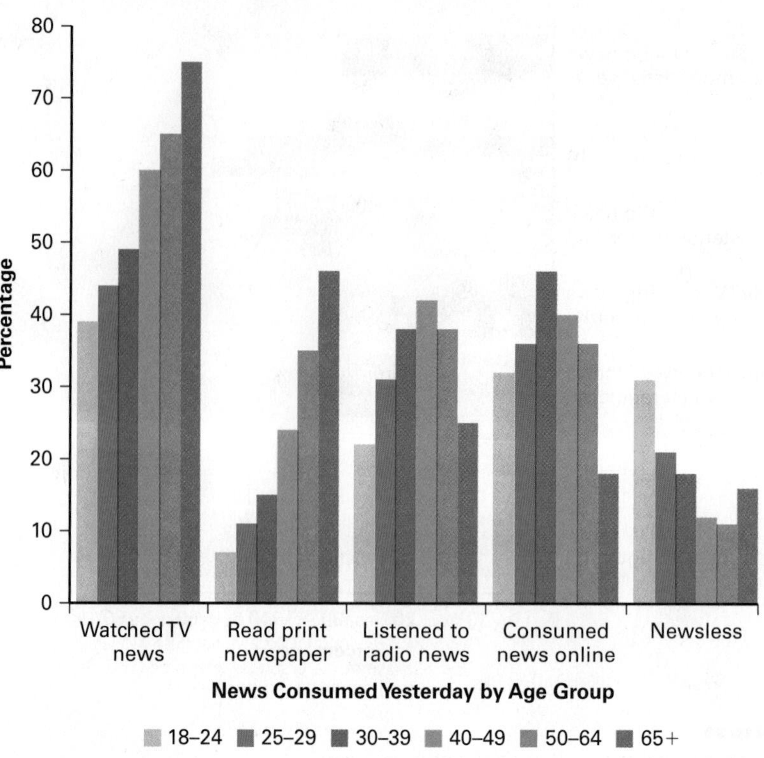

FIGURE 5–2 THE NEWS GENERATION GAP, 2010

News consumption and consumption patterns by news sources vary across age groups, with older Americans consuming more news than younger Americans. News sources also vary by age group.

Source: Pew Research Center for the People & the Press, *Pew Research News Consumption Survey*, September 12, 2010.

in Austin and KERA in Dallas, which offer regular state and local political coverage. KUT's local resources are enhanced by its reporting partnership with *The Texas Tribune*, the online newspaper mentioned earlier in this chapter. KUT and KERA also are part of the National Public Radio network. Few other radio stations have sufficient news staffs to cover major events in Austin. They rely on wire stories or feeds from a news service such as the Texas State Network, which has an Austin bureau. A handful of news talk stations—including WOAI in San Antonio, KRLD in Dallas, and KTRH in Houston—broadcast their own news coverage and commentary on political events and public issues. This commentary includes talk show programs that include primarily conservative viewpoints.

Television and radio often take their cues about what to cover from the print media. Most stations do not have large enough reporting staffs to do the extensive background work required to develop many complex stories. However, once a story broken by a newspaper has grabbed attention, the electronic media usually will join in pursuit.

THE INTERNET AND SOCIAL MEDIA Facebook and Twitter received much acclaim for helping antigovernment protesters in Tunisia and Egypt organize and spread the word about massive Arab Spring demonstrations that helped topple autocratic governments in both of those Middle Eastern countries in 2011. But many people who rely on blogs, Twitter, or YouTube for most of their news may not be getting a complete picture of current events or political options, suggested the results of another study by the Pew Research Center's Project for Excellence in Journalism.

This study examined the blogosphere and social media by tracking the news items linked to on millions of blogs and social media pages between January 2009 and January 2010. The study concluded that these online media embraced different agendas from the mainstream press. Twitter users linked to technology stories more than anything else, and to a much greater degree than the coverage afforded technology issues

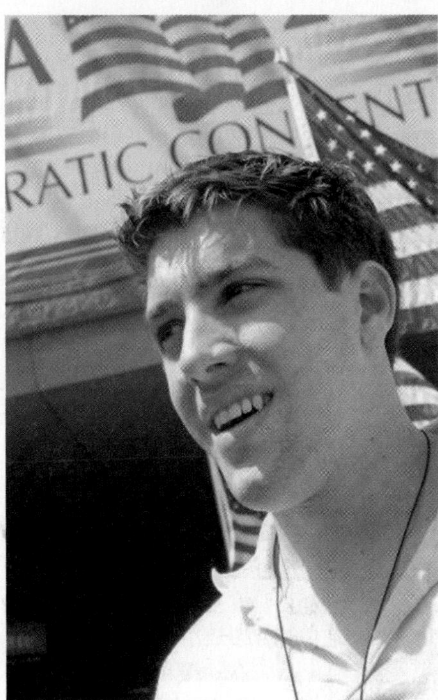

AN EARLY BLOGGER

Byron LaMasters, an early political blogger in Texas, is now a Democratic political consultant in Washington, D.C. He was one of the first bloggers to be credentialed to cover the 2004 Democratic National Convention.

by the traditional media. Blogs and YouTube shared a greater interest in politics (see *Talking Texas: Some Texas Political Bloggers*). Politics accounted for 21 percent of all top stories on YouTube during a given week and 17 percent of the top five linked-to stories in a given week in the blogosphere. (In this survey, the blogosphere does not include reporter-bloggers writing for newspaper websites or other traditional media.) Political links on blogs, the Pew Center noted, were "often accompanied by emphatic personal analysis or evaluations."

Talking ★ TEXAS Some Texas Political Bloggers

Bloggers come and go, and some post items more often than others. Some also are better writers and more authoritative than others. But here, in no particular order, is a small sample of some of Texas's political bloggers, representing both ends of the political spectrum.

Liberal

Burnt Orange Report:
www.burntorangereport.com

Off the Kuff:
http://offthekuff.com

Grits for Breakfast:
http://gritsforbreakfast.blogspot.com

Eye on Williamson County:
http://eyeonwilliamson.org

South Texas Chisme:
http://stxc.blogspot.com

In the Pink Texas:
www.inthepinktexas.com

Conservative

North Texas Conservative:
http://collincountyink.blogspot.com

Blog Houston:
www.bloghouston.net

Texas Conservative Republican News:
http://hardincountyconservatives.blogspot.com

The Conservative Cloakroom:
http://caseybrownmyers.blogspot.com

CRITICAL THINKING QUESTIONS

1. Although few bloggers do much original reporting, do they have an obligation to be as factual as possible as they spin their viewpoints? Or, is that a contradictory proposition?
2. Do you read many politically oriented blogs? If so, which are your favorites and why?

5.1
5.2
5.3
5.4
5.5
5.6
5.7

Even if they have a different agenda than the mainstream media, these bloggers still rely heavily on traditional media outlets for their information. More than 99 percent of the stories linked to in blogs tracked in the Pew study came from outlets such as newspapers and broadcast networks.[35] Unless they work for a traditional media organization, most bloggers do little, if any, original reporting, and many seldom discuss news events without including their own personal or partisan spin.

With these changes has come increased concern about the role of television and the Internet in shaping our view of politics and setting the agenda for public policies. Declining levels of news literacy among Americans, particularly young Americans, compound these concerns.

□ Growing Media Conglomerates

Several newspapers and broadcast outlets in Texas are owned by large corporate conglomerates, as are major media properties elsewhere. The New York–based Hearst Corp. owns six daily newspapers in Texas—including the *Houston Chronicle* and the *San Antonio Express-News*—as well as other newspapers and television stations throughout the country. Hearst also publishes numerous magazines, including *Cosmopolitan, Esquire, Seventeen,* and *Road & Track*, and has a 20 percent ownership interest in ESPN, the sports network, whose major owner is ABC Inc., parent company of the ABC television network. Hearst Texas's newspapers have separate staffs, but in recent years they have significantly reduced their staffs and begun sharing many stories and editing functions to save money. Two reporters cover state government and political news in Austin for both the Houston and San Antonio papers. Dallas-based A. H. Belo Corp., owner of *The Dallas Morning News,* also owns television stations in Dallas, Houston, San Antonio, and Austin and in several cities in other states. San Antonio–based Clear Channel Communications owns several hundred radio stations around the country.

The large conglomerates that own major television networks, which provide national political news to millions of Texas households, also own newspapers, movie distribution companies, and theme parks. ABC is an indirect subsidiary of the Walt

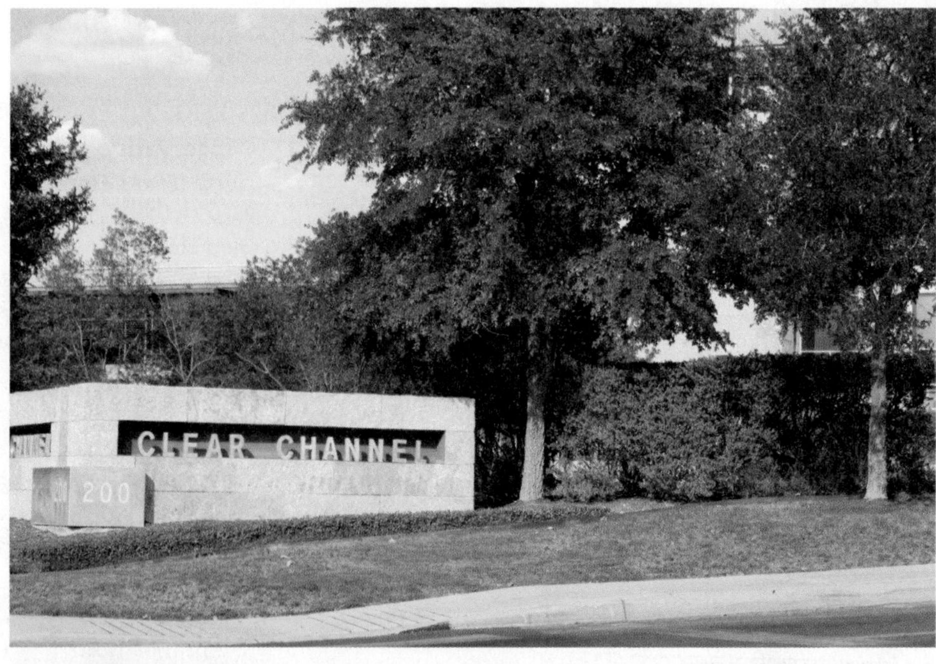

A DOMINANT FORCE IN THE RADIO INDUSTRY

Clear Channel Communications, headquartered in San Antonio, owns several hundred radio stations around the country.

Disney Co. The NBC television network is part of NBC Universal, which also includes, among other entities, Universal Pictures; Universal theme parks; and Fandango, the online source of movie reviews and tickets. CBS Corp. includes the television network as well as the Showtime cable channel and Simon & Schuster, the publishing company. One of the largest media conglomerates is Rupert Murdoch's News Corp., which owns several newspapers in Great Britain and Australia as well as the *Wall Street Journal*, the *New York Post,* and the Fox Broadcasting Co. in the United States. News Corp. also owns 20th Century Fox and HarperCollins Publishers.

These are only some of the mergers that link, at least indirectly, major newspapers and television news divisions to entertainment and other non-journalistic pursuits. As a result, there has been debate over how much independence news outlets may be losing with these consolidations. "The worry is not that there are fewer media outlets—the opposite is true—but that few people have ultimate control over them," Felicity Barringer wrote in the *New York Times*. "Critics wonder if news judgments will be bent, with executives suppressing news deemed harmful to corporate interests. They wonder if companies will use their journalists to promote their other interests, be they movies, television shows or sports teams." Media experts interviewed by the newspaper, however, offered different opinions about those potential problems. "Defenders of the news divisions point out that plenty of media outlets would be eager to pick up on a story suppressed by a competitor. Top media executives also know and have argued to their corporate bosses that cheap or compromised journalism costs the enterprise both trust and profits," the newspaper story noted.[36]

Many of the radio stations held by national conglomerates no longer provide local news. Some are basically remote facilities in which the programming is formatted in another city, and the reporters or disc jockeys speak from a studio miles away. Another potential source of local news is being lost to corporate consolidation and the homogenization of news. Although it is difficult to foresee all the implications of the recent technological advances and high-stakes mergers, one can speculate that there will continue to be changes in how voters receive information about politics and government—and the way the media will be exploited by officeholders and candidates.

Capitol press corps
Representatives of Texas newspapers, television and radio stations, and wire services who are assigned to Austin full time to report on state government and politics.

The Capitol Press Corps

5.5 Evaluate the consequences of the shrinking size of the Capitol press corps.

Most of the state's major newspapers, the Associated Press, and a radio network are represented at the Texas State Capitol by reporters who cover state government and politics full time. However, as noted at the start of this chapter, the **Capitol press corps** has been shrinking in Austin, as has coverage of statehouses throughout the country. More than fifty reporters and television correspondents were assigned to the Texas Capitol in 2000. By 2012, the full-time number had dwindled to about half that. Most newspaper bureaus are smaller—the *Fort Worth Star-Telegram*'s bureau closed in 2012—and the only television stations that regularly cover events at the Capitol are the Austin stations. Several "insider" subscriber newsletters and Internet bloggers focusing on state government also operate in Austin.[37]

The muckraking *Texas Observer,* mentioned earlier, still publishes fortnightly in Austin and has a faithful following among Texas liberals. The slick magazine *Texas Monthly* offers limited coverage of state government, including an online blog by senior editor Paul Burka and its ranking of what it considers to be the ten best and ten worst legislators after each regular session. Harvey Kronberg's *Quorum Report*, available to subscribers online, offers a daily compilation of newspaper headlines and "Daily Buzz" alerts of breaking news throughout the day. It also has a small staff of reporters who post stories online about statehouse events. Kronberg also operates the online *Texas Energy Report,* which carries news about the energy industry.

The news organizations with the biggest Austin staffs are the *Austin American-Statesman* and *The Texas Tribune*, the online newspaper. Both are headquartered in Austin. The largest bureaus representing out-of-town media companies are *The Dallas Morning News* and the Associated Press. Each has four reporters. Other newspapers have downsized to only one or two reporters each.

The small newspaper bureaus often give priority to covering members of their local legislative delegations and events of particular interest to their communities; the large papers and the wire service provide more general coverage. But even the large papers find it impossible to cover more than a fraction of state government activities, and that task has become even more difficult with the contraction of the newspaper industry and reductions in Capitol staffs.

"The concern about statehouse coverage—indeed, about newspaper retrenchment in general—is not just the declining number of reporters, but deterioration in the quality of journalism," wrote Professor Paul Starr in the *New Republic*, "As the editorial ranks are thinned, internal checks on accuracy are being sacrificed. As reporters with years of experience are laid off, newspapers are losing the local knowledge and relationships with trusted sources that those reporters had built up, which enabled them to break important stories."[38]

The statehouse bureaus are generally considered prestigious assignments and attract capable and aggressive reporters. Nevertheless, in addition to the staff reductions, there has been considerable turnover on Capitol news staffs in recent years. Only a dozen or so of the reporters covering the legislature in 2011 had more than ten years of experience on the Capitol beat. This means many reporters have limited historical perspective for comparing the administrations of different governors or the performance of the legislature over a sustained period.

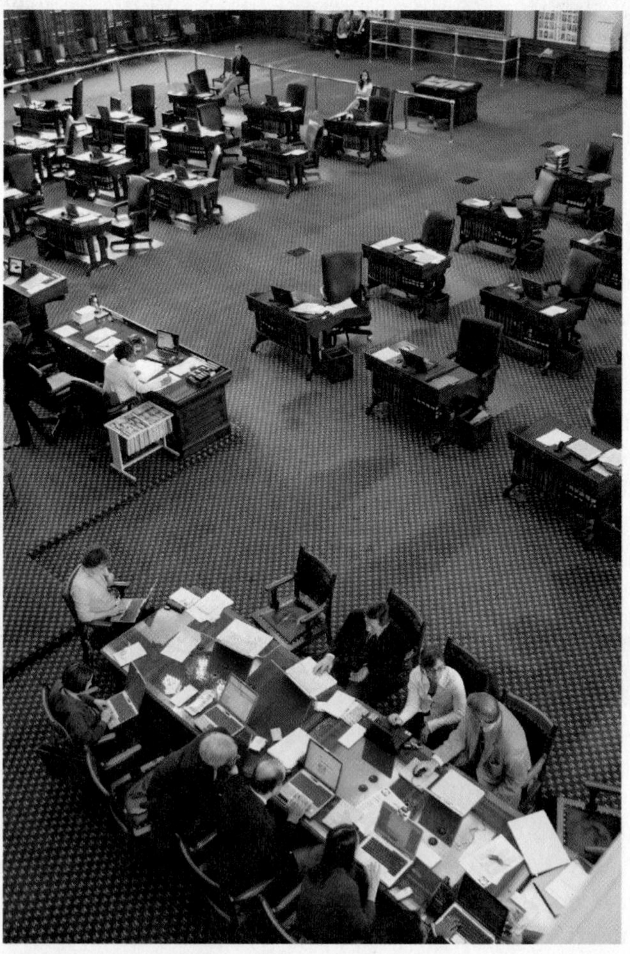

KEEPING "TABS" ON THE LEGISLATURE

Members of the Capitol press corps are shown working at the press table (foreground) in the state Senate chamber during a recent session.

There is no typical pattern to the careers of Capitol reporters. Some were promoted from their organizations' local staffs; others were hired from competing bureaus or from out-of-state newspapers. In recent years, relatively few Capitol reporters have chosen to retire in those jobs, but only a handful have gone on to become editors in their home offices. Some have moved to news bureaus in Washington or jobs in other media markets, whereas others have become press secretaries or information specialists for elected officeholders, state agencies, or interest groups.

spin
The presentation of information in the best possible light for a public official or political candidate. It usually is provided by a press secretary, campaign consultant, or another individual representing the officeholder or candidate.

Most news bureaus lease private office space near the Capitol for their main offices and lease smaller, additional workspace from the state in an underground addition to the Capitol. With proper credentials, media representatives are granted access to the floors of the House and the Senate when the legislature is in session. Special worktables at the front of each chamber are provided for reporters, and the House and the Senate set standards for credentials.

Despite new online tools and research capabilities, sound news judgment and perseverance are still the basic tools of the successful Capitol reporter, just as they are for thousands of newspeople elsewhere. Statehouse reporters usually have to dig out the best stories, frequently using confidential sources to develop tips or hunches. Legislators, other elected officials, members of their staffs, bureaucrats, and lobbyists love to tell secrets about one another. Such sources, of course, often have their own political or personal agendas, and the smart reporter is wary.

Campaigns for state office are notorious for whispered accusations or innuendoes directed against opposing camps. Sometimes a legislator, without allowing his or her name to be used, will leak a controversial proposal to a reporter as a trial balloon to see how other lawmakers and the general public react to the idea before deciding whether to actively promote it. Similar anonymous leaks, cast in a negative light, can be used to kill someone else's proposal before he or she has had a chance to gather support for it. Although reporters run the risk of being used in such situations, they also can be put on the trail of significant stories. A newsperson has to evaluate each tip on its own merits, although he or she often is pressured by the knowledge that competitors also get similar tips.

Governmental Public Relations

5.6 List the ways elected officials and interest groups use public relations personnel and resources.

Most of the state's top elected officials and administrators of major agencies spend thousands of tax dollars each year on press secretaries and public relations operations to help disseminate public information and to promote themselves and their agencies. News releases, websites, social media messages, press conferences, background briefings, slick reports, and videotapes are designed to maintain the visibility of state agencies, cultivate general goodwill, announce new programs, and anticipate budgetary attacks or program changes. In a dispute with the legislature or another state agency, a public official's media specialists often try to put a **spin** on a story that presents information in the best possible light for their boss.

The House and the Senate also provide media services for their members. Taxpayers pay for websites, written news releases, newsletters, and radio and television feeds to local stations. These resources can be used by a legislator to maintain a flow of information to constituents that, in effect, amounts to a continuous political campaign.

Some governors have used political funds to purchase statewide television satellite time to communicate directly with the public on major policy issues or proposals. Websites give governors and other officeholders an excellent opportunity—unfiltered by the media's critical eye—to promote their proposals directly to the public and tout what they claim to be their accomplishments.

Most of the Austin-based trade associations and other special interest groups have public relations specialists to promote their causes and keep their members informed of developments at the Capitol. Interest groups are at the center of the policymaking process, and their proposals and efforts to get them enacted are inherently newsworthy. Lobbyists also provide a wealth of insider information to reporters, but newspeople must carefully evaluate it because of the large stakes that special interests have in the workings of state government.

How Well Informed Are Texas Citizens?

5.7 Assess the consequences of an uninformed citizenry in Texas politics.

Despite the media's efforts, only a small percentage of Texans attempt to keep up with what their elected officials in Austin are doing. A few high-profile issues, such as taxes or firearms regulation, attract a lot of attention. But many taxpayers, particularly those who live in metropolitan areas that have numerous legislators, do not even know who their state representatives or state senators are, much less how they have voted on significant issues.

This may be the media's fault in part. Many small newspapers carry only brief wire service stories about news events in Austin, and others give an incomplete picture by concentrating primarily on issues of local interest. The major newspapers provide more complete coverage, although it is shrinking, but they seldom publish recorded votes of legislators within their readership areas.

However, as noted, the media are only partly to blame for the uninformed and under-informed state of many Texas citizens. There are ample information sources by which anyone, with minimal effort, can stay informed of major developments in state government. The distractions and demands on a person's time are great in today's fast-paced world, and a person who wants to know what is going on in the governmental and political arena often has to juggle priorities. But the opportunities are there, and they have been expanded by the Internet. It is up to the individual to make the time and the effort to become informed and to take care to differentiate fact from opinion.

Ignorance among the general electorate plays right into the hands of the special interests, who not only stay abreast of developments in Austin, but also spend millions of dollars on political donations and legislative lobbying to influence those developments to their advantage, not to the benefit of the general public. Most governmental actions, whether taken by the legislature or a state regulatory board, eventually will affect the pocketbooks or quality of life of thousands, perhaps millions, of Texans, most of whom will be caught by surprise. If recent patterns of policy making continue, the influence of special interests over the public's business will become even greater in the future.[39]

For more than three decades, Americans have been reporting that they were consuming less news than in the past, a disturbing pattern for those concerned with the information literacy required of citizens to make informed judgments about politics and public policy. Significant declines were reported in the consumption of print, network, and local television news, but the digital age has transformed the mass media, and online consumption of news and information continues to grow. The Pew Research Center for the People & the Press reported in 2010 that "there are many more ways to get news these days [and] Americans are spending more time with the news than over much of the past decade." Although the report is not glowing, it suggests that the decline in news consumption may have been arrested with prospects for increased interest in the news provided by online sources.[40]

According to the same survey, younger Americans though were keeping up with the news far less than older people. Newspaper readership was highest among those age 65 and older, and very low among those age 18 to 24. News consumption from television also increased with age, although older respondents were less likely to obtain their news online. Some 31 percent of young people reported that they were "newsless" the previous day, the highest percentage of any age group. These findings supplemented earlier studies showing that young people were less likely than their parents to be able to identify major newsmakers.

Researchers have attributed part of the blame to deficiencies in public education, which Texas and other states are trying to resolve.[41] Another likely factor is the increased number of entertainment alternatives competing for young people's time. It has been suggested that many young people believe that they cannot make a difference, do not link the actions of governments to their lives, and have tuned out the political process.

Whatever the reason, the prospects for a quality state government sensitive to the public interest in the next generation are somewhat discouraging. If the surveys accurately reflect the news consumption patterns of young Americans, their levels of knowledge about government and politics, and their attitudes toward participation and involvement in the political process, state and local governments will be controlled for years to come by special interests. There will be limited opposition or scrutiny by the general public. It remains to be seen whether the expansion of online news sources will make a positive difference for young people and the future of political participation.

On MyPoliSciLab

Review the Chapter

Listen to Chapter 5

The Mass Media and the Policy Agenda

5.1 Explain the role of the mass media in the policy agenda process, emphasizing the strengths and weaknesses of its influence, p. 122.

The news media are the primary information link between those who govern and those who are governed. The news media affect the development of public policy by influencing the election of policymakers and informing and educating the public on policy alternatives. They can make the causes of a few individuals the concerns of many. This role has remained basically unchanged in this country since the adoption of the First Amendment to the U.S. Constitution more than 200 years ago, but vast changes in technology have transformed the dissemination of information and challenged the media's traditional role.

The Mass Media and the Electoral Process

5.2 Describe the various features of mass media coverage of elections and the use of the mass media by campaigns in Texas, p. 124.

Candidates for public office depend on the mass media to develop name identification and convey information about their policy positions to the public. Although the media devote some coverage to substantive policy issues and candidates' positions on them, much media coverage is on the "horse race" aspects of campaigns—who is running ahead in the polls and who has raised the most money. Most voters get their news about political campaigns from television, but increasingly the Internet is emerging as a major source of political news. Much of the online reporting is highly partisan and opinionated. Candidates cannot control what is reported in the mainstream media, but they try to influence coverage through news releases and staged news or pseudo-news events.

Most serious candidates for statewide office and some local and district offices in metropolitan areas spend large amounts of money on advertising, which allows candidates to control the message. The use of negative or attack ads against opponents has become common in political campaigns. Voters indicate that they do not like the harsh, often vicious attacks, but political consultants say attack ads work.

The Mass Media and Public Ethics

5.3 Outline the mass media's role as a guardian of open government and describe the problems of combating media bias, p. 129.

Media organizations are persistent guardians of the public's access to governmental business through the state's Open Meetings and Public Information Acts, but the fight against government secrecy is a never-ending battle. Some public officials do not want the public to know what they are doing and who might have influenced their decisions. Often, the press has to go to court to obtain records of public agencies. The media function, in part, to establish disclosure and public ethics.

Thanks to major government scandals and the passing of former publishers who had helped run the conservative Texas establishment, the media today are much more independent of officialdom and much more eager to challenge those in power. Nevertheless, they must still fight charges of bias in presentation of the news, in part because the subtle, subjective decisions of a relatively few reporters, editors, and news directors have a major impact on which stories are covered and how prominently they are presented

The Development of the Media in Texas

5.4 Trace the development of the news media in Texas, from frontier newspapers to the Internet, p. 132.

Texans have seen many changes in how they obtain their news since the frontier era, when many settlers had access only to published political opinions in primitive newspapers. For much of the twentieth century, influential newspaper publishers in Texas were part of the state's business-oriented political establishment and had close ties to elected officials. In the 1970s, Texas newspapers began to more eagerly challenge public officials and governmental decisions, in part because out-of-state corporate owners, who had only limited interest in local Texas politics, replaced establishment-oriented publishers. The expanded coverage also reflected a changing state political system, and newspapers began covering issues of particular concern to minority groups and low-income Texans. In the late twentieth century, many Texans started to get more of their news from television, rather than newspapers.

Today, both newspapers and TV stations are losing news consumers to the Internet. Newspapers, in particular, are struggling with reduced readership and lost advertising dollars and have reduced staff, including the number of reporters assigned to cover the state Capitol. Newspapers still publish print editions, but they also have websites, as do television stations. The Internet continues to grow as a news source, but it provides more immediacy than depth. Most media outlets, including local radio, television, and newspapers, now are owned by large media conglomerates often headquartered in other parts of the country.

The Capitol Press Corps

5.5 Evaluate the consequences of the shrinking size of the Capitol press corps, p. 141.

Changes in the mass media, including financial problems, have resulted in a dramatic reduction in the number of reporters assigned to the state Capitol. Coverage of state politics has been reduced because the decreased reporter ranks force the remaining newspeople to be more selective in which stories they cover. Some historical perspectives on state politics also have been lost.

Governmental Public Relations

5.6 List the ways elected officials and interest groups use public relations personnel and resources, p. 143.

Officeholders and state agencies use websites, emails, newsletters, and other information tools to inform the public, in the best possible light, about their work. They also employ communications specialists. This effort is designed, in part, to sustain public support for their programs, counter criticism, or prepare for a subsequent reelection bid. Interest groups also use the mass media in numerous ways to shape public opinion on their policy objectives. The large, well-funded organizations have paid media specialists who constantly monitor news stories and decisions of policymakers that potentially will impact their interests. From the press release to a well-orchestrated statewide public relations campaign using various media, these organizations are prepared to use the mass media in offensive or defensive strategies.

How Well Informed are Texas Citizens?

5.7 Assess the consequences of an uninformed citizenry in Texas politics, p. 144.

One of the greatest ironies of the so-called "information age" is that young people apparently are paying less attention than their parents to governmental news and other substantive events occurring in the world around them. This dims the prospects for a quality state government in the next generation because ignorance among the general public plays right into the hands of the special interests who make it their business to influence public policy.

Learn the Terms

Study and **Review** the Flashcards

agenda setting, p. 122
agenda building, p. 123
issue-attention cycle, p. 124
sound bite, p. 124
negative television ads, p. 127
Open Meetings and Public Information Acts, p. 130
media bias, p. 130
editorial autonomy, p. 134
Capitol press corps, p. 141
spin, p. 143

Test Yourself

Study and **Review** the Practice Tests

1. All of the following are criteria the media use to select which political events and subjects to cover EXCEPT that the story

a. must have a significant impact on its audience.
b. must generate considerable interest.
c. must be about an unusual or unfamiliar situation or individual.
d. should occur in some proximity to the readers and viewers.
e. should be timely.

2. The ability of conservative activists to minimize the influence of the media in the 2011 debate over the budget is an example of failed

a. agenda setting.
b. generation of interest.
c. timeliness.
d. agenda building.
e. investigation.

3. What does covering the "horse race" refer to?

- **a.** news coverage of campaign polls instead of legitimate polls
- **b.** news coverage of campaign strategies and personalities instead of substantive policy issues
- **c.** paid television advertising instead of news coverage
- **d.** negative attack ads instead of positive ads
- **e.** news media fact checking of campaign accuracy

4. When thinking about the role of television in election campaigns, we can say that

- **a.** voters trust campaign ads more than they do news analyses of those ads.
- **b.** the candidate who spends the most money on television ads always wins the election.
- **c.** local and national television stations broadcast an average of ten minutes a night of discussion or debate by candidates.
- **d.** paid television advertising does a better job of covering complex issues than print newspaper reporting.
- **e.** "horse race" coverage is more expensive than issue coverage.

5. Which of the following statements is NOT true about media coverage of recent gubernatorial campaigns in Texas?

- **a.** Governor Rick Perry boycotted all meetings with newspaper editorial boards in 2010.
- **b.** Most people said they believed the TV ads that George W. Bush and Ann Richards used in their 1994 race more than they believed the accuracy views that newspapers published about the ads.
- **c.** Republican candidate Clayton Williams saw his campaign fall apart with increased news media scrutiny in 1990.
- **d.** In 2002, Rick Perry used television spots to link opponent Tony Sanchez to the murder of a federal law enforcement officer.
- **e.** In 2010, Governor Rick Perry debated his Democratic opponent, former Houston Mayor Bill White, in an unprecedented five televised debates.

6. Which act requires a governmental body to post advance notices of all its meetings?

- **a.** Open Meetings Act
- **b.** Open Hearings Act
- **c.** Public Information Act
- **d.** Freedom of Information Act
- **e.** Freedom of the Press Act

7. Which act allows the state attorney general's office to decide disputes over whether specific governmental records can be kept confidential?

- **a.** Open Meetings Act
- **b.** Open Hearings Act
- **c.** Public Information Act
- **d.** Freedom of Information Act
- **e.** Freedom of the Press Act

8. One reason that governmental bodies can hold closed-door meetings is to

- **a.** debate overrides of the governor's vetoes.
- **b.** discuss lawsuits in which they are involved.
- **c.** deliberate over border security issues.
- **d.** investigate charges of ethical malfeasance.
- **e.** plan political strategy.

9. When it comes to media bias, we can say that

- **a.** television reporters are more liberal and newspaper reporters are more conservative.
- **b.** corporate media ownership tends to skew news decisions in a more liberal direction.
- **c.** the process of selecting what will be covered and how is uncontroversial.
- **d.** the fact that media outlets are businesses has no impact on news coverage decisions.
- **e.** the new world of online blogging has made media coverage of politics more susceptible to viewpoint biases.

10. The news media in Texas began to challenge the political and business establishment with the

- **a.** decline of frontier newspapers.
- **b.** censure of Joe McCarthy.
- **c.** runoff election between conservative Allan Shivers and liberal Ralph Yarborough.
- **d.** Sharpstown stock fraud scandal.
- **e.** consolidation of media ownership.

11. Because of the consolidation of media ownership across the country

- **a.** frontier newspapers disappeared.
- **b.** newspapers lost their editorial autonomy.
- **c.** more newspapers opened for business than closed.
- **d.** concerns were raised about the loss of diversity of editorial viewpoints.
- **e.** newspapers expanded their staffs.

12. What does research about Americans' consumption of news find?

a. Radio is a more frequently used medium for news than television.

b. Younger Americans rely more on the Internet than traditional media outlets.

c. Twitter users link more to political stories than bloggers.

d. Talk radio programs are evenly balanced between liberal and conservative commentary.

e. The print media tend to take their cues about what to cover from television and radio.

13. What can we say about the Capitol press corps in recent years?

a. Even large papers can cover only a fraction of state government activities.

b. Turnover in staff has led to a larger percentage of reporters with more than ten years of experience.

c. Dallas and Houston newspapers have the biggest Austin bureau staffs.

d. With news media consolidation, the Capitol press corps has expanded in size.

e. Thinning editorial staffs have led to increased accuracy in political reporting.

14. Which of the following is the best example of spin?

a. the use of websites by legislators to keep constituents informed about legislations

b. the purchase of television airtime by a governor to communicate directly to the public

c. the use by special interest groups of public relations specialists to promote their causes

d. the effort by lobbyists to provide insider information to reporters

e. a public official's media specialist trying to present information or a news story in the best possible light

15. When it comes to the problem of ignorance of public affairs, we can say that

a. there are fewer opportunities to learn what is going on in the political arena than ever before.

b. Americans actually consume more news now than ever before.

c. increased entertainment alternatives compete for young people's time.

d. the Internet has led young people to consume more news than those who are older.

e. ignorance of public affairs is a problem for special interest groups as much as it is for the general public.

Explore Further

Burka, Paul, "The Capitol Press Corpse," *Texas Monthly*, January 2008. Provides an extended discussion and lament of the decline of the Capitol press corps in Austin.

Cash, Wanda Garner, and Ed Sterling, *The News in Texas: Essays in Honor of the 125th Anniversary of the Texas Press Association*. Austin: University of Texas Press, 2005. Recounts "the stories of courageous publishers who used their columns to challenge inequities and injustices" in Texas.

Christ, W. G., Harry Haines, and Robert Huesca, "Remember the Alamo: Late Night Local Newscasts in San Antonio, Texas," in *The Electronic Election: Perspectives on the 1996 Campaign Communication*, Vol. 1, edited by L. Kaid and D. Bystrom. Mahwah, NJ: Lawrence Erlbaum Associates, 1998. Focuses on content and patterns of local news coverage in the city of San Antonio.

Cox, Patrick, *The First Texas News Barons*. Austin: University of Texas Press, 2005. Highlights the work of early Texas newspapers that did more than report news and current events; major newspaper owners such as A. H. Belo and George B. Dealey played a key role in the industrialization and urbanization of Texas.

Friedenberg, Robert V., *Communications Consultants in Political Campaigns: Ballot Box Warriors.* Westport, CT: Praeger Publishers, 1997. Commences with a brief history of campaign consultants in the United States; the author "examines the principal communication specialties used in contemporary campaigns."

Graber, Doris A., *Mass Media and American Politics*, 8th ed. Washington, DC: Congressional Quarterly Press, 2010. Uses up-to-date information to focus on news dissemination through different media venues; written by a nationally recognized scholar.

Jackson, Brooks, and Kathleen Hall Jamison, *Un-Spun: Finding Facts in a World of [disinformation].* New York: Random House, 2007. Offers practical advice to help discern fact from fiction in a media environment where distortion is common; written by the founders of FactCheck.org.

Jamieson, Kathleen Hall, *Dirty Politics: Deception, Distraction and Democracy*. New York: Oxford University Press, 1993. Gives clues as to how to assess political ads and speeches in political campaigns; written by a nationally recognized expert on political campaigns.

Mayer, Vicki, *Producing Dreams, Consuming Youth: Mexican Americans and Mass Media*. Piscataway, NJ: Rutgers University Press, 2003. Provides a perspective on the mass media in San Antonio and its influence and role in shaping the Hispanic culture of the city.

Subervi, Federico, *The Mass Media and Latino Politics: Studies of U.S. Media Content, Campaign Strategies and Survey Research: 1984–2004*. New York: Routledge, 2008. Focuses on Hispanic media coverage of national elections.

6

Listen on MyPoliSciLab

The Party System in Texas

Political parties created democracy and modern democracy is unthinkable save in terms of party.

—E. E. Schattschneider, 1960

The common and continual mischiefs of the spirit of party are sufficient to make it the interest and duty of a wise people to discourage and restrain it.

—George Washington, Farewell Address to the People of the United States, September 17, 1796

The Texas Republican Party has always been conservative, and it has had firm control of state government since Republicans won a majority in the Texas House of Representatives in 2002. Republicans captured control of the state Senate several years earlier, and they have won every statewide election since 1996. The party's conservatism became even more potent after the 2010 elections, when ultraconservatives aligned with the tea party movement became a driving force in GOP primary elections. In several legislative races around the state, they unseated moderate Republican incumbents, and in November they helped boost the House Republican margin to 101 to 49, a modern Republican record. They also were instrumental in helping Governor Rick Perry defeat more moderate challengers, U.S. Senator Kay Bailey Hutchison in the GOP primary and former Houston Mayor Bill White in the general election.

6.1 Explain what political parties are and why Texas has a two-party system, p. 153.

6.2 Describe the different functions of political parties in Texas, p. 157.

6.3 Trace the partisan history of Texas, focusing on the transformation from one-party to two-party politics, p. 159.

6.4 Outline the basic structure of the party organization in Texas, from the precinct level to the state convention, p. 171.

6.5 Assess why political parties in Texas do not produce cohesive, policy-oriented coalitions in government, p. 177.

ANTI-TAX PROTESTERS register for a tea party rally in Houston. One woman wears a sign expressing her feelings.

6.1

6.2

6.3

6.4

6.5

The result was a legislative session in 2011 that was one of the most conservative in recent Texas history. In an email campaign led by Michael Quinn Sullivan and Empower Texans (a tea party–type group), conservative activists were unsuccessful in trying to pressure House members to unseat moderate Republican Speaker Joe Straus in favor of a more conservative presiding officer. But Empower Texans and other advocates intent on cutting spending and shrinking the size of government ruled the budget-setting process. Conservative lawmakers formed a Tea Party Caucus and had an advisory committee of tea party leaders around the state. They kept the pressure on and applauded as Governor Perry and the Republican legislative majority closed a $27 billion revenue shortfall with billions of dollars in spending cuts to education, health care, and other public services. At the insistence of tea party advocates, they did so while leaving more than $6 billion of taxpayers' money unspent in the state's emergency Rainy Day Fund. When some Senate Republicans proposed spending $3 billion in Rainy Day money to reduce the spending cuts, tea party activists hammered them with protests, and they abandoned the idea.

State Senator Dan Patrick, a Republican from Houston and chairman of the Tea Party Caucus, praised the budget-cutting work as a "huge success."[1] But others warned that the Texas Republican Party, by embracing "extremist" views, was shooting itself in the foot and compromising its own future as a force in Texas politics. Although the Republican Party is likely to remain in control of Texas government for several more years, changing demographics—most notably the strong growth of the Hispanic population in Texas—ultimately will swing the political pendulum back to the Democratic Party. Most Hispanics traditionally have voted for Democrats. Many Hispanics have low incomes, and they strongly support government services such as health care and education as critical to improving their future. They may not consider the Republican-engineered cuts to those services as an overture for their support.

"If you think a (political) party is better off not being dominated by its extremes, and I do, then this is not a good thing for the GOP," wrote William McKenzie, an editorial columnist for *The Dallas Morning News*. He added, "In the short term, the party may win by letting the tea party take over. But, in the end, I think it will limit [its] ability to sustain winning coalitions."[2]

The tea party is not an organized political party. Although comparisons may be drawn to the Religious Right, which helped antiabortion activists and other social conservatives take over Texas Republican Party leadership positions in 1994, the tea party does not seem to be as well organized. Instead, the tea party is a political movement involving a loose coalition of ultraconservatives who may have other differences but generally share a strong disdain for government. Some activists are social conservatives, and some are not. Most members of the tea party movement, though, if they gravitate toward a real political party at all, are likely to be more attracted to the Republican Party or the Libertarian Party, which shares many of their extreme, limited-government views. How the tea party will continue to affect the political landscape—and political party structure—in Texas and across the country remains to be seen. Will it evolve into a new, real political party; will it make permanent changes in the Republican Party; or will it eventually disappear? Time will tell. (See *Talking Texas: The Religious Right and the Tea Party Paint the GOP Landscape.*)

Although relatively few people are active in political parties, some voters are convinced that parties are essential to developing and maintaining a democratic society. A political party, these individuals believe, is one of the few mechanisms available to the general public for reviewing and possibly repudiating the actions of governmental leaders. With all of their weaknesses, including internal dissension, political parties provide a democratic process for choosing leaders and for developing and clarifying policy alternatives. They bring large numbers of people together under one umbrella with some degree of consensus.

For much of the century after the Civil War, Texas was a one-party Democratic state. There was no organized opposition party available to mobilize the interests of those who felt neglected or excluded from the Democratic Party. Electoral politics were based on factions and personalities, and the interests of the lower socioeconomic classes, especially minorities, were blatantly neglected. Since the 1980s, however, Texas, along with many other states that were part of the Confederacy, has witnessed

Talking ★ TEXAS The Religious Right and the Tea Party Paint the GOP Landscape

The Religious Right has long been part of the Texas political landscape. Although its influence was occasionally manifested in conservative Democratic politics, it has found far greater potential for shaping electoral politics in the Republican Party. It has strong religious overtones, is strongly antiabortion, and draws strong support from evangelical groups. Some scholars attribute much of its success to its ability to mobilize voters who had traditionally been inactive and bring them into the Republican Party. The Republicans' difficulty in attracting minority groups gave the social conservative wing greater influence in the party.

By 1994, the Religious Right was instrumental in a takeover by social conservatives of the Republican state convention and the party leadership. The Religious Right also was instrumental in the election of Republican George W. Bush over Democrat Ann Richards in the 1994 gubernatorial race. According to an exit poll of voters reported in *The Dallas Morning News*, 20 percent of the 4.4 million Texans who voted in that election identified themselves as white Christian fundamentalists. Of those, 84 percent said they voted for Bush. They also voted heavily for other Republican candidates.

Republican Governor Rick Perry has actively courted the Religious Right as an important part of his electoral base. In 2005, on the eve of his 2006 reelection campaign, he successfully promoted a state constitutional amendment banning same-sex marriages in Texas, a proposition that attracted large numbers of social conservatives to the polls.

The Religious Right remains influential in Republican primary elections in Texas, but, beginning in 2011, the tea party movement also began to have a huge impact on these elections. There is some common membership between the Religious Right and the tea party, but many members of the tea party movement are not social conservatives. Instead, they are more motivated by their unhappiness with government. It is still unknown if participants in the tea party movement will attempt to take over Republican Party leadership positions in Texas and remain a strong force within the party in future elections.

CRITICAL THINKING QUESTIONS

1. Do you think many moderate Republicans are discouraged from voting in their party's primaries? Why or why not?
2. How representative are Republican primary voters of the state's population as a whole?

the emergence of a strong Republican Party and the decline of the Democratic Party. During this period of change, the electoral power of minorities also has increased dramatically, and minority groups that once were excluded now play a significant role in Democratic Party politics.

Political Parties and a Democratic Society

6.1 Explain what political parties are and why Texas has a two-party system.

As long as a few individuals rule a society and the interests or concerns of the general population have no political significance or influence, leaders have little reason to be concerned with what the masses think or want. But democratic societies are based on the principle that those who rule have a fundamental obligation to consider the preferences, interests, and opinions of those who are governed. Because it is impossible for every individual to participate in every public policy decision, we have chosen to construct representative governments in the United States. We choose individuals to act on our behalf, which makes it necessary

6.1 6.2 6.3 6.4 6.5

political party
A group that seeks to elect public officeholders under its own name.

for us to find mechanisms to ensure that these individuals are selected fairly and are responsive and responsible. We try to accomplish this objective through several means, including elections, interest groups, and political parties.[3]

☐ What Are Political Parties?

Although political parties share their representative roles with other institutions, scholars tend to agree that parties perform critical functions that other institutions cannot. There is considerable debate about formal definitions of parties, their characteristics, organizational and membership criteria, and the relationship of the parties to the governing institutions and the social system.[4] Our purpose is to focus on that part of the debate that would help us understand the political parties in Texas.

We find the party definition given by political scientist Leon D. Epstein to be best suited to Texas. A **political party** is "any group, however loosely organized, seeking to elect governmental officeholders under a given label."[5] Although we tend to think only in terms of Democrat and Republican, other political parties that meet this definition have emerged at both the state and local levels in Texas history. Although political parties share some characteristics of other groups that function in the political arena, they are distinguished from these organizations by their primary preoccupation with contesting elections and the fact that "it is only parties that run candidates on their own labels."[6]

Political parties are complex structures that relate to most other facets of government and politics. V. O. Key suggested that parties are social structures that are best understood from three perspectives: the party in the electorate, the party as an organization, and the party in government. The party in the electorate involves the party's relationship to voters and election activities. The party organization includes a wide range of activities, officials, and workers from the precinct to the state level that are necessary to support the party's structure. The party in government covers the activities of those elected individuals who take office at the local, national, and state levels and carry out the functions of government (see Figure 6–1).

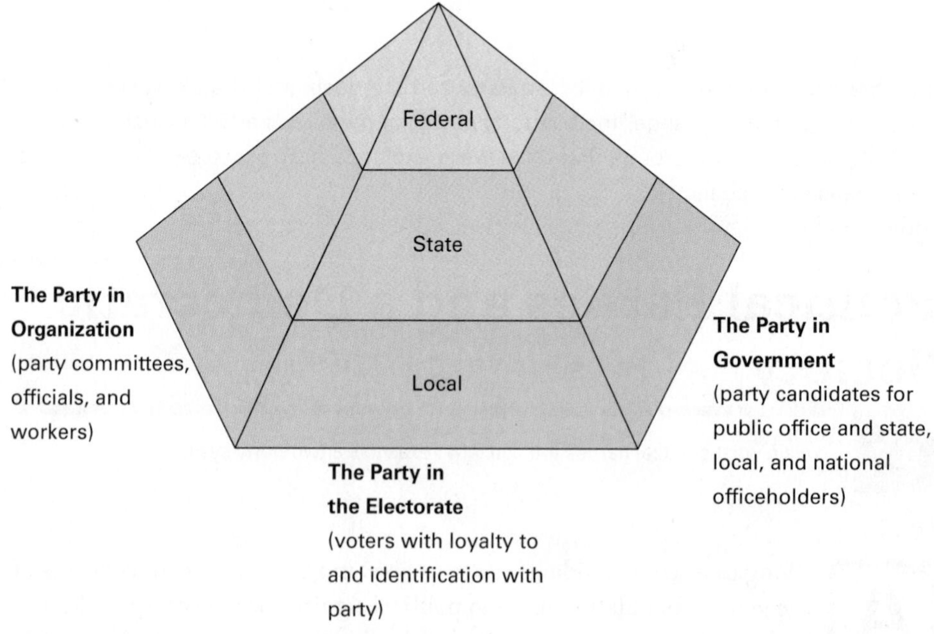

FIGURE 6–1 THE THREE-PART POLITICAL PARTY

V. O. Key put forward the view that parties are social structures best understood from three perspectives: the party in the electorate, the party as an organization, and the party in government. These three functions can be found at the federal, state, and local levels.

Source: Based on V. O. Key, *Politics, Parties, and Pressure Groups* (New York: Cromwell, 1958); and Paul Allen Beck, *Party and Politics in America* (New York: Longman, 1997).

☐ Parties versus Interest Groups

At first glance, political parties and interest groups often appear indistinguishable, but there are differences. Interest groups are concerned with shaping public policy by influencing the actions and decisions of public officials, regardless of the officials' party affiliation. Political parties are structured under a "common label to recruit, nominate, and elect candidates for public office" under specific partisan labels.[7] An interest group usually focuses on a narrow range of policy issues. It can attempt to influence the outcome of elections, but it does not nominate candidates or take responsibility for the day-to-day management of government.[8] These are functions of the political parties and officials elected under their banners.

Studies conducted during the years of one-party Democratic domination in Texas concluded that the interest groups were especially powerful.[9] Some expected the relative power balance between interest groups and parties to change in a two-party Texas, but that remains to be seen.

☐ Two-Party System

Why are there only two major political parties in Texas and the United States? Many other democratic countries have multiparty systems that function quite well. Given the economic, regional, and social diversification of this nation and this state, one might conclude that multiple parties would be better able to translate the interests of their members and supporters into public policy. Yet, the United States has a 200-year history of two-party politics.

By historical accident and certainly not by design, the first national party system in this country was configured around two identifiable coalitions of interests that articulated two alternative views of American government. Some have suggested that there was a natural dualism in American politics and parties aligned along these fundamental differences. By itself, that is not a very convincing argument in that it glosses over complex social and economic divisions among the electorate, but subsequent generations have been politically socialized or educated to think that two parties are inevitable and preferred over any alternatives. Democrats and Republicans can fight over a wide variety of issues, but one will hear spokespersons of both parties extolling the virtues of two-party politics. Democrats and Republicans just do not talk about multiparty politics.

State election laws, which are written by Democratic and Republican legislators, also contribute to the persistence of a two-party system. Unlike the party primaries, where runoffs are held—if necessary—to select a nominee by majority vote, general elections are won by a simple plurality. The candidate who gets more votes than any other candidate, regardless of how many are in the race, is elected. There are no runoffs. Governor Rick Perry was reelected in 2006 with less than a majority over three major opponents—a Democrat and two independents. Governor Dolph Briscoe also won election with less than a majority in 1972, when La Raza Unida candidate Ramsey Muniz siphoned off traditional Democratic votes. Without a runoff, third-party candidates have little chance of winning office over major party nominees. Election laws also impose specific requirements that make it difficult for third parties to get their candidates listed on the ballot.

Most Texans do not have the intense ideological positions that may prompt the formation of a third party. Winning elections takes precedence over ideological purity, and only a relatively few individuals are "true believers" with a highly cohesive, systematic set of beliefs shaping their political behavior.[10] A conservative Republican may support marketplace economics and deregulation but oppose a ban on abortion. A liberal Democrat who is a Catholic may favor greater economic regulation and expanded social services but oppose government programs subsidizing family planning or sex education.

Although class and race shape politics and public policy debates, other issues and concerns cut across these groupings. There is a tendency of one party to attract more

third party
A minor political party. There have been many in Texas over the years, but none has had significant success on a statewide level.

of one group of citizens than the other party, but no party has a monopoly on key segments of the electorate. There are Hispanics, Anglos, and African Americans in both major parties. Labor divides its support between the two parties, as do religious, economic, and educational groups. The multiclass and heterogeneous base of support for the two major parties minimizes the potential for third parties.[11]

☐ Third Parties in Texas

Over the years, Texas has had a number of **third parties**, including Grangers, Populists, Progressives, Socialists, Dixiecrats, the American Independent Party, La Raza Unida, the Natural Law Party, and Libertarians. None has had statewide electoral success. But both the Populists in the 1890s and La Raza Unida in the early 1970s were perceived to be a significant threat to the established state party structure and those who controlled political and economic power.

Major third-party movements surfaced when Texas was still a one-party Democratic state, and, in some respects, they suggested an alternative to the then-weak Republican Party. But from both a state and a national perspective, they were movements of crisis or discontent.[12] The Democratic Party, particularly its conservative wing, either co-opted these movements by making minor public policy concessions to them or by getting restrictive legislation, such as the poll tax, enacted to reduce their electoral base. In some instances, economic recriminations were the price individuals paid for participating in these third-party movements.[13]

La Raza Unida (People United) raised a particularly interesting prospect of a political party built upon an ethnic group. In the 1960s, young Hispanic leaders began to develop student organizations across the state that became the organizational framework on which this party developed.[14] Low-income Hispanics historically had been excluded from any major role in the Democratic Party by restrictive voter registration laws, at-large elections, and racial gerrymandering of political districts designed to minimize Hispanic voting strength. An even more fundamental problem was that state public policy in those days was not responsive to the educational and economic needs of Hispanics because conservative Democrats refused to enact legislation that would benefit that major part of the population.

La Raza Unida, led by Jose Angel Gutierrez and Mario Compean, began in 1969 to organize in Crystal City in Zavala County and then extended its efforts to Dimmit, La Salle, and Hidalgo Counties.[15] Overwhelmingly Hispanic and poor, these counties were characteristic of many South Texas counties, in which the Anglo minority controlled both the political and economic institutions and showed little sensitivity to the needs of low-income residents.

The struggle for access to the ballot box and fair elections in Zavala County parallels the experience of African Americans throughout the South. The Anglo minority used manipulation of the election laws, economic reprisals, and intimidation by the police and Texas Rangers to try to retain control. La Raza Unida, however, won control of local and county offices in Crystal City and Zavala County in 1972, the same year that Ramsey Muniz ran as the party's gubernatorial candidate. During the general election campaign, there was considerable speculation in the press and apprehension among conservative Democrats that La Raza would drain a sufficient number of votes away from Dolph Briscoe, the Democratic nominee, to give Henry (Hank) Grover, a right-wing Republican, the governorship. Briscoe won the election, but without a majority of the votes. The subsequent growth of liberal and minority influence within the Democratic Party, internal dissension within La Raza Unida, and legal problems encountered by Muniz contributed to the demise of this third party after 1978.

The most successful third party in Texas in recent years has been the Libertarian Party. Libertarians have qualified for a place on the ballot in every Texas general election since 1986 because the party has won at least 5 percent of the vote in at least one statewide race during each election year. But the party has never won an elected office in Texas.

In addition to statewide third parties, local political organizations connected to neither the Democratic nor the Republican Parties have been influential in some cities. Elections for city offices are nonpartisan, and most are held during odd-numbered years when there are no state offices on the ballot. Cities such as San Antonio and Dallas developed citizens' associations, which had all of the characteristics of political parties. Many of these local organizations controlled city governments for decades and maintained a virtual monopoly over city elections, but these groups have disappeared in recent years due to the changing economic and population characteristics of the cities they dominated.

The Functions of Political Parties

6.2 Describe the different functions of political parties in Texas.

The more than 25 million people who live in Texas have a wide range of interests and needs that they expect their governments to fulfill. Samuel Huntington, an influential American political scientist, noted that political parties, although they share some characteristics with other social and political institutions, have a unique function in modern societies "to organize participation, to aggregate interests, and to serve as the link between social forces and the government."[16] Simply stated, the political parties link diverse segments of the population to government and thus contribute to the stability and legitimacy of the government.

☐ Recruit and Nominate Candidates

There are thousands of partisan officeholders in Texas, ranging from constable to governor. Except for city, school board, and special district elections, which are nonpartisan, the parties have a virtual monopoly on nominating candidates. It is possible to place an independent on the ballot with no party affiliation, but an independent is not likely to be elected, as Carole Keeton Strayhorn and Kinky Friedman, two highly publicized independents, discovered in the 2006 gubernatorial election. Under Texas law, an individual who runs for an office in the primary election of one of the two major parties wins that party's nomination if he or she receives the majority vote in either the primary or a runoff.

Many local elected positions do not pay well and are not politically attractive, and, in some areas of the state, it is difficult to convince people to run for them. In some counties, the parties aggressively recruit candidates. In other counties, they do not. In some counties, one party may be nothing more than a shell or paper organization. In other counties, the parties are competitive, with sophisticated organizations and paid professional staffs capable of providing prospective candidates with considerable campaign resources. Most candidates, though, are self-recruited, raise their own funds, and hire their own campaign managers.

Parties have not always used the primary to nominate candidates. Prior to reforms enacted in the Terrell Election Laws of 1903 and 1905, party conventions attended by the party faithful nominated candidates.

☐ Contest Elections and Mobilize Voters

Although candidate-centered campaigns built on modern media-oriented technology have reduced the role of the political parties in elections, parties still are the most important institutions for mobilizing voters for specific candidates. Even though most Texans are not active in party affairs, approximately 60 percent of Texas voters identify with either the Republican or the Democratic Party, which have a near monopoly on the votes cast. Given the size of the state, the number of people who participate in elections, the diversity of interests, and the variety of political subcultures within the state, the political parties have had considerable success in mobilizing voters in Texas.[17]

☐ Organize and Manage the Government

Once elected, officeholders use their party affiliations in carrying out their public responsibilities, and with the development of a competitive party system in Texas, the parties have taken on a more significant role in the organization and management of government. Governor Ann Richards, a Democrat, appointed primarily Democrats to hundreds of positions on policymaking state boards and commissions and to vacancies on state courts. Her successors, Republicans George W. Bush and Rick Perry, appointed primarily Republicans.

After taking office in 1979 as Texas's first Republican governor in more than 100 years, Bill Clements appointed many Republicans to state boards, but he also named some Democrats, in part to encourage conservative Democrats to switch parties. His successful strategy was instrumental in adding to the strength and influence of the Republicans (often referred to as the Grand Old Party [GOP]) in Texas.

Despite the growth of the Republican Party and increased GOP representation in the legislature, the organizational structure of the legislature remains bipartisan. In the last quarter of the twentieth century, Democratic leaders built coalitions by appointing Republicans as well as Democrats as chairs of major committees. Republican leaders continued this bipartisan approach.

Although the bipartisan tradition, shaped by political philosophy and local interests cutting across party lines, continues, party caucuses now appear to be more influential in defining policy positions and possibly legislative strategies. Voting along party lines has increased in both the House and the Senate in recent legislative sessions. The ideological positions dividing the two parties in the legislature have been sharper, and there has been less willingness to compromise on selected, major issues. The partisan divisions were particularly evident and strident in 2011, when most Republicans voted for deep budget cuts and most Democrats voted against them. Some legislative battles also have become highly personalized. Trust that had crossed party lines consequently has suffered. If partisanship continues to increase, the majority party in the legislature may begin to use its organizational powers to further reduce the influence of the minority party.

☐ Mediate the Effects of Separation of Powers

The political parties also help bridge the inherent conflicts between the executive and legislative branches of government. The governor needs legislative support for key programs, and, in turn, legislators often need the governor's support and assistance to enact their bills. The chances of such cooperation are enhanced if the governor and a majority of the legislature are of the same party. Republican Governor George W. Bush usually worked well with Democratic lawmakers and shared many of their priorities. But his successor, Governor Rick Perry, has had a stormier relationship with most Democratic legislators. Bush had a more accommodating style than Perry, he was less ideological, and he had to seek Democratic support because key legislative leaders were Democrats and Democrats still held a majority in the Texas House. With Republican majorities in both the House and the Senate, Perry has used partisanship and ideology to marginalize Democratic influence in the legislative process.

☐ Provide Accountability

One of the fundamental problems of a democratic government is how to keep public officeholders responsive and accountable to the people. Elected officials can abuse power. They can engage in graft and corruption. They can pursue policies that conflict with the interests of most of their constituents or pursue foolish or shortsighted policies that produce adverse results. The political parties, in their criticisms of each other and their electoral competitiveness, serve to inform the voters of the shortcomings and failures of elected officials. This process provides alternatives for the voters and gives them an opportunity to "turn the rascals out."

☐ Manage Conflict and Aggregate Interests

The United States generally has had a stable political system that manages conflict among competing groups and interests, and the political parties have played a major role in that process. A party tries to find common ground among varied interests within the electorate so that successful coalitions of voters can be put together to support that party's candidates on Election Day. The Texas Democratic Party, for example, is built on a diverse coalition of African Americans, Hispanics, lower socioeconomic groups, labor, some professionals, and rural interests, to name a few. The Republican Party's base is markedly different from that of the Democrats, but party leaders and candidates also work to build stable coalitions of voters. To build durable support for its candidates, the party must find common interests, structure compromises, and develop accommodations among groups of voters. As interests within the party agree to support a variety of programs and common principles, the party succeeds in resolving conflict.[18]

☐ Set the Policy Agenda

Public policy does not just happen. It is the result of groups organizing around issues and keeping pressure on elected officials to respond. Some issues are long-standing problems that have produced sharp differences of opinion and will take years to resolve. Others emerge rapidly, perhaps as a result of a catastrophic event. A deadly school bus accident in the Rio Grande Valley in 1989, for example, produced an immediate outcry for safety barriers between public roadways and open, water-filled gravel pits like the one in which many young bus passengers drowned. Groups seeking change often try to build support for their programs through the political parties.

The parties also play a role in establishing policy priorities. Candidates running for public office under a party's banner announce their support or opposition to specific policies and, once elected, are expected to use the resources of their offices to try to achieve those objectives. In anticipation of future elections, officeholders will spend much time and energy trying to carry out policies that will solidify their support among the voters.

The Party in the Electorate

6.3 Trace the partisan history of Texas, focusing on the transformation from one-party to two-party politics.

The Texas party system has been restructured by the social and economic changes that the state has experienced since the 1970s. Texas now has a strong Republican Party, and although Democrats still hold many local offices, Republicans dominate statewide politics. From the 1870s through the 1970s, however, Texas was a one-party Democratic state.

☐ One-Party Democratic Politics

Texas's long domination by the Democratic Party can be traced to the period immediately after the Civil War, when the Republican Party was able to capture control of Texas government for a short period. The Reconstruction administration of

Jim Crow laws
Legislation enacted by many states after the Civil War to limit the rights and power of African Americans.

Radical Republican Governor Edmund J. Davis generated strong anti-Republican feelings, and the Republican Party was perceived by most Texans of that era to be the party of conquest and occupation. By the time the Constitution of 1876 was approved, the Republican Party's influence in state politics was negligible. From 1874 to 1961, no Republican won a statewide office in Texas, and in only a few scattered areas were Republicans elected to local offices.

The state voted for Herbert Hoover, the Republican presidential candidate, in 1928. For many Texans, the key issue in that election was that Al Smith, the Democratic nominee from New York, was a Catholic and favored the repeal of Prohibition. Anti-Catholicism and support for Prohibition had deep roots among many fundamentalist religious groups in Texas during that period.

The anti-Republicanism that evolved from the Civil War and Reconstruction, however, is only a partial explanation for the Democratic Party's longtime domination of Texas politics. V. O. Key, in his classic study *Southern Politics,* presents the provocative thesis that Texas politics might be better understood in terms of "modified class politics."[19]

As Texas's conservative agricultural leaders attempted to regain control over the state's political system after Reconstruction, the postwar economic devastation divided Texas along class lines. Small farmers, African Americans, and an emerging urban labor class suffered disproportionately from the depression of this period. They turned their discontent into support for agrarian third parties, particularly the Populist Party, which began to threaten the monopoly of the traditional Texas power structure.

To protect their political power, the established agricultural leaders moved to divide the lower class social groups by directing the discontent of the lower income whites against the African Americans. The rural elites, who manifested traditionalistic political values and wanted to consolidate power in the hands of the privileged few, also created alliances with the mercantile, banking, and emerging industrial leaders, who reflected the individualistic view of a limited government that served to protect their interests. These two dominant forces consolidated political power and merged the politics of race with the politics of economics. Then, for more than eighty years, the conservative Texas establishment pursued policies that best served its interests rather than those of the general population.

The elites were able to institutionalize their control through the adoption of constitutional restrictions and the enactment of legislation designed to reduce the number of voters. The effect of these actions was to reduce the potential of a popular challenge to the establishment's political monopoly.[20] Segregation legislation, called **Jim Crow laws**, stripped African Americans of many economic, social, and political rights and eliminated most of them from the political process. Restrictive voter-registration laws, including a poll tax, which also were designed to exclude African Americans, reduced the participation of low-income whites in the political process as well. In addition, the costs of statewide political campaigns boosted the electoral prospects of candidates financed by the establishment.[21] The result of all this was a one-party Democratic system dominated by influential conservatives.

☐ Factionalism in the Democratic Party

The Texas Democratic Party, however, was not homogeneous. Factions, regional differences, and personal political rivalries caused splits within it. Initially, there were no sustained, identifiable factions, as voting coalitions changed from election to election through much of the first third of the twentieth century. The onset of the Great Depression in 1929, the election of President Franklin Roosevelt in 1932, and the policies of the New Deal reshaped Texas politics in the 1930s.

State party systems are linked to the national party system, and developments in the Texas party system must be understood as part of this relationship. During the period from the Civil War to Franklin Roosevelt's election, the Republican Party dominated the national party system. The elections from 1928 to 1936, however, produced a major national party realignment, and the Democratic Party, capitalizing on the devastation of the Great Depression, replaced the Republicans as the dominant national party.

Roosevelt's administrations articulated and developed a radically different policy agenda than that of the Republican Party. Government was to become a buffer against economic downturns as well as a positive force for change. Under Roosevelt, the regulatory function of the federal government was expanded to exercise control and authority over much of the nation's economy. The federal government also enacted programs such as Social Security, public housing, and labor legislation to benefit lower socioeconomic groups.

These national policies had a direct impact on many Texans and produced an active philosophical split within the Texas Democratic Party that was to characterize Texas politics for the next two generations. A majority of Texas voters supported Roosevelt in his four elections, and the Democratic Party maintained its monopoly over Texas politics. But competing economic interests clearly—and often bitterly—divided Texas Democrats along liberal and conservative lines.

A strong Republican Party did not emerge at this time in Texas or any other southern state because "southern conservative Democratic politicians, who would have been expected to lead such a realignment, or any politicians for that matter, did not relish jumping from a majority-status party to one in the minority."[22] Furthermore, the restrictive voter-registration laws designed to reduce participation by minorities and poor whites continued to limit the electoral prospects of liberal Democrats and allowed conservatives to remain largely in control of the state party: "As long as the conservative Democrats remained dominant, they served as a check on the potential growth of the Republican Party."[23] There also were residual feelings from the Civil War and an antipathy toward the Republican Party that required generations to die off before new voters were willing to change party allegiances.

Despite some liberal successes under Governor James Allred, who was elected in 1934 and again in 1936, the conservative wing of the party prevailed in state elections from the 1940s to the late 1970s. Democratic presidential candidates carried Texas in 1944, 1948, 1960, 1964, 1968, and 1976, even though some of them were too liberal to suit the tastes of the state's conservative Democratic establishment.

By 1941, the conservative Democrats began to lay the groundwork for an all-out attack on the New Deal, or liberal, Democrats in the 1944 presidential election. Roosevelt won the nomination and election for a fourth term, but in Texas there was a bitter intraparty battle between conservative Democrats and liberal Democrats (loyal to Roosevelt) for control of the party organization and delegates to the Democratic National Convention. This election was followed by three successive presidential elections in which conservative Democrats bolted the party to support either third-party candidates or the Republican nominee.[24]

The harbinger of this conservative-liberal split in a statewide political race was the 1946 Democratic gubernatorial race between Homer Rainey and Beauford Jester. Rainey, a former University of Texas (UT) president who had been fired after a bitter fight over the UT governing board's censorship of books and efforts to force him to dismiss liberal faculty members, ran as a liberal, or progressive, candidate supporting academic freedom, labor legislation, and civil rights.

He was challenged by four conservatives who attacked him on the university issue, suggested there was rampant atheism at the university, and unleashed antilabor, anticommunist, and anti–African American attacks. Jester, in a well-financed campaign, eventually defeated Rainey two to one in a runoff. Many of the allegations raised against Rainey were designed to inject demagoguery into the race and divert attention from the substantive social and economic issues of importance to the lower economic classes. The tactics served the economic and political objectives of the state's corporate establishment.

Similar volatile allegations emerged during many subsequent state elections, and the conservative Democrats capitalized on them. In 1944, the U.S. Supreme Court had declared the white primary—party elections in which only whites could vote—unconstitutional in *Smith* v. *Allwright*. Subsequently, a number of candidates appealed to the sentiments of white supremacists. Texas also had its own brand of "McCarthyism" initiated by right-wing groups that alleged communist conspiracies throughout the state.[25]

6.1

6.2

6.3

6.4

6.5

bifactionalism
The presence of two dominant factions organized around regional, economic, or ideological differences within a single political party. For much of the twentieth century, Texas functioned as a one-party system with two dominant factions.

one-party politics
The domination of elections and governmental processes by a single party, which may be split into different ideological, economic, or regional factions. In Texas, the phrase is used to describe the period from the late 1870s to the late 1970s, when the Democratic Party claimed virtually all elected, partisan offices.

□ Modified One-Party Democratic Politics

At first glance, it might appear that the **bifactionalism** in the Democratic Party partially compensated for the lack of a competitive two-party system in Texas. In his study of southern politics, however, V. O. Key argued against that perception. He concluded that factionalism resulted in "no-party politics." Factionalism produces discontinuity in leadership and group support, so that the voter has no permanent reference point from which to judge the performance of the party or selected candidates. Because there are no clear distinctions between who holds power and who does not, the influence of pressure groups increases.[26] In one-party Democratic Texas, state government and public policy were conducive to control by wealthy and corporate interests.

A number of factors tested this bifactional pattern of state Democratic politics, including the national party's increased commitment after 1948 to civil rights and social welfare legislation. These liberal developments alienated segments of the white population and eventually prompted many voters to leave the Democratic Party and to align with the Republicans.

Efforts by Texas oil interests to reestablish state control over the oil-rich tidelands off the Texas coast also played a key role in the demise of **one-party politics** and the development of a two-party system. President Harry Truman, concerned about national security and federal access to these offshore oil resources, refused to accede to state demands and vetoed legislation favorable to Texas oil interests in 1952. That veto prompted a series of maneuvers orchestrated by Democratic Governor Allan Shivers to move the support of conservative Democrats to the Republican Party.

Promising to support the Democratic Party, Shivers and his allies captured control of the Texas delegation to the 1952 Democratic National Convention. The Democrats nominated Adlai Stevenson for president, and the Republicans nominated Dwight Eisenhower. When the Texas Democratic Party convened its fall convention, Shivers succeeded in winning the party's endorsement of Eisenhower. The "Shivercrats," as they were called, were successful in carrying Texas for the Republican nominee. This

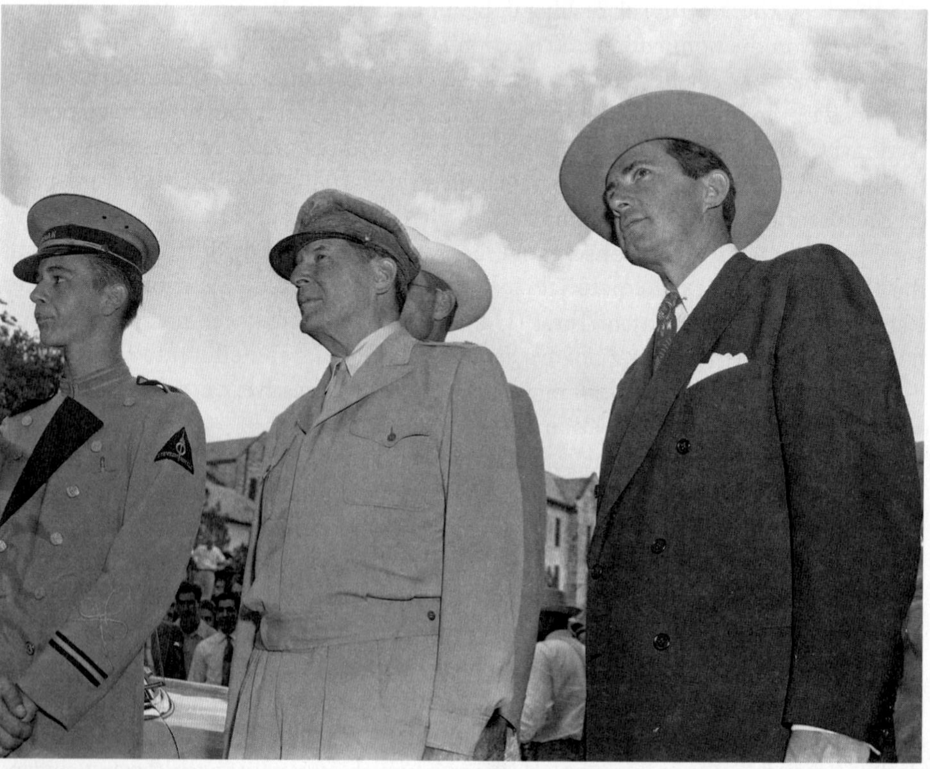

LEADER OF THE SHIVERCRATS

Texas Governor Allan Shivers, right, a leader of conservative Democrats in the 1950s, stands with General Douglas MacArthur, center, in a ceremony greeting the World War II leader in Austin in June 1951.

election helped establish a pattern of Texas retaining its Democratic leanings at the state and local levels but voting for Republicans for president.[27]

For years, the Republican Party's limited presence in Texas basically had been a patronage base for leaders who were more interested in an occasional appointment than in winning elections.[28] The 1952 election marked a change in the party's state leadership and led to efforts to create a party capable of winning local and statewide elections.[29] It took years to develop the necessary organization, but the process would accelerate after the 1964 election.

In 1960, Democrat Lyndon B. Johnson ran both for vice president and for reelection to the U.S. Senate from Texas—a dual candidacy permitted under state law—and won both offices. His Republican opponent in the Senate race was John Tower, a relatively unknown college professor from Wichita Falls, who received 41 percent of the vote. After Johnson won the vice presidency and resigned from the Senate, a special election to fill the Senate seat was called in 1961. It attracted seventy-one candidates, including Tower, who defeated conservative Democrat William Blakely with 50.6 percent of the vote in a runoff.[30]

There is some evidence that liberal Democrats, in retaliation for having been locked out of the power centers of their party and in anticipation of an ideological realignment of the party system, supported Tower in this election.[31] The *Texas Observer*, an influential liberal publication, endorsed Tower with an argument for a two-party system. "How many liberals voted for Tower will never be known, nor will it be known how many 'went fishing' (and didn't vote)," wrote Republican campaign consultant and author John R. Knaggs, who was a volunteer worker for Tower during the 1961 race. He added, "But in reviewing Tower's razor-thin 10,343-vote margin out of 886,091 cast, it must be concluded that the liberal element was pivotal in electing the first Republican United States senator to represent Texas during the twentieth century."[32] Texas Republicans, incidentally, had not even held a primary in 1960.

Tower was reelected in 1966, 1972, and 1978, but no other Texas Republican won a statewide office until 1978, when Bill Clements was elected governor. Nevertheless, many students of Texas politics regard Tower's election in 1961 as a key factor in the development of the state's **two-party system**.[33]

two-party system
A political system in which each of the two dominant parties has the possibility of winning national, statewide, or county elections.

Although Republicans made some gains in suburban congressional districts and local elections in the 1960s—including the election to Congress of a Houston Republican named George Herbert Walker Bush—the numbers were inconsequential. Most significant election battles continued to take place for a while longer within the Democratic Party.

The only liberal Democratic candidate who was successful on a statewide basis during this period was Ralph Yarborough. After several losing campaigns, he was elected to the U.S. Senate in a special election in 1957 and held that office until his defeat in 1970 by conservative Democrat Lloyd Bentsen. Yarborough, who had a distinguished legislative career, was "the mainstay of the liberal wing until his primary defeat in 1970 and comeback failure in 1972."[34]

Despite some indications of an energized Republican Party and the increased mobilization of minorities in support of the liberal wing of the Democratic Party, conservative Democrats controlled state politics until 1978. Conservatives dominated the nominating process in the Democratic primaries through well-financed and well-executed campaigns. In the general elections, liberal Democrats had little choice but to vote for a conservative Democrat against a candidate who was usually perceived to be an even more conservative Republican.[35] During this period of Democratic factionalism, Texas Democrats played major roles in the U.S. Congress and national politics. Sam Rayburn, the longtime speaker of the U.S. House of Representatives and regarded as one of a handful of great speakers in U.S. history, came from a rural congressional district in Northeast Texas. Before moving on to the vice presidency and then the White House, Lyndon B. Johnson was majority leader in the U.S. Senate. Other members of Congress from Texas, as a result of the seniority system used in the selection of committee chairs in the U.S. Congress, had influential committee posts and used their positions to funnel large sums of federal dollars to the state.

realignment
A major shift in political party support or identification, which usually occurs around a critical election. In Texas, this was a gradual transformation from a one-party system dominated by Democrats to a two-party system in which Republicans became the dominant party statewide.

□ Two-Party Politics in Texas

On the national level, **realignment** of political parties often is associated with a critical election in which economic or social issues cut across existing party allegiances and produce a dramatic, permanent shift in party support and identification.[36] Realignment did not occur in one single election in Texas, but over several decades. The early stages of this transformation often are hard to identify, but by the mid-1990s, it was clear that one-party politics had given way to a two-party system.

The civil rights movement was a major factor contributing to the transformation of the state's party system. African Americans and Hispanics went to federal court to attack state laws promoting segregation and restricting minority voting rights. Successful lawsuits were brought against the white primary, the preprimary endorsement, the poll tax, and racial gerrymandering of political districts. Then minorities turned to the U.S. Congress for civil rights legislation, a process that produced the 1965 Voting Rights Act, which Congress extended to Texas after 1975. African Americans and Hispanics challenged electoral systems throughout the state using federal law and a growing body of U.S. Supreme Court decisions prohibiting the dilution of minority voting power in the drawing of congressional, legislative, and other political districts. Minorities were successful in their long, tortuous effort to increase electoral equity. But the creation of more political districts from which African Americans and Hispanics could win election also resulted in the creation of more districts from which Republicans could win public office. As the number of minority elected officials increased, the number of Republican elected officials also increased.

Economic factors also contributed to two-party development. African Americans and Hispanics are disproportionately low-income populations and generally support such governmental services as public housing, public health care, day care, and income support. Many people associate these policies with the liberal wing of the Democratic Party. Minority organizations made concerted efforts to register, educate, and mobilize the people in their communities. Approximately 90 percent of the African American vote in Texas is Democratic, and although there is less cohesion among Hispanic voters, approximately 75 percent of the Hispanic vote goes to Democrats. As the numerical strength of minorities increased, conservative Anglo Democrats found their position within the party threatened and began to look to the Republican Party as an alternative.

The large numbers of people who migrated to Texas from other states, particularly when the Sun Belt economy of the 1970s and early 1980s was booming and many northern industrial states struggled, also contributed to the two-party system. Many of these new arrivals were Republicans from states with strong Republican parties, and many of them settled in high-income, suburban, Anglo areas in Texas.[37] Other significant factors included President Ronald Reagan's popularity in the 1980s and the 1978 election of Republican Governor Bill Clements, who encouraged many conservative Democratic officeholders to switch parties. Some scholars see an earlier outline of these changes in the so-called "southern strategy" of Richard Nixon in 1968. Simply stated, the national Republican Party made calculated efforts to peel off whites using wedge issues that were likely to resonate within the southern political culture.[38]

During the 1970s, the Texas Republican Party had an organizational edge on the Democrats. As the minority party, the only way the GOP could successfully challenge the Democrats' numerical strength was to develop local party organizations capable of mobilizing membership, providing continuity between elections, and providing candidates with campaign resources. After the defeat of Republican presidential nominee Barry Goldwater in 1964, the national Republican Party began rebuilding using modern campaign technology. The national party assisted state parties, and Texas Republicans applied the new campaign technology to state and local elections. Moreover, Republican candidates appeared to more readily adapt technology to their campaigns than did the Democrats. For a short period in the late 1980s and early 1990s, Texas Democrats tried to catch up by using money provided by the national party organization, but the Democratic leadership seemed incapable of making maximum use of these resources to reenergize state and local party organizations.

Other events of the 1970s and the 1980s demonstrated that the transformation of the Texas party system was well on its way. After the Sharpstown stock fraud scandal rocked state government in 1971, the Texas House elected a liberal Democrat, Price Daniel Jr., as speaker in 1973. Three other moderate-to-liberal Democrats were elected to statewide office in the early 1970s: Bob Armstrong as land commissioner in 1970, John Hill as attorney general in 1972, and Bob Bullock as comptroller in 1974. These men initiated and carried out policies that were more equitable in the treatment of lower socioeconomic Texans.[39]

In 1978, John Hill defeated Governor Dolph Briscoe, a conservative, in the Democratic primary, and Bill Clements, then a political unknown, defeated Ray Hutchison, a former state legislator who had the endorsement of most Republican state leaders, in the Republican primary. Hill neglected to mend fences with conservative Democrats, and Clements, a multimillionaire, used much of his own money on an effective media campaign to defeat Hill for governor by 17,000 votes in the general election. Four years later, Clements lost to Democratic Attorney General Mark White, but in 1986 he returned to defeat White in an expensive, bitter campaign.

In the 1982 election, Democratic candidates who were considered liberal won additional statewide offices. Ann Richards was elected state treasurer; Jim Mattox, attorney general; Jim Hightower, agriculture commissioner; and Garry Mauro, land commissioner.

The 1990 election further demonstrated how far the realignment process had gone. Democratic gubernatorial nominee Ann Richards defeated conservative businessman Clayton Williams, who had spent $6 million of his own money to win the Republican primary. But Republican Kay Bailey Hutchison was elected state treasurer, and Republican Rick Perry unseated Hightower to become agriculture commissioner. Republicans also retained one of the U.S. Senate seats from Texas when Phil Gramm easily won reelection to the seat once held by John Tower, and the GOP claimed eight of the twenty-seven congressional seats that Texas then had in Congress.

In a special election in 1993 to fill the U.S. Senate seat vacated by Democrat Lloyd Bentsen when President Bill Clinton appointed him secretary of the treasury, Kay Bailey Hutchison defeated Democrat Bob Krueger to give the Republicans both U.S. Senate seats from Texas. Hutchison easily won reelection in 1994, despite a political and legal controversy over her administration of the state treasurer's office.

Also in 1994, Republican nominee George W. Bush, the son of former President George H. W. Bush and a future president himself, unseated Governor Ann Richards. Republicans that year also captured four other statewide offices that had been held by Democrats, marking the most statewide gains by Texas Republicans in any single election since Reconstruction. Meanwhile, Republicans also were increasing their share of seats in the Texas legislature. In the same election, Republicans posted sweeping victories across the country, cashing in on anger over President Bill Clinton's policies, and gaining control of both houses of Congress and a majority of the nation's governorships.

☐ Republican Dominance

The political transformation of Texas accelerated even more in 1996, when Republicans swept all statewide offices on the general election ballot and captured a majority of the state Senate for the first time since Reconstruction. Republican presidential nominee Bob Dole even carried the Lone Star State, despite a poor national showing against President Clinton. Republicans also increased their numbers in the Texas House and in the Texas congressional delegation. When the electoral dust had cleared, Republicans held twenty of Texas's twenty-nine statewide elected offices, including the top three. That number increased to twenty-one in 1997, when Presiding Judge

6.1

6.2

6.3

6.4

6.5

Michael McCormick of the Texas Court of Criminal Appeals switched from the Democratic to the Republican Party.

Lieutenant Governor Bob Bullock and Attorney General Dan Morales, both Democrats, chose not to seek reelection or any other office in 1998, and Republicans cashed in on the opportunity. With Governor Bush winning reelection in a landslide, Republicans again swept all statewide offices. A few weeks after the 1998 election, the GOP secured all statewide offices in Texas for the first time since Reconstruction when Texas Supreme Court Justice Raul A. Gonzalez, a Democrat, retired in midterm and was replaced by Bush's Republican appointee. Republicans did not capture control of the Texas House, but they picked up four seats to narrow the Democratic margin to six seats. In the governor's race, Bush won 69 percent of the vote against Democratic challenger Garry Mauro, the longtime land commissioner.

Democrats fielded candidates for only three of the nine statewide offices up for election in 2000. They lost all three but held their ground in state legislative races. Republicans also swept all statewide races in 2002, including Governor Rick Perry's victory over Democratic nominee Tony Sanchez and former Texas Attorney General John Cornyn's victory over former Dallas Mayor Ron Kirk in a race to succeed retiring U.S. Senator Phil Gramm. Republicans also finally gained control of the Texas House of Representatives in 2002, capturing 88 of the 150 seats after the Legislative Redistricting Board in 2001 had drawn new districts that favored Republicans. In addition, the GOP increased its margin in the state Senate by winning nineteen of the thirty-one seats. All statewide elected officials remained Republican.

The statewide losses in 2002 were particularly disappointing for Democratic leaders, who had carefully assembled a racially diverse ticket with an eye toward increasing minority turnout. Kirk, the U.S. Senate candidate, was African American, and Sanchez, a wealthy businessman from Laredo, was Hispanic. The Democratic nominee for lieutenant governor, John Sharp, a former state comptroller, was Anglo. Former Texas Attorney General Dan Morales unexpectedly challenged Sanchez in the Democratic primary. The race was historic because it was the first gubernatorial contest in Texas between two Hispanics, and it was extremely contentious. Most party leaders supported Sanchez because the party was banking on his wealth to help finance the Democrats' general election campaign.

Republicans achieved still another long-sought goal in 2004—a majority of Texas's congressional delegation—after the legislature, in a bitter partisan fight in 2003, redrew congressional district boundaries to favor GOP candidates.

Republican Governor Rick Perry was reelected in 2006 over three major opponents, including Democratic nominee Chris Bell, a former congressman and former city councilman from Houston. Republican Comptroller Carole Keeton Strayhorn and musician-author Kinky Friedman challenged Perry as independents. Republicans also won all other statewide offices against a Democratic ticket that was less experienced and more poorly financed than the party's slate of candidates in 2002. Texas Republicans in 2006 kept their majorities in the legislature and in the congressional delegation.

Republicans also won all statewide races in 2008 and 2010, including Rick Perry's reelection to a third full term as governor in 2010. A strong Republican sweep that same year, boosted by the tea party movement, gave Republicans a 101 to 49 supermajority in the Texas House. Republicans had a 19 to 12 majority in the state Senate and held 23 of Texas's 32 seats in the U.S. House after the 2010 elections.

The GOP also has made significant gains across Texas at the county level. In 1974, Republicans held 53 county offices but had claimed 1,862 by 2008, paralleling the dramatic statewide realignment. The Texas Republican Party reported the election of 234 additional Republicans to county offices in 2010 (see Table 6–1).

☐ Changing Party Identification

The changes in party affiliations over the past forty years illustrate Texas's political realignment. Belden Associates of Dallas reported in a 1952 survey that 66 percent of Texans called themselves Democrats, and only 6 percent claimed to be Republicans, a

TABLE 6–1 GROWTH OF REPUBLICAN OFFICEHOLDERS IN TEXAS, 1974–2010

Year	U.S. Senate	Other Statewide	U.S. Congress	Texas Senate	Texas House	County Offices*	District Offices**	Total
1974	1	0	2	3	16	53	-	75
1976	1	0	2	3	19	67	-	92
1978	1	1	4	4	22	87	-	119
1980	1	1	5	7	35	166	-	215
1982	1	0	5	5	36	191	79	317
1984	1	0	10	6	52	287	90	446
1986	1	1	10	6	56	410	94	578
1988	1	5	8	8	57	485	123	687
1990	1	6	8	8	57	547	170	797
1992	1	8	9	13	58	634	183	906
1994	2	13	11	14	61	734	216	1051
1996	2	18	13	17	68	938	278	1334
1998	2	27	13	16	72	1,108	280	1,518
2000	2	27	13	16	72	1,233	336	1,699
2002	2	27	15	19	88	1,443	362	1,956
2004	2	27	21	19	87	1,608	392	2,156
2006	2	27	19	20	82	1,814	379	2,343
2008	2	27	20	19	76	1,862	379	2,385
2010	2	27	23	19	101	-	385	-

*County offices include county judge, commissioners, constables, county attorneys, county clerks, district clerks, county judicial positions, treasurers, surveyors, justices of the peace, sheriffs, tax assessor/collectors, and other local offices.
**District offices include court of appeals, district judges, and district attorneys.
- Incomplete data

SOURCE: Republican Party of Texas.

pattern that changed little from 1952 to 1964.[40] During the next decade, Republican Party identification increased to 16 percent and Democratic Party identification declined to 59 percent (see Figure 6–2). Between 1975 and 1984, a dramatic decline in voter identification with the Democratic Party and a significant increase in Republican Party identification took place. By 2012, approximately 33 percent of Texas voters called themselves Republicans and 33 percent identified as Democrats (see *Talking Texas: Where Have All the Yellow Dogs Gone?*). The remainder called themselves independents, third-party affiliates, or undecided. Of the independents, more than half leaned toward the Republican Party, illustrating reasons for Republicans electoral successes.[41] This shift in party identification is further proof that Texas, at least on a statewide basis, is now Republican dominant, but party identification does not always translate into winning elected offices at the county level.

A large number of voters identify themselves as independents. Independents do not have their own party, and their choices in most elections are limited to candidates from the two major parties. Surveys of Texas voters, moreover, suggest that most self-proclaimed independents tend to vote for Republican candidates.[42]

ticket splitting
The decisions of voters to divide their votes among candidates of more than one political party in the same election.

Ticket splitting, a practice associated with the realignment process, has been common in recent Texas elections. It explains, in part, why Democrats have been able to keep most local offices despite Republican sweeps statewide. Many Texans cast their votes selectively as they go down the general election ballot.

Voting differences and party identification sometimes are based on gender. Nationally, differences in the voting patterns of men and women have been significant. These differences usually are not as pronounced in Texas politics but on occasions, they have been. The gubernatorial election of 1990 produced one of the largest gaps between women and men in recent Texas political history. According to surveys

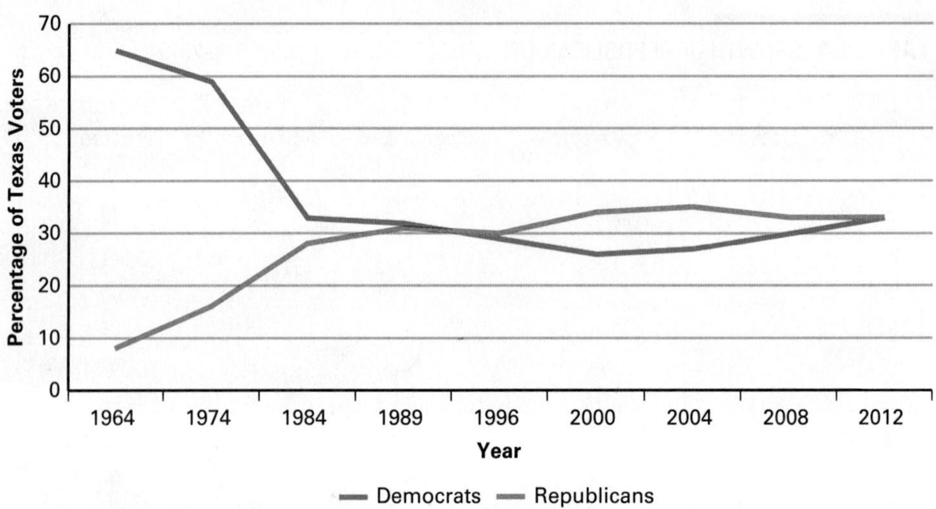

FIGURE 6–2 CHANGING PARTY AFFILIATION IN TEXAS, 1964–2012

Although Republicans hold all statewide offices and control the legislature, this figure shows a near parity between Republicans and Democrats in Texas. Many independent voters, who are believed to account for about one-third of the state electorate, split their ballots on Election Day, voting mainly for Republicans in statewide races and for Democrats for many county offices.

Source: The Texas Polls, 1993–2004; Pew Research Center, "Fewer Voters Identify as Republicans," March 20, 2008; and University of Texas/*The Texas Tribune* Poll, February 2012.

of voters leaving the polls, Democrat Ann Richards enjoyed a lead of as much as 20 percent among women voters in some precincts in her defeat of Republican Clayton Williams. Part of that difference was believed to have been attributable to Williams's clumsy outspokenness, including a rape joke gaffe, which prompted a negative reaction among women across the state. Voter polls in the 1994 gubernatorial race indicated that Richards held a more modest lead among women over Republican George W. Bush, who unseated her.[43]

Talking ★ TEXAS Where Have All the Yellow Dogs Gone?

For a long-time Democrat (that is, a person 50 or older), there is a bit of nostalgia when someone asks, "Where have all the yellow dogs gone?" To a newcomer to the state, this probably conjures up an image of a mangy, brownish-yellow mutt that is used for raccoon hunting or running the dogs at night while its keeper drinks hard liquor around the campfire. But to a real Democrat, it is a code word for those party members, often white conservatives, who swore by the phrase, "I'd vote for a yellow dog if he ran on the Democratic ticket." Moreover, those "yellow dogs" also would encourage voters to "pull one lever"—that is, vote straight Democratic.

Yellow-dog, one-party voters are a dying breed. Historically, there were counties in Texas that had never elected a Republican to local office. Some had never had a Republican Party organization or seen a Republican challenge a Democrat in a local election. With the transformation of the state to one-party Republican dominance, there are fewer and fewer yellow dogs. Franklin County, which is in deep East Texas, had not elected a member of the GOP from 1875 to 2000. But in 2002, three Republicans won elections to local offices.[a]

So, where have all the yellow dogs gone? The answer is rather clear. Many of them have died. Many others have converted to the Republican Party and are now voting the straight GOP ticket. Some of those yellow dogs have now become pedigree Republicans.

CRITICAL THINKING QUESTIONS

1. **Should one-party, straight-ticket voting be abolished? Should voters have to cast individual votes for candidates on the ballot? Why or why not?**
2. **Why was it unfashionable or objectionable for so many years to vote for Republicans in many parts of conservative, rural Texas?**

[a] John Williams, *The Houston Chronicle Online*, November 17, 2002.

There also is evidence that older and younger voters in Texas view the world in markedly different ways, a difference reflected in how they vote. According to survey data, younger voters, for example, are more tolerant of candidates who have experienced problems with alcohol or drug abuse. Many younger voters also are more tolerant of various lifestyles, which can create problems for conservatives who campaign against homosexuality and gay rights. Unlike older voters, fewer 18- to 29-year-olds express any party identification. Moreover, younger people vote at much lower rates than older citizens.[44]

In 1992, Republican President George H. W. Bush carried Texas while losing his reelection bid to Democrat Bill Clinton. That election marked the first time a Democratic candidate won the White House without winning Texas's electoral votes, a feat that Clinton repeated in 1996 and Barack Obama accomplished in 2008. The 1992 and 1996 elections also included the independent candidacy of Ross Perot, a billionaire computer magnate from Dallas, who attracted a lot of attention but finished third in Texas each time, as he did nationwide.

☐ Differences between Republicans and Democrats

Social scientists make a strong effort to classify voters according to party identification and voting patterns. When reviewing a survey or a poll, it is critical to know the specific population from which the sample is drawn. A pollster could sample all Texans who are age 18 and older or could focus on registered voters. If a pollster were trying to determine the relationship of party identification with actual voting, samples would be drawn from those who are likely to vote in an upcoming election. And, of course, one could use exit polling on Election Day to ascertain party identification and voting preferences. One is likely to reach a variety of conclusions about partisan preferences, depending on the group that is sampled.

As noted thus far, we have relied primarily on election results to support our conclusion that Texas has become a Republican-dominant state, but there have been recent Democratic victories at the county level as well. Although polls generally indicate that the state is split one-third Republican, one-third Democratic, and one-third independent in party identification, most individuals who call themselves "independent" vote for Republican candidates, especially in statewide elections. In some areas of the state, Democrats do well at the polls and win legislative and county offices. The successes of Republicans are based to a large extent on independents who lean toward the Republican Party. What is one to make of this when Texas voters continue to elect Republicans to all statewide offices and in 2008 cast 56 percent of their ballots for Republican presidential nominee John McCain and only 44 percent for Democratic winner Barack Obama?

There are many exceptions in each party, but some broad generalizations about differences between Democrats and Republicans can be made. The Texas Republican Party is composed disproportionately of people who are college educated, higher income, Anglos, newcomers to Texas, and suburban residents. More men identify with the Republican Party than women, and support for the Republican Party increases with age. Republicans tend to classify themselves as conservative to moderate with significant numbers reporting frequent church attendance.

Democrats are more likely to have lower incomes and to be younger, African American or Hispanic, and less educated. More women identify themselves as Democrats than do men. Democrats tend to classify themselves as moderate to liberal and attend church less regularly.[45]

☐ Are Parties Realigning or Slowly Disappearing?

Although the party system has been transformed in Texas, there is considerable disagreement about what these changes will mean in the long run. V. O. Key, writing in the 1940s, concluded that race was becoming less important and the electorate was

dealignment
A view that the party system is breaking up and the electoral influence of political parties is being replaced by interest groups, the media, and well-financed candidates who use their own media campaigns to dominate the nomination and election process.

party activist
Member of a political party involved in organizational and electoral activities.

dividing along liberal and conservative lines. He concluded that a "modified class politics seems to be evolving."[46] More than a half century later, the parties appear, in part, to be aligning around economic issues that are manifested in liberal and conservative philosophies, but issues involving race continue to shape attitudes.

Chandler Davidson argues that "the Republican Party's hard-line racial policy" attracted large numbers of conservative Democrats as well as supporters of George Wallace, the conservative American Independent Party's 1968 presidential nominee, and "strengthened the commitment of African Americans and Mexican Americans to the Democratic Party."[47] Some Texas African Americans and Hispanics, primarily well-educated, well-to-do individuals, have become Republicans. But the vast majority remain Democrats, and Sunday morning visits to African American churches in Houston and Dallas and appearances at South Texas *pachangas* (cookouts) are practically mandatory for Democratic candidates serious about winning statewide office.

Seeking to expand the Republican Party's base, Governor George W. Bush made a strong appeal to Hispanics during his 1998 reelection campaign and, according to some estimates, was rewarded with about 40 percent of the Hispanic vote. Some Republican strategists have been arguing for years that the GOP must strengthen its appeal to the growing Hispanic population—and chip away at Hispanics' traditional support for the Democratic Party—if the GOP is to continue to maintain its control over state politics. Anglo Protestants, who form the core of the Republican Party, are declining in proportion to the increased number of Hispanics in Texas. To maintain dominance, it has been argued, Republicans must embrace issues that are central to Hispanic voting interests, such as improved health care and educational opportunities. According to this argument, they also may need to develop a more tolerant attitude toward immigration. Both parties will battle for the Hispanic vote over the next two decades. Republicans also have spoken about the need to appeal to African American Texans who share their core values, but the GOP has had little success attracting African Americans from the Democratic Party.

An alternative view to realignment is that the party system is undergoing disintegration or **dealignment**.[48] This view is supported by the decline of the parties' electoral functions, their general organizational weaknesses, and voter indifference toward partisan labels, as manifested in ticket splitting and the increasing numbers of people calling themselves independents. Since the 1980s, some 40 percent of Texans of voting age have not identified themselves as either Democrats or Republicans. According to these arguments, political parties no longer perform their traditional functions because other institutions—including interest groups, the media, and the candidates themselves—control the political process, and the number of persons who identify with neither party will continue to grow.

A well-financed candidate, for example, can ignore party leaders and still win a party's nomination by using effective campaign and media tactics in the primary. Interest groups, which offer sophisticated organizations to shape public policy, may provide more access to policymakers than do the parties, and the media play a much greater role in screening candidates and shaping public opinion. The dealignment arguments, however, were more prominent in the last two decades of the twentieth century. Although they still may have some validity, other evidence suggests that the party doomsayers were somewhat premature.

A contrary view in Texas is that the parties are undergoing a process of revitalization, attempting to reclaim basic party functions, especially in the areas of elections and campaigns.[49] **Party activists** are attempting to adapt modern campaign technology to the party organization. If the parties are able to provide strong support in fund-raising, campaign advertising, phone banks, and other campaign functions, some candidates likely will become more dependent on the party organization. The massive infusion of money from corporations, labor unions, and other interest groups into the state and local party organizations by the national parties was one factor in this new vitality of state political parties. There also has been considerable collaboration between the state parties and the national parties in voter identification, voter mobilization, funding of campaigns, and organizational development. Increasingly, money is coming from various sources to support the parties' efforts to provide increased campaign services.

precinct
A specific, local voting area created by county commissioners court. The state election code outlines detailed requirements for drawing up these election units.

The Party Organization

6.4 Outline the basic structure of the party organization in Texas, from the precinct level to the state convention.

precinct chair
A local officer in a political party who presides over the precinct convention and serves on the party's county executive committee. Voters in each precinct elect a chair in the party's primary election.

To carry out their functions, the two major parties in Texas have developed permanent and temporary organizations, structured by state law, state and national party rules, and a series of court decisions protecting voters' rights. Party organizations are built around geographic election districts.[50] Party organization, however, has no hierarchical arrangement. V. O. Key described the party structure as a "system of layers of organization," with each level—county, state, and federal—concentrating on the elections within its jurisdiction.[51] There is a great deal of autonomy at each party level, based on the limited sanctions that one level can impose on another, and the fact that each level of the party needs the others to carry out electoral functions.[52]

county executive committee
A panel responsible on the local level for the organization and management of a political party's primary election. It includes the party's county chair and each precinct chair.

county chair
The presiding officer of a political party's county executive committee. Voters in the party primary elect him or her by countywide election.

There are no membership requirements for either the Democratic or the Republican Party. Party members do not have to pay dues, attend meetings, campaign for candidates, or make contributions. When people register to vote in Texas, they are not required to state their party preference as they do in many other states. The right to participate in a party's electoral and nominating activities is based simply on voting in that party's primary election. When a person votes in one of the major party primaries, his or her voter registration card is stamped "Democrat" or "Republican."

☐ The Permanent Organizations

Election **precincts**—an estimated 8,150 in Texas in 2010—are created by the county commissioners of each of Texas's 254 counties. Population, political boundaries, and available voting sites help determine the number of precincts within a county. Voters in each precinct elect a **precinct chair** in the party primary (see Figure 6–3). Any eligible voter within the precinct can file for this position, and the names of write-in candidates can be added to the ballot. (One of this book's authors was elected a precinct chair with two write-in votes.)

Although there are many contested precinct chair elections, often no one runs for the office, leaving many precinct vacancies throughout the state. This problem has contributed to the parties' organizational decline. The chair calls the precinct convention (which is discussed later) to order and serves as a member of the county executive committee. Precinct chairs also can mobilize party supporters to vote. Many people do nothing with the position; others contribute much time and energy and have successfully delivered the precinct for their party's candidates in the general election. In some counties, the precinct chair is responsible for staffing the polling places on Election Day, but increasingly the county election administrator does this.

The second level of the party organization is the **county executive committee**, which includes each precinct chair and the **county chair**, who is elected to a two-year term by primary voters countywide. A major responsibility of the county chair and the executive committee is the organization and management of the primary election in their county. The county executive committee accepts filings by candidates for local offices and also is responsible for planning the county or district conventions. Funds for the management of primary elections are provided to the county party by the state through the secretary of state's office.

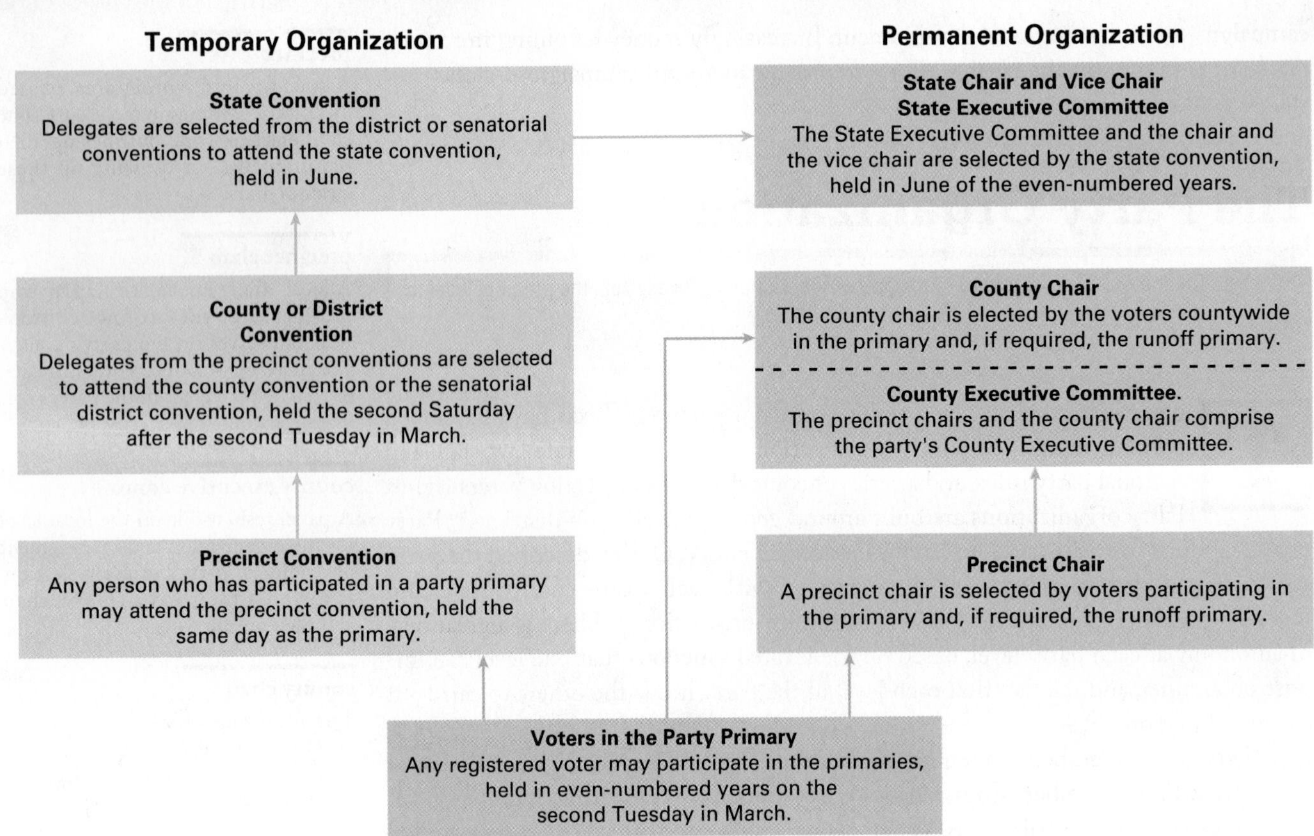

Temporary Organization
Permanent Organization
State Convention
Delegates are selected from the district or senatorial conventions to attend the state convention, held in June.
State Chair and Vice Chair
State Executive Committee
The State Executive Committee and the chair and the vice chair are selected by the state convention, held in June of the even-numbered years.
County or District Convention
Delegates from the precinct conventions are selected to attend the county convention or the senatorial district convention, held the second Saturday after the second Tuesday in March.
County Chair
The county chair is elected by the voters countywide in the primary and, if required, the runoff primary.
County Executive Committee.
The precinct chairs and the county chair comprise the party's County Executive Committee.
Precinct Convention
Any person who has participated in a party primary may attend the precinct convention, held the same day as the primary.
Precinct Chair
A precinct chair is selected by voters participating in the primary and, if required, the runoff primary.
Voters in the Party Primary
Any registered voter may participate in the primaries, held in even-numbered years on the second Tuesday in March.

FIGURE 6–3 ORGANIZATION OF TEXAS POLITICAL PARTIES

The rules of both Texas political parties provide for a permanent organization that serves to carry out party functions throughout the year. The party rules also provide for a temporary organization that functions for a short period of time during the nominating process.

state executive committee
The statewide governing board of a political party. It includes a man and a woman elected by party members from each of the thirty-one state senatorial districts and the state chair and vice chair.

state chair and vice chair
The two top state leaders of a political party, one of whom must be a woman. Delegates to the party's state convention select them every two years.

County committees may be well organized and actively work to carry out a wide range of organizational and electoral activities, or they may meet irregularly and have difficulty getting a quorum of members to attend. The county chair is an unpaid position. Party organizations in some counties have successful fund-raising operations, and they support a party headquarters, retain professional staff, and are engaged in various party activities between elections.

The Texas Election Code provides for other district committees that correspond to a state senatorial, state representative, judicial, or congressional district. District committees that are solely within a county include precinct chairs, whereas multicounty district committees include representatives of all affected counties. These committees select candidates for vacancies in local and district offices if they occur between the primary and general election.

At the state level, a party's permanent organization is the **state executive committee**, which has sixty-four members, including the party's **state chair and vice chair**. When the parties meet in their biennial state conventions, delegation caucuses from each of the thirty-one state senatorial districts select two committee members—a man and a woman. The state chair and the vice chair, one of whom must be a woman, also are selected by the convention. The two top state party leaders and other executive committee members serve two-year, unpaid terms.

Statewide candidates file for office with the executive committee, which also is responsible for planning and organizing the party's state convention and helps raise funds for the ongoing operations of the party. The committee serves to establish party policy, but day-to-day party operations are entrusted to the party's executive director and professional staff. The Texas Democratic Party and the Texas Republican Party have permanent staffs and headquarters in Austin.

Sometimes, the state committees are highly effective with strong, energetic leadership that carries over into the development and retention of a competent professional staff.

At other times, however, the state committees have been divided along ideological, factional, or personal lines, producing conflict that sometimes has become open warfare. In those instances, a party finds it difficult to raise funds, maintain a highly qualified staff, and carry out its electoral functions.

platform
A set of principles or positions on various issues adopted by a political party at its state or national convention.

Religious Right
An ultraconservative political faction that draws considerable support from fundamentalist religious groups and economic conservatives.

☐ The Temporary Organizations

The temporary organizations of the political parties are the series of conventions that are held every two years, beginning on the day of the party primaries. They are particularly significant in presidential election years because they—together with the presidential preference primary—help select the state's delegates to the national party conventions, which nominate the presidential candidates. The convention system also helps organize the permanent party structure and brings party activists together to share common political concerns and shape party policies. Most Texans, however, have little knowledge of the convention system, and few participate in it.

☐ The Precinct Convention

Anyone who votes in a party primary, normally held on the first Tuesday in March of even-numbered years, is eligible to participate in that party's precinct convention, normally held in the same place as the primary after voting stops at 7 P.M. (In 2012, because of lawsuits over the redistricting of legislative and congressional districts, the primaries were delayed until May 29. Temporary delegate selection procedures, which differ from what we discuss here, were put in place for that year alone).

After the convention is organized and selects its permanent officers—chair, vice chair, and secretary—it begins its real business, the selection of delegates and alternate delegates to the county or senatorial district convention. Each precinct is assigned a specific number of delegates, based on the party's voting strength. Since 1972, the Democrats have used complex procedures designed to ensure broad-based delegate representation by ethnicity, gender, and age. A precinct convention also can adopt resolutions to be submitted at the county or district conventions for possible inclusion in the party's **platform**.

In presidential election years, the presidential preference primary and the precinct conventions are the first steps in the selection of delegates to the national conventions. Before 1988, when Texas's participation in the first regional "Super Tuesday" presidential preference primary changed the delegate selection process, the precinct conventions were extremely crucial to presidential candidates because a candidate had to have strong support among delegates at the precinct level to ultimately capture a significant number of Texas delegates to the national convention. Now, much of that luster has been stolen by the primary, although the conventions still play a role in the Democratic Party's presidential nominating process.

Precinct conventions held in nonpresidential election years often are poorly attended, and, in many precincts, no one shows up. The precinct meeting may last fifteen minutes, and those attending may not be able to get enough people to volunteer to be delegates to the upcoming county or senatorial convention. Those who conclude that the political parties are in decline cite such low participation rates.

In the past, highly motivated political and ideological movements have been able to capture precinct conventions and advance candidates who had little in common with mainstream party voters. Supporters of Barry Goldwater used this strategy in 1964 to help win the Republican presidential nomination for their candidate, as did supporters of Democrat George McGovern in 1972. Both men were soundly defeated in the general election. In recent years, the **Religious Right** used a similar strategy to extend its influence in the Republican Party and was successful for the first time in Texas in 1994. Republican candidates nominated with the support of the Religious Right and other social conservatives were highly successful in general elections in Texas. The tea party movement became a major force in Republican primary races in

6.1

6.2

6.3

6.4

6.5

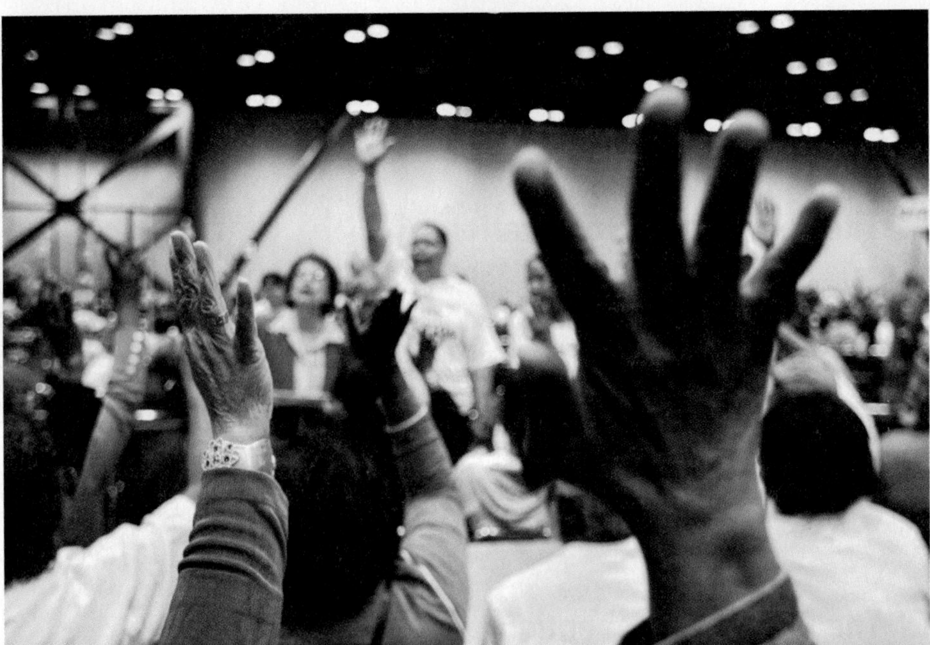

THE TEXAS TWO-STEP
Delegates conduct business at the Democratic District 6 state senatorial convention in Houston in 2008. Supporters of Barack Obama and Hillary Clinton fought to win support for their candidates for the Democratic presidential nomination. In the two-step nomination process, delegates also cast their votes in the party primary.

Texas in 2010, but it remains to be seen if the movement will become a major factor in the Republican Party's organization and leadership.

In 2008, the presidential campaigns of Democrats Barack Obama and Hillary Clinton went to great lengths organizing their support in the precinct conventions during their fight for the presidential nomination (see *Talking Texas: Texas Democrats Dance the Two-Step*).

☐ The County or Senatorial District Conventions

County or senatorial district conventions are held two weeks after the precinct conventions. District conventions are held in the larger urban counties, such as Harris, Dallas, Tarrant, and Bexar, which include more than one state senatorial district. Delegates elected at the precinct conventions constitute the membership of this second level of the convention process, which, in turn, elects delegates to the state convention.

Conventions are about politics, selection of candidates, and control of the party apparatus. There have been intermittent periods of lackluster conventions, but during Texas's one-party, Democratic era, frequent, bitter convention fights took place between conservatives and liberals for control of the Democratic Party. Although those fights were most evident at the state convention, they also permeated the precinct, county, and district conventions. As Texas Republicans have increased in number and developed more diversified interests, similar intraparty struggles have surfaced.

☐ State Conventions

The two major parties hold their state conventions in June of even-numbered years. Convention delegates certify to the secretary of state the names of those individuals who were nominated to statewide offices in the March primaries; adopt a party platform; and elect the state party chair, the vice chair, and the state executive committee. Although the primary elections were delayed until late May in 2012 because of

Talking ★ TEXAS Texas Democrats Dance the Two-Step

Democratic officials were delighted but also overwhelmed by the extraordinary response to the March 2008 Texas Democratic primary and related precinct conventions, the so-called "Texas Two-Step" that helped decide the tight race between Barack Obama and Hillary Clinton for the 2008 Democratic presidential nomination.

Texas was not even supposed to be in play in the presidential nominating campaign in 2008. Both Democratic and Republican nominations were expected to be all but decided by the time the March 4 Texas primary was held, following, as it did, the better-known caucuses in Iowa, the New Hampshire and South Carolina primaries, and a host of "Super Tuesday" contests stretching from New York to California. But the Democratic battle between Obama and Clinton was still wide open, focusing national attention on the Texas Democratic Party's bifurcated system of picking delegates that had been put to the test only once before–in 1988, when Michael Dukakis had won the nomination over the Rev. Jesse Jackson.

More than 2.8 million Texans (a record) voted in the 2008 Democratic primary, and about 1 million of them (also a record) returned after the polls closed for their precinct conventions. Clinton won the primary by about 101,000 votes over Obama and was awarded 65 delegates to Obama's 61. Another 67 delegates were awarded on the basis of support demonstrated in party caucuses, beginning with more than 8,000 precinct conventions held that evening after the primary vote had ended. A preliminary count of precinct convention results indicated that Obama would get most of those delegates, 37, and Clinton would get 30, a count that was made official at the state Democratic convention in June.

Both the primary and the caucuses drew criticism. Delegates based on the primary vote were allocated according to the 31 state senatorial districts. Furthermore, some districts were worth proportionately more delegates than others because they had had a higher Democratic turnout in the 2006 and 2004 elections. Senatorial districts, for example, in heavily Hispanic South Texas, where Clinton had a strong lead in the primary vote, did not have as many delegates as some districts in Houston and Dallas, where Obama received more votes. Most of the criticism, however, was leveled at the caucus system. Some participants complained of long lines and confusion. Others said that delegates for the opposing candidate had locked them out of their meeting places. Other people argued that it was "undemocratic" to allow caucus attendees to, in effect, vote twice for their candidates, once in the primary and again in the caucus.

CRITICAL THINKING QUESTIONS

1. Should Texas Democrats have been allowed to vote twice for the same candidate, once in the primary and again in the caucus? Was that undemocratic? Why or why not?
2. Should the lengthy, confusing system of state-by-state presidential primaries and caucuses be replaced with one national presidential primary for each major party? Why or why not?

lawsuits over congressional and legislative redistricting, the state conventions were still held in June of that year. The delegate selection process, however, was revised.

In presidential election years, the state conventions also select delegates to their respective parties' national nominating conventions, elect members to their parties' national committees, and choose presidential electors. Electors from the party that carries Texas in the presidential race will formally cast the state's electoral votes for that party's candidate in December after the general election.

The allocation among the candidates of Texas delegates to the Republican National Convention is determined by the presidential primary, but the actual delegates are selected at the state convention. Texas delegates to the Democratic National Convention are determined through a more complicated process, based both on the primary vote and on candidate support from attendees at the series of party conventions, beginning at the precinct level.

☐ The Party Activists

Texans participate in party politics for a variety of reasons, including some that are similar to reasons people join and participate in interest groups. Some see their

THE PARTY'S BUSINESS IS CONDUCTED HERE

State party conventions are held in June of even-numbered years in one of the major Texas cities. In addition to attending to the business of the party organization, these conventions are the critical final stage in delegate selection to the national nominating conventions. Seen here is the 2008 Texas Democratic Convention in Austin.

participation in party organizational and campaign activities as a way to help shape or influence public policy.[53] Some are brought into party activities through issues or specific candidates running for office. Others, influenced by politically active families, have absorbed party loyalty and interest in the political process. Some hope that party activism will serve as a stepping-stone to public office or political appointments. Political campaigns have a social component to them, and many activists enjoy the social contacts and friendships that come with actively working for the party or a candidate.

Texans who participate in the organizational activities of the political parties have characteristics that vary, to some extent, from other voters who support their respective political parties. In general terms, party activists tend to be more ideological than the voters who regularly support their party. Republican activists tend to be more conservative than most Republicans, and Democratic activists tend to be more liberal than most Democrats in the electorate. Activists tend to be better informed about candidates and issues than the general electorate, and they have "the time and financial resources to afford political activity, the information and knowledge to understand it, and the skills to be useful in it."[54]

Demographic and social characteristics of activists also differ between the two major parties. Democratic activists include more Hispanics, African Americans, union members, and Catholics. But despite differences in backgrounds and political views, activists of both parties tend to be better educated, to have higher incomes, and to hold higher status occupations than the general population.[55]

Approximately four decades ago, noted Washington columnist David Broder published *The Party's Over,* in which he linked the decline in party loyalties and weakened party organizations to the failure of governments in the United States to be more responsive in dealing with many social, economic, and political issues.[56] Although Broder was writing about the national political system, one can make similar observations about Texas's political parties. Broder noted that there was something fundamentally wrong with the American party system. As a debate emerged over the relevance and role of political parties, some scholars turned their attention to the parties' loss of control over the nomination of candidates, the candidate-centered campaign, the development of an extensive campaign consulting industry, candidate reliance on interest group contributions, the high costs of campaigns, and the weakened party organization. Elections, it seemed, were in the hands of professionals, and there appeared to be little need for party activists.

Other scholars focused on the decline in voting and its relationship to personal contacts by party workers or campaign volunteers. Study after study concluded that voter turnout increased with personal contacts, with numerous examples of voter turnout increasing by 5 percent to 10 percent because of organized grass-roots efforts.[57] Obviously, party activists did not disappear, but it has taken a series of elections at all levels to reestablish an emphasis on the importance of grass roots or local campaign and party activity. The 2008 presidential campaign demonstrated how technology and new media could be used to mobilize large numbers of volunteers to contact voters effectively. Other parties and candidates can be expected to follow suit, and increased emphasis is likely to be given to the mobilization of party activists.

The Party in Government

6.5 Assess why political parties in Texas do not produce cohesive, policy-oriented coalitions in government.

As part of V. O. Key's three-part perspective on political parties, we have begun our discussion of the political party in the electorate. In the next chapter, we will expand on this analysis by looking more closely at voting behavior, partisan attitudes, and the party activists. We also have presented a brief summary of the party organization. We will discuss the party in government in later chapters on the legislature, the executive branch, the bureaucracy, and the judiciary.

Political parties in Texas, however, do not produce cohesive, policy-oriented coalitions in government and have been unable to hold their elected officials accountable or responsive to those supporting the party. Under ideal circumstances, some students of government believe, the two major parties would lay out clearly defined political philosophies and policies they would pursue if their candidates were elected. Once elected, persons supported by the party would be committed to these programs, giving the voters a clear standard by which to evaluate their performance in office. This perspective is often referred to as the "responsible party model."

Texas parties are incapable of functioning in this manner for several reasons, none of which lessens the disenchantment and disgust that many voters have felt toward political parties and politicians. First, the political parties in Texas are highly decentralized and unable to discipline members who pursue goals that conflict with the parties' stated objectives. The large number of elected officials at both the state and the local levels serves to diffuse party leadership.

Moreover, the coalitions that parties form with groups harboring different objectives, interests, and agendas make it next to impossible to develop clearly stated positions that would always differentiate one party from another. Philosophical, ideological, and programmatic differences among members and supporters of the same party result, for example, in ideological voting patterns in the legislature that sometimes cross party lines.

Another explanation for the lack of partisan accountability is the long-standing antiparty tradition of American politics. Many voters are ambivalent, even outright hostile, toward political parties and make little, if any, effort to become informed on political and public issues. In addition, the parties make only limited efforts to include a large number of individuals in their organizational activities.

On MyPoliSciLab

Review the Chapter

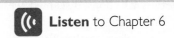

Political Parties and a Democratic Society

6.1 Explain what political parties are and why Texas has a two-party system, p. 153.

A political party is a group of individuals who organize to elect candidates to office under their banner for purposes of enacting a broad array of public policies. Although it was not always the case, Texas now has a two-party system. Third parties have developed from time to time, but their impact on the outcome of elections has been negligible. The pattern of two-party politics has been shaped by a long tradition of American politics that developed early in the nation's history. Other factors that have helped preserve a two-party system include plurality elections in which the candidate with the largest number of votes wins, state election laws that restrict third parties, the absence of intense ideological differences among most Texans, and issues that cut across race and economic class.

The Functions of Political Parties

6.2 Describe the different functions of political parties in Texas, p. 157.

Political parties build broad electoral coalitions and serve as intermediaries between the voters and the government. Parties recruit and nominate candidates, contest elections, attempt to mobilize voters, organize and manage governments, mediate the effects of separation of powers, provide accountability, resolve conflicts among diverse groups, and set the policy agenda.

The Party in the Electorate

6.3 Trace the partisan history of Texas, focusing on the transformation from one-party to two-party politics , p. 159.

Significant changes in the state's party structure have occurred over the past four decades, transforming Texas from a one-party Democratic state to a two-party state dominated by the Republican Party. Party realignment in the state reflects patterns that have occurred in most other southern states. Realignment has occurred for a number of reasons, including in-migration of residents from states with strong Republican parties, changes in the ethnic and racial composition of the state, the impact of the Voting Rights Act, and policy shifts of the national political parties. Republicans have won all statewide races in Texas since 1996. They captured a majority of the Texas Senate in 1997 and a majority of the Texas House in 2002. Democrats, however, still hold many county offices throughout Texas. Historically, politics in Texas were configured around class and race, and despite all of the partisan changes, these two factors still are significant in party alliances.

The Party Organization

6.4 Outline the basic structure of the party organization in Texas, from the precinct level to the state convention, p. 171.

State laws outline the formal party structure, but the vitality and strength of local party organizations vary widely from one area of the state to another. The permanent organization of the parties begins with the voting precinct and moves from the county party organization to the state organization. All of these levels elect party officials who serve to carry out party functions. There are no membership requirements, and any voter can opt to participate in the organizational activities of one or the other party.

Every two years, the parties hold conventions. These conventions begin with the precinct and are followed by a county or senatorial district convention and then the state convention. In presidential election years, the focus of the state convention is on the selection of delegates to the national nominating conventions. Conventions, which are described as the temporary organizations of the parties, also serve other functions, including the mobilization of party activists and the development of party platforms.

The Party in Government

6.5 Assess why political parties in Texas do not produce cohesive, policy-oriented coalitions in government, p. 177.

Political parties in Texas do not produce cohesive, policy-oriented coalitions in government because they have few resources with which to hold elected officials accountable. Elected officials are self-recruited and usually raise funds for their campaigns with minimal party assistance. With candidate-centered campaigns, the parties have lost much of their control over those elected under party labels. Legislators and other elected officials are somewhat like free agents, taking sides on issues with little concern of recrimination from their political parties.

The parties are highly decentralized, and party leadership is diffused across the state. Legislative alliances have cut across party labels with leaders from both parties appointing members of the opposite party to be chairs of committees. Voting in the legislature tends to follow philosophical rather than partisan lines. Persistent antiparty attitudes on the part of many Texans also have weakened the parties' efforts at disciplining their elected officials.

Learn the Terms

 **Study** and **Review** the Flash

political party, p. 154
third party, p. 156
Jim Crow laws, p. 160
bifactionalism, p. 162
one-party politics, p. 162
two-party system, p. 163
realignment, p. 164
ticket splitting, p. 167
dealignment, p. 170
party activist, p. 170
precinct, p. 171
precinct chair, p. 171
county executive committee, p. 171
county chair, p. 171
state executive committee, p. 172
state chair and vice chair, p. 172
platform, p. 173
Religious Right, p. 173

Test Yourself

 **Study** and **Review** the Practice Tests

1. What is a political party?

a. a special type of interest group
b. a group that represents a narrower range of policy interests than an interest group
c. any group that opposes those who hold political power
d. an organization that seeks to elect officeholders under a given label
e. a group that always seeks objectives that are contrary to the common good

2. La Raza Unida became a major force as a third party in 1972 because

a. the Democratic Party expanded voter registration.
b. the Democratic Party was not responsive to the concerns of Hispanic voters.
c. the Republican Party was not sensitive to the needs of low-income voters.
d. the Democratic Party at the time was too liberal.
e. Texas outlawed the poll tax.

3. Why has the Texas Libertarian Party been successful in recent years?

a. It has been able to win at least 5 percent of the vote in at least one statewide race each election cycle.
b. It has won at least one statewide office each election cycle.
c. It has allied itself with La Raza Unida to form a more powerful third-party movement.
d. It has focused its efforts on building support in different ethnic groups.
e. It has prompted a change in the law to allow for runoffs in the general election.

4. What is one reason why Texas has a two-party system?

a. The state is not diverse enough to have more than two parties.
b. State law bans the formation of third parties.
c. The large number of interest groups makes third parties unnecessary.
d. Texans tend to be too ideological for third parties.
e. The simple plurality election system inhibits the success of third parties.

5. Political parties increase accountability of elected officials to the people by

a. allowing independent candidates to get on the ballot.
b. encouraging bipartisanship in the legislature.
c. giving voters an opportunity to vote out failed officeholders.
d. allowing for runoff elections in primaries.
e. encouraging the proliferation of third parties.

6. Which of the following is TRUE about the function of political parties to organize and manage government in recent years?

a. Split party control of the legislature has led to an increase of bipartisan lawmaking.
b. Republican majorities in the legislature have led to a weakening of the bipartisan tradition.
c. Democratic governors have been successful in convincing Republican lawmakers to switch parties.
d. Smaller percentages of voters are turning out for elections.
e. Voter anger has led to persistent alternation in party control of the legislature.

7. Democratic Party dominance over Texas politics can be traced to

a. independence from Mexico.
b. state politics in the Confederacy.
c. Republican-dominated Reconstruction government.
d. the New Deal.
e. the election of the first president from Texas.

8. What is one of the arguments of the "class politics" thesis of Democratic Party dominance?

a. Established agricultural leaders allied themselves with banking and industrial leaders to preserve their power.
b. Oppressive Reconstruction government generated anti-Republican sentiments.
c. Republican leaders tried to forge alliances with white farmers and African Americans.
d. Republican support for Prohibition created anti-Republican sentiments.
e. The Populist Party supported restrictive voter registration laws.

9. Factionalism in the Democratic Party in Texas

a. was caused by a resurgence of the Republican Party during the New Deal.
b. was caused by Franklin Roosevelt's decision to run for a third term.
c. compensated for the lack of a competitive two-party system.
d. allowed the Republican Party to win the governorship in the 1950s.
e. led to internal party battles over race, religion, and Communism.

10. Who were the "Shivercrats"?

a. liberal Democrats who opposed the conservative establishment
b. Republicans who voted for Democrats in the general election
c. liberal Democrats led by Ralph Yarborough
d. Democrats who supported the election of Republican Dwight Eisenhower
e. minorities who voted for Republicans in the New Deal era

11. All of the following are factors contributing to the rise of a two-party system in Texas EXCEPT

a. the popularity of southern President Jimmy Carter in the 1970s.
b. the creation of minority-dominated electoral districts.
c. low-income minority support for liberal economic policies.
d. the stronger organization of the Republican Party.
e. the election of Republican Governor Bill Clements in 1978.

12. Which of the following statements is TRUE concerning the extent of Republican Party dominance in Texas today?

a. Republicans control the Texas House but not the Texas Senate.
b. Republicans control the governor's mansion but not the legislature.
c. Republicans have never controlled a majority of the state's congressional delegation.
d. Republicans control only one of the state's two U.S. Senate seats.
e. Republicans have won every statewide race since 1996.

13. Which of the following is TRUE about the partisan alignment of Texas voters?

a. Republicans now outnumber Democrats two to one in party identification.
b. Democrats continue to maintain some parity with Republicans in party identification.
c. Republicans have been successful in winning a majority of Hispanic votes in recent years.
d. A majority of Texans are registered independents.
e. The tea party now outnumbers the Republican Party in party identification.

14. Precinct conventions

a. elect delegates directly to the state convention.
b. choose presidential electors.
c. adopt resolutions for possible inclusion in the party's state platform.
d. elect county chairpersons.
e. elect members to the party national committee.

15. Which of the following statements is TRUE about the party organization in Texas?

a. There are roughly 500 election precincts in the state.
b. Precinct conventions are held only in presidential election years.
c. If no one shows up to a precinct convention, its votes are transferred to a neighboring precinct.
d. State convention delegates certify the names of party nominees to the secretary of state.
e. Several small counties may be combined into one senatorial district convention.

Explore Further

Anders, Evan, *Boss Rule in South Texas: The Progressive Era.* Austin: University of Texas Press, 1982. Analyzes the political machines of South Texas that developed in the late nineteenth and early twentieth centuries and the leading roles of James B. Wells, Archer (Archie) Parr, Manual Guerra, and John Nance Garner in the creation and operation of these organizations.

Barnes, Ben. *Barn Burning, Barn Building.* Albany, TX: Bright Sky Press, 2002. Provides an insider's assessment of political changes and party realignment in Texas; written by a former Texas lieutenant governor.

Black, Earl, and Merle Black, *The Rise of Southern Republicans.* Boston: Harvard University Press, 2002. Assesses the Republican realignment in southern states systematically.

Davidson, Chandler, *Race and Class in Texas Politics.* Princeton, NJ: Princeton University Press, 1990. Adapts V. O. Key's earlier analysis of Texas politics through the 1980s and assesses the dimensions of race, class, and a governing elite in Texas.

———, and Bernard Grofman, eds. *Quiet Revolution in the South: The Impact of the Voting Rights Act, 1965–1990.* Princeton, NJ: Princeton University Press, 1994. Analyzes the impact of the Voting Rights Act on the political systems of southern states with a chapter covering Texas.

Garcia, Ignacio, *United We Win: The Rise and Fall of La Raza Unida Party.* Tucson: Mexican American Studies and Research Center at the University of Arizona, 1989. Traces the development of La Raza Unida, a Hispanic third party, based on its origins with the formation of the Mexican American Youth Organization (MAYO) to its demise in the early 1980s; written from the perspective of an activist.

Hershey, Marjorie Randon, *Party Politics in America*, 15th ed. White Plains, NY: Pearson Longman, 2012. Introduces American political parties comprehensively.

Key, V. O., *Southern Politics.* New York: Vintage Books, 1949. Details the politics in each of the states of the Confederacy and provides a historical framework for understanding the development of political changes in Texas and other southern states; this is a classic study of southern politics.

Knaggs, John R., *Two Party Texas: The John Tower Era, 1961–1984.* Austin, TX: Eakin Press, 1986. Provides a history of the early development of the modern Republican Party in Texas.

Navarro, Armando, *La Raza Unida: A Chicano Challenge to the U.S. Two-Party Dictatorship.* Philadelphia, PA: Temple University Press, 2000. Assesses the La Raza Unida Party grounded in third-party literature.

7

Listen on MyPoliSciLab

Elections, Campaigns, and Political Behavior in Texas

People never lie so much as after a hunt, during a war and before an election.

—Otto von Bismarck

Politics is show business for ugly people.

—Bill Miller, political consultant, 1991

The next time you decide to skip voting in an election because you are convinced your vote will not count, think about Donna Howard and Dan Neil. Donna Howard is a Democratic state representative who represents Texas House District 48 in northern and western Austin, only a short drive from the state Capitol. Neil was Howard's Republican challenger in 2010, and he would be the state representative today were it not for four votes—four votes out of more than 51,000 cast in that race. That was Howard's final margin after a recount and an election contest supervised by a Texas House

7.1 List the basic functions of elections in a democratic society, p. 184.

7.2 Compare and contrast the types of elections held throughout Texas, p. 185.

7.3 Explain the measures taken to keep some Texans from voting and the countermeasures employed to curtail these discriminatory practices, p. 192.

7.4 Assess the political gains made by minorities and women in Texas politics in recent years, p. 197.

7.5 Describe some of the applications of marketing technology to political campaigns, p. 200.

7.6 Differentiate between controlled and uncontrolled media in election campaigns and explain how they fit into the larger advertising strategy of campaigns, p. 203.

7.7 Evaluate the impact of money in campaigns in Texas and assess to what extent campaign finance laws are effective, p. 206.

7.8 Outline the process of acquiring political views and attitudes toward politics and describe the various ways in which Texans participate politically, p. 211.

Hobby
VOTER'S GUIDE TO
POLITICIANS
Ben Barnes
Bloodshot eyes from meeting in smoke-filled rooms.
"Winning Smile" dental caps. (Also suitable for biting invectives.)
TEXAS UNDER THE CARPETBAGGER
W. C. NUNN

A YARDSTICK OF DEMOCRACY?

Fair and free elections are one yardstick of a democratic society. For a good part of its history, Texas has struggled with issues related to suffrage and access to the ballot box.

7.1
7.2
7.3
7.4
7.5
7.6
7.7
7.8

committee.[1] In other words, had five more individuals who would have voted for Neil—maybe a business associate, a couple of straight-ticket Republican voters, or friends who were out of town—showed up on Election Day, Neil would be District 48's state representative. Howard, meanwhile, was grateful that four of her voters—any four— did not skip the election.

Votes count. That is why millions of people around the world have spilled blood and made other great sacrifices to eliminate authoritarian political systems and win free and open elections. Yet, Texans congratulate themselves if one-third of the eligible population votes. Such a poor turnout cannot be blamed on a lack of opportunity. After decades of denying voting rights to large parts of the population, Texas now has one of the more progressive voter registration laws in the United States. Contemporary political campaigns, especially those for national and statewide offices, have high media visibility. People are bombarded by television and Internet advertising, direct mail, email, Twitter feeds, social networking messages, phone bank solicitations for candidates, and daily news coverage. But something fundamental is turning off Texas voters, as well as voters across the nation. Statewide election turnout rates in Texas are consistently low, and turnout rates in many local elections are downright appalling.

Some suggest that Texans do not care about what happens in government as long as their own selfish interests are being met. Other people argue that there is a sense of disenchantment, disillusionment, or alienation among Texas voters. Voters, they believe, feel disconnected from government and elected officeholders. They do not trust public officials to do what they said they were going to do in their election bids, and they believe politicians are using their offices to line their own pockets. Other Texans care about politics, government, and public policy but believe that a single vote will make no difference.

Elected officials, moreover, are perceived to be increasingly insulated from the popular will. This especially has been the case in recent years in Washington, where partisanship, at times, has all but crippled government. Although they articulate a commitment to elections and political participation, some officeholders ignore their constituents' wishes as they make policy decisions. Some observers also have argued that different elections scheduled throughout the year, as they are in Texas and other states, are designed to reduce voter participation. The real brokers of politics and public policy, they believe, are the interest groups, lobbyists, political action committees, and the "fat cats" who contribute large sums of money to candidates and parties. With the decline of political parties, many candidates seem to become free agents ready to sell their services to the highest bidders—the biggest campaign contributors. When voters read or hear that candidates are taking hundreds of thousands of dollars from political action committees or individual donors, it is difficult to convince them that politicians are not on the take or that they really care about the average citizen.

Much has been written indicting contemporary elections in Texas and the United States. Elections were designed to give the people the opportunity to direct public policy through chosen officials who would then be held accountable at the next election, but the system will not work properly if people do not vote. Elections are clearly imperfect instruments, but we have found no other vehicle for translating the needs, interests, and expectations of the public into public policy.

The Functions of Elections

7.1 List the basic functions of elections in a democratic society.

or more than 200 years, we in the United States have been debating electoral issues. Who should participate? Should individuals who cannot read at a certain level be permitted to vote? When should elections be held? What percentage of the popular vote should be required to win an election—a majority or a plurality? What are the policy consequences of elections? Does it really make any difference who gets elected? Although these questions are significant, the most important issue is the relationship of elections to our definition of a democratic society. In the most fundamental terms, "elections are used to assure popular support and legitimacy for those who make governmental decisions."[2] A stable political system depends on popular support, and people freely participating in the process of choosing those who make public policy are more likely to accept and support policy without coercion or force.

suffrage
The right to vote.

Although elections provide broad statements of the voters' expectations for future public policy and a prospective judgment on the performance of elected officials, they seldom articulate or direct precise programs. Successful political parties and candidates build broad-based campaign coalitions, and the competing demands of the diverse groups courted by candidates make it difficult for candidates to specify in detail the policies they plan to pursue once elected. Most people seeking public office, therefore, prefer to speak in general concepts and try to avoid answering hypothetical "what if" questions posed by reporters, such as, "What if there isn't enough money in the budget to raise teachers' pay or improve health care? Will you support a tax increase or cut back on other programs?"

Nevertheless, after an election, a successful candidate is likely to indicate that the people have spoken and claim a mandate to pursue specific public policies of his or her choosing. If there is a mandate, it is for the person elected, not for a specific program.[3]

Elections enable voters to replace public officials or force officeholders to change their policies.[4] They are, in effect, the one institution that a democratic society can use to control its leaders and provide a retrospective judgment of the past actions of elected officials. But this role is based on the assumptions that (1) there is universal **suffrage**, (2) voters are offered clear alternatives, (3) large segments of the population are informed about those aspiring to hold public office and determine public policy, and (4) voter participation is significant. Throughout Texas's history, elections often have been manipulated for the advantage and interests of the few.

Texas's political culture has unwritten rules as to how elections should be conducted and what candidates should and should not do. For example, we expect a candidate to shake the hand of his or her opponent even after a bitter defeat or attack. That is why Republican Clayton Williams's snub of the handshake offered by Democrat Ann Richards during one joint appearance in the 1990 gubernatorial campaign received much media attention. Candidates can attack, counterattack, make charges and countercharges against each other and still be considered politically acceptable and civilized. Such election rituals are manifestations of the way in which we have institutionalized conflict.

Some would argue that elections and election rituals have only a symbolic function that serves to "quiet resentments and doubts about particular political acts, reaffirm belief in the fundamental rationality and democratic character of the system, and thus fix conforming habits of future behavior."[5] Although this position may be extreme, the trivialization of elections may ultimately result in even more disenchantment, disdain, and disgust with politics and government.[6]

State and Local Elections

7.2 Compare and contrast the types of elections held throughout Texas.

Texans have numerous opportunities to vote, often as many as three or four times a year, in a variety of elections. Voters in Texas and other states, in fact, vote on more candidates and issues than citizens of any other democracy.[7] Turnout and interest are highest in the general election in

primary election
An election in which the Democratic or Republican Party chooses its nominees for public offices. In presidential election years, the primary also plays a key role in selecting Texas delegates to the parties' national nominating conventions.

presidential election years, but they can be abysmally low in elections for constitutional amendments, school boards, and the governing bodies of single-purpose districts, such as hospital and water districts.

☐ Election Cycles

Except for some constitutional amendment elections, which are set by the legislature, and emergency elections set by the governor to fill vacancies in specific offices, elections are held at regular, predictable intervals mandated by state law. There has been a systematic effort to separate elections and thereby minimize the convergence of issues in state and local races.[8] Most city and school board elections are held in May of odd-numbered years to separate them from party primaries held in March of even-numbered years and general elections held in November. Some city and school board elections, however, are held in November, but on separate ballots from state and federal races. Many constitutional amendment elections are scheduled for the same day as the general election, but they can be held separately. There are all kinds of explanations and justifications for this election scheduling, but there is evidence to suggest that it contributes to "voter fatigue," reduced voter turnout, and the disproportionate influence of a few individuals in many of the local and special elections for which voter turnout usually is the lowest. While some experts believe that many voters have tired of elections and tuned them out, others challenge this view.[9]

These election cycles also shape the policymaking process. A tax increase, for example, is likely to take place soon after an election, not immediately prior to one. Voter dissatisfaction, officeholders hope, would be dissipated by the time the next election takes place after their tax vote. This is a double-edged sword. It insulates public officials from immediate voter retaliation when hard and unpopular decisions must be made. It also makes it difficult to punish elected officials for pursuing questionable or highly unpopular programs.

☐ Primary Elections

Texas and most other states use the direct **primary election** to nominate major party candidates for public office. Prior to the adoption of the primary in 1903, the political parties nominated their candidates in party conventions, but changes were made for two basic reasons. Throughout the country during that era, a Progressive reform movement criticized the conventions as undemocratic, corrupt, and dominated by a few of the party elites. That movement advocated the party primary as an alternative. Second, the personal rivalries and factional disputes that erupted at nominating conventions threatened the monopoly that the Democratic Party had over Texas politics during that era, and the primary elections were a solution to excessive intraparty conflict. Under current law, any party that received 20 percent of the vote in the previous gubernatorial election is required to nominate candidates by the primary method. Other parties can continue to use the nominating convention.

Primaries are now held on the second Tuesday in March in even-numbered years, a change that was made in 1988 as part of the strategy of southern states to increase the region's influence in the presidential nominating process. The 2012 Texas primaries, however, were delayed until May 29 because of lawsuits over the redistricting of legislative and congressional districts.

For practical purposes, the primaries in Texas are open because no party membership is designated on an individual's voter registration card. A voter does not register as a Republican or a Democrat. Only after a person has voted in a party's primary is the party's name stamped on the card, which restricts a person to voting only in that party's runoff, if there is one.

Some students of Texas politics suggest that the structure of the state's primary delayed the development of the two-party system and contributed to the conservative establishment's long domination of state politics.[10] Comparisons between earlier primary elections and general elections suggest that many Republicans voted for the most conservative candidates in the Democratic primaries and then voted for Republicans in the general elections. This practice helped ensure that conservative candidates usually were nominated by both parties and conservatives were elected in the general election.[11] During the period of one-party Democratic politics, the person who won the Democratic primary usually won the general election. One early student of the Texas primaries noted, "The only campaigning, therefore, to which the state is usually subjected comes in connection with the Democratic primaries, and it is largely taken up with personalities."[12]

Voter turnout in contemporary primary elections is significantly lower than in the general election, but this has not always been the case. From 1904, when the primary was first used for nominations, through 1950, turnout in the primary matched or exceeded that of the general election, except for the elections of 1924 and 1944. From the 1920s through 1970, the rate of turnout for the Democratic primary never exceeded 35 percent of the voting-age population.

Participation in party primaries has eroded since the 1970s, as a result, in part, of partisan realignment, the weak party organization, and the candidate-centered campaigns. About 28 percent of the voting-age population (persons 18 or older) voted in a hotly contested Democratic gubernatorial primary in 1972 (see Table 7–1). After

TABLE 7–1 DEMOCRATIC AND REPUBLICAN PRIMARY TURNOUT, 1970–2010

		REPUBLICAN PARTY			DEMOCRATIC PARTY		
Year	Race	Primary Vote	Percentage Turnout of Voting-Age Population	Percentage Turnout of Registered Voters	Primary Vote	Percentage Turnout of Voting-Age Population	Percentage Turnout of Registered Voters
1970	Governor	109,021	1.5	2.6	1,011,300	**14.1**	**24.4**
1972	President/ Governor	114,007	1.5	2.9	2,192,903	**28.4**	**56.6**
1974	Governor	69,101	0.8	1.3	1,521,306	**18.4**	**28.4**
1976	President	356,307	4.0	6.6	1,529,168	**17.3**	**28.5**
1978	Governor	158,403	1.7	3.1	1,812,896	**19.4**	**35.8**
1980	President	526,769	5.3	9.8	1,377,767	**13.8**	**25.7**
1982	Governor	265,794	2.5	4.4	1,318,663	**12.3**	**21.6**
1984	President	336,814	3.0	4.9	1,463,449	**12.9**	**21.3**
1986	Governor	544,719	4.6	6.9	1,096,552	**9.3**	**13.8**
1988	President	1,014,956	8.3	13.1	1,767,045	**14.4**	**22.8**
1990	Governor	855,231	6.8	10.3	1,487,260	**11.9**	**18.0**
1992	President	797,146	6.2	10.0	1,482,075	**11.5**	**18.6**
1994	Governor	557,340	4.3	6.2	1,036,944	**7.9**	**11.5**
1996	President	1,019,803	**7.4**	**10.5**	921,256	6.7	9.5
1998	Governor	596,839	4.2	5.4	664,532	**4.7**	**6.0**
2000	President	1,126,757	**7.8**	**9.7**	786,890	5.4	6.9
2002	Governor	622,423	4.0	5.1	1,003,388	**6.5**	**8.2**
2004	President	687,615	4.3	5.6	839,231	**5.2**	**6.8**
2006	Governor	655,919	**3.9**	**5.2**	508,602	3.1	4.0
2008	President	1,362,322	7.7	10.7	2,874,986	**16.2**	**22.5**
2010	Governor	1,484,542	**8.0**	**11.4**	680,548	3.6	5.2

*Bold percentages note party with the larger turnout.

SOURCE: Texas Secretary of State, Elections Division.

runoff election

A required election if no candidate receives an absolute majority of the votes cast in a primary race or in many nonpartisan elections. The runoff is between the top two vote getters.

Voting Rights Act

A federal law designed to protect the voting rights of minorities by requiring the Justice Department's approval of changes in political districts and certain other electoral procedures. The act, as amended, has eliminated most of the more restrictive state laws that limited minority political participation.

that year, turnout in Democratic primaries fell below 20 percent with a low point of 3.1 percent of the voting-age population in the 2006 gubernatorial primary. However, the battle between Barack Obama and Hillary Clinton for the 2008 Democratic presidential nomination sparked a record turnout of more than 2.8 million voters in the Democratic primary that year. Almost 1.4 million voters cast ballots in the Republican primary for a record total primary turnout of more than 4.2 million.

Prior to 1980, participation in the Republican primaries never exceeded 5 percent of the voting-age population or more than 7 percent of the registered voters.[13] That rate has increased somewhat since then, but the percentage of Texans voting in a Republican primary has never reached the levels of participation that the Democratic Party experienced when it dominated state politics. Since 1980, the Republicans' share of the voting-age population participating in their primaries has never exceeded 10 percent. One million voters, or 8.3 percent of voting-age Texans, cast ballots in the 1988 Republican presidential primary, when Texan George H. W. Bush was on the ballot. That is the highest turnout percentage in a Republican primary in Texas so far. More voters participated in the 2008 Republican primary, but the participation rate was lower as the total population and number of registered voters had increased.

A number of generalizations can be drawn from these data. Only a small percentage of the population normally participates in the selection of the political parties' nominees. Those who do participate in party primaries tend to be more ideological than the general population. This often prompts candidates to take more extreme positions on issues during their primary campaigns, only to try to move to the center in the general election campaign to appeal to more moderate voters.

A candidate must receive an absolute majority of votes cast for a specific state or local office in a primary to receive a party's nomination. If no candidate receives a majority in multi-candidate races, the two top vote getters must face each other in a **runoff election**. Voter turnout rates for runoffs are consistently lower than those for the first primary.

Minority groups have argued that the absolute majority requirement discriminates against African American and Hispanic candidates. Although there has been no successful challenge to the requirement in the party primaries, runoff elections have been successfully challenged under the **Voting Rights Act** in many elections for local governments, in which candidates usually are elected on a nonpartisan ballot. When challenges have been successful, candidates who receive a plurality of votes (more votes than any other candidate) are elected.

Texas and a handful of other states give the political parties the responsibility of administering the primary elections. A party's county chair and the county executive committee are responsible for printing the ballots, locating polling places, providing for voting machines, hiring the election judges and clerks, and canvassing the election returns. In recent years, however, the parties have had increasing difficulty managing their elections, prompting party officials in some counties to contract with the counties to administer their primary elections.

Before 1972, the costs of the primaries were borne by the political parties, which paid for them primarily with filing fees paid by candidates running for office. Those fees could be extremely high. This system was perceived by many as a way of eliminating potential candidates from running for public office, and the system was successfully challenged in the federal courts in 1970.[14] Under current law, modest filing fees are still permitted, and the parties still conduct the primaries, but the state picks up most of the cost. Administrative costs for the 2008 primaries were more than $11.8 million, including about $1.25 million in Harris County (Houston) and $1.5 million in Dallas County.[15] A person can get a place on the primary ballot without paying a filing fee by submitting a designated number of registered voters' signatures on petitions to party officials.

Although the primary has helped make the nominating process more democratic than the party conventions, some scholars and party advocates argue that the primary has contributed to the decline of the political parties.[16] The parties no longer control the nomination process because any eligible individual can be listed on a primary ballot by paying the required filing fee or submitting the required petitions. Also, potential officeholders, organizing and funding their own campaigns, have little allegiance to the parties. A person who is even hostile toward the party's leadership, the party's platform, or its traditional public policy positions can win the party's nomination. In addition, primary contests can be vicious with personal attacks between candidates that can weaken the eventual winner and lead to a loss in the general election.

Parties function primarily to win elections, but the primaries may result in an unbalanced ticket that for ideological or other reasons has limited appeal to voters in the general election. This imbalance minimizes the party's electoral strength. Bitter primary battles also can increase conflict within a party organization, and an expensive primary race can leave a candidate underfunded for a general election campaign. Moreover, a primary can nominate a weak candidate who will fare poorly in the general election.[17]

general election
An election for state, federal, and county offices held in November of even-numbered years. The ballot includes nominees of the two major political parties plus other candidates who meet certain legal requirements.

local election
An election for city council, the school board, and certain other local offices. Most of these are nonpartisan.

☐ General Elections

General elections for state and federal offices are held on the first Tuesday after the first Monday in November in even-numbered years. Unlike the primaries, the administration and costs of the general election are the responsibility of the county. The names of the candidates nominated in the primaries by the two major parties are placed on a ballot, along with the names of third-party candidates who have submitted petitions bearing the names of registered voters equal to 1 percent of the vote in the previous gubernatorial election.

In the election of 1896, the turnout rate was more than 80 percent of the eligible voting-age population, but only twelve years later in 1908, turnout had fallen to approximately 35 percent. During much of the period from 1910 to 1958, turnout rates in nonpresidential, general elections were less than 20 percent, mainly because the outcome already had been determined in the Democratic primaries. Presidential elections generated a higher turnout, but in very few instances did the turnout rate exceed 40 percent of eligible voters.[18]

In more recent years, turnout rates in presidential elections have been considerably higher than in years when the governor and other statewide officials are elected. Since 1970, the average turnout in gubernatorial elections in Texas has been 28 percent of the voting-age population and approximately 43 percent of registered voters. By contrast, average turnout in presidential elections has been 45 percent of the voting-age population and 63 percent of registered voters. These turnout rates are significantly higher than turnout in the primaries, but it still is evident, if not distressing, that many Texans do not participate in the selection of their leaders (see Table 7–2).

State officials quoted in the news media often will refer to the voter turnout in terms of a percentage of registered voters. Turnout of registered voters will produce a higher rate and sounds better than the percentage of the voting-age population, but it omits critical information about voter participation. If we compare voter registration figures with census data identifying the population eligible to vote, it is clear that a large part of the population does not even register to vote. Rates of participation are important to our efforts to establish the vitality of democratic values or norms.

☐ City, School Board, Single-Purpose Districts

Most local elections, which are nonpartisan, are held in May in odd-numbered years to minimize the convergence of issues in national, state, and local races. Across the state, wide variations exist in the competitiveness of these elections, campaign costs, and turnout.

Although turnout rates in **local elections** rarely match those in the general elections, competition for control of local governments became more intense in the 1970s and 1980s, in part because of the increased political mobilization of minority voters.

special election
An election set by the legislature or called by the governor for a specific purpose, such as voting on constitutional amendments or filling a vacancy in a legislative office. Local governments also can call special elections.

TABLE 7–2 TURNOUT IN TEXAS GENERAL ELECTIONS, 1970–2010

Year	Type of Election	Total Registered Voters	Total Votes Cast	Percentage Turnout of Voting-Age Population	Percentage Turnout of Registered Voters
1970	Governor	4,149,250	2,235,847	31.1	53.9
1972	President	3,872,462	3,471,281	44.9	66.6
1974	Governor	5,348,393	1,654,984	20.0	30.9
1976	President	6,281,149	4,071,884	46.1	64.8
1978	Governor	5,681,875	2,369,764	25.3	41.7
1980	President	6,639,661	4,541,637	45.6	68.4
1982	Governor	6,414,988	3,191,091	29.8	49.7
1984	President	7,900,167	5,397,571	47.6	68.3
1986	Governor	7,287,173	3,441,460	29.1	47.2
1988	President	8,201,856	5,427,410	44.3	66.2
1990	Governor	7,701,449	3,892,746	31.1	50.6
1992	President	8,439,874	6,154,018	47.6	72.9
1994	Governor	8,641,848	4,396,242	33.6	50.9
1996	President	10,540,678	5,611,644	41.0	53.3
1998	Governor	11,538,235	3,738,078	26.5	32.4
2000	President	12,365,235	6,407,637	44.3	51.8
2002	Governor	12,563,459	4,553,979	29.4	36.2
2004	President	13,098,329	7,410,749	46.1	56.6
2006	Governor	13,074,279	4,399,068	26.4	33.6
2008	President	13,575,062	8,077,795	45.6	59.5
2010	Governor	13,269,233	4,979,870	27.2	37.5

SOURCE: Texas Secretary of State, Elections Division.

More recently, however, participation seems to have declined. Contested local campaigns in large urban areas can be as expensive as state legislative and congressional races.

But most elections for school boards or single-purpose districts, such as hospital or water districts, have abysmally low rates of voter participation. It is not uncommon for many seats to go uncontested, and turnout rates, even in large urban districts, can be as low as 2 percent to 5 percent. Candidates often spend little, if any, money on these elections, and their campaigns usually are informal. Recent state legislation permits local governments to cancel an election if no offices are contested, and numerous communities in recent years have canceled elections for this reason. Some fifteen towns and cities in Navarro County, for example, cancelled their 2012 elections because of a lack of competition.[19]

☐ Special Elections

Most constitutional amendments are placed on the general election ballot in November of odd-numbered years, a few months after a regular legislative session ends, or they are scheduled for a **special election**. In either case, voter turnout normally is low, which results in most amendments being approved.

In constitutional amendment elections since 1991, average turnout of registered voters has been 12.1 percent, but this was only 8.3 percent of the voting-age population. A few of those were special elections. Most, however, were held on the general election date in November of odd-numbered years, when the only other significant races on the ballot were in Houston for mayor and city council. Unlike most Texas cities, Houston holds its municipal elections in November. Consequently, the turnout in Houston is heavier than in the rest of the state for constitutional amendment elections and usually is a major factor in determining the outcome. It is somewhat disturbing that in most years, fewer than 10 percent of Texas citizens care enough to vote for constitutional amendments. The low turnout also means that special interest groups can mount well-organized campaigns to place provisions favoring them into the constitution with little public scrutiny or interest.

Local governments also conduct special elections for bond issues, local initiatives and referenda, and the recall of local officials. Although occasional high-interest, emotionally charged elections are held, turnout rates in these elections still are extremely low. People who do vote tend to be those with higher incomes and educational levels. The governor also can call special elections to fill vacancies in certain offices, including legislative and congressional seats.

absentee (or early) voting
A period before the regularly scheduled election date during which voters are allowed to cast ballots. With recent changes in election law, a person does not have to offer a reason for voting absentee.

☐ Extended Absentee Balloting

In 1988, Texas made a major change in the requirements for absentee voting. Prior to that time, if a voter was not going to be in the county on Election Day or was incapacitated, he or she could vote absentee at a designated polling place or by mail before Election Day. Now, anyone can vote early without having to state an excuse during an extended period for **absentee (or early) voting**. Urban counties, in particular, now maintain multiple voting places, including stations conveniently located in shopping malls, during the extended voting period, which runs from the twentieth day to the fourth day before the scheduled Election Day. The result has been a notable increase in the number of votes cast early—20 percent to 30 percent of all votes in some areas.

The extended early voting, now used in thirty-one states, has radically changed campaign strategies and tactics.[20] A candidate now has to communicate earlier to that part of the population that has a high likelihood of voting prior to Election Day. With a large portion of votes cast early, a candidate might well carry the Election Day totals but lose the early vote and lose the election. A candidate also has to mobilize those voters who cast their votes on Election Day. Thus, a campaign must "peak" twice.

☐ Straight Ticket Voting

The election ballot is styled in such a way as to permit straight party voting by pulling one lever, marking one block, punching one hole, or selecting the straight party ticket option.[21] In campaigns, candidates and political leaders often urge voters to "pull one lever" in support of one party's entire slate of candidates. Many voters claim to be independent, to vote for the individual, not the party. Yet, evidence suggests that many Texas voters do not split their tickets.[22] Even a casual review of voting returns indicates congruence in votes cast down ballot for the more obscure offices. There is a drop off in total number of votes cast down ballot, but the division of the party vote tends to be consistent.

☐ Ballot Security and the Voter ID Law

Although some governments in Texas still use paper ballots and mechanical voting machines, many other governments use punch cards, mark-sense ballots, or touch-screen voting machines that permit the election returns to be counted by computer.[23] In the aftermath of the ballot problems in Florida in the 2000 presidential election, ballot security and the accurate tabulation of votes received more attention in Texas as well as in other states. Historic allegations of voter fraud included "stuffing" ballot boxes, votes from people who were dead or nonexistent, persons voting more than one time, lost ballots, and failure to count ballots. Relatively little voting fraud has been proven in recent years, but electronic voting does not eliminate these potential problems, and there are legitimate concerns that tabulation software can be hacked or electronic voting devices manipulated.

After several years of trying, Republicans in the Texas legislature enacted a voter identification law in 2011, which requires voters to present photo identification in

7.1
7.2
7.3
7.4
7.5
7.6
7.7
7.8

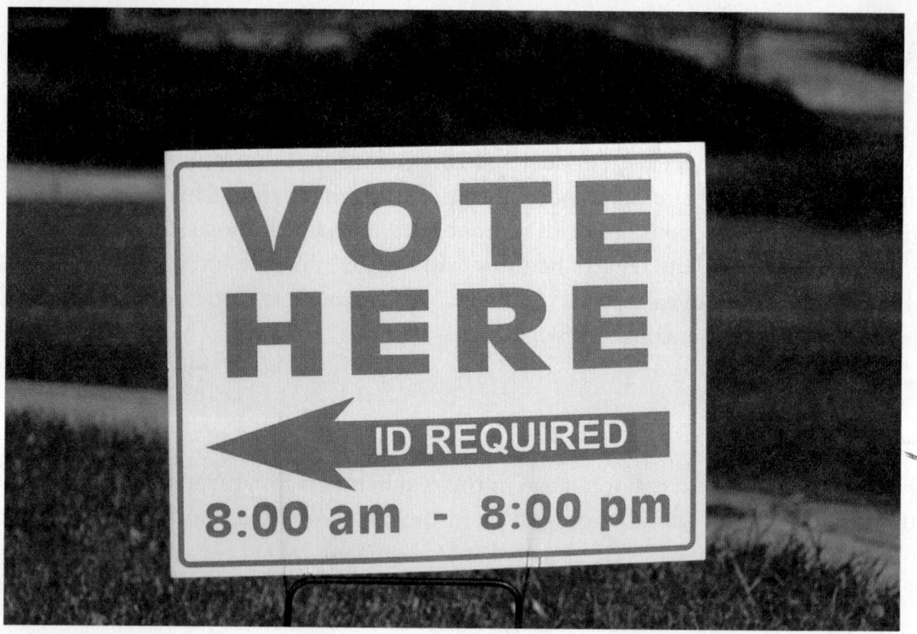

BRING YOUR ID
This sign, posted in another state, reminds voters to bring a form of photo identification to the polls. The fate of Texas's new voter ID law was being fought in the courts when this book went to press.

order to cast a ballot. Republican legislators insisted the step would reduce voter fraud. But Democrats argued that the requirement would intimidate many minority and elderly voters who were likely to vote for Democratic candidates. In March 2012, the U.S. Department of Justice refused to "preclear," or approve, the photo identification law under the Voting Rights Act. The department said Texas had not proved that the requirement would not discriminate against minority voters. It said Hispanic voters were much more likely than non-Hispanic voters to lack a driver's license or a personal identification card. About 2.8 million of Texas's 12.8 million registered voters are Hispanic.

More than a dozen states have either passed voter identification requirements or tightened other election rules in recent years, primarily the result of Republican initiatives. In December 2011, the Obama administration's Justice Department also blocked a voter ID law in South Carolina, which, like Texas, is covered by the Voting Rights Act. Both states have histories of suppressing minority voting. In 2008, the U.S. Supreme Court ruled that a similar voter ID law in Indiana did not violate the U.S. Constitution. Indiana is not covered by the Voting Rights Act because it does not have a history of suppressing minority voting.

Texas Attorney General Greg Abbott, a Republican, went to federal district court in Washington, D.C., in an effort to overturn the Justice Department's ruling and put the law into effect. That lawsuit was still pending in early July 2012. Abbot indicated there had been about fifty convictions related to voter fraud in Texas during the previous ten years. Some, he said, included fraudulent voter impersonation.[24]

Political Suffrage in Texas: A Struggle for Minorities and Women

7.3 Explain the measures taken to keep some Texans from voting and the countermeasures employed to curtail these discriminatory practices.

Despite the rhetoric of democratic theory in the state's constitution and the somewhat venerable view that people have of elections and voting, Texas has a dark history of voter disfranchisement. For many years, African Americans, Hispanics, and low-income whites were systematically excluded from the political process. Texas had a political system in which the interests of a few could prevail over the interests of the majority. Many people paid a high price for this early legacy of discrimination.

After the Civil War, the state initiated efforts to organize a civilian government that would reestablish Texas's full statehood in the Union. The Constitutional Convention of 1866 accepted the supremacy of the national government and eliminated slavery, but it refused to adopt the Thirteenth Amendment, which gave African Americans the right to vote and hold public office.[25] This constitution was rejected by the Radical Reconstructionists in U.S. Congress in 1867, and subsequent Texas constitutions extended full voting rights to African Americans. Forty-one African Americans served in the Texas legislature from 1868 to 1894.[26] Even though the Texas Constitution extended political rights to them, African Americans were threatened with physical violence and economic recriminations, such as loss of their jobs, that reduced their political participation well into the twentieth century. In addition, several state laws were enacted to block their access to the ballot.

poll tax
A tax that Texas and some other states used to require people to pay before allowing them to vote. The purpose was to discourage minorities and poor whites from participating in the political process. The tax was declared unconstitutional in the 1960s.

white primary
A series of state laws and party rules that denied African Americans the right to vote in the Democratic primary in Texas in the first half of the twentieth century.

☐ The Poll Tax

The conservative Texas establishment's reaction to the Populist movement and its potential for building a coalition between African Americans and low-income whites resulted in the legislature's adoption of a **poll tax**, which went into effect in 1904.[27] It was a tax of $1.50 to $1.75 that had to be paid each year before a person could vote. In the early 1900s, that was a large sum of money for low-income people. It was to be paid between October 1 and January 31, three months before the primaries were then held and nine months before the general elections, long before most people even began to think about voting. Consequently, the tax eliminated large numbers of voters who were likely to support the Populist Party and undermine the political establishment.[28]

The poll tax was in effect for more than sixty years in Texas. It was outlawed for federal elections by the Twenty-fourth Amendment to the U.S. Constitution, adopted in 1964, but Texas retained the poll tax for state and local elections, thus requiring two sets of registered voters and separate ballots when a federal election also was at the same time. In November 1966, Texas voters approved an amendment to the state constitution eliminating the poll tax for state elections and implementing annual voter registration. By that time, the U.S. Supreme Court had already ruled that the state poll tax was unconstitutional.[29]

☐ The White Primary

Texas, along with several other southern states, also created the **white primary**, which was designed to eliminate African American participation in the elections that really counted during the years of one-party, Democratic control.[30] In 1923, the Texas legislature enacted a law that denied African Americans the right to vote in the Democratic primary. The U.S. Supreme Court declared that law unconstitutional in 1927 on the basis of the Fourteenth Amendment.[31] Almost immediately, the legislature authorized the state party executive committee to establish the qualifications for voting in the primaries, and the Democratic Party adopted a resolution that only whites could vote. This was challenged in the federal courts, and again, in 1932, the Supreme Court declared the white primary unconstitutional.[32]

Acting through its state convention and without legislative authorization, the Democratic Party then proceeded in May 1932 to exclude African Americans from the primary again. The issue was taken a third time to the Supreme Court, which this time ruled that the party, as a voluntary organization and not a government entity, had the authority to determine membership and the right of participation.[33] But African Americans continued to use the courts to attack the white primary. Finally, in the case

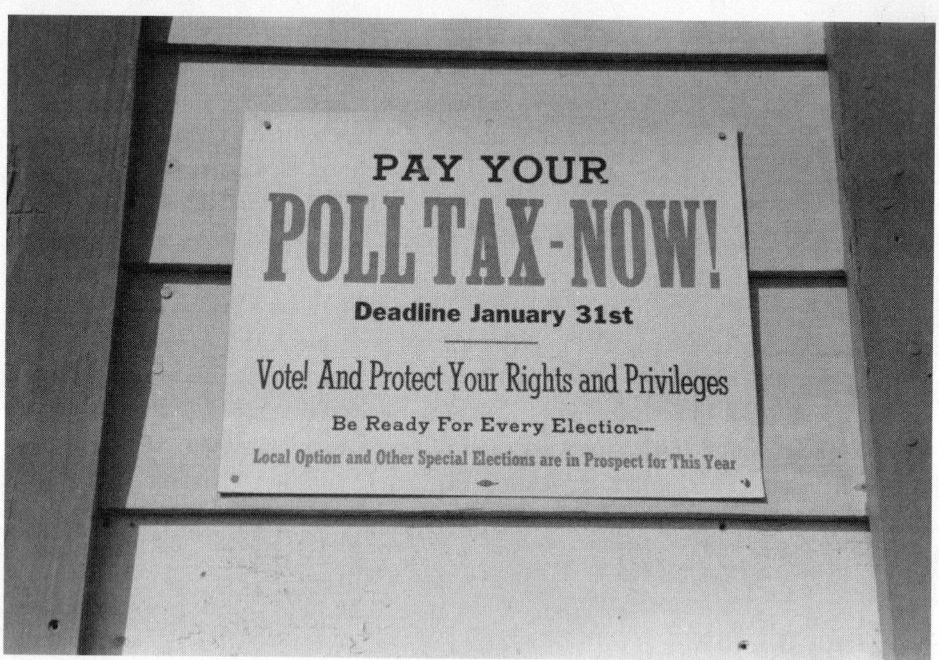

ANTI-POPULIST MOVEMENT TACTIC

The poll tax was a requirement for voting until it was eliminated by a constitutional amendment in 1966. The voter would register to vote by paying the tax yearly—$1.50 to $1.75—at the courthouse. Given the value of a dollar in 1904, the tax was hefty.

of *Smith* v. *Allwright* in 1944, the Supreme Court reversed its earlier decision and declared the white primary unconstitutional.[34]

Those who persisted in excluding African Americans from participation were extremely imaginative in their efforts to circumvent the court's decisions. They substituted a restrictive, preprimary selection process through the private Jaybird Democratic Association—open only to whites—to choose candidates, who then were formally nominated in the Democratic primary and subsequently elected in the general election. In 1953, the U.S. Supreme Court also declared this arrangement unconstitutional.[35]

□ Restrictive Registration Law

Until 1971, Texas had one of the most restrictive voter-registration systems in the nation. Voters had to register annually between October 1 and January 31. If voters did not register in person at the county courthouse but with deputy registrars, these officials could deliver or mail in only one registration form at a time, thus minimizing the possibilities of coordinated voter-registration drives. These restrictions discouraged voter registration across the state, especially among the African American, Hispanic, and low-income populations.[36]

More court intervention forced major changes in the voter-registration law in 1971.[37] The highly restrictive system was transformed, in a relatively short time, into one of the most progressive systems in the country. Annual registration was replaced with permanent registration. An individual now can register by mail or in person up to thirty days prior to an election. Persons working individually or with a political campaign can be deputized to register voters, and large voter-registration drives are encouraged. County voter registration officials now must send out cards to voters, automatically renewing their registrations, every two years. Officials also are restricted in how soon they can remove the names of voters who have moved from registration lists.

Property Ownership and the Right to Vote

From colonial times, one requirement for the right to vote was property ownership, a practice that continued in modified form through the 1970s in many states, including Texas. Property ownership was not required to vote in primaries and most other elections, but it was required in bond elections that were used by local governments to win financing of new buildings, roads, sewer systems, and other infrastructure needs. The exclusion of non–property owners from these elections was based on the argument that revenue from property taxes was used to repay these bonds, and if a person did not own property on which to pay a tax, he or she should not have the right to vote for the bonds.

Landlords, however, passed on their property taxes to renters, and many renters, therefore, had a direct interest in the outcome of bond elections. Many urban areas, moreover, had large numbers of rental property and many residents who were barred from participating in those elections. Eventually, the federal courts declared property ownership as a requirement for voting in bond elections unconstitutional.

gerrymandering
Drawing of political district lines in such a way that they favor a particular political party or racial group.

single-member district
A system in which legislators, city council members, or other public officials are elected from specific geographic areas.

Women and the Right to Vote

The national movement for women's suffrage, or the right to vote, was a long struggle fought in state capitals as well as in Washington. In 1915, the Texas legislature considered a constitutional amendment extending the right to vote to women but rejected it. In 1918, women were given the right to vote in primary elections and party conventions. Then, in 1919, Texas became the first southern state to approve the Nineteenth Amendment to the U.S. Constitution, which, by late 1920, was approved by the required number of states to grant women's suffrage in all elections.[38]

Extension of the Vote to Those Eighteen Years of Age and Older

A long-standing debate over the age at which a person should be permitted to vote became more intense during the Vietnam War. Many people believed that individuals who were required to comply with the draft and risk death in battle should no longer be denied the right to vote. The Twenty-sixth Amendment, which lowered the voting age from twenty-one to eighteen, was adopted in 1971, and the first election in which eighteen-year-olds could vote was in 1972. Perhaps because of the political activism of many college students during the Vietnam era, young people were expected to vote at higher rates than older adults, but this never has happened. The lowest voter turnout rates, in fact, are among voters eighteen to twenty-nine years old.

Other Discriminatory Aspects of Election Systems

Even after the most obvious discriminatory practices against minorities were eliminated, there were more subtle, but just as pervasive, techniques for reducing the political power and influence of these same groups. One technique is racial **gerrymandering** of political boundaries. State legislators and many city council members are elected from **single-member districts**, each of which represents a specific number of people in a designated area. After the 2010 census, for example, each member of the Texas House ideally represented 167,637 people, and each member of the state Senate, 811,147 people. To minimize the possibility of minority candidates being elected, policymakers could divide minority communities and attach them to predominantly nonminority communities—a tactic called *cracking*. Minority communities also could be consolidated into one district, a tactic called *packing*, with an 80 percent to 90 percent minority population, which would reduce the number of other districts in which minorities might have a chance

7.1

7.2

7.3

7.4

7.5

7.6

7.7

7.8

at-large election
A system under which city council members or other officeholders are elected by voters in the entire city, school district, or single-purpose district. Many of these election systems have been struck down by the federal courts or by the U.S. Justice Department under the Voting Rights Act as discriminatory against minorities.

motor voter registration
Term referring to federal and state laws that allow people to register to vote at offices where they receive their drivers' licenses.

of winning office. The federal Voting Rights Act forbids such practices, but minority groups continue to go to court to challenge redistricting plans.

At-large elections also have been used to reduce minority representation. At one time, members of the Texas House who came from urban counties were elected in multimember districts, which required candidates to win election in countywide races, a difficult prospect for many minority candidates. The practice was eliminated in legislative races in the 1970s as a result of federal lawsuits. But many cities, school districts, and special districts across Texas continue to use at-large elections, requiring candidates to run for office citywide or districtwide. This system dilutes minority representation in most communities in which it is used. In addition to the increased costs of running in at-large elections, which discourage minority candidates, a minority group that may account for 60 percent of a city's total population and 52 percent of the voting-age population may account for only 45 percent of the registered voters. With the possibility of polarized voting, whereby minorities vote for the minority candidates and the nonminorities vote for the white candidates, there is a high likelihood that no minority could get elected in many at-large systems. At-large elections have come under increasing attack under the Voting Rights Act, and many local governments have adopted some form of single-member districting.

□ The Voting Rights Act

In 1965, the U.S. Congress enacted the Voting Rights Act, which was extended to Texas in 1975. This law has been central to efforts by minorities in challenging discriminatory election systems and practices. Under the Voting Rights Act, minority groups can challenge state and local election systems in the federal courts. The burden of proof in such challenges is on the government. An election system that dilutes minority voting strength is illegal, even without a clear intent to discriminate against minorities. Furthermore, any changes in the election systems of state or local governments, including redistricting plans, must be precleared (or approved) by the U.S. Department of Justice or must be approved by the U.S. District Court in Washington, D.C. This legislation has produced changes in election systems across the state and has helped increase minority representation in the Texas legislature and on local governing bodies.

By the mid-1990s, however, the Voting Rights Act was under attack by conservatives. The U.S. Supreme Court, in "reverse discrimination" cases from Texas and Georgia, ruled that some congressional districts had been illegally gerrymandered to elect minority candidates. In the Texas case, three federal judges held that the Texas legislature had violated the U.S. Constitution by designing two districts in Houston and one in the Dallas area to favor the election of African American or Hispanic candidates. The court redrew thirteen congressional districts in Texas—the three minority districts and ten districts adjoining them—and ordered special elections to fill the seats.

Despite the redrawn boundaries, two incumbent African American congresswomen in the affected districts were reelected. In effect, recent court cases have held that race or ethnicity can be considered in drawing legislative boundaries but cannot be the predominant factor. Representatives of minority groups fear that these recent cases will reduce the number of potentially winnable legislative districts for African American and Hispanic candidates. They also are concerned that the Voting Rights Act will be significantly modified whenever temporary sections are scheduled to expire. Lawsuits over the 2011 redistricting maps in Texas will be another test for the Voting Rights Act. The U.S. Supreme Court, a more conservative body than it was when the Voting Rights Act was initially enacted, will make the final decisions in those lawsuits, including interpretations of the Voting Rights Act.

□ Motor Voter Registration

The **motor voter registration** law was passed by the U.S. Congress in 1993 and signed by President Bill Clinton, despite the opposition of Republicans, who apparently feared it would benefit the Democratic Party. The first President Bush had vetoed an earlier version of the bill in 1992. The federal law, similar to a 1991 Texas law, requires states to provide eligible citizens the opportunity to register to vote when they apply for or renew a driver's license. The law also requires states to make voter registration forms available at certain agencies that provide welfare benefits or assist the disabled.[39] From 2006 through 2008, elections administrators in Texas's 254 counties received approximately 5 million registration applications. Some 27 percent of these, or more than 1.3 million applications, came from the Department of Public Safety's drivers' licenses offices.[40] The law has expedited the voter registration process for many Texans.

☐ Facilitating Voter Participation

Since the 1980s, efforts have been made across the nation to reduce administrative barriers to political participation. Several states have adopted procedures for online registration. Other states have adopted "same day" registration, allowing people to register to vote on Election Day. Others have provided for online voting. Following the lead of Texas and a handful of other states, extended early voting has been allowed. Some people advocate longer hours for voting, and others push for making Election Day a holiday, among other recommendations. Some of these proposals eventually may be adopted. Eliminating barriers can increase voter registration and increase turnout, but they will not resolve voter indifference, problems of getting transportation to the polls, and health issues that deter voting.

Political Gains by Minorities and Women

7.4 Assess the political gains made by minorities and women in Texas politics in recent years.

Since the mid-1970s, African Americans and Hispanics have made substantial gains in the electoral process. Elimination of restrictive voting laws, the adoption of a more liberal state voter-registration system, and changes mandated by the National Voter Registration Act of 1993 have contributed to an increase in minority voters across the state. Voter registration and mobilization drives coordinated by groups such as the National Association for the Advancement of Colored People and the Southwest Voter Registration Education Project have contributed to increased participation, as has an increase in the number of minority candidates and elected officials. When minority candidates run and have a good chance of winning, minority voters have a stronger incentive to vote. Yet, it would be premature to conclude that the state's election system is now "color blind." The contentious debate over the 2011 photo identification law pushed by Texas Republicans is a case in point. As noted earlier in this chapter, the U.S. Justice Department refused to approve the law under the Voting Rights Act because Texas had failed to prove the law would not discriminate against minority voters. The federal agency determined that a disproportionately large number of minority voters in Texas lacked drivers' licenses or other government-issued IDs that included photos, as required by the voting law.

☐ Hispanics

According to the 2010 census, Hispanics make up 37.6 percent of Texas's population, but the Hispanic population is younger than the Anglo and African American populations, and Hispanics account for only 33.6 percent of Texans of voting age (see Table 7–3).

7.1 7.2 7.3 7.4 7.5 7.6 7.7 7.8

TABLE 7–3 RACIAL AND ETHNIC DIFFERENCES IN THE TOTAL POPULATION OF TEXAS, THE VOTING AGE OF ALL TEXANS, AND CITIZENS OF VOTING AGE.

	Population	Percentage of Total Population	Population Age 18+	Percentage of Population Age 18+	Citizens Age 18+	Percentage of Citizens Age 18+
Anglo	11,397,345	45.3	9,074,684	49.6	8,932,021	56.7
Hispanic	9,460,921	37.6	6,143,144	33.6	4,131,145	26.2
Black	2,886,825	11.5	2,123,923	11.6	2,048,643	13.0
Other	1,400,470	5.6	937,986	5.1	652,454	4.1
Total	25,145,561	100.0	18,279,737	100.0	15,764,263	100.0

SOURCE: U.S. Census Bureau, *2010 Census.*

Hispanics also include many immigrants who are not citizens, thus reducing to approximately 26 percent the Hispanic portion of adults eligible to register and vote. The percentage of Hispanics who actually register and vote is even smaller.

In the 2004 presidential election, the U.S. Census Bureau estimated that 22 percent of registered voters in Texas were Hispanic and 20 percent of those voting were Hispanic. By comparison, Anglos comprised 65 percent of those voting and African Americans, 12 percent.[41]

The 2008 presidential election produced a similar pattern of turnout and influence for the Hispanic population, with an estimated 20 percent of the Texas votes cast by Hispanic citizens. African Americans comprised 16.5 percent of the votes cast in the state.[42] Election studies conducted in the early 1990s concluded that Hispanics accounted for only 12 percent to 15 percent of Texans casting ballots.[43] The recent turnout shows improvement but certainly not the full potential for the state's Hispanic population.

Voter registration and turnout are not simply explained by racial or ethnic factors. Study after study of registration and turnout demonstrate a direct relationship between education and income.[44] Across racial and ethnic groups, people with more education and higher incomes are more likely to vote than those at the lower end of the scales. Low income and educational levels serve to deter voter participation among Hispanics.

Approximately 44 percent of Hispanic adults interviewed in the 2003 to 2004 *Texas Polls* identified with the Democratic Party, but the story is more complex.[45] Until Governor George W. Bush made substantial inroads into the Hispanic vote in 1998, Democratic candidates for president and governor consistently received more than 70 percent of the Hispanic vote in Texas.[46] Using state exit polls, the Pew Hispanic Center estimated that George W. Bush, as president, received 49 percent of the Hispanic vote in 2004. Barack Obama received 63 percent of the Hispanic vote in 2008.[47]

Hispanic voters played a major role in the 2002 Democratic primary, which for the first time featured two Hispanic gubernatorial candidates, Laredo businessman Tony Sanchez and former Attorney General Dan Morales. One of the three major candidates for the party's U.S. Senate nomination also was Hispanic—Victor Morales, a schoolteacher who had shocked party leaders by winning the 1996 senatorial nomination. The William C. Velasquez Institute, which specializes in Hispanic-related voting activity, reported that Hispanics cast a record 33 percent of the 2002 Democratic primary votes.[48] Spending heavily from his wealth on television advertising, Sanchez easily defeated Dan Morales for the gubernatorial nomination. And tapping into the Hispanic vote, Victor Morales participated in a runoff for the Senate nomination with former Dallas Mayor Ron Kirk, an African American. Each received about one-third of the vote. But Kirk, who was supported by most party leaders, swamped Morales in fund-raising and won the Senate runoff, when Hispanic voter turnout had fallen off. Both Sanchez and Kirk later lost their general election races to Republicans.

TABLE 7–4 LATINO ELECTED OFFICIALS IN TEXAS, 1974–2011

	1974	1996	2001	2011
Federal	2	5	6	6
State	13	35	36	38
County	102	203	213	298
Municipal	251	536	555	632
Judicial/Law Enforcement	172	323	280	472
School Board	—	536	701	1,025
Special District	—	51	37	49
Total	540	1,689	1,828	2,520

SOURCES: Juan A. Sepulveda Jr., *The Question of Representative Responsiveness for Hispanics,* Harvard College, Honors Thesis, March 1985; National Association of Latino Elected and Appointed Officials, *National Roster of Hispanic Elected Officials,* 1996, 2001; and NALEO Educational Fund, *2011 National Directory of Latino Elected Officials.*

The increased electoral strength of the Hispanic population is borne out in Table 7–4, which compares the number of elected Hispanic officials in Texas in 1974 to those holding office in 2011. Some 540 Hispanics held elected office in 1974. By 2011, there were 2,520 Hispanic elected officials, the highest in any state. The marked increase can be attributed to a more equitable apportionment of city, county, and school district political boundaries, the growth of the Hispanic population, and increased organizational efforts among Hispanics.

By 2012, only seven Hispanics had been elected to statewide office in Texas. Four were Texas Supreme Court Justices Raul A. Gonzalez, Alberto R. Gonzales, David M. Medina, and Eva Guzman. The others were Attorney General Dan Morales and Texas Railroad Commissioners Tony Garza and Victor Carrillo. Other Hispanic candidates, such as Victor Morales and Tony Sanchez, have made serious statewide races. With changing demographics and the increased political sophistication of the Hispanic population, Hispanics will win additional statewide and local offices in the future.

☐ African Americans

African Americans constitute approximately 11 percent of the state's population, 11 percent of the voting-age population, and 10 percent to 12 percent of those who vote. Approximately 61 percent of Texas African Americans call themselves Democrats, but 80 percent to 90 percent of the African American vote normally is cast for Democratic candidates. Voting cohesively as a group, African Americans, like Hispanics, have considerable potential to influence the outcome of both primaries and general elections.

The increased political clout of the African American population also is manifested in the number of African American elected officials (Table 7–5). In 1970, there were only twenty-nine African Americans elected to public office in Texas. The number increased to 196 in 1980 and 466 in 2002. Only four African Americans have been elected to statewide office in Texas: former Railroad Commissioner Michael Williams, Texas Supreme Court Chief Justice Wallace Jefferson, and Texas Supreme Court Justice Dale Wainwright, all Republicans, and former Texas Court of Criminal Appeals Judge Morris Overstreet, a Democrat.

☐ Women

Historically, the world of Texas politics has been dominated by men, but that is changing. Prior to Ann Richards's election as state treasurer in 1982, only two women had been elected to statewide office. Richards was elected governor in 1990, and Kay Bailey Hutchison, who had succeeded Richards as state treasurer, was elected to the

7.1

7.2

7.3

7.4

7.5

7.6

7.7

7.8

TABLE 7–5 AFRICAN AMERICAN ELECTED OFFICIALS IN TEXAS, 1970, 1980, AND 2002*

	1970	1980	2002
Federal	—	1	2
State	3	14	17
County	—	5	21
Municipal	16	75	285
Judicial/Law Enforcement	—	21	47
School Board	10	78	94
Special District	—	2	—
Total	29	196	466

**2002 was the last year for which this information was reported by the Joint Center for Political and Economic Studies.*

SOURCE: Metropolitan Applied Research Center and Voter Regional Council, *National Roster of Black Elected Officials*; and Joint Center for Political and Economic Studies, *National Roster of Black Elected Officials,* 1980, 1998, and 2002.

U.S. Senate in 1993. As governor, Richards also appointed more women than her predecessors to key positions on state boards and commissions.

In 2012, nine women held statewide offices in Texas, including Hutchison, who served her last year in the U.S. Senate before retiring; state Comptroller Susan Combs; two members of the Texas Supreme Court; and five members, a majority, of the Texas Court of Criminal Appeals. That same year, six women served in the state Senate and thirty-two in the Texas House. As recently as 1981, only one woman was in the Senate and eleven in the House.

Women play an increasing role in local government as well, and this pattern can be expected to continue. Since the 1970s, the state's three largest cities—Houston, Dallas, and San Antonio—have had women mayors. A 2006 survey by the Texas Municipal League counted 198 women mayors (or 16 percent) in the state's 1,211 cities. The 6,021 council members in the cities included 1,588 women, or 26 percent of the total.[49] Of the 254 county judges in 2006, 24 (or 9.5 percent) were women, and women held 65 (or 6.4 percent) of 1,016 county commissioner posts.[50] Women also held a large number of other county offices. Of the 7,207 elected school board trustees in 2008, some 1,835 (or 25 percent) were women. There were 1,036 school superintendents in 2008, and 166 (or 16 percent) were women.[51]

The New Campaign Technology

7.5 Describe some of the applications of marketing technology to political campaigns.

When Texas was a one-party Democratic state during much of the twentieth century, the only state elections that counted were the Democratic primaries, and they often would include five or six candidates for a single office. In statewide or local campaigns, candidates seldom ran as a ticket or coalition. Each candidate developed his or her own campaign organization, thus precluding the development of party organizations. Individuals who became involved in a campaign were primarily motivated by their personal loyalties to a candidate and not to the political party.

With low rates of voter participation in the primaries and the absence of viable Republican challengers in the general elections, Democratic candidates stumbled through the election process with loose coalitions that often disintegrated after

Election Day. Although there was competition in the Democratic primaries, conservative candidates, tied to the establishment, generally prevailed. Despite differences in personality and style, these conservative candidates were fundamentally committed to the policy agendas of the economic elites of the state.

By today's standards, political campaigns through the 1950s were amateurish and unsophisticated. A number of factors have reshaped modern political campaigns, including an expanded and highly mobile electorate, the growing dominance of the Republican Party, the organizational weaknesses of both political parties, the continuation of the candidate-centered campaign, the increased reliance on the electronic media for news and political information, and the emergence of the Internet and social networking sites.[52] Today's successful campaigns rely on sophisticated public opinion polling, slick campaign ads, analyses of demographics, and targeting of selected populations through direct mail, phone banks, and online resources—all orchestrated by professional **campaign consultants**.

Such consultants have been around in Texas in some form or another for a long time. W. Lee "Pappy" O'Daniel, the owner of a flourmill that produced Hillbilly Flour and master of ceremonies of a daily radio talk show, ran for governor in 1938, exploiting a rustic image couched in religious, evangelical language that had a wide appeal in the rural areas of the state. His speeches were designed to create identification with the "common folks," but he was a wealthy businessman who had ties to Texas's corporate leaders. His homespun style was contrived, and O'Daniel relied heavily throughout his campaign on public relations expert Phil Fox of Dallas.[53] What is different about contemporary campaign consulting is that it is an identifiable industry with diversified expertise. More significantly, few candidates for statewide office or major local offices now run without using the services of campaign consultants.

campaign consultant
A professional expert who helps political candidates plan, organize, and run their campaigns.

public opinion polling
The scientific compiling of people's attitudes toward business products, public issues, public officeholders, or political candidates. It has become a key ingredient of statewide political campaigns and is usually conducted by telephone, using a representative sample of voters.

□ Public Opinion Polling

In a society based on mass consumption, it is no wonder that techniques were developed to measure public attitudes and opinions. The origins of the industry usually are linked to George Gallup, who conducted a statewide poll in 1932 for his mother-in-law, who was running for secretary of state in Iowa. Survey research or public opinion polling has a variety of applications, most of which are nonpolitical; market research is now a multibillion-dollar industry.[54]

Public opinion polling is used in political campaigns for a number of purposes. As would-be candidates consider running for office, they often will hire pollsters to conduct benchmark surveys of people who are likely to vote in the upcoming election. Using well-tested sampling techniques, the pollster will conduct either a telephone survey or a face-to-face survey of a representative sample of voters. The length and type of the survey usually are determined by available funds and the information desired by the candidate and those developing the campaign. Surveys are expensive and can consume a significant chunk of a campaign budget.

Surveys also are used to develop campaign strategy, monitor or track the progress of the campaign, and modify the campaign as changes take place in the attitudes, perceptions, or mood of the electorate. The benchmark survey, often taken some time before the official campaign gets underway, is rather lengthy and attempts to assess public opinion relating to the office a candidate seeks. Issues are identified, perceptions of candidates are probed, and trial heats with potential opponents are tested. A wide range of demographic questions permits the segmentation of the electorate into small groups whose specific interests or concerns can be identified and targeted.

As the campaign proceeds, tracking surveys are used to determine shifts in attitudes, perceptions, and support for the candidate. Does the candidate now have greater name identification? Do more people perceive the candidate positively and express their support with greater intensity? Is there a particular event or emerging campaign issue that might spell defeat? This information is used to adjust the campaign to changing conditions. Toward the end of the campaign, surveys often are taken nightly to permit further fine-tuning of the campaign in the final days.

A variation on the survey is the focus group. As television advertisements are developed, the campaign staff may choose to test them before they are aired. A series of focus groups, each including eight to twelve persons recruited for specific demographic characteristics, will be asked to review these ads and provide their impressions and reactions. An experienced staff will watch these proceedings to identify subtle responses to the ads, the theme, or the message. On the basis of these qualitative assessments, the media consultants will decide which ads to use or discard.

Some campaigns have resorted to "push polls," a practice that most scholars and reputable pollsters consider a violation of research ethics. The survey is presented to the voter as an effort to solicit perceptions and attitudes toward candidates, but as the interviewer moves through the questions, a controversial or negative position or attribute of a potential candidate is introduced. Finally, this attribute is linked to a specific candidate, and the voter is then asked if this fact would change his or her vote.

□ Segmentation and Targeting of the Electorate

A political campaign is fundamentally an organized effort to communicate with the electorate with the goal of convincing a majority of those who participate to vote for a specific candidate. But effective communication is difficult for a number of reasons. One is the low voter turnout in most elections. Voter turnout rates also vary among different ethnic, income, and education-level groups, and some of these voters will not support a particular candidate no matter what he or she says or does. In a partisan election, many people will vote for or against a candidate strictly on the basis of party identification. Obviously, not every voter shares a candidate's concerns and priorities.

Candidates use census data, surveys, and previous election returns with turnout and party voting patterns to divide voters into segments. Some research specialists organize this information to permit the campaign to target its messages to small, well-defined populations. Psycho-demographics, a technique used by some opinion specialists, combines survey and census data to divide populations by lifestyles rather than party identification. Whether direct mail, social networking, television, radio, newspapers, phone banks, or block walking is used to reach its audience, the modern campaign directs a specific, relevant message to these segmented populations based on sophisticated market research.

For example, survey data may suggest that a disproportionate number of women between the ages of 45 and 54 have not heard of the candidate but are concerned about health care and medical insurance. Based on demographic data and television program ratings, the media specialist knows that a large number of these women watch daytime television programs. To get a specific message to these voters, television spots with a health care message oriented to the specific concerns of women ages 45 to 54 will be developed and aired during these times of the day. Most populations can be identified and targeted in this manner, increasing the likelihood that a desired message gets to the specific voters whose perceptions and attitudes the consultant wants to influence. The use of the Internet for political communications has made some aspects of segmentation and targeting even more sophisticated as large amounts of data on users can be captured and analyzed to determine the messages that should be sent to specific populations.

The segmentation of the electorate may well lead to a fracturing of the political debate. Various segments of voters are exposed to narrow slices of the candidate's image, personality, and concerns. The campaign hopes that each group of voters will respond favorably to its own limited knowledge of the candidate, but some critics argue that this segmentation "further diminishes the importance of language, logic, and reason in the articulation of campaign issues."[55]

Media and Advertising

7.6 Differentiate between controlled and uncontrolled media in election campaigns and explain how they fit into the larger advertising strategy of campaigns.

It is easy to assume that a campaign can market a candidate much like a pack of cigarettes or a box of soap, and our increasing cynicism often leads to this facile conclusion. But voter response to candidates, the progress of the campaign, and the various ads and messages that voters receive form an extremely complex decision-making process. Scholars in various disciplines have attempted to unravel the effects of news reports, campaign advertising, and campaign strategies and tactics on voter behavior. But the conclusions are only tentative because it is difficult to demonstrate that a specific event, news story, or campaign ad results in the final decision of a voter.

Controlled Media

Candidates can communicate their messages to the voters through numerous media. For those media that can be purchased commercially, the only limitations are availability and finances. Candidate-purchased media often are referred to as the **controlled media**. The candidate controls decisions concerning which media to use, when to purchase advertisements, and what message to convey. Some technical and legal questions pertain to campaign advertising, but the candidate has a wide range of options.

Billboards, bench signs, advertisements on buses and cabs, and electronic signs can be purchased to establish voter awareness and name identification. Although such ads are not likely to convert or mobilize voters, they establish the candidate's visibility.

Although candidates talk about "pressing the flesh" and making direct contact with the voters, it is simply impossible to talk personally to the number of people necessary to win an election, particularly in a statewide or urban race. Candidates stage block walks and rallies in which they personally participate and meet with supporters, but many of these are **media events** they hope the press will cover. Campaigns also shoot their own videos of these events for posting on candidates' websites, for distribution through social media and for coordinating with the paid media campaign, direct mail, and other tactics.

In many local elections across Texas, it is too costly or inefficient to use radio and television advertising. But it is almost impossible to run a viable statewide campaign without the use of the electronic media. Texas is large and diverse and has about twenty-three separate media markets. Candidates often spend half of the campaign budget for television and radio advertising, and media specialists—ranging from creative staff to time buyers—have taken on increased importance in modern campaigns. Candidates also are increasingly using Internet advertising, either to save money or to supplement the more expensive TV advertising.

The thirty-second spot is the standard for television advertising, and the candidate's consultants attempt to carefully craft advertisements that address concerns, perceptions, and expectations of varied segments of the electorate.[56] The media blitz usually picks up steam as the campaign moves closer to Election Day because it is assumed that it takes several exposures to a given ad for a voter to respond, and, in many cases, allegations raised in an opponent's advertisements must be addressed.

Campaign advertising in the 1990 and 2002 gubernatorial races is still considered some of the ugliest, most negative in Texas history. In 1990, "gay-bashing" advertisements were used against Democratic nominee Ann Richards after she received the endorsement of groups alleged to be linked to lesbian rights, and a fund-raising letter from the national Democratic chairman attempted to link Republican nominee Clayton Williams with neo-Nazism and racism.[57] Most observers agreed that advertisements in the 1990 gubernatorial race were more vitriolic, aired with more frequency, and were seemingly

controlled media
Paid advertising in the media whose content and presentation are determined by a political candidate or campaign.

media event
An event staged by an officeholder or political candidate that is designed to attract media—especially television coverage.

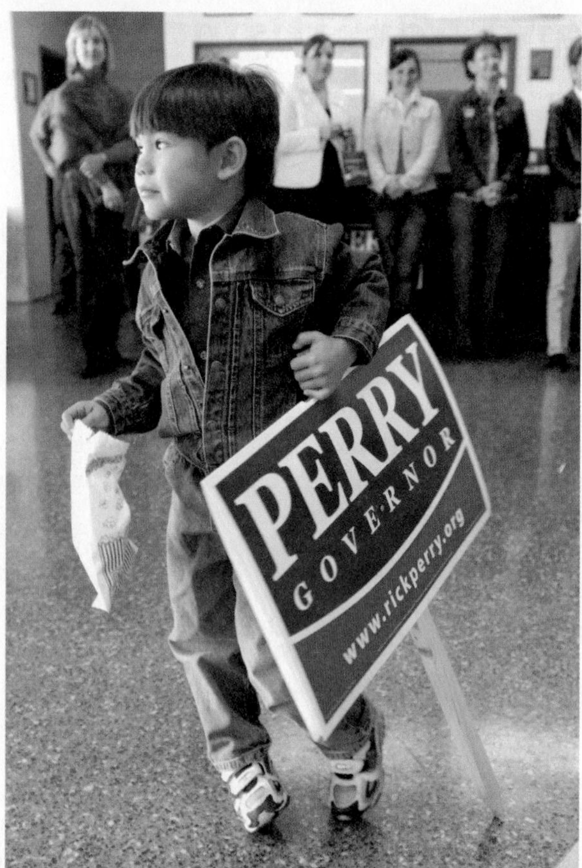

ADVERTISING HIS CANDIDATE

John Levy, then 5, waited for Governor Rick Perry to speak to supporters in Wichita Falls a few days before Perry was re-elected in 2006. The boy carried a sign in support of Perry. Signs such as these help to establish voter awareness and name recognition.

more irrelevant to the issues facing the state than most ads had been in the past. As the advertisements continued, newspapers began to analyze their themes and veracity, and voters indicated that they were displeased with them. But consultants continued to convince their clients that negative attacks worked and that people, although objecting to negative ads, had higher recall of them than of many other television spots.

The 2002 gubernatorial race, in which Republican Rick Perry and Democrat Tony Sanchez spent almost $100 million, much of it bashing each other over the airwaves, was equally vicious. Sanchez tried to blame Perry for high electric bills and homeowners' insurance rates, which the state partly regulated. Perry tried to link Sanchez, a wealthy Laredo businessman, to drug dealers. Perry's allegation was based on a federal investigation that had determined that a savings and loan owned by Sanchez in the 1980s had unwittingly been used to launder drug money. Sanchez never was implicated in any wrongdoing, and he and other officials of the savings and loan, which later folded, said they did not know the depositors were connected to the illegal drug trade.

Computers and smart phones also are major vehicles for campaign communications. Officeholders and candidates communicate with volunteers, supporters, the news media, and the general public through email, Twitter feeds, Facebook pages, and updates on campaign websites. This, in part, is a further extension of the controlled media, although a candidate cannot control how a message may be used—or misused—after it hits cyberspace.

☐ Uncontrolled Media

Positive news stories—or blog posts—about a candidate are potentially more valuable than paid advertising and do not cost the campaign money. Candidates and their handlers thus attempt to exploit the press (the old media as well as the new) by getting positive coverage and reducing as much as possible any negative slants in campaign stories. But the relationship between political candidates and the press—as well as much of the blogosphere—is adversarial. The news media, ever alert for weaknesses in a candidate and tips spread by political opponents, can make or break a candidate by the coverage and slant given to the candidate's personality, reputation, view of the issues, and campaign activities. A candidate's mistakes or "oops" moments spread instantaneously on the Internet, and often a candidate is unable to recover from them.

Many campaigns hire press secretaries who specialize in media relations. One author has suggested that a successful media strategy entails the following: "Keeping the candidate away from the press; feeding the press a simple, telegenic political line of the day; and making sure the daily news line echoes [*magnifies* may be the better word] the images from the campaign ads, thus blurring the distinction between commercials and 'reality.'"[58] It is common to hear consultants speak of "staying on message" as they attempt to influence media coverage.

Members of the press are keenly aware of these efforts to manipulate them, and the best reporters usually are able to resist. But the hectic, irrational nature of statewide campaigns, the online pressure of constant news deadlines, the propensity for pack journalism—a group of reporters chasing the same news source - and the fear of being beaten on a major story by a competitor often work against a reporter's sincere efforts to get the "straight skinny" on the candidate's abilities, leadership potential, and stand on the issues.

□ Direct Mail and Fund-Raising

People like to receive mail. Some people even like to receive junk mail, experts say, and direct mail has become a highly sophisticated component of modern campaigns. Direct-mail specialists provide campaigns with a technique for "persuasion and fundraising."[59] As a further refinement of the segmentation and targeting of voters, this technique permits the campaign to craft a specific message for a narrowly defined population and ensure, with high probability, that households with the specified demographic or psychographic characteristics will receive the campaign message. In a sense, it is "narrow casting" a specific message to an identifiable audience.

Direct mail is big business in the United States, and it has been easily adapted to political campaigns. As new innovations are developed with direct Internet communications, we are seeing its increased use for communicating with voters and fund-raising. In many instances, the campaign messages and appeals are emotional, designed to push the voters' "hot buttons" on specific issues. They are crafted by specialists who have studied the emotional appeals of such communications, and the attention to detail often astonishes the uninitiated. The length of a letter, the color of the paper on which it is printed, the underlining and highlighting of specific words or phrases, and teasers on the envelope to convince the recipient to open the letter receive the specialist's critical attention. Evidence indicates that people respond to direct-mail appeals, and if the technique is integrated with phone banks, block walks, and the media campaign, it becomes an extremely valuable campaign tool.[60]

Direct mail also has become a major tool in campaign fund-raising. Massive mailing lists targeting virtually every population group in the state have been developed, and computers can easily extract names of persons with probable political attitudes and beliefs from these files. Successive mailings to probable supporters have a high likelihood of producing campaign dollars. The continued use and refinement of these lists increase the rate of return. Although campaigns still rely on large contributions, the more modest contributions received from direct-mail solicitation have taken on increased importance.

Large amounts of money also can be raised using the Internet, and both of the state's major political parties encourage online contributions.[61] A campaign that merges modern technology, the knowledge of segmentation and targeting, and

grass roots
A term used to describe a wide range of political activities designed to organize and mobilize the electorate at the local level. Modern campaigns are increasingly dominated by the campaign consultants, but such support can prove crucial for political candidates, particularly for those with limited financial resources.

well-developed appeals that speak to the interests or "hot buttons" of groups of voters can raise money from a vast number of small contributors giving less than $200 apiece. A great deal of information can be conveyed electronically. The potential contributor can be given ongoing information about the direction and success of the campaign. The campaign can go back again and again to those who demonstrate a predisposition to contributing.

Many campaigns for minor, down-ballot offices cannot afford the technologies just discussed. Nor do they have the technical staff available to develop and implement these new tools. Candidates do the best they can with what they have. But the Internet has offered some modestly funded candidates for lesser-known offices less expensive alternatives to communicate with voters.

☐ Grass Roots

Over the past few decades, many political candidates and consultants often have neglected **grass-roots** campaigning in favor of mass media. They believed the mass media were more efficient because large numbers of voters could be contacted in a short period. If attacked by an opponent, a quick response could be aired. Repeated contacts also could be used to mobilize voters. Messages could be targeted to specific segments of the electorate. The campaign did not have to engage in the time-consuming process of recruiting and managing volunteers. Although grass-roots campaigns never went away, they often were conducted on a shoestring budget with little careful thought as to how volunteers could be effectively integrated into the overall campaign.

As noted earlier, however, effective grass-roots activities can make a difference, especially in closely contested elections. Traditional grass-roots activities include door-to-door campaigning (block walking), neighborhood gatherings, recruiting other volunteers, addressing and stuffing envelopes, making signs, staffing phone banks, staffing the polls on Election Day, and a host of other tasks. Whether the grass-roots organization staff is paid or unpaid, a telephone call, letter, postcard, personal email, or visit from a campaign worker who demonstrates an intense commitment to a candidate still can have a strong impact on voters. But it takes a great deal of planning and resources to successfully coordinate these activities.

Money and Campaigns

7.7 Evaluate the impact of money in campaigns in Texas and assess to what extent campaign finance laws are effective.

No one knows precisely how much is spent on political campaigns in Texas because there is no single place where all this information is collected. Candidates for state office file campaign finance reports with the Texas Ethics Commission, but candidates for city councils, county offices, and school boards file reports with the jurisdictions in which they run. Campaign costs vary widely among the different contested offices, but it is evident that costs, even at the local level, continue to increase.

☐ Campaign Costs and Fund-Raising

City council races in major cities such as San Antonio, Houston, Fort Worth, and Dallas can easily cost $50,000 to $100,000, and they can go higher. Multimillion-dollar races for mayor in the big cities are rather common. Bob Lanier spent $3 million to be elected mayor of Houston in 1991, and eight candidates spent more than $6.6 million in the 1997 race to succeed him. The 1997 winner, Lee Brown, spent more than $2.1 million alone, and the second-place finisher, businessman Rob Mosbacher, spent more than $3.5 million.[62] These figures, however, paled in comparison to the nearly $9 million that businessman Bill White spent to win the 2003 Houston mayor's race.[63] Reports have indicated that candidates for county commissioner have spent $100,000 or more and district judges in metropolitan counties have spent more than $150,000. Historically, school board elections have been low budget, but it is not uncommon for slates of candidates in large urban school districts to spend $10,000 to $15,000 in low-turnout elections.

In the 2010 election cycle, 333 major party candidates for statewide and legislative offices reported raising $202 million. Candidates for governor, including unsuccessful primary candidates, raised almost $82.2 million. Republican Rick Perry, the winner, raised $39.3 million of that total. Some $76.8 million was raised in races for the Texas House, in which all 150 seats were on the ballot. The winning candidates averaged $371,000 in money raised for a job that pays $7,200 a year, and some winners were unopposed in the primary and the general election. State Senate incumbents and challengers reported $21.5 million in contributions, and that included $9.5 million raised by 15 senators who were not even up for reelection in 2010. The average Senate winner raised more than $684,000, and several of those were incumbents who ran unopposed (see Table 7–6).[64]

Heading the list of biggest spending, but losing candidates in a Texas gubernatorial race is Democrat Tony Sanchez, who spent more than $50 million from his own pocket in losing to Rick Perry in 2002.[65] There are a number of explanations for such high campaign finance figures. The population has increased, requiring more money to be spent to reach more voters. Candidates increasingly rely on the electronic media, which are very costly. So is the increased use of consultants to organize and run political campaigns. Meanwhile, the growing number of interest groups and political action committees (PACs) has made more money available to candidates (see *Talking Texas: PACs: A Growth Industry in Texas*).

Unspent funds raised for a campaign can be carried over as a "war chest" for the successful candidate's next election. Even unopposed officeholders will attempt to raise large amounts of money to discourage potential opponents in the future. A significant question about House and Senate fund-raising is why a person would go to such lengths to raise such huge sums of money to win an office that pays only $7,200 a year.

TABLE 7–6 CAMPAIGN CONTRIBUTIONS TO CANDIDATES SEEKING STATE OFFICES, 2010 ELECTION CYCLE

Office	Totals for Winner in General Election	Totals for Loser in General Election	Totals for Primary Losers	Total Number of Candidates
Governor	$39,328,540	$26,298,865	$16,565,395	8
Lt. Governor	10,635,480	949,944	56,772	4
Comptroller	2,716,730	—	—	1
Attorney General	5,828,869	910,779	—	2
Land Commissioner	863,307	98,758	2,270	3
House	56,155,371	15,367,175	5,328,930	271
Senate*	10,951,410	110,780	897,362	44
Totals	$126,479,707	$43,736,301	$22,850,729	333

* Sixteen of the thirty-one Senate seats were up for election in 2010. All House seats were up for election.

SOURCE: Texans for Public Justice, *Money in PoliTex*, 2010.

7.1

7.2

7.3

7.4

7.5

7.6

7.7

7.8

Talking ★ TEXAS PACs: A Growth Industry in Texas

Political action committees (PACs) are big business in Texas, and they continue to get bigger. According to Texans for Public Justice, a record 1,302 active PACs in Texas spent $133 million trying to influence election results during the two-year 2010 election cycle, a 12 percent increase over the 2008 election campaign period. The spending was an almost threefold increase over the previous decade, during which the number of active PACs had grown by 50 percent.

Leading the PACs in spending were business and ideological (or single-issue) committees, with labor committees ending up a distant third. Business PACs spent $68 million, but if you count the $6.7 million spent by Texans for Lawsuit Reform (TLR), the business total becomes almost $75 million. TLR is business oriented, but because its goal is winning additional limits on civil lawsuits and damage judgments, it is classified as a single-issue PAC. The second and third highest-spending ideological PACs were the Texas Democratic Trust ($5.3 million) and Back to Basics ($4.2 million), which plaintiffs' attorney Steve Mostyn of Houston funded almost exclusively.

Another ideological PAC, the National Rifle Association, spent $630,771, including a $2,500 donation to Governor Rick Perry.[a]

CRITICAL THINKING QUESTIONS

1. **With all the heavy spending by political action committees, should people of modest means bother making $50 or even $500 campaign contributions to state candidates? Why or why not?**
2. **What are the odds of the legislature ever imposing limits on spending by political action committees? Explain your answer.**

[a]Texans for Public Justice, "Texas PACs: 2010 Cycle Spending," August 10, 2011.

☐ Why People Contribute to Campaigns

Soaring campaign costs have raised considerable concern about campaign fundraising and contributions in Texas, as they also have nationally. There is concern that elections are being bought and that major campaign contributors are purchasing influence in the policymaking process. Some critics of contemporary campaigns have argued that current practices are a form of legalized bribery, implying that public officials are available to the highest bidder. Other critics have asserted that some officeholders engage in "shaking down" organizations for campaign contributions with implied threats.

Money is critical to most successful campaigns for public office because it permits the candidate to purchase advertising and other resources for communicating with the voters. But money is not the only factor affecting an election. Incumbency, existing party loyalties, the availability of party or campaign activists, the public's perceptions of a candidate, and a candidate's campaign skills or expertise also help determine electoral success. In numerous elections, well-financed candidates have been defeated by opponents with far fewer dollars. This may suggest that there are genuine limits on what money can accomplish in a campaign.[66]

Contributions are made to influence the outcome of an election and, subsequently, to shape public policy by electing persons who share similar political views with or who will be sympathetic or accessible to those making the contributions. Reports of large campaign contributions often prompt remarks that Texas has the "best Supreme Court that money can buy" or the "best legislature that money can buy." These remarks are given credence if key policy votes seem to be influenced by an officeholder's relationship to his or her political contributors.

Some people undoubtedly make contributions to candidates out of a sense of civic duty, general concern for good public policy, partisan loyalty, or personal friendship. But contributions of hundreds of thousands of dollars, either from individuals or political action committees, raise different questions about intent and purpose. For example, James Leininger, a wealthy businessman from San Antonio, is known for his support of conservative causes, particularly a proposal to spend tax dollars on private school vouchers. When a voucher proposal was defeated in the 2005 session of the legislature with the support of five Republicans, he then gave more than $2 million to their opponents in the 2006 Republican primaries.

Rarely will anyone admit publicly that he or she is attempting to buy a candidate. Individuals and PACs making large political contributions usually say they are doing so for the purpose of "gaining access" to elected officials.[67] Since officeholders have limited time to consider and assess competing interests, lobbyists representing interest groups and their PACs contend that campaign contributions are necessary to give them an opportunity to present their cases on specific legislation.

Political scientists and others have attempted to prove that a relationship exists between campaign contributions and public policy, but so far the research is inconclusive. Multiple factors shape the decisions of public policymakers, including an officeholder's personal views, the views of his or her constituents, legal and technical issues, and the merits of the requests made by specific individuals or groups.[68] Nevertheless, the strong appearance of a relationship between money and public policy exists, and advocates of campaign finance reform can make strong arguments for change.

political action committee (PAC)
Often referred to as a PAC, a committee representing a specific interest group or including employees of a specific company that raises money from its members for distribution to selected officeholders and political candidates.

fat cat
An individual who contributes a large amount of money to political candidates.

☐ PACs, Fat Cats, and the Really Big Money

Just as they have nationally, **political action committees (PACs)** have increased their importance at the state and local levels by bringing sophisticated fund-raising skills to political campaigns. Representing special interest groups or individual companies, PACs collect money from their members and are a ready source of campaign dollars. They are in the business of influencing elections. A record 1,302 Texas political action committees spent $133 million during the two-year, 2010 election cycle, a 12 percent increase over the 2008 cycle. Texas PAC spending increased by nearly threefold, and the number of active PACs grew by 50 percent between 2000 and 2010, according to Texans for Public Justice, which tracks money in Texas politics.[69]

Unlike the federal government, Texas places no limits on the amount of money an individual or political action committee can contribute to most political candidates, and there are no limits on how much a candidate can contribute to his or her own campaign. The only exceptions in Texas are campaign contribution limits in judicial races, which were imposed by the legislature in 1995. Large contributions have long played a role in Texas politics, and, over the years, most large contributions have gone to the conservative candidates, both Democratic and Republican. The role of large money may be mitigated in the future through the use of direct mail and the Internet to solicit small campaign donations. From the available data, however, it is still too early to discern such a pattern. For now, large donors—including PACs and a relatively small number of super-wealthy individuals, sometimes called **fat cats**—still dominate the contributions to Texas political campaigns (see *Talking Texas: Bob Perry: Homebuilder and Mega Donor*).

Political action committees are an extension of interest groups. These committees, which collect money from their members for redistribution to candidates, have increased their importance at the state and local levels by bringing sophisticated fund-raising skills to political campaigns. PACs are in the business of influencing elections, and they are key players in the fund-raising game. Many PACs are organized by corporations and are a major source of business funding to political candidates in Texas. Corporations also can influence elections by spending money on issue advertising, provided they do not endorse a specific candidate. Many company executives also make individual contributions to candidates.

7.1 7.2 7.3 7.4 7.5 7.6 7.7 7.8

Talking ★ TEXAS Bob Perry: Homebuilder and Mega Donor

For Governor Rick Perry and many other Republican officeholders, candidates, and causes, multimillionaire Houston homebuilder Bob Perry is the gift that keeps on giving. Bob Perry (no relation to Rick Perry) tries to maintain a low public profile, but his prolific political check writing has attracted considerable media attention in Texas and around the country. One associate told *The New York Times*, in a 2010 interview, that Perry had contributed "well over $20 million" in recent years.[a] He has been the single biggest political donor in Texas over the past decade and is one of the biggest contributors to Governor Perry.

Bob Perry was the primary financer of the Swift Boat Veterans attack ads against John Kerry, the 2004 Democratic presidential nominee. He also has given millions of dollars to independent Republican groups attacking Democrats or supporting Republican candidates in a number of states. Recipients of his largesse have included the Republican Governors Association and American Crossroads, the conservative group that political strategist Karl Rove helped to establish.

Bob Perry rarely gives media interviews or attends political events. Some of his admirers say he never asks for favors. But his voice obviously is heard. He is believed to have been influential in the Texas legislature's creation in 2003 of a new state agency, the Residential Construction Commission, to develop performance standards for builders and discourage lawsuits against builders by unhappy homebuyers. Governor Perry appointed an executive of Bob Perry's company to the new agency's board, less than one month after the governor received a $100,000 contribution from Bob Perry. The governor's office said the appointment was not influenced by the contribution—neither the governor's first nor his last contribution from the homebuilder—but by the appointee's experience in the homebuilding industry.

The legislature abolished the Residential Construction Commission in 2009, following numerous consumer complaints that it did little but protect the homebuilding industry. Bob Perry, however, continues giving.

CRITICAL THINKING QUESTIONS

1. **What do you think motivates an individual to give millions of dollars to political candidates and causes?**
2. **How much influence do you think Bob Perry has over state government in Texas? Explain your answer.**

[a]Eric Lichtblau and Michael Luo, "Big Gifts to G.O.P. Groups Push Donor to New Level," *The New York Times*, October 21, 2010.

The biggest PAC spenders in Texas are business oriented. Texans for Lawsuit Reform, whose members include businesspeople, has played a leading role in recent years in a successful lobbying effort that has produced significant restrictions on damage lawsuits filed against doctors and businesses. Other major PACs include the Texas Association of Realtors and the Texas Medical Association.

☐ Attempts at Reform

On the heels of the Sharpstown scandal, in which high-ranking state officials were given preferential treatment in the purchase of stock in an insurance company, the legislature enacted a major campaign finance disclosure law in 1973. The Texas Ethics Commission now administers this law, with some changes. Although the law did not limit the size of political contributions, for the first time it required candidates to list the addresses as well as the names of donors and the amounts and dates of contributions. It also required PACs contributing to candidates or officeholders to report the sources of their donations, which in the past usually had been hidden. Also for the first time, officeholders were required to file annual reports of their political contributions and expenditures—even during years when they were not seeking reelection—and candidates were required to report contributions and other financial activity that occurred after an election. A candidate also had to formally designate a campaign treasurer before he or she could legally accept political contributions. Campaign finance reform, however, remains a difficult and seemingly endless struggle as officeholders, individuals, and organizations resist efforts to reduce the influence of money and require the fund-raising process to be more transparent.

Political Participation

7.8 Outline the process of acquiring political views and attitudes toward politics and describe the various ways in which Texans participate politically.

political socialization
The process that begins in early childhood whereby a person assimilates the beliefs, attitudes, and behaviors of society and acquires views toward the political system and government.

Several years ago, a small group of protesters pitched tents and erected a series of crude displays outside the offices of what then was known as the Texas Water Commission in Austin. They came from a small town south of Dallas where, they claimed, an industrial plant was polluting the environment with cancer-causing agents. People living in the community had experienced disproportionately high cancer rates and immunity and respiratory problems. These were middle-aged Texans who had never before participated in, much less organized, a demonstration. They appeared to be uncomfortable, but there was a sense of desperation as they talked about their families and friends.

A month or so later in San Antonio, several thousand antiabortionists organized a three-mile-long demonstration along a major highway. The demonstration took place after church on a Sunday, and many of the well-groomed protesters carried Bibles and had their young children in tow. Waving placards, singing songs, and praying, they used tried and true tactics that have been implemented by other antiabortion groups across the nation.

On any given day, Texas newspapers publish hundreds of letters to the editor addressing a wide range of state and local political issues. People contact public officials every day about stop signs, public facilities, garbage collection, and a multitude of governmental functions and responsibilities. Thousands of people are involved in politics as they attempt to shape the actions of public officials.

Voting and running for office are the first two activities that may come to mind when we think of political participation. But they are just a small part of the ongoing process necessary to sustain a democratic political system, translate the interests and demands of the public into specific policies, and ensure governmental responsiveness.

Most people who participate in politics engage in what scholars call conventional political behavior. This includes voting, running for office, contributing to and campaigning for candidates, writing letters, gathering petitions, participating in other grass-roots activities, and lobbying.

Fewer individuals participate in what is considered unconventional political behavior—acts that may offend many people. They can include boycotts, protest marches, and other nonviolent demonstrations, although many individuals consider any lawful, peaceful demonstration a conventional means of exercising their constitutional rights. To most people, however, destruction of property, personal injury, assassination, and other forms of violence are totally unacceptable forms of political behavior.[70]

Not everyone, of course, participates in politics at the same level. Why some people get actively involved in politics and public life whereas others seem totally uninterested in government, current events, or public policy is a question that has challenged scholars, candidates, journalists, and reform groups for years and has generated much research.

From the day a person is born, he or she is subject to a socialization or a learning process. The process is complex, lifelong, and structured by the interaction of the individual with the environment in which he or she lives. As the person approaches adulthood, the process includes the shaping of political attitudes, beliefs, and behavior.

Political socialization, the process by which people learn to behave politically, "transmits a broad array of values and opinions, from general feelings about trust in government to specific opinions" about the economy, political leaders, and institutions.[71] The agents of political socialization include the family, through which the young child first learns the views and attitudes of parents and relatives toward government, the political process, and leaders. The process is expanded through schools, where children are exposed to national and state history, government, heroes, and values. Civics lessons

activists
A small segment of the population that is engaged in various political activities.

7.1

7.2

7.3

7.4

7.5

7.6

7.7

7.8

and courses are taught to further shape commitment to the dominant values of the society. Other institutions, such as the church and the mass media, contribute to this molding process. So do a person's peers and life experiences. Individuals tend to validate their perceptions and attitudes through the opinions of friends and acquaintances, and a major life experience, such as a tour of duty in the military or extended unemployment, has a potential effect on one's political behavior.

Political behavior is complex and changes over time. The limited space dedicated to this topic here is insufficient to flesh out its nuances and complexities, and we warn you to avoid drawing hard-and-fast conclusions. But a few broad generalizations about political behavior are in order.

A number of scholars have developed classifications of political behavior that run from high levels of involvement in a wide range of activities to virtual passivity. Sidney Verba and Norman H. Nie, well-known American political scientists specializing in political socialization, identified six categories of political participation.[72] At one end of the spectrum are the complete **activists** (approximately 11 percent of the population), who engage in all types of political activity. Not only are these individuals involved in political campaigns, but they also participate in almost every other arena of community life. At the other end are the *inactives* (22 percent), who participate rarely, if at all, in the political life of the community. Some scholars refer to the first group as *political gladiators* and the second group as *apathetics*.[73]

Another group that is relatively inactive and shares many of the characteristics of the inactives are the *voting specialists* (21 percent). These individuals vote regularly in presidential and local elections but seldom engage in other organizational activities or attempt to contact policymakers personally.

A small number of *parochial participants* (4 percent) vote but do not engage in collective activity or campaigns. Nevertheless, they do contact policymakers over specific issues that affect their personal lives.

The *communalists* (20 percent) demonstrate a high rate of participation in community life but a low level of campaign activity. These people participate in community activities such as church, PTA, and neighborhood associations but rarely engage in the high-conflict game of political campaigns.

The *campaigners* (15 percent) are just the opposite. They participate regularly in political campaigns but rarely in community activities. This group appears to be attracted to the conflict of campaigns.[74]

Although we have limited survey data for Texas, some generalizations emerge from national studies to provide insights into the patterns of political participation in the state:

1. **Income.** Individuals with higher income levels are more likely to be active participants in a wider range of political activities than those with low incomes. Affluent people have more time and resources to engage in political activities. They have a better understanding of the process, and they are acquainted with other participants and public officials.
2. **Education.** Participation increases as the level of education increases. People with college degrees are more likely to participate in politics than those less educated. Education also is correlated with income. Knowledge of political issues, public policies, the political process, and public officials makes a person aware of the importance and potential benefits of political participation.
3. **Gender.** Historically, men had participated in politics at higher rates than women. In recent years, women and men have been participating at comparable levels, and in some areas of the country, women now participate at higher rates than men. More women now run for and win public office. In recent years, evidence has pointed out differences between men and women in support of the major political parties, which often is referred to as the "gender gap."[75]
4. **Age.** Young people are far less likely to engage in politics than older people. The highest rates of participation are among middle-aged people. Younger adults tend to be in a transitory stage of their lives in which they do not identify with the

issues or politics of the communities in which they live. Younger voters engage in a wide range of volunteer activities, but these tend not to be political.

5 **Race and ethnicity.** Rates of participation among Anglos are highest among all ethnic groups. African Americans, despite historical patterns of discrimination, now are moving toward the Anglo level of participation. Hispanics tend to participate at much lower rates than either Anglos or African Americans. Explanations for these variations include educational and income differences, citizenship status, and the degree to which Hispanics have been assimilated into the political culture.

6 **Political efficacy.** Complex psychological attributes contribute to one's sense of having an impact on others or on political events. Political activists believe that they can influence the outcome of events. The more intense this sense of efficacy, the more likely one is to become involved politically.

In Texas and elsewhere, there is a great deal of concern about decreased political participation. Election turnout has declined, and it often is difficult to get strong candidates to run for public office. Public discourse has lost its civility, and citizens do not seem to have learned the lessons of the benefits and logic of collective action.[76] Surveys indicate much distrust of elected officials, and many people believe that government is for sale to the highest bidder. Moreover, some people just do not care. These findings lead many to conclude that an erosion of democratic practices has taken place in the state and the nation.

On MyPoliSciLab

Review the Chapter

Listen to Chapter 7

The Functions of Elections

7.1 List the basic functions of elections in a democratic society, p. 184.

Elections in a democratic society link citizens to their political leaders and institutions. Elections provide the general population with an opportunity to shape public policy indirectly through the selection of leaders. They serve to keep public officials accountable, and they provide the electorate with opportunities of replacing one set of leaders with another. For elections to achieve their ideal purpose under democratic theory, voters must be well informed, be attentive to the actions of their leaders, and care about the outcome of elections.

State and Local Elections

7.2 Compare and contrast the types of elections held throughout Texas, p. 185.

Texans have ample opportunities to exercise their right to vote; with frequent elections, it often appears that the election cycle is endless. Candidates for partisan state and county offices are nominated in the party primaries and run-off elections, normally held in March and April of even-numbered years. Statewide general elections are held in November of even-numbered years, and candidates nominated in the primaries and runoffs compete in these elections. Vacancies in some offices require special elections to fill unexpired terms. Partisan elections include high levels of straight ticket voting.

Each regular session of the Texas legislature proposes several constitutional amendments, which normally are on the general election ballot in odd-numbered years. Constitutional amendment elections also can be held at other times, if the legislature chooses. Candidates for city, school board, and special district offices run for election on nonpartisan ballots. Most local governments hold their elections in May of odd-numbered years, although some cities and school boards have elections in May of even-numbered years or November in either odd- or even-numbered years. Local governments also hold special elections at various times to seek voter approval of charter changes or bond issues.

Political Suffrage in Texas: A Struggle for Minorities and Women

7.3 Explain the measures taken to keep some Texans from voting and the countermeasures employed to curtail these discriminatory practices, p. 192.

Constitutional amendments following the Civil War extended full citizenship to African Americans, but Texas, along with the other southern states, engaged in a long history of denying full voting rights to minority residents. Texas used a variety of discriminatory legislation, including the poll tax, white primary, restrictive registration laws, and property ownership as a requirement for voting. Eventually, U.S. Supreme Court decisions and constitutional amendments eliminated all of these restrictions. In 1971, Texas replaced a highly restrictive voter registration law with a system, still in place, making it much easier for large numbers of voters to be registered by minority groups and political campaigns. However, the enactment in 2011 of a Texas law requiring photo identification for voting (not registration) was potentially a huge step backward. The U.S Department of Justice refused to approve the new voting law under the Voting Rights Act and a federal lawsuit was still pending as of July 2012.

The federal Voting Rights Act, extended to Texas in 1975, also has helped Hispanics and African Americans fight discriminatory redistricting of congressional, legislative, and local political districts and replace discriminatory countywide or district-wide election requirements with single-member districts. That struggle, however, continues.

Women won the right to vote in Texas party primaries in 1918, and the ratification of the Nineteenth Amendment to the U.S. Constitution in 1920 gave women the right to vote in all elections throughout the country. The Twenty-sixth Amendment lowered the voting age from twenty-one to eighteen in 1971, and eighteen-year-olds voted for the first time in 1972.

Political Gains by Minorities and Women

7.4 Assess the political gains made by minorities and women in Texas politics in recent years, p. 197.

Since the 1970s, Hispanics and African Americans have realized substantial gains in the electoral process with an increased number of elected officials at the state and local levels of government. These groups have developed established relationships with the political parties, particularly the Democratic Party, and play an increasingly identifiable role in the outcomes of elections. Although approximately 58 percent of the eligible voting-age population is Anglo, minority voters' share of the electoral base will continue to increase. Seven Hispanics and four African Americans have been elected to statewide office in Texas. Thirty-seven Hispanics and nineteen African Americans served in the Texas House or Senate in 2011. The House also included two Asian Americans.

Women also are playing an increased role in state and local politics. Nine women held elected statewide office in Texas in 2012. Six women served in the state Senate and thirty-two in the Texas House in 2011. Two women have been elected governor, and several of Texas's largest cities have or recently have had women mayors.

The New Campaign Technology

7.5 Describe some of the applications of marketing technology to political campaigns, p. 200.

Political parties once played a major role in elections, but now candidates increasingly rely on paid campaign consultants, who have taken over many of the traditional party functions. Candidates contract with campaign specialists for a wide variety of campaign-related functions, including public opinion polling, demographic studies, and segmentation of the electorate into identifiable groups of people with shared interests or concerns. The consultants then target tailored advertising and other communications efforts to specific groups. The consultants' primary objective is to win campaigns, and they appear to give little consideration to the subsequent effects of campaigns on governance and policymaking.

Media and Advertising

7.6 Differentiate between controlled and uncontrolled media in election campaigns and explain how they fit into the larger advertising strategy of campaigns, p. 203.

Candidates must communicate an array of messages to win support and mobilize voters to turn out and vote for them on Election Day. To do this, candidates use both controlled and uncontrolled media. The controlled media include those messages that are paid for by the candidate. They include advertising on television, radio, the Internet and other paid media. Candidates also maintain their own websites, on which they control the message, and they pay for direct mail, door-to-door canvassing, telephone banks, and a variety of grass-roots activities. The candidates also attempt to manipulate and use uncontrolled media. They try to garner free and, they hope, positive coverage by issuing news releases, holding press conferences, and staging pseudo-news events to attract media coverage.

Money and Campaigns

7.7 Evaluate the impact of money in campaigns in Texas and assess to what extent campaign finance laws are effective, p. 206.

The costs of statewide campaigns, as well as of many regional and local campaigns, have escalated since the late 1970s. Candidates receive much of their money in large campaign contributions from political action committees ar individuals. Although money may not buy publ it certainly buys access to them, and it creates t sion that well-organized interests, corporations, individuals have a disproportionate influence on ers. Texas law prohibits corporations and labor unions from making contributions directly to political candidates. However, except for modest limits on judicial campaigns, Texas law puts no limits on the amount of money that can be contributed in political races by individuals and political action committees. Texas law, however, does require fairly thorough and timely reporting of campaign contributions and expenditures.

Political Participation

7.8 Outline the process of acquiring political views and attitudes toward politics and describe the various ways in which Texans participate politically, p. 211.

The process by which people acquire their political values and interest in political participation is called political socialization. Several factors, including education and family interest in politics, help determine the degree of a person's political participation. People in the higher socioeconomic groups are more likely to participate in a wider range of political activities, such as making political contributions, attending political conventions, or joining special interest groups. They have more influence on the policymaking process than people in the lower socioeconomic groups. One of the most disturbing aspects of the contemporary Texas political system is the low voter turnout in most elections, despite the elimination of discriminatory election laws, the creation of an extended voting period, and easy voter registration. Many people may be too uninformed about governmental actions to care to vote. Other people may be turned off by a belief that public officials put their own interests and special interests before the public interest.

Learn the Terms

Study and **Review** the Flashcards

suffrage, p. 185
primary election, p. 186
runoff election, p. 188
Voting Rights Act, p. 188
general election, p. 189
local election, p. 189
special election, p. 190
absentee (or early) voting, p. 191
poll tax, p. 193
white primary, p. 193
gerrymandering, p. 195
single-member district, p. 195
at-large election, p. 196
motor voter registration, p. 196
campaign consultant, p. 201
public opinion polling, p. 201
controlled media, p. 203
media event, p. 203
grass roots, p. 206
political action committee (PAC), p. 209
fat cat, p. 209
political socialization, p. 211
activists, p. 212

Test Yourself

Study and Review the Practice Tests

1. The notion that elections allow a democratic society to control its leaders and judge their actions assumes that

a. voters are offered clear alternatives.
b. at least half the population has the right to vote.
c. candidates answer all questions posed to them by the news media.
d. there is 100 percent voter turnout.
e. voters are resentful of politics.

2. Elections in Texas are separated and scheduled at different times in order to

a. increase voter turnout.
b. maximize accountability of elected officials to the public.
c. maximize the level of democracy in the state.
d. minimize the convergence of issues in state and local races.
e. keep voters interested in public issues.

3. Direct primaries in Texas

a. are usually held on the second Tuesday in April in even-numbered years.
b. are optional for the Democratic and Republican Parties.
c. do not require formal party membership.
d. allow members from one party to vote in the other party's runoff election.
e. usually have a higher voter turnout than general elections.

4. If no candidate in a primary election receives a majority of votes, the

a. election is run a second time.
b. top three vote getters face one another in a runoff election.
c. plurality winner wins the nomination.
d. party convention chooses a nominee.
e. top two vote getters face each other in a runoff election.

5. Party primaries

a. draw more voters than general elections.
b. are paid for by the state.
c. draw more moderate and independent voters than general elections.
d. are required for every party appearing on the general election ballot.
e. give the party more control over the nomination process than party conventions.

6. General elections for state and federal offices

a. usually are held on the second Tuesday in March in even-numbered years.
b. are held on the first Tuesday after the first Monday in November in even-numbered years.
c. do not allow split ticket voting.
d. do not allow straight ticket voting.
e. permit only one third party per ballot.

7. Most local elections

a. usually are held on the second Tuesday in March in even-numbered years.
b. usually are held on the first Tuesday after the first Monday in November in even-numbered years.
c. allow for split ticket voting.
d. are nonpartisan.
e. do not allow for early voting.

8. The poll tax in Texas

a. was instituted to prevent African Americans from building coalitions with low-income whites.
b. was a tax of 1 percent of a person's income.
c. was levied on wealthy voters to help pay for the cost of running elections.
d. replaced the white primary.
e. was declared unconstitutional by the Texas Supreme Court.

9. All of the following are reforms that addressed restrictive registration in Texas EXCEPT

a. permanent registration.
b. automatic registration renewal.
c. same-day registration.
d. registration deadline thirty days prior to an election.
e. encouragement of voter registration drives.

10. The tactic of dividing minority communities and attaching them to predominantly nonminority communities in redistricting is known as

a. packing.
b. stacking.
c. fracking.
d. tracking.
e. cracking.

11. All of the following are true about political gains of minorities and women in Texas EXCEPT that

a. Hispanic voting turnout is less than the proportion of Hispanics in the state.

b. there are more Hispanic elected officials in Texas than in any other state.

c. African Americans comprise a larger percentage of the voting population in Texas than Hispanics.

d. more African Americans elected to statewide office in Texas have been Republicans than Democrats.

e. a majority of the Texas Court of Criminal Appeals is made up of women.

12. One of the dangers of sophisticated targeting of voters by campaign consultants is that

a. voters are less likely to turn out to vote.

b. partisans are more likely to switch party allegiances.

c. polled citizens are more likely to lie to consultants.

d. voters will acquire too much information about the candidates.

e. political debate will become fractured by the segmentation of the electorate.

13. Which of the following is an example of controlled media?

a. news coverage by the press

b. debate coverage

c. press conferences

d. billboards

e. appearance on a radio talk show

14. Which of the following is an example of uncontrolled media?

a. newspaper articles

b. block walking

c. direct mail

d. thirty-second spots

e. yard signs

15. Which of the following statements is TRUE about campaign finance laws in Texas?

a. Texas places the same limits on campaign contributions that the federal government does.

b. Texas places campaign contribution limits in judicial races.

c. There are no limits on the amount of money an individual can contribute to any race in Texas.

d. Candidates must disclose the amounts of contributions, but not the names of the donors.

e. PACs, but not individuals, are limited in what they can contribute to campaigns.

Explore Further

Bailey, Chuck, with Bill Crawford, *Texas Political Memorabilia: Buttons, Bumper Stickers, and Broadsides.* Austin: University of Texas Press, 2007. Presents "the most exceptional, most memorable, and most informative examples of Texas political memorabilia"; drawn from the author's personal collection.

Bridges, Kenneth, *Twilight of the Texas Democrats: The 1978 Governor's Race.* College Station: Texas A&M University Press, 2008. Details the watershed governor's election of 1978, which reflected the forces of realignment and the eventual ascendency of the Texas Republican Party.

Bryson, Conrey, *Dr. Lawrence A. Nixon and the White Primary*, rev. ed. El Paso: Texas Western Press, 1992. Provides an account of the role of Dr. Lawrence Nixon, an El Paso physician and activist in the black community, in challenging the Texas white primary.

David, Chandler, and Bernard Grofman, eds., *Quiet Revolution in the South: The Impact of the Voting Rights Act, 1965–1990.* Princeton, NJ: Princeton University Press, 1994. Constitutes a "must read" for those who want to understand the impact of the Voting Rights Act.

Erikson, Robert S., and Kent L. Tedin, *American Public Opinion*, 8th ed. New York: Longman, 2010. Covers topics including political socialization, the impact of the media on public opinion, and the role of public opinion in the electoral process, in addition to presenting data from the 2008 election.

Flanigan, William H., and Nancy H. Zingale, *Political Behavior of the American Electorate*, 12th ed. Washington, DC: Congressional Quarterly Press, 2009. Introduces political behavior in an informative manner; rooted in an extensive body of research.

Kinch, Sam, *Crapshoot Politics: Money and the Texas Judiciary.* Austin, TX: Eakin Press, 2003. Focuses on the impact of money in judicial races in Texas; based on interviews with lawyers and former judges.

Maisel, L. Sandy, and Mark D. Brewer, *Parties and Elections in America*, 6th ed. Lanham, MD: Rowman and Littlefield Publishers, 2012. Provides a highly readable treatment of political parties in the United States with an emphasis on elections.

Texans for Public Justice, *Money in PoliTex: Who Bankrolls Your Representative, 2010.* Austin: TX: Texans for Public Justice, 2011. Analyzes the millions of dollars raised by major-party candidates in the 2010 elections; part of a biennial series of reports on campaign finances and expenditures in Texas.

Traugott, Michael W., and Paul J. Lavrakas, *The Voter's Guide to Election Polls*, 4th ed. Lanham, MD: Rowman and Littlefield Publishers, 2008. Guides the voter through the morass of polling data that are generated in each election cycle; the authors provide direction in assessing data produced from polls.

8

Listen on MyPoliSciLab

The Texas Legislature

Leadership by encouragement can be more successful than leadership by full frontal force.

—Joe Straus, Speaker of the Texas House of Representatives, 2009

When Republicans swept to an unprecedented (at least in modern times) supermajority of the Texas House during the 2010 elections, conservatives immediately began to flex their political muscles, and one of their first targets was the Republican House speaker, Joe Straus. Although it may sound strange for Republicans to try to unseat another Republican from one of the most influential posts in state government, conservative activists wanted to reap the maximum benefit, in terms of their legislative priorities, from a new 101 to 49 GOP House margin. Moreover, several of the new Republican House members were ultraconservatives who, with the support of tea party voters, had unseated more moderate Republican incumbents in the party primary.

Many conservative GOP members of the House and their constituents had never been comfortable with Straus. He was perceived as being too moderate. He had unseated Republican Speaker Tom Craddick in 2009 with the key backing of most of the House's Democratic members when Republicans had held only a razor-thin 76 to 74 House majority.

Craddick had been the first Republican speaker elected in Texas in modern times in 2003, but after three terms of strong-handed, autocratic leadership, he had worn out his welcome with many of his fellow Republicans. So, his enemies from both parties had taken advantage of the near-equal partisan lineup in 2009 to replace Craddick with the less-autocratic Straus. But the House dynamic had changed substantially on the eve of the 2011 session. Conservatives had not forgiven Straus for his previous Democratic support or forgotten that the speaker had let the same Democrats later outmaneuver him in 2009 and kill a major Republican priority, a bill to require voters to have a form of photo identification at the polls.

8.1 List the major functions of the Texas legislature, p. 220.

8.2 Describe the basic organizational structure of the Texas legislature and the professional characteristics of its members, p. 222.

8.3 Explain redistricting and the impact of court-ordered redistricting changes on the composition of the Texas legislature, p. 227.

8.4 Contrast the leadership and committee structure of the Texas House with that of the Texas Senate, p. 229.

8.5 Outline how a bill becomes a law in Texas and the various obstacles that exist in the lawmaking process, p. 241.

8.6 Trace the changes in partisanship of the Texas legislature, from Democratic to Republican Party dominance, p. 245.

8.7 Assess the various influences on Texas lawmakers' decision making, p. 248.

8.8 Analyze and explain recent efforts to reform the legislative process in Texas, p. 251.

THE TEXAS STATE CAPITOL, completed in 1888 and now surrounded by state office buildings, is a prominent landmark in downtown Austin. The part-time, bicameral legislature meets in the State Capitol in odd-numbered years.

institutionalization
The complex process of institutional change and adaptation in the organization and operations of the legislature.

House members, not their constituents or special interest groups, elect the speaker. Immediately after the November 2010 elections, however, conservative activists began pressuring Republican House members to unseat Straus. The pressure included a public email and telephone campaign orchestrated by Empower Texans, an extreme, antitax group seeking to shrink the size of government. Two other Republican legislators launched campaigns against Straus during the two months between the elections in November and the January opening of the 2011 regular session. Straus fought back and held on to his base of support. On the day before the session convened, 70 of the 101 House Republicans endorsed Straus in a nonbinding vote. His two opponents then withdrew from the race, and his fellow House members reelected Straus to a second term, 132 to 15, on opening day.[1]

Many legislators were unhappy with the outside pressure exerted on them, including threats that conservative activists would recruit opponents for Straus's supporters in the 2013 Republican primary. Nevertheless, after Straus's reelection, the House joined the Republican-dominated Senate in passing a conservative agenda, including deep cuts in the state budget, a law requiring photo identification for voting, and another law requiring doctors to conduct a sonogram on patients before performing an abortion. Although Straus may have been a moderate at heart, he chose to ride an overwhelming conservative tide rather than be drowned in it.

The contentious circumstances surrounding Straus's reelection reflect some of the enormous changes in the political environment in which the Texas legislature functions. Until the late 1960s, a rural-dominated legislature operated within the context of one-party Democratic control and an interest group system dominated by oil, finance, and agriculture. Legislative leaders tied to conservative factions in the Democratic Party pursued selected policies that benefited those sectors of the Texas economy. Speaker's races were influenced—and won—by conservatives, but at the time they called themselves Democrats. Only a handful of Republicans served in the legislature then, certainly not enough to influence a speaker's race.

Today, Texas is the country's second most populous state and is more than 80 percent urban. The ethnic and racial characteristics of its population have changed, and still more changes in social composition are projected. The Republican Party now dominates Texas, its economy is diversifying, and more demands now are placed on the legislature than in the past. The issues and policy questions that confront lawmakers are more complex, and the special interests demanding attention are more numerous and diverse. Despite Texas's major demographic and political changes, however, lawmakers still have to operate under outdated constitutional restrictions—including strict limits on when they can meet—that were written for a rural state in a bygone era.

Legislative Functions

8.1 List the major functions of the Texas legislature.

The Texas legislature has undergone significant institutional changes over the past 130 years. Some changes have resulted from external factors, such as the development of a two-party system, changes in the state's interest group system, and complex social and economic problems. Other changes have been internal. They include the increased tenure of the legislative membership, changing career and leadership patterns, expanded workload, the development and enforcement of complex rules and procedures, the evolution of professional staffs, and the emergence of partisan divisions. Political scientists describe these developments as **institutionalization**.[2]

Institutionalization varies throughout the fifty states. Some state legislatures are highly professional, whereas others are not.[3] In some states, salaries are high, turnover is limited, and legislators think in terms of legislative careers. Similarly, some legislatures have developed sophisticated staff and support services. In other legislatures members are poorly paid, turnover is high, legislative service is regarded as a part-time activity, and support services are limited. The Texas legislature falls somewhere between those state legislatures that can be classified as highly professional and those that can be classified as amateur or citizen lawmaking bodies (see Table 8–1). The institutionalization process has produced a more professional legislature in Texas, and this development is likely to continue in the future.

Although it is generally assumed that a "professional" state legislature is a more effective policymaking body, there are some indications that this is not always true. In recent years, California, Pennsylvania, New York, and Illinois—states with professional legislatures—have witnessed ugly partisan confrontations, ethical violations, and the decline of civility among legislators.

The Texas legislature, whose members are elected from districts throughout Texas, is the chief policymaking branch of state government. Its basic role is similar to that of the U.S. Congress at the federal level, although there are major differences between the two institutions. The Texas legislature performs a variety of functions, but its primary task is to decide how conflicts between competing groups and interests are to be resolved. Although often taken for granted, this orderly, institutionalized process of conflict management and resolution is critical to a stable political system.[4]

☐ Enacting Laws

Every two years, the legislature enacts several hundred laws governing Texans' behavior; allocating resources, benefits, and costs; and defining the duties of those institutions and bureaucrats responsible for putting these laws into effect. From local legislation that affects one city or county to general statewide policies and proposals for constitutional amendments, literally thousands of ideas are advanced for new laws

TABLE 8–1 PROFESSIONALISM IN THE LEGISLATURE

Professional—Full Time, Large Staff, High Pay, Low Turnover		
Alaska	Massachusetts**	Ohio*
California*	Michigan*	Pennsylvania
Florida*	New Jersey	Wisconsin
Illinois	New York	
Professional-Citizen—Moderate Time, Staff, Pay, and Turnover		
Alabama	Kentucky	Oregon**
Arkansas*	Louisiana*	South Carolina
Arizona*	Maryland	Tennessee
Colorado*	Minnesota	Texas
Connecticut	Missouri*	Virginia
Delaware	Nebraska*	Washington**
Hawaii	North Carolina	
Iowa**	Oklahoma*	
Citizen—Part Time, Small Staff, Low Pay, High Turnover		
Georgia	Montana*	South Dakota*
Idaho	New Hampshire	Utah**
Indiana	New Mexico	Vermont
Kansas	Nevada*	West Virginia
Maine*	North Dakota	Wyoming**
Mississippi	Rhode Island	

*States currently with term limits (15 total).
**States in which term limits have been repealed by legislative or court action (6 total).

SOURCE: National Conference of State Legislatures, unpublished report, 1998; U.S. Term Limits, "State Legislative Term Limits" (website); National Conference of State Legislatures, "The Term Limited States," June, 2009 (web site); "Three Kinds of State Legislatures," *State Legislatures*, July/August 2004; James D. King, "Changes in Professionalism in U.S. State Legislatures," *Legislative Studies Quarterly* 25 (May 2000), pp. 327–43.

every legislative session. The legislative arena includes a wide range of players in addition to legislators, and lawmaking requires compromise and accommodation of competing ideas and interests.

Budgeting and Taxes

The legislature establishes programs providing a variety of public services and sets priorities through the budgetary process. It sets the budgets for the governor, the bureaucracy, and the state courts. It decides whether state taxes should be increased and, if so, how much they should be increased and how the tax burden should be distributed. Its actions indirectly affect local tax rates as well.

Overseeing State Agencies

Hundreds of laws are passed each legislative session, and the legislature assigns specific state agencies and local governments the responsibility of carrying out the laws on a day-to-day basis. It is ultimately the legislature's responsibility to make sure agencies and bureaucrats are doing what they are charged with by law, and this review, or "oversight," process is achieved through legislative budget hearings, other committee investigations, and program audits. The Senate further influences policy by confirming or rejecting the governor's appointees to hundreds of state boards and commissions that administer public programs.

Educating the Public

The 181 members of the Texas legislature certainly do not speak with one voice, and on major policy issues, it is inevitable that there will be a variety of opinions and proposed solutions. Individual lawmakers try to inform the public about their own actions and the collective actions of the legislature. They use speeches, letters to constituents, news releases, telephone calls, newsletters, websites, emails, social media, and other techniques to explain the legislative process and substantive policy issues.

Representing the Public

The legislature is a representative body whose members are chosen in free elections. This process provides legitimacy to legislative actions and decisions. People may disagree over how "representative" the legislature is in terms of race, ethnicity, gender, or class. Furthermore, many Texans may be indifferent toward or ignorant about public policy. Successful lawmakers must demonstrate concern for the attitudes and demands of their constituents. Legislators use many methods to learn what their constituents think, including public opinion polls, questionnaires, phone calls, town hall meetings, and personal visits.

Organization of the Texas Legislature and Characteristics of Members

8.2 Describe the basic organizational structure of the Texas legislature and the professional characteristics of its members.

Following the oppressive efforts of Governor Edmund J. Davis and the Radical Reconstructionists to centralize power and authority in Texas after the Civil War, the rural delegates who dominated the Constitutional

Convention in 1875 were distrustful, even fearful, of the excesses and abuses of big government. They created a part-time, **bicameral legislature** that included a 31-member Senate and a 150-member House of Representatives. All other states also have bicameral legislatures, except Nebraska, which has a unicameral system with only one lawmaking body of 49 members. The sizes of other state senates range from 20 in Alaska to 67 in Minnesota, whereas houses of representatives vary in size from 40 in Alaska to 400 in New Hampshire.[5]

bicameral legislature
A lawmaking body, such as the Texas legislature, that includes two chambers.

regular legislative session
The 140-day period in odd-numbered years in which the legislature meets and can consider laws on any issue or subject.

special sessions
Legislative sessions that can be called by the governor at any other time than the regular legislative session. They are limited to thirty days and can consider only subjects or issues designated by the governor.

8.1 8.2 8.3 8.4 8.5 8.6 8.7 8.8

☐ Legislative Sessions

To curb lawmakers' power, the Texas constitutional framers limited the **regular legislative session** to a maximum of 140 days every two years but gave the governor the authority to call special sessions when necessary. Lawmakers convene in regular session on the second Tuesday of January in odd-numbered years. **Special sessions** are limited to thirty days each and to subjects submitted by the governor, and the governor can call an unlimited number of special sessions.

There have been periods of frequent special sessions. From midsummer 1986 through midsummer 1987, for example, during a lingering budgetary crisis spawned by a depressed oil industry, the legislature convened for its regular 140-day session and four special sessions, two of which lasted the maximum thirty days. The seventy-first legislature in 1989–1990 held six special sessions to deal with school funding and medical expenses for workers injured on the job. The seventy-second legislature had two special sessions in the summer of 1991 to write a new budget, pass a tax bill, make changes in the criminal justice system, and redraw the boundaries of congressional districts. The seventy-eighth legislature had three special sessions in the summer and early fall of 2003 in a protracted, partisan fight over the drawing of congressional districts. Governor Rick Perry called one special session in the spring of 2004 and two more in the summer of 2005 to try to lower school property taxes and change the educational funding system, but all three were unsuccessful. The legislature finally met those goals in still another special session in the spring of 2006, but only after the Texas Supreme Court had declared the school finance system unconstitutional and given lawmakers a deadline.

Some state officials and government experts believe the Texas legislature should have annual regular sessions, at least for budgetary purposes. Only six other state legislatures do not. The change, however, would require a constitutional amendment.

☐ Terms of Office and Qualifications

Article 3 of the Texas Constitution establishes the structure, membership, and selection of the Texas legislature. Representatives serve two-year terms; senators are elected to four-year, staggered terms. A senator has to be a qualified voter, at least twenty-six years old, a resident of Texas for five years preceding his or her election, and a resident of the district from which elected for at least one year. A representative must be a qualified voter, at least twenty-one years old, a Texas resident for two years, and a resident of the district represented for one year.[6] There is no limit on the number of terms an individual can serve in the legislature.

☐ Pay and Compensation

Members of both the House and the Senate and their presiding officers have a base pay of $7,200 per year. This figure is set by the state constitution and can be raised only with voter approval. This is one of the lowest legislative pay levels in the country and was last increased in 1975 by a constitutional amendment that also set lawmakers' per diem, or personal expense allowance, at $30 a day while the legislature is in session.

Legislators proposed a constitutional amendment in 1989 to increase their salaries to more than $20,000 a year, but the voters turned the proposal down by a two-to-one margin.

The amendment also would have removed voter control over legislative pay and given lawmakers the power to give themselves raises by setting their pay at one-fourth the governor's salary, which the legislature sets and periodically increases.

In 1991, Texas voters approved a constitutional amendment creating a state Ethics Commission that could recommend legislative pay raises to the voters and change per diem on its own. The commission set per diem at $150 per day for the 2011 legislative session.

By 2011, only Alabama, Texas, New Hampshire, and Rhode Island had limits on legislative pay that could be changed only by constitutional amendment. Compensation commissions now recommend legislative pay levels in some states, whereas legislatures in other states set their own salaries, often with the approval of the voters. In 2011, legislative pay ranged from a high of $95,261 in California, where lawmakers set their own salaries and are considered members of a full-time legislature, to a low of $200 a year in New Hampshire, which has annual sessions but a constitutional limit on salaries.[7]

Advocates of higher legislative pay in Texas say raising the salary is necessary because legislative service has become much more than a part-time job for many lawmakers, particularly during periods of frequent special sessions. They argue that the present low compensation level restricts legislative service to wealthy individuals or those who have law practices or own businesses in which partners or employees can help take up the slack while they are in Austin. They believe higher pay would broaden the potential pool from which legislators are drawn—and perhaps improve the prospects for quality—by encouraging more salaried working people to run for legislative office. A wider pool of candidates also could broaden the perspectives from which policy issues are viewed and addressed.

The outside personal income of many legislators obviously does suffer while they are in office, but legislative service also can enhance business and professional connections. Critics of higher legislative pay also note that candidates, many of whom spend thousands of dollars to get elected to the legislature, know the pay level before they run for the office. Texas lawmakers also have provided themselves one of the best legislative retirement plans in the country, and they can increase their retirement benefits without voter approval.

Retirement benefits are computed on the basis of state district judges' salaries, which legislators raise periodically, thereby increasing their own retirement benefits as well. Many former legislators receive pensions that are much larger than their paychecks were while they were in office. In 1991, legislators sweetened their retirement plan even more by quietly amending a state employee retirement bill to allow former legislators to receive full retirement benefits at age fifty instead of fifty-five, as set in earlier law, and reduce the required time for service in office. The sponsor of the amendment, Representative Nolan "Buzz" Robnett, a Republican from Lubbock, who, incidentally, was fifty at the time, helped make himself eligible for $1,780 a month in retirement pay, almost triple his legislative salary.[8]

□ Physical Facilities

The House chamber and representatives' offices traditionally have been located in the west wing of the Texas State Capitol, and the Senate chamber and senators' offices are in the east wing (see Figure 8–1). The pink granite building was completed in 1888, but the growth of state government and periodic renovations created a hodgepodge of cramped legislative offices. After one visitor died in a fire behind the Senate chamber in 1983, it also became obvious that the building was unsafe. So the state launched a $187 million Capitol building restoration and expansion project in 1990 that included a four-story underground addition to the building. Legislative committee hearing rooms and many lawmakers' offices were relocated from the main building to the underground extension, which is connected to the original Capitol and nearby office buildings by tunnels.

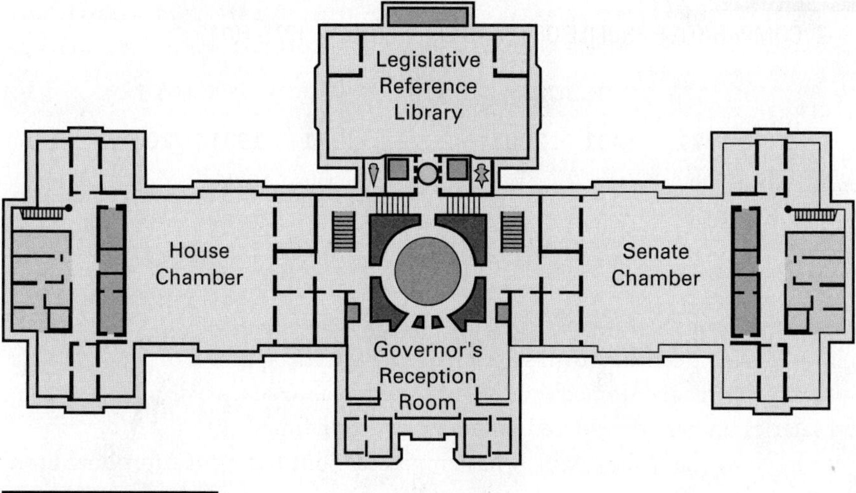

FIGURE 8–1 CORRIDORS OF POWER IN THE TEXAS CAPITOL

The second floor of the Texas Capitol, shown here, houses the Senate and House chambers, the Legislative Reference Library, and the Governor's Reception Room.

When the legislature is in session, access to the floor of each chamber on the second floor of the Capitol building is restricted to lawmakers, certain other state officials, some staff members, and accredited media representatives. The galleries, to which the public is admitted, overlook the chambers from the third floor of the Capitol. In both the House and Senate chambers, members' desks face the presiding officer's podium, which is flanked by desks of the clerical staff. Unlike the U.S. Congress, where seating is arranged by party affiliation, seats are assigned to state legislators by seniority.

☐ Membership

In 1971, the Texas legislature was overwhelmingly white, male, and Democratic. Two African Americans served in the 150-member House and one in the 31-member Senate. The one African American senator, Barbara Jordan of Houston, also was the only woman in the Senate. Two years later, she would begin a distinguished career in the U.S. Congress. Frances Farenthold of Corpus Christi was the only woman in the House. A reform-minded lawmaker, she often was referred to as the "Den Mother of the Dirty Thirty," a coalition of liberal Democrats and conservative Republicans who challenged the power of House Speaker Gus Mutscher during a major stock fraud scandal involving the speaker. In 1972, Farenthold ran a strong race for governor in the Democratic primary but lost a runoff election to Uvalde rancher Dolph Briscoe. In 1971, only one Hispanic served in the Senate and eleven Hispanic members served in the House, and only twelve legislators were Republicans—ten in the House and two in the Senate.

By 2011, changing political patterns and attitudes, redrawn political boundaries, and court-ordered single-member districts for urban House members had altered significantly the composition of the legislature (see Table 8–2). That year, Republicans had a 19 to 12 majority in the Senate. The Senate also had two African American members, seven Hispanics, and six women. The House in 2011 had a 101 to 49 Republican majority, the largest Republican majority of modern times. The 150 House members in 2011 included seventeen African Americans, thirty Hispanics, two Asian Americans, and thirty-two women. Representation from the urban and suburban areas of the state also had grown, reflecting the population shifts accommodated by redistricting.

In recent years, business has been the dominant occupation of serving legislators, followed by law. Low legislative pay and increasing demands on legislators' time, even when they are not formally in session, preclude many salaried people from serving. Consequently, most legislators are business owners or attorneys, who have employees and partners back home to look out for their business interests while they are in Austin.

8.1

8.2

8.3

8.4

8.5

8.6

8.7

8.8

TABLE 8–2 COMPARATIVE PROFILE OF TEXAS LEGISLATORS, 1971–2011

	HOUSE				SENATE			
	1971	**1981**	**2001**	**2011**	**1971**	**1981**	**2001**	**2011**
Democrats	140	112	78	49	29	24	15	12
Republicans	10	38	72	101	2	7	16	19
Males	149	139	120	118	30	30	27	25
Females	1	11	30	32	1	1	4	6
Hispanics	11	17	28	30	1	4	7	7
African Americans	2	13	14	17	1	0	2	2
Asian Americans	0	0	0	2	0	0	0	0
Anglos	137	120	108	101	29	27	22	22

SOURCE: Texas House and Senate rosters, 1971, 1981, 2001, 2011.

Legislators in 2011 also included four physicians, one pharmacist, a retired firefighter, and a radio talk-show host.

☐ Legislative Careers

Various career patterns lead to election to the Texas legislature.[9] Lawmakers include former members of city councils and school boards, former prosecutors, former legislative aides, and long-time Democratic and Republican Party activists. Fifteen of the thirty-one senators in 2011 had previously served in the House. Many first-term legislators, however, arrive in Austin with relatively little political experience.

☐ Legislative Turnover

Compared to other states, turnover in the Texas legislature is generally low, but in occasional elections, such as that in 2010, the turnover rate is higher than in previous years.[10] Yet, few individuals who serve can be considered career legislators. In 2011, the average tenure of incumbents was 14.7 years in the state Senate (combining Senate and House experience) and 8 years in the Texas House.[11]

In addition to the effects of redistricting of legislative seats after every U.S. census, turnover is due to the low pay and the personal costs involved in running for public office. While in session, many legislators lose income from their regular sources of employment. Political ambition also is a factor. Many lawmakers who want to move up the political ladder serve only a few terms in the Texas House before running for the Texas Senate, the U.S. Congress, or other state or local offices. Other legislators quit after a few sessions to become lobbyists.

Five senators, including three of the chamber's more senior members, ended their legislative careers in 2006, taking with them a cumulative 112 years of experience in the House and the Senate. Democrats Ken Armbrister of Victoria and Gonzalo Barrientos of Austin and Republican Jon Lindsay of Houston voluntarily retired. Democrat Frank Madla of San Antonio was unseated in his party's primary, and Republican Todd Staples of Palestine was elected state agriculture commissioner. In the House, former speaker Pete Laney, a Democrat, also retired after thirty-four years in the legislature. In addition, twenty-six other House members did not return for the 2007 legislative session. Madla died in a house fire in San Antonio a few months after leaving office, and Armbrister joined Governor Rick Perry's staff as legislative liaison for the 2007 session.

Representation and Redistricting

8.3 Explain redistricting and the impact of court-ordered redistricting changes on the composition of the Texas legislature.

redistricting
The process of redrawing legislative and other political district boundaries to reflect changing population patterns. Districts for the Texas House, state Senate, State Board of Education, and U.S. Congress are redrawn every ten years by the legislature.

any European legislatures use a system of proportional representation, in which legislative seats are allocated on the basis of each party's vote. In effect, the number of legislative seats held by a party reflects the proportion of votes cast for the party by voters. By contrast, the Texas legislature and most other American legislatures allocate seats geographically on the basis of single-member districts, whereby the candidate with the most votes wins, a process often referred to as "winner take all." The long legal and political battles over the allocation of legislative seats address some of the fundamental questions of who should be represented and how they should be represented.

The Texas Constitution of 1876 provided that the legislature redraw state representative and senatorial districts every ten years, "at its first session after the publication of each United States decennial census," to reflect changing population patterns; this is a process known as **redistricting**. Nevertheless, members of earlier rural-dominated legislatures ignored the constitutional requirement to apportion the legislative seats equitably to reflect the increased urbanization of the state. Since there were no mechanisms to force compliance at the time, inequities grew. In 1948, Texas voters approved a constitutional amendment creating the Legislative Redistricting Board to carry out redistricting responsibilities if the legislature failed to do so during the

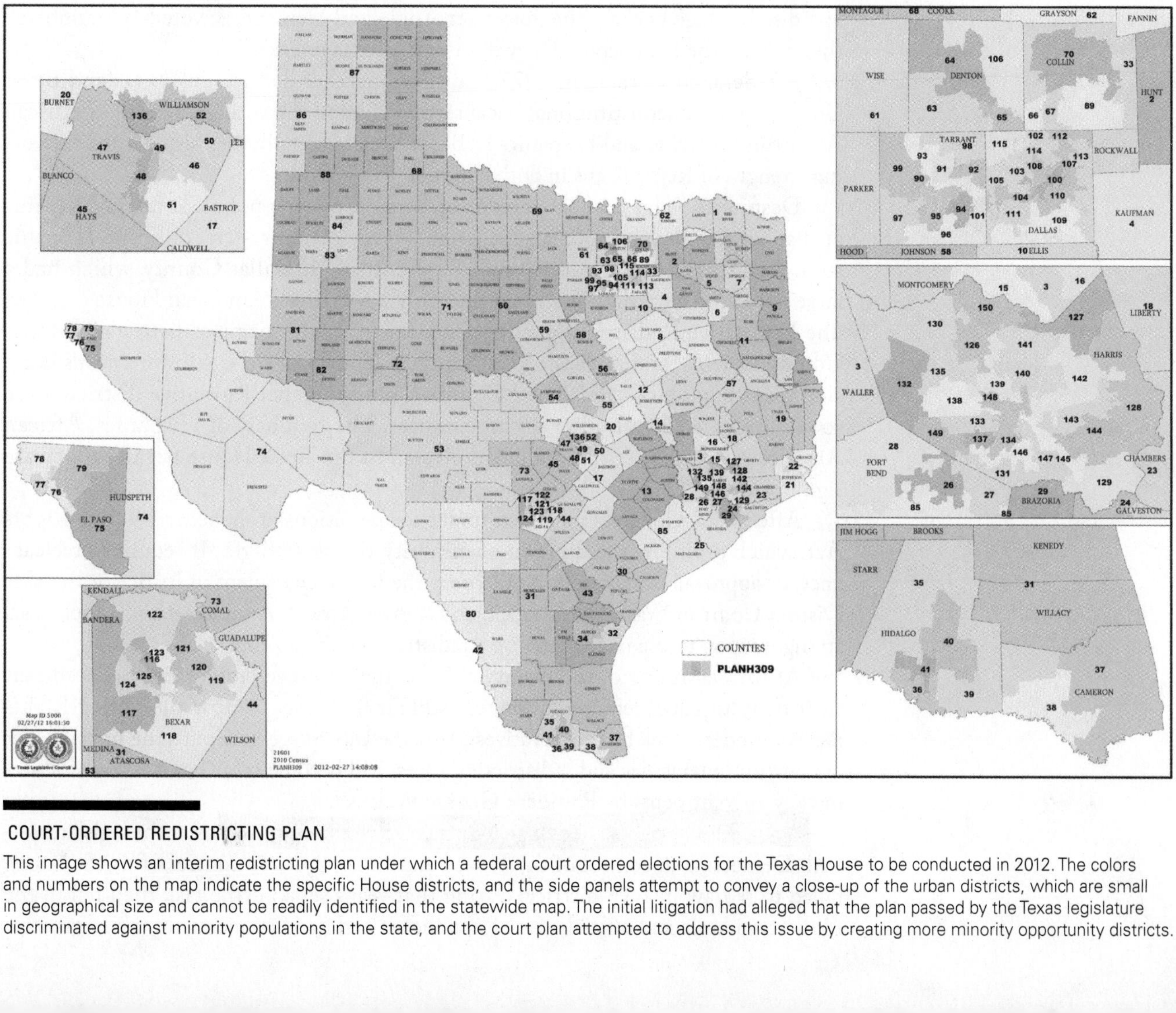

COURT-ORDERED REDISTRICTING PLAN

This image shows an interim redistricting plan under which a federal court ordered elections for the Texas House to be conducted in 2012. The colors and numbers on the map indicate the specific House districts, and the side panels attempt to convey a close-up of the urban districts, which are small in geographical size and cannot be readily identified in the statewide map. The initial litigation had alleged that the plan passed by the Texas legislature discriminated against minority populations in the state, and the court plan attempted to address this issue by creating more minority opportunity districts.

gerrymandering
Drawing of political district lines in such a way that they favor a particular political party or racial group.

required session. The board includes the lieutenant governor, the speaker of the House, the attorney general, the comptroller, and the commissioner of the General Land Office.

Even so, the urban areas of the state still were denied equality in representation for many more years. In 1960, the House districts ranged in size from 23,602 to 155,393 persons, and Senate districts from 131,970 to 1,243,158.[12] With those disparities in population, it was possible for approximately 33 percent of the state's rural population to elect a majority of both the Texas House and the Senate.[13] Rural legislators tended to neglect urban problems.

In 1962, the federal courts finally ordered equality in redistricting. The U.S. Supreme Court, in *Baker* v. *Carr*, applied the principle of equality to congressional redistricting. Then, in *Reynolds* v. *Sims*, the Court held that state legislative districts had to be apportioned on the "one person, one vote" principle. Litigation in 1965 (*Kilgarlin* v. *Martin*) extended this ruling to Texas, and the "reapportionment revolution" soon began to produce dramatic changes in the composition of the Texas legislature.[14] To a large degree, the increased representation of minorities and Republicans in Texas's lawmaking body is a result of the legal and political redistricting battles. But issues such as **gerrymandering**—the drawing of political district lines to favor a particular political party or racial group—continue to be fought today.

The Texas Senate has always been elected by single-member districts, and after the 1970 census, the application of the equality principle to the Senate resulted in districts that were comparable in size. Rural members of the Texas House also were elected from single-member districts, but elections were held in multimember districts in the urban counties that had been allocated more than one representative. Candidates in those races had to run countywide, which put ethnic and political minorities at a disadvantage because the dominant Anglo and Democratic voters outnumbered their voters. The Democratic Party dominated Texas politics then.

A federal court ruled in 1972 that multimember districts in Dallas and Bexar Counties were unconstitutional because they diluted the voting strength of African Americans in Dallas and Hispanics in Bexar. Coincidentally, they also diluted the voting strength of Republicans in both counties.

Despite the fact that 50 percent of Bexar County's population was Hispanic at that time, under the countywide, or at-large, election system, only one Hispanic from Bexar had served in the Texas House in 1971. Dallas County, which had a large African American population, had only one African American House member. The Legislative Redistricting Board had drawn single-member districts in Harris County in 1971, and after the U.S. Supreme Court upheld the lower court's decision regarding Dallas and Bexar Counties, multimember legislative districts were soon eliminated in all other urban counties. The numbers of Hispanics, African Americans, women, and Republicans elected to the Texas House began to increase significantly.

After 1975, Congress put Texas under the provisions of the federal Voting Rights Act, which prohibits the dilution of minority voting strength. It requires preclearance, or approval, of redistricting plans by the U.S. Department of Justice or the U.S. District Court in Washington, D.C., and it gives African Americans and Hispanics a strong weapon to use in challenging a redistricting plan in court.

At the beginning of the twenty-first century, however, minorities believed that their fight for equal representation was still far from over because the Voting Rights Act was under attack by conservatives. Also, the U.S. Supreme Court, the final decider of constitutional issues and redistricting cases, had become more conservative following key appointments by President George W. Bush.

Texas Republicans scored huge redistricting victories in 2001 after the legislature—with Democrats in control of the House and Republicans in control of the Senate—failed to redraw its own districts during that year's session. The task then fell to the five statewide elected officials, four Republicans and one Democrat, on the Legislative

Redistricting Board. The board drew new legislative maps for the 2002 elections that helped increase Republican strength in the thirty-one-member Senate to nineteen senators. It also enabled Republicans to capture their first majority of modern times in the 150-member Texas House.

In the 2002 elections, the GOP increased its strength in the House from seventy-two seats to eighty-eight seats, a net gain of sixteen seats that cleared the way for state Representative Tom Craddick of Midland, a Republican, to be elected speaker after the regular session convened in 2003. The GOP takeover of the Texas House also allowed Republicans to redraw the lines for Texas's congressional districts later that year. They prevailed after a bitter partisan fight that included two walkouts by Democratic legislators. The new congressional map gave Republicans a 21 to 11 majority among members of the U.S. Congress elected from Texas in 2004 and ended the congressional careers of several veteran Democratic incumbents. The U.S. Supreme Court later upheld most of the plan but ordered the redrawing of some district lines in South Texas to protect minority voting rights. Those changes led to the unseating of a Republican incumbent in 2006, trimming the GOP majority to 20 to 12 (see *Talking Texas: Redistricting: A Partisan Drama*).

By 2011, the next redistricting year, Republicans had increased their margin in the state's congressional delegation to 23 to 9. According to the 2010 U.S. Census, Texas's population had grown during the previous decade from 21 million people to approximately 25 million, and most of the growth occurred among Hispanics. As a result, Texas was awarded four additional congressional seats, and Hispanic leaders believed most of the new districts should be drawn to give Hispanics the opportunity to elect the new congressional members. But the Republican-dominated Texas legislature drew maps that retained strong Republican majorities in the legislature and the congressional delegation. Anglos also dominated the new districts. In 2011, Democrats and minority groups filed a lawsuit in federal court in San Antonio to overturn the redistricting plans, contending they violated the Voting Rights Act. The U.S. Department of Justice and the federal district court in Washington, D.C., delayed action on preclearing the legislature's maps, and both sides prepared for a lengthy redistricting fight that ultimately would be decided by the U.S. Supreme Court. The federal court in San Antonio, meanwhile, issued interim redistricting plans under which races for the Texas legislature and Congress would be held in 2012. The plans slightly reduced the number of Republican districts approved by the legislature but failed to give Democratic plaintiffs as many districts as they wanted. Only one of the four new congressional districts in the interim plan was considered likely to elect an Hispanic candidate, and Republicans seemed likely to retain strong majorities in the Texas congressional delegation and both the Texas House and Senate. The lengthy litigation also delayed for several weeks the primary elections, which had to be postponed from the March 6 date set by state law to May 29th, a date ordered by a federal court.[15]

Legislative Leaders and Committees

8.4 Contrast the leadership and committee structure of the Texas House with that of the Texas Senate.

Detailed and restrictive provisions of the Texas Constitution dictate the organization of the Texas legislature and the rules adopted each legislative session by the House and the Senate. These rules concern both the legislative leaders of the House and the Senate and the committee structure.

8.1

8.2

8.3

8.4

8.5

8.6

8.7

8.8

Talking ★ TEXAS Redistricting: A Partisan Drama

The contentious, nationally publicized fight over congressional redistricting in 2003 was not the Texas legislature's finest hour. The drama of Democratic lawmakers fleeing across state lines to shut down legislative business in Austin, the bitter partisan rhetoric, and the persistence of the eventual Republican victors vividly illustrated the huge political stakes that were involved.

The Republican takeover of the Texas House in 2003 gave the GOP control of state government, but Democrats still held a 17 to 15 edge among members of the U.S. Congress elected from Texas. A federal court, not the legislature, had redrawn the lines for congressional districts to reflect new census data in 2001 because the Texas House, which still had a Democratic majority in 2001, could not agree on a new map with the Republican-dominated Senate. Once Republicans had control of both legislative chambers, the Republican leader of the U.S. House, Congressman Tom DeLay, began urging Texas Republican leaders to redraw the congressional lines to favor more Republican candidates and help their party maintain its narrow majority of the entire U.S. House.

However, a redistricting bill died late in the regular legislative session in the spring of 2003 when more than fifty Democratic members of the Texas House fled to Ardmore, Oklahoma, to break a House quorum and prevent the body from conducting business for four days—long enough to miss a deadline for action on the redistricting measure. The Democrats, outnumbered 88 to 62, did not have enough votes in the House to defeat the bill outright, but they had enough members to shut down work because a quorum required two-thirds of the members to be present. The Democrats left the state in order to avoid being arrested by state troopers and forced to return to the Capitol. In their absence, Speaker Tom Craddick and the remaining members had placed a "call" on the House, authorizing the sergeant-at-arms to enlist the aid of law enforcement officers to round up the missing members.

Republican leaders, most notably DeLay and Governor Rick Perry, did not give up. Perry called the legislature back into a thirty-day special session in June to tackle redistricting again. This time, Democrats stayed, and the House easily approved the bill. But the measure died in the Senate, where Democratic senators used the two-thirds rule to block action on it.

At the end of the first special session, Republican Lieutenant Governor David Dewhurst announced that he would bypass the two-thirds rule during a second special session. That prompted eleven Democratic senators to fly to Albuquerque, New Mexico, breaking a Senate quorum, only minutes before Perry issued a proclamation calling the second special session. The Democrats remained holed up in New Mexico for more than a month, outlasting the entire second session. The only Democratic senator who did not flee was Ken Armbrister of Victoria, who represented a strongly Republican district.

While the national media listened and watched, the Democrats in Albuquerque and the Republicans in Austin exchanged a barrage of partisan charges and countercharges. The dissident Democrats—who included nine minorities and two Anglos who represented predominantly minority districts—accused the Republicans of trying to redraw congressional districts to dilute the voting strength of Hispanics and African Americans. Dewhurst and the Republican senators denied the charges. They said redistricting would enhance minority voting strength. They argued that Republicans, with a majority in Texas, were entitled to a majority of congressional seats from the state.[a]

The stalemate finally ended when one of the Democrats, state Senator John Whitmire of Houston, returned to Texas, announcing that he would continue the fight on the Senate floor. Because Whitmire's return restored the Senate's two-thirds quorum, the remaining dissidents returned as well. Perry called a third special session in September, and Republican majorities in the House and the Senate approved different versions of a redistricting map. Final approval, however, was delayed for several days because House and Senate Republicans, ironically, continued to fight among themselves over a handful of districts. DeLay had to visit Austin personally to negotiate a final map.

The third special session ended on October 12, and Perry quickly signed the new redistricting plan. Democrats filed suit in federal court to block the law, but a three-judge federal panel approved it in time for the 2004 elections, which gave Republicans twenty-one of Texas's thirty-two congressional seats. Ruling in 2006, the U.S. Supreme Court upheld most of the plan. The Court, however, held that one South Texas district was unconstitutional because it failed to protect the voting rights of Hispanics. Subsequent revisions in the plan led to the defeat of one Republican congressman in 2006.

CRITICAL THINKING QUESTIONS

1. A few states have created bipartisan or nonpartisan commissions to conduct congressional redistricting. Would this be a better alternative for Texas than leaving redistricting in the hands of the partisan legislature? Why or why not?
2. Is it unethical for legislators to boycott a session and shut down important business when the issue being debated is supported by most of their colleagues? Why or why not?

[a] R. G. Ratcliffe, "Stalemate Speaks to Hard Core—Neither Side Wants to Lose Face by Giving in on Remap Ruckus," *Houston Chronicle*, August 14, 2003, p. 27A

☐ Legislative Leadership

The highly institutionalized leadership structure found in the U.S. Congress is beginning to emerge in the Texas legislature only now—and only to a limited extent. The Texas legislature is a part-time institution that, until recently, was dominated by a small group of Democratic lawmakers. With no significant party opposition or minority representation until recent years, legislative leadership remained highly personal and dependent on the political relationships between the presiding officers and key legislators. Republican growth in the statehouse in recent years, however, is forcing changes.

speaker
The presiding officer of the House of Representatives.

HOUSE LEADERSHIP The presiding officer of the House of Representatives is the **speaker**, who is elected by the House from among its membership. With the long tenures of Gib Lewis and his immediate predecessor in the speaker's office, Bill Clayton, a contested speaker's race did not occur from 1975 to 1991 (see Table 8–3). Lewis decided not to seek reelection in 1992, and he was succeeded by veteran Democratic Representative James E. "Pete" Laney, a farmer-businessman from Hale Center, a small town in West Texas. Several other House members also had announced for the post, but Laney secured the support of the necessary majority of House members several weeks before the 1993 legislature convened and ran unopposed by the time of the speaker's election.

TABLE 8–3 PRESIDING OFFICERS OF THE TEXAS LEGISLATURE, 1951–2011

Lieutenant Governors	Party	When Served	Home
Ben Ramsey	Democrat	1951–1961*	San Augustine
Preston Smith	Democrat	1963–1969	Lubbock
Ben Barnes	Democrat	1969–1973	DeLeon
Bill Hobby Jr.	Democrat	1973–1991	Houston
Bob Bullock	Democrat	1991–1999	Hillsboro
Rick Perry	Republican	1999–2000	Haskell
Bill Ratliff	Republican	2001–2003	Mt. Pleasant
David Dewhurst	Republican	2003–	Houston
Speakers	**Party**	**When Served**	**Home**
Reuben Senterfitt	Democrat	1951–1955	San Saba
Jim T. Lindsey	Democrat	1955–1957	Texarkana
Waggoner Carr	Democrat	1957–1961	Lubbock
James A. Turman	Democrat	1961–1963	Gober
Byron M. Tunnell	Democrat	1963–1965	Tyler
Ben Barnes	Democrat	1965–1969	DeLeon
Gus Mutscher	Democrat	1969–1972	Brenham
Rayford Price	Democrat	1972–1973	Palestine
Price Daniel Jr.	Democrat	1973–1975	Liberty
Bill Clayton	Democrat	1975–1983	Springlake
Gib Lewis	Democrat	1983–1993	Fort Worth
James E. "Pete" Laney	Democrat	1993–2003	Hale Center
Tom Craddick	Republican	2003–2009	Midland
Joe Straus	Republican	2009–	San Antonio

*Ben Ramsey resigned as lieutenant governor on September 18, 1961, upon his appointment to the Railroad Commission. The office was vacant until Preston Smith took office in 1963.

SOURCES: Texas Legislative Council, *Presiding Officers of the Texas Legislature,* 1846–1982 (Austin: Texas Legislative Council, 1982); Texas Legislature Online.

Laney served five terms as speaker, and, although he was a Democrat, enjoyed the support of many Republican House members. Continuing Lewis's bipartisan tradition, he appointed several Republicans to chair House committees. After winning a House majority in the 2002 elections, however, Republicans elected state Representative Tom Craddick, a Republican from Midland, to succeed Laney in 2003. A House member since 1969, Craddick became the first Republican speaker of modern times.

As did his predecessors, Craddick gave his key supporters choice leadership positions when he exercised one of his most significant formal powers as speaker and made his committee assignments. The earlier legislators join a winning campaign in a speaker's race, the better chance they have of getting their preferred committee assignments or the opportunity to advance their legislative programs. But choosing a winning candidate sometimes can be difficult because the campaigning occurs largely behind the scenes with candidates making personal pleas to individual legislators.

Until the 1950s, it was unusual for a speaker to serve more than one 2-year term. The position then circulated among a small group of legislators who dominated the House. But multiple terms have been the norm for more recent speakers. Gib Lewis and Pete Laney are tied for the longevity record with five terms each. Unlike most of their predecessors, recent speakers have devoted long hours to the job and kept large staffs.

During Laney's speakership, the state completed a multibillion-dollar expansion of its prison system, overhauled criminal justice laws, and enacted a school finance law to provide more equity in education spending among school districts. In a bipartisan endeavor, Laney actively supported many of Republican Governor George W. Bush's priorities. He also encouraged opposing sides to find common ground on other major issues, but one of his own priorities was to improve the way the House conducted its business. Laney won significant changes in House rules that produced, in the view of many House members, a more democratic lawmaking process than under some of his predecessors. But Craddick, his successor, exercised an iron-fisted leadership style.

Backed by a Republican majority, Craddick insisted on spending cuts in many state programs to help bridge a $10 billion revenue shortfall in 2003. He opposed raising state taxes, but he insisted the legislature enact a law allowing university governing boards to raise college tuition. Craddick also played a key role in the enactment of a redistricting bill in 2003 to increase the number of Republicans elected to Congress from Texas. He was a consistently tough negotiator with Lieutenant Governor David Dewhurst and the Senate.

By 2007, Craddick's speakership came under attack from some Republicans as well as Democrats. Many blamed his authoritarian style for the defeat of several incumbent Republican House members in 2006. Critics accused the speaker of forcing the lawmakers to vote against the best interests of their districts on such important issues as education, thus making them vulnerable to challengers. Craddick survived a challenge at the beginning of the 2007 session, when he was reelected to a third term as presiding officer. In the closing days of the session, however, he faced an open rebellion on the House floor and hung on to the speaker's post by refusing to recognize motions to depose him. By the time the 2007 session adjourned, several Republican and Democratic House members had announced they would challenge Craddick for speaker when the next regular session convened in January 2009.

Craddick's speakership was all but over when Democrats won additional House seats in the 2008 elections, trimming the Republican majority to 76 to 74. Several weeks later, eleven anti-Craddick Republicans met behind closed doors and selected Republican Joe Straus of San Antonio as their choice for speaker. Straus then won the endorsement of sixty-four Democrats to easily win the speakership when the 2009 session convened.

Straus, then forty-nine, faced two major obstacles. Beginning only his third term in the House, he was the most inexperienced speaker in recent Texas history, and he was a Republican who owed his election primarily to Democrats. The House's work got off to a slower-than-normal start in 2009, thanks to the leadership turnover and

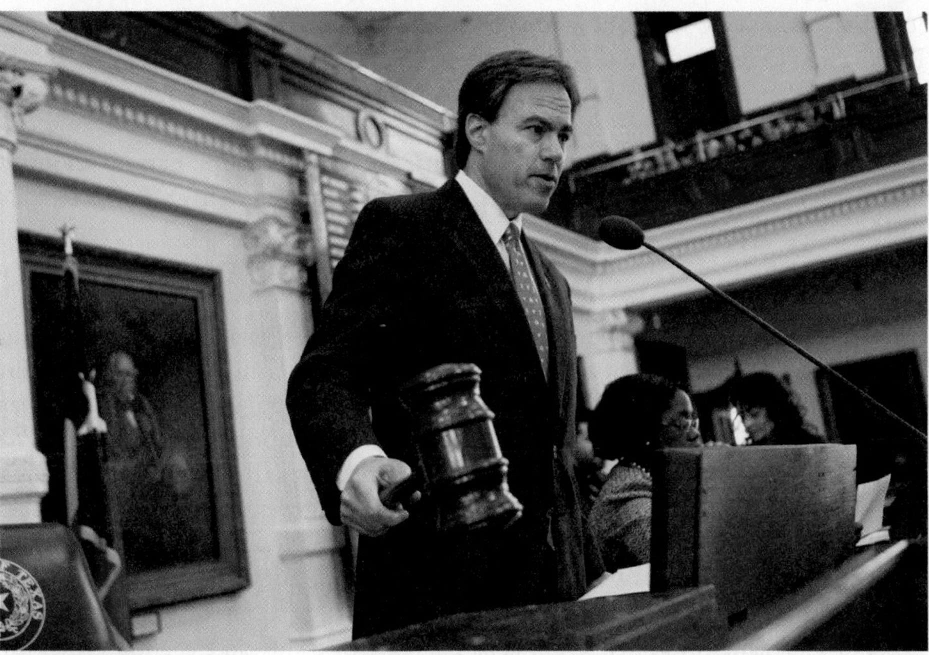

A BIPARTISAN SPEAKER?

Joe Straus (R-San Antonio) challenged Tom Craddick for speaker at the beginning of the 2009 legislative session. His election was atypical in that much of his support came from Democratic members of the House. He solidified his support with Republicans to win reelection in 2011.

Straus's inexperience and more relaxed leadership style. The new speaker appointed Democrats to leadership positions but named Republicans to chair most of the major committees. Outmaneuvered by Democrats in a late-session parliamentary fight, Straus failed to win House approval of the Republicans' top legislative priority, a bill that would have required voters to show photo identification cards.

Straus nevertheless was well liked personally by his House colleagues, both Democrats and Republicans, and received generally favorable marks when the session ended. Despite the loss of the voter ID bill, Straus helped unite the House's Republican caucus.[16] But questions about his leadership style, particularly among members of Craddick's former team, lingered.

Assessing his own leadership at the end of the 2009 session, Straus said he believed he had restored civility to the House. "There may be a few voices out there who want to rewind the clock," he said, "They miss the point that leadership by encouragement can be more successful than leadership by full frontal force."[17]

As noted in the opening of this chapter, strong Republican gains during the 2010 election cycle, including the unseating of moderate Republicans by ultraconservatives in the Republican primary, prompted a move to replace Straus with a more conservative Republican at the beginning of the 2011 session. Although the effort failed, Straus, presiding over an overwhelming 101 to 49 Republican margin, subscribed to the conservative Republican agenda. The House joined the Senate in making deep cuts to the state budget to bridge a huge revenue shortfall without raising taxes, passed a law requiring doctors to perform sonograms before conducting abortions, and passed a law requiring photo identification for voting, the same proposal that House Democrats had killed two years earlier.

The speaker appoints a speaker pro tempore, or assistant presiding officer. In 1981, Speaker Clayton named the first African American, Representative Craig Washington of Houston, to the post. Clayton was a rural conservative and Washington was an urban liberal, but Washington proved to be a critical member of the speaker's team. He also exercised considerable influence on numerous issues of importance to minorities. Ten years later, Gib Lewis named another African American, Representative Wilhelmina Delco of Austin, as the first woman speaker pro tempore. Speaker

lieutenant governor
The presiding officer of the Senate. This officeholder also becomes governor if the governor dies, resigns, becomes incapacitated, or is removed from office.

Joe Straus, who owed his election in 2009 to the key support of Democrats, appointed Democratic Representative Craig Eiland of Galveston to the post that year. But in 2011, after Republicans increased their House margin to 101 to 49, Straus appointed a Republican, Beverly Woolley of Houston, as speaker pro tempore.

The membership of most House committees is determined in part by seniority. The speaker has total discretion, however, in naming committee chairs and vice chairs and in appointing all the members of procedural committees, including the influential Calendars Committee, which will be described in more detail later in this chapter.

SENATE LEADERSHIP The presiding officer of the Senate is the **lieutenant governor**, who is elected statewide to a four-year term. Unlike the vice president of the United States—the office's counterpart in the federal government, who has only limited legislative functions—the lieutenant governor has traditionally been the Senate's legislative leader. This office, elected independently of the governor, often has been called the most powerful office in state government because it offers the opportunity to use a statewide electoral base to develop a dominant legislative role.[18] Lieutenant governors, however, get most of their power from rules set by the senators, not from the constitution.

The lieutenant governor's power is based, in part, on the same coalitions that the speaker uses through committee assignments and relationships with interest groups. But the lieutenant governor traditionally has had more direct control over the Senate's agenda than the speaker has over the House's. Under long-standing Senate rules, the lieutenant governor determines when—and if—a committee-approved bill will be brought up for a vote by the full Senate. In the House, the Calendars Committee determines the order of floor debate. Although that panel is appointed by the speaker and is sensitive to the speaker's wishes, it represents an intermediate step that the lieutenant governor does not encounter.

The lieutenant governor also has more formal control over the membership of Senate committees than the speaker has over House panels. The Senate's rules traditionally have allowed the lieutenant governor to appoint members of all standing committees without regard to seniority or any other restrictions.

The Senate has a president pro tempore, or assistant presiding officer, who is chosen by senators from among their membership on a seniority basis. The president pro tempore is third in line of succession to the governorship. Traditionally, the governor and the lieutenant governor both allegedly "leave" the state on the same day so that the president pro tempore can serve as "governor for a day" at one point during his or her limited term.

Bill Hobby, a quiet-spoken media executive, served a record eighteen years as lieutenant governor before voluntarily leaving the office in January 1991. He patiently sought consensus among senators on most major issues and rarely took the lead in promoting specific legislative proposals. One notable exception occurred in 1979, when Hobby tried to win Senate approval of a presidential primary bill opposed by most Democratic senators. After Hobby announced that he would change the Senate's traditional operating procedure to give the bill special consideration, twelve Democratic senators, dubbed the "Killer Bees," hid out for several days away from the Capitol to break a quorum and keep the Senate from conducting business. They succeeded in killing the bill and reminding Hobby that the senators set the rules.

Hobby's successor, Bob Bullock, had demonstrated strong leadership and a mercurial personality during sixteen years as state comptroller. On taking office as lieutenant governor, he had major policy changes in mind and was ready to see them enacted. Bullock took the lead in making proposals and then actively lobbying for them. During his first session in 1991, he reportedly had shouting matches with some lawmakers behind closed doors and one day abruptly adjourned the Senate when not enough members were present for a quorum at the scheduled starting time. Even so, his experience and knowledge of state government and his tireless work habits won the respect of most senators and their support for most of his proposals.

Bullock, a Democrat, strengthened his leadership role during the 1993 and 1995 sessions. Recognizing that increases in Republican strength after the 1992 and 1994 elections made the Senate more conservative than it had been in several years, and eager to strengthen his support in the business community, Bullock engineered closed-door compromises on several major issues, including some long sought by business. This approach kept controversy to a minimum and defused partisanship, but it distressed consumer advocates and environmentalists, who felt excluded. It also prompted remarks that the Senate had abandoned democracy. There were so many unanimous or near-unanimous votes in the Senate in 1993 that some House members joked that those senators who wanted to show dissent voted "aye" with their eyes closed.[19]

Bullock helped Republican Governor George W. Bush enact some of his key proposals in 1995, but he played a less active role during the 1997 session, after Republicans had won a Senate majority for the first time since Reconstruction. He supported some legislation, including a statewide water conservation and management plan, but he did little to promote a property tax relief effort that Governor Bush had made his highest priority for the session. One key part of Bush's proposal, an increase in state taxes as a partial trade-off for lower school district taxes, died primarily because of strong Senate opposition, which Bullock did not try to defuse.

A few days after the 1997 session ended, Bullock surprised the Texas political world by announcing that he would not seek reelection in 1998. Bullock, who had a history of health problems, was later diagnosed with lung cancer, and he died in June 1999.

After defeating Democrat John Sharp in a hard-fought race in 1998, former Agriculture Commissioner Rick Perry became Texas's first Republican lieutenant governor of modern times in 1999. Although Perry had to follow in Bullock's legendary footsteps, he had the advantage of entering the 1999 session with a $6 billion state budgetary surplus and a rare absence of emergencies. Perry lost one of his priorities, a pilot program to allow students in low-performing public schools to use state-paid vouchers to transfer to private schools. However, he received generally high marks for his performance during the session, from both Democrats and Republicans. "He might not have used the Bullock style of cracking heads or the woodshed" to force legislative solutions, one senator observed, but "he did effectively bring people together and kept us from having any meltdowns."[20] Perry was more low key than Bullock, perhaps choosing to learn more about the Senate before plunging into potential controversies. Nevertheless, he was credited with helping Republican and Democratic lawmakers negotiate a compromise on one of the key legislative packages of the session—a series of tax cuts, teacher pay raises, and other increased education spending.

Perry was elected to a lieutenant governor's term set to expire in January 2003. But after Bush resigned the governorship in December 2000 to become president, Perry was promoted to governor and vacated the lieutenant governor's office. Acting under a constitutional amendment adopted in 1999 in anticipation of such an eventuality, senators elected state Senator Bill Ratliff, Republican of Mount Pleasant, to serve as lieutenant governor during the 2001 session.

Ratliff, a former chairman of the Senate Education and Finance Committees, was businesslike in his role as presiding officer, and he received generally favorable reviews. He appointed the first African American, state Senator Rodney Ellis, Democrat of Houston, to chair the budget-writing Finance Committee. He also opposed most Republican senators and supported Ellis's bill to strengthen the state law against hate crimes, which passed that session. At the end of the session, Ratliff announced that he would seek election to the lieutenant governor's post in 2002. But several days later, admitting he did not have the stomach for the compromises often involved in a statewide race, Ratliff announced that he had changed his mind and would seek reelection to his Senate seat instead. "I do love policy-making, but I do not love politics," he said.[21] After winning reelection to the Senate in 2002 and serving during the regular and special sessions in 2003, Ratliff resigned in early 2004, expressing weariness after fifteen years in the legislative arena.

Republican David Dewhurst won the 2002 lieutenant governor's race over Democrat John Sharp, who had narrowly lost to Rick Perry in 1998. A wealthy businessman, Dewhurst had no legislative experience. His only time in elected office had been his four previous years as state land commissioner, but he moved quickly to establish credibility as the Senate's new leader. He appointed respected legislative insiders to key staff positions and spent hours studying issues and meeting with individual senators. Although Republicans held a 19 to 12 Senate majority, he continued the tradition of appointing both Republicans and Democrats as committee chairs.

Dewhurst agreed with Governor Rick Perry and Speaker Tom Craddick that the legislature would bridge a $10 billion revenue shortfall and write a new state budget without increasing state taxes. He and the Senate helped minimize some of the spending cuts by insisting that lawmakers tap into nontax revenue, such as the state's Rainy Day Fund savings account. On such budgetary details and other matters, Dewhurst sometimes differed with Perry and Craddick. Their differences stemmed partly from Dewhurst's independent nature, which was bolstered by the fact that he—not special interest groups—had largely funded his election to the state's powerful number two office. The Senate's rules also required the lieutenant governor to seek more consensus among senators than the speaker normally has to do in the House. Legislation traditionally was not approved in the Senate without the consent of two-thirds of the senators, which meant that the twelve Democratic senators had enough clout to force some budgetary concessions.

Dewhurst's leadership was severely challenged during the bitter partisan fight over congressional redistricting that took three special sessions in the summer and fall of 2003 to resolve. The flight of eleven Democratic senators to Albuquerque, N.M., to break a quorum and delay a vote on the redistricting bill for more than a month received national media coverage. It also severely damaged the Senate's tradition of personal and partisan cooperation. Democratic and Republican senators exchanged verbal attacks across state lines, with Dewhurst catching much of the Democrats' anger. The boycotting senators eventually returned to Austin, and the legislature approved the Republicans' redistricting bill. Dewhurst immediately began working behind the scenes to restore the Senate's ability to conduct business in a civil fashion.

Dewhurst was instrumental in the accomplishment of several legislative goals in 2007, but he lost one of his and fellow Republicans' top priorities, a bill that would have required Texas voters to have photo identification cards before voting. That bill, which sparked a major partisan fight, was approved by the House but died in the Senate when Democratic senators used the two-thirds rule to block it. Dewhurst then angered Democrats during the 2009 session when he and Republican senators bypassed the two-thirds rule to win Senate approval of a similar bill. Ironically, the measure died in the House that session. Dewhurst and Republican senators again bypassed the two-thirds rule to pass another voter identification bill in 2011, and this time the House, with a 101 to 49 Republican majority, also passed it (see *Talking Texas: A Three-Session War over Voter ID*).

Dewhurst also bypassed the two-thirds rule in 2011 to win Senate approval of a state budget, strongly opposed by Senate Democrats, that made deep cuts in education and other state programs in order to bridge a multibillion-dollar revenue shortfall without raising state taxes. The budget also left more than $7 billion unspent in the state's Rainy Day Fund, much to the dismay of teachers, school superintendents, and public health care advocates but much to the delight of conservative activists intent on reducing state spending.

Dewhurst's insistence on winning approval of the voter ID bill, even to the point of changing the Senate's rules to do so, and his conservative approach to the budget and other issues in 2011 were widely viewed as political. Soon after the legislature adjourned, Dewhurst announced his campaign for the Senate seat of retiring U.S. Senator Kay Bailey Hutchison.

Talking ★ TEXAS A Three-Session War over Voter ID

Republicans had a strong majority in the Texas legislature during the 2007 session, but one of their top priorities—a bill to require Texas voters to produce a form of photo identification before casting ballots—died, because of the Senate's two-thirds rule and two ailing Democratic senators. An effort to revive the measure in 2009 failed as well, this time in the House, before Republicans finally prevailed in 2011—maybe.

Republicans said the voter ID bill was an essential protection against voter fraud, but Democratic opponents argued that it was an effort to discourage minority and elderly voters, who primarily vote for Democratic candidates, from going to the polls. The bill won easy approval in the Republican-dominated House in 2007 but ran aground in the Senate, where eleven Democratic senators, the minimum needed to block legislation, remained steadfast against it.

The Senate's rules require two-thirds of the senators present to approve debate on any bill. The Senate had only eleven Democrats that year, and one of them, Senator Mario Gallegos of Houston, missed much of the session, recuperating from a liver transplant. Republican Lieutenant Governor David Dewhurst could have won approval of the bill in Gallegos's absence, but he agreed to give Gallegos advance notice and time to get to Austin before taking a vote on the controversial measure.

After Gallegos returned to Austin, Dewhurst tried to win Senate approval of the bill one day when another Democratic senator, Carlos Uresti of San Antonio, was out of action (or so Dewhurst thought) with a stomach virus. Notified by other Democrats of the pending vote, Uresti rushed to the Senate chamber in time to cast a vote against the bill and then hurried to the senators' private lounge to vomit.[a]

Uresti soon recovered, but it took longer for the voter ID bill to wage a comeback. During the 2009 session, Dewhurst and Republican senators bypassed the two-thirds rule to win Senate approval of another voter identification measure. That bill died in the House late in the session, as a result of parliamentary wrangling by Democratic legislators.

Finally in 2011, after Republicans had increased their margin in the House to 101 to 49, both chambers succeeded in passing the bill, and Governor Rick Perry signed it. But the new law still had one more hurdle. Under the federal Voting Rights Act, it had to be precleared, or approved, by the U.S. Department of Justice.

In March 2012, that agency refused to approve the new law because it said that Texas had failed to prove the law would not discriminate against minority voters. Texas Republicans continued to fight, as Attorney General Greg Abbott sued the federal government to try and put the law into effect.[b]

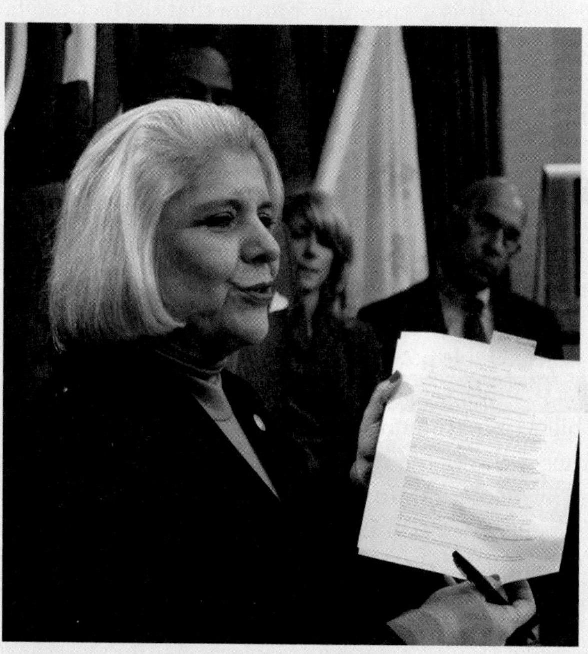

Senator Judith Zaffirini of Laredo (foreground) and other Democratic senators discuss their opposition to a bill requiring people to show photo identification and prove their eligibility before voting. Senators in the background are Royce West of Dallas, Wendy Davis of Fort Worth, and John Whitmire of Houston.

CRITICAL THINKING QUESTIONS

1. **What do you think is the real purpose of the voter ID law?**
2. **Should a minority of senators be allowed to block major legislation? Should the state Senate abolish the two-thirds rule? Why or why not?**

[a]Gary Scharrer, "Dewhurst: Voter ID Bill Most Likely Dead," *Houston Chronicle*, May 17, 2007, p. 10B.

[b]Julian Aguilar, "Voter ID Mudslinging Continues," *The Texas Tribune*, January 26, 2012; Gary Scharrer, "Court to Decide Fate of Voter ID," *San Antonio Express-News*, March 13, 2012, p. 1A.

☐ Control over the Legislative Process

In the Senate, the lieutenant governor can vote only to break a tie. The speaker can vote on any issue in the House but normally abstains from voting except to break a tie or to send a signal to encourage reluctant or wavering House members to vote a particular way on an issue. The speaker and the lieutenant governor derive tremendous

8.1

8.2

8.3

8.4

8.5

8.6

8.7

8.8

standing committees
Legislative committees that specialize in bills by subject matter. A bill has to win committee approval before the full House or Senate can consider it.

influence over the lawmaking process from their power to appoint and assign legislation to committees and their application of legislative rules, including those set in the state constitution and those adopted by the House and the Senate. A parliamentarian advises each presiding officer on procedures.

The speaker and the lieutenant governor do not participate in House or Senate debate on bills and usually attempt to present an image of neutral presiding officers. Their formal powers are strengthened by their relationships with their committee leaders and interest groups. With the notable exceptions of the separate walkouts by House and Senate Democrats during the 2003 redistricting battle, the presiding officers rarely lose control of the process.

Traditionally, there has been no formal division along party lines or a formal system of choosing floor leaders in either the Texas House or the Senate. The longtime, Democratic-dominated legislative system with the speaker's and lieutenant governor's control of committee appointments did not produce a leadership structure comparable to that of the U.S. Congress. The committee chairs constitute the speaker's and lieutenant governor's teams and usually act as their unofficial floor leaders in developing and building support for the leadership's legislative priorities. Most chairs are philosophically, if not always politically, aligned with the presiding officers.

☐ The Committee System

The backbone of the legislative process is the committee system, molded by the lieutenant governor and the speaker.[22] It is a screening process that decides the fate of most legislation. Committees are where technical errors and oversights in bills can be corrected and where compromise can begin for those bills that eventually do become law. Typically, about a fourth of the bills proposed during a regular session win final legislative approval. In 2011, 1,379 of the 5,796 bills and constitutional amendments filed during the regular session became law. Most that do not make it die in a Senate or a House committee, many without ever being heard. A committee occasionally may kill a bill on an outright vote, but there are other, less obvious ways to scuttle legislation. A bill can be gutted or so drastically amended or weakened that its sponsor may abandon it, or a bill simply can be ignored.

Committee chairs have considerable power over legislation assigned to their committees. They may kill bills by simply refusing to schedule them for a hearing. After a hearing, a chair may send a bill to a subcommittee that he or she stacks with members opposed to the legislation, thus allowing the bill to die slowly and quietly in a legislative deep freeze. Even if a majority of committee members want to approve a bill, the chair can simply refuse to recognize such a motion. Most chairs, however, are sensitive to the wishes of the presiding officers. If the speaker or the lieutenant governor wants a bill to win committee approval or another measure to die in committee, a chair usually will comply.

Referral to a subcommittee does not always mean the death of a bill. Subcommittees also help committees distribute the workload. They work out compromises, correct technical problems in bills, or draft substitute legislation to accommodate competing interests.

STANDING COMMITTEES The number and names of committees are periodically revised under House and Senate rules, but there have been relatively few major changes in the basic committee structure in recent years. During the 2011 regular and special sessions, the Senate had nineteen **standing committees**, varying in membership from five to fifteen. The House had thirty-nine standing committees, with memberships ranging from five to twenty-seven (see Table 8–4).

Most of these committees are substantive. They hold public hearings and study bills related to their particular subject areas, such as public education, public health, transportation, or insurance. A few committees are procedural, such as the Rules and

TABLE 8–4 SENATE AND HOUSE STANDING COMMITTEES, EIGHTY-SECOND LEGISLATURE, 2011 REGULAR SESSION

Senate Committees	Number of Members
Administration	7
Agriculture and Rural Affairs	5
Business & Commerce	9
Criminal Justice	7
Economic Development	5
Education	9
Finance	15
Government Organization	7
Health & Human Services	9
Higher Education	7
Intergovernmental Relations	5
International Relations and Trade	7
Jurisprudence	7
Natural Resources	11
Nominations	7
Redistricting	15
State Affairs	9
Transportation and Homeland Security	9
Veteran Affairs & Military Installations	6

House Committees	Number of Members
Agriculture & Livestock	9
Appropriations	27
Border and Intergovernmental Affairs	9
Business & Industry	9
Calendars	15
Corrections	9
County Affairs	9
Criminal Jurisprudence	11
Culture, Recreation, and Tourism	9
Defense & Veterans Affairs	9
Economic and Small Business Development	7
Elections	9
Election Contest	9
Energy Resources	9
Environmental Regulation	9
General Investigating & Ethics	5
Government Efficiency and Reform	7
Higher Education	9
Homeland Security and Public Safety	9
House Administration	11
Human Services	9
Insurance	9
Judiciary & Civil Jurisprudence	11
Land & Resource Management	9
Licensing & Administrative Procedures	9
Local & Consent Calendars	11
Natural Resources	11
Pensions, Investments & Financial Services	9
Public Education	11
Public Health	11
Redistricting	17
Rules & Resolutions	11
State Affairs	13
State Sovereignty	7
Technology	5
Transportation	11
Urban Affairs	11
Voter Identification and Voter Fraud	9
Ways & Means	11

SOURCE: Texas Legislature Online, *Legislative Reports for the 82nd Legislature, Regular Session, 2011.*

Resolutions Committee, which handles many routine congratulatory resolutions, such as congratulating a high school football team on a state championship or a prominent constituent on her 100th birthday, and the Calendars Committee, which schedules bills for debate by the full House.

Some committees play more dominant roles than others in the lawmaking process, particularly in the House. The House State Affairs Committee, for example, handles many more major statewide bills than the Committee on Culture, Recreation and Tourism or the Committee on Agriculture and Livestock. The House Urban Affairs and County Affairs Committees handle several hundred bills of importance to local governments each session. The importance of a committee is determined by the area of public policy over which it has jurisdiction or by its role in the House's operating procedure.

Calendars Committee
A special procedural committee in the Texas House of Representatives that schedules bills that already have been approved by other committees for floor debate.

The House **Calendars Committee** historically has had more life-and-death power over legislation than any other committee because it sets the order of debate on the House floor. During each regular session, it kills hundreds of bills that have been approved by substantive committees by refusing to schedule them for debate by

conference committee
A panel of House members and senators appointed to work out a compromise on a bill if the House and the Senate passed different versions of the legislation.

select committee
A special committee—usually appointed by the governor, the lieutenant governor, and the speaker—that studies a specific issue and makes recommendations to the legislature. This panel usually includes private citizens as well as legislators.

the full House or scheduling them so late in the session they do not have time to win Senate approval. This committee traditionally works closely with the speaker and is one means by which the speaker and the speaker's team control the House. Although legislators may complain about the committee killing their bills, some lawmakers appreciate the fact that the panel can keep controversial legislation—on which many members would rather not have to cast votes—from reaching the House floor.

The state budget is the single most important bill—the only one that absolutely has to pass every other year—because, through it, lawmakers determine how much money is spent on the state's public programs and services. In the House, the Appropriations Committee takes the lead in drafting state budgets, and the House Ways and Means Committee normally is responsible for producing any tax or revenue measures necessary to balance the budget. The two most important committees in the Senate are the Finance Committee, which handles the budget and, usually, tax bills, and the State Affairs Committee, which, like its House counterpart, handles a variety of major legislation.

Although committees are responsible for general subject areas, legislative rules allow the lieutenant governor and the speaker some latitude in assigning legislation. The presiding officer can ensure the death of a bill by sending it to a committee known to oppose it or can guarantee quick approval by referring a bill to a receptive, or friendly, panel.

CONFERENCE COMMITTEES To become law, legislation must be passed in exactly the same form by the House and the Senate. If one chamber refuses to accept the other's version of a bill, a **conference committee** can try to resolve the differences. The presiding officers appoint conference committees of five senators and five representatives. If at least three senators and three House members on a conference committee approve a compromise bill, it is sent back to the full House and the full Senate for approval or rejection. Neither chamber can amend the compromise bill. Over the years, some conference committees have drafted legislation dramatically different from earlier House or Senate versions, even though a conference panel is supposed to do no more than adjust the differences between the House and the Senate bills. Legislative rules now require both chambers to pass a concurrent resolution to allow a conference committee to add significant new language.

SELECT COMMITTEES Special or **select committees** are occasionally appointed by the governor, the lieutenant governor, and the speaker to study major policy issues, usually during the interims between legislative sessions. These panels sometimes include private citizens as well as legislators, and they usually recommend legislation. Standing legislative committees also study issues in their assigned areas during the interims, and the presiding officers can ask them to conduct special investigations or inquiries pertaining to governmental matters.

☐ Legislative Staff

A legislator's staff can help determine his or her success, and both the quality and quantity of legislative staffs have been significantly enhanced over the past forty years.[23] This change reflects the development of a professional approach to lawmaking. As Texas's population has grown, the state has become increasingly urban and its problems more complex. During recent regular sessions, the House has had about 900 employees and the Senate about 800. These figures include Capitol and district office staff for individual senators and representatives, committee staffs, assistants to the lieutenant governor and the speaker, and other support staff hired directly by the House and the Senate.

Other staff members are assigned to the Legislative Budget Board, the legislature's financial research arm; the Legislative Council, which researches issues and drafts bills and resolutions for introduction by legislators; and the Legislative Reference Library, which provides resource materials for lawmakers, their staffs, and the general public.

Other support staff members are assigned to the Sunset Advisory Commission, which assists the legislature in periodic reviews of state agencies, and to the state auditor, who is chosen by and reports to the legislative leadership.

Legislative staffers range from part-time secretaries and clerks to lawyers and other professionals who conduct research and draft bills that become major state laws. There are limits on the number of staff members and funds allocated for legislators' personal staffs. Senators, who represent more constituents, have larger staffs than House members. Staffing levels are usually reduced between sessions, but most lawmakers maintain offices both in Austin and in their home districts.

A key support group in the House is the House Research Organization, which was organized as the House Study Group in the 1970s by a group of primarily liberal lawmakers. The group's name was later changed, and its structure was reorganized to represent the entire House, but it still fills a strong research role. Funds from the House budget support the group, which is governed by a steering committee that represents a cross section of Democratic and Republican House members. During legislative sessions, its staff provides detailed analyses, including pro and con arguments, of many bills on the daily House calendar. During interims between sessions, it provides periodic analyses of proposed constitutional amendments and other issues. The Senate formed a similar organization, the Senate Research Center, in 1991.

The quality of other resources available to lawmakers also has improved in recent years. Legislators and their staffs can routinely check the status or texts of bills online, and so can the public. The Legislative Council maintains a website that includes committee schedules, bill texts and analyses, and other legislative information. Members of the public also can use the website to identify their state representatives and senators and learn what legislation they are sponsoring. They also can view House and Senate floor debate and committee meetings online. The House and the Senate maintain individual websites.

reading
The first step of law-making. Bills are required to go through three readings in both houses of the legislature. The first reading occurs with the introduction of a bill in the House or the Senate and its referral to a committee by the presiding officer. The second reading is the initial debate by the full House or Senate on a bill that has been approved by a committee. The third occurs with the final presentation of a bill before the full House or Senate.

Rules and the Lawmaking Process

8.5 Outline how a bill becomes a law in Texas and the various obstacles that exist in the lawmaking process.

Laws are made in Texas according to the same basic process followed by the U.S. Congress and other state legislatures.[24] But, as the discussion of the committee system already has indicated, the rules that determine how and when legislation is considered are complex and loaded with traps whereby legislation can be killed. One often hears the remark around the Capitol that "there are a lot more ways to kill a bill than to pass one." Legislators and lobbyists who master the rules can wield a tremendous amount of influence over the lawmaking process. The House and the Senate both have a detailed set of rules governing the disposition of legislation, and each has a parliamentarian to help interpret them.

□ The Lawmaking Process

The simplified outline of the process by which a bill becomes a law starts with the introduction of a bill in the House or the Senate and its referral to a committee by the presiding officer, which constitutes first **reading** (see Figure 8–2). That is the only reading that most bills will ever get.

A bill that wins committee approval and clears procedural hurdles (the Calendars Committee in the House and the two-thirds rule, explained below, in the Senate) can be considered on second reading by the full House or Senate, where it is debated and often amended. Some amendments are designed to improve a bill, whereas others are

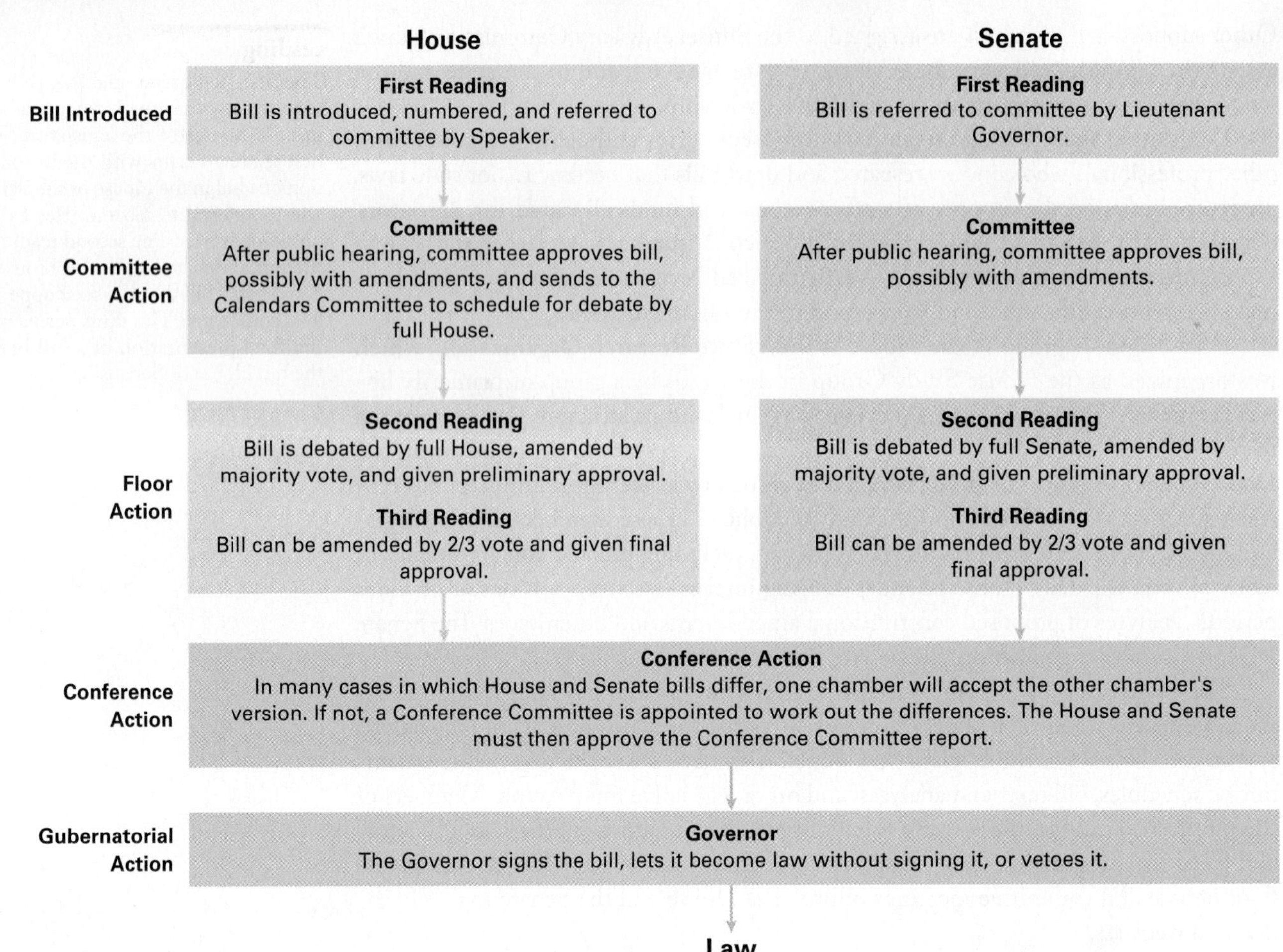

House
Senate
Bill Introduced
First Reading
Bill is introduced, numbered, and referred to committee by Speaker.
First Reading
Bill is referred to committee by Lieutenant Governor.
Committee Action
Committee
After public hearing, committee approves bill, possibly with amendments, and sends to the Calendars Committee to schedule for debate by full House.
Committee
After public hearing, committee approves bill, possibly with amendments.
Floor Action
Second Reading
Bill is debated by full House, amended by majority vote, and given preliminary approval.
Third Reading
Bill can be amended by 2/3 vote and given final approval.
Second Reading
Bill is debated by full Senate, amended by majority vote, and given preliminary approval.
Third Reading
Bill can be amended by 2/3 vote and given final approval.
Conference Action
Conference Action
In many cases in which House and Senate bills differ, one chamber will accept the other chamber's version. If not, a Conference Committee is appointed to work out the differences. The House and Senate must then approve the Conference Committee report.
Gubernatorial Action
Governor
The Governor signs the bill, lets it become law without signing it, or vetoes it.
Law

FIGURE 8–2 BASIC STEPS IN THE TEXAS LEGISLATIVE PROCESS

Approximately one-fourth of all legislative proposals make it through the legislative process, which is filled with obstacles, potential delays, and opposition.

veto
The power of the governor to reject, or kill, a bill passed by the legislature.

appropriations bill
A legislative action authorizing the expenditure of money for a public program or purpose. A general appropriations bill approved by the legislature every two years is the state budget.

line-item veto
The power of the governor to reject certain parts of an appropriation, or spending, bill without killing the entire measure.

designed to kill it by loading it down with controversial or objectionable provisions that will prompt legislators to vote against it. Still other amendments that may be punitive toward particular individuals or groups are sometimes offered. Such an amendment, which may be temporarily added to a bill only to be removed before the measure becomes law, is designed to give a group or perhaps a local official a message that the sponsoring legislator expects his or her wishes to be heeded on a particular issue. Lawmakers also may offer amendments that they know have little chance of being approved merely to make favorable political points with constituents or interest groups.

If a bill is approved on second reading, it has to win one more vote on third reading before it goes to the other chamber for the same process, beginning with its referral to a committee. If the second chamber approves the bill without any changes or amendments, it then goes to the governor for signature into law or **veto.** The governor also can allow a bill to become law without his or her signature. This procedure is just the opposite of the pocket veto power afforded the president of the United States. If the president does not sign a bill approved by Congress by a certain deadline, it is automatically vetoed. If the governor of Texas does not sign or veto a bill by a certain deadline, it becomes law. A veto can be overridden and the bill allowed to become law by a two-thirds vote of both houses, although this process is rarely attempted given that the legislature has usually adjourned when the governor exercises most vetoes.

The governor has to accept or reject a bill in its entirety, except for the general **appropriations bill**, or state budget, from which the governor can delete specific spending proposals while approving others. This power is called a **line-item veto.** The budget or any other bill approved by the legislature that appropriates money has to be certified by the comptroller before it is sent to the governor. Texas has a pay-as-you-go state government, and the comptroller has to certify that there will be enough available revenue to fund the bill.

If the second chamber amends the bill, the originating house has to approve, or concur in, the changes or request a conference committee. Any compromise worked out by a conference committee has to be approved by both houses, without further changes, before it is sent to the governor. All bills except revenue-raising measures can originate in either the House or the Senate. Tax bills must originate in the House.

two-thirds rule
A rule under which the Texas Senate has traditionally operated that requires approval of at least two-thirds of senators before a bill can be debated on the Senate floor. It allows a minority of senators to block controversial legislation.

tag
A rule that allows an individual senator to postpone a committee hearing on any bill for at least forty-eight hours, a delay that can be fatal to a bill during the closing days of a legislative session.

filibuster
A procedure that allows a senator to speak against a bill for as long as he or she can stand and talk. It can become a formidable obstacle or threat against controversial bills near the end of a legislative session.

☐ Procedural Obstacles to Legislation

Pieces of legislation encounter other significant procedural obstacles. In addition to the House's Calendars Committee (discussed earlier in this chapter), the **two-thirds rule** for debating bills on the Senate floor has been a strong obstacle to controversial bills. The rule means that only eleven senators, if they are determined enough and one is not absent at the wrong time, can keep any proposal from becoming law. This rule also is a source of the lieutenant governor's power. After a committee approves a bill, its sponsor can have it placed on the daily intent calendar. If the lieutenant governor recognizes the sponsor, he or she will seek Senate permission to consider the bill. A sponsor can have majority Senate support for a measure but will watch it die if he or she cannot convince two-thirds of the senators to let the body formally debate the measure.

The two-thirds tradition also gives a senator the opportunity to vote on both sides of an issue. Sometimes a senator will vote to bring up a bill for discussion and then vote against the measure when it actually comes up for a vote, as only a majority vote is required for approval. This procedure enables the senator to please the bill's supporters, give the sponsor a favor that can be repaid later, and, at the same time, tell the bill's opponents that he or she voted against the measure.

Lieutenant Governor David Dewhurst and Republican senators have bypassed the two-thirds rule on selected, partisan-charged issues, such as redistricting and voter identification. Although the procedure still enjoys strong support among senators—a proposal to change it at the beginning of the 2007 session was defeated 30 to 1—efforts to suspend the two-thirds rule on highly divisive, partisan issues may become more prevalent in the future.

The Senate rules also provide for **tags** and **filibusters**, both of which can be effective in killing bills near the end of a legislative session. A tag allows an individual senator to postpone a committee hearing on any bill for at least forty-eight hours, a delay that often is fatal in the crush of unfinished business during a session's closing days. The filibuster, a procedure that allows a senator to speak against a bill for as long as he or she can stand and talk, usually is little more than a nuisance to a bill's supporters early in a session, but it, too, can become a potent and ever-present threat against controversial legislation near the end of a session. Sometimes several senators will engage in a tag-team filibuster, taking turns speaking against a bill. Often, the mere likelihood of a senator speaking against a bill is sufficient to kill a measure. Late in a session, the lieutenant governor may refuse to recognize the sponsor of a controversial bill for fear a filibuster will fatally delay other major legislative proposals. State Senator Bill Meier of Euless spoke for forty-three hours in 1977 against a bill dealing with the public reporting of on-the-job accidents. In so doing, he captured the world's record for the longest filibuster, which he held for years.

☐ Shortcuts, Obfuscation, and Confusion

Sponsors of legislation languishing in an unfriendly committee or subcommittee often try to resurrect their proposals by attaching them as amendments to related bills being debated on the House or Senate floor. Such maneuvers may be successful, particularly if opponents are absent or if the sponsor succeeds in "mumbling" his amendment through without challenge. Nevertheless, the speaker or the lieutenant governor must

8.1

8.2

8.3

8.4

8.5

8.6

8.7

8.8

calendars
Agendas or the lists of bills to be considered by the House or the Senate on a given day.

record votes
Votes taken in the House or the Senate for which a permanent record is kept, listing how individual legislators voted. By contrast, with voice votes, legislators simply voice ayes or nays on an issue without being permanently recorded.

find that such amendments are relevant to the pending bill if an alert opponent raises a point of order against them.

To facilitate the passage of noncontroversial and local pieces of legislation, which affect one city or one county, the House and the Senate have periodic local and consent or local and uncontested **calendars**, which are conducted under special rules that enable scores of bills to be routinely and quickly approved by the full House or Senate without debate. Bills of major statewide significance, even controversial measures, sometimes get placed on these calendars, but it takes only one senator or three representatives to have any bill struck. Legislators will sometimes knowingly let a controversial bill slip by on a local calendar without moving to strike it so as not to offend the sponsor or the presiding officer. But to protect themselves politically should the bill become an issue later, they will quietly register a vote against the measure in the House or Senate journal.

Compromises on controversial legislation often are worked out behind closed doors long before a bill is debated on the House or Senate floor or even afforded a public committee hearing. It can be argued that this approach to consensus building is an efficient, businesslike way to enact legislation, but it also serves to discourage the free and open debate that is so important to the democratic process.

Recent speakers also have discouraged the taking of **record votes** during House floor debate on most bills. A constitutional amendment approved by Texas voters in 2007 requires record votes on final House or Senate passage of all legislation, except local bills. But many important amendments in the House are decided with "division" votes, which are taken on the computerized voting machine but leave no formal record of how individual legislators voted once the voting boards are cleared (see *Talking Texas: Dead Man Voting*). This approach saves the taxpayers some printing costs and can give lawmakers some respite from lobby pressure. However, it also serves to keep the public in the dark about significant decisions made by their elected representatives. The fewer record votes that legislators have to make, the more easily they can dodge accountability to their constituents.

Legislators often have their minds made up on an issue before the matter is debated on the floor, but there are many bills that most lawmakers will have little

Talking ★ TEXAS Dead Man Voting

When record votes are taken, House rules prohibit members from punching the voting buttons on other members' desks, but the practice occurs regularly. Sometimes, members will instruct their desk mates or other legislators to cast specific votes for them if they expect to be absent when the votes are called for. Other legislators make a habit of punching the voting buttons at all the empty desks within easy reach. This practice is normally challenged only in cases of close votes, when members of the losing side request a roll-call verification of the computerized vote, and the votes of members who do not answer the roll call are struck.

The House was embarrassed in 1991 when a dead lawmaker was recorded as answering the daily roll call and voting on several record votes. The legislator had died in his Austin apartment, but his body was not discovered for several hours. Meanwhile, colleagues had been pushing his voting button. This practice is not a problem in the Senate, where the secretary of the Senate orally calls the roll on record votes.

CRITICAL THINKING QUESTIONS

1. There is no penalty for a legislator who punches another lawmaker's voting button. Should there be a penalty? If so, what sort of penalty would make the most sense?
2. Is punching another lawmaker's voting button a breach of ethics? Why or why not?

or no interest in and will not bother to study. When legislators are not familiar with a bill, they often simply vote the way the sponsor votes or the way the House or Senate leadership wants them to vote. Despite what tourists in the gallery may think, legislators who raise their fingers above their heads when a vote is taken are not asking the presiding officer for a rest break. They are signaling their vote and encouraging other lawmakers to vote the same way. One finger means yes; two fingers mean no.

In part because of the rules under which the legislature operates, in part because of the heavy volume of legislation, and in part because of political maneuvering, the closing weeks of a regular session are hectic. Legislators in both houses are asked to vote on dozens of conference committee reports they do not have time to read. With hundreds of bills being rushed through the legislature to the governor's desk, mistakes occur. Deliberate attempts also are made—often successfully—to slip in major changes in law through the confusion. For every surprise bill or special interest amendment that is caught, many others slip through and become law.

norms
Unwritten rules of institutional behavior that are critical to the stability and effectiveness of the institution.

☐ Legislative Norms

In addition to the formal rules of each legislative body, there are unwritten rules, or **norms**, that shape the behavior of legislators and other actors in the lawmaking process.[25] The legislature is like most other social institutions in that its members have perceptions of the institution and the process as well as the way they are expected to behave or carry out their responsibilities. Other participants also impose their views and expectations on lawmakers.

The legislative process is designed to institutionalize conflict, and the rules and norms of the legislature are designed to give this conflict an element of civility. Debate is often intense and vigorous, and it may be difficult for some lawmakers to separate attacks on their positions from attacks on their personalities. But most legislators have learned the necessity of decorum and courtesy. Even if lawmakers believe some of their opponents in the House and Senate are deceitful, personal attacks on other legislators are considered unacceptable. Such attacks, even to the point of fistfights, occasionally occur, but they are rare.

The Emerging Party System

8.6 Trace the changes in partisanship of the Texas legislature, from Democratic to Republican Party dominance.

Unlike the U.S. Congress, the Texas legislature is not organized along party lines, with rules automatically giving leadership positions to members of the majority party. The Texas arrangement is due primarily to the absence or near-absence of Republican legislators for almost a century and the more recent practice—before Republicans gained a House majority in 2003—of rural Democrats aligning with a Republican minority to produce a conservative coalition. As recently as 1971, the year before a federal court declared urban, countywide House districts unconstitutional, there were only ten Republicans in the House and two in the Senate. As Republicans increased their numbers, they aligned themselves with conservative Democrats to attempt to control or influence the lawmaking process. This ideological coalition became increasingly important as single-member districts boosted not only the number of Republican lawmakers but also the number of moderate and liberal Democratic legislators elected from urban areas. It enabled conservative Democrats to maintain some control as the base of power shifted in their own party.

Republicans and conservative Democrats formally organized the Texas Conservative Coalition in the House in the 1980s. The coalition remained a strong force in the 1990s, chaired for several years by Representative Warren Chisum of Pampa, a highly effective legislator, who switched from the Democratic to the Republican Party in 1995.

□ The Growth of Partisanship

With the growth of the Republican Party in Texas in the 1980s, Speaker Gib Lewis, a conservative urban Democrat, appointed Republicans to chair some of the major House committees. But partisan divisions increased in 1987 when Lewis, Democratic Lieutenant Governor Bill Hobby, and Republican Governor Bill Clements fought over a new state budget in the face of a huge revenue shortfall. On one side of the debate were moderate and liberal Democratic legislators, including urban and South Texas minorities whose constituents had the most to gain from a tax increase and the most to lose from deep cuts in spending on education and human services. On the other side were a handful of conservative, primarily rural Democrats and a number of Republicans with middle- and upper-middle-class suburban constituents who insisted on fiscal restraint. Clements eventually gave in and supported a tax increase, but most of the House Republicans continued to fight the tax bill until it was approved in a summer special session.

In 1989, Republicans formed their first caucus in the House, and soon both parties had active caucuses in both the House and the Senate. These partisan organizations began to marshal legislative support on selected issues and become active in legislative races, as Republicans began to wage well-financed challenges of Democratic incumbents.

During the 1995 legislative session, when Democrats still held a majority of House and Senate seats, Lieutenant Governor Bob Bullock and Speaker Pete Laney, both Democrats, continued the practice of naming Republicans, as well as Democrats, to be committee chairs. Bullock and Laney also were strongly supportive of Republican Governor George W. Bush's legislative priorities. They were instrumental in helping Bush make major changes in public education and juvenile justice and set limits on civil liability lawsuits.

After many bitterly contested legislative races, Republicans won their first majority in the Senate in modern times during the 1996 elections and gained four seats in the House to narrow the Democratic majority in that body to 82 to 68. Bipartisanship still prevailed for the most part in the 1997 session. Bullock, the Democratic lieutenant governor, gave Republicans some new leadership positions in the Senate although he named Democrats to chair most committees. However, legislative fights with strong partisan overtones increased in 1997 and subsequent sessions over such issues as abortion and gay rights and whether tax dollars should be spent to pay for private school tuition.

Another partisan-charged issue in 1999 and 2001 was an attempt by some Democrats to strengthen the state law against hate crimes after three white men in East Texas were accused—and later convicted—of dragging an African American man, James Byrd Jr., to death behind a pickup truck. Most of the Republican opposition to the bill stemmed from the fact that it increased penalties for crimes motivated by prejudice against homosexuals as well as prejudice related to race or religion. Social conservatives opposed that provision and, in 1999, Governor Bush—who did not want to anger conservatives on the eve of his race for the Republican presidential nomination—called the bill unnecessary. The measure, which sponsors named for Byrd, died in the Senate in 1999 but passed in 2001.

□ Republicans Take Control

Aided by the GOP-controlled 2001 redistricting process discussed earlier in this chapter, Republicans made major gains in the 2002 elections. They increased their majority in the state Senate to 19 to 12; captured an 88 to 62 majority in the Texas House, their first since Reconstruction; and elected Republican Tom Craddick as speaker. Those victories, along with Governor Rick Perry's and Lieutenant Governor David Dewhurst's elections, gave Republicans control of all the points of power in the statehouse. They made significant budgetary cuts to close a $10 billion revenue shortfall without raising state taxes, enacted significant new restrictions on civil lawsuits, and won the contentious fight over congressional redistricting. Partisanship was stronger that year than it had been since Republicans became competitive in Texas.

Craddick and Dewhurst appointed Democrats, as well as Republicans, to chair committees and serve in other leadership positions. Democrats chaired six of the Senate's fifteen standing committees and thirteen of the forty-two committees in the House. Craddick also appointed a Democrat, state Representative Sylvester Turner of Houston, as speaker pro tempore. But Craddick stacked the chairs of key committees and the membership of the budget-writing House Appropriations Committee with Republicans who clearly reflected his conservative viewpoint. After winning a change in House rules that removed seniority as a factor in appropriations appointments, the new speaker bumped from the panel three outspoken Democrats who opposed budget cuts.

Democrats regained some of their lost House seats in subsequent elections and cut the Republican majority in the House to 76 to 74 in 2009. However, Republicans came roaring back in the 2010 elections, capturing a 101 to 49 House majority. In the future, it seems likely that Democrats will eventually recapture majorities in the House and Senate, primarily because of the growing Hispanic, Democratic-leaning population, and the legislature even may organize itself along the same partisan lines as the U.S. Congress—with distinct party positions, such as floor leaders, caucus leaders, and whips. If this happens, the legislative rules and powers of the presiding officers discussed earlier in this chapter would change significantly. But this development will depend on how long Republicans continue to dominate the statehouse, on how Democrats react, and on the future leadership personalities that emerge in both parties. Another factor will be how well the two factions in the Republican Party—the traditional fiscal conservatives and the social conservatives—accommodate each other's interests.

☐ Other Legislative Caucuses

In addition to Republican and Democratic **caucuses** in the Texas House and Senate, other groups, including Hispanic and African American House members, have formed caucuses as their numbers have increased in the wake of redistricting and the creation of urban single-member districts. Their cohesive voting blocs have proved influential in speaker elections and the resolution of major statewide issues, such as health care for the poor, public school finance, and taxation. Their ability to broker votes has won committee chairs and other concessions they may not otherwise have received.

Some urban delegations, such as the group of legislators representing Harris County, the state's most populous county, have formed their own caucuses to discuss and seek consensus on issues of local importance. In Harris County's case, however, consensus is rarely found on major local controversies because of the political, ethnic, and urban-suburban diversity within the delegation. Twenty-five House members—one-sixth of the body's membership—represent various parts of Houston and Harris County, and eight senators have districts that are wholly within or include part of the county. On many occasions, debate in committees and on the House or Senate floor has bogged down into fights among legislators from Houston over mass transportation, annexation, or fire and police civil service.

caucuses
Groups of legislators who band together for common political or partisan goals or along ethnic or geographic lines.

Legislative Behavior

8.7 Assess the various influences on Texas lawmakers' decision making.

lthough representative government is an essential component of American society, debates continue over how people elected to public office should identify the interests and preferences of the people they represent.[26] Political theorists as well as legislators struggle with the problem of translating the will of the people into public policy. Most legislators represent diverse groups and interests in their districts. During a normal legislative session, there are thousands of proposed laws to consider, and legislators must constantly make decisions that will benefit or harm specific constituents.

□ Legislators and Their Constituents

Except for an occasional emotional issue—such as whether motorcycle riders should have to wear safety helmets or whether private citizens should be allowed to carry pistols—most Texans pay little attention to what the legislature is doing. That is why they often are surprised to discover they have to pay a few extra dollars to register their cars or enter a state park. Very few Texans—particularly in the large cities that are divided among numerous lawmakers—can identify their state representatives or senators by name, and far fewer can tell you what their legislators have voted for or against. This public inattention gives a legislator great latitude when voting on public policies. It also is a major reason why most incumbent lawmakers who seek reelection are successful. With occasional, notable exceptions—such as the Republican surge in 2010, fueled, in part, by the conservative tea party movement—most legislative turnover is the result of voluntary retirements, not voter retribution.

Media coverage of the legislature is uneven. The large daily newspapers with reporters in Austin make commendable efforts to cover the major legislative issues and players and provide both spot news accounts and in-depth interpretation of the legislature's actions. All too frequently, however, they are limited by insufficient space, and they rarely publish individual voting records or attempt to evaluate the performances of individual legislators. Most newspapers also have significantly reduced their state Capitol staffs in recent years because of the newspaper industry's financial struggles. Most television and radio news shows provide only cursory legislative coverage.

Although legislators are aware of latent public opinion, they tend to be more responsive to the interest groups or to attentive members of the public who operate in their individual districts or statewide.[27] People who are well informed and attentive to public policy issues are a relatively small portion of the total population, but they can be mobilized for or against an individual legislator. In some instances, these are community opinion leaders, such as mayors and prominent businesspeople, who, directly or indirectly, are able to communicate information to other individuals about a legislator's performance. Or they may belong to public interest and special interest groups that compile legislative voting records on selected issues of importance to their memberships. Although these records are disseminated only sporadically by the news media to the general public, they are posted on the sponsoring groups' websites, emailed to their members, or disseminated through social media.

Many special interest groups contribute thousands of dollars to a legislator's reelection campaign or to the campaign of an opponent. But politically astute legislators duly take note of all the letters, phone calls, petitions, emails, and visits by their constituents—plus media coverage—lest they lose touch with a significant number of voters with different views on the issues and become politically vulnerable.

A favorite voter-contact tool of many legislators is a newsletter they can mail to households in their districts at state expense. These mailings usually include photos of the lawmaker plus articles summarizing, in the best possible light, his or her accomplishments in Austin. Sometimes, legislators also include a public opinion survey seeking constituent responses on a number of issues. Lawmakers also maintain individual websites.

☐ Legislative Decision Making

With about 5,700 pieces of legislation introduced during a regular session—the level reached in 2011—no legislator could possibly read and understand each bill, much less the hundreds of amendments offered during floor debate. Despite moments of high drama when issues of major, statewide importance are being debated, most of the legislative workload is tedious and dull and produces little direct political benefit for most senators and representatives. But many of those bills contain hidden traps and potential controversies that can haunt a legislator later, often during a reelection campaign. So legislators use numerous information sources and rely on the norms of the process to assist them in decision making.

To make the process work, legislators must accommodate the competing interests they represent and achieve reciprocity with their fellow legislators. An individual legislator usually will have no direct political or personal interest in most bills because much legislation is local in nature and affects only a limited number of lawmakers and constituents. A legislator accumulates obligations as he or she supports another lawmaker's bill, with the full expectation that the action will be returned in kind (see Table 8–5).

A number of other factors, however, help shape lawmakers' decisions on major legislation.[28] The wishes of constituents are considered, particularly if there is a groundswell of dominant opinion coming from a legislator's district. Legislators also exchange information with other lawmakers, particularly with members of the same caucus, members who share the same political philosophy, and colleagues from the same counties or regions of the state. Lawmakers often take their cues from the sponsors of a bill or the speaker's and lieutenant governor's leadership teams. As the political parties develop more formal legislative structures,

TABLE 8–5 SOME INFLUENCES ON LEGISLATORS' VOTES

1. Personal political philosophies and policy interests
2. Personal and political friends
3. Other legislators
4. Committee chairs
5. Their staffs
6. Interest groups and lobbyists
7. The governor
8. Other elected administrators and state agency heads
9. Legislative leaders
10. Party leaders
11. Local elected officials
12. The media
13. Court decisions
14. Regional blocs within the state
15. County delegations
16. Legislative caucuses
17. National and state trends
18. Programs that have worked in other states

identifiable patterns of giving and taking cues are likely to emerge along party lines. This has started to happen to a significant extent on budgetary, taxation, and redistricting issues.

A legislator's staff also assists in the decision-making process, not only by evaluating the substantive merits of legislation but also by assessing the political implications of a lawmaker's decisions. The Legislative Budget Board and the Legislative Council provide technical information and expertise that also can be weighed by legislators.

Interest groups are major sources of information and influence. Although an individual legislator will occasionally rail against a specific group, most lawmakers consider interest groups absolutely essential to the legislative process. Through their lobbyists, interest groups provide a vast amount of technical information and can signal the level of constituency interest, support, or opposition to proposed laws. A senator or representative can use interest groups to establish coalitions of support for a bill, and some legislators become closely identified with powerful interest groups because they almost always support a particular lobby's position.

The governor also can influence the legislature in several ways. He or she can raise the public's consciousness of an issue or need and can promote solutions through speeches and through the media. The governor can communicate indirectly to individual lawmakers through the governor's staff, party leaders, and influential persons in a lawmaker's district. The governor also can appeal personally to lawmakers in one-on-one meetings or in meetings with groups of legislators. At the beginning of each regular session, the governor outlines his or her legislative priorities in a State of the State address to a joint session of the House and the Senate. Throughout the session, the governor usually has frequent meetings with the lieutenant governor and the speaker.

The governor also may visit the House or the Senate chamber in a personal show of support when legislation that he or she strongly advocates is being debated. Unlike most recent governors, Governor Ann Richards personally testified before legislative committees on several of her priorities, including ethics reform and government reorganization, during her first year in office. The severity of a governor's arm-twisting often is in the arm of the beholder, but it can include appeals to a lawmaker's reason or conscience, threats of retaliation, appeals for party support, and promises of a quid pro quo. The greatest threat that a governor can hang over a legislator is the possible veto of legislation or a budget item of importance to the lawmaker. In special sessions, the governor also can negotiate with a lawmaker over whether to add a bill that is important to the legislator to the special session's agenda, which is controlled by the governor.

Legislators also get information and support from other elected statewide officeholders, such as the attorney general, the comptroller, or the land commissioner. These officials and lawmakers can assist one another in achieving political agendas. In addition, the news media provide information and perspective on issues in broader political terms. In part, the policy agenda is established by those issues the media perceive to be important.

The relative importance of any groups or actors on decision making is difficult to measure and varies from lawmaker to lawmaker and from issue to issue. Outside influences can be tempered by a legislator's own attitude and opinion. On many issues, legislators get competing advice and pressure. As much as lawmakers may like to be all things to all people, they cannot be. One cannot please both a chemical lobbyist—who is seeking a tax break for a new plant on the Gulf Coast and also happens to be a large campaign contributor—and environmentalists who fear the facility would spoil a nearby wildlife habitat. Nor can one please the governor promoting casino gambling as a new state revenue source and most of the voters in the lawmaker's district who have consistently voted against gambling. The ultimate decision and its eventual political consequences are the legislator's.

Should lawmakers cast votes on the basis of the specific concerns of their districts, their personal convictions, the position of political parties, or the wishes of the special interest groups that helped fund their campaigns? These criteria reflect complex relationships between the legislator and the people represented. Because the overriding consideration for most lawmakers is to get reelected, the legislator must balance them carefully.

Sharpstown stock fraud scandal
After rocking state government in 1971 and 1972, the scandal helped produce some far-reaching legislative and political changes. It involved the passage of banking legislation sought by Houston financier Frank Sharp and quick profits that some state officials made on stock purchased in an insurance company owned by Sharp with unsecured loans from Sharp's Sharpstown State Bank.

☐ Legislative Styles

Some legislators become known for their commitment to producing good legislation. These "workhorses" spend endless hours developing programs and are repeatedly turned to by the presiding officers to handle tough policy issues. Other lawmakers tend to look to their leadership for direction and cues, further enhancing the power of leaders.

Some legislators earn reputations as grandstanders. Almost every legislator has shown off for the media or the spectators in the gallery at one time or another, but there are a number who develop a distinct reputation for this style of behavior. They appear to be more interested in scoring political points with their constituents or interest groups—in order to be reelected or to seek higher office—than with mastering the substance of legislation. Many of these lawmakers are lightweights who contribute little to the legislature's product. Although they may introduce many bills during a session, they are not interested in the details of the lawmaking process and are unable to influence other legislators to support their legislation.

The legislature also has a number of opportunists, including members who pursue issues to produce personal or political benefits for themselves. They may sponsor legislation or take a position on an issue to curry favor with a special interest group or bring benefit to their personal businesses or professions. Legislative rules prohibit legislators from voting on issues in which they have a personal monetary interest, but individual lawmakers can interpret that prohibition as they see fit. Many lawmakers will try to cash in on their legislative experience by becoming lobbyists after they leave office at considerably higher pay than they received as legislators.

Still other legislators appear to be little more than spectators. They enjoy the receptions and other perks of the office much more than the drudgery of committee hearings, research, and floor debate. Some quickly weary of the legislative process and, after a few sessions, decide against seeking reelection.[29]

Legislative Ethics and Reform

8.8 Analyze and explain recent efforts to reform the legislative process in Texas.

The majority of legislators are honest, hard-working individuals. But the weaknesses of a few and the millions of dollars spent by special interests to influence the lawmaking process undermine Texans' confidence in their legislature and their entire state government. Although legislators cannot pass laws guaranteeing ethical behavior, they can set strong standards for themselves, other public officials, and lobbyists and provide stiff penalties for those who fail to comply. Such reform efforts are periodically attempted, but, unfortunately, they usually are the result of scandals and fall short of creating an ideal ethical climate.

Fallout from the **Sharpstown stock fraud scandal** rocked the Capitol in 1971 and 1972 and helped produce some far-reaching legislative and political changes.[30] It involved banking legislation sought by Houston banker-developer Frank Sharp that was approved by the legislature in a special session in 1969, only to be vetoed by Governor Preston Smith. A lawsuit filed in 1971 by the federal Securities and Exchange Commission broke the news that Smith, House Speaker Gus Mutscher, and Representative Tommy Shannon of Fort Worth, who had sponsored the bills, and others had profited from stock deals involving Sharp's National Bankers Life Insurance Company. Much of their stock was purchased with unsecured loans from Sharp's Sharpstown State Bank.

Mutscher, Shannon, and an aide to the speaker were convicted of conspiracy to accept bribes. Mutscher, who had consolidated power in the House and often was regarded as ironhanded and arbitrary, was forced to resign. Later, the House moved to limit the speaker's power through a modified seniority system for committee appointments. Subsequent speakers still exercised a great deal of power, but it was constrained by expectations that the speaker would be more responsive to the membership. The media also began giving greater scrutiny and coverage to the activities of the speaker. Fallout from the Sharpstown scandal helped outsider Uvalde rancher Dolph Briscoe win the 1972 gubernatorial race, and it also resulted in a large turnover in legislative elections in that year, one of the rare examples in Texas political history of "kicking the rascals out."

In 1973, the legislature responded with a series of ethics reform laws, including requirements that lobbyists register with the secretary of state and report their total expenditures in their attempts to influence legislation. State officials were required to file public reports identifying their sources of income, although not specific amounts.

Weaknesses in those laws, however, were vividly demonstrated in 1989. Wealthy East Texas poultry producer Lonnie "Bo" Pilgrim distributed $10,000 checks to several senators in the Capitol building while lobbying them on workers' compensation reform. The Travis County district attorney could find no law under which to prosecute Pilgrim. Some senators had angrily rejected Pilgrim's checks on the spot; others returned them after the media pounced on the story. But the very next year, Pilgrim—a long-time political contributor—again contributed thousands of dollars to several statewide officeholders and candidates. This time, the checks were more traditionally sent through the mail, and they were gratefully accepted.

There also were published reports that lobbyists had spent nearly $2 million entertaining lawmakers during the 1989 regular session without having to specify which legislators received the "freebies," thanks to a large loophole in the lobby registration law. News stories about lobbyists treating lawmakers to golf tournaments, ski trips, a junket to Las Vegas for a boxing match, and limousine service to a concert created an uproar.

Despite all the headlines over ethical problems, legislative turnover was minimal in 1990. But in early December, about a month after the general election, a Travis County grand jury began investigating Speaker Gib Lewis's ties to a San Antonio law firm, Heard, Goggan, Blair, and Williams. The firm had made large profits collecting delinquent taxes for local governments throughout Texas under a law that allowed it to collect an extra 15 percent from the taxpayers as its fee. For several years, it had successfully defeated legislation that would have hurt its business. The *Fort Worth Star-Telegram* reported that Heard Goggan had paid about half of a $10,000 tax bill owed to Tarrant County by a business that Lewis partly owned.[31] The *Houston Chronicle* reported that the grand jury also was looking into a trip that Lewis had taken to a Mexican resort during the 1987 legislative session with four Heard Goggan partners and a lobbyist (all males) and six women (including a waitress from a topless nightclub in Houston).[32] The trip occurred while a bill opposed by Heard Goggan was dying in a House committee.

On December 28, only twelve days before the 1991 regular legislative session was to convene and Lewis was to be reelected to a record fifth term as the House's presiding officer, grand jurors indicted Lewis on two misdemeanor ethics charges. He was accused of soliciting, accepting, and failing to report an illegal gift from Heard Goggan—the partial payment of the tax bill. Lewis insisted he was innocent and vowed to fight the charges. He said the tax payment was the settlement of a legal dispute. He also angrily accused Travis County District Attorney Ronnie Earle, who headed the prosecution and had been publicly advocating stronger ethics laws, of using the grand jury to "influence the speaker's election." Lewis said Earle was guilty of "unethical and reprehensible behavior."[33] Lewis won a postponement of his trial under a law that automatically grants continuances to legislators when they are in session. The grand jury investigation, which prosecutors said would include other legislators or former legislators, continued for several more weeks, but no more indictments were issued.

Meanwhile, Governor Ann Richards urged the legislature to pass a law imposing tougher ethical requirements on state officials and lobbyists. The Senate approved an ethics bill fairly early in the session, but the House did not act on its version until late in the session. The final bill was produced by a conference committee on the last night of the session in a private meeting and was approved by the House and the Senate only a few minutes before the legislature adjourned at midnight. There was no time to print and distribute copies, and very few legislators knew for sure what was in the bill.

Despite the secrecy and complaints that the bill was not strong enough, Richards signed it. She called the new law a "very strong step in the direction of openness and ethics reform in this state." The new law required more reporting of lobbyists' expenditures and conflicts of interest between lobbyists and state officials, prohibited special interests from treating legislators to pleasure trips, prohibited lawmakers from accepting honoraria—or fees—for speaking before special interest groups, and created a new state Ethics Commission to review complaints about public officials.

But the new law did not put any limits on financial contributions to political campaigns, nor did it prohibit legislator-attorneys from representing clients before state agencies for pay. The new law also provided that complaints filed with the Ethics Commission would remain confidential unless the commission took action, a provision that would allow the commission to dismiss or sit on legitimate complaints without any public accounting.

In January 1992, Lewis announced that he would not seek reelection to another term in the House. In a plea bargain later the same month, prosecutors dropped the two ethics indictments against Lewis in return for the speaker's "no contest" plea to two minor, unrelated charges. Lewis paid a $2,000 fine for failing to publicly disclose a business holding in 1988 and 1989, for which he had already paid a minor civil penalty to the secretary of state.

The legislature enacted other significant changes in ethics laws in 2003. The new provisions required officeholders and candidates to identify the occupations and employers of people who contribute more than $500; required financial reports to be filed with the Ethics Commission electronically; increased penalties for people who filed their reports late; and required—for the first time—officeholders and candidates for municipal offices in the large cities to file personal financial disclosure statements, similar to those already filed by state officeholders.

Also in 2003, Travis County District Attorney Ronnie Earle began a lengthy investigation of how corporate contributions were used to affect several legislative elections in the Republican takeover of the Texas House. Republicans accused Earle, a Democrat, of playing politics, but Earle said that he was investigating the possibility that corporate funds had been spent illegally on political activity.

The investigation produced several criminal indictments, including charges against Tom DeLay of Sugar Land, the then-powerful Republican leader of the U.S. House of Representatives. DeLay and two associates were charged with money laundering and conspiracy relating to alleged improper campaign fund-raising for Republican legislative candidates. DeLay and the other defendants said they were innocent, but the politically charged controversy raged for months. The 2002 legislative elections had been crucial because they not only gave Republicans a majority of the Texas House, but they also gave Republicans enough clout to redraw congressional district lines in Texas, at DeLay's urging, to favor GOP candidates.

A state district judge dismissed the conspiracy indictment against DeLay and his two associates, political consultants John Colyandro and Jim Ellis. But the judge let the money laundering charge against the three men stand. The Texas charges and ethical questions in Washington took a political toll on DeLay. He stepped down from his leadership position in January 2006 and resigned from Congress later that year. DeLay finally went to trial on the money laundering charge in late 2010 and was convicted by a jury of illegally funneling $190,000 in corporate donations to seven Republican legislative candidates in Texas through a money swap with the Republican National Committee. The trial judge sentenced DeLay to three years in prison, but the former congressman remained free on appeal through mid-2012.

Review the Chapter

Listen to Chapter 8

Legislative Functions

8.1 List the major functions of the Texas legislature, p. 220.

Lawmaking is the central function of the Texas legislature, and the performance of the legislature is assessed in terms of the policies it enacts and the consequences of these policies. The legislative process includes enacting laws, budgeting for and financing public programs, overseeing the performance of state agencies, and educating the public about public policy changes.

Organization of the Texas Legislature and Characteristics of Members

8.2 Describe the basic organizational structure of the Texas legislature and the professional characteristics of its members, p. 222.

Texas, the nation's second most populous state, has a part-time, low-paid legislature that operates under restrictions drafted by nineteenth-century Texans in the wake of the repressive Reconstruction era. There are serious questions about the legislature's ability to respond readily to modern needs and crises. Because lawmakers meet in regular sessions every other year, emergencies sometimes require special legislative sessions. On a continuum from a highly professional legislature to a citizen or amateur lawmaking body, the Texas legislature is somewhere in between, and turnover is moderate.

As recently as 1971, only a handful of African Americans, Hispanics, Republicans, and women served in the 150-member House of Representatives and the 31-member Senate. But political realignment and federal court intervention in redistricting, particularly the ordering of single-member House districts for urban counties in 1972, have significantly increased the number of women, ethnic minorities, and Republicans in the legislature. Prior to the 2012 elections, Republicans had a majority in both the Texas House and the state Senate.

Representation and Redistricting

8.3 Explain redistricting and the impact of court-ordered redistricting changes on the composition of the Texas legislature, p. 227.

After every U.S. decennial census, redistricting of the Texas House and Senate districts is required. A long history of litigation initially established standards that the districts must be equal in size (one person, one vote). After 1975, Texas was covered by the Voting Rights Act, which prohibits the dilution of the voting effectiveness of the minority populations in legislative districts. Early court cases centered on the under-representation of the urban areas of the state, and the more recent court cases have focused on issues of minority political interests. The redistricting process has become increasingly contentious, as demonstrated by the walkouts of Democratic legislators in 2003 and extended litigation in the federal courts in 2012.

Legislative Leaders and Committees

8.4 Contrast the leadership and committee structure of the Texas House with that of the Texas Senate, p. 229.

Unlike the U.S. Congress, the Texas legislature is not organized along party lines and has only the tentative beginnings of an institutionalized leadership structure. The presiding officer of the House is the speaker, who is elected by the other House members. The presiding officer of the Senate is the lieutenant governor, who is elected by the voters statewide. Leadership in both the House and the Senate has been highly personal, centering on the presiding officers and their legislative teams. The lieutenant governor is potentially more powerful than the speaker because of his or her statewide election, but in practical terms, differences depend on who holds the offices.

The most significant powers of the speaker and the lieutenant governor are the appointment of House and Senate members to committees that screen and draft legislation and the assignment of bills to committees. The fate of most pieces of legislation is decided at the committee level. The presiding officers also play key roles in the development of major legislative proposals and, to a great extent, depend on their handpicked committee chairs to sell their legislative programs to House and Senate colleagues.

Rules and the Lawmaking Process

8.5 Outline how a bill becomes a law in Texas and the various obstacles that exist in the lawmaking process, p. 241.

Any legislator can introduce a bill or resolution, but once it has been filed with the clerk of the House or the Senate, it is subject to a potentially long, arduous process that requires a legislator's continuous attention. Tax bills must originate in the House. All other bills can originate in either chamber. To be sent to the governor for signature into law, a bill must be approved on three readings in both the House and the Senate. Hurdles to legislation are the Calendars Committee in the House and the two-thirds rule in the Senate. To become law, a bill has to be approved in exactly the same form by both chambers. A conference committee of House and Senate members often has to work out a compromise when the versions passed by the two chambers differ. The governor can sign a bill, veto it, or let it become law without his or her signature. The legislative rules and heavy volume of bills considered sometimes enable lawmakers to sneak major, controversial proposals into law by adding little-noticed amendments to other bills.

The Emerging Party System

8.6 Trace the changes in partisanship of the Texas legislature, from Democratic to Republican Party dominance, p. 245.

From the post–Civil War period to the last quarter of the twentieth century, Texas was a one-party Democratic state in which few Republicans were elected to the Texas legislature. Conservative Democrats dominated the legislature, organizing both houses to ensure a conservative legislative agenda. Factions within the Democratic Party were evident, but there was no Democratic-Republican division of any consequence. As party realignment emerged in the last part of the twentieth century, increasing numbers of Republicans were elected to the legislature, and the growth of Republican strength has increased partisan activity in the legislature and fueled speculation that, sooner or later, attempts may be made to organize the legislature along the partisan lines of the U.S. Congress. Both major parties already have active legislative caucuses.

Legislative Behavior

8.7 Assess the various influences on Texas lawmakers' decision making, p. 248.

Legislators show considerable diversity in their style and work habits. Their decisions are influenced by a number of factors, including constituents, interest groups, colleagues, staff, the governor, and the media.

Legislative Ethics and Reform

8.8 Analyze and explain recent efforts to reform the legislative process in Texas, p. 251.

Although most legislators are honest, hard-working individuals, the weaknesses of a few and the millions of dollars spent by special interests to influence the lawmaking process serve to undermine Texans' confidence in state government. Lawmakers make periodic efforts to strengthen their ethical standards, but usually only after well-publicized scandals, such as the Sharpstown stock fraud scandal. Reforms affecting the organization of the legislature or the salaries paid legislators can come only through constitutional amendments, and there currently is no widespread interest in these types of reforms.

Learn the Terms

Study and **Review** the Flashcards

institutionalization, p. 220
bicameral legislature, p. 223
regular legislative session, p. 223
special sessions, p. 223
redistricting, p. 227
gerrymandering, p. 228
speaker, p. 231
lieutenant governor, p. 234
standing committees, p. 238
Calendars Committee, p. 239
conference committee, p. 240
select committee, p. 240
reading, p. 241
veto, p. 242
appropriations bill, p. 242
line-item veto, p. 242
two-thirds rule, p. 243
tag, p. 243
filibuster, p. 243
calendars, p. 244
record votes, p. 244
norms, p. 245
caucuses, p. 247
Sharpstown stock fraud scandal, p. 251

Test Yourself

Study and **Review** the Practice Tests

1. The Texas legislature

a. convenes in annual sessions that match congressional sessions.
b. meets every other year in even-numbered years.
c. is limited to one special session per year.
d. meets biannually in 140-day sessions.
e. has not held a special session since 1948.

2. Members of the Texas House

a. must serve two-year staggered terms.
b. must be at least 21 years old.
c. can serve no more than four terms in a row.
d. have a base pay of $20,000 per year.
e. serve four-year staggered terms.

3. Members of the Texas Senate

- **a.** must serve six-year staggered terms.
- **b.** must be at least 30 years old.
- **c.** can serve no more than four terms in a row.
- **d.** must be a Texas resident from birth.
- **e.** have a base pay of $7,200 per year.

4. Members of the Texas legislature

- **a.** tend to be independently wealthy because the low annual salary prevents salaried workers from running for office.
- **b.** have become more Democratic since the social upheavals of the 1960s.
- **c.** experience frequent turnover due to strict term limits.
- **d.** earn an annual salary second only to California's legislature.
- **e.** enjoy no retirement benefits.

5. All of the following can be said about redistricting in Texas EXCEPT that

- **a.** district sizes varied dramatically before the 1960s court cases.
- **b.** in the 1960s, the U.S. Supreme Court ordered all districts to be apportioned on the "one person, one vote" principle.
- **c.** urban areas always have been represented by single-member districts.
- **d.** court decisions have led to a dramatic increase in the number of women and minorities in the legislature.
- **e.** Republicans have used the redistricting process to strengthen their position in the legislature.

6. Redistricting for state legislative seats in Texas

- **a.** is managed by an independent nonpartisan commission.
- **b.** is managed by the Legislative Redistricting Board if the legislature fails to carry out its responsibilities.
- **c.** is done every five years, coinciding with the federal census.
- **d.** has rarely been affected by partisan gerrymandering.
- **e.** never involves elected officials, who would benefit from control of the process.

7. The speaker of the Texas House of Representatives

- **a.** is elected statewide.
- **b.** can vote only to break a tie.
- **c.** has no power over the chamber's committee membership.
- **d.** always staffs the committee leadership with members of his or her own party.
- **e.** is elected by the House from among its members.

8. The lieutenant governor

- **a.** is appointed to office by the governor.
- **b.** is always elected by the Senate from among its members.
- **c.** is seen by many as the most powerful position in state government.
- **d.** has less control over the Senate's agenda than the speaker has over the House's.
- **e.** is banned by the Texas Constitution from voting.

9. In the committee system

- **a.** committee chairs are typically allied with the House and Senate leadership.
- **b.** committees are staffed on a partisan basis, similar to the U.S. Congress.
- **c.** committee chairs have little power to control legislation.
- **d.** committee chairs must follow the will of the majority on the committee.
- **e.** committees usually operate independently of the House and Senate leadership.

10. All of the following are true of the legislative process EXCEPT that

- **a.** a bill must survive three readings before being sent to the other chamber.
- **b.** a veto can be overridden by a two-thirds vote of both houses.
- **c.** the governor can veto specific lines of spending bills.
- **d.** the governor can use the line-item veto on any bill.
- **e.** all tax bills must originate in the House.

11. One of the procedural obstacles to legislation is the

- **a.** two-thirds rule, which allows any eleven House members to kill a controversial bill.
- **b.** tag, which allows senators to postpone committee hearings for at least 48 hours.
- **c.** filibuster, which allows House members to bypass the committee structure.
- **d.** line-item veto, which allows the lieutenant governor to delete specific lines from bills.
- **e.** two-thirds rule, which requires both chambers to pass bills by a two-thirds vote.

12. Which of the following best describes the place of partisanship in the Texas legislature?

- **a.** The legislature still is not organized along party lines.
- **b.** The rules of the legislature automatically give leadership positions to members of the majority party.
- **c.** As Republicans grew in force, Democratic leaders blocked them from serving as committee chairs.
- **d.** Republicans took majorities in both chambers with Governor George W. Bush's 1998 reelection.
- **e.** Current Republican leaders have blocked Democrats from serving as committee chairs.

13. Which of the following best describes the legislative process in Texas?

a. Texans pay closer attention to legislation than residents of most other states.
b. News media outlets hold legislators accountable for every vote they take.
c. Interest groups play a relatively unimportant role in the legislative process.
d. Lawmakers often take their cues from other lawmakers.
e. The governor generally stays out of the legislative process.

14. One of the governor's important influences in the lawmaking process is the power to

a. filibuster a bill.
b. grandstand in front of the media.
c. ban interest groups from testifying in committee hearings.
d. help legislators identify bills that will reward them financially.
e. threaten a veto.

15. One of the accomplishments of modern reform efforts was to

a. place limits on financial contributions to political campaigns.
b. prohibit legislators from representing clients before state agencies for pay.
c. prohibit lawmakers from accepting payment for speaking to special interest groups.
d. require full disclosure of major campaign contributions in statewide races.
e. prevent candidates from spending their own money in campaigns.

Explore Further

Ansolabehere, Stephen, and James M. Snyder Jr., *The End of Inequality: One Person, One Vote and the Transformation of American Politics.* New York: W. W. Norton, 2008. Provides an engaging analysis of the "reapportionment revolution" and its impact on the American political system.

Barnes, Ben, with Lisa Dickey, *Barn Burning, Barn Building: Tales of a Political Life, from LBJ through George W. Bush and Beyond.* Albany, TX: Bright Sky, 2006. Chronicles political events of the last quarter of the twentieth century that contributed to the transformation of Texas from a solid Democratic state to Republican domination of state politics.

Fenno, Richard F., *Home Style: House Members in Their Districts.* Boston: Little, Brown, 1978. Helps scholars and students assess the various ways in which legislators balance their "home styles" and "hill styles"; Fenno's classic was reissued in 2002.

Hamm, Robert, and Robert Harmel, "Legislative Party Development and the Speaker System: The Case of the Texas House," *Journal of Politics* 55 (November 1993), pp. 1140–51. Traces the development of the Republican Party in the Texas House, emphasizing the potential for the reduction of the power of the speaker.

Jones, Nancy Baker, and Ruthie Winegarten, *Capitol Women: Texas Female Legislators, 1923–1999.* Austin: University of Texas Press, 2000. Provides a compilation of the biographies and biographic sketches of the eighty-six females who served in the Texas legislature from 1923 to 1999, with a focus on their impact on the legislative process and public policy.

Kousser, Thad, *Term Limits and the Dismantling of State Legislative Professionalism.* New York: Cambridge University Press, 2005. Discusses term limits and professionalism in state legislatures. Reform advocates advanced term limits across the nation as corrective measures for poor-performing and unresponsive state legislatures. The author identifies few dramatic changes in the composition and organization of legislatures but observes less specialization, a reduced role in the development of state budgets, and less innovative policies.

Kubin, Jeffrey C., "The Case for Redistricting Commissions," *Texas Law Review* 75 (March 1997), pp. 837–72. Assesses the potential of redistricting commissions to mitigate the political and judicial conflicts that plague the state's redistricting processes, against the backdrop of the legislative and judicial quagmires that surrounded redistricting in the 1990s.

McNeely, Dave, and Jim Henderson, *Bob Bullock: God Bless Texas.* Austin: University of Texas Press, 2008. Profiles Bob Bullock, who served as comptroller and lieutenant governor and is generally regarded to have been the most powerful Texas political leader in the last quarter of the twentieth century, shaping most of the major public policy initiatives during this period.

Moncrief, Gary F., Joel A. Thompson, and Karl T. Kurtz, "The Old Statehouse, It Ain't What It Used to Be," *Legislative Studies Quarterly* 21 (February 1996), pp. 57–72. Reports the survey results of 330 state legislators from across the nation on significant changes such as increased workloads and ever-increasing partisan polarization.

Rosenthal, Alan, *Engines of Democracy: Politics & Policymaking in State Legislatures*. Washington, DC: Congressional Quarterly Press, 2009. Provides a comparative perspective on state legislatures, from one of the foremost authorities on the subject, focusing on topics such as the unappreciated legislatures, legislators and their districts, and the influence of the parties and interest groups on the legislatures and legislative behavior.

Listen on MyPoliSciLab

9 The Texas Executive

The executive power of the State may with truth be said to be represented by the Governor, although he enjoys but a portion of its rights.

—Alexis de Tocqueville, 1835

The Governor's office is not the primrose path of pleasure. Every time you throw yourself in opposition to what somebody wants, you immediately become the target for many a poisoned arrow.

—Governor Pat M. Neff, 1921

Constitutionally, Texas has one of the weakest governors in the country. But Governor Rick Perry probably has done more than any other Texas chief executive in recent history to loosen the formal restraints on the office. Much of Perry's success in stamping his own conservative, business-oriented brand on state government stems from his record longevity. After more than eleven years in office (at the beginning of 2012), he had made more than 5,000 appointments to policy-setting state boards and commissions, and it was no secret that the governor demanded political loyalty from his appointees. Moreover, many of his former staffers have become influential administrators in state agencies or powerful lobbyists whose relationships with Perry remain strong.

Even during the many years of one-party Democratic control, conservatives dominated state government, and Perry tapped into that conservatism in a big way. His administration rode the wave of a sustained period of Republican control in which Perry and GOP legislative leaders made it a priority to promote a low-tax, anti-regulatory, anti-lawsuit, pro-business climate. As a result, Perry has reaped millions of dollars in political support from wealthy, influential business executives and has appointed a number of those donors to state boards and commissions.

9.1 Trace the evolution of the Texas governor from a strong unified executive to a plural executive, p. 262.

9.2 Outline the basic constitutional and structural features of the plural executive branch, p. 263.

9.3 Explain the legislative, budgetary, appointive, judicial, and military powers of the Texas governor, p. 269.

9.4 Evaluate the informal resources at the governor's disposal to advance his or her political objectives, p. 273.

9.5 Contrast the different leadership styles of recent Texas governors, p. 276.

9.6 List and describe the basic duties and responsibilities of the other offices of the executive branch, p. 285.

I, RICK PERRY, DO SOLEMNLY SWEAR...
Governor Rick Perry took the oath of office for his third full term in January of 2011.

governor
The state's top executive officeholder.

Critics accuse the governor of being too cozy with his political contributors and other business interests, but this criticism, if anything, probably reinforces Perry's business support. Perry also successfully combined his establishment-oriented business support with the support of conservative ideologues intent on shrinking state government. He was one of the first political figures in Texas to tap into the rising influence of the tea party, even if, ironically, he has spent most of his adult life in public office and, by most definitions, would be the professional, career politician that many members of the tea party claim to despise.

Despite strong business support, Perry has suffered some major legislative defeats, including the loss of his proposed Trans Texas Corridor, a futuristic, cross-state transportation network that would have relied heavily on toll roads. Nevertheless, he frequently enforces his will by vetoing legislation. In 2011, only a few months before launching his unsuccessful campaign for the 2012 Republican presidential nomination, Perry won several legislative priorities, including deep cuts in the state budget, more regulation of abortion, and further restrictions on consumer lawsuits against businesses.

Some political observers believe Perry's presidential campaign may have been the beginning of the end of his strong hold on state government. The campaign, haunted by a series of poor debate performances and other gaffes, included a nationally televised "oops" moment, when Perry could not remember the names of all three federal agencies he would abolish. Some 51 percent of Texas voters responding to a University of Texas/*Texas Tribune* Poll taken a few weeks after Perry ended his White House bid said they would not likely vote to reelect him, if he ran for another term as governor in 2014. "It's not that Perry is dead," said Daron Shaw, a government professor and codirector of the poll, "But the notion that he's invulnerable is dead."[1]

The office of governor is the most visible office in the state of Texas, and most Texans probably associate it with power. But as Perry and others elected to the position have discovered, the office is institutionally weak. The term "chief executive" is almost a misnomer, thanks to constitutional restrictions meant to ensure that no governor can repeat the oppressive abuses of the Reconstruction administration of Governor Edmund J. Davis.

Unlike the president of the United States, the governor of Texas has no formal appointive cabinet through which to impose policy on the governmental bureaucracy. Independently elected officers, including such key players as the attorney general and the comptroller, head several other major state agencies. The governor appoints hundreds to boards and commissions that set policy for numerous other state agencies, but most of those boards are structured in such a way that a new governor has to wait until halfway through his or her first term to appoint a majority of panel members.

All of this is not to suggest that the governor is merely a figurehead. The governor can veto legislation and has the exclusive authority to schedule special sessions of the legislature and set their agendas. In addition, as Perry has demonstrated, the appointments power offers the opportunity to make a strong mark on state government. The high visibility of the office also offers a governor a ready-made public forum. So, although the state constitution limits the formal powers of the office, a governor's personality, political adroitness, staff appointments, and ability to define and sell an agenda that addresses broad needs and interests all shape his or her influence.

A Historical Perspective on the Executive Function in Texas

9.1 Trace the evolution of the Texas governor from a strong unified executive to a plural executive.

The **governor,** the top executive officeholder in Texas, has not always had such limited authority. In the 1836 Constitution of the Republic, the powers of the president of Texas "closely resembled the powers of the

American president, except he was forbidden to lead armies without the consent of Congress."[2] The constitution adopted after Texas was annexed to the United States in 1845 continued the office of a strong single or unified executive and gave the governor significant powers, including the appointment of other executive officials.[3] The revised constitution Texas adopted upon joining the Confederacy in 1861 reflected only minor reductions in the powers of the governor. The new charter called for the election of two other executive officeholders: the state treasurer and the comptroller of public accounts.[4]

The governor also retained extensive powers under the Constitution of 1866, written at the end of the Civil War. Although the treasurer and the comptroller continued to be elected, the line-item veto over budget bills (a power that still exists today) expanded the legislative power of the governor. The Constitution of 1866 was short lived, however, and was replaced by the Constitution of 1869 to bring the state into compliance with the Reconstruction policies of the Radical Republicans who had taken over the U.S. Congress. Jacksonian democracy influenced the Constitution of 1869, which led to the diffusion of the executive function among eight officeholders, six of whom were to be elected statewide.[5]

But Radical Reconstruction policies and the abuses of Governor Edmund Davis's administration prompted Texans to put strict limits on the power of the governor in the Constitution of 1876, which still forms the basic framework of state government. The new constitution retained the **plural executive** structure of independently elected officeholders. The only executive officer the governor appoints is the secretary of state. The constitution limits the terms of the governor and other elected members of the executive branch to two years. The constitution also sets their salaries and specifies in great detail the duties of each office, thus limiting executive officeholders' discretionary powers. In addition, the constitution places restrictions on outside employment and the holding of any other office or commission.[6]

Although constitutional amendments loosened a few restrictions on the executive branch over the years, the changes have not significantly enhanced the governor's authority. In 1954, voters approved an amendment giving the legislature the authority to raise the governor's salary.[7] Another amendment, in 1972, expanded the term of office for the governor and most other statewide executive officeholders to four years. In 1980, the governor was given the power, with the approval of the state Senate, to remove persons from boards and commissions whom the governor had personally appointed.[8] But when Governor Ann Richards in 1991 tried to revive interest in giving the governor cabinet-style appointment powers over major state agencies, she met with only limited success.

plural executive
A fragmented system of authority under which most statewide, executive officeholders are elected independently of the governor. This arrangement, which is used in Texas, places severe limitations on the governor's power.

lieutenant governor
The presiding officer of the Senate. This officeholder also becomes governor if the governor dies, becomes incapacitated, or is removed from office.

The Plural Executive

9.2 Outline the basic constitutional and structural features of the plural executive branch.

Article 4, Section 1, of the 1876 Constitution created the executive branch, which "shall consist of a Governor, who shall be the Chief Executive Officer of the State, a **Lieutenant Governor**, Secretary of State, Comptroller of Public Accounts, Treasurer, Commissioner of the General Land Office, and Attorney General." Added later to the executive branch were the agriculture commissioner, the three-member Railroad Commission, and the fifteen-member State Board of Education. Only the secretary of state is appointed by the governor (see Figure 9–1). Members of the education board are elected from districts, and the other officeholders are elected statewide. The constitution requires most of these officials to be at least thirty years old and a resident of Texas for at least five years.[9]

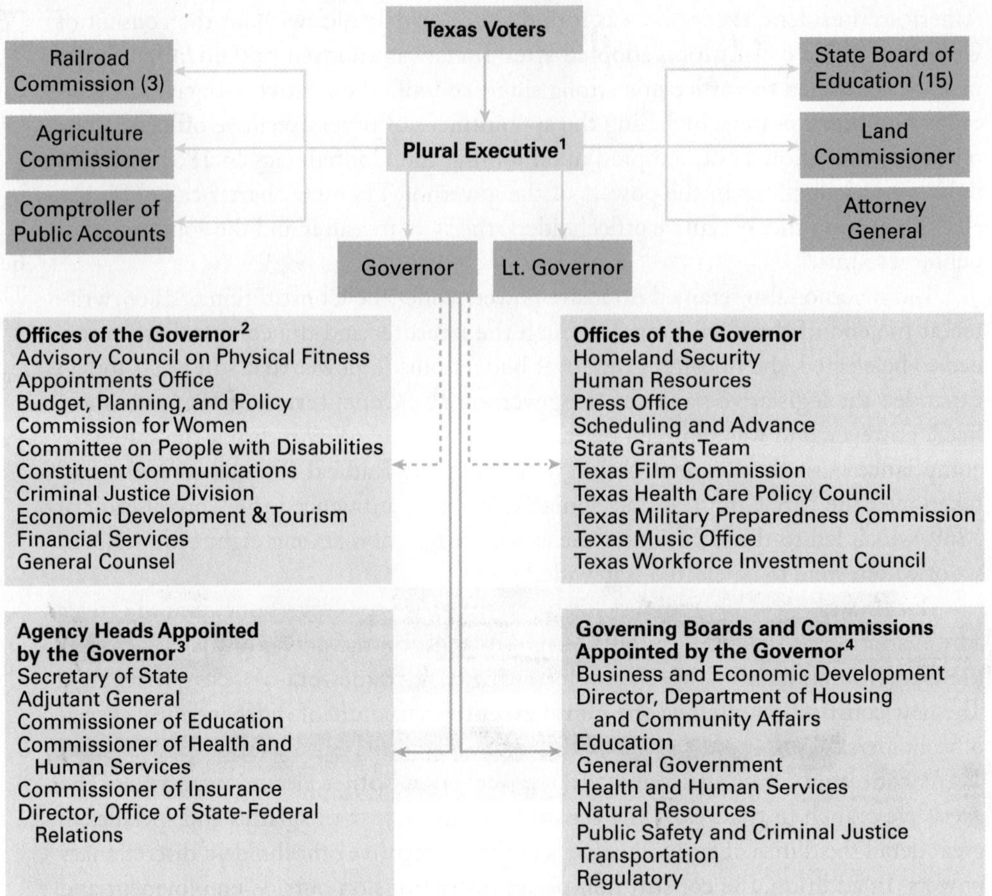

[1] Defined by the constitution or statutory law, the heads of these agencies are elected independently of the governor.

[2] The Offices of the Governor are created under statutory authority and serve to assist the governor in policy development, budgeting and planning, and coordination of policy among agencies and governments. Some 200 persons serve in these offices and are appointed by the governor.

[3] With the exception of the Secretary of State, which is authorized under the Texas Constitution, these administrative positions were created under statutory law giving the appointment authority to the governor.

[4] Some two hundred state agencies, including universities, are assigned by statutory law the responsibilities for the administration of public policy in these areas. The members of the governing bodies are appointed by the governor with the approval of the legislature. In turn, the agency executives are appointed by the governing boards.

FIGURE 9–1 STRUCTURE OF THE EXECUTIVE BRANCH IN TEXAS

This figure illustrates the structure of the Texas executive branch. The governor appoints only the secretary of state. The other members of the plural executive are elected independently of the governor.

☐ The Potential for Conflict in the Plural Executive

Agencies headed by these officials are autonomous and—except for limited budgetary review—independent of the governor. In a confrontation with the governor over policy, agency heads can claim their own electoral mandates. For many years, there were only "scattered incidents of hostility within the executive branch," and elected officials generally "cooperated remarkably well with their chief executives."[10] This observation was based on the period during which Texas was a one-party Democratic state. Conservatives dominated party politics, and statewide elected officials generally reflected those conservative interests and believed it was in their own best political interests to cooperate with one another.

The potential for conflict between the governor and other executive officials increased as Texas became a two-party state, and conflict is likely to become more common in the future, even among officials within the same party. During Republican Governor Bill Clements's first term (1979–1983), the other elected officers in the executive branch were Democrats, including Attorney General Mark White, who frequently feuded with the governor and jockeyed for the political advantage that allowed him to unseat Clements in 1982.

In 2003, budgetary differences erupted between Republican Comptroller Carole Keeton Strayhorn and other Republican officeholders, including Governor Perry. These differences resulted in the legislature's approval of a bill, signed by Perry, transferring two key programs from the comptroller's office to the Legislative Budget Board. The political animosity between Strayhorn and Perry intensified, and in 2006 the comptroller challenged the governor's reelection as an independent candidate. Perry ultimately won the election, but in the months leading up to it, official actions and pronouncements by both officeholders often had sharp political edges.

Conflict may also occur between other members of the executive branch. In 1994, for example, Perry, who at the time was agriculture commissioner, opposed a coastal management plan promoted by Democratic Land Commissioner Garry Mauro. In 2012, with Lieutenant Governor David Dewhurst running for the U.S. Senate, three other Republican officeholders—Comptroller Susan Combs, Land Commissioner Jerry Patterson, and Agriculture Commissioner Todd Staples—began jockeying for the next lieutenant governor's election in 2014. How their ambitions will affect their working relationships remains to be seen, but the potential for conflict on policy issues may occur.

Some argue that the effect of the plural executive on state politics and the governor's control of the executive branch is minimal because, for the most part, rancorous conflict among these elected officials still appears to be infrequent. But others argue that the governor, in an effort to avoid conflict with officials over whom he or she has no control, often pursues policies that are not likely to be disruptive, innovative, or responsive to pressing contemporary issues. It is difficult to develop coordinated policies if those holding office in a plural executive system have sharply different or competing agendas. However, proponents of the plural executive contend that it does what it was intended to do: control and constrain the governor. Although collegial or collective decision making often is inefficient and potentially leads to deadlock, the advocates of the plural executive contend that democracy, in most instances, is to be preferred over efficiency.

☐ Qualifications and Backgrounds of Texas Governors

The Texas Constitution has few requirements for a person who desires to run for governor. A governor must be at least thirty years old, a U.S. citizen, and a resident of Texas for at least five years. There also is a requirement that no individual can be excluded from office for religious beliefs, "provided he acknowledges the existence of a Supreme Being."[11] The constitution, however, does not spell out all the roadblocks to winning the office.

Until the election of Bill Clements in 1978, every governor since 1874 had been a Democrat (see Table 9–1). Clements served two terms (1979–1983 and 1987–1991). Republican George W. Bush was elected to the office in 1994 and again in 1998, and Republican Rick Perry was elected in 2002, 2006, and 2010, as Republican strength increased in Texas.

Most governors have been well-educated, middle-aged, and affluent white male Protestants. In many cases, their families were active in public life and helped shape their careers. No minorities and only two women have been elected to the office: Miriam A. "Ma" Ferguson, whose husband, James E. "Pa" Ferguson, earlier served as governor for two terms (1925–1927 and 1933–1935), and Ann Richards who served for one term (1991–1995). By the time Richards became governor, only three women had ever been elected to statewide executive office in Texas. Richards, a Democrat, served two terms as state treasurer before being elected governor, and Republican Kay Bailey Hutchison succeeded her as treasurer. From 1919 to 1923, Annie Webb Blanton served as the state superintendent of schools, an elective office that no longer exists.

With the rising costs of statewide political campaigns, a candidate's personal wealth or ability to raise large sums of money has taken on increased importance.

9.1

9.2

9.3

9.4

9.5

9.6

TABLE 9–1 GOVERNORS OF TEXAS SINCE 1870

	Party Affiliation	Years Served
Edmund J. Davis	Republican	1870–1874
Richard Coke	Democrat	1874–1876
Richard B. Hubbard	Democrat	1876–1879
Oran M. Roberts	Democrat	1879–1883
John Ireland	Democrat	1883–1887
Lawrence Sullivan Ross	Democrat	1887–1891
James Stephen Hogg	Democrat	1891–1895
Charles A. Culberson	Democrat	1895–1899
Joseph D. Sayers	Democrat	1899–1903
Samuel W.T. Lanham	Democrat	1903–1907
Thomas Mitchell Campbell	Democrat	1907–1911
Oscar Branch Colquitt	Democrat	1911–1915
James E. Ferguson*	Democrat	1915–1917
William Pettus Hobby	Democrat	1917–1921
Pat Morris Neff	Democrat	1921–1925
Miriam A. Ferguson	Democrat	1925–1927
Dan Moody	Democrat	1927–1931
Ross S. Sterling	Democrat	1931–1933
Miriam A. Ferguson	Democrat	1933–1935
James V. Allred	Democrat	1935–1939
W. Lee O'Daniel	Democrat	1939–1941
Coke R. Stevenson	Democrat	1941–1947
Beauford H. Jester	Democrat	1947–1949
Allan Shivers	Democrat	1949–1957
Price Daniel	Democrat	1957–1963
John Connally	Democrat	1963–1969
Preston Smith	Democrat	1969–1973
Dolph Briscoe Jr.**	Democrat	1973–1979
Williams P. Clements, Jr.	Republican	1979–1983
Mark White	Democrat	1983–1987
William P. Clements Jr.	Republican	1987–1991
Ann Richards	Democrat	1991–1995
George W. Bush	Republican	1995–2000
Rick Perry	Republican	2000–present

* Only governor of Texas to be impeached and convicted.

** Prior to 1974, governors were elected for two-year terms of office.

SOURCE: Texas State Library & Archives Commission, *Portraits of Texas Governors.*

Otherwise-qualified prospects are dissuaded from running for governor and other offices because of the difficult burden of fund-raising. Bill Clements and fellow Republican Clayton Williams, a Midland businessman who lost the 1990 gubernatorial race to Ann Richards, spent millions of dollars out of their own pockets on gubernatorial races that were their first bids for elective office. Similarly, Democrat Tony Sanchez, a wealthy Laredo businessman, spent more than $50 million of his personal fortune on an unsuccessful race for governor against Perry in 2002. Their experience raises the possibility that personal wealth and the willingness to spend it on one's own election campaign will continue to take on more importance in future races.

Previous public service often provides gubernatorial aspirants with public visibility and links to party leaders, interest groups, and public officials around the state. Such relationships help candidates develop broad electoral support. Texas governors previously have served in local and statewide offices, the state legislature, and the U.S. Congress, but a few have served without any previous elected experience. Preston Smith (1969–1973) was a legislator and lieutenant governor prior to being elected governor. Dolph Briscoe (1973–1979) also served in the legislature. Mark White (1983–1987) served as secretary of state and then as attorney general. Ann Richards was a county commissioner and then state treasurer. Although he had never previously held elective office, Bill Clements was a deputy U.S. secretary of defense prior to winning his first gubernatorial race. George W. Bush was elected governor in 1994 without any previous formal government experience. However, he served as an unofficial adviser to his father, former President George H. W. Bush. Rick Perry served as a state representative, agriculture commissioner, and lieutenant governor before becoming governor.

□ Impeachment and Incapacitation

A governor can be removed from office through impeachment proceedings initiated in the state House of Representatives and conviction by the state Senate in a trial of the impeachment charges. Only one Texas governor, James E. "Pa" Ferguson in 1917, has been removed from office through impeachment (see *Talking Texas: Impeaching a Governor*).

Across the country, the most recent governor to be removed from office through the impeachment process was Rod Blagojevich of Illinois, who was impeached in early 2009 after being indicted on federal corruption charges.[12] Some states, such as California, can remove a governor through recall as well as impeachment. Through a process initiated by a petition of voters, a special election is held on the question of the removal of the governor. If the people vote to remove the governor, a new governor is then elected. This occurred in late 2003 in California, when Democrat Gray Davis was recalled as governor and voters, in the same election, selected Arnold Schwarzenegger, a Republican, to replace him. In 2012, Wisconsin voters forced a recall election against Republican Governor Scott Walker over legislation he promoted to eliminate most collective bargaining rights for public employee unions. Walker survived the recall election in June 2012, garnering national attention and financial support from conservative groups. Unions, teachers, and public employees from other states were mobilized by his opponents.

Texas does not have a recall process for statewide officeholders. If a Texas governor dies, is incapacitated, is impeached and convicted, or voluntarily leaves office in midterm,

Talking ★ TEXAS Impeaching a Governor

Texas is one of only a few states that have removed a governor by impeachment. In 1917, a controversy erupted over Governor James E. "Pa" Ferguson's efforts to remove five University of Texas faculty members. The governor vetoed the university's appropriations, and when he called a special legislative session to consider other funding, he faced articles of impeachment based primarily on the misuse of public funds. He ultimately was convicted and removed from office, but for two more decades, the husband-and-wife team of Ma and Pa Ferguson, and the controversy that continued to surround them, dominated a great deal of Texas politics.[a]

CRITICAL THINKING QUESTIONS

1. Is it possible to remove political considerations from the impeachment process? Why or why not?
2. Do governors, who sign state budgets, have the right to try to influence state university decisions over faculty members? Why or why not?

[a]Fred Gantt Jr., *The Chief Executive in Texas* (Austin: University of Texas Press, 1964), pp. 229–30.

9.1
9.2
9.3
9.4
9.5
9.6

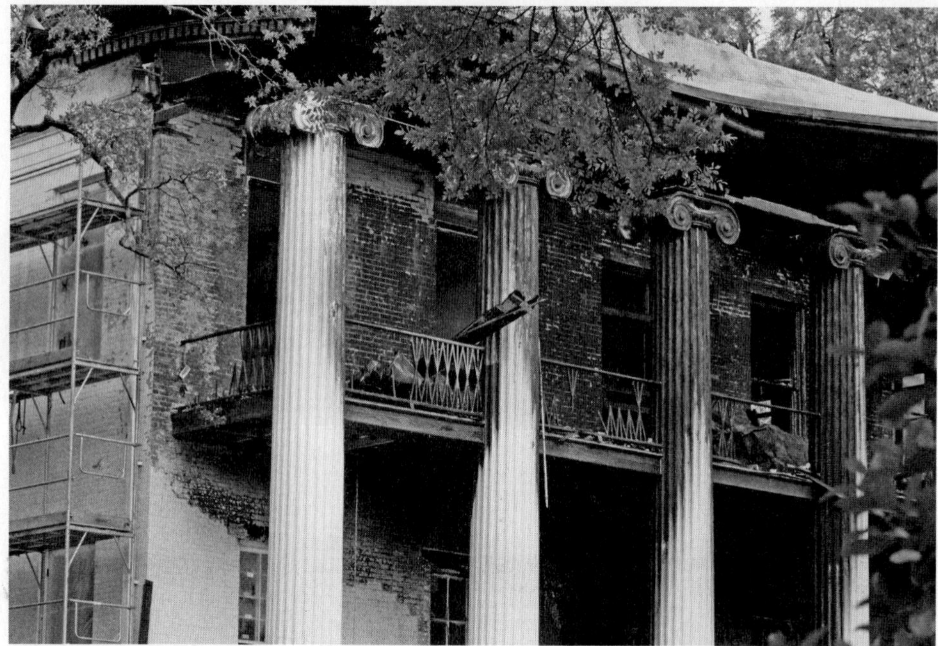

TORCHED

The 152-year-old Governor's Mansion, located across the street from the Capitol building in Austin, was torched by an arsonist on June 8, 2008. The mansion, under renovation and unoccupied at the time, suffered extensive damage.

the lieutenant governor replaces the governor until the next general election. Whenever the governor leaves the state, the lieutenant governor serves as acting governor.

The Salary and "Perks" of the Governor's Office

In 2012, the governor of Texas was paid $150,000 a year (see *Talking Texas: Rick Perry: Double Dipper*). The state also provides the governor with housing, a security detail, travel expenses, and access to state-owned planes and cars. For many years, governors and their families had lived in the Governor's Mansion in downtown Austin near the Capitol. That historic structure was severely damaged by an arsonist in 2008 while it was closed for renovations. Governor Rick Perry and his family already had relocated to a rental house elsewhere in Austin before the fire, and they remained there while the state rebuilt the mansion.

Talking ★ TEXAS Rick Perry: Double Dipper

Both in pronouncements at home and along the national trail in his short-lived presidential campaign, Governor Rick Perry frequently criticized Social Security and other government "safety-net" programs. He also, in his frequent attacks against Washington, criticized "perks" enjoyed by members of Congress. So, many Texans may have been surprised to learn that the governor, while still in office, is double dipping, collecting both his $150,000 annual salary and retirement benefits worth another $90,000-plus a year.

Perry began collecting his retirement pay in January 2011, but that did not become public until late in the year when the governor had to include the information on a disclosure form that presidential candidates are required to file with the Federal Election Commission. "Rick Perry has done something his opponents have been hoping he'd do for years: retire. But it's not what the governor's detractors had in mind," wrote reporter Jay Root in *The Texas Tribune* after learning about the disclosure entry.

Was Perry being inconsistent?

No, said spokesman Ray Sullivan. He said Perry's early collection of retirement benefits was "consistent with Texas state law and Employee Retirement System rules." The governor's retirement credits included his service in the Air Force before he entered politics, Sullivan noted. He also said that Perry, even while collecting pension benefits, still contributed 6.5 percent of his salary to Employees Retirement System premiums. Perry also will get additional credit—and higher benefits—for his continued service as governor, and he is eligible for lifetime, state-provided health care and—you guessed it—Social Security.[a]

CRITICAL THINKING QUESTIONS

1. Was Governor Perry's decision to collect retirement benefits while still in office and collecting a full-time salary inconsistent with his political pronouncements? Why or why not?
2. Should governors be allowed to double dip? Explain your answer.

[a]Jay Root, "Perry 'Retires' to Boost Pension Pay," *The Texas Tribune*, December 16, 2011.

The Powers of the Governor

9.3 Explain the legislative, budgetary, appointive, judicial, and military powers of the Texas governor.

Views of the chief executive's functions have changed over time. Early state constitutions limited gubernatorial powers, and governors in many states found themselves in a subordinate position to their legislatures. Throughout the nineteenth century, those relationships often were redefined. At times, the governors' powers were increased and those of the legislatures reduced. During other periods, such as the era of Jacksonian democracy, the powers of both institutions were subjected to strong restrictions to ensure greater responsiveness to the public.

Reform movements of the early twentieth century, responding to political corruption, focused on management and efficiency in the governors' offices. In some states, the office of governor was restructured around the organizational principles of an executive cabinet. Events such as the Great Depression contributed to a further redefinition of executive leadership, with an emphasis in some states on policy initiatives, administrative control and coordination, and expanded political leadership.[13] The Texas Constitution of 1845, adopted when the state was admitted to the Union, modeled the governor's authority on the strong executive principle found in the U.S. Constitution. Later Texas constitutions reduced the powers of the office, however, reflecting apprehension of strong executive and political authority.

For many years, scholars have ranked state governors on their formal constitutional and legal powers, such as budgetary authority, appointment and veto powers, and term limitations.[14] From the earliest to the latest studies, the governor of Texas has ranked consistently with the weaker state governors (see Table 9–2).

Texans, nonetheless, appear to have high expectations of their governor. They evaluate governors in terms of their policy agendas and the leadership they exercise in achieving those goals. But how does a governor meet such expectations when the formal powers of the office are limited? The sections that follow analyze both the formal powers and informal resources at the governor's disposal.

☐ Legislative Powers

The governor has the opportunity to outline his or her legislative priorities at the beginning of each regular biennial session through the traditional "state of the state" address

TABLE 9–2 COMPARISON OF THE FORMAL POWERS OF THE GOVERNORS

Strong (4.0 and above)			
Alaska (4.1)	Massachusetts (4.3)	New York (4.1)	West Virginia (4.1)
Maryland (4.1)	New Jersey (4.1)	Utah (4.0)	
Moderately Strong (3.5–3.9)			
Arkansas (3.6)	Iowa (3.8)	Nebraska (3.8)	Tennessee (3.8)
Colorado (3.9)	Maine (3.6)	New Mexico (3.7)	Washington (3.6)
Connecticut (3.6)	Michigan (3.6)	North Dakota (3.9)	Wisconsin (3.5)
Delaware (3.5)	Minnesota (3.6)	Ohio (3.6)	
Florida (3.6)	Missouri (3.6)	Oregon (3.5)	
Illinois (3.8)	Montana (3.5)	Pennsylvania (3.8)	
Moderate (3.0–3.4)			
Arizona (3.4)	Idaho (3.3)	Nevada (3.0)	**Texas (3.2)**
California (3.2)	Kansas (3.3)	New Hampshire (3.2)	Virginia (3.2)
Georgia (3.2)	Kentucky (3.3)	South Carolina (3.0)	Wyoming (3.1)
Hawaii (3.4)	Louisiana (3.4)	South Dakota (3.0)	
Weak (2.9 and below)			
Alabama (2.8)	North Carolina (2.9)	Oklahoma (2.8)	Vermont (2.5)
Mississippi (2.9)	Indiana (2.9)	Rhode Island (2.6)	

SOURCE: Based on Thad Beyle, "The Governors," at http://www.unc.edu/~beyle/gubnewpwr.html. Beyle's rankings are based on a six-point scale using the structure of the executive branch, tenure, appointment powers, budget powers, veto powers, and governor's party control. The governor of Texas ranks thirty-fifth using this scale.

to the legislature. The governor also can communicate with lawmakers—collectively or individually—throughout the session. In this fashion, the governor can establish a policy agenda, recommend specific legislation, and set the stage for negotiations with legislative leaders, other state officials, and interest groups. The media cover the governor's addresses and other formal messages to the legislature, giving the governor the opportunity to mobilize the public support that may be essential to the success of his or her initiatives.

The governor's effectiveness also may be enhanced by the office's two major constitutional powers over the legislature—the authority to call and set the agenda for special legislative sessions and the ability to veto proposed legislation. The governor may call any number of special sessions, each of which can last as long as thirty days, and designate the subjects to be considered during a session. Sometimes, the mere threat of a special session can be enough to convince reluctant lawmakers to approve a priority program of the governor or reach an acceptable compromise during a regular session. Most legislators, who are paid only part-time salaries by the state, dislike special sessions because they interfere with their personal livelihoods and disrupt their family lives. Governor Rick Perry called three special sessions in 2003 to overcome Democratic opposition—including a month-long walkout by Democratic senators—and win approval of a congressional redistricting bill that favored Republican candidates. The bill would not have passed without Perry's persistence. In 2011, Perry called a special session when the legislature failed to finalize a school funding measure.

It can be risky for the governor to call special sessions. The governor's influence and reputation are on the line, and further inaction by the legislature can become a political liability. In some instances, the legislative leadership has broadly interpreted the subject matter of a governor's special session proclamation and considered bills not sought by the governor. The speaker and the lieutenant governor make the parliamentary rulings that determine whether a specific piece of legislation falls within the governor's call; therefore, the governor has to be very careful in drafting a proclamation setting a special session's agenda. Once a special session is called, the governor can increase his or her bargaining power by adding legislators' pet bills to the agenda in exchange for the lawmakers' support of the governor's program.

The governor of Texas has one of the strongest **veto** powers of any governor. When the legislature is in session, the governor has ten days (excluding Sundays) to veto a bill, sign it, or let it become law without his or her signature. A veto can be overridden by a two-thirds vote of both the House and the Senate. During the past fifty years, Governor Clements has been the only governor to have a veto overridden. It was a local game-management bill the legislature, then dominated by Democrats, voted to override during the Republican governor's first term. The governor has twenty days after the legislature adjourns to veto bills passed in the closing days of a session, which is when most legislation receives final passage. So, most gubernatorial vetoes are issued after the legislature has adjourned and no longer has the opportunity to attempt an override. The governor also has **line-item veto** authority over the state budget. This means the governor can delete specific spending items without vetoing the entire bill. All other bills have to be accepted or rejected in their entirety.

veto
The power of the governor to reject, or kill, a bill passed by the legislature.

line-item veto
The power of the governor to reject certain parts of an appropriation, or spending, bill without killing the entire measure.

A governor may veto a bill for a number of reasons, including doubts about its constitutionality, objections to its wording, concerns that it duplicates existing law, or opposition to its policy. A governor's threat of a veto also can be effective because such threats can prompt legislators to make changes in their bills to meet a governor's objections.

Historic records on gubernatorial vetoes are not complete, but Governor Bill Clements issued 184 vetoes, and Governor Dan Moody (1927–1931) issued 117. Governor Ann Richards vetoed 36 bills and resolutions in one regular and two special sessions in 1991 and allowed 228 bills to become law without her signature that same year.

Governor Rick Perry, the longest-serving governor in Texas history, is believed to hold the record for vetoes—259 through 2011. He vetoed 82 bills, also believed to be a record, at the end of the 2001 legislative session alone. One of the 2001 vetoes, which struck down a bill that would have banned the execution of mentally retarded convicts, received international attention. The veto was sharply criticized by death penalty opponents but drew praise from crime victims' advocates. Soon afterward, however, the U.S. Supreme Court, ruling in a case from another state, imposed a national ban on the execution of mentally retarded convicts. In 2011, Perry enraged many parents and other public safety advocates by vetoing a bill that would have banned texting while driving.

☐ Budgetary Powers

The governor of Texas has weaker budgetary authority than the governors of most states and the president of the United States. These budgetary constraints limit the governor's ability to develop a comprehensive legislative program. The legislature has the lead in budget setting, with a major role played by the Legislative Budget Board (LBB), a ten-member panel that includes the lieutenant governor, the speaker, and eight key lawmakers. Both the LBB and the governor make budgetary recommendations to the legislature, but lawmakers usually give greater attention to the LBB's proposals. To meet emergencies between legislative sessions, the governor and the LBB can transfer appropriated funds between programs or agencies. Either the governor or the LBB can initiate the proposal, but the other must agree to it.

☐ Appointive Powers

One indication of a strong governor is the power to hire and fire the persons responsible for implementing public policy. But as we discussed earlier in this chapter, the Texas

9.1

9.2

9.3

9.4

9.5

9.6

staggered terms

A requirement that members of state boards and commissions appointed by the governor serve terms that begin on different dates. This is to assure that a board maintains a level of experience by guarding against situations in which all board members leave office at the same time.

senatorial courtesy

An unwritten policy that permits a senator to block the confirmation of a gubernatorial appointee who lives in the senator's district.

governor's administrative authority is severely limited by the plural executive structure under which independently elected officeholders head several major state agencies.

Most of the remainder of the state bureaucracy falls under more than 200 boards and commissions that oversee various agencies created by state law. Most of these are part-time, unpaid positions whose occupants are heavily dependent on agency staffs and constituents for guidance. Although members of these boards are appointed by the governor and confirmed by the Senate, the structure creates the potential for boards and commissions to become captives of the narrow constituencies they are serving or regulating and reduces their accountability to both the governor and the legislature.

Most board members serve six-year **staggered terms**. That means it takes a new governor at least two years to get majorities favoring his or her policies on most boards. Resignations or deaths of board members may speed up the process, but a governor cannot remove a predecessor's appointees. A governor, with the approval of two-thirds of the Senate, can fire only his or her own appointees. Governor Perry has been in office long enough to have a lock on these board appointments and a strong influence on their policy.

The governor appoints individuals to boards and commissions with the approval of two-thirds of the Senate. **Senatorial courtesy**, an unwritten norm of the Senate, permits a senator to block the governor's nomination of a person who lives in that senator's district. The governor and staff members involved in appointments spend considerable time clearing potential nominees with senators because political considerations are as important in the confirmation process as a nominee's qualifications.

Individuals seek gubernatorial appointments for a variety of reasons, and the appointments process can be hectic, particularly at the beginning of a new governor's administration. The governor's staff screens potential nominees to determine their availability, competence, political acceptability, and support by key interest groups. Although most governors would deny it, campaign contributions also are a significant factor for governors of both parties. A number of Governor Clements's appointees made substantial contributions to his campaign.[15] Governors Richards, Bush, and Perry also appointed major contributors to important posts. Governor Perry made the most controversial appointment of his first year in office, former Enron Corporation executive Max Yzaguirre as chairman of the Public Utility Commission, one day before receiving a $25,000 political donation from then-Enron Chairman Ken Lay in 2001. Perry insisted the timing was coincidental, but it generated much controversy after Enron filed for bankruptcy a few months later, prompting Yzaguirre's resignation from the post. Then, in 2003, less than one month after receiving a $100,000 contribution from homebuilder Bob Perry of Houston, Governor Perry appointed a top executive of the homebuilder's company to a new state commission charged with developing building performance standards. The legislature created the commission, the Texas Residential Construction Commission, to reduce consumer lawsuits against builders. A few years later, the legislature took the rare step of abolishing the agency, following numerous consumer complaints. Bob Perry, who is not related to the governor, remains one of his biggest contributors. According to an analysis by a campaign finance watchdog group, Texans for Public Justice, about one-fifth of the $83.2 million that Perry raised during his first nine and one-half years as governor came from appointees or their spouses.[16]

The governor appoints individuals to fill vacancies on all courts at the district level or above. If a U.S. senator dies or resigns, the governor appoints a replacement. When a vacancy occurs in another statewide office, except for that of the lieutenant governor, the governor also appoints a replacement. All of these appointees must later win election to keep their seats. If a vacancy occurs in the lieutenant governor's office, the state senators choose someone from among their membership to preside over the Senate as lieutenant governor until the next general election.

Governor Richards was particularly sensitive to constituencies that historically have been excluded from full participation in the governmental process and appointed a record number of women and minorities to state posts. About 41 percent of Richards's appointees during her four-year term were women, and about 33 percent were minorities. Governor Bush appointed the first African American, Michael Williams, to the Texas Railroad Commission, and, at different times during his administration, he appointed two Hispanics—Tony Garza and Alberto R. Gonzales—secretary of state. Bush later appointed Gonzales to fill a vacancy on the Texas Supreme Court. Governor Perry appointed the first African American, Wallace Jefferson, to the Texas Supreme Court, and his appointments, through late 2011, included 36 percent who were women, 15 percent Hispanic, and 9 percent African American.[17]

☐ Judicial Powers

Texas has a seven-member Board of Pardons and Paroles, appointed by the governor.[18] This panel decides when prisoners can be released early, and its decisions do not require action by the governor. The governor, however, can influence the board's overall approach to paroles, as Governor Richards did when she convinced her appointees to sharply reduce the number of paroles, even though the state was struggling with an overcrowding crisis in its prisons. Despite the crisis, Richards responded to citizen outrage over crimes committed by parolees.

The governor has the authority to grant executive clemency—acts of leniency or mercy—toward convicted criminals. One is a thirty-day stay of execution for a condemned murderer, which a governor can grant without a recommendation of the parole board. The governor, on the recommendation of the board, can grant a full pardon, a conditional pardon, or the commutation of a death sentence to life imprisonment.[19]

If a person flees a state to avoid prosecution or a prison term, the U.S. Constitution, under the extradition clause, requires that person, upon arrest in another state, to be returned to the state from which he or she fled. The governor is legally responsible for ordering state officials to carry out such extradition requests.[20]

☐ Military Powers

The Texas Constitution authorizes the governor to function as the "commander-in-chief of the military force of the state, except when they are called into actual service of the United States."[21] The governor appoints the adjutant general to carry out this duty. Texas cannot declare war on another country, and the president of the United States has the primary responsibility for national defense. When riots or natural disasters occur within the state, the governor can mobilize the Texas National Guard to protect lives and property and keep the peace. Should the United States go to war, the president can mobilize the National Guard as part of the national military forces. After the September 11, 2001, terrorist attacks on the World Trade Center and the Pentagon, some National Guard members from Texas were activated to temporarily bolster security at airports. Others went overseas to assist in the wars in Afghanistan and Iraq. And some were assigned to support the U.S. Border Patrol along the U.S.-Mexico border after President George W. Bush ordered the National Guard's assistance in securing the border during political debate over illegal immigration.

Informal Resources of the Governor

9.4 Evaluate the informal resources at the governor's disposal to advance his or her political objectives.

overnors can compensate for the constitutional limitations on their office with their articulation of problems and issues, leadership capabilities, personalities, work habits, and administrative styles (see Table 9–3). Some

TABLE 9–3 THE GOVERNOR'S LEADERSHIP RESOURCES

Formal Constitutional Powers
1. Veto legislation
2. Exercise a line-item veto over the state budget
3. Call and set the agenda for special legislative sessions
4. Make recommendations on the budget
5. Propose emergency budgetary transfers when the legislature is not in session
6. Appoint hundreds of members of policymaking boards and commissions, subject to Senate confirmation
7. Remove his or her own appointees from boards, with Senate approval
8. Fill vacancies in U.S. Senate seats and certain elective state offices
9. Proclaim acts of executive clemency, including stays of execution, for convicted criminals
10. Mobilize the Texas National Guard to protect lives and property during natural disasters and other emergencies
Informal Resources
1. Governor's electoral mandate
2. A large staff to help develop and sell policy proposals
3. Ability to communicate to the public through the mass media
4. Public's perception and opinions about the governor's job performance
5. The governor's political party and relationships with legislative leaders
6. Support and mobilization of interest groups

governors want to be involved in the minutiae of building policy coalitions and spend much of their time trying to develop agreements with legislators and other political players. Other governors find such hands-on involvement unpleasant, inefficient, and time consuming and leave such detailed work to subordinates. When things go well, the governor may receive credit that belongs to others, but during times of trouble, the governor may be blamed for problems beyond his or her control.

□ The Governor's Staff

The earliest governors had only three or four people to help them, but staffs have grown as the growing state has increased demands on the governor's time. By 1963, under John Connally, the governor's staff had grown to sixty-eight full-time and twelve part-time employees.[22] Under Dolph Briscoe in the 1970s, the staff expanded to more than 300, but staffs have been smaller in most subsequent administrations. Governor Perry has about 200 employees.

The staff's organization reflects the governor's leadership style. Some governors create a highly centralized office with a chief of staff who screens the governor's contacts and the information the chief executive receives. Other governors want greater personal contacts with numerous staff members. The critical question is whether the governor obtains enough information with which to produce good public policy and minimize the potential for controversy, conflict, or embarrassment. Under ideal circumstances, the staff enhances the governor's work. Some governors, however, have permitted their staffs to insulate them by denying access to people with significant information or recommendations.

Governors generally choose staffers who are loyal and share their basic political attitudes. Because communication with the governor's various constituencies is essential for success, some staffers are chosen for their skills in mass communications and public relations. Others are hired for their expertise in specific policy areas.[23] In many respects, staff members function as the governor's surrogates. If one makes a mistake, particularly a serious mistake, the public will perceive it as the governor's error.

The staff collects, organizes, and screens information; helps decide who sees the governor; and otherwise schedules the governor's time. Staffers also work to win support for the governor's proposals from legislators, agencies, interest groups, and the public. Key staff members often represent the governor in meetings and in lobbying lawmakers. Sometimes the governor will become personally involved, particularly if his or her participation is needed to break an impasse and produce a solution.[24]

The Governor and the Mass Media

The mass media help shape the governor's political and policy options. Governors who have failed to understand the media's influence often have courted disaster. A governor can develop a good working relationship with the media by being reasonably accessible to reporters and understanding the deadlines and other constraints under which they work. But success with the media requires more than being accessible and friendly, it also involves being honest—or, at least, the avoidance of being caught in a lie—offering policies that are credible, and demonstrating an ability to enact them.

Governors sometimes call press conferences to announce new policies or explain their positions on pending issues. They stage pseudo "news events," such as visiting a classroom to discuss educational quality or a high-tech facility to talk about creating jobs. Their staffers sometimes leak information to selected reporters to embarrass the opposition, put an action of the administration in the best possible light, or float a trial balloon to gauge legislative or public reaction to a proposal. Some governors spend political funds to purchase radio or television time to try to mobilize public opinion in support of pet proposals before the legislature. In addition, the use of social media has become increasingly important. Governor Perry often sends Twitter alerts to supporters and members of the media. Overall, the timely use of the media can contribute significantly to the power and influence of a governor. Periodic statewide public opinion polls commissioned by media organizations often include questions about the governor's performance. Those ratings are widely monitored by players in the political arena.

The Governor and the Political Party

The historic political factions within one-party Democratic Texas were somewhat ill-defined. There were liberal and conservative factions, as well as political differences between urban and rural Texans and between Texans who lived in different regions of the state. There also were differences between economic classes. Democratic governors built political coalitions around these various factions, but the coalitions usually were short lived, and most governors realized only limited power from their position as party leader.

Under the two-party system, however, the political party has become more important in providing support for the governor (see Figure 9–2). During his second term in the late 1980s, Bill Clements often had enough Republican votes in the House to thwart the will of the Democratic majority. After Republicans gained legislative control, Rick Perry received strong support from Republican lawmakers and party officials during the budgetary and redistricting battles of 2003 and for controversial policies, including deep budget cuts, enacted in 2011.

In 1995, during his first year as governor, Republican George W. Bush enjoyed the support of party leaders for his priorities—changes in education, civil and juvenile justice, and welfare. Initially, he kept his distance from much of the agenda advocated by the social conservatives who had taken control of the Texas Republican Party in 1994. But in 1999, while preparing for a presidential race and the conservative voters in Republican primaries across the country, Bush strengthened his antiabortion credentials by endorsing one of the social conservatives' major priorities—a law requiring parents to be notified before their minor daughters could have abortions.

Governor Perry courted social conservatives from the beginning of his administration. He solidified their support for his 2006 reelection race with enactment of a state constitutional amendment banning same-sex marriages and a law that required parental approval, not just notification, for minors to obtain abortions. Perry, however, faced strong

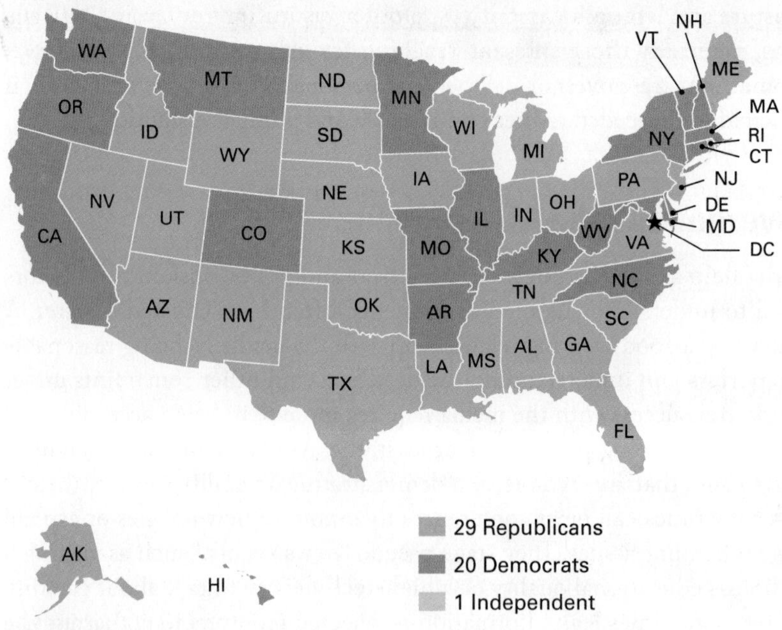

FIGURE 9–2 PARTY CONTROL OF THE GOVERNOR'S OFFICE

This map shows the political party in control of the governorships of the 50 states as of January 2012. Republicans outnumbered Democrats 29 to 20 with one Independent heading Rhode Island.

Source: National Governors Association, "Governors Roster 2012."

opposition from many conservatives in 2007 when he issued an order that schoolgirls be vaccinated against a virus linked to cervical cancer. Opponents, who convinced the legislature to overturn the order, said the governor was interfering with parental rights. Perry patched up those differences, in part, by heating up his rhetoric against President Obama and the federal government, in time to handily win reelection again in 2010.

☐ The Governor and Interest Groups

Successful governors must be full-time political animals who continually nurture relationships throughout the political system. A gubernatorial candidate solicits the endorsements and contributions of various groups. These groups, in turn, develop stakes in gubernatorial elections and usually assume that the candidates they support will be responsive to their interests. A governor's policy initiatives often include legislation of benefit to key support groups, which maintain active roles throughout the policy process. Business groups have been major political donors to Governor Perry, and the governor has strongly supported business priorities throughout his record tenure.

Leadership Styles of Recent Texas Governors

9.5 Contrast the different leadership styles of recent Texas governors.

ubernatorial leadership styles have been as varied as the personalities that molded the chief executives' approaches to their jobs. Some governors have come to the office with well-defined policy agendas and attempted to exploit every resource available to them. Other governors have taken a more limited view of the office. They adopted an administrative or

managerial posture and left policy initiatives to other institutions or elected officials. New programs, especially those with far-reaching tax or social implications, were pursued with considerable caution.

Some governors have thrived on the constant attention and political and social interactions that go with the office. They have worked long hours and continually engaged in public relations and coalition building. Strange as it may seem, however, other governors were introverted and apparently found many aspects of the office distasteful. They often insulated themselves from the public and other political officials through their staffs and seemed detached from the activities necessary to influence public policy.[25]

☐ Bill Clements (1979–1983, 1987–1991)

Clements, a self-made multimillionaire who had founded an international oil-drilling firm, personally funded much of his first campaign in 1978, effectively using a sophisticated media strategy. The man who shocked the Democratic establishment by defeating Attorney General John Hill by 17,000 votes had held no previous elected office. His only governmental experience had been as deputy secretary of defense under Presidents Richard Nixon and Gerald Ford. He was an outsider, a Republican, highly opinionated and blunt, and he had a reputation for solid management skills. All the other elected statewide officials were Democrats, as were the vast majority of legislators, although many lawmakers shared Clements's conservative views.

On arriving in Austin, Clements did not understand the limitations of the powers of the governor.[26] In his election campaign, he had tapped a rather widely held view that state government was wasteful and had proposed that 25,000 state jobs be eliminated. He also appealed to popular notions of limited government and proposed that the Texas Constitution be amended to allow private citizens to propose laws through the initiative and referendum processes. Gradually, however, he learned that he could not single-handedly run the statehouse and the bureaucracy the way he had the corporate boardroom, and he did not accomplish either of those goals.

Clements eagerly exercised his veto power. During his first legislative session in 1979, he vetoed a near-record fifty-one bills.[27] He also struck $252 million from the $20.7 billion state budget for 1980–1981.[28]

THE SECOND TIME AROUND

Republican Bill Clements campaigns in Houston in 1986 during his successful race to unseat Democrat Mark White and return to the governor's office.

Clements generally received high marks for the quality of his staff and board appointments during his first term. The governor appointed Republicans, who for years had been shut out of appointments, to boards and commissions. Clements also appointed many conservative Democrats. In part, his appointment strategies were designed to convert conservative Democrats to the Republican Party, thus extending and consolidating Republican gains across the state. Clements made many judicial appointments during his two terms, including the first two women to the Texas Supreme Court and the first African American to the Court of Criminal Appeals.

Clements never developed effective public relations with the legislature, the news media, and the general public, and he often found himself at odds with other elected officials and interest groups, primarily because of his outspokenness. He was often portrayed as insensitive, as someone inclined to "shoot from the lip" and worry about the consequences later. After learning at a meeting at Texas A&M University that scuba diving by a pregnant woman could damage a fetus, he angered many women by saying, in jest, that diving could serve as a form of birth control. After an offshore Mexican oil well blew out and threatened Texas beaches in 1979, Clements advised coastal residents against "crying over spilt milk." The insensitive remark was compounded by revelations that SEDCO, the drilling firm he had founded, had leased the drilling equipment used on the blown-out well.

By the end of his first term in 1982, Clements's job performance rating had dropped, his image had suffered, and the Texas economy had begun to show signs of weakness. A revitalized Democratic statewide political effort helped Mark White unseat Clements in a bitterly fought campaign.

In 1986, Clements became only the second person in Texas history to regain the governor's office after losing it. Although his motivation for staging a comeback effort was not totally clear, it was widely believed that his main interest was revenge. His hostility toward White remained so intense that he snubbed White's offer of a handshake on Inauguration Day, a clear violation of the unwritten rules of American politics.

Clements spent his first six months back in Austin battling Lieutenant Governor Bill Hobby and Democratic legislators over the state budget. Clements insisted on deep service cuts that would have enabled him to keep a 1986 campaign promise against higher taxes, but he finally gave in during a summer special session in 1987 and signed a record $5.6 billion tax increase.

The public's opinion of Clements, meanwhile, plummeted, and his negative ratings remained high throughout the remainder of his term. By the time he left the governor's office the second time, in 1991, he was widely viewed more as an obstructionist who would rather fight the Democratic majority in the legislature than as a leader who was ready to seek solutions to significant state problems.

Clements's two terms converged with the emergence of a two-party system in Texas that soon would be dominated by the Republican Party, and he contributed significantly to this historic development. By proving that a Republican could win the governorship, Clements made the party attractive to conservative Democrats, and many switched to the Republican Party.

In an interview in late 1990, he assessed his contribution to the development of a two-party system: "The electorate out there breaks down into about one-third Democrats, one-third Republicans, and one-third independents. Well, that is a significant change in the political profile of Texas. That's a historic change, and I guess I'd like to say that I put a brick in place to bring that about."[29] Clements died in 2011.

□ Ann Richards (1991–1995)

Taking her oath in January 1991, Governor Ann Richards attempted to convince the public that her election marked the emergence of a "New Texas." She invited supporters to join her in a march up Congress Avenue to symbolically retake the Capitol for "the people." Hitting on the progressive Democratic themes of her campaign, she promised in her inaugural address a user-friendly, compassionate state government that would expand opportunities for everyone, particularly minorities and women. She promised to clean up the environment, improve education, attack crime, cut red tape, and boost ethical standards for public officeholders.

But the euphoria of the day was tempered by the reality of a $4 billion-plus potential deficit, a court order for school finance reform that could make the shortfall even greater, and a grand-jury investigation into legislative behavior that had further eroded public confidence in state government.

Richards moved quickly to establish herself as an activist governor. The day after her inauguration, she marched over to a meeting of the State Board of Insurance to speak against a proposed increase in auto insurance premiums. Unlike her recent predecessors, she also testified before House and Senate committees, ensuring that her legislative priorities would receive maximum media coverage, and she used the media to attack the state bureaucracy.

Richards also quickly fulfilled a campaign promise to appoint more women and minorities to key positions in state government. She appointed the first African American to the University of Texas System Board of Regents, the first African American woman to the Texas A&M University governing board, and the first Hispanic to the Texas Court of Criminal Appeals. Twenty-five percent of the appointees during her first three months in office were Hispanic, 21 percent were African American, and 49 percent were women. Richards also named a disabled person to the Board of Human Services and a crime victim to the Board of Criminal Justice.[30]

With the state facing a revenue crunch, Richards took the lead in successfully lobbying legislators for a constitutional amendment to create a state lottery. Polls indicated the lottery had strong support among Texans as a new source of revenue for state government.

Most other major issues before the legislature during Richards's first year in office, however, were not so simple, and the new governor was less willing to take specific policy positions on them. She preferred to support the initiatives of Democratic legislative leaders or take the best bill they were willing to give her, rather than demand that legislators enact a specific plan. Richards outlined strong provisions for a new ethics law for legislators and other public officials, but she ended up signing a much weaker bill rather than trying to force a showdown. Detractors would say Richards's leadership wilted in the heat of legislative battle. Supporters would say she was a pragmatist who knew the limits of her office and recognized the necessity of political compromise.

The progressive goals that Richards had outlined in her campaign also were tempered by the reality that Texas was a predominantly conservative state. Despite promoting a vision of a "New Texas" that offered more compassion for the poor, improved health care for the sick, and greater educational opportunity for all, Richards took pains to establish credentials for fiscal restraint. She opposed a proposal for a personal income tax, even though it could have provided a big boost in health and human services programs and education spending.

Although Richards entered the 1993 legislative session with one of the highest public approval ratings of any governor in Texas history, she remained cautious during the entire session, apparently to save political capital for a 1994 reelection race. She joined Lieutenant Governor Bob Bullock and Speaker Pete Laney in insisting that a new state budget be written without an increase in state taxes. Without a tax bill, the new budget did not enable the legislature to give teachers a pay raise, which had been a Richards priority, and it did not keep up with growing caseloads in health and human services.

In one of the most emotional issues of the session, Richards sided with police chiefs, mayors, physicians, and members of the clergy—and against a majority of the legislature—in killing a proposal to allow private citizens to legally carry handguns. (It was revived and approved under Governor George W. Bush two years later.) She successfully advocated an immunization program for children and actively promoted the legislature's efforts to meet a Texas Supreme Court order for a constitutional school finance system but did not propose a plan of her own.

Richards supported a huge prison expansion program and made economic development a major goal. She actively recruited companies to locate or expand in Texas and was instrumental in lobbying the U.S. Congress for approval of the North American Free Trade Agreement (NAFTA), even though organized labor, one of her key supporters, bitterly opposed NAFTA.

Richards was a national figure who was readily welcomed on Wall Street, at Hollywood parties, and in corporate boardrooms throughout the country. Many analysts believed her role as Texas's chief ambassador was her greatest contribution, along with the appointments that opened up the state policymaking process to a record number of women, Hispanics, and African Americans.

Richards, who had no legislative experience, did not seem to relish the often bloody give-and-take of the legislative process but obviously enjoyed her celebrity role as governor. During the 1993 session, Richards told reporters she wasn't the kind of leader who could force results. Instead, she said, she tried to contribute to "an atmosphere in which good things can happen."[31]

Although Republican George W. Bush unseated Richards in 1994, polls indicated she remained personally popular with her constituents. Most conservative, independent voters, however, had never been comfortable with Richards politically. Her defeat coincided with voter discontent with the Democratic Party that swept the country that year. A number of other Democratic governors also were defeated, and Republicans captured control of both houses of the U.S. Congress. Richards's opposition to the handgun bill during the 1993 legislative session was another factor, particularly in key conservative areas of the state. After leaving office, Richards was a lobbyist in Washington and remained in the public eye as a frequent television commentator. She died of cancer in 2006.

☐ George W. Bush (1995–2000)

George W. Bush, son of former President George H. W. Bush, had never held public office before being elected governor, but he had gained valuable political experience campaigning for and serving as an unofficial adviser to his father. The younger Bush became Texas's second Republican governor in modern times by conducting an effective campaign for improvements in the public schools, tougher penalties for juvenile offenders, and changes in the welfare and civil justice systems. He succeeded in winning approval of all four programs during the 1995 legislative session, the first of his term.

Bush's public style was low key. He seemed to go out of his way to avoid controversy during his first year in office, but he remained focused on his four primary goals with the assistance of conservative, Democratic legislative leaders who shared his views and sensed that public sentiment was on the governor's side. Although Democrats had majorities in both the House and the Senate in 1995, conservatives of both major parties dominated the Texas legislature, and Democrats had already initiated work on some of the reforms the new governor wanted.

While keeping a low public profile during his first legislative session, Bush actively worked with legislators behind the scenes, making minor compromises when necessary on his policy priorities. The governor had frequent private meetings with House and Senate members and would sometimes drop by their Capitol offices unannounced. He had weekly breakfast meetings with Lieutenant Governor Bob Bullock and Speaker Pete Laney, two Democrats whose work was crucial to the governor's program. "We disagree, but you'll never read about it," Bush said of his meetings with the two legislative leaders, "The way to forge good public policy amongst the leadership of the legislative branch and executive branch is to air our differences in private meetings that happen all the time. The way to ruin a relationship is to leak things [to the media] and to be disrespectful of meeting in private."[32]

Bush also believed his decisive victory in the 1994 election helped his cause in the legislature. "I won by 352,000 votes," he told reporters the day after the 1995 session adjourned, "And when you stand up in front of the legislature and outline a legislative agenda that was endorsed by the will of the people, that helps remind people that this is what Texans want."[33]

Unlike Governors White, Clements, and Richards before him, Bush did not face budgetary problems in state government that could have distracted lawmakers' attention from his priorities. Unlike Richards, Bush supported legislation that gave adult Texans the right to carry concealed handguns. The gun bill was not one of Bush's major priorities, but it had been an issue in his victory over Richards. Bush signed the gun bill approved by lawmakers in 1995.

Bush faced a tougher challenge during the 1997 legislative session, when he made school property tax reform a major goal. Bush said he wanted to lower property taxes because they had become so high they were making home ownership difficult for many Texans. He proposed that state government assume a larger share of the cost of funding the public schools by lowering local school taxes by about $3 billion a year. To replace the lost revenue, he proposed an increase in the state sales tax, the enactment of a new business tax, and the transfer of $1 billion in state budgetary savings to the public schools. The House rejected most of Bush's proposal and approved a controversial tax trade-off that would have increased numerous state taxes in exchange for major cuts in local school taxes. Bush lobbied Republican legislators for the House plan and helped convince about half of the sixty-eight Republicans in the House to vote for it. Assured that Bush was actively backing the plan, Speaker Laney helped persuade a large number of Democratic House members to vote for it. The bipartisan balancing act was necessary because many Republican legislators had campaigned against higher taxes of any kind, and Republicans had previously targeted many Democratic lawmakers over the tax issue.

Despite the success in the House, the Senate, which had a Republican majority, refused to approve a large increase in state taxes. Bush remained mostly in the background while the Senate debated the issue. After it became obvious that the House and the Senate were in a stalemate, legislative negotiators requested the governor's active participation once again. But Bush was unable to forge any compromise that raised state taxes. The governor managed to salvage only a modest amount of property tax relief—about $150 a year for the average homeowner—by convincing the legislature to increase homestead exemptions, a form of tax break that homeowners get on their school taxes. The legislature used $1 billion in state budgetary savings to repay school districts for the revenue they lost from the higher exemptions.

In failing to win more substantial property tax relief, Bush could not overcome two major obstacles. One was strong opposition from business lobbyists to the proposed state tax increases. The other was the absence of a state budgetary crisis that would have forced the legislature to increase taxes.

Bush easily won reelection over Democratic challenger Garry Mauro in 1998 and entered the 1999 legislative session amidst widespread speculation that he was preparing for a presidential race. With his pending White House campaign obviously on his mind, he convinced the legislature to enact some additional tax cuts and increase education spending. He also accepted a priority of Democratic lawmakers to give schoolteachers a $3,000-a-year pay raise. Bush's biggest legislative defeat in 1999 was the rejection of a pilot program to allow students from low-performing public schools to use tax-backed vouchers to attend private schools. However, in an effort to shore up support among religious and social conservatives in the Republican Party, Bush won approval of a law to require parents to be notified before their minor daughters could receive abortions. It was the most significant piece of abortion-control legislation to be passed by Texas lawmakers since the U.S. Supreme Court had legalized abortion twenty-six years earlier.

Bush officially launched a successful campaign for the 2000 Republican presidential nomination in June 1999. He was elected president in the 2000 election, resigned as governor in December, and was succeeded by Rick Perry, the lieutenant governor.

☐ Rick Perry (2000–)

Republican Rick Perry came to the governor's office with much more governmental experience than his immediate and more famous predecessor, George W. Bush. He had served six years as a state representative, eight years as state agriculture commissioner, and almost two years as lieutenant governor before succeeding Bush as governor in December 2000, after Bush had resigned to become president. However, Perry was not blessed with Bush's politically powerful name or his popularity, and he had not been elected governor. He inherited the job. Moreover, the 2001 legislative session, with which Perry immediately had to deal, promised to be contentious because of political redistricting and a worrisome budgetary outlook.

Perry, however, survived his first session mostly unscarred. He did not have to sign or veto any redistricting bills because Republicans and Democrats in the legislature were unable to agree on new political boundaries for themselves or Texas's congressional delegation. The legislative impasse put legislative redistricting in the hands of the Legislative Redistricting Board and deferred congressional redistricting—for the time being, anyway—to a federal court. Lawmakers wrote a new state budget without having to raise taxes and, at Perry's urging, even found enough money to triple funding for a grant program to help thousands of young Texans from low-income families attend college, a program that would suffer significant cuts later in Perry's administration.

Some legislators criticized Perry's mostly low-key style during the 2001 session and complained that he did not let them know early enough and clearly enough what he wanted. Shortly after the legislative session had ended, however, Perry flexed his muscles and vetoed a record eighty-two bills, including a measure that would have banned the execution of mentally retarded convicts in Texas. Aware that international attention was focused on his decision, Perry invited relatives of murder victims to join him at a state Capitol news conference announcing the veto. A year later, though, the U.S. Supreme Court, acting on a case from another state, prohibited the execution of mentally retarded inmates throughout the country.

Despite his rural roots—Perry grew up in Paint Creek, a tiny town in West Texas—the governor was acutely aware of the clogged freeways that plagued the daily lives of urban and suburban Texans. Early on, he sought to make improved transportation a signature issue of his administration. In early 2002, he proposed a massive $175 billion transportation network for Texas, which would include toll roads, railroads, and underground utility tunnels grouped in corridors stretching across the state. The plan, which Perry called the Trans Texas Corridor, would generate controversy for years, in part because rural landowners viewed it as a "land grab" and as a way of enriching toll road operators. The legislature finally scuttled the plan.

Perry defeated Democratic nominee Tony Sanchez, a multimillionaire Laredo businessman, in a bruising campaign to win a full term in the governor's office in 2002. Perry's victory and the first Republican takeover of the Texas House in modern times put the GOP in undisputed control of state government, and Perry acted accordingly. The governor joined Republican legislative leaders in demanding that a $10 billion revenue shortfall be bridged by cutting spending, not raising state taxes, and Republicans prevailed. Advocates of health care programs and other services protested the spending reductions, and many of the state's daily newspapers editorialized for limited tax increases to help minimize the cuts in services. The legislature raised some state fees and enacted legislation to allow university governing boards to increase tuition, but Perry refused to budge on taxes, apparently convinced that most middle-class Texans agreed with him. He also argued that the state's relatively low tax burden had to be protected to keep the state attractive to businesses looking for places to expand. Perry also won from the legislature a special economic development fund that could be used to provide financial incentives for business recruitment. In addition, the governor advocated and won significant new restrictions on medical malpractice claims and other civil lawsuits.

Perry played a dominant role in a bitter, partisan fight over congressional redistricting in 2003. He supported an effort, initiated by U.S. House Majority Leader

Tom DeLay of Sugar Land, to increase the number of Republicans elected to the U.S. House from Texas, and he called three special sessions that summer to force the result.

Facing a Texas Supreme Court order for changes in the state's school finance system, Perry called the legislature into another special session in 2006. He endorsed a plan for cutting local school property taxes by about one-third and replacing most, but not all, of the lost revenue with an expanded business tax and an increase in the state cigarette tax. With Republicans still holding a legislative majority and a court deadline looming, Perry succeeded in getting the plan passed. Democrats and educator groups criticized the tax trade-off because it did not increase funding for education. In fact, as would become obvious later, it reduced overall school funding by about $5 billion a year. But Perry, who was running for reelection that year, bragged about cutting school property taxes, even though he overstated the significance of the tax reductions for most Texans. The plan, nevertheless, satisfied the court order.

Perry already had strengthened his support among conservative Republican voters in preparation for his 2006 reelection race. In 2005, he advocated a state constitutional amendment banning same-sex marriage, which Texans overwhelmingly approved with strong support from fundamentalist churches. He also backed a new state law to require minors to have their parents' permission before obtaining an abortion.

Perry attracted three high-profile reelection opponents, an unusually high number, in 2006. They included Democratic nominee Chris Bell, a former congressman and former city councilman from Houston, and independents Carole Keeton Strayhorn, the state comptroller, and Kinky Friedman, an author-musician whose campaign was punctuated with satirical one-liners. Strayhorn, who had openly feuded with Perry on budgetary matters, ran as an independent because she knew she could not unseat the governor in the Republican primary. Perry was reelected, but with only 39 percent of the vote.

That low margin probably contributed to the rocky relationship the governor had with many lawmakers, including Republicans, during the 2007 and 2009 legislative sessions. In 2007, Perry infuriated many conservatives by issuing an executive order to require schoolgirls to be vaccinated against a virus linked to cervical cancer. Perry said his order was an important health care initiative, but opponents said it interfered with parental rights and questioned the governor's authority to issue it. With Republicans taking the lead, legislators overwhelmingly approved a bill to rescind it. Many Republican lawmakers, particularly from rural areas, also fought the governor over the expanded use of toll roads. Several toll road projects were allowed to continue, but lawmakers placed new limits on privately financed toll projects.

In 2009, the Republican-led Senate rejected one of Perry's appointees to the Board of Pardons and Paroles as unqualified for the job and rejected his choice for chair of the State Board of Education, following complaints that the individual had tried to impose his religious beliefs on educational policies. The Texas Department of Transportation, headed by Perry appointees, again came under legislative attack. However, Perry already was preparing for his 2010 reelection campaign by aiming most of his political criticisms at President Barack Obama and the federal government.

To help balance a new state budget, Perry and the legislature readily accepted several billion dollars of federal economic recovery stimulus money, which had been championed by Obama. But Perry refused to accept $555 million in extra federal unemployment compensation money under the stimulus package. The governor argued that the federal money came with too many "strings attached," including a requirement that Texas make more jobless workers eligible for benefits. By rejecting the money, Perry sought to strengthen his support among conservative Republican voters in anticipation of a reelection challenge from U.S. Senator Kay Bailey Hutchison in the 2010 Republican primary. Perry's anti-Washington rhetoric became so inflamed that he received national attention for failing to repudiate secession at an antitax protest rally (see *Talking Texas: Secession Is Not an Option*).

In addition to winning the fight over the unemployment money, Perry claimed several other victories at the end of the 2009 session, including tax cuts for small business owners and replenishing two economic development funds from which he awarded tax dollars to businesses promising to create new job opportunities in Texas.

9.1

9.2

9.3

9.4

9.5

9.6

In the face of Perry's opposition, the 2009 legislature refused to expand the Children's Health Insurance Program for low-income families, even though Texas had more children without health insurance than any other state.

As anticipated, Senator Hutchison challenged Perry in the 2010 Republican primary. Perry tapped into the strong support of conservatives, including members of the tea party movement, by attacking Hutchison as a "Washington insider" who did not know what was best for Texas. Perry won the primary and the November general election against Democratic challenger Bill White, a former mayor of Houston. Republicans also won an overwhelming majority of the Texas House in 2010, and Perry advocated and won a strongly conservative agenda during the 2011 legislative session. At Perry's insistence, the legislative majority slashed billions of dollars from education and other public services to cover a $27 billion revenue shortfall without raising state taxes and, with his support, enacted new regulations for abortion and a law mandating that voters show photo identification in order to cast ballots.

A few months after the legislature adjourned, Perry launched a race for the 2012 Republican presidential nomination. His campaign had been highly anticipated by conservative Republicans but ended after only five months, following a series of highly publicized gaffes by the governor. It was the first political race Perry had ever lost. After cruising over the Texas political landscape for so long, he obviously was not prepared for the much greater scrutiny of a national campaign. On returning to Austin, Perry served notice that he would try to regain his political clout at home and perhaps even run for president again in 2016.[34] Some observers wondered, though, if he was simply trying to avoid being tagged a "lame duck" before the 2013 legislative session convened.

Talking ★ TEXAS Secession Is Not an Option

The Civil War may have determined that a state cannot withdraw from the Union, but *secession* remains a popular word with many disgruntled American citizens, including some conservative Republican primary voters whom Governor Rick Perry tried to impress in preparation for his 2010 reelection campaign.

Seeking to bolster his image as a Washington "outsider" and distinguish himself from a popular future opponent, U.S. Senator Kay Bailey Hutchison, Perry courted right-wing voters by attending a handful of antitax "Tea Parties" in April 2009. But he stirred up more controversy than he intended when a reporter in Austin asked him about the "secede" signs that were held aloft by some participants in the events.

"Texas is a unique place," the governor replied,

> When we came into the Union in 1845, one of the issues was that we would be able to leave if we decided to do that. My hope is that America, and Washington in particular, pays attention. We've got a great Union. There's absolutely no reason to dissolve it. But if Washington continues to thumb [its] nose at the American people, you know, who knows what might come out of that? But Texas is a very unique place, and we're a pretty independent lot, to boot."[a]

Although Perry did not endorse secession, he failed to strongly repudiate it either, and that failure sparked a political firestorm. Democrats criticized him, late-night TV hosts joked about him, and experts corrected him. The terms under which Texas was admitted to the Union did not allow for secession. They instead gave Texas the option of dividing into as many as five states.

After several weeks of trying to downplay the controversy, Perry finally took steps to try to repair the damage. In letters to Texas newspapers, he attacked the expansion of the federal government but took pains to also note that he would never advocate secession. And in an interview with the *Los Angeles Times*, he said: "We live in a great country. I'm not in favor of Texas seceding."[b]

CRITICAL THINKING QUESTIONS

1. What would be some of the advantages and disadvantages of Texas dividing into five states?
2. Take another look at Governor Perry's response to the secession question. Was the criticism over his response fair? Why or why not?

[a]Anna M. Tinsley, "At Rally, Perry Says Secession Is on Minds of Many in the State," *Fort Worth Star-Telegram*, April 16, 2009, p. B1.

[b]Mark Z. Barabak, "In Texas, Even Taking Sides Is Bigger," *Los Angeles Times–Washington Post News Service*, May 18, 2009.

Other Offices of the Plural Executive

9.6 List and describe the basic duties and responsibilities of the other offices of the executive branch.

Under the Texas Constitution of 1836, the executive branch resembled the structure of the American presidency with an elected president and vice president. The Constitution of 1845 replaced the office of vice president with an elected lieutenant governor. This constitution also introduced the plural executive, giving the governor the power to appoint the attorney general and the secretary of state; however, the comptroller and treasurer were to be elected every two years by a joint session of the legislature. Subsequent constitutions created new offices to be elected statewide, producing the constitutional legacy of the plural executive.

☐ Lieutenant Governor

The lieutenant governor, the second highest-ranking official in Texas, has only limited executive powers. Were the governor to die, be incapacitated, removed from office, or voluntarily leave office midterm, the lieutenant governor would become governor. That eventuality has occurred only four times. In 1917, William P. Hobby replaced James E. Ferguson, who was impeached. Governor W. Lee O'Daniel resigned in 1941 to enter the U.S. Senate and was succeeded by Coke Stevenson. Governor Beauford Jester died in office in 1949 and was replaced by Allan Shivers. Most recently, George W. Bush resigned in December 2000 after being elected president and was succeeded by Rick Perry.

The office of lieutenant governor is primarily a legislative office in Texas. Because of the lieutenant governor's key legislative role and statewide constituency, many experts consider this position to be the most powerful office in state government. The lieutenant

THE PLURAL EXECUTIVE

Governor Rick Perry, right, and other Republican officials talk with reporters in Austin about the upcoming 2012 presidential and state elections after voting early in a recent election. Also shown are U.S. Senator John Cornyn and state Agriculture Commissioner Todd Staples, to Perry's right, and state Attorney General Greg Abbott, bottom. Most members of the plural executive are elected independently of the governor, which places severe limitations on the governor's power.

9.1

9.2

9.3

9.4

9.5

9.6

attorney general

The state's chief legal officer. He or she represents the state in lawsuits; is responsible for enforcing the state's antitrust, consumer protection, and other civil laws; and issues advisory opinions on legal questions to state and local officeholders. This elected official has little responsibility for criminal law enforcement.

governor is elected independently of the governor and does not have to belong to the same party as the governor. He or she is the presiding officer of the Senate, and Senate rules give the lieutenant governor enormous power over the legislature. The office's legislative powers far exceed those of the vice president on the federal level. The lieutenant governor controls the flow of legislative business in the Texas Senate. He or she also chairs the Legislative Budget Board, which plays a key role in the state budgetary process. In contrast, the vice president's legislative role in the U.S. Senate is largely ceremonial. He or she rarely presides over the Senate. The only real power of the vice-presidential office in the U.S. Senate is to cast a vote, if necessary, to break a tie.

Democrat Bill Hobby, son of the former governor, served a record eighteen years as lieutenant governor before retiring in 1991. He was succeeded by Bob Bullock, a former state comptroller and one of the most influential state officials in recent history. Bullock, who chose not to seek reelection in 1998 and died the next year, was succeeded by Republican Rick Perry, a former state agriculture commissioner.

Perry presided over the Senate for only one session, 1999, before succeeding Bush as governor. The senators elected state Senator Bill Ratliff, Republican of Mt. Pleasant, to complete Perry's term and preside over the Senate during the 2001 session. Republican David Dewhurst was elected lieutenant governor in 2002 and reelected in 2006 and 2010. He campaigned for the U.S. Senate in 2012 and, if elected to that body, the state senators would choose one of their own to complete his four-year term as lieutenant governor and preside over the state Senate during the 2013 session. At least three other Republican officeholders—Comptroller Susan Combs, Land Commissioner Jerry Patterson, and Agricultural Commissioner Todd Staples—have begun jockeying for the 2014 lieutenant governor's race.

☐ Attorney General

The **attorney general** is the state's chief legal officer and is called upon to defend state laws enacted by the legislature and orders adopted by regulatory agencies. The office also enforces the state's antitrust and consumer protection laws and helps collect child-support payments from delinquent noncustodial parents. Recent attorneys general also have been called on to defend the state or negotiate settlements in federal and state court lawsuits challenging the constitutionality of state prisons, the school finance system, redistricting laws, and other major policies. In addition, the attorney general gives opinions on the legality of actions of other state and local officials.[35]

Unlike counterparts in the federal government and some other states, the Texas attorney general is primarily a civil lawyer. Except for representing the state in the appeals of death penalty cases and assisting local prosecutors, the position has relatively little responsibility for criminal law enforcement. Many candidates for the office like to campaign on tough law-and-order platforms, but responsibilities for criminal prosecution are vested in locally elected county and district attorneys.

Dan Morales, a former Democratic state representative from San Antonio, was elected attorney general in 1990, becoming the second Hispanic elected to statewide office in Texas. He won reelection in 1994 but chose not to run for a third term in 1998. In a major policy decision made independently of the governor, the legislature, and other state officials, in 1996 Morales filed a multibillion-dollar damage suit against tobacco companies, seeking reimbursement for public health care costs associated with smoking. Morales acted within his authority as the state's chief legal officer, and the lawsuit resulted in a $17.3 billion settlement for the state. The tobacco suit also sparked a controversy over legal fees. Several years after Morales left office, he was sentenced to federal prison for four years for mail fraud and filing a false income tax return.

Morales was succeeded by former Texas Supreme Court Justice John Cornyn, Texas's first Republican attorney general in modern times. Cornyn was elected to the U.S. Senate in 2002 and was succeeded by Greg Abbott, a Republican and another former Texas Supreme Court justice. Abbott created a "cyber crimes unit," which went online to crack down on sexual predators prowling Internet chat rooms and posing as teenagers to lure young victims into personal meetings. His unit, assisted by local law enforcement officers, has made numerous arrests. Abbott was reelected in 2006 and 2010.

☐ Comptroller of Public Accounts

The **comptroller of public accounts** is Texas's primary tax collector, accounting officer, and revenue estimator. Texas functions under a **pay-as-you-go** principle, which means that the legislature cannot adopt an operating budget that exceeds anticipated revenue. The comptroller is responsible for providing the revenue estimates on which the legislature drafts biennial state budgets. A budget cannot become law without the comptroller's certification that it falls within the official revenue projection, developed by using sophisticated models of the state's economy.[36] If the revenue estimate is below the legislature's budget proposals, appropriations must be reduced or taxes must be raised. In a volatile, changing economy, it is difficult to accurately project revenues two years in the future. In the mid-1980s, then-Comptroller Bob Bullock had to adjust his revenue estimate downward several times to account for plunging oil prices.

The comptroller's powerful role in budgetary affairs was enhanced by the legislature in 1990 with the additional authority to conduct management audits of local school districts, and again in 1991 with similar oversight authority over other state agencies. Comptroller John Sharp and his successor, Republican Carole Keeton Strayhorn, used this process to identify billions of dollars of potential savings for legislative budget writers and local school boards.

Strayhorn reaped favorable publicity from the management audits. However, the legislature, in a 2003 special session, transferred those programs to the Legislative Budget Board after she became involved in a series of budgetary disputes with legislators and other Republican leaders. Strayhorn surprised the governor and the legislature with a larger-than-anticipated revenue shortfall of $10 billion at the beginning of the 2003 regular session and threatened—but only briefly—not to certify the new state budget drafted by lawmakers. Finally, to make matters worse, she announced that the no-new-taxes budget about which the governor and Republican lawmakers had bragged actually included $2.7 billion in higher fees to be paid by millions of Texans. Strayhorn blamed Governor Rick Perry for the decision to strip the management audit programs from her agency. The governor's office denied the allegation, but Perry had signed the bill. Strayhorn was so angry—or ambitious—that she (unsuccessfully) challenged Perry's reelection in 2006 as an independent candidate.

Republican Susan Combs, a former agriculture commissioner, was elected comptroller in 2006 and reelected in 2010. During the recession that preceded the 2011 legislative session, Combs frequently reported declining tax revenues, resulting in a $27 billion revenue shortfall that the legislature handled, at Governor Perry's insistence, with deep budget cuts. Combs suffered a huge embarrassment and potential political liability when she discovered in 2011 that Social Security numbers and other personal information for 3.5 million people—including current and retired teachers and state employees—had accidentally been left exposed for a year or more on a publicly accessible computer server at her agency. She apologized and offered free credit monitoring and Internet surveillance to those affected. She also offered to spend her political funds for "identity restoration services" for anyone whose personal information was misused because of the breach.[37]

☐ Commissioner of the General Land Office

The state of Texas retains ownership, including mineral rights, to approximately 22 million acres of public lands, which are managed by the **commissioner of the General Land Office**. Revenues generated by mineral leases and other land uses are earmarked for education through the Permanent University Fund and the

comptroller of public accounts
The state's primary tax administrator and revenue estimator. It is an elective position.

pay-as-you-go
A constitutional prohibition against state government borrowing money for its operating budget.

commissioner of the General Land Office
An elected official who manages the state's public lands and administers the Veterans Land Program, which provides low-interest loans to veterans for the purchase of land and houses.

commissioner of agriculture
An elected state official responsible for administering laws and programs that benefit agriculture.

secretary of state
Administers state election laws, grants charters to corporations, and processes the extradition of prisoners to other states. The governor appoints this officeholder.

Permanent School Fund. This agency also is responsible for the Veterans Land Program, which provides low-interest loans to veterans for the purchase of land and houses.

During sixteen years in office, Land Commissioner Garry Mauro, a Democrat, developed several environmental initiatives, including beach cleanup efforts and a program for cleaning up oil spills off the Texas coast. After Mauro unsuccessfully ran for governor in 1998, the next land commissioner, Republican David Dewhurst, a businessman from Houston, continued the beach cleanup efforts. Dewhurst also administered a program to replenish beaches and protect them from erosion. Dewhurst was elected lieutenant governor in 2002 and was succeeded as land commissioner by Jerry Patterson, a former state senator from Harris County. Patterson's priorities also included beach protection as well as development of new nursing homes for veterans and new veterans' cemeteries. He was reelected in 2006 and 2010.

Patterson angered environmentalists by proposing to sell the remote, undeveloped Christmas Mountains in the Big Bend area of far West Texas to private interests, an issue that remained unresolved for several years. Finally, in 2011, the land commissioner agreed to give the mountains, some 9,000-plus acres, to the Texas State University System to use as a study site for archaeology, biology, geology, and wildlife management. The university agreed to provide public access to the site, and environmentalists endorsed the transfer.[38]

☐ Commissioner of Agriculture

This office, created by statute rather than by the constitution, is responsible for carrying out laws regulating and benefiting Texas agriculture. The agency supports agricultural research and education and administers consumer protection laws in the areas of weights and measures, packaging and labeling, and marketing. Republican Rick Perry aggressively promoted Texas agricultural products during two terms as commissioner. Republican Susan Combs, a former state representative from Austin who succeeded Perry, also urged Texans to buy more produce grown in the Lone Star State.

Republican Todd Staples, a former state senator from Palestine, was elected agriculture commissioner in 2006 and reelected in 2010. He promoted Texas produce and nutrition campaigns for children and, during the 2011 drought, publicized the devastating effects on farmers and ranchers.

☐ Secretary of State

The **secretary of state**, the only constitutional official appointed by the governor, has a variety of duties, including granting charters to corporations and processing the extradition of prisoners to other states. The primary function of this office, however, is to administer state election laws. That responsibility includes reviewing county and local election procedures, developing statewide policies for voter registration, and receiving and tabulating election returns.

☐ Elected Boards and Commissions

Only two—the Texas Railroad Commission and the State Board of Education—of the more than 200 boards and commissions that head most state agencies are elected.

TEXAS RAILROAD COMMISSION Originally designed to regulate intrastate (within Texas) operations of railroads and trucking companies, the Texas Railroad Commission now regulates oil and natural gas production and lignite mining in Texas. The commission includes three elected members who serve six-year, staggered terms and rotate the position of chair among themselves. The oil and gas industry has historically focused much attention on this agency and made large campaign contributions to commission members. Many critics claim the commission is a prime example of a regulatory body that has been co-opted by those interests it was created to regulate.

In recent years, the **Texas Railroad Commission** also has become a staging area for opportunistic politicians who seek election to the commission primarily as a stepping-stone to higher office. A commissioner does not have to resign in the middle of his or her six-year term to seek another office and, as an incumbent regulator, has little trouble collecting large contributions from the oil and gas industry that can be used to further political ambitions. Both Democrat John Sharp and Republican Carole Keeton Strayhorn used seats on the commission to strengthen their political bases for successful races for state comptroller in 1990 and 1998, respectively. One commissioner, Tony Garza, resigned in midterm to accept President George W. Bush's appointment as ambassador to Mexico.

The turnover has prompted calls for the commission to be abolished and its duties transferred to other agencies appointed by the governor, including the Public Utility Commission, which already has oversight over electric utilities, and the Texas Commission on Environmental Quality, the state's main environmental protection agency. Democrat Hector Uribe, a former state senator, ran for the commission in 1996, promising to work to abolish it. But Strayhorn, his Republican opponent, argued that the agency was important and needed to be retained. Strayhorn defeated Uribe for a six-year term on the commission, but two years later she ran for and won election to the comptroller's office.

Texas Railroad Commission
A three-member, elected body that regulates oil and natural gas production and lignite mining in Texas.

State Board of Education
A fifteen-member body, whose members are elected by districts, has responsibility over textbook selection, curriculum standards for public schools, and Permanent School Fund investments.

STATE BOARD OF EDUCATION Debate on public education in Texas has not been limited to educational quality and financing. It also has focused on how best to carry out and manage public education programs. The state has bounced back and forth between an elected state education board and an appointed one.

Prior to educational reforms enacted in 1984, the **State Board of Education** had twenty-seven members elected from then-existing congressional districts. At the urging of reformers dissatisfied with student performance, the legislature provided for a new education board of fifteen members to be appointed by the governor and confirmed by the Senate. The idea was to reduce the board's independence while education changes ordered by the legislature were being carried out. But the law also provided that the board would again become an elected body within a few years. Some state leaders later proposed that the board remain appointive and put the question to the voters, who opted for an elected board in 1986. The present board has fifteen members elected from districts established by the legislature.

Those districts are so large that most voters know little, if anything, about candidates for board seats, and, until recently, races for the board received little media attention. Social conservatives wanting to influence education policies started targeting the board and became successful in winning Republican primary races for several board seats. Philosophical and partisan bickering on the board then became so strident that the legislature reduced its powers. The panel's main remaining duties include investment of education dollars in the Permanent School Fund and some oversight over textbook selection and curriculum standards.

However, the political and philosophical battles continue. A major fight in 2010 over the history curriculum for Texas's public schools attracted national attention and ridicule. Several conservatives on the board succeeded in rewriting some of the curriculum standards to conform to their own religious or philosophical beliefs. The changes downplayed the role of Hispanics in Texas history and attempted to diminish Thomas Jefferson's historical standing because of his belief in the separation of church and state.[39]

The Texas Education Agency, the agency responsible for the daily administration of public education, is directed by the commissioner of education, who is appointed by the governor.

Review the Chapter

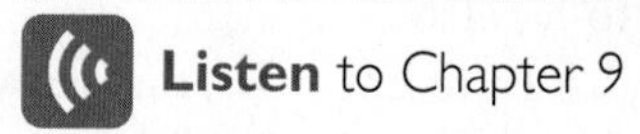
Listen to Chapter 9

A Historical Perspective on the Executive Function in Texas

9.1 Trace the evolution of the Texas governor from a strong unified executive to a plural executive, p. 262.

In Texas's formative period, the executive function was similar in structure to that of the president of the United States, but through the progression of the state's constitutions, the power of the governor was weakened through the creation of the plural executive and other constitutional constraints. The current structure of the executive branch was a reaction to the abuses of the Davis administration during the Reconstruction era. Although more recent constitutional changes have been adopted, such as the extension of the governor's term from two to four years and legislative control over the governor's salary, the constitutional restrictions have created a weak "institutional governor."

The Plural Executive

9.2 Outline the basic constitutional and structural features of the plural executive branch, p. 263.

Texas has a "plural executive," which includes several independently elected statewide officeholders. The governor shares administrative and policy authority with other statewide officials, including the lieutenant governor, secretary of state, comptroller of public accounts, commissioner of the general land office, attorney general, agriculture commissioner, the three-member Texas Railroad Commission, and a fifteen-member State Board of Education. Except for the secretary of state, who is appointed by the governor, all of these officials are elected. Candidates for these offices do not run with the governor on a partisan ticket, and sometimes they are from a different political party than the governor. Reform advocates argue that the plural executive diminishes the ability of the executive branch to respond to modern-day problems.

The Powers of the Governor

9.3 Explain the legislative, budgetary, appointive, judicial, and military powers of the Texas governor, p. 269.

Although it is the most visible office in state government and the public believes it has considerable power, the office of governor is weak in formal powers. As part of their legislative responsibilities, governors propose legislation; call special sessions when necessary; set the agenda for the special sessions; and exercise the veto, including the line-item veto over the budget. The governor has limited influence over the administrative responsibilities of the other elected state officials, but the governor appoints members of more than 200 policy-setting state boards and commissions authorized by statutory law. The governor's control over these agencies is diluted by board members' staggered terms, the need for senatorial approval of the governor's appointments, and legal requirements relating to the composition of these boards. The governor shares budget responsibilities with the Office of Comptroller and the Legislative Budget Board. The governor calls up the National Guard when there is an emergency but has limited administrative responsibilities for the state's military. With frequent vacancies on the state courts, the governor can shape the philosophy of the courts through his or her appointments to the bench.

Informal Resources of the Governor

9.4 Evaluate the informal resources at the governor's disposal to advance his or her political objectives, p. 273.

Although the constitution potentially constrains a governor in his or her efforts to exercise leadership, governors compensate for these limitations with their ability to articulate problems and issues facing the state, their leadership skill in building coalitions in support of their policies, the appeal of their personalities, personal work habits, and administrative styles. Governors have used their staffs, their access to the mass media, their party roles, and their relationships to key interest groups to influence the legislature and other elected officials. A governor can be quite effective and compensate for the institutional limitations with the adroit use of the informal resources available to the office.

Leadership Styles of Recent Texas Governors

9.5 Contrast the different leadership styles of recent Texas governors, p. 276.

Some governors have relished tough policy negotiations and have used cajoling, intimidation, and intense bargaining to achieve their goals. By temperament or design, other governors have worked quietly behind the scenes, letting others do the heavy lifting. Some governors have been highly partisan, others, bipartisan. Some governors have come to the office with a rather extensive policy agenda; others have opposed expanding government. Some governors have exploited the mass media to achieve their objectives; others have had difficult relationships with the press. In recent years, though, governors of Texas have demonstrated that effective leadership can be exercised through a careful blending of both the formal powers and informal resources of the office.

Other Offices of the Plural Executive

9.6 List and describe the basic duties and responsibilities of the other offices of the executive branch, p. 285.

The lieutenant governor serves as governor when the governor is out of state, but this officeholder serves primarily a legislative role as presiding officer of the Texas Senate. The attorney general is the state's chief legal officer and advises state and local agencies and represents the state in lawsuits in state and federal courts. The comptroller of public accounts is the state's chief budget officer, tax collector, and revenue estimator. The state land commissioner oversees millions of acres of public land and administers mineral leases on them. The agriculture commissioner has some regulatory and promotion authority over the agriculture industry. The three-member Texas Railroad Commission regulates intrastate oil and gas production, and the fifteen-member State Board of Education has limited responsibility over public education. The secretary of state is the state's chief elections officer.

Learn the Terms

Study and **Review** the Flashcards

governor, p. 262
plural executive, p. 263
lieutenant governor, p. 263
veto, p. 271
line-item veto, p. 271
staggered terms, p. 272
senatorial courtesy, p. 272
attorney general, p. 286
comptroller of public accounts, p. 287
pay-as-you-go, p. 287
commissioner of the General Land Office, p. 287
commissioner of agriculture, p. 288
secretary of state, p. 288
Texas Railroad Commission, p. 289
State Board of Education, p. 289

Test Yourself

Study and **Review** the Practice Tests

1. The transformation of the Texas executive from a strong unified institution to a divided and plural institution began with the

- **a.** 1836 Constitution of the Republic.
- **b.** 1845 state constitution.
- **c.** 1861 Confederate state constitution.
- **d.** post–Civil War Constitution of 1866.
- **e.** Reconstruction Constitution of 1869.

2. Which of the following executive branch officials does the governor have the power to appoint?

- **a.** Secretary of state
- **b.** Lieutenant governor
- **c.** Comptroller of public accounts
- **d.** Attorney general
- **e.** Commissioner of the General Land Office

3. Some argue that one of the advantages of a plural executive in Texas is that it

- **a.** allows the governor to pursue innovative policymaking.
- **b.** decreases conflict between the executive and legislative branches.
- **c.** constrains the governor.
- **d.** facilitates the coordination of public policy.
- **e.** reduces the disruptive influence of personal ambition among officeholders.

4. In order to qualify to run for governor, a person must be

- **a.** at least 35 years old.
- **b.** a resident of Texas for at least five years.
- **c.** a natural-born citizen.
- **d.** an adherent of the Christian religion.
- **e.** someone who has had previous experience in public service.

5. A governor can be removed from office

- **a.** by a vote of no confidence in the legislature.
- **b.** by a vote of censure in both the House of Representatives and the Senate.
- **c.** by a recall election.
- **d.** through impeachment proceedings initiated in the House of Representatives.
- **e.** through an impeachment trial conducted by other members of the plural executive.

6. The governor's power to call special legislative sessions

- **a.** is limited to two special sessions per year.
- **b.** increases the power of the legislature because it can determine the agenda of the special session.
- **c.** increases the power of the governor because he or she can add items to the special session agenda.
- **d.** is limited to one 30-day session per year.
- **e.** is used only when the governor is too weak to get his or her agenda passed during the regular legislative session.

7. The governor's veto power is strong because

a. he or she has thirty days to veto any bill.
b. a veto can be overridden only by a three-fourths vote of both the House and the Senate.
c. a veto can be overridden by a simple majority of the House.
d. he or she has line-item veto authority over all bills passed by the legislature.
e. most vetoes are issued after the legislature has adjourned, making an override vote impossible.

8. All of the following are offices a governor can appoint EXCEPT

a. vacant U.S. Senate seats.
b. the lieutenant governor.
c. secretary of state.
d. vacant Railroad Commission seats.
e. vacant Texas Supreme Court seats.

9. Which of the following describes why the governor's appointment powers are limited?

a. It takes years for a governor to get majorities favoring his or her policies because of staggered terms.
b. Vacancies can be filled only by popular election.
c. Senatorial courtesy requires the Senate to defer to the governor's preferences.
d. Campaign finance laws in Texas bar any campaign contributor from holding appointive office.
e. A governor can fire his or her own appointees only with the approval of two-thirds of both houses of the legislature.

10. The Texas governor has the unilateral power to

a. fire a predecessor's appointees upon accession to office.
b. grant a full pardon to a criminal.
c. commute a death sentence to life imprisonment.
d. grant a thirty-day stay of execution for a condemned murderer.
e. declare war on a bordering country in a time of national emergency.

11. Which of the following best describes the various informal resources the governor has at his or her disposal?

a. The governor's staff remains too small to handle the increased demands on the governor's time.
b. The mass media remain an undeveloped source of influence for the governor.
c. Political parties were a more important resource for the governor when Democrats dominated the state.
d. Political parties have become a more important resource as Republicans have gained power in the legislature.
e. Campaign finance laws have prevented business groups from having a significant influence in state policymaking.

12. Which of the following is TRUE about the leadership of recent Texas governors?

a. Bill Clements contributed to the development of a two-party system in Texas.
b. Ann Richards used her influence with the conservative legislature to enact a law allowing private citizens to legally carry handguns.
c. George W. Bush succeeded in enacting his policy agenda because Republicans had captured control of both houses of the legislature.
d. Rick Perry successfully enacted Texas's first state income tax.
e. Rick Perry became the first person to win three successive gubernatorial elections with more than 50 percent of the vote.

13. Which of the following can be said about the leadership of recent Texas governors?

a. Bill Clements's exhaustive experience in statewide office enabled him to forge a healthy working relationship with the Democratic legislature.
b. Ann Richards made a priority of appointing more women and minorities to key positions in state government.
c. George W. Bush's background as a businessman helped him overcome business opposition to state tax increases.
d. George W. Bush successfully lobbied state lawmakers for the creation of a state lottery.
e. Rick Perry used his influence with the business community to enact a plan for a massive transportation network called the "Trans Texas Corridor."

14. The lieutenant governor

a. is required to be from the same party as the governor.
b. is the running mate of the governor.
c. presides over the Texas Senate.
d. presides over the Texas House of Representatives.
e. chairs the Texas Railroad Commission.

15. Which of the following can be said about the various offices of the executive branch in Texas?

a. The attorney general serves as the state's chief criminal law enforcement officer.
b. The comptroller can authorize deficit spending for the state's operating budget.
c. The position of land commissioner was eliminated by constitutional amendment in 1991.
d. The Railroad Commission has fifteen members elected from districts established by the legislature.
e. The Railroad Commission deals mainly with oil and gas regulation.

Explore Further

Beyle, Thad L., "Governors: The Middlemen and Women in Our Political System," in *Politics in the American States: A Comparative Analysis*, 6th ed., edited by Virginia Gray and Herbert Jacob. Washington, DC: Congressional Quarterly Press, 1996. Provides a comparative analysis of the formal and informal powers of U.S. governors.

Childs, William R., *The Texas Railroad Commission: Understanding Regulation in America to the Mid-Twentieth Century*. College Station: Texas A&M University Press, 2005. Chronicles the history of one of the most powerful state regulatory commissions and analyzes, from multiple perspectives, its national and international influence.

Connally, John, with Mickey Herskowitz, *In History's Shadow: An Odyssey*. New York: Hyperion Books, 1994. Supplies Connally's perspective on the assassination of John F. Kennedy and includes detailed reflections on his governorship and other phases of his public life.

Gantt, Fred, Jr., *The Chief Executive in Texas: A Study of Gubernatorial Leadership*. Austin: University of Texas Press, 1964. Analyzes the governorship of Texas, including the development of the office and leadership roles played by governors in the administrative and policy processes.

Hendrickson, Kenneth E., *Chief Executives of Texas: From Stephen F. Austin to John B. Connally, Jr.* College Station: Texas A&M Press, 1995. Sketches brief biographies of the political careers of forty-three individuals who held the office of governor or president of the Republic of Texas.

Hill, John L., Jr., with Eric Stromberger, *John Hill for the State of Texas*. College Station: Texas A&M University Press, 2008. Focuses on some of the most contentious issues that faced Texas in the 1970s and the response of the Attorney General's Office to these issues.

Lipson, Leslie, with an introduction by Marshall E. Dimock, *The American Governor from Figurehead to Leader*. Chicago: University of Chicago Press, 1939. Analyzes the development of the office of the American governor.

Reston, James, Jr., *The Lone Star State: The Life of John Connally*. New York: Harper & Row, 1989. Focuses on several controversial aspects of the governor's long business and political career, including the events surrounding the assassination of President John F. Kennedy; this is an unauthorized biography.

Rosenthal, Alan, *The Best Job in Politics: Exploring How Governors Succeed as Policy Leaders*. Washington, DC: Congressional Quarterly Press, 2012. Explores the successes and failures of governors who served during the past thirty years; written by one of the foremost authorities on American legislators.

Texas General Land Office, *The Land Commissioners of Texas*. Austin: Texas General Land Office, 1986. Provides brief biographical sketches of past land commissioners.

10

The Texas Bureaucracy and Policy Implementation

Public service is a public trust. As public servants we take pride in the service we provide for our fellow citizens.

—Texas Governor's Office, 2003

Government is going to be seen as bigger, dumber and slower than ever before if we don't become smaller, smarter and faster.

—Carole Keeton Strayhorn, State Comptroller, 2003

hether public services are performed by state employees or farmed out to private companies under contracts that are supposed to save money and promote efficiency, the cost of running a state bureaucracy for Texas's 25 million residents can be staggering. So can the cost of compiling and securing the millions of pieces of information generated by that bureaucracy and its clients. Consider the experience of the Texas Department of Information Resources, which was ordered by the Texas legislature in 2005 to upgrade the state's outdated information technology system, improve the security of state information, and consolidate the data collection centers of twenty-eight state

10.1 List the basic characteristics of bureaucracies, p. 297.

10.2 Trace the growth of state and local government employment in Texas, p. 298.

10.3 Assess the dynamics of and obstacles to policy implementation by state bureaucrats, p. 301.

10.4 Describe the various ways by which the Texas legislature attempts to increase its control over state agencies, p. 304.

10.5 Explain the use of the whistle-blower protection law to counteract corruption and intentional wrongdoing in the Texas bureaucracy, p. 308.

10.6 Outline the various ways state and local governments regulate economic activity in Texas, p. 309.

10.7 Differentiate among the personnel systems used by governments in Texas, p. 310.

WHERE SOME BUREAUCRATS WORK
Viewed from the Capitol looking north toward the campus of the University of Texas, these are office buildings housing a number of state agencies. Most state employees, however, work in other facilities scattered throughout Texas.

agencies into two high-quality facilities. In 2006, the agency hired IBM to manage the huge job at a cost of $863 million over seven years.

By early 2012, IBM had been paid about $758 million of its contract, and some of the work, including one new data center in Austin, had been completed. But the state complained that most of the work was still undone, and the company was behind schedule. With each party blaming the other for the problem, the state negotiated a settlement with IBM to end the contract and found other private contractors to complete the work.[1]

Texans who happened to read or hear news reports about the apparent loss of taxpayer money on the information contract doubtlessly were angered or, at the very least, concerned. The debacle certainly did nothing to dispel the popular notion that governmental bureaucracy is bloated and entwined in a gigantic ball of expensive red tape. Efforts to provide services to millions of people certainly can produce mistakes, sometimes costly ones. But everyone—those people who imagine government waste behind every computer screen or service counter and those who do not—relies almost daily on the routine services that public employees provide. They take for granted that the water flowing through their taps will not cause dysentery, that their garbage will be picked up regularly, that potholes in their neighborhood streets will be fixed, that their children will have good public schools to attend, and that a truck and crew will be on duty at the nearest fire station if they have to call 911.

Most Texans know someone who works for a government. Public employees are our friends, neighbors, members of our religious congregations, and people we see in the park every weekend. We tend to have positive perceptions of those public employees we know or interact with, but we also can be ambivalent about public employees as a group and the agencies for which they work.

Moreover, as noted, many people associate bureaucrats and bureaucracies with red tape, waste, inefficiency, indifference, or incompetence. Many candidates for elected office campaign on promises to reduce governmental waste and spending, streamline government, and reduce the number of people on public payrolls. Such talk plays well with many voters, and it creates few potential liabilities for the candidates. Once elected, however, public officials soon realize that governments do not run on rhetoric but on the work of the same public employees, or bureaucrats, against whom they campaigned.

Government employees, meanwhile, are not exempt from the regulations, programs, and policies they administer, and they have to pay the same taxes that some of them collect. They do not have special privileges because they are public employees.

Since the early 1990s, the number of people working in the executive branch of the federal government has declined due, in part, to the cuts in the Department of Defense following the end of the Cold War and the increased use of private contractors to carry out many governmental functions.[2] The number of Texas state and local employees in 2010, meanwhile, increased to the equivalent of more than 1.4 million full-time workers. Almost 318,000 people (based on full-time equivalency) worked for the state, and more than 1.1 million for local governments in Texas.[3] As a result of the 2011 state budget cuts, about 25,000 public school jobs in Texas were lost during the 2011–2012 school year, and a state auditor's report published in the spring of 2012 indicated that some 7,700 state jobs were eliminated.[4]

State agencies have an aging workforce with many workers nearing retirement, and the political bureaucrat bashing undoubtedly has convinced many young people that a career in public service is undesirable. Effective administration of public services requires competent employees, but some scholars argue that we have created an environment of "bureaucrat bashing" in which governments at all levels will have a difficult time recruiting new employees who are among the best and the brightest of their generation.[5]

The sheer size of state government and the fragmented structure of the executive branch also contribute to problems in the state bureaucracy. No single, elected official is ultimately responsible for the quality of public services performed by thousands of state workers. A loosely connected and often confusing network of more than 200 state agencies and universities is responsible for carrying out programs and policies approved and funded by the legislature and the governor. Programs often are developed and agencies established with little thought for policy coordination between departments. The organization of many agencies also is influenced by interest groups, which believe agencies should serve their needs, not those of the general public.

Fragmentation also extends to local governments. With thousands of school districts, cities, counties, and special districts in Texas—many with overlapping jurisdictions—people often are confused about where to turn for help with public services. The legislature and the governor develop and enact the broad outlines of public policy, but the hundreds of state agencies and local governments must transform those policies into specific programs, based on rules and procedures set by the agencies and local governments. The legislature meets in regular session only five months every other year, and the systematic review and oversight of every state agency is impossible. Moreover, the governor has only limited administrative control over most of the agencies in the executive branch. At the federal level, the president of the United States has the Office of Management and Budget to assist in reviewing federal agencies and their regulations, but the governor of Texas has no comparable resource.[6] The part-time boards and commissions that oversee most state agencies can exercise considerable independence in interpreting policies and determining the character and the quality of public services. Many boards, moreover, depend heavily on the guidance of veteran administrators and career bureaucrats within their agencies.

Modern, interdependent societies require large bureaucracies to provide the range of services demanded by citizens. These bureaucracies, through the uniform application of rules and procedures, designed to provide comparable treatment to everyone, contribute to the maintenance of a democratic society. Unlike people in other political systems in which bribery is widespread, we have come to expect routine public services without having to slide money under the table, in part because we have laws providing strong criminal penalties for bribery. The power and influence of agencies and bureaucrats, however, must be checked by legislative review and oversight. Abuse and malfeasance can be found in some governmental agencies, but most agencies effectively carry out the policy mandates of legislative bodies.

bureaucracies
The agencies of government and their employees responsible for carrying out policies and providing public services approved by elected officials.

Characteristics of the Texas Bureaucracy

10.1 List the basic characteristics of bureaucracies.

Max Weber, a German sociologist writing in the early part of the twentieth century, regarded **bureaucracies** as efficient means of organizing large numbers of people to carry out the required tasks for accomplishing specific goals.[7] Bureaucratic structures are inevitable in large, complex societies that have a lot of individual and group interdependence. To a large extent, these complex organizations are "superior to other methods of organizing people to perform tasks."[8]

Scholars have identified a number of characteristics of bureaucracies, the first of which is size. Whether defined in terms of the number of employees, size of budgets, or number of programs administered, size suggests complex relationships among the people working for an organization. Employees of some large state agencies are scattered among many cities, and both the size and geographic dispersion of these agencies contribute to their organizational hierarchy.[9]

Within governmental organizations, specific positions are assigned specific responsibilities or given specific authority in a hierarchical arrangement. Most agency staffs have one individual at the top, with the organization divided into bureaus, divisions, field offices, or other units. The organization develops rules for supervision, management, and reporting of activities.

Bureaucracies require a division of labor among employees and encourage the development of expertise based on experience and education. State agencies break down the responsibilities given to them by the legislature into narrowly defined tasks for their employees. Thousands of workers become specialists in a limited number of activities.

The specialization and division of labor in large organizations require rules and procedures to coordinate the activities of many individuals. Rules reduce the need for continued supervision of employees, and they lay the foundation for standardized behavior.[10] Rules define how tasks are to be carried out, who is responsible for carrying them out, and who qualifies for the organization's or agency's services.

Contemporary bureaucracies also are characterized by impersonal relationships, which is why people often complain about having to deal with "faceless" bureaucrats. Responsibilities within an agency are assigned to positions, which can be held by several workers who are supposed to be able to provide the requested service. When you obtain a voter-registration card or have your driver's license renewed, the name of the person assisting you should make no difference. People come and go in large organizations, and the ongoing functions of organizations do not depend on specific individuals.[11]

The Growth of Government Employment in Texas

10.2 Trace the growth of state and local government employment in Texas.

In 1972, Texas had 504,000 full-time state and local government employees (see Table 10–1). By 2007, as reported in the latest *Census of Governments*, the total was 1,344,442.[12] Three years later, the total had increased by another 100,000, although it is unknown how much the figure might have been reduced by subsequent government cutbacks during the most recent recession.

By 2008, the state had 662 full-time state and local government employees per 10,000 residents. The state government alone had only 153 employees per 10,000 people, which was forty-second among the states. With 509 local government workers per 10,000 people, Texas ranked eighteenth.[13] Local governments have a larger number of public employees per capita because they are responsible for a wide range of services, including the public schools.

TABLE 10–1 EMPLOYMENT BY TYPE OF GOVERNMENT, 1972–2007*

	Full-Time Equivalent Employees				
Unit of Government	**1972**	**1982**	**1992**	**2002**	**2007**
State	**124,560**	**175,660**	**238,974**	**269,674**	**290,451**
Total Local	**380,038**	**557,082**	**744,325**	**979,164**	**1,053,991**
Counties	37,302	67,228	94,145	120,885	133,722
Municipalities	93,107	127,794	147,812	172,846	175,635
School Districts	223,646	335,855	460,212	634,589	690,712
Special Districts	25,983	26,205	42,156	50,844	53,922
Total for Texas	**504,598**	**732,742**	**983,299**	**1,248,838**	**1,344,442**

*The U.S. Census Bureau conducts a Census of Governments of all state and local government organization units every 5 years, for years ending in 2 and 7.

SOURCE: U.S. Department of Commerce, Bureau of the Census, *Census of Governments, 1972,* vol. 3, no. 2, table 14; *Census of Governments, 1982,* vol. 3, no. 2, table 13; *Census of Governments, 1992,* vol. 3, no. 2, table 14; *Census of Governments, 2002,* vol. 3, table 9; and *Government Employment and Payroll Data,* 2007, http://www.census.gov/govs/apes/ (latest Texas data via Build-a-Table).

In addition, more privatization of government has occurred over the past two decades. Governments continue to raise taxes, but they contract with private companies to carry out some services. Contractors' employees are not public employees and are not counted in the public employment census data. Supporters of privatization say it can reduce governmental costs by promoting efficiency. Critics, however, argue that contracting out governmental functions can be more costly. They cite examples such as the information technology contract discussed at the beginning of this chapter, in which privatization failed, despite the expenditure of large amounts of tax dollars on vendors. Some private contract employees may not be as familiar with state programs as were the state employees they replaced. It also can result in less public scrutiny and control and fewer benefits for workers.

State spending in Texas almost doubled between 2000 and 2010, with the legislature appropriating $182 million for the 2010–2011 budget period. Although the rate of spending growth outpaced growth in the state's population, Texas still ranked low in per capita expenditures. Texas was forty-eighth among the states in per capita spending by state government alone—$3,703 per person—in 2010. When combined state and local spending are compared, Texas's ranking rose slightly, thanks in part to the large share of public school costs borne by local taxpayers. In such key areas as per capita state spending on public health, education, and welfare, Texas ranked below many other states.[14]

Except for budget crises in 2003 and 2011, efforts to curtail government growth and spending have met with only marginal success. Texas citizens have come to expect a wide range of public services, and these expectations increase as the population grows. The federal government also has imposed mandates on state and local governments that require additional expenditures and personnel. The success of interest groups in winning approval of new programs adds to the growth of public employment. In 2003, though, the legislature reduced spending on many programs to help bridge a $10 billion revenue shortfall. That same year, it also ordered a major reorganization of health and human services agencies with the goal of privatizing some services (see *Talking Texas: Privatization Hits a "Black Hole"*).

Talking ★ TEXAS Privatization Hits a "Black Hole"

The Texas legislature in 2003 ordered a controversial restructuring of Texas's health and human services agencies with an eye toward privatizing some functions, such as screening applicants for public assistance, which had previously been done by state employees. Republican state leaders predicted the changes would promote efficiency and save money for taxpayers, but the reorganization and privatization got off to a rough start. Within a few years, thousands of children had been dropped from Medicaid and the Children's Health Insurance Program (CHIP), to the dismay of health care advocates who blamed the problem on changes in eligibility rules and problems with the transition to private contractors.

Accenture LLP—a company given an $899 million state contract to screen applicants for children's health coverage and other welfare benefits—came under fire from legislators and advocates angry that Texans in need were losing benefits because of inadequate staffing and training at private call centers operated by the company. Eventually, the contract was terminated.

In 2006, the *Houston Chronicle* reported that for three months, dozens of documents from applicants seeking food stamps and other public assistance in Texas were mistakenly routed to a fax machine in a warehouse in Seattle, Washington, because a wrong phone number had been listed on an information memo. The applicants thought they were sending their faxes, which included personal financial information, to the Texas Health and Human Services Commission or to its private contractor in Midland.

"There was a black hole in Seattle, Washington," a clerk at the warehouse told the newspaper. "People

(*continued*)

10.1

10.2

10.3

10.4

10.5

10.6

10.7

send us check stubs. They send us bills. We've gotten letters from people asking why they haven't been approved for food stamps yet. They were faxing in their personal information."[a]

CRITICAL THINKING QUESTIONS

1. State government does not have to make a profit. Private contractors do. How can a private contractor save the state money by performing services normally handled by state employees?
2. Can the public hold private, contract employees accountable for accidental releases of personal client information or other mistakes that result in lost services for program clients or wasted tax dollars? If so, how?

[a]Polly Ross Hughes, "Needy Texans' Applications Faxed into a Black Hole," *Houston Chronicle*, June 2, 2006, p. 1A.

In 2011, the legislature cut spending by several billion dollars to address another shortfall in revenue. The legislature reduced state aid to public school districts alone by $5.4 billion. The total impact on public employment was not immediately known. However, many state agencies trimmed employees, and school district payrolls statewide were reduced by about 25,000 employees, including almost 11,000 teachers during the 2011–2012 school year. That was an overall school employment reduction of 3.8 percent. Additional layoffs were anticipated for the 2012–2013 school year because the legislature spread the reduction in state aid over two years.[15]

Eighty-two percent of state government employees work in higher education, public safety and corrections, and social services (see Table 10–2). Eighty-six percent of county government employees work in three areas: social services, public safety and corrections, and general governmental administration. About 38 percent of city employees are engaged in fire and police protection, and another 30 percent work for city utilities and in housing, sanitation, parks and recreation, and natural resources departments. Elementary and secondary schoolteachers are employees of local school districts. Almost 30 percent of the employees of special districts work in utilities, and more than 50 percent work in social services, including public hospitals.

TABLE 10–2 STATE AND LOCAL EMPLOYMENT BY GENERAL FUNCTIONS, 2007 (IN PERCENTAGES)*

Service or Function	State Employees	County Employees	City/Town Employees	School District Employees	Special District Employees
Education	**39.8****	1.0	3.0	**100.0**	0.1
Social Services	**25.4**	**30.2**	4.8		**52.5**
Public Safety and Corrections	**17.0**	**33.2**	**38.4**		0.7
Transportation	5.5	7.5	9.0		3.1
Government Administration	6.1	**22.6**	**14.1**		0.1
Environment/ Housing	4.0	2.1	8.9		**14.1**
Utilities		0.1	**15.6**		**28.0**
All Other Functions	2.3	3.4	6.3		1.4
Total Number of Employees	**290,451**	**133,722**	**175,635**	**690,712**	**53,922**

*The U.S. Census Bureau conducts a Census of Governments of all state and local government organization units every 5 years, for years ending in 2 and 7.
**The top functions are bolded for each level of government.

SOURCE: U.S. Department of Commerce, Bureau of the Census, *Government Employment & Payroll*, 2007, http://www.census.gov/govs/apes (latest Texas data via Build-a-Table).

Bureaucrats and Public Policy

10.3 Assess the dynamics of and obstacles to policy implementation by state bureaucrats.

The bureaucracy does more than carry out the policies set by the legislature. It is involved in virtually every stage of the policymaking process. The legislature usually broadly defines a program and gives the affected agency the responsibility for filling in the details.[16] Administrative agencies can sometimes interpret a vaguely worded law differently from its original legislative purpose. Although the legislature can use oversight committees and the budgetary process to exercise some control over the bureaucracy, agencies often have resources and political influence that protect their prerogatives. Many appointed agency heads have political ties to interest groups affected by the work of their agencies, and these officials help develop policy alternatives and laws because legislators depend on their technical expertise.

Policy Implementation

Implementation is the conversion of policy plans into reality.[17] Although one state agency may be primarily responsible for translating legislative intent into a specific program, other governmental bodies also are involved. The courts, for example, shape the actions of the bureaucrats through their interpretation of statutes and administrative rules. Jurisdictional and political battles may occur between different agencies over program objectives. Such conflicts often result from Texas's plural executive system of government, in which the governor and several other statewide officials are elected independently and appointed boards and commissions head numerous other agencies.

In some cases, a new agency may have to be organized and staffed to carry out the goals of a new law. More often, however, the new responsibilities are assigned by the legislature to an existing agency, which develops the necessary rules, procedures, and guidelines for operating the new program. Additional employees are hired if the legislature provides the necessary funding. If not, responsibilities are reassigned among existing personnel. Sometimes tasks are coordinated with other agencies. Ultimately, all this activity translates into hundreds of thousands of daily transactions between governmental employees—or an agency's private contractors—and the public.

Establishing rules and standards at the agency level for carrying out programs enacted by the legislature is a complex process that also involves the legislative sponsors, interest groups, sometimes specific businesses, and other interested parties. Rules and procedures are not just hatched in a vacuum. The task is highly political, subject to intense negotiations, often contentious, and often requiring a lot of political adroitness by administrators to ensure a program's success.

Almost everyone has heard horror stories about persons who have suffered abuse or neglect at the hands of public employees and agencies. Whether they involve an indigent family that fell through the cracks of the welfare system or a county jail prisoner who was lost in the administrative processes of the judicial system, these stories tend to reinforce the suspicion and hostility that many people have toward bureaucracies and public employees. Unquestionably, such abuses deserve attention and demand correction, yet thousands of governmental programs are successfully carried out with little or no fanfare and are consistent with the purpose of the authorizing legislation.

Most public employees take pride in what they do and attempt to be conscientious in translating policy objectives into workable public services. They are citizens and taxpayers who also receive services from other state and local agencies. A complex, interdependent state with 25 million people depends on the effectiveness and efficiency

10.1

10.2

10.3

10.4

10.5

10.6

10.7

Talking ★ TEXAS Negotiating Bureaucracies

We have studied the actions of bureaucracies for more than thirty years, and one of us has served on a government commission. Like many other people, we have had to negotiate through red tape to resolve issues that personally affected us or our families. In so doing, we have concluded that the best defense is a good offense. That is, learn how an agency works and then develop the appropriate strategy and tactics to achieve your objective. Here are our rules for "working the bureaucracy":

- *Remember you are dealing with people.*
  Bureaucracies are composed of individuals. Many of them are overworked, but most want to be successful in carrying out their tasks. Approach them in a cooperative spirit, not as if you are looking for a fight.

- *Find the right agency and the right person or persons authorized to provide solutions.*
  Bureaucracies also operate under organizational structures that divide responsibilities among employees. The first person you call or meet at an agency may not be the person who can deal with your issue. You may believe you are "getting the runaround" if you are transferred from person to person or agency to agency. But you can save yourself some time and frustration by making your needs or request clear in your first encounter with a governmental employee.

- *Be patient.*
  Employees of large organizations often do not know every service their agencies perform. Most public workers are specialists. They have specific areas of responsibility and specific tasks and often know little about other offices or divisions within their agency.

- *Be tenacious.*
  Dealing with bureaucracies can be frustrating, but persistence is imperative. The more questions you ask, the more you are going to understand the organization and the more quickly you are going to find someone who can help you.

- *Know your rights and act on them.*
  Governments exist for you. You do not exist for governments. The more you learn about governmental procedures, the more likely you are to be successful. If an employee of a state agency dismisses your inquiry or claim in a cavalier manner, go above that person's head to the next person in the chain of command. If the obstruction persists at the higher levels of the agency, call your legislator's office with a detailed summary of what occurred. (It also will help to know which state representative and which state senator represent you.) Not all legislators will respond to your complaint, particularly if you have dealt with the agency erratically. But many will, and agencies normally respond to inquiries from legislators, who set their budgets and pass the laws under which the agencies operate.

- *Occasionally, you may have to be adversarial.*
  Sometimes, unfortunately, governmental agencies and their employees misinterpret the law or refuse to do what the law requires. In those cases, your only recourse may be to file a lawsuit against the agency. Corporations and well-organized interest groups usually have the financial resources for such a fight. Most citizens, however, do not. So, concentrate on the previous steps, and do everything you can to avoid getting to this one.

CRITICAL THINKING QUESTIONS

1. Does the Texas legislature leave too much discretion and control over important state policies and programs in the hands of bureaucrats? If so, why or why not?
2. Are there additional obstacles that arise as a result of the fact that many governmental services are now online? If so, what are they?

of governmental agencies. That activity appears, on the whole, to be mutually satisfactory or beneficial to most parties (see *Talking Texas: Negotiating Bureaucracies*).

☐ Obstacles to Policy Implementation

When things go wrong in state government and problems go unresolved, the tendency is to blame the bureaucrats for excessive red tape, inefficiency, mismanagement, or incompetence. As noted earlier in this chapter, bureaucrat bashing plays well politically,

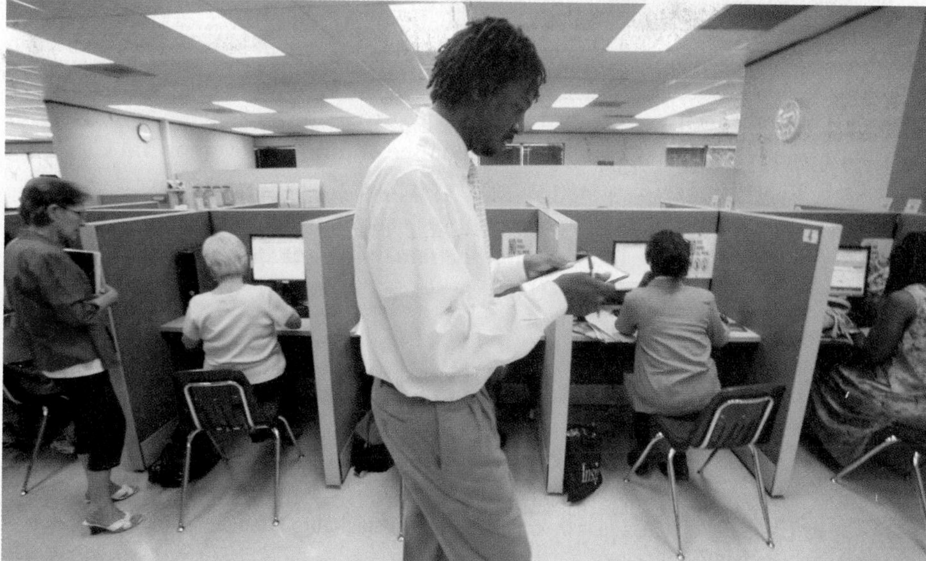

DID AVAILABLE RESOURCES IMPACT AN EFFECTIVE JOB SEARCH?
State agencies anticipate a normal workload as they serve Texans, but circumstances may develop that place additional demands on agencies, their staffs, and funding. The Texas unemployment rate peaked in December of 2009 at 8.2 percent, and many job seekers turned to the Texas Workforce Commission for assistance in their search for employment. Seen here is an agency supervisor, David Serrell, monitoring applicants' time on the computers as they search for employment in a Richardson job resource center.

co-optation
Influence over state regulatory boards by the industries they are supposed to regulate, often to the detriment of the general public.

and many candidates for public office run on such campaigns. But in many cases they unfairly blame government employees for complex problems that policymakers have been unable—or unwilling—to resolve. One high-profile issue is the perennial struggle to improve the quality of the public education system. Some of the criticism directed at educational bureaucrats has been justified, but ultimately the legislature and the governor are responsible for the enactment of sound educational policies and the development of a sufficient and equitable system of paying for them.

Some legislative policies may be misdirected, with little potential for producing the intended results. Or economic and social conditions may change, making programs inappropriate. Administrators also may find that approaches different from those outlined by the legislature would have worked better. The legislature also frequently fails to fund programs adequately. In some cases, those charged with carrying out a new policy may not have the knowledge or the resources to make it work.[18] Finally, programs often produce unanticipated results.[19]

Other factors also affect the accountability and responsiveness of state and local agencies, including the influence of special interests. Thanks to the clout of special interest lobbyists with the legislature, boards that head regulatory agencies often include a majority of members from the professions or industries they are supposed to regulate. Many taxpayers may think that this system is merely a legalized way of letting the foxes guard the henhouse. It is an extension of the "iron triangles" concept, whereby special interests seek to influence not only the legislators responsible for enacting laws but also the agencies responsible for enforcing them.

Appointment to State Agencies

Business and professional groups argue that their professions can be effectively regulated only by individuals knowledgeable of them. Although that argument has some validity, it also increases the potential for incestuous relationships that mock the regulatory process. The possibility—and often the likelihood—always exists that industry representatives serving on boards or commissions will be inclined to protect their industries against the best interests of consumers. This pattern of influence and control often is referred to as **co-optation**, underscoring the possibility that agencies may be captured by the industries they are supposed to regulate. Licensing agencies also may seek to adopt unfair regulations designed to restrict new competitors from entering an industry.

Governor Ann Richards highlighted the "fox in the henhouse" approach to state regulation when she demanded that the Texas Department of Health crack down on deplorable conditions in some nursing homes. State inspectors had repeatedly found unsanitary conditions in three nursing homes partly owned by a member of the Texas Board of Health. The board member, an appointee of former Governor Bill Clements, denied any allegations of improper care but resigned after moving to another state.[20] Texas law then required that one member of the eighteen-member health board be involved in the nursing home industry, and the remaining board members be appointed from other health care professions. The board has since been restructured.

Political Control and the Responsiveness of the Bureaucracy

10.4 Describe the various ways by which the Texas legislature attempts to increase its control over state agencies.

The Texas legislature has taken several steps over the years to increase its control over state agencies, including limited budgetary oversight, performance reviews, sunset legislation, and restrictions on the "revolving door" between government and industry employment.

☐ Legislative Budgetary Control

Every two years, the legislature sets the budgets for state agencies, but its review over spending between legislative sessions is limited. The Legislative Budget Board (LBB), which includes the lieutenant governor, the speaker of the House, and eight other legislators, has some oversight. The LBB can join with the governor to transfer appropriated funds between programs or agencies, if necessary to meet emergencies when the legislature is not in session. Legislative committees also can hold hearings between sessions and question agency administrators about spending. When drafting state budgets, legislators include a number of line items that give agencies specific spending instructions or impose specific spending restrictions (see Table 10–3).

☐ Performance Reviews

Facing a large revenue shortfall in 1991, the legislature directed Comptroller John Sharp to conduct performance reviews of all state agencies to determine ways to eliminate mismanagement and inefficiency and to save tax dollars. Sharp recommended $4 billion worth of spending cuts, agency and funds consolidations, accounting changes,

TABLE 10–3 HOW TO CONTROL BUREAUCRATS

Taking a cue from political scientist Robert Lineberry, Texas policymakers can use several strategies to control bureaucracies and help ensure that policies are carried out as intended:

1. Change the law or make legislation more detailed to reduce or eliminate the discretionary authority of an agency.
2. Overrule the bureaucracy and reverse or rescind an action of an agency. With the independence of many agencies, boards, and commissions at the state level, the governor can reverse few agency decisions, so this step often requires legislative action.
3. Transfer the responsibility for a program to another agency through administrative reorganization.
4. Replace an agency head who refuses to or is incapable of carrying out program objectives. The governor can directly exercise such authority over only a few agencies in Texas.
5. Cut or threaten to reduce the budget of an agency to force compliance with policy objectives.
6. Abolish an agency or program through sunset legislation.
7. Pressure the bureaucracy to change, using legislative hearings and public disclosures of agency neglect or inadequacies.
8. Protect public employees who reveal incompetence, mismanagement, and corruption through whistleblower legislation.
9. Enact revolving-door restrictions to reduce or eliminate the movement of former state employees to industries over which they had regulatory authority.

SOURCE: Based on information found in Robert Lineberry, *American Public Policy* (New York: Harper & Row, 1977), pp. 84–85.

Talking ★ TEXAS Texas Receives High Marks for Open Government

In its third annual report ranking the transparency of state governments in their public spending, U.S. PIRG (Public Interest Research Group) gave Texas an A. In the not-too-distant past, Texas had a poor record for open government and public access to its finances, but this has changed. Many, including state Comptroller Susan Combs, can share credit for these changes:

- **The report makes the point that if citizens are to exercise some control over their government, it is essential that they be able to "see how government uses the public purse." It also notes, "Transparency in government spending promotes fiscal responsibility, checks corruption, and bolsters public confidence."[a]**
- **Citizens can visit the state's TexasTransparency.org website, which includes information on revenues and expenditures by specific agencies.[b] The site also tracks the transparency initiatives of cities, counties, school districts, and other special districts in Texas and encourages local governments to adopt best practices in making their budgets and other financial information available to the public. The comptroller reported that the data posted on the site have led to cost savings in state agencies.**

CRITICAL THINKING QUESTIONS

1. **Is transparency in government finances enough to assure most voters that their tax dollars are being spent wisely? Why or why not?**
2. **Is public information about government revenues and expenditures likely to influence the decisions of policymakers when they enact budgets and allocate funds for programs? Why or why not?**

[a]U.S. PIRG, *Following the Money, 2012*, http://www.uspirg.org/reports/usp/following-money-2012.

[b]Texas Transparency, http://www.texastransparency.org/local/index.php?id=pageID.

some minor tax increases, and increases in various state fees to more accurately reflect the costs of providing services. Pressure from special interests killed many of the recommendations, but the legislature adopted about $2.4 billion of them. Sharp produced follow-up reports in 1993, 1995, and 1997, and his successor, Carole Keeton Strayhorn, continued the performance reviews after she took office. At the beginning of the 2003 session of the legislature, she made sixty-four recommendations for further restructuring state agencies and their operations, some of which were adopted by lawmakers. The comptroller also conducted performance reviews of some local school districts.

These reviews generally were considered to be instrumental in improving administrative practices. After a series of budgetary disputes between the comptroller and other state leaders in 2003, the legislature, with Governor Rick Perry's approval, transferred the responsibility for performance reviews from the comptroller's office to the Legislative Budget Board, and subsequent reviews have not been as far-reaching. Under the leadership of Susan Combs, the comptroller's office, meanwhile, has turned its attention to comprehensive disclosure of the expenditures of state and local governments, providing online access to detailed agency information (see *Talking Texas: Texas Receives High Marks for Open Government*).

☐ Sunset Legislation

Texas was one of the first states to require formal, exhaustive reviews of how effectively state agencies are doing their jobs. The sunset process, enacted in 1977, was so named because most agencies have to be periodically re-created by the legislature or automatically go out of business.[21] Relatively few agencies—except for a number of inactive ones such as the Pink Bollworm Commission and the Stonewall Jackson Memorial Board—have been abolished, but the review has produced some significant structural and policy changes in the state bureaucracy that the legislature may not

sunset review
The process under which most state agencies have to be periodically reviewed and re-created by the legislature or eliminated.

have otherwise ordered. It also has expanded employment opportunities for lobbyists because special interest groups have much at stake in the sunset process. Sometimes, special interests have succeeded in protecting the status quo.

Each agency is usually up for **sunset review** every twelve years under a rotating order set out in the sunset law. The review begins with the Sunset Advisory Commission, which includes four state representatives, four senators, and two members from the public, appointed by the Speaker and the lieutenant governor. The commission employs a staff that studies each agency up for review during the next legislative session and reports its findings to the panel, which makes recommendations to the legislature.

In a few cases, the commission will propose that an agency—usually a minor one—be terminated or consolidated with another agency. In most cases, however, the commission recommends the continuation of an agency and proposes changes in its organization and operations. The agency's future is then decided by the full legislature. If lawmakers fail to approve a sunset bill for any agency by September 1 of the year the agency is scheduled for review, the agency will be phased out of existence over the next year. It will be terminated abruptly on September 1 if the legislature refuses to approve a new budget for the agency. In recent years, however, the legislature has postponed controversial sunset decisions by passing special laws to allow some agencies to stay open past their review dates. In 2011, for example, the legislature extended the life of the Public Utility Commission for an additional two years after lawmakers failed to agree on a new sunset law for the agency.

The Texas Higher Education Coordinating Board is subject to sunset review, but individual universities are not. Also exempted from sunset review are the courts and state agencies created by the constitution, such as the governor's office, the attorney general, the comptroller, and the General Land Office.

The sunset process has not reduced the size of the state bureaucracy. By 2010, there were almost 318,000 state employees, compared to about 164,000 in 1977, the year the sunset law was approved. Although more than sixty agencies have been terminated or merged, others have been created (see Table 10–4). But supporters of the sunset process believe it has served to slow down the creation of new agencies.

The sunset review process has helped rid state government of some obsolete agencies, modernized state laws and bureaucratic procedures, and made some agencies more responsive to the public. For example, under sunset review provisions, members of the public have been added to the boards of numerous small regulatory agencies that previously included only representatives of the professions or industries that they regulated. The Sunset Advisory Commission concluded:

> Boards consisting only of members from a regulated profession or group affected by the activities of an agency may not respond adequately to broad public interests. This potential problem can be addressed by giving the general public a direct voice in the activities of the agency through representation on the board.[22]

The largest agencies and those with influential constituencies usually are the most difficult to change because special interests work hard and make large political contributions to protect their turf. In 1993, for example, the insurance lobby succeeded

TABLE 10–4 SUNSET ACTION FROM 1979 TO 2011, 66TH TO 82ND LEGISLATIVE SESSIONS

Actions Taken by Commission	Total	Percentage
Agencies Reviewed	451*	
Agencies Continued	339	81
Agencies Abolished Outright	37	9
Agencies Abolished and Functions Transferred	41	10

*This includes agencies subject to sunset review but not abolishment and agencies reviewed but whose sunset dates then were removed from the law.

SOURCE: Texas Sunset Advisory Commission, *Sunset in Texas*, January 2012.

in weakening some pro-consumer provisions in the Department of Insurance sunset bill. In another case that year, there was such a high-stakes war involving telephone companies, newspaper publishers, electric utilities, and consumers over the Public Utility Commission (PUC) sunset bill that the legislature postponed action on PUC sunset for two years. The lobby's influence prompted Governor Ann Richards and some legislators to suggest that the sunset process should be changed or repealed because it was being abused by special interests. But consumer advocates, who value the sunset process, blamed the problem on legislators who had difficulty saying no to special interest lobbyists.

A major sunset battle erupted in 2009 over the Texas Residential Construction Commission, which had been created several years earlier with the strong support of homebuilders. The agency supposedly had been created to establish uniform building standards and crack down on shoddy construction in exchange for giving the homebuilding industry legal protections against lawsuits from unhappy customers. But consumer advocates complained that the agency functioned mainly to protect homebuilders. The Sunset Advisory Commission recommended that the agency be re-created with new consumer protections, but the legislature let the agency die.

revolving door
The practice of former members of state boards and commissions or key employees of agencies leaving state government for more lucrative jobs with the industries they used to regulate. It raises questions of undue industry influence over regulatory agencies.

□ The Revolving Door

Before the legislature started clamping down, many regulatory agencies had become taxpayer-financed training grounds for young attorneys and other professionals just out of college or law school. They would work for state agencies for a few years for relatively low pay but make influential contacts and gain valuable experience in a particular regulatory area. Then they would leave state employment for higher-paying jobs in the industries they had regulated and would represent their new employers before the state boards and commissions for which they had once worked. In other cases, they would become consultants or join law firms representing regulatory clients. Former gubernatorial appointees to boards and commissions, as well as hired staffers, participated in this **revolving-door** phenomenon, which raised ethical questions about possible insider influence over regulatory decisions.

An early step in slowing the revolving door was part of the 1975 law that created the Public Utility Commission. This law prohibited PUC commissioners and high-ranking staffers from going to work for regulated utilities immediately after leaving the agency. A 1991 ethics reform law expanded the restriction to other agencies.

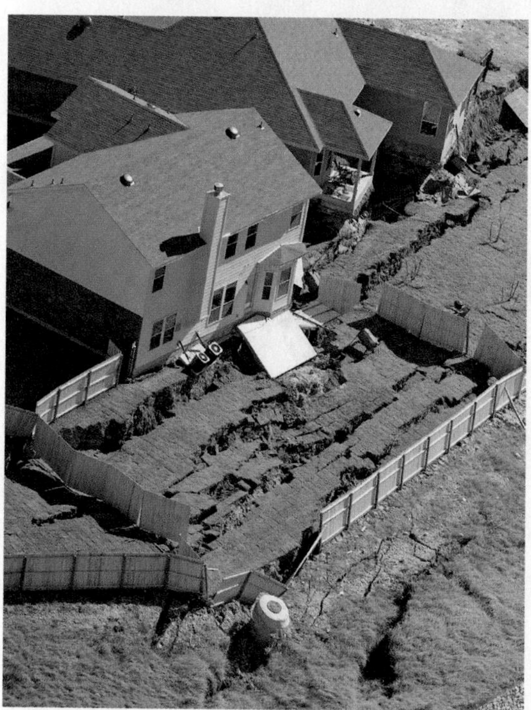

FAILED REGULATORY POLICIES

Construction problems pictured here show what can happen when building codes are weak or ineffectively enforced.

whistle-blower
A government employee who publicly reports wrongdoing or unethical conduct within a government agency.

Whistle-Blowing

10.5 Explain the use of the whistle-blower protection law to counteract corruption and intentional wrongdoing in the Texas bureaucracy.

Governmental agencies make mistakes that often can be costly in terms of financial waste or regulatory neglect and may endanger the public's health or safety. As agencies spend large sums of money for supplies, construction, and services the potential exists for public officials or employees to be offered kickbacks or bribes to influence decisions benefiting particular vendors or contractors.

To encourage public employees to report mistakes and intentional wrongdoing in their agencies, Texas has a **whistle-blower** protection law. If an employee is subjected to retaliation after having come forward, the law permits the worker to file a lawsuit against the offending agency. It is difficult to determine, though, how effective that law has been in weeding out governmental waste and corruption because many public workers still may be intimidated by supervisors. As major tests of the law have shown in recent years, a whistle-blower's journey can be very rough, even with legal protections.

Anne Mitchell and Vickilyn Galle, two nurses in the tiny West Texas town of Kermit, were prosecuted in 2010 after they sent a letter to the Texas Medical Board, questioning the standard of care provided by a physician working for the county hospital, where they were employed, and the county's rural health clinic. They contacted the medical board after the hospital's administration had failed to act on their complaints about the doctor's practices, which included selling herbal supplements to patients in the county facilities.

When the doctor learned that he was being investigated by the state board, he complained of "harassment" to Winkler County Sheriff Robert Roberts, a friend and associate in his herbal supplement business. The sheriff began investigating hospital employees and found the letter to the medical board on a computer used by the two nurses. The evidence was presented to Winkler County Attorney Scott Tidwell, a political ally of the sheriff and, according to testimony in the case, the doctor's personal lawyer. The nurses lost their jobs and were charged with "misuse of official

VINDICATED AFTER A LONG ORDEAL

Nurses Anne Mitchell, right, and Vickilyn Galle, left, who blew the whistle on questionable medical practices in a county hospital, are seen at the Andrews County Courthouse in February 2010, after winning their fight against retaliation from local officials.

information," a third-degree felony that could have resulted in a ten-year prison sentence and $10,000 fine for each woman.[23]

The case prompted charges of political cronyism and divided the residents of Kermit. It also attracted national attention and mobilized outside support for the nurses. The Texas Nursing Association and the American Nursing Association provided legal and financial assistance. The defendants also received small contributions from people around the state and country.[24]

Mitchell was acquitted by a jury, and the charges against Galle were dropped. The sheriff and the county attorney later were indicted for misuse of official information and retaliation and were forced out of office. The doctor about whom the nurses had complained eventually lost his medical license. Mitchell and Galle received $750,000 from Winkler County to settle a federal lawsuit they had filed over First Amendment rights violations and vindictive prosecution.[25]

The nurses eventually won because their attack on substandard care and the obvious unfairness of their prosecution resonated with nurses and other people throughout the country. But their case demonstrates that whistle-blowers, despite the protection of state law, can still face huge obstacles.

Several years earlier, under different circumstances, a similarly stressful ordeal involved another whistle-blower. George Green, a state architect in Austin, was fired and threatened with prosecution on trumped-up charges after complaining of shoddy construction, kickbacks, and noncompliance with contracts at the Texas Department of Human Services.

Green sued the state under the whistle-blower law and won a $13.6 million judgment from a Travis County jury in 1991. The amount included $3.6 million in actual damages that Green had suffered and $10 million in punitive damages to punish the state for the way he had been treated. Even after losing a lengthy appeal, the state initially refused to appropriate the money to pay Green's judgment. Finally, in 1995, Green negotiated a $13.8 million settlement, which included only a fraction of the interest he was owed on the four-year-old judgment, with legislative leaders. Then-Lieutenant Governor Bob Bullock apologized to Green and called his ordeal a "black mark on the history of Texas."[26]

The legislature also took steps to ensure that there never would be such a large whistle-blower judgment again. It changed the law to limit all whistle-blower–suit damages against the state to $250,000.

licensing
A key regulatory function of government that seeks to ensure that individuals and companies providing critical professional services to the public are properly trained or qualified.

Regulation

10.6 Outline the various ways state and local governments regulate economic activity in Texas.

The legislature delegates much authority for carrying out state policy to regulatory agencies, and regulation, in turn, takes many forms. Economic regulation affects the practices of some businesses, including the prices they can charge for their services. Major state regulators in this area include the Department of Insurance, which oversees rates that can be charged for automobile and homeowners insurance, and the Public Utility Commission, which has authority over some practices of electric utilities and telephone companies.

A second regulatory function is the **licensing** of professions and franchising of corporations. Under state law, some occupations require formal training, testing, and subsequent licensing from a state agency. These include doctors, nurses, accountants, lawyers, and a host of other professions. Individuals and companies also must have state licenses to be a barber or operate a funeral home or a nursing home, among other businesses. Licensing implies regulation, and the acceptance of a license implies a willingness to comply with state controls. On the local level, contractors are required to meet building codes established by city councils.

political patronage
The hiring of government employees on the basis of personal friendships or favors rather than ability or merit.

merit employment system
A personnel system under which public employees are selected for government jobs through competitive examinations and the systematic evaluation of job performance.

State agencies also regulate the allocation of natural resources and safeguard their quality. The Texas Commission on Environmental Quality is charged with enforcing state laws protecting air and water quality. Water districts throughout the state regulate the conservation of groundwater supplies, although their regulatory powers may be subject to change following a major Texas Supreme Court decision in early 2012. The court's decision may result in a curtailment of the districts' authority to set strict conservation limits on the amount of water that landowners can pump from aquifers beneath their property. In another crucial conservation area, the Texas Railroad Commission establishes the rate at which a well can pump oil from the ground.

State and local governments also are involved in regulation by providing operating subsidies to businesses, including tax breaks that are subject to limitations imposed by the legislature. These incentives are usually offered for specified periods to encourage businesses to locate or expand in a specific community. In return, the businesses may agree to conditions imposed on them by the participating government. Cities grant franchises to cable television systems, which agree to provide a specific level of service in return for the operating rights.

State agencies also regulate companies for fairness and competition. Although many federal laws deal with price fixing, monopolies, and unfair competition, state statutes also relate to the competitiveness of the state's economy. The Texas State Securities Board, for example, regulates the investment industry. Additionally, the state is involved in what some writers call social regulation.[27] This type of regulation is much broader than the economic regulation just described. Social regulations affect "the conditions under which goods and services are produced and the physical characteristics of products that are manufactured."[28] Although the federal government has preempted many state policies in these areas, some state agencies are involved in regulating workplace safety and consumer protection.

Merit Systems and Professional Management

10.7 Differentiate among the personnel systems used by governments in Texas.

arlier in Texas history, public employees were hired on the basis of **political patronage**, or the personal relationships and friendships they had with elected or appointed public officials. Little consideration was given to their skills, competence, or expertise. There were few rules concerning terms of employment, advancement, or the rights or conduct of public employees, and wide variations in wages and salaries existed from agency to agency. Employee turnover rates also were high.

To better serve the public and state workers, some reform advocates pushed for a **merit employment system** based, in part, on the Civil Service Commission created by the federal government for its workers in 1883. Although other states have developed comprehensive, statewide employment or personnel systems administered by a single agency, the reform movement in Texas has not been as successful. Improvements have been made, but state government in Texas continues to function under a decentralized personnel system.[29]

Merit-based public employment was inconsistent with the individualistic views of government, politics, and public administration evolving from the dominant political subcultures of Texas. The plural executive system worked against efforts to centralize and coordinate personnel policies because the various elected executive officeholders jealously guarded their prerogatives to hire and fire the people who worked for them.

Governmental functions have expanded in modern times, and carrying out public policy has become more complex and technical.[30] Many programs require highly specialized skills, not political hacks who have no formal training or expertise for technical jobs. Furthermore, the public has gradually developed higher expectations of its government and reacts unfavorably to incompetent public workers. Additional pressure for merit employment has come from the federal government. Since the 1930s, numerous federal grants have required the state to enact a merit system for state employees administering them. In more recent years, federal laws prohibiting hiring discrimination on the basis of sex, age, disability, race, ethnicity, or sexual orientation have been extended to state and local governments. These requirements, in turn, have forced Texas government to pay more attention to employment practices.[31]

Even so, politics has not been totally eliminated in the hiring and promotion of public employees. State government's personnel "system" is not a merit system but a highly fragmented system with different agencies assigned various personnel responsibilities. Ultimately, the legislature has the legal authority to define personnel practices, and the biennial budget is the major tool used by legislators to establish several hundred job classifications and corresponding salary schedules. The technical work on the state's classification schedule is assigned to the State Classification Office, a division of the State Auditor's Office. This is an agency of the legislature, not the executive branch, supervised by the Legislative Audit Committee. The legislature also establishes policies on vacations, holidays, and retirement.

Within this highly decentralized personnel system, the primary responsibility for carrying out personnel policies is still delegated to the various state agencies. An administrator can develop specific policies for an agency as long as the agency works within the general framework defined by the legislature. Some agencies have developed modern personnel plans—including employee grievance procedures and competitive examinations for placement and advancement—whereas others have not.

All state job openings are required to be listed with the Texas Workforce Commission. Agencies also advertise for workers through the mass media and college placement centers. But many jobs still are filled as a result of friendships, personal contacts, and the influence of key political players.

Higher and public education employees are subject to different employment policies, which are determined by individual university governing boards and local school districts. Unlike state government, many cities across Texas have adopted centrally administered merit systems organized around the accepted principles of modern personnel management. Their personnel departments include independent civil service commissions that have some rule-making authority and hear appeals of personnel matters. These changes, which resulted from the urban reform movement, were designed to recruit quality employees and to insulate them from external political pressures. They have led to a high level of professionalism in some cities. Large metropolitan counties also have tried to structure their employment systems on the basis of merit, but the partisan election of county officials thwarts the full implementation of merit systems.

On MyPoliSciLab

Review the Chapter

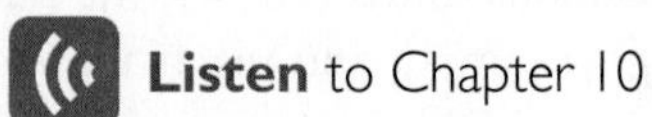

Characteristics of the Texas Bureaucracy

10.1 List the basic characteristics of bureaucracies, p. 297.

Bureaucracies are administrative organizations created to carry out the policies of legislative bodies. They are complex, hierarchical organizations of varying sizes, with an emphasis on division of labor, specialization, and policy expertise. Bureaucracies develop comprehensive rules defining different jobs and establishing procedures for carrying out assigned responsibilities.

The Growth of Government Employment in Texas

10.2 Trace the growth of state and local government employment in Texas, p. 298.

Despite their historical ambivalence toward government, Texans have come to expect a wide range of public services. With the growth of the state's population, government programs have been added or expanded, resulting in an increase of public employees at all levels of government. More than 1.3 million Texans now are employed either full or part time by state and local governments. Most work for local governments. Although some reduction in public employment has occurred with more recent recessions, the number of public employees is likely to continue to increase with the future growth of the state's population.

Bureaucrats and Public Policy

10.3 Assess the dynamics of and obstacles to policy implementation by state bureaucrats, p. 301.

The bureaucracy has the primary responsibility of carrying out public policies adopted by the legislature and the local governing bodies. Administrative agencies also are involved in virtually every stage of the policymaking process. Legislators depend on administrative agencies for counsel and advice when they draft public policies, and they rely on them to help assess the success or failure of policies.

When things go wrong and problems go unresolved, the tendency is to blame bureaucrats, but government employees often are unfairly blamed for complex problems that elected policymakers have been unwilling or unable to resolve. The fragmented structure of the executive branch of state government is, in itself, a major obstacle to the efficient, responsive delivery of public services. The potential also exists for agencies headed by appointed boards to become unaccountable to the voters and susceptible to the influence of special interest groups.

Political Control and the Responsiveness of the Bureaucracy

10.4 Describe the various ways by which the Texas legislature attempts to increase its control over state agencies, p. 304.

The legislature has a number of ways to control administrative agencies. These include budgetary restrictions, performance reviews, sunset legislation, restructuring agencies, changing programs assigned to agencies, and revolving-door restrictions on agency board members and key employees. Although candidates for the legislature and other state offices campaign on reducing the number of public employees, campaign rhetoric has not resulted in significant reductions in the government workforce.

Whistle-Blowing

10.5 Explain the use of the whistle-blower protection law to counteract corruption and intentional wrongdoing in the Texas bureaucracy, p. 308.

Government agencies make wasteful and harmful mistakes, sometimes unintentionally and sometimes under the unethical or illegal influence of interest groups or contractors. The state has a whistle-blower law designed to encourage public employees to report such mistakes or corruption within their agencies. Nevertheless, whistle-blowers sometimes find that the law does not protect them from retaliation. So, some public employees still may be reluctant to reveal problems within agencies.

Regulation

10.6 Outline the various ways state and local governments regulate economic activity in Texas, p. 309.

The legislature enacts laws to control or regulate specific industries or economic activities in the state. Regulation responsibilities are assigned to government agencies. They include regulation of some public utilities, licensing of some professions and occupations, protection of natural resources, promotion of fairness and nondiscrimination in business and public practices, and social regulation.

Merit Systems and Professional Management

10.7 Differentiate among the personnel systems used by governments in Texas, p. 310.

Many cities and other local governments have adopted merit-based employment systems with rules for screening potential employees in order to hire competent workers cal interference. However, state government h a centralized, comprehensive merit systen ees, although some agencies use merit-bas state's employment practices are fragmente largely free to set its own personnel policie

Learn the Terms

Study and **Review** the Flashcards

bureaucracies, p. 297
co-optation, p. 303
sunset review, p. 306
revolving-door, p. 307
whistle-blower, p. 308
licensing, p. 309
political patronage, p. 310
merit employment system, p. 310

Test Yourself

Study and **Review** the Practice Tests

1. All of the following are reasons why the state bureaucracy faces problems EXCEPT that

a. the fragmented executive branch means no single elected official is responsible for the quality of public services.
b. the part-time legislature makes systematic review and oversight impossible.
c. the workforce of state agencies is young and inexperienced.
d. part-time boards and commissions have considerable independence in interpreting policies.
e. many boards are dependent on the guidance of veteran administrators and career bureaucrats.

2. One of the basic characteristics of a bureaucracy is its

a. small size.
b. flat organizational structure.
c. broadly defined tasks for employees.
d. flexible rules and standards.
e. impersonal relationships.

3. Which of the following statements about government employment in Texas is TRUE?

a. There are more local government workers than state government workers.
b. Texas has more government employees per 10,000 people than any other state.
c. The majority of local government employees work for the cities and counties.
d. The majority of city and county employees work in the areas of education and social services.
e. Privatization of health and human services by the state has been successful in reducing a large number of public jobs.

4. Policy implementation

a. never involves the judicial branch.
b. requires rule making that involves government officials and interest groups.
c. is dictated by the governor to lower-level officials in state agencies.
d. is a nonpolitical, neutral process.
e. is marred by systematic corruption of public officials.

5. One of the obstacles to the bureaucracy's policy implementation is

a. the absence of the expertise brought by interest groups.
b. high rates of turnover of the most competent employees.
c. high failure rates on promotion exams.
d. lack of adequate funding by the legislature.
e. the absence of iron triangles.

6. Co-optation refers to the

a. influence on policy implementation by corrupt legislators.
b. ability of state agencies to interpret the law how they see fit.
c. influence on agency management by the governor.
d. influence on state agencies by the industries they are supposed to regulate.
e. authority of the Sunset Commission to recommend the abolishment of a state agency.

[illegible] Legislative Budget Board is made up of the

[illegible] governor, lieutenant governor, and speaker of the House.
[illegible] lieutenant governor, comptroller, and speaker of the House.
c. lieutenant governor, speaker of the House, and eight legislators.
d. comptroller and chairs of the House and Senate Budget Committees.
e. governor, lieutenant governor, and chief justice of the Texas Supreme Court.

8. Which process examines state agencies to determine ways to eliminate mismanagement and inefficiency?

a. legislative budget control
b. performance review
c. outcomes review
d. revolving door restrictions
e. legislature's removal of ineffective administrators

9. Which process requires most state agencies to be periodically examined and re-created by the legislature or eliminated?

a. legislative budget control
b. performance review
c. revolving door
d. bureaucratic co-optation
e. sunset review

10. Which of the following is one accomplishment of sunset review?

a. modernization of state laws and procedures
b. reduction in the size of the bureaucracy
c. a one-quarter reduction in the number of state agencies
d. limitation of the influence of lobbyists
e. speeding up of the revolving-door phenomenon

11. The practice of leaving a government job for a more lucrative job with the industry one used to regulate is known as

a. sunsetting.
b. whistle-blowing.
c. revolving door.
d. licensing.
e. promotion.

12. A public employee who reports mistakes and intentional wrongdoing is known as a

a. sunsetter.
b. whistle-blower.
c. performance reviewer.
d. licenser.
e. bureaucrat revolving door.

13. All of the following are examples of state regulation EXCEPT

a. oversight of automobile insurance rates.
b. licensing of barbers.
c. pumping rate of oil.
d. economic incentives to businesses.
e. interstate commerce.

14. The hiring of public employees based on personal relationships and friendships is known as

a. political patronage.
b. revolving door.
c. merit system.
d. civil service system.
e. state classification.

15. Why is the personnel system in Texas fragmented and decentralized?

a. A merit-based system is inconsistent with the state's moralistic views of politics.
b. Turnover rates are high.
c. The Texas Workforce Commission was sunsetted.
d. The plural executive system gives power to hire and fire to executive officeholders.
e. Political patronage has been successful in hiring competent and skilled experts.

Explore Further

Alexander, Kate, "Battle Brewing Over Texas Public Pensions," *Austin American-Statesman*, August 28, 2011. Discusses the creation of the Texas for Public Pension Reform by a group of Houston business leaders to assess public employee pension plans across Texas with an eye toward modifications or reforms.

Barrett, Katherine, and Richard Greene, "Grading the States 2008: The Mandate to Measure," The Pew Center on the States, March 2008. Assesses the quality of management in the fifty states.

Beal, Ronald L., *Texas Administrative Practice and Procedure*. Charlottesville, VA: Michie, 1998. Provides a wide range of technical information on Texas administrative procedures.

Castillo, Juan, "CPS Struggling with Staffing Shortage, Backlog of 1,000 Cases in Travis County," *Austin American-Statesman*, March 26, 2012. Discusses personnel shortages and problems retaining newly hired investigators that caused the Texas Child Protective Services to face difficulties in managing its caseload in a timely manner.

Molina, Mario, and Patricia M. Shields, "The Treatment of Bureaucracy in Texas Government Textbooks," Department of Political Science, Texas State University, Faculty Publications, 1998. Assesses differences in coverage of the Texas bureaucracy by authors of Texas government textbooks.

Kettl, Donald F., *The Politics of the Administrative State*, 5th ed. Washington, DC: Congressional Quarterly Press, 2011. Provides an engaging introduction to public administration that places bureaucracies and public employees within the framework of the policy processes.

Sunset Advisory Commission, *Summary of Sunset Legislation, 82nd Legislature.* Austin, TX: Sunset Advisory Commission, July 2011). Details sunset action taken by the Sunset Advisory Commission and the legislature during 2010 and 2011; similar reports follow each regular legislative session.

Sunset Advisory Commission, *Sunset in Texas*. Austin, TX: Sunset Advisory Commission, 2012. Summarizes sunset action taken since the Sunset Advisory Commission's creation and outlines the sunset process.

Thurmaier, Kurt M., and Katherine G. Willoughby, *Policy and Politics in State Budgeting.* Armonk, NY: M.E. Sharpe, 2001. Compares budgeting and the roles of budgeting officials in state governments.

Wilson, James Q., *Bureaucracy: What Government Agencies Do and Why They Do It*. New York: Basic Books, 1991. Covers a range of government agencies and describes what those in public agencies do, why they do what they do, and how they could do it better.

11

Listen on MyPoliSciLab

The Judicial System in Texas

The Texas (judicial) system is a hodgepodge of courts.

—**Anthony Champagne, 1997**

I am concerned by the public's perception that money in judicial races influences outcomes. This is an area where perception itself destroys public confidence.

—**Texas Supreme Court Chief Justice Wallace B. Jefferson, 2009**

lthough most people would like to think that justice in Texas is blind and that everyone has a level playing field in the state's courts, this is not the case. Litigation, whether civil or criminal, is expensive, and many Texans do not have the resources to pay for legal assistance. Most judges try to be fair, but, even so, their political and ideological views, life experiences, ethnicity, and gender mold their decisions. In recent years, moreover, a series of controversies has beset the Texas courts, severely straining the notion that the scales of justice are weighed in an atmosphere that is above reproach. Large campaign contributions to elected state judges, from lawyers who practice before them and from other special interests, fuel an ongoing high-stakes war for philosophical and political control of the judiciary and raise questions in the media and many advocacy groups about whether Texas courtrooms are "for sale."

11.1 Explain how the Texas judicial system fits within the constitutional framework of federalism, p. 318.

11.2 Outline the structure of the Texas court system, focusing on the jurisdiction of each level and qualifications of judges serving on the courts, p. 319.

11.3 Describe the roles of the different participants in the Texas court system, p. 324.

11.4 Summarize the procedures required for cases to move to the Texas Supreme Court and the Texas Court of Criminal Appeals, p. 329

11.5 Trace the growth of minority representation in the Texas judiciary, p. 330.

11.6 Characterize the controversies centering on the state's courts and their impact on public perceptions of the courts, p. 332.

11.7 List the legal and constitutional rights of suspects and the different classes of crimes and punishments in the Texas penal code, p. 339.

11.8 Provide examples of the increased policy role of the state courts, p. 344.

HISTORIC CHAMBER OF THE COURT OF CRIMINAL APPEALS
The Court of Criminal Appeals met in this room in the Texas Capitol until December of 1959, when the court was relocated to its current chamber in the Texas Supreme Court Building.

11.1

11.2

11.3

11.4

11.5

11.6

11.7

11.8

Penal Code
A body of law that defines most criminal offenses and sets a range of punishments that can be assessed.

Minorities and women remain underrepresented among the ranks of Texas judges. Even the basic structure of the judicial system—an assortment of more than 2,700 courts of various, often overlapping, jurisdictions—is so outdated that many experts believe it should be overhauled. But change does not come easily, and some influential people have a vested interest in maintaining the status quo.

State courts resolve civil disputes over property rights and personal injuries. They also determine guilt or innocence and set punishment in criminal cases involving offenses against people, property, and public institutions. To a more limited extent than the federal judiciary, they help set policy by reviewing the actions of the executive and legislative branches of government. A civil dispute may stem from something as simple as a tenant breaking an apartment lease to something as complex and potentially expensive as a manufacturer's liability for defective tires that contribute to the deaths or injuries of dozens of motorists. Criminal cases range from traffic offenses, punishable by fines, to capital murder, for which the death penalty can be imposed.

Texas streamlined some of its judicial processes, especially at the appellate level, in 1981. But the Texas judiciary, particularly in urban areas, has become overloaded by criminal cases and an increasingly litigious approach to civil disputes. It can take months for a civil or a criminal case—one that is not settled out of court or in a plea bargain with prosecutors—to make it to trial.

Texas Courts in the Federal Framework

11.1 Explain how the Texas judicial system fits within the constitutional framework of federalism.

Like people in every state, Texans are subject to the jurisdiction of both state and federal courts. The federal judiciary, created by Article 3 of the U.S. Constitution, has jurisdiction over violations of federal laws, including criminal offenses that occur across state lines, and over banking, securities, and other activities regulated by the federal government. Federal courts also have had major effects on state government policies and Texas's criminal justice system through interpretations and applications of the U.S. Constitution and federal laws, including the Bill of Rights.

Although Texas has a bill of rights in its constitution, the federal courts have taken the lead in protecting many civil and political rights, such as when the U.S. Supreme Court declared the white primary election unconstitutional in *Smith* v. *Allwright* (1944).[1] Federal court intervention continues in the redistricting of legislative and congressional district lines. The federal judiciary also ordered far-reaching improvements in the state prison system. When police officers read criminal suspects their rights, the officers comply with constitutional requirements determined by the U.S. Supreme Court in the *Miranda* case.[2] Nevertheless, estimates indicate that more than 95 percent of all litigation is based on state laws or local ordinances.[3] Thus, anyone involved in a lawsuit is likely to be found in a state rather than a federal court.

The U.S. and Texas constitutions form the basic legal framework of the Texas court system. Building on that framework, the Texas legislature has enacted codes of criminal and civil procedure to govern conduct in the courtroom and statutory laws for the courts to apply.

The Texas **Penal Code** defines most criminal activities and their punishments. In criminal cases, the state, often based on charges made by another individual, initiates action against a person accused of a crime. The most serious criminal offenses, for which prison sentences can be imposed, are called *felonies*. More minor offenses, punishable by fines or short sentences in county jails, are called *misdemeanors*. Many property crimes and drug offenses are classified as state jail felonies and are punishable by community service work or time in a state jail, a prison-like facility operated by the state. Sentences in state jails are shorter than most sentences served in prisons, which are reserved for more serious offenders. The state operates both types of facilities.

Civil lawsuits, which can be initiated under numerous statutes, involve conflicts between two or more parties—individuals, corporations, governments, or other entities. Civil law governs contracts and property rights between private citizens, affords individuals an avenue for relief against corporate abuses, and determines liability for personal injuries. Administrative law includes government enforcement powers over many aspects of the state's economy. This may include a lawsuit brought by the state against an oil company that violates a drilling permit or an environmental violation.

An individual with a grievance has to take the initiative of going to court. A person can be having problems with a landlord who refuses to return a deposit, a dry cleaner that lost a suit, or a friend who has borrowed and wrecked a car. In such a civil dispute, no legal issue can be resolved unless a lawsuit is filed. An injured person filing a lawsuit is a plaintiff. Because even the most minor disputes in the lowest courts can require professional assistance from a lawyer, a person soon will discover that the pursuit of justice can be very costly and time consuming.

Statutes and constitutional laws are subject to change through legislative action and popular consent of the voters, and over the years significant changes have been made in what is legal or illegal, permissible or impermissible. At one time, for example, state law provided for a potential life prison sentence for the possession of a few ounces of marijuana. Small amounts are now considered a misdemeanor punishable by a fine. The legal drinking age was lowered to 18 for a few years but was reestablished at 21 after parents and school officials convinced the legislature that the younger age had led to an increase in alcohol abuse among teenagers.

civil lawsuits
Noncriminal legal disputes between two or more individuals, businesses, governments, or other entities.

original jurisdiction
The authority of a court to try to resolve a civil lawsuit or a criminal prosecution being heard for the first time.

appellate jurisdiction
The authority of a court to review the decisions of lower courts to determine if the law was correctly interpreted and legal procedures were correctly followed.

bifurcated court system
Existence of two courts at the highest level of the state judiciary. The Texas Supreme Court is the court of last resort in civil cases, and the Court of Criminal Appeals has the final authority to review criminal cases. Texas and Oklahoma are the only two states that use this system.

commissioners court
The principal policymaking body for county government. It includes four commissioners and the county judge, all elected offices. It sets the county tax rate and supervises expenditures.

The Structure of the Texas Court System

11.2 Outline the structure of the Texas court system, focusing on the jurisdiction of each level and qualifications of judges serving on the courts.

There are five levels of courts in Texas, but some courts at different levels have overlapping authority and jurisdiction (see Figure 11–1). Some courts have only **original jurisdiction**; that is, they try or resolve only those cases being heard for the first time. They weigh the facts presented as evidence and apply the law in reaching a decision, or verdict. Other courts have only **appellate jurisdiction**; that is, they review the decisions of lower courts to determine if constitutional and statutory principles and procedures were correctly interpreted and followed. Appellate courts are empowered to reverse the judgments of the lower courts and to order cases to be retried if constitutional or procedural mistakes were made. Still other courts have both original and appellate jurisdiction.

At the highest appellate level, Texas has a **bifurcated court system** with the nine-member Texas Supreme Court serving as the court of last resort in civil cases and the nine-member Texas Court of Criminal Appeals functioning as the court of last resort in criminal cases. Only one other state, Oklahoma, has a similar structure.[4]

Unlike federal judges, who are appointed by the president to lifetime terms, state judges, except for those on municipal courts, are elected to limited terms in partisan elections. Midterm vacancies, however, are filled by appointment. County **commissioners courts** fill vacancies on justice of the peace and county courts, whereas the governor fills vacancies on the district and appellate benches.

Judicial reform remains a recurring issue in Texas politics. Small, incremental changes have been made since the 1970s, but many jurists and scholars continue to push

11.1
11.2
11.3
11.4
11.5
11.6
11.7
11.8

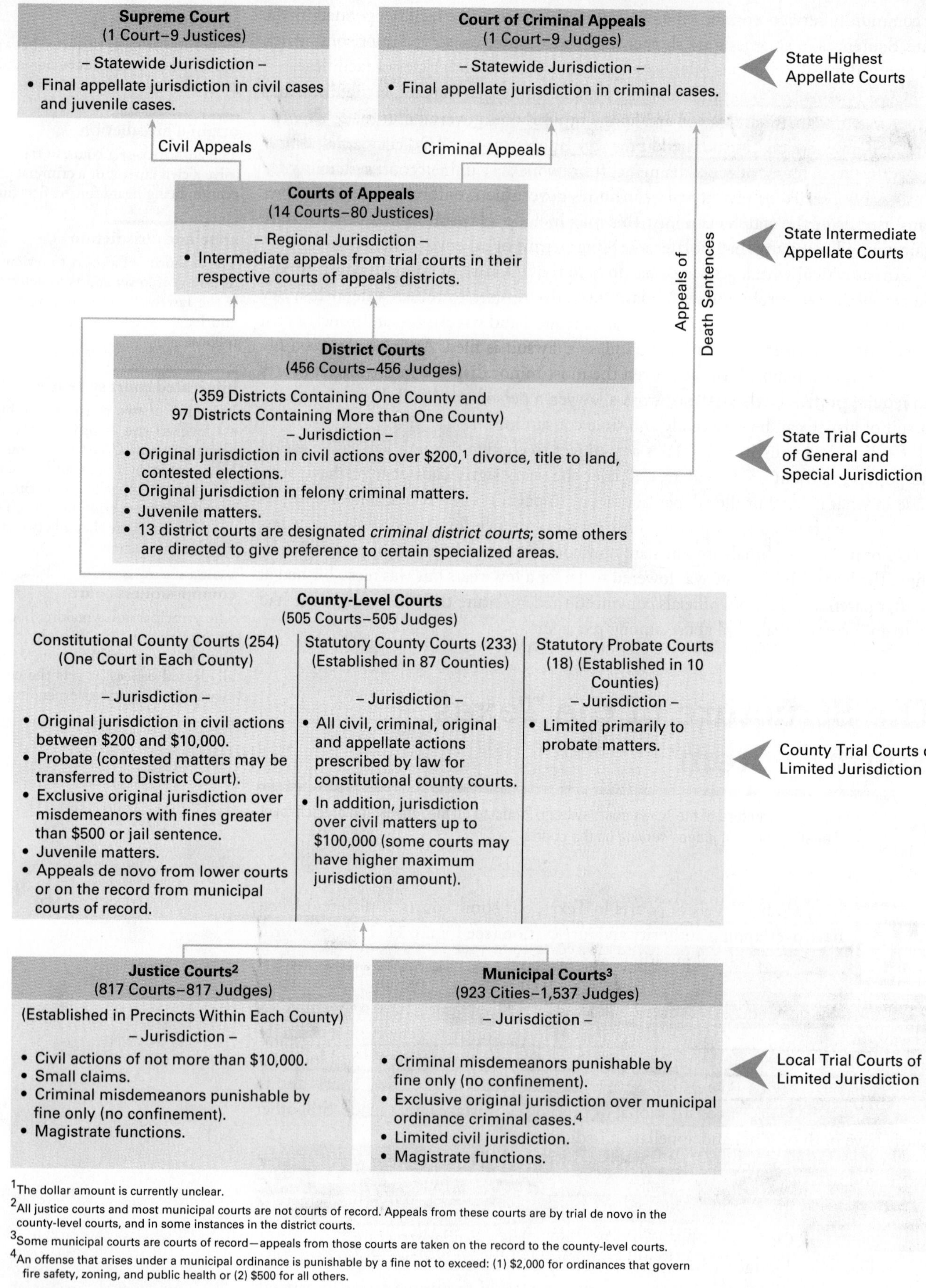

Supreme Court
(1 Court–9 Justices)
– Statewide Jurisdiction –
• Final appellate jurisdiction in civil cases and juvenile cases.
Court of Criminal Appeals
(1 Court–9 Judges)
– Statewide Jurisdiction –
• Final appellate jurisdiction in criminal cases.
State Highest Appellate Courts
Civil Appeals
Criminal Appeals
Courts of Appeals
(14 Courts–80 Justices)
– Regional Jurisdiction –
• Intermediate appeals from trial courts in their respective courts of appeals districts.
State Intermediate Appellate Courts
Appeals of Death Sentences
District Courts
(456 Courts–456 Judges)
(359 Districts Containing One County and 97 Districts Containing More than One County)
– Jurisdiction –
• Original jurisdiction in civil actions over $200,[1] divorce, title to land, contested elections.
• Original jurisdiction in felony criminal matters.
• Juvenile matters.
• 13 district courts are designated criminal district courts; some others are directed to give preference to certain specialized areas.
State Trial Courts of General and Special Jurisdiction
County-Level Courts
(505 Courts–505 Judges)
Constitutional County Courts (254)
(One Court in Each County)
– Jurisdiction –
• Original jurisdiction in civil actions between $200 and $10,000.
• Probate (contested matters may be transferred to District Court).
• Exclusive original jurisdiction over misdemeanors with fines greater than $500 or jail sentence.
• Juvenile matters.
• Appeals de novo from lower courts or on the record from municipal courts of record.
Statutory County Courts (233)
(Established in 87 Counties)
– Jurisdiction –
• All civil, criminal, original and appellate actions prescribed by law for constitutional county courts.
• In addition, jurisdiction over civil matters up to $100,000 (some courts may have higher maximum jurisdiction amount).
Statutory Probate Courts (18) (Established in 10 Counties)
– Jurisdiction –
• Limited primarily to probate matters.
County Trial Courts of Limited Jurisdiction
Justice Courts[2]
(817 Courts–817 Judges)
(Established in Precincts Within Each County)
– Jurisdiction –
• Civil actions of not more than $10,000.
• Small claims.
• Criminal misdemeanors punishable by fine only (no confinement).
• Magistrate functions.
Municipal Courts[3]
(923 Cities–1,537 Judges)
– Jurisdiction –
• Criminal misdemeanors punishable by fine only (no confinement).
• Exclusive original jurisdiction over municipal ordinance criminal cases.[4]
• Limited civil jurisdiction.
• Magistrate functions.
Local Trial Courts of Limited Jurisdiction

[1] The dollar amount is currently unclear.

[2] All justice courts and most municipal courts are not courts of record. Appeals from these courts are by trial de novo in the county-level courts, and in some instances in the district courts.

[3] Some municipal courts are courts of record—appeals from those courts are taken on the record to the county-level courts.

[4] An offense that arises under a municipal ordinance is punishable by a fine not to exceed: (1) $2,000 for ordinances that govern fire safety, zoning, and public health or (2) $500 for all others.

FIGURE 11–1 COURT STRUCTURE OF TEXAS, SEPTEMBER 1, 2011

The structure of the Texas court system, which is composed of five levels of courts, is based on provisions of the Texas Constitution, state statutes, and city ordinances.

Source: Texas Office of Court Administration.

for an overhaul of the structure and jurisdiction of state courts. In September 1989, Texas Supreme Court Chief Justice Thomas R. Phillips requested an in-depth study of the Texas judiciary by the Texas Research League, a privately financed, nonprofit organization specializing in studies of state government. The League concluded that the court system was fundamentally flawed and sorely in need of an overhaul. It made twenty-seven recommendations, including that the legislature rewrite the judiciary article of the state constitution to provide a fundamental framework for a unified court system.

Despite a series of similar studies and reports, reform of Texas courts has been difficult. The public may have a lot to gain from judicial restructuring, but the primary stakeholders—the judges; the attorneys; the court administrative personnel; and litigants who benefit from delays, confusion, and inefficiency—resist change. In the absence of spontaneous popular demand, there will be few structural changes in the judiciary until some or all of these participants perceive some advantages from it.[5]

municipal courts
Courts of limited jurisdiction that hears cases involving city ordinances and primarily handle traffic tickets.

justice of the peace courts
Low-ranking courts with jurisdiction over minor civil disputes and criminal cases.

Municipal and Justice of the Peace Courts

The lowest ranking trial courts in Texas are **municipal courts** and **justice of the peace courts**. You or someone you know probably has appeared before a judge in one of these courts because both handle a large volume of traffic tickets. Some of these courts are big sources of revenue for local governments, and they often are accused of subordinating justice and fairness to financial considerations.

State law authorizes cities to create municipal courts, but not all cities have enacted ordinances to create such courts, relying, instead, on justice of the peace courts. Some 923 cities do have municipal courts, and a number of those have multiple judges.[6] Individual cities determine the qualifications, terms of office, and method of selecting municipal judges, but they generally are appointed by the city council. Municipal courts have original and exclusive jurisdiction over city ordinances, but most of these courts are not courts of record, in which a word-for-word transcript is made of trial proceedings. Most of these courts record only very rudimentary information, and any appeal from them is heard *de novo* by a higher court. That is, the second court has to conduct a new trial and hear the same witnesses and evidence all over again because no official record of the original proceedings was kept. The informality of these proceedings and the absence of a record add to the confusion and cost of using the system.[7] In response to these problems, the legislature in recent years has created municipal courts of record for some cities.

Each county in Texas must have one justice of the peace court, and each county government in the larger metropolitan areas may create sixteen. There are 817 of these courts in Texas. Justices of the peace are elected to four-year terms from precincts, or subdivisions of the county, drawn by the commissioners court, which also sets their salaries. Justices of the peace are not required to be licensed attorneys, which has generated much criticism of these courts.

Although their duties vary from county to county, justice of the peace courts, with certain restrictions, have original jurisdiction in civil cases when the amount in dispute is $10,000 or less, and they have original jurisdiction over criminal offenses that are punishable by fines only. In some areas of criminal law, they have overlapping jurisdiction with municipal courts. Justices of the peace also sit as judges of small claims courts, and in many rural counties, they serve as coroners. They also function as state magistrates with the authority to hold preliminary hearings to determine if there is probable cause to hold a criminal defendant. Each justice of the peace court has an elected constable to serve warrants and perform other duties for the court.

County-Level Courts

Any confusion about the authority and jurisdiction of municipal and justice of the peace courts is compounded by the county courts. They were created by the Texas Constitution to serve the needs of the sparsely populated, rural society that existed

constitutional county court
The Texas Constitution provides for 254 courts with limited jurisdiction. The county judge, who is also the presiding officer of a county's commissioners court, which is a policy-making body, performs some limited judicial functions in some counties.

statutory county court
A court created by the legislature that exercises limited jurisdiction over criminal and/or civil cases. The jurisdiction of these courts varies from county to county.

district court
Court with general jurisdiction over criminal felony cases and civil disputes.

when the charter was written in 1875. But population growth and urbanization have placed enormous demands on the judicial system, and rather than modernize the system, the state has added courts while making only modest changes in the structure and jurisdiction of the existing courts.

Each county has a **constitutional county court**. The holder of this office, the county judge, is elected countywide to a four-year term. This individual is the chief executive officer of the county and presides over the county commissioners court, the policymaking body of county government. Most urban county judges do not perform judicial duties, but county judges in many rural counties perform both executive and judicial functions, a dual responsibility that some experts believe is inconsistent with the Texas Constitution's separation of powers doctrine. Although a large number of county judges are lawyers, they are not required to be. They are required only to be "well informed in the law" and to take appropriate courses in evidence and legal procedures.

The constitutional county court shares some original civil jurisdiction with both the justice of the peace and district courts. It has original criminal jurisdiction over misdemeanors punishable by fines of more than $500 and jail sentences of one year or less. These courts also probate wills and have appellate jurisdiction over cases tried originally in justice of the peace and municipal courts.

Over the years, the legislature also has created 251 **statutory county courts**, or county courts-at-law, in more than ninety counties. Some specialize in probate cases and are called probate courts. These courts were designed to deal with specific local problems and, consequently, have inconsistent jurisdictions. Judges on these courts are elected countywide and have to be lawyers, but the authority of a particular court is defined by the legislation by which it was created. Some statutory county courts cannot hear civil disputes involving more than $2,500, whereas others can hear disputes involving as much as $100,000. Drunken driving cases are the primary criminal cases tried before these courts, but some also hear appeals *de novo* from lower courts.

County courts across the state disposed of more than 742,000 civil and criminal cases during the 2011 fiscal year but saw more than 812,000 cases added to their dockets. At the end of the year, more than 828,000 cases were pending before the county courts.[8]

District Courts

The primary trial court in Texas is the **district court**. Although there is some overlapping jurisdiction with county courts, district courts have original jurisdiction over civil cases involving $200 or more in damages, divorce cases, contested elections, suits over land titles and liens, suits for slander or defamation, all criminal felony cases, and misdemeanors involving official misconduct. In recent years, the legislature has created district courts with specialized jurisdictions over criminal or civil law or over such specialties as family law—divorces and child custody cases. In some large metropolitan counties that have numerous district courts, informal agreements among judges determine the jurisdictions of the respective courts. District court judges are elected to four-year terms, must be at least twenty-five years old, and must have practiced law or served as a judge of another court for four years prior to taking office.

The Texas Constitution gives the legislature the responsibility to define judicial districts, and as the expanding population produced greater caseloads, new district courts were created. In 1981, there were 328 district courts. In 2011, the number was 456. A single county may be allocated more than one district court with overlapping geographical jurisdiction. Harris County, the state's most populous county, has fifty-nine district courts, each covering the entire county. By contrast, one rural district court may include several counties. As these courts evolved, the respective workloads of individual courts received little systematic consideration, and great disparities now exist in the number of people whom district courts serve.

Many urban counties suffer from a heavy backlog of cases that can delay a trial date in civil lawsuits and even some criminal cases for months or years. The district courts disposed of 864,000 civil and criminal cases during the 2011 fiscal year, but new cases were added, and the courts began fiscal 2012 with 846,000 pending cases.[9]

Delays in criminal cases have prompted a widespread use of **plea bargains**. In plea bargaining, a criminal defendant, through a lawyer, negotiates with prosecutors a guilty plea that will get a lesser sentence than he or she could expect to receive if convicted in a trial. The process saves the state the time-consuming expense of a full-blown trial and has become an essential tool in clearing urban court dockets.

Former District Attorney John B. Holmes, Jr., estimated that 90 percent of the thousands of felony cases filed in Harris County (Houston) each year were disposed of through plea bargains. Without plea bargains, the caseload would simply overwhelm the twenty-two Harris County district courts that handle criminal cases. Many civil lawsuits are resolved through negotiations between the opposing parties, but those that are tried and appealed can take several years to be resolved.

The wide disparities in populations and caseloads of the various district courts prompted the adoption of a constitutional amendment in 1985 that created the Judicial Districts Board, which is responsible for redrawing judicial districts with an eye toward a more equitable distribution of the workload. But in 1994, yielding to pressure from incumbent judges who did not want to lose their offices, it issued recommendations that primarily preserved the status quo. Extensive changes by the legislature were considered unlikely.

Although the district court is the state's primary trial court and the state pays the district judges' base salaries, the counties pick up virtually all the other district court expenses. The counties provide courtrooms, pay the courts' operating expenses, and supplement the judges' state pay.

plea bargain
A procedure that allows a person charged with a crime to negotiate a guilty plea with prosecutors in exchange for a lighter sentence than he or she would expect to receive if convicted in a trial.

courts of appeals
Intermediate-level courts that review civil and criminal cases from the district courts.

Texas Supreme Court
A nine-member court with final appellate jurisdiction over civil lawsuits.

☐ Courts of Appeals

There are fourteen intermediate **courts of appeals** covering thirteen multicounty regions that hear appeals of both civil and criminal cases from the district courts. Two courts, the First Court of Appeals and the Fourteenth Court of Appeals, are based in Houston and cover the same area. The Texas Constitution provides that each court shall have a chief justice and at least two other justices, but the legislature can add to that number and has done so for most courts. Each Houston court has nine judges, and the Fifth Court of Appeals in Dallas has thirteen judges. Five of these intermediate courts, however, have only three members. Appellate judges are elected to six-year terms. They must be at least thirty-five years old and have at least ten years of experience as an attorney or a judge on a court of record.

All courts of appeals combined disposed of more than 11,900 cases during fiscal 2011 with approximately 7,700 other cases still pending on their dockets at the end of that year.[10] Disparities, nevertheless, exist in the caseloads among individual courts, with those in Houston and Dallas handling the lion's share. The Texas Supreme Court partially balances the load by transferring cases among courts. The courts of appeals normally decide cases in panels of three judges, but an entire court can hear some appeals *en banc*—when all of the judges of an appellate court sit to hear a case.

☐ Supreme Court and Court of Criminal Appeals

The creation of separate courts of last resort for civil and criminal cases was part of the effort by the constitutional framers of 1875 to fragment political power and decentralize the structure of state and local governments. It also was based on the rationale that criminal cases should be handled more expeditiously, and the way to accomplish this was through a separate appellate court.[11]

Although it decides only civil appeals, the **Texas Supreme Court** is probably viewed by most Texans as the titular head of the state judiciary, and it has been given

11.1

11.2

11.3

11.4

11.5

11.6

11.7

11.8

Texas Court of Criminal Appeals
A Texas nine-member court with final appellate jurisdiction over criminal cases.

SITTING "EN BANC" IN THE TEXAS HOUSE OF REPRESENTATIVES

Members of the Texas Supreme Court and the Texas Court of Criminal Appeals listen to a State of the State speech by the governor in the House of Representatives chamber in Austin.

some authority to coordinate the state judicial system.[12] The Supreme Court is charged with developing administrative procedures for the state courts and rules of civil procedure. It appoints the Board of Law Examiners, which is responsible for licensing attorneys, and has oversight of the State Bar, the professional organization to which all lawyers in Texas must belong. The Supreme Court also has disciplinary authority over state judges through recommendations of the State Commission on Judicial Conduct.

The Texas Supreme Court includes a chief justice and eight justices who serve staggered, six-year terms. Three members are up for election every two years on a statewide ballot. Members must be at least thirty-five years old and must have been a practicing attorney, a judge of a court of record, or a combination of both for at least ten years.

The **Texas Court of Criminal Appeals**, which hears only criminal cases on appeal, includes a presiding judge and eight other judges elected statewide to staggered, six-year terms. The qualifications for members of this court are the same as those for the Supreme Court.

Under the federal system, some decisions of the Texas Supreme Court and the Texas Court of Criminal Appeals can be appealed to the U.S. Supreme Court. Those cases have to involve a federal question or a constitutional right assured under the U.S. Constitution.

Participants in the Judicial System

11.3 Describe the roles of the different participants in the Texas court system.

Although judges and lawyers may be the first people we think of when discussing the courts, the judicial process in Texas also includes thousands of law enforcement officers and administrative and support personnel who assist judges, as well as thousands of ordinary Texans who play critical roles in the administration of justice by serving on juries.

NO LONGER DOMINATED BY MALE JURISTS

In 2012, five women, including Sharon Keller (bottom row, center), the presiding judge, served on the state's highest court for criminal appeals.

Texas Judges

Many judges on the intermediate and highest appellate courts previously served on lower courts. Most district judges came to their offices from a private law practice or from a prosecutor's office. Figure 11–2 highlights the judicial qualifications and selection process in Texas.

With the partisan realignment of Texas, Republicans saw election gains and more appointments to judicial vacancies. A number of judges also switched from the Democratic Party. By 2003, almost two-thirds of the judges at the district court level and higher were Republicans, but by 2006, Democrats were making a comeback. Democrats swept all judicial races on the ballot in Dallas County that year and made a strong showing in Harris County two years later. In 2012, however, Republicans still held all nine seats on the Texas Supreme Court and all nine seats on the Texas Court of Criminal Appeals.

Most Texas judges are white males. More women, Hispanics, and African Americans are entering the legal profession and running for judicial offices, but they still are disproportionately underrepresented in the judiciary. As will be discussed later in this chapter, advocates for minorities have pressed for changes in the judicial selection process to enhance their chances to serve on the bench.

Judicial elections have been diluted by a large number of appointments to judicial vacancies. The governor appoints judges to fill midterm vacancies on the district and appellate courts. County commissioners courts fill midterm vacancies on county court-at-law and justice of the peace courts. Appointees are required to run for office in the next general election to keep their seats, but their incumbency can enhance their election chances.

Prosecuting Attorneys and Clerks

County attorneys and district attorneys prosecute criminal cases. Both positions are elected. Some counties do not have a county attorney. In those that do, the county attorney is the chief legal adviser to county commissioners, represents the county in civil lawsuits, and may prosecute misdemeanors. The district attorney prosecutes

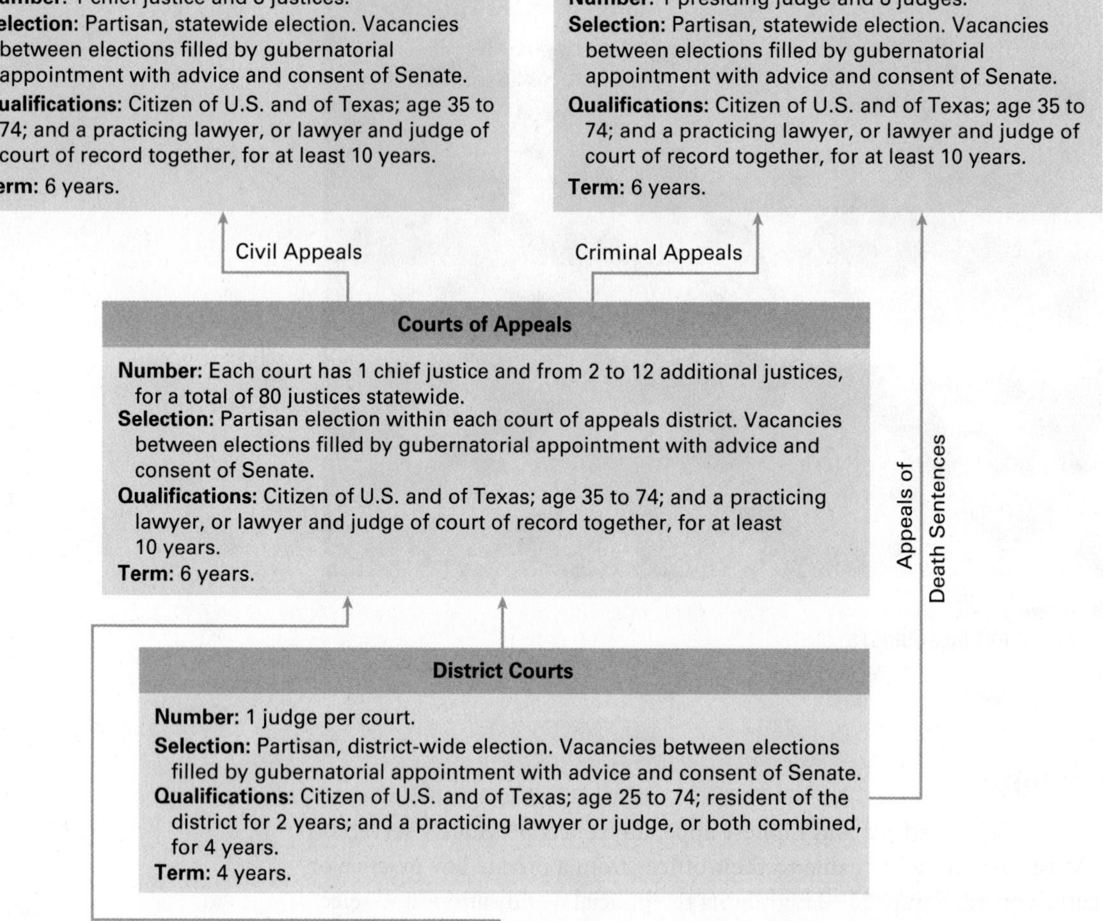

Supreme Court
Number: 1 chief justice and 8 justices.
Selection: Partisan, statewide election. Vacancies between elections filled by gubernatorial appointment with advice and consent of Senate.
Qualifications: Citizen of U.S. and of Texas; age 35 to 74; and a practicing lawyer, or lawyer and judge of court of record together, for at least 10 years.
Term: 6 years.
Court of Criminal Appeals
Number: 1 presiding judge and 8 judges.
Selection: Partisan, statewide election. Vacancies between elections filled by gubernatorial appointment with advice and consent of Senate.
Qualifications: Citizen of U.S. and of Texas; age 35 to 74; and a practicing lawyer, or lawyer and judge of court of record together, for at least 10 years.
Term: 6 years.
Civil Appeals
Criminal Appeals
Appeals of Death Sentences
Courts of Appeals
Number: Each court has 1 chief justice and from 2 to 12 additional justices, for a total of 80 justices statewide.
Selection: Partisan election within each court of appeals district. Vacancies between elections filled by gubernatorial appointment with advice and consent of Senate.
Qualifications: Citizen of U.S. and of Texas; age 35 to 74; and a practicing lawyer, or lawyer and judge of court of record together, for at least 10 years.
Term: 6 years.
District Courts
Number: 1 judge per court.
Selection: Partisan, district-wide election. Vacancies between elections filled by gubernatorial appointment with advice and consent of Senate.
Qualifications: Citizen of U.S. and of Texas; age 25 to 74; resident of the district for 2 years; and a practicing lawyer or judge, or both combined, for 4 years.
Term: 4 years.

County-Level Courts

Constitutional County Courts

Number: 1 judge per court.

Selection: Partisan, county-wide election. Vacancies between elections filled by appointment by county commissioners.

Qualifications: "Shall be well informed in the law of the State." (Law license not required.)

Term: 4 years.

Statutory County Courts/Probate Courts

Number: 1 judge per court.

Selection: Partisan, county-wide election. Vacancies between elections filled by appointment by county commissioners.

Qualifications: Age 25 or older; resident of county for at least 2 years; and licensed attorney who has practiced law or served as a judge for 4 years.

Term: 4 years.

Justice Courts

Number: 1 judge per court.

Selection: Partisan, precinct-wide election.

Qualifications: No specific statutory or constitutional provisions apply.

Term: 4 years.

Municipal Courts

Number: Generally, 1 court per incorporated municipality and 1 judge per court. Statutes allow some city governing bodies to establish more than 1 court and/or more than 1 judge per court.

Selection: Elected or appointed by the governing body of the city as provided by city charter or ordinance.

Qualifications: Determined by the governing body of the city.

Term: Most appointed for 2-year terms and serve at the will of the governing body of the city.

FIGURE 11–2 JUDICIAL QUALIFICATIONS AND SELECTION IN THE STATE OF TEXAS

Qualifications for judges vary among the courts but are higher for district and appellate judges. Legal training and some professional experience as either a practicing attorney or a judge is required for the judges of district and appellate courts. A similar requirement applies to statutory county courts and probate courts. However, the county judges and justices of the peace are not required to have a law license. Cities set the qualifications of their judges. With the exception of municipal judges who are appointed, all other judges in the state are elected in partisan elections.

Source: Texas Office of Court Administration.

felonies and, in some counties, also handles misdemeanors. The district attorney exercises considerable power in the criminal justice process by deciding which cases to take to a grand jury for an indictment, whether to seek the maximum penalty for an offense, or whether to plea-bargain with a defendant for a reduced sentence. The office represents one county in metropolitan areas and several counties in less populated areas of the state.

County and district clerks, both elected officials, are custodians of court records. Bailiffs are peace officers assigned to the courts to help maintain order and protect judges and other parties. Other law enforcement officers play critical roles in the arrest, detention, and investigation of persons accused of crimes.

☐ The Jury Systems

Other important players in the judicial process are the private citizens who serve on grand juries and trial, or petit, juries. Although some people may doubt the competency of a jury of ordinary people to make reasonable decisions in complex and technical cases, no one has yet come up with a better system.

THE GRAND JURY The **grand jury**, in theory, functions to ensure that the government has sufficient reason to proceed with a criminal **prosecution** against an individual. It includes twelve persons selected by a district judge from a list proposed by a jury commission appointed by the local district judge or judges. Although the grand jury evolved to protect the individual against arbitrary and capricious behavior by governmental officials, a district attorney can exercise great control over a grand jury through deciding which evidence and which witnesses jurors will hear. Allegations have been made over the years that grand juries overrepresent the interests of upper social and economic groups and underrepresent minorities. Grand jury meetings and deliberations are conducted in private, and the accused is not allowed to have an attorney present during grand jury questioning.

A grand jury usually meets on specified days of the week and serves for the duration of the district court's term, usually from three to six months. If at least nine grand jurors believe there is enough evidence to warrant a trial in the case under investigation, they will issue an **indictment**, or a "true bill," a written statement charging a person or persons with a crime. A grand jury investigation also may result in no indictment, or a "no bill."

In some cases, grand juries will issue indictments alleging misdemeanors. That often happens after an investigation fails to produce a strong enough case for a felony indictment. Most misdemeanors, however, are not handled by grand juries; instead, they are handled by the district or county attorney, who prepares an **information**—a document formally charging an individual with a misdemeanor—on the basis of a complaint filed by a private citizen.

THE PETIT JURY The jury on which most people are likely to be called to serve is the trial or **petit jury**. Citizens who are at least eighteen years old and meet other minimal requirements are eligible for jury duty, and anyone refusing to comply with a jury summons can be fined for contempt of court (see *Talking Texas: Skipping Jury Duty Can Be Costly*). Persons older than seventy, individuals with legal custody of young children, and full-time students are exempted from jury duty.

The legislature in 1991 increased the likelihood of an individual's being called to jury duty by providing that county and district clerks prepare jury summonses from lists of Texans holding driver's licenses or Department of Public Safety identification cards. Previously, prospective jurors were chosen from voter registration lists, and it was believed that some Texans had not been registering to vote in order to avoid jury duty.

grand jury
Panel that reviews evidence submitted by prosecutors to determine whether to indict, or charge, an individual with a criminal offense. A grand jury can hear witnesses; all its meetings are held behind closed doors.

prosecution
The conduct of legal proceedings against an individual charged with a crime.

indictment
A written statement issued by a grand jury charging a person or persons with a crime or crimes.

information
A document formally charging an individual with a misdemeanor.

petit jury
A panel of citizens that hears evidence in a civil lawsuit or a criminal prosecution and decides the outcome by issuing a verdict.

11.1

11.2

11.3

11.4

11.5

11.6

11.7

11.8

Talking ★ TEXAS Skipping Jury Duty Can Be Costly

If you ever are tempted to ignore a jury summons, you may want to think about what happened to Douglas Maupin. Maupin, a masonry contractor, spent eighty-three days in jail for skipping jury duty. It may have been the largest penalty ever for neglecting a basic duty of citizenship and an important part of Texas's justice system.

Police stopped Maupin for speeding in Collin County on February 15, 2009, and discovered a warrant had been issued against him for failing to appear for jury duty six years prior. So, Maupin, then 34, was locked up. Since he could not afford to pay a $1,500 bond, and, he said, a jail clerk denied his attempt to get a public defender, there he stayed. Maupin was released only after writing a letter to *The Dallas Morning News*, which began an inquiry into his plight.

"He should not have spent that much time. This is unacceptable," said District Judge Chris Oldner, after ordering Maupin's release in May. "I don't know why the process failed to notify us."

Maupin had fallen through the cracks of that bureaucratic process. The judge who signed the original warrant against him six years earlier had retired, and Oldner said he had not known Maupin was in jail until after the prisoner had written the letter to the newspaper. "I understand I am partially responsible, but I just want my day in court," Maupin said. "I do know I have the right to due process and a speedy trial. I've had neither. It's not right."[a]

CRITICAL THINKING QUESTIONS

1. How often do you think people jailed for minor offenses get "lost" by the bureaucracy? What steps can be taken to guard against such incidences?
2. Is it possible for people who do not want to serve on a jury to be fair in their deliberations? Why or why not?

[a]Katie Fairbank, "83 Days—for Missing Jury Duty—Collin Man's Case Fell Through Cracks After He Was Jailed on '03 Warrant," *The Dallas Morning News*, May 9, 2009, page 1A.

veniremen
Persons who have been called for a jury panel.

Six persons make up a jury in a justice of the peace or county court, and twelve in a district court. Attorneys for both sides in a criminal or civil case screen the prospective jurors, known as **veniremen**, before a jury is seated. In major felony cases, such as capital murder, prosecutors and defense attorneys may take several days to select a jury from among hundreds of prospects.

Attorneys for each side in a criminal case are allowed a certain number of peremptory challenges, which allow them to dismiss a prospective juror without having to explain the reason, and an unlimited number of challenges for cause. In the latter case, the lawyer has to state why he or she believes a particular venireman would be unable to evaluate the evidence in the case impartially. The judge decides whether to grant each challenge for cause but can rule against a peremptory challenge only if he or she believes the prosecutor is trying to exclude prospective jurors because of their race, such as keeping African Americans off a jury that is to try an African American defendant. If that happens, the defendant is entitled to a new group, or panel, of prospective jurors.

In civil cases, attorneys for both sides determine whether any persons on the jury panel should be disqualified because they are related to one of the parties, have some other personal or business connection, or could otherwise be prejudiced. For example, a lawyer defending a doctor in a malpractice suit probably would not want to seat a prospective juror who had been dissatisfied with his or her own medical treatment. Attorneys' careful screening and questioning of veniremen discover such potential conflicts.

Unanimous jury verdicts are required to convict a defendant in a criminal case. Agreement of only ten of the twelve members of a district court jury and five of the six on a county court jury, however, are necessary to reach a verdict in a civil suit. In a criminal case, jurors have to be convinced "beyond a reasonable doubt" that a defendant is guilty before returning a guilty verdict.

Judicial Procedures and Decision Making

11.4 Summarize the procedures required for cases to move to the Texas Supreme Court and the Texas Court of Criminal Appeals.

Civil litigants and criminal defendants (except those charged with capital murder) can waive their right to a jury trial, if they believe it would be to their advantage to have their cases decided by a judge. Following established procedures, which differ between civil and criminal cases and are enforced by the judge, the trial moves through the presentation of opening arguments by the opposing attorneys, examination and cross-examination of witnesses, presentation of evidence, rebuttal, and summation. Some trials can be completed in a few hours, but the trial of a complex civil lawsuit or a sensational criminal case can take weeks or months. Convicted criminal defendants or parties dissatisfied with a judge or jury's verdict in a civil lawsuit may then appeal their case to higher courts.

The procedure in the appellate courts is markedly different from that in the trial courts. There is no jury at the appellate level to rehear evidence. Instead, judges review the decisions and the procedures of the lower court for conformance to constitutional and statutory requirements. The record of the trial court proceedings and legal briefs filed by attorneys are available for appellate judges to review.

Most civil and criminal appeals are initially made to one of the fourteen intermediate courts of appeals. Parties dissatisfied with decisions of the courts of appeals can appeal to the Texas Supreme Court or the Court of Criminal Appeals.

Cases reach the Texas Supreme Court primarily on **petitions for review**, usually filed by the losing parties, claiming that lower courts made legal or procedural mistakes. The petitions are divided among the nine justices for review. The justices and their briefing attorneys then prepare memoranda on their assigned cases for circulation among the other court members. Meeting in private conference, the court decides which petitions to reject outright—thus upholding the lower court decisions—and which to schedule for attorneys' oral arguments. A case will not be heard without the approval of at least four of the nine justices.

Lawyers present oral arguments, in which they relate their perspectives on the legal points that are at issue in their cases and answer questions from the justices in open court. The responsibility for writing the majority opinions that state the court's decisions is determined by lot among the justices. It often takes several months after oral arguments before a decision is issued. Justices debate legal points and their judicial philosophies behind the closed doors of their conference room, but differences sometimes spill out for public view through split decisions and strongly worded dissenting opinions.

Most cases taken to the Texas Supreme Court on appeal are from one of the courts of appeals, but occasionally the Supreme Court receives a direct appeal from a district court. In recent years, the court has been hearing about 10 percent of the petitions for review it receives.

The Texas Supreme Court also acts on petitions for **writs of mandamus**, or orders directing a lower court or another public official to take a certain action. Many involve disputes over procedure or evidence in cases still pending in trial courts.

The Texas Court of Criminal Appeals has appellate jurisdiction in criminal cases that originate in the district and county courts. Death penalty cases are appealed directly to the Court of Criminal Appeals. Other criminal cases are appealed first to the intermediate courts of appeals. Either the defendant or the prosecution can appeal the courts of appeals' decisions to the Court of Criminal Appeals by filing **petitions for discretionary review**, which the high court may grant if at least four judges agree. The court sets one day a week aside for lawyers' oral arguments in the cases it agrees to review. The task of writing majority opinions rotates among the nine judges.

petition for review
Petition to Texas Supreme Court stating that legal or procedural mistakes were made in the lower court, thus meriting a hearing before the court.

writs of mandamus
Court orders directing a lower court or a public official to take a certain action.

petition for discretionary review
Petition to the Texas Court of Criminal Appeals stating that legal or procedural mistakes were made in the lower court, thus meriting a hearing before the court.

Changing the Face of the Judiciary

11.5 Trace the growth of minority representation in the Texas judiciary.

In relation to their share of the Texas population, minorities and women are underrepresented among the ranks of Texas judges. As will be discussed in more detail, minority activists have thus far failed to force changes in the judicial selection process to favor the election of more minority judges. Slowly, however, the face of the Texas judiciary is changing, thanks in part to midterm appointments by recent governors.

Minorities

Democratic Governor Mark White appointed the first Hispanic, Raul A. Gonzalez, the son of migrant workers, to the Texas Supreme Court in 1984 to fill a vacancy created by a resignation. Gonzalez made history a second time in 1986 by winning election to the seat and becoming the first Hispanic to win a statewide election in Texas. A native of Weslaco in the Rio Grande Valley, Gonzalez was a state district judge in Brownsville before being appointed to the Thirteenth Court of Appeals in Corpus Christi by Republican Governor Bill Clements in 1981.

Despite his background, Gonzalez, a Democrat, was one of the most conservative members of the Supreme Court during his tenure. Consequently, he came under frequent attack from trial lawyers and, ironically, from many of the constituent groups within his own party who advocated increasing the number of minority judges. Gonzalez's reelection race in 1994 was one of the most bitterly contested Supreme Court races in recent memory. He defeated a strong challenge in the Democratic primary from Corpus Christi attorney Rene Haas, who was supported by trial lawyers, women's groups, consumer advocates, several key Democratic legislators, and a number of African American and Hispanic leaders in the Democratic Party. Gonzalez drew heavy financial support from business interests, insurance companies, and defense attorneys.

Raul Gonzalez resigned from the Supreme Court in midterm in late 1998 and was replaced by Alberto R. Gonzales, a Republican appointee of Governor George W. Bush and only the second Hispanic to serve on the high court. As had Raul Gonzalez, Alberto Gonzales came from a modest background. His parents were migrant workers when he was born in San Antonio, but they soon moved to Houston, where his father became a construction worker. The young Gonzales, one of eight children, joined the Air Force after graduating from high school and earned degrees from Rice University and Harvard Law School. He had never been a judge before Governor Bush named him to the Supreme Court. However, he had been a partner in one of Houston's largest law firms. In addition, he was Bush's top staff lawyer, and he served under Bush as Texas secretary of state.

Alberto Gonzales's appointment came at a time when Governor Bush was actively trying to increase the Republican Party's appeal to Hispanics, and Bush acknowledged that it was important to him that Gonzales was Hispanic. "Of course, it mattered what his ethnicity is, but first and foremost what mattered is: I've got great confidence in Al. I know him well. He's a good friend. He'll do a fine job," Bush said.[13] Bush's confidence in Gonzales continued after Bush became president in 2001. He appointed Gonzales White House counsel and later U.S. attorney general.

On succeeding Bush, Republican Governor Rick Perry named minorities to the first two vacancies he had the opportunity to fill on the Texas Supreme Court in 2001. One was Wallace Jefferson, an appellate lawyer from San Antonio who became the first African American to serve on the high court. Perry named Jefferson to succeed Alberto Gonzales, who had resigned to take the White House job. Jefferson, a

Republican, was the great-great-great grandson of a slave. Later the same year, Perry appointed Xavier Rodriguez, a San Antonio labor lawyer, to the Supreme Court to succeed former Justice Greg Abbott, who had resigned to run for Texas attorney general. Rodriguez became the third Hispanic to serve on the court, but he was unseated in the 2002 Republican primary by Austin lawyer Steven Wayne Smith, an Anglo. Jefferson was elected in 2002 to keep his seat on the high court, and a second African American, Republican Dale Wainwright, a state district judge from Houston, was elected to an open Supreme Court seat the same year. By 2012, the court also included two Hispanic justices—Eva Guzman and David Medina, who had initially been appointed by Governor Perry.

Governor Ann Richards appointed the first Hispanic, Fortunato P. Benavides, to the Texas Court of Criminal Appeals to fill a vacancy in 1991. Benavides had been a justice on the Thirteenth Court of Appeals and a district judge and a county court-at-law judge in Hidalgo County. But Benavides's tenure on the statewide court was short lived. He was narrowly unseated in 1992 by Republican Lawrence Meyers of Fort Worth, an Anglo, who became the first Republican elected to the criminal court. President Clinton later appointed Benavides to the Fifth U.S. Circuit Court of Appeals.

Governor Bill Clements appointed the first African American, Louis Sturns, a Republican state district judge from Fort Worth, to the Texas Court of Criminal Appeals on March 16, 1990. Because the vacancy that Sturns filled had occurred after the filing deadline for the 1990 party primaries, the State Republican Executive Committee put Sturns on the general election ballot as the GOP nominee for the seat. The State Democratic Executive Committee nominated another African American, Morris Overstreet, a county court-at-law judge from Amarillo. Overstreet narrowly defeated Sturns in the November general election to become the first African American elected to a statewide office in Texas. Overstreet served on the court until 1998, when, instead of seeking reelection, he lost a race for the Democratic nomination for Texas attorney general.

One Hispanic, Judge Elsa Alcala, served on the Court of Criminal Appeals in 2012. Governor Perry appointed her in 2011 to fill a vacancy.

□ Women

The first woman to serve as a state district judge in Texas was Sarah T. Hughes of Dallas, who was appointed to the bench in 1935 by Governor James V. Allred and served until 1961, when she resigned to accept an appointment by President John F. Kennedy to the federal district bench. Ironically, Hughes is best known for swearing a grim-faced Lyndon B. Johnson into office aboard Air Force One on November 22, 1963, following Kennedy's assassination in Dallas.

Ruby Sondock of Houston was the first woman to serve on the Texas Supreme Court. She had been a state district judge before Governor Bill Clements named her to the high court on June 25, 1982, to fill a temporary vacancy. Sondock chose not to seek election to the seat and served only a few months. She later returned to the district bench. Barbara Culver, a state district judge from Midland, became the second female Supreme Court justice when Clements appointed her in February 1988 to fill another vacancy. Culver also served less than a year. Democrat Jack Hightower unseated her in the 1988 general election.

Democrat Rose Spector, a state district judge from San Antonio, became the first woman elected to the Texas Supreme Court when she defeated Republican Justice Eugene Cook in 1992. She was unseated in 1998 by Republican Harriet O'Neill. Two women—Justices Eva Guzman and Debra Lehrmann—served on the Texas Supreme Court in 2012.

In 1994, Republican Sharon Keller, a former Dallas County prosecutor, became the first woman elected to the Texas Court of Criminal Appeals and the first female presiding judge of the court in 2001. Five women, including Keller, served on the nine-member court in 2012, and 274 women were serving judges at the county court level or higher in Texas by 2012.[14]

Judicial Controversies and the Search for Solutions

11.6 Characterize the controversies centering on the state's courts and their impact on public perceptions of the courts.

For more than thirty years, Texas courts have been beset with conflict and controversy. Large campaign contributions from lawyers and other special interests to judges and judicial candidates periodically raise allegations that Texas has the best justice that money can buy. With millions of dollars at stake in crucial legal decisions, the Texas Supreme Court has been a philosophical and political battleground. Meanwhile, minorities, who hold a disproportionately small number of judicial offices, continue to press for greater influence in electing judges. Lengthy ballots, particularly in urban areas, make it increasingly difficult for most voters to choose intelligently among judicial candidates. Although these issues and concerns may seem unrelated, they all share one important characteristic: they cast a cloud over the Texas judiciary. Each, in its own way, undermines public confidence in the state courts and makes many Texans question how just their system of justice really is.

☐ Judicial Activism

In earlier chapters, we noted that state politics and policies historically have been dominated by the conservative, business-oriented establishment. Until the mid-1970s, that domination also applied to the judiciary, as insurance companies, banks, utilities, and other large corporate entities became accustomed to favorable rulings from a Democratic, but conservative, Texas Supreme Court.

Establishment-oriented justices, usually elected with the support of the state's largest law firms, tended to view their role as strict constructionists. They believed the legislature enacted public policy and that the courts narrowly interpreted and applied the law. Judges did not engage in setting policy but honored legal precedent and prior case law, which in general favored the interests of corporations over those of consumers, laborers, and the lower social classes.

The establishment began to feel the first tremors of a philosophical earthquake in the mid-1970s. The Texas Trial Lawyers Association, whose members represent consumers in lawsuits against businesses, doctors, and insurance companies, increased its political activity. In 1973, the legislature, with increased minority and female membership from single-member House districts ordered by the federal courts, enacted the Deceptive Trade Practices–Consumer Protection Act, which encouraged injured parties to take their grievances to court. Among other things, the new law allowed consumers to sue for attorneys' fees as well as compensatory and punitive damages.

Trial, or plaintiffs', attorneys, who usually receive a healthy percentage of the monetary damages awarded their clients, began contributing millions of dollars to successful Texas Supreme Court candidates, and judicial precedents began falling. A revamped court issued significant decisions that made it easier for consumers to win large judgments for medical malpractice, faulty products, and other complaints against businesses and their insurers. The new activist, liberal interpretation of the law contrasted sharply with the traditional record of the court.

The business community and defense lawyers accused the new court majority of exceeding its constitutional authority by trying to write its own laws. Some business leaders contended that the court's activism endangered the state's economy by discouraging new businesses from moving to Texas, a fear that was soon to be put to partisan advantage by Republican leaders.

☐ Judicial Impropriety

Controversy over the Texas Supreme Court escalated into a full-blown storm in 1986 when the Judicial Affairs Committee of the Texas House investigated two justices, Democrats C. L. Ray and William Kilgarlin, for alleged improper contact with attorneys practicing before the court. The two justices denied the allegations, made largely by former attorneys on the Supreme Court staff, but never testified before the legislative panel. Both justices had consistently sided with plaintiffs' lawyers and had received considerable campaign support from them, and they contended the investigation was politically motivated and orchestrated by defense lawyers and corporate interests opposed to their judicial activism.

The committee eventually concluded its investigation without recommending any action against the justices. But in June 1987, the State Commission on Judicial Conduct issued public sanctions against both. Ray was reprimanded for seven violations of the Code of Judicial Conduct, including the acceptance of free airplane rides from attorneys practicing before the court and improper communication with lawyers about pending cases. Kilgarlin received a milder admonishment because two of his law clerks had accepted a weekend trip to Las Vegas from a law firm with cases pending before the court. Both justices were cited for soliciting funds from attorneys to help pay for litigation the justices had brought against the House Judicial Affairs Committee and a former briefing attorney who testified against them.

Later in 1987, the Texas judiciary, particularly the Texas Supreme Court, received negative publicity on a national scale when the high court upheld a record $11 billion judgment awarded Pennzoil Company in a dispute with Texaco Inc. Several members of the Texas Supreme Court were even featured on a network television program that questioned whether justice was "for sale" in Texas.

The record judgment awarded to Pennzoil came after a state district court jury in Houston had determined that Texaco had wrongfully interfered in Pennzoil's attempt to acquire Getty Oil Company in 1984. Texaco, which sought protection under federal bankruptcy laws, later reached a settlement with Pennzoil, but it also waged a massive public relations campaign against the Texas judiciary.

In a segment on CBS-TV's program, *60 Minutes*, correspondent Mike Wallace pointed out that plaintiff's attorney Joe Jamail of Houston, who represented Pennzoil, had contributed $10,000 to the original trial judge in the case and thousands of dollars more to Texas Supreme Court justices. The program also generally criticized the elective system that allowed Texas judges to legally accept large campaign contributions from lawyers who practiced before them. The program presented what already had been reported in the Texas media, but after the national exposure, Governor Bill Clements and other Republicans renewed attacks on the activist, Democratic justices. Some Texas newspapers published editorials calling for changes in the judicial selection process, but to no avail.

☐ Campaign Contributions and Republican Gains

Supreme Court Chief Justice John L. Hill, a former attorney general who had narrowly lost a gubernatorial race to Clements in 1978, had been a strong supporter of electing state judges and had spent more than $1 million winning the chief justice's seat in 1984. As did his colleagues on the court, he accepted many campaign contributions from lawyers. But in 1986, Hill announced that the "recent trend toward

11.1

11.2

11.3

11.4

11.5

11.6

11.7

11.8

merit selection
A proposal under which the governor would appoint state judges from lists of potential nominees recommended by committees of experts. Appointed judges would have to run later in retention elections in which voters would simply decide whether a judge should remain in office or be replaced by another gubernatorial appointee.

excessive political contributions in judicial races" had prompted him to change his mind.[15] He now advocated a so-called **merit selection** plan of gubernatorial appointments and periodic retention elections. But the other eight Supreme Court justices—like Hill, all Democrats—still favored the elective system, and the legislature ignored pleas for change.

Hill resigned from the court on January 1, 1988, to return to private law practice and lobby as a private citizen for changing the judicial selection method. His resignation and the midterm resignations of two other Democratic justices before the 1988 elections gave Republicans a golden opportunity to make historic inroads on the high court. The resignations also helped the business community begin to regain control of the court from plaintiffs' attorneys.

Party realignment and midterm judicial appointments by Clements already had increased the number of Republican judges across the state, particularly on district court benches in urban areas. But only one Republican had ever served on the Texas Supreme Court in modern times. Will Garwood was appointed by Clements in 1979 to fill a vacancy on the court but was defeated by Democrat C. L. Ray in the 1980 election.

GOP leaders had already been planning to recruit a Republican slate of candidates for the three Supreme Court seats that normally would have been on the ballot in 1988. Now, six seats were contested, including those held by three new Republican justices appointed by Clements to fill the unexpected vacancies. Even though a full Supreme Court term is six years, the governor's judicial appointees have to run in the next election to keep their seats. Clements appointed Thomas R. Phillips, a state district judge from Houston, to succeed Hill and become the first Republican chief justice since Reconstruction.

The competing legal and financial interests in Texas understood that the six Texas Supreme Court races on the 1988 ballot would help set the philosophy of the court for years to come. Consequently, these were the most expensive court races in Texas history, with the twelve Republican and Democratic nominees raising $10 million in direct campaign contributions. Much of the money was spent on television advertising.

Contributions to the winners averaged $836,347. Phillips, one of three Republican winners, spent $2 million, the most by a winning candidate. The smallest amount spent by a winner was $449,290. Some individual donations to candidates were as large as $65,000.[16] Reformers argued that such large contributions created an appearance of impropriety and eroded public confidence in the judiciary's independence.

But the successes of Republicans and conservative Democrats in the 1988 races probably hindered, more than helped, the cause of reforming the judicial selection process. The business and medical communities, which had considerable success fighting the plaintiffs' lawyers under the existing rules with large campaign contributions of their own, were pleased with the election results. "I'm a happy camper today," said Kim Ross, lobbyist for the Texas Medical Association, whose political action committee had supported two conservative Democratic winners and the three Republican victors.[17] In several key liability cases over the next few years, the Supreme Court began to demonstrate a rediscovered philosophy favoring business defendants over plaintiffs.[18]

Republicans won a fourth seat on the Texas Supreme Court in 1990 and a fifth in 1994, to give the GOP a majority for the first time since Reconstruction. In straight-party voting, Republican challengers in 1994 also unseated nineteen incumbent Democratic district judges in Harris County. Republicans completed their sweep of the high court in 1998.

Phillips, the chief justice since 1988, resigned in midterm in 2004 to accept a temporary appointment as a visiting professor at the South Texas College of Law in Houston. He later reentered private law practice. Phillips believed the court's reputation had been enhanced during his tenure, but, as his predecessor had done on stepping down sixteen years earlier, he criticized the money-driven, partisan election system for judges. He said it "creates great instability in the judiciary and erodes public confidence in the fairness of our decisions."[19]

Wallace B. Jefferson, who succeeded Phillips as chief justice, also has called for replacing partisan judicial elections with appointments and retention elections.[20] But the legislature has refused to change the system.

tort reform
Changes in state law to put limits on personal injury lawsuits and damage judgments entered by the courts.

Legislative Reaction to Judicial Activism

The business community also moved its war against the trial lawyers to the legislature, which in 1987 enacted a so-called **tort reform** package that attempted to put some limits on personal injury lawsuits and damage judgments entered by the courts. A *tort* is a wrongful act over which a lawsuit can be brought. Insurance companies, which had been lobbying nationwide for states to set limits on jury awards in personal injury cases, were major proponents of the legislation. The Texas Civil Justice League, an organization of trade and professional associations, cities, and businesses formed in 1986 to seek similar changes in Texas tort law, joined them. Governor Bill Clements enthusiastically supported the high-stakes campaign for change, but consumer groups and plaintiffs' lawyers, who had been making millions of dollars from the judiciary's new liberalism, opposed it.

Cities, businesses, doctors, and even charitable organizations had been hit with tremendous increases in insurance premiums, which they blamed on greedy trial lawyers and large court awards in malpractice and personal injury lawsuits. Trial lawyers blamed the insurance industry, which, they said, had started raising premiums to recoup losses the companies had suffered in investment income after interest rates fell.

Among other things, the 1987 tort reform laws limited governmental liability, attempted to discourage frivolous lawsuits, and limited the ability of claimants to collect damages for injuries that were largely their own fault. They also set limits on punitive damages, which are designed to punish whoever caused an accident or an injury and often are awarded in addition to an injured party's compensation for actual losses.

Later legislative sessions, including those in 1995, 2003, and 2011, enacted other limits on lawsuits. The 1995 changes, major priorities of then-Governor George W. Bush, imposed even stricter limits on punitive damages and limited the liability of a party who is only partially responsible for an injury. The 2003 legislation, actively sought by Governor Rick Perry and a new Republican majority in the Texas House, set new restrictions on class action lawsuits—which are brought on behalf of large groups of people—and imposed new limits on money that could be awarded for noneconomic damages—such as pain, suffering, or disfigurement—in medical malpractice cases. The 2011 tort law requires some plaintiffs who sue and lose to pay court costs and attorney fees for the defendants they sue. It also provides for expedited court cases for civil lawsuits involving less than $100,000 in damages. A leading proponent for civil justice restrictions in recent years has been Texans for Lawsuit Reform (TLR), a Houston-based business group whose political action committee has given millions of campaign dollars to legislators and legislative candidates.

Winners and Losers

In a study released in 1999, Texas Watch, a consumer advocacy group, said that doctors, hospitals, and other business-related litigants had been big winners before the Texas Supreme Court during the previous four years and that consumers had fared poorly. The group studied more than 625 cases in which the court had written opinions between January 1, 1995, and April 14, 1999. That was a period during which most court members received substantial campaign funding from doctors, insurers, and other business interests. Most of the opinions were issued after the Texas legislature had enacted tort reform laws setting limits on civil lawsuits.

The study determined that physicians and hospitals had won 86 percent of their appeals, most of which involved medical malpractice claims brought by injured patients or their families. Other consistent winners were insurance companies

(73 percent), manufacturers (72 percent), banks (67 percent), utilities (65 percent), and other businesses (68 percent). Insurance policyholders, injured workers, injured patients, and other individual litigants won only 36 percent of the time.[21] "Individuals are the lowest link in the legal food chain that ends in the Texas Supreme Court," said Walt Borges, who directed the study. "The study raises a question about the fairness of the Texas Supreme Court and state law," he added.[22]

CBS-TV's *60 Minutes*, which had turned the national spotlight on plaintiffs' lawyers and their political contributions to Texas judges in 1987, revisited the Texas judiciary in a follow-up program in 1998. Noting that the partisan system of electing judges had remained unchanged, the new *60 Minutes* segment suggested that justice may still be for sale in Texas, but with different people—the business community—now wielding the influence. The Texas legislature in 1995 imposed modest limits on campaign contributions to judges and judicial candidates and restricted the periods during which judges and their challengers could raise funds. A judge, however, still could receive as much as $30,000 from members of the same law firm and as much as $300,000 in total contributions from special interests through political action committees. The 1996 races for the Texas Supreme Court—the first conducted under the new law—demonstrated how weak the new reforms were. Four Republican incumbents still raised a combined $4 million, easily swamping fund-raising efforts by their unsuccessful challengers.

In 2012, Texas Watch, the consumer advocacy group, issued a follow-up report, analyzing the Texas Supreme Court's record from 2000 to 2010. During that period, the report said, consumer-plaintiffs lost in 79 percent of the cases decided by the high court when the defendants were corporations or governmental entities. The report also found that the Supreme Court overturned 74 percent of decisions in which local juries had found in favor of consumers. "The Texas Supreme Court has become a reliable friend to those who seek to escape the consequences of their actions; its justices are the ultimate guardians for the moneyed and powerful who wish to shirk responsibility," the consumer group declared.[23]

□ Minorities' Fight for Representation

As high-stakes battles waged over the Texas Supreme Court's philosophical and political makeup, minorities actively sought more representation in the Texas judiciary. But instead of pouring millions of dollars into judicial races, Hispanics and African Americans filed lawsuits to try to force change through the federal courts.

Throughout Texas history, Hispanics and African Americans have had difficulty winning election to state courts. The high cost of judicial campaigns, polarized voting along ethnic lines in the statewide or countywide races that are required for most judges, and low rates of minority participation in elections have minimized their electoral successes, although that may be starting to change, at least for elections to the highest courts. Another factor limiting minority participation is a proportional shortage of minority attorneys, from whose ranks judges are drawn.

In 1989, a few months before a major lawsuit went to trial over the issue, only 35 of 375 state district judges were Hispanic, and only seven were African American. Only three Hispanics and no African Americans were among the eighty judges on the fourteen intermediate courts of appeals. Although they constituted at least one-third of the Texas population, African Americans and Hispanics held only 11.2 percent of the district judgeships and less than 4 percent of the intermediate appellate seats.[24]

In a lawsuit tried in September 1989 in federal district court in Midland, attorneys for the League of United Latin American Citizens (LULAC) and other minority plaintiffs argued that the countywide system of electing state district judges violated the federal Voting Rights Act by diluting the voting strength of minorities. This case, *League of United Latin American Citizens et al.* v. *Mattox et al.*, took almost five years and two appeals to the U.S. Supreme Court to resolve. Although the case did not change Texas's judicial selection system, a summary of the case and its bumpy journey through the judicial process highlights the political stakes involved in the issue.

In November 1989, U.S. District Judge Lucius Bunton ruled that the countywide system of electing state district judges was illegal in nine of the state's largest counties—Harris, Dallas, Tarrant, Bexar, Travis, Jefferson, Lubbock, Ector, and Midland. Those counties elected 172 district judges, almost half of the state's total, but had only a handful of minorities serving on the district courts. Bunton did not order an immediate remedy but strongly urged the legislature to address the issue in a special session. After the legislature failed to act, the next year, Bunton ordered judges in the nine counties to run for election from districts in nonpartisan elections. But the state won a stay of Bunton's order from the Fifth U.S. Circuit Court of Appeals, and partisan, countywide judicial elections were held as scheduled in 1990.

Ironically, one minority judge was outspoken in his opposition to district elections. State District Judge Felix Salazar of Houston did not seek reelection in 1990, at least in part because he disliked the prospect of having to run from a district rather than countywide. A Democrat, Salazar lived in a predominantly non-Hispanic, white Houston neighborhood and in previous elections had been endorsed by a diversity of groups. He claimed that small districts could work against the interests of minorities because a judge from a conservative Anglo district could feel political pressure to sentence minority criminal defendants more harshly than whites. "The judge will have to espouse the feeling of the community. His district may think that's all right, and it will be hell unseating him," he told the *Houston Chronicle*.[25]

Other opponents of district elections argued that district elections could lead to minority communities putting undue pressure on judges. But Jesse Oliver, a former African American legislator and judge who had been unseated in a countywide race in Dallas, did not agree that judicial districts would distort the administration of justice any more than countywide elections. "For one thing, if the community does exert pressure, then the white community is exerting all the pressure now because they are electing the judges in Dallas County," he said.[26]

After several more legal twists and turns, the Fifth Circuit Court rejected an attempt to settle the lawsuit in favor of district elections, holding in August 1993 that the "evidence of any dilution of minority voting power [in countywide judicial elections] is marginal at best."[27] The Fifth Circuit said partisan affiliation was a more significant factor than ethnicity in judicial elections. Then, in January 1994, the U.S. Supreme Court brought the lawsuit to an end by upholding the Fifth Circuit's opinion.

The U.S. Supreme Court's decision placed the issue of judicial selection in the hands of the Texas legislature, which has left the countywide elective system unchanged. Despite this, minority representation on the courts has slowly increased. In 1989, prior to the litigation, Hispanics held only 9 percent of state district judgeships, and African Americans held 2 percent. By 2011, according to the most complete data available, about 14 percent of the state judges at the county court level and higher were Hispanic and about 5 percent were African American.[28]

☐ Searching for Solutions

The debates and lawsuits over judicial elections and representation in Texas emphasize the significant role of the courts in policymaking as well as day-to-day litigation. The composition of the courts makes a difference. Although some may argue that the role of a judge is simply to apply the law to the facts and issues of a specific case, judges bring to the courts their own values, philosophical views, and life experiences, and these factors serve to filter their interpretations of the law—and determine the shape of justice for millions of people.

There is no one simple solution to all the problems and inequities in the judicial system. Stricter limits on the amount of campaign funds that judges and judicial candidates could raise from lawyers and other special interests, for example, could reduce

retention elections
Elections in which judges run on their own records rather than against other candidates. Voters cast their ballots on the question of whether the incumbent judge should stay in office.

the appearance of influence peddling in the judiciary and temper the high-stakes war between the trial lawyers and the business community for philosophical control of the courts. Campaign finance reform also could help build or restore public confidence in the impartiality of the judiciary. Such reform, however, may not improve opportunities for more minorities to win election to the bench. Nor would it shorten the long election ballots that discourage Texans from casting informed votes in judicial races.

The same shortcomings could be anticipated with nonpartisan judicial elections or a merit selection system—two frequently mentioned alternatives to Texas's system of partisan judicial elections. In nonpartisan elections, judges and judicial candidates would not run under Democratic, Republican, or other party labels. This would guard against partisan bickering on the multimember appellate courts and eliminate the possibility that a poorly qualified candidate could be swept into office by one-party, straight ticket voting.

Under the merit selection plan (sometimes referred to as the "Missouri Plan"), the governor would appoint judges from lists of nominees recommended by nominating committees. The appointed judges would have to run later in **retention elections** to keep their seats, but they would not have opponents on the ballot. Voters would simply decide whether a judge should remain in office or be removed—and replaced by another gubernatorial appointee.

Texas was one of only seven states in 2012 with a partisan election system for judges (see Figure 11–3). Thirteen states had nonpartisan judicial elections, and about half used some form of judicial nominating commission, usually in conjunction with a gubernatorial appointment. Only sixteen states, however, combined the use of nominating commissions with retention elections, as provided in the Missouri Plan. Each alternative has its advantages, but none would necessarily eliminate undue political influences on the judiciary.[29]

Under a merit selection system, interest groups still could apply pressure on the governor and the members of the committees making recommendations for

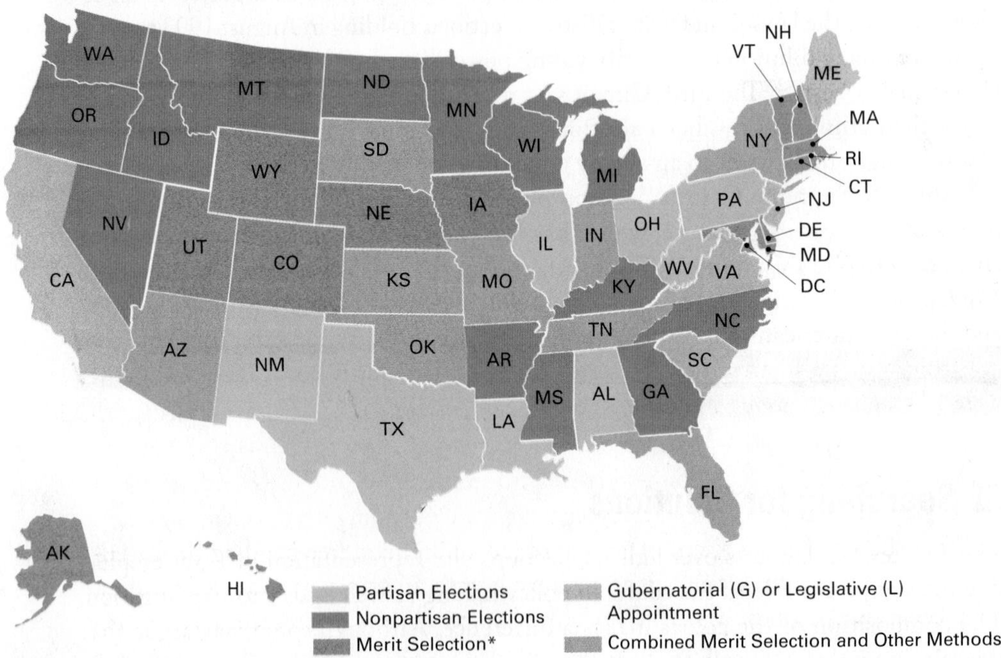

*The following ten states use merit plans only to fill midterm vacancies on some or all levels of court: Alabama,Georgia,Idaho,Kentucky, Minnesota,Montana,Nevada,New Mexico,North Dakota,and West Virginia.

FIGURE 11–3 SELECTION PROCESS FOR APPELLATE JUDGES IN THE FIFTY STATES

There is no uniformity in the manner states select judges. In an effort to reduce the impact of politics and campaign contributions, many states have moved toward nonpartisan elections or gubernatorial appointments with retention elections. With the exception of municipal judges, Texas selects judges by partisan election. This map shows how states select their appellate judges.

Source: Data from the American Judicature Society, "Judicial Selection in the States: Appellate and General Jurisdiction Courts." Updated 2010.

appointments. Although a merit selection plan could be written to require the nominating panels to make ethnically diverse recommendations to the governor, that would not answer the question of how to structure the retention elections. Minority appointees still could be at a disadvantage in retention elections if they had to run countywide, rather than in smaller geographic districts. Despite their popularity among minorities, district elections for judges still are viewed by many decision makers as a form of **ward politics** that may be appropriate or desirable for legislative seats but not for judges. Judges, they argue, do not represent a particular constituency.

ward politics
Term, often with negative connotations, that refers to partisan politics linked to political favoritism.

Miranda ruling
A far-reaching decision of the U.S. Supreme Court that requires law enforcement officers to warn a criminal suspect of his or her right to remain silent and have an attorney present during questioning.

nolo contendere
A plea of no contest to a criminal charge.

Crime and Punishment

11.7 List the legal and constitutional rights of suspects and the different classes of crimes and punishments in the Texas penal code.

Much of the Texas judiciary's time is spent deciding the guilt or innocence of individuals accused of crimes and meting out punishment to those convicted. Criminal justice is a multistep process designed to reduce the risk of innocent people being punished for crimes they did not commit. Even though judges and other criminal justice officials operate under numerous constitutional restrictions, mistakes sometimes occur.

☐ Rights of Suspects

Under both the U.S. Constitution and the Texas Constitution, a person charged with a crime is presumed innocent until the state can prove guilt beyond a reasonable doubt to a judge or a jury. The state also has the burden to prosecute fairly and to follow principles of procedural due process outlined in constitutional and statutory law and interpreted by the courts. Even persons charged with the most heinous crimes retain these fundamental rights. Although a public outcry about "coddling" criminals often erupts, the process is designed to protect an individual from governmental abuses and to lessen the chance that an innocent person will be wrongly convicted of a crime.

In Texas, as well as in other states, these rights have sometimes been violated. Over the years, however, the federal courts, in particular, have strengthened their enforcement. Through a case-by-case process, the U.S. Supreme Court has applied the Bill of Rights to the states by way of the "due process of law" and the "equal protection of law" clauses of the Fourteenth Amendment to the U.S. Constitution. The failure of police or prosecutors to comply with specific procedures for handling a person accused of a crime may result in charges against an individual being dropped or a conviction reversed on appeal.

Arrested suspects must be taken before a magistrate—usually a justice of the peace or a municipal court judge—to be formally informed of the offense or offenses with which they are charged and told their legal rights. Depending on the charges, a bond (bail) may be set to allow them to get out of jail and remain free pending their trials. They have the right to remain silent, to consult with an attorney, and have an attorney present during questioning by law enforcement officers or prosecutors and to be warned that any statement they make can be used against them in a trial. Defendants who cannot afford to hire a lawyer must be provided with court-appointed attorneys at taxpayer expense. The U.S. Supreme Court extended many of these protections to the states in the landmark **Miranda ruling** in 1966.

All criminal defendants have the right to a trial by jury but—except in capital murder cases—may waive a jury trial and have their cases decided by a judge. Defendants may plead guilty, not guilty, or **nolo contendere** (no contest). Prosecutors and defense attorneys settle many cases through plea bargaining, a process described

11.1

11.2

11.3

11.4

11.5

11.6

11.7

11.8

capital murder
Murder committed under certain circumstances for which the death penalty or life in prison must be imposed.

earlier in this chapter. The trial judge does not have to accept the plea bargain but usually does. When defendants choose to have their guilt or innocence determined by a judge, the judge also determines the punishment, if the defendant is convicted. A jury can return a guilty verdict only if all jurors agree that the defendant is guilty beyond a reasonable doubt. If the jury cannot reach a unanimous verdict—even after lengthy negotiations and prodding from the judge—the judge must declare a mistrial. In that case, the prosecution has to seek a new trial with another jury or drop the charges. In a jury trial, a defendant may choose to have the punishment set by the jury. If not, the judge determines the punishment.

In 1991, the Texas Court of Criminal Appeals took the major step of ordering, for the first time, an official definition of "reasonable doubt" that was to be submitted to every jury deciding a criminal case. According to the definition, evidence against a criminal defendant must be so convincing that jurors would be willing to rely upon it "without hesitation" in the most important events in their own lives.[30] Reflecting a change in philosophy, however, a more conservative Court of Criminal Appeals eliminated that definition in 2000, to the dismay of some criminal defense lawyers. "We find the better practice is to give no definition of reasonable doubt at all to the jury," said the new opinion written by Judge Mike Keasler.[31]

☐ Punishment of Criminals

Jury trials are required in **capital murder** cases, which are punishable by death or life in prison without parole. Executions in Texas used to be carried out by electrocution at the state prison unit in downtown Huntsville. Some 361 individuals were executed in Texas from 1924 to 1964, when executions were suspended because of legal challenges. In 1972, the U.S. Supreme Court halted executions in all the states by striking down all the death penalty laws then on the books as unconstitutional. The high court held that capital punishment, as then practiced, violated the constitutional prohibition against cruel and unusual punishment because it could be applied in a discriminatory fashion. Not only could virtually any act of murder be punished by death under the old Texas law, but so could rape and certain other crimes.

In 1973, the Texas legislature rewrote the death penalty statute to try to meet the Supreme Court's standards by defining capital crimes as murder committed under specific circumstances. The list was expanded later and now includes the murder of a law enforcement officer or firefighter who is on duty, murder committed during the course of certain other major crimes, murder for hire, murder of more than one person, murder of a prison guard or employee, murder committed while escaping or attempting to escape from a penal institution, or murder of a child younger than six.

A jury that has found a person guilty of capital murder must answer certain questions about the defendant before choosing between death or life imprisonment, the only punishments available. Jurors must consider whether a convicted murderer will be a continuing danger to society as well as mitigating circumstances, including evidence of mental retardation, before deciding punishment.[32]

The first execution under the 1973 Texas law was carried out in 1982. By then, the legislature, acting in 1977, had changed the method of execution from the electric chair to the intravenous injection of a lethal substance. By 2012, more than 470 men and three women had been executed in Texas by lethal injection. Karla Faye Tucker, the first woman executed in Texas since the Civil War, was put to death in 1998 for killing two people with a pickax almost fifteen years prior. The second woman was executed in early 2000 for the murder of her husband and the third in 2005 for the murder of her husband and two children.

After considerable controversy in Texas and other states, the U.S. Supreme Court in June 2002 banned the execution of mentally retarded convicts. Death penalty opponents had argued that before the high court ruling that Texas had executed at least six inmates who were demonstrably retarded.

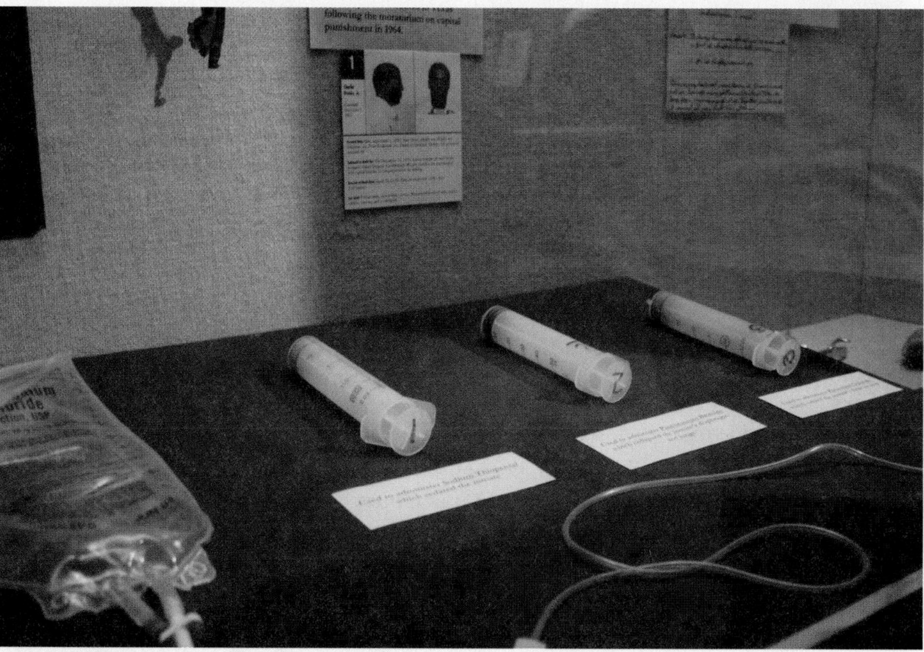

TOOLS OF LETHAL INJECTION.

Texas uses lethal injections for executions. Condemned prisoners are strapped to a gurney, two needles are inserted, and the inmate is injected with three solutions that produce an anesthetic overdose and respiratory and cardiac arrest.

In 2008, the nation's high court, deciding two appeals from Kentucky, ruled that the chemicals used in lethal injections did not amount to cruel and unusual punishment and did not violate the U.S. Constitution. Death penalty opponents had argued that the chemicals might cause the condemned to feel intense pain. Texas uses the same chemicals as Kentucky (see *Talking Texas: Slamming the Courthouse Door on a Last-Gasp Appeal*).

Talking ★ TEXAS

Slamming the Courthouse Door on a Last-Gasp Appeal

Despite the controversy it provokes, the death penalty still has strong political support in Texas, which has executed more than 470 convicts by lethal injection—more than all other states combined—since 1982. Few, if any, public officials in Texas are stronger supporters of the death penalty than is Sharon Keller, presiding judge of the Texas Court of Criminal Appeals, which upholds the vast majority of the death sentences it reviews. However, in the view of many lawyers and other Texans as well, Keller went too far when she cut off a condemned inmate's attempt to file a last-gasp appeal only a few hours before he was executed.

Lawyers for Michael Richard, a convicted murderer and rapist, attempted to halt his execution by lethal injection on September 25, 2007, following the U.S. Supreme Court's decision earlier that day to accept for review two Kentucky cases challenging the constitutionality of chemicals used for lethal injection. Death penalty opponents had argued that the execution method might amount to cruel and unusual punishment, prohibited by the U.S. Constitution, because the condemned might feel intense pain as the mixture of drugs is administered. Texas uses the same chemicals as Kentucky.

Richard's attorneys tried to get a stay of execution for their client until the nation's high court decided the Kentucky cases, but computer problems at one lawyer's office slowed the preparation of their appeal. When they asked the Court of Criminal Appeals for more time, Keller ordered the court clerk's office to close at the normal time, 5 p.m. Richard's lawyers did not have time to file his appeal, and he was executed later that evening.

After the controversy over Keller's decision erupted during subsequent days, three other judges on the nine-member court said they had been available for work on the evening of Richard's execution and could have handled his appeal had they known about it. Twenty lawyers from across Texas, including many prominent names, later filed a formal complaint against Keller with the State Commission on Judicial Conduct. The complaint accused the judge of violating the constitutional due process of a condemned man, stating that "Judge Keller's actions denied Michael Richard two constitutional rights, access to the courts and due process, which led to his execution."

Keller blamed Richard's lawyers. "I think the question ought to be why didn't they file something on time. They had all day," she said.[a] A few weeks later, the Court of Criminal Appeals announced it would accept emergency email filings of appeals in death penalty cases in an effort to avoid something like the Richard's case from occurring again.

In 2008, the State Commission on Judicial Conduct filed misconduct charges against Keller over her handling of the Richard's case. It eventually issued a "public warning" against the judge, but a special court of review vacated the sanction in 2010, ruling that the option was not available to the commission. The commission, the court said, instead could have issued a "public censure" or recommended Keller's removal from office. The commission did neither. Ultimately, after completing its review of the lethal chemicals used in executions, the U.S. Supreme Court upheld their constitutionality.

CRITICAL THINKING QUESTIONS

1. **Should the State Commission on Judicial Conduct have recommended Presiding Judge Keller's removal from office? Why or why not?**
2. **Judge Keller and several other members of the Texas Court of Criminal Appeals are former prosecutors. Can former prosecutors be fair in deciding appeals of death row inmates? Why or why not?**

[a]R. G. Ratcliffe and Polly Ross Hughes, "Questions Raised on Sept. 25 Execution—Lawyers Say Appellate Judge Violated Rights of Condemned Man," *Houston Chronicle,* October 11, 2007, page 1A; and R. G. Ratcliffe, "Court Says It Will Take e-filings in Death Cases," *Houston Chronicle,* November 7, 2007, page 1A.

felony
A criminal offense that can be punished by imprisonment and/or a fine. This is a more serious offense than a misdemeanor.

misdemeanor
A minor criminal offense punishable by a fine or a short sentence in the county jail.

probation
A procedure under which a convicted criminal is not sent to prison if he or she meets certain conditions, such as restrictions on travel and with whom he or she associates.

parole
The early release of an inmate from prison, subject to certain conditions.

After capital murder, the most serious criminal offense is a first-degree **felony** (e.g., aggravated sexual assault or murder), punishable by a prison sentence of five to ninety-nine years or life. Second-degree felonies, such as burglary of someone's home and bribery, are punishable by two to twenty years in prison. Third-degree felonies, including intentional bodily injury to a child and theft of trade secrets, are punishable by two to ten years in prison. State jail felonies, which include many property crimes such as burglary of an office building and drug offenses, are punishable by up to two years in a state-run jail or time in a community corrections program, each of which is supposed to emphasize rehabilitation as well as punishment.

The most minor crimes are classified as Class A, B, or C **misdemeanors**. Crimes such as public lewdness and harboring a runaway child are examples of Class A misdemeanors and are punishable by a maximum $4,000 fine and one year in a county jail. The unauthorized use of television cable decoding equipment and falsely claiming to be a police officer are examples of Class B misdemeanors and carry a maximum sentence of 180 days in a county jail and a $2,000 fine. Class C misdemeanors include illegal gambling and the issuing of bad checks. They are punishable by a maximum $500 fine.

People convicted of crimes can be sentenced to **probation** (also called community supervision). They are not sent to prison but must meet certain conditions, such as restrictions on where they travel and with whom they associate. Except for those under the death penalty and some capital murderers serving life sentences, convicted felons sentenced to prison can become eligible for **parole**—early release under supervisory restrictions—after serving a portion of their sentences. Capital murderers sentenced to life in prison before a significant change in state law in 2005 can be considered for parole after serving forty years. Those sentenced after the 2005 law, which imposed life without parole for capital murderers who are not sentenced to death, cannot be paroled. The Board of Pardons and Paroles, which is appointed by the governor, makes all parole decisions.

☐ The Politics of Criminal Justice

The Texas Court of Criminal Appeals must try to balance the constitutional rights of convicts against the public welfare—a role that puts the court at the center of major philosophical and political battles. The combatants on one side of the debate are the prosecutors—the elected district and county attorneys—who do not like to see the convictions they have won reversed, in part because too many reversals could cost them reelection. Judges of the trial courts, who periodically face the voters, also are sensitive to reversals. So are the police and sheriff's departments that arrest the defendants and provide the evidence on which criminal convictions are based (see *Talking Texas: Almost Twenty-five Lost Years for a Crime He Didn't Commit*).

On the other side of the debate are defense attorneys, who have an obligation to protect the rights and interests of their clients and who in their appeals often attack procedures used by police, prosecutors, and trial judges. Also on this side are civil libertarians, who insist that a criminal defendant's every right—even the most technical—be protected, and minority groups, which have challenged the conduct of trials in which minorities have been excluded from juries weighing the fate of minority defendants.

Throughout much of its early history, the Texas Court of Criminal Appeals was accused of excessive concern with legal technicalities that benefited convicted criminals.[33] The court reversed 42 percent of the cases appealed to it during the first quarter of the twentieth century, when Texas and many other states had a harsh system of criminal justice that often reflected class and racial bias. By 1966, the reversal rate had

Talking ★ TEXAS

Almost Twenty-five Lost Years for a Crime He Didn't Commit

For Michael Morton, it was horrible enough going through the experience of his wife, Christine, being bludgeoned to death in their Georgetown home in 1986 while he was away. But that agony was compounded when he was charged with her murder, convicted, and sentenced to life in prison for a crime he did not commit. He served almost twenty-five years behind bars before attorneys, including members of the New York–based Innocence Project, won a protracted legal fight to obtain DNA testing on a blood-stained bandanna, which had been found near the crime scene. DNA tests pointed to another man as the likely suspect, and Morton was released in 2011.

But his story was not over. The attorneys who won his freedom then began an investigation to determine if prosecutors had deliberately withheld evidence from his defense lawyers at the time of his trial that could have exonerated him. Prosecutors in Texas are required to provide defendants with any evidence that could be used to support their innocence. DNA testing was not available at the time Morton's wife was murdered, but his attorneys said other evidence was, and it never was disclosed to his defense team. The undisclosed evidence, they said, included a transcript of a taped interview in which Christine Morton's mother had told a sheriff's investigator that the Morton's three-year-old son apparently witnessed the attack on his mother and said his father was not home when it happened. Other documents that had been withheld from Michael Morton's defense team at the time of his trial indicated that his wife's credit card had been used, and a check made out to her was cashed soon after she was killed.

Morton was 57 when he won his freedom, and his son was grown. To make the miscarriage of justice even worse, the same suspect implicated in Christine Morton's death also was implicated in the murder of another woman, Debra Masters Baker, who was bludgeoned to death in her bed two years later, about twelve miles away in a central Austin neighborhood, while Michael Morton was in prison.

Ken Anderson, the district attorney who prosecuted Morton, was a state district judge when Morton was released from prison. He issued a public apology to Morton but denied any misconduct in prosecuting the case against him. Nevertheless, state District Judge Sid Harle of San Antonio, who had been assigned to review the Morton case, recommended that a court of inquiry be convened to investigate allegations of possible prosecutorial misconduct against Anderson. Texas Supreme Court Chief Justice Wallace Jefferson agreed and appointed state District Judge Louis Sturns of Fort Worth to lead the court of inquiry.[a]

CRITICAL THINKING QUESTIONS

1. How often do you think innocent people get sentenced to prison in Texas? What additional safeguards can Texas take to keep this from occurring?
2. Is there any way for society to adequately compensate an innocent person who has spent almost twenty-five years behind bars? Why or why not?

[a]Brandi Grissom, "Ft. Worth Judge to Lead Ken Anderson Court of Inquiry," *The Texas Tribune*, February 16, 2012.

dropped to 3 percent, but changes in the court's makeup and changes in political attitudes produced fluctuations in that record in subsequent years.

The court signaled a shift toward a conservative philosophy after the 1994 elections of Judges Sharon Keller and Steve Mansfield increased the number of Republicans on the court to three. During the first thirteen months the new judges were in office, the court ordered the reinstatement of two death sentences it had reversed before Keller's and Mansfield's arrival.

The Republican sweep of all three court seats on the 1996 ballot solidified the court's conservatism. A 6–3 Democratic majority became a 6–3 Republican majority, the first GOP majority on the court since Reconstruction. Republicans increased their majority to 7–2 in 1997, when longtime Presiding Judge Mike McCormick, one of the court's most conservative members, switched from the Democratic to the Republican Party. The Republican takeover of the court was completed in 1998, when Democrats lost their last two seats on the panel. McCormick did not seek reelection in 2000 and was replaced as presiding judge by Sharon Keller, a former prosecutor.

After the GOP takeover, the Court of Criminal Appeals quickly began compiling a strong, pro-prosecutorial record, particularly in death penalty cases. The court upheld a number of death sentences that later were overturned by federal courts. In one case, it affirmed a capital conviction even though the defendant's attorney had slept through part of his trial. In another case, it upheld a death sentence despite the fact that a prosecution witness had argued improperly that the defendant was a future danger to society, partly because he was Hispanic. That ruling prompted then–Texas Attorney General John Cornyn, a Republican and strong law-and-order advocate, to admit to the U.S. Supreme Court that the prosecution had committed reversible error in the case. Such rulings led defense lawyers and civil libertarians to heap much criticism upon the court. "They're so far gone they're barely even a court anymore," lawyer Jeff Blackburn of Amarillo said in a 2003 interview with the *Houston Chronicle*.[34]

Increased Policy Role of the State Courts

11.8 Provide examples of the increased policy role of the state courts.

The federal judiciary has traditionally had more influence than the state courts in molding public policy. Over the years, it has been at the center of political debate over the proper role of the judiciary in the policymaking process. This debate, often framed in terms of judicial activism versus judicial restraint, attempts to address the question of where judicial interpretation of the law and the Constitution ends and legislating from the bench begins. It is a question often answered only in terms of subjective, political philosophy. Much of the Texas Supreme Court's time is spent refereeing civil disputes among individuals and businesses, rather than far-reaching policy issues. In recent years, however, this court has increasingly played an active role in shaping broader public policies and addressing significant constitutional issues.

☐ The Courts and Education

In one of its most significant and best-known rulings, the Texas Supreme Court, in the Edgewood school finance case in 1989, unanimously ordered major, basic changes in the financing of public education to provide more equity between rich and poor school districts. Poor districts brought the lawsuit against the state after years of legislative inaction against a property tax–based finance system that had produced huge disparities in local resources and the quality of local schools.

The unanimous opinion, written by then-Justice Oscar Mauzy, a Democrat, held that the school finance law then on the books violated a constitutional requirement for an efficient education system. The ruling was the product of considerable compromise among the nine justices, but from the beginning, compliance did not come easily. Subsequent litigation has continued periodically to this day.

A 1990 school finance law failed to meet the court's standards. So the court issued another order in 1991 and a third order in 1992, after the legislature had again come up short. The legislature responded with still another school finance law in 1993. This "Robin Hood" law, as it was dubbed, gave wealthier school districts several options for sharing revenue with poor districts, and both rich and poor districts challenged the law. The rich districts objected to sharing their property wealth; the poor districts argued that the new law was inadequately funded and did not sufficiently reduce the funding gap between rich and poor districts. The Texas Supreme Court upheld the law in a 5–4 decision in January 1995. By that time, a majority of the court's members were Republicans. In the majority opinion, Justice John Cornyn, a Republican, wrote:

> Children who live in property-poor districts and children who live in property-rich districts now have substantially equal access to the funds necessary for a general diffusion of knowledge. . . . It is apparent from the court's [previous] opinions that we have recognized that an efficient system does not require equality of access to revenue at all levels.[35]

By 2003, the school finance law came under attack again, this time from school districts contending that the share-the-wealth requirement and inadequate state aid were forcing many districts to raise local school maintenance tax rates to the maximum $1.50 per $100 valuation. They argued that this fee amounted to an unconstitutional statewide property tax. In the fall of 2005, the Texas Supreme Court, in a subsequent decision, agreed. This time, the court gave the state until June 1, 2006, to correct the problem, which the legislature did in a special session that spring. Lawmakers enacted Governor Rick Perry's plan to cut school maintenance tax rates by as much as one-third over the next two years. Lawmakers replaced part, but not all, of the lost revenue with money from a budgetary surplus, an expanded business tax, a $1 per pack increase in the cigarette tax, and tightened collections of sales taxes on used cars.

However, the school finance fight was still far from over. After the legislature made deep cuts in the public school budget in 2011 to help bridge a revenue shortfall without raising state taxes, several hundred school districts and other plaintiffs went back to court. They filed four new lawsuits against the state, contending again that the school finance system was inequitable and inadequate.

In 1992, a state district judge in Brownsville ruled that the state's system of funding higher education also was unconstitutional because it shortchanged Hispanics in South Texas. However, the Texas Supreme Court reversed that decision and upheld the higher education system.[36]

In another education case with major implications, the Texas Supreme Court in 1994 upheld the right of Texas parents to educate their own children. Ending a ten-year legal battle, the court overturned a Texas Education Agency ruling that home schools were illegal. The court held that a home school was legitimate if parents used books, workbooks, or other written materials and met "basic education goals" by teaching basic subjects.[37]

☐ The Courts and Water Policy

In February 2012, the Texas Supreme Court, in a major water rights case, ruled in favor of two farmers who had challenged governmental restrictions on how much water they could pump from a well on their own land. In a major change from existing regulatory practice, the court held that the owner of the property above the water source

11.1

11.2

11.3

11.4

11.5

11.6

11.7

11.8

also owns that groundwater. The ruling was viewed as a major victory for landowners. But environmentalists greeted it with concern; they feared the ruling would curtail state water conservation efforts at a time when the state's water resources were rapidly being depleted in the face of continued population growth.[38]

The Courts and Abortion Rights

In 1998, dealing with another controversial issue, the Texas Supreme Court upheld $1.2 million in damages against antiabortion protesters who had staged massive demonstrations at Houston abortion clinics during the 1992 Republican National Convention. Some clinics had been vandalized and patients harassed. The high court also upheld most of the restrictions a lower court had set on demonstrations near the clinics and the homes of several doctors who performed abortions. The court said it was trying to balance free speech rights with the rights of the clinics to conduct business, the rights of women to have access to pregnancy counseling and abortion services, and privacy rights of physicians. The court prohibited demonstrators from blocking access to clinics, intimidating patients, and engaging in other forms of aggressive behavior.[39] In a case from Florida, the U.S. Supreme Court had ruled in 1994 that judges could limit demonstrations near abortion clinics but that restrictions on protestors had to be strictly limited.[40]

The Texas Supreme Court became embroiled in the abortion issue again in 2000 after a state law went into effect requiring parents to be notified by the doctors before their minor daughters could have abortions. The law included a "judicial bypass" provision, giving a young woman who did not want her parents to be told an opportunity to convince a judge that she was mature and well informed enough to make an abortion decision by herself or that notifying her parents would be harmful. Acting on several early cases, the Texas Supreme Court set guidelines for district judges to follow in making bypass decisions.

In another abortion case, decided in 2002, the Texas Supreme Court held that the state's refusal to pay for medically necessary abortions for poor women did not violate the Texas Constitution. The court ruled that the restriction on funding abortions for women on Medicaid did not discriminate by gender and advanced a legitimate governmental interest of favoring childbirth over abortion.[41]

Review the Chapter

Texas Courts in the Federal Framework

11.1 Explain how the Texas judicial system fits within the constitutional framework of federalism, p. 318.

Many Texans will have some experience with a state court during their lifetimes, but relatively few will find themselves in federal court. Federal courts, nevertheless, play an important role in Texas. Ruling on constitutional guarantees in the Bill of Rights and requirements in federal law, they make decisions affecting state policies. They adjudicate disputes over mandates imposed by the federal government on state and local governments, and decisions in some lawsuits in state court can be appealed to federal court.

The Structure of the Texas Court System

11.2 Outline the structure of the Texas court system, focusing on the jurisdiction of each level and qualifications of judges serving on the courts, p. 319.

Texas has a confusing array of courts, many with overlapping jurisdictions and varying qualifications for judges. It is one of only two states with a bifurcated court system at the highest appellate level. The Texas Supreme Court is the court of last resort in civil cases, and the Texas Court of Criminal Appeals in criminal cases. District courts have general unlimited jurisdiction in both civil and criminal cases. There are 254 constitutional county courts that have limited jurisdiction, but the judges of these courts serve primarily in an administrative capacity. Statutory county courts, including probate courts, have limited jurisdiction in civil and criminal matters. Justices of the peace and municipal courts have very limited jurisdiction in civil or criminal matters, handling large numbers of traffic violations and other misdemeanors. All state judges, except those on municipal court benches, are elected in partisan elections. In practice, however, Texas has a mixed judicial selection system because many judges quit or retire in midterm, allowing the governor or a county commissioners' court to appoint their successors. Justices of the peace and constitutional county judges are not required to have law degrees, but all other judges have to be lawyers.

Participants in the Judicial System

11.3 Describe the roles of the different participants in the Texas court system, p. 324.

The main participants in the court system are judges at the trial and appellate levels. Lawyers representing plaintiffs and defendants in civil lawsuits and district and county attorneys representing the state in criminal proceedings (and criminal defense lawyers representing individuals accused of crimes) also are integral participants. County and district clerks are custodians of court records. Law-enforcement officers serve as bailiffs, protecting judges and other courtroom participants and helping maintain order. Private citizens play a crucial role in the judicial process by serving on juries. A grand jury determines if there is just cause for a criminal proceeding against a defendant, based on evidence presented by prosecutors. A petit (or trial) jury hears evidence in both civil and criminal trials and issues verdicts. In some cases, it also sets punishment in criminal cases and recommends damage awards in civil lawsuits.

Judicial Procedures and Decision Making

11.4 Summarize the procedures required for cases to move to the Texas Supreme Court and the Texas Court of Criminal Appeals, p. 329.

The state code describes in detail civil and criminal procedures to be used in the state courts. Trials move through the presentation of opening arguments by the opposing attorneys, examination and cross-examination of witnesses, presentation of evidence, rebuttal, and summation. If a party in the case is dissatisfied with the verdict of the judge or a jury, the case can be appealed to a higher court.

No juries are used in the appellate courts. Appellate court judges review the decisions and procedures of trial courts for conformity to constitutional and statutory requirements. Most civil and criminal cases are first appealed to an intermediate court of appeals. The next and final state level of appeal for civil cases is the Texas Supreme Court, and the next and final state level of appeal for criminal cases is the Texas Court of Criminal Appeals. Death penalty cases are appealed directly from district court to the Court of Criminal Appeals. In all other cases, both civil and criminal, the two highest courts have discretion over whether to accept appeals. Most appeals are not accepted at this level.

Changing the Face of the Judiciary

11.5 Trace the growth of minority representation in the Texas judiciary, p. 330.

Most Texas judges are white males. Although they have made progress in recent years, in part through midterm gubernatorial appointments, women and minorities are still underrepresented on most courts. Five women make up a majority of the nine-member Texas Court of Criminal

Appeals. Two women now serve on the nine-member Texas Supreme Court, which also includes two African American and two Hispanic justices. Countywide election systems for lower court judges, however, make it difficult for many minority candidates to win election. In the late 1980s, minority plaintiffs filed a federal lawsuit to try to force single-member district elections for local judges but lost before the U.S. Supreme Court.

Judicial Controversies and the Search for Solutions

11.6 Characterize the controversies centering on the state's courts and their impact on public perceptions of the courts, p. 332.

Large campaign contributions to judges from lawyers and other parties with interests before the courts have helped create a cloud over the Texas judiciary. Much of this has been driven by a long-running war for control of the Texas Supreme Court between plaintiff's attorneys, on one side, and businesses, doctors, and insurance companies on the other. The legislature has imposed limited restrictions on political contributions to judges, but it has refused to change the money-driven, partisan election system. Over the years, media reports have raised the question of whether justice in Texas is "for sale." In addition, despite recent inroads, minorities remain underrepresented in the Texas judiciary as a whole. Finally, urban Texas counties have dozens of judicial offices, and most voters know little about the candidates. This has resulted in the election of some underqualified candidates, in part because of straight ticket, partisan voting.

Crime and Punishment

11.7 List the legal and constitutional rights of suspects and the different classes of crimes and punishments in the Texas penal code, p. 339.

The state's Bill of Rights and the federal Bill of Rights spell out the rights of those accused of crimes. Persons are entitled to be informed of their rights when arrested. They are entitled to be arraigned before a magistrate following well-defined rules. They are entitled to an attorney, even when they cannot afford one. They have the right to a jury trial, but many choose to waive this right. Many defendants negotiate lower sentences through plea bargains with prosecutors. A guilty jury verdict in a criminal case has to be unanimous. The state's schedule of criminal offenses ranges from misdemeanors—punishable by fines and short jail sentences—through felonies, for which long prison sentences can be imposed. The most serious offense is capital murder, punishable by death or life in prison without parole.

Increased Policy Role of the State Courts

11.8 Provide examples of the increased policy role of the state courts, p. 344.

The federal judiciary traditionally has had more influence than the state courts in molding public policy. But in recent years the Texas Supreme Court has increasingly played an active role in addressing significant constitutional issues, such as school funding, water policy, and abortion.

Learn the Terms

Study and **Review** the Flashcards

Penal Code, p. 318
civil lawsuits, p. 319
original jurisdiction, p. 319
appellate jurisdiction, p. 319
bifurcated court system, p. 319
commissioners court, p. 319
municipal courts, p. 321
justice of the peace courts, p. 321
constitutional county court, p. 322
statutory county court, p. 322
district court, p. 322
plea bargain, p. 323
courts of appeals, p. 323
Texas Supreme Court, p. 323
Texas Court of Criminal Appeals, p. 324
grand jury, p. 327
prosecution, p. 327
indictment, p. 327
information, p. 327
petit jury, p. 327
veniremen, p. 328
petitions for review, p. 329
writs of mandamus, p. 329
petition for discretionary review, p. 329
merit selection, p. 334
tort reform, p. 335
retention elections, p. 338
ward politics, p. 339
Miranda ruling, p. 339
nolo contendere, p. 339
capital murder, p. 340
felony, p. 342
misdemeanor, p. 342
probation, p. 342
parole, p. 342

Test Yourself

Study and **Review** the Practice Tests

1. What percentage of litigation is based on state or local laws and ordinances, rather than federal law?

a. 95 percent
b. 80 percent
c. 50 percent
d. 35 percent
e. 10 percent

2. The Texas Supreme Court

a. has jurisdiction only in criminal cases.
b. has jurisdiction only in civil cases.
c. has jurisdiction in both criminal and civil cases.
d. has original jurisdiction, but not appellate jurisdiction.
e. hears appeals from the Texas Court of Criminal Appeals.

3. Most state judges are

a. elected to lifetime terms in nonpartisan elections.
b. appointed to lifetime terms by the governor, with the advice and consent of the Senate.
c. appointed to limited terms by the governor, with the advice and consent of the Senate.
d. elected to limited terms in partisan elections.
e. selected by a state lottery of all qualified lawyers.

4. Which type of court does not require its judges to be lawyers?

a. Texas Supreme Court
b. Texas Court of Criminal Appeals
c. district courts
d. intermediate courts of appeals
e. county courts

5. Plea bargains are used to

a. appeal convictions in municipal court cases to the district court.
b. dispute the results of a field sobriety check.
c. clear a crowded district court docket by negotiating guilty pleas.
d. negotiate whether a dispute goes to a criminal court or a civil court.
e. appeal a decision in the Texas Supreme Court to the U.S. Supreme Court.

6. Which of the following statements best reflects the description of Texas judges as of 2012?

a. Despite partisan realignment in favor of Republicans, Democrats still hold a majority on the state's two highest courts.
b. Demographic changes in Texas have resulted in white males comprising a minority of Texas judges.
c. Republicans control every seat on the state's two highest courts.
d. Republicans control a majority on the Texas Supreme Court, but Democrats control a majority on the Texas Court of Criminal Appeals.
e. Women and ethnic groups are represented in the Texas court system in numbers proportional to their numbers in the population as a whole.

7. Which of the following is one difference between a grand jury and a petit jury?

a. Grand juries deal with felonies and petit juries deal with misdemeanors.
b. Eighteen persons make up a grand jury; only six make up a petit jury.
c. Grand juries require unanimous verdicts to convict; petit juries require only ten of twelve members to convict.
d. Grand juries issue indictments; petit juries issue verdicts.
e. Grand juries deal with violations of state law; petit juries deal with violations of city and county law.

8. Which of the following is TRUE of the judicial process in Texas?

a. At least four justices must agree to hear a case for it to get to the Texas Supreme Court.
b. Death penalty cases are appealed directly to the Texas Supreme Court.
c. Appellate courts empanel new juries to rehear evidence from lower-level courts.
d. The Texas Court of Criminal Appeals hears appeals from the Texas Supreme Court.
e. The Texas Supreme Court hears about half of the petitions for review that it receives.

9. Which of the following is TRUE about minority representation in the Texas judicial system?

a. Democratic governors have appointed more ethnic minorities to the highest courts than Republican governors.
b. As of 2012, a majority of judges on the Texas Court of Criminal Appeals were women.
c. Governor George W. Bush appointed the first Hispanic to the Texas Supreme Court.
d. Minority judges on the highest courts tend to be more liberal than conservative.
e. No woman appointed to the highest courts has ever won election to that office.

10. What is the central criticism about money and the Texas Supreme Court?

a. Wealthy interests have less influence in the judicial process than they once did.
b. The state ban on campaign contributions impairs the free speech rights of business interests.
c. Republicans have not won their fair share of judicial seats.
d. The legislature in recent years has tended to support the trial lawyers.
e. Popular election of judges has increased the influence of money in the judicial system.

11. All of the following are reasons for the small number of minority judges serving on the Texas courts EXCEPT

a. the high cost of judicial campaigns.
b. the low rates of minority participation in elections.
c. a shortage of minority attorneys from whose ranks judges are drawn.
d. single-member judicial districts that fragment minority voting power.
e. countywide elections that dilute minority voting strength.

12. Complaints about the inequities in the Texas judicial system have prompted the state to

a. enact modest limits on campaign contributions to judges and judicial candidates.
b. shorten the election ballot so that citizens can cast informed votes.
c. change from a system of partisan elections to nonpartisan elections.
d. move to a system in which nominating committees recommend individuals for appointment by the governor.
e. ban all campaign contributions by businesses.

13. Capital punishment in Texas is

a. carried out by electrocution.
b. in violation of the prohibition against cruel and unusual punishment.
c. not used as a punishment for women.
d. only used for those who commit multiple murders.
e. not used as a punishment for mentally retarded convicts.

14. Unauthorized use of television cable decoding equipment is an example of a

a. first-degree felony.
b. capital murder.
c. Class B misdemeanor.
d. third-degree felony.
e. state jail felony.

15. The "Robin Hood" law upheld by the Texas Supreme Court in 1995

a. raised cigarette taxes to pay for increased funding for poor school districts.
b. required wealthier school districts to share revenue with poor districts.
c. forced landowners with large amounts of groundwater to give a portion to owners of drier property.
d. required the state to pay for abortions for poor women.
e. raised taxes on businesses to increase funding in poor school districts.

Explore Further

Champagne, Anthony, and Judith Haydel, eds., *Judicial Reform in the States*. New York: University Press of America, 1993. Analyzes judicial reform in seven states including Texas from an interest group perspective.

Cheek, Kyle, and Anthony Champagne, *Judicial Politics in Texas: Partisanship, Money, and Politics in State Courts*. New York: Peter Lang Publishing, 2004. Examines judicial politics in Texas. Historically, judicial elections in Texas were low key and generally received little attention. Dramatic changes have occurred with increased ideological rhetoric and partisanship, and many judicial elections have become the battlegrounds for competing interest groups in the state.

Campbell, Randolph B., ed., and compiled by William S. Pugsley and Marilyn P. Duncan, *The Laws of Slavery in Texas: Historical Documents and Essays*. Austin: University of Texas Press, 2010. Compiles fifty years of slave laws in Texas, focusing on legal views that treated slaves as property.

Hill, John, "Taking Texas Judges Out of Politics: An Argument for Merit Election," *Baylor Law Review* 40 (1988). Argues for nonpartisan selection of Texas state judges; written by a former chief justice of the Texas Supreme Court.

Horton, David M., and Ryan Kellus Turner, *Lone Star Justice: A Comprehensive Overview of the Texas Criminal Justice System*. Austin, TX: Eakin, 1999. Provides a compendium of information covering the history of Texas courts, crime, law enforcement, corrections, and juvenile justice.

Schulze, Enika, and Susan Patterson, *Texas Courts*, 8/e. Upper Saddle River, NJ: Prentice Hall, 2006. Introduces the structure and organization of the Texas Court System.

Texans for Public Justice, *Interested Parties: Who Bankrolled Texas' High-Court Justices in 2008*. Austin: Author, 2009. Assesses campaign contributions made to three justices of the Texas Supreme Court who successfully ran for reelection in 2008.

Texas Court Records Preservation Task Force, "A History of Texas in 21 State Court Records," *Texas Bar Journal*, 75 (March 2012), pp. 190–219. Demonstrates the value of state court documents in the analysis of major historical events in the state; issued by a task force created by the Texas Supreme Court.

Texas Judicial Council, Office of Court Administration, *Texas Judicial System, 82nd Annual Report, 2011*. Austin, TX: Office of Court Administration 2011. Compiles data annually on the activities of Texas state courts.

Willett, Jim, and Ron Rozelle, *Warden: Prison Life and Death from the Inside Out*. Albany, TX: Bright Star Press. 2004. Relates personal events, including those that surrounded the execution of prisoners; based on author's thirty-year career with the Texas prison system.

12

Listen on MyPoliSciLab

Local Government in Texas

The best school of democracy and the best guarantee of its success is the practice of local self-government.

—James Bryce, 1921

The American system, which divides the local authority among so many citizens, does not scruple [hesitate] to multiply the functions of the town officers.

—Alexis de Tocqueville, 1835

Austin, like fast-growing cities across the United States, was being overwhelmed by household garbage, much of it in the form of plastic bags that residents brought home by the thousands each day from grocery stores and other retailers. After a recycling program made only a modest dent in the problem, Austin became the first major city in Texas to impose a ban on disposable plastic and paper bags at retail checkout counters, to begin in March 2013. The ban included some limited exceptions, but for the vast majority of transactions, retailers would be allowed to offer customers only reusable bags.

Environmentalists applauded the ban, but some Austin residents were not so sure. The Austin City Council delayed the effective date of the new ordinance for a year to give residents time to get used to the idea and begin changing their shopping habits.[1] The delay also may have given the Texas Retailers Association, which opposed the ban, an opportunity to appeal to the Texas

12.1 Trace Texas's transition from an agrarian state to an urban one, p. 354.

12.2 Compare and contrast the forms of government, election systems, sources of revenue, and issues facing Texas cities, p. 357.

12.3 List the officials involved in and the consequences of the fragmented nature of county government, p. 369.

12.4 Explain the functions and problems associated with single-purpose districts, p. 375.

12.5 Describe the governance structure and inequities of independent school districts, p. 378.

12.6 Assess the various proposed solutions to the problems of local government, p. 380.

OVER 4,800 GOVERNMENTS SPREAD ACROSS MORE THAN 260,000 SQUARE MILES

Texas has 254 counties and three of the nation's ten largest cities. Among the states, it is second only to Alaska in physical size and second only to California in population.

legislature to try to nullify or weaken the ordinance with an overriding state law when the legislature convened in January 2013.

Texas has a strong tradition of local government, and these governments—cities, counties, and special districts—handle a wide array of issues, many not nearly as attention getting as a plastic bag ban. These local governments increasingly are finding their policy options complicated by requirements and limitations imposed by state and federal governments.

Texas has more than 4,800 local governments, of all sizes, many with overlapping jurisdictions. Some operate with a handful of employees and budgets of $100,000 or $200,000 a year; others have tens of thousands of employees with billion dollar-plus budgets. Some special districts perform one basic function, whereas cities perform any number of services that are limited only by budgetary and legal restraints. Loving County in remote West Texas has fewer than 90 residents; across the state, Harris County, the state's largest, has approximately 4.1 million residents. One school district, San Vicente ISD, in West Texas, has only about 20 students; the Houston Independent School District has more than 200,000. Three of the ten largest cities in the United States are in Texas, but many cities across the state have fewer than 1,000 residents.

The key to understanding local governments in Texas is to understand what responsibilities the Texas Constitution and statutory law have assigned to them. Once the institutional structures and functions of local governments have been studied, we will look at a number of core problems confronting them and their political capacities to address these issues. Two themes underlie this analysis: what changes can make local governments more effective, and is it possible or desirable to reduce the fragmentation in local governments?

Urban Texas

12.1 Trace Texas's transition from an agrarian state to an urban one.

Despite popular images of wide-open spaces dotted with cattle and oil wells, Texas is an urban state. Some areas, particularly in West Texas, still offer much room to roam, but more than 80 percent of Texans live in cities or urban areas. First-time visitors to the state often express surprise at the size and diversity of Houston and Dallas and the more relaxed charm of San Antonio, whose river walk reminds many tourists of some European cities. Austin, the seat of state government and location of a world-class university, is highly attractive to young professionals and high-technology businesses.

When the Texas Constitution was adopted in 1876, the state was rural and agrarian. Less than 10 percent of the population lived in cities. According to the 1880 census, Galveston was the largest city with a population of 22,248, followed by San Antonio with 20,550. Dallas, a relatively new settlement, had 10,358 residents, and Houston, 16,513. For most of the period from 1880 to 1920, San Antonio was Texas's largest city, but since the 1930 census, Houston has held that distinction.[2] In 1940, only 45 percent of Texans lived in urban areas, but by 1960, some 60 percent of the population resided in cities. Since the 1970 census, eight of every ten Texans have been living in cities. More recent data indicate that more than 88 percent of Texans live in urban areas.[3]

Houston, San Antonio, and Dallas are among the ten largest cities in the United States. According to the 2010 census, Houston had a population of 2,099,451; San Antonio, 1,327,407; and Dallas, 1,197,816. Six additional Texas cities—El Paso, Fort Worth, Austin, Corpus Christi, Arlington, and Plano—each had more than 250,000 residents. Growth rates, however, have varied widely from city to city, thanks to differences in economic expansion, annexation policies, in-migration from other areas, and

population density
Number of persons residing within a square mile.

12.1 12.2 12.3 12.4 12.5 12.6

A SYMBOL OF A HIGHLY URBANIZED STATE

Almost 90 percent of Texans live in urban or suburban areas. Shown here is the skyline of downtown Dallas.

fertility and mortality rates. In some instances, the growth rate for the central city has been relatively modest, whereas growth in surrounding suburban areas has been quite high, reflecting continued urban sprawl.

Compared with many other parts of the country, Texas cities have a relatively low ratio of population to incorporated area. Texas cities are relatively young and had a lot of inexpensive land available to them during their early development. So, unlike older cities in other states, they tended to expand outward rather than upward. Texas cities also have used liberal annexation powers granted by the legislature to block the development of nearby, small municipalities that would curb their expansion. Houston covers approximately 600 square miles, the largest landmass of any city in the state, and has a **population density** of approximately 3,500 persons per square mile. Population density affects policy and budgetary issues relating to virtually every public service provided by the city. Land use, zoning laws, police and fire protection, the location of libraries and parks, and the development of water and sanitation systems all relate to the density of a city's population.

The racial and ethnic composition of Texas cities also is a major factor in urban diversity. Plano, located north of Dallas, reported in the 2010 census a combined minority population of approximately 39 percent with an Asian population of 17 percent (see Table 12–1). By contrast, Hispanics comprised more than 95 percent of the population of Laredo. Other cities along the Texas-Mexico border showed very high numbers of Hispanics. Brownsville was 93 percent Hispanic; Harlingen, 80 percent; McAllen, 85 percent; and El Paso, 81 percent. In 2010, the African American population in Dallas was 25 percent. Houston's African American population was 23 percent, and Fort Worth's, 18.5 percent. In contrast, the African American population in El Paso was less than 3 percent; in Corpus Christi, 4 percent; and San Antonio, 6.3 percent.[4]

The 1,214 incorporated municipalities in Texas are diverse, as urban life, politics, and government have developed different styles across the state. Statutory and constitutional laws define the basic forms of city government, but cities vary in their demographic makeup, their economies, the historical experiences that shaped their development, and their quality of life.[5]

TABLE 12–1 SELECT CHARACTERISTICS FOR THE TEN LARGEST CITIES IN TEXAS, 2010

City	Total Population in 2010	Percentage over age 65	Percentage under age 18	Median Age	Percentage African American	Percentage Hispanic	Percentage Asian	Median Household Income 2010	Percentage of Persons Below Poverty Level 2010	Percentage of Children Below Poverty Level 2010
Houston	2,099,451	9.0	25.9	32.2	23.1	43.8	5.9	$42,355	22.8	34.5
San Antonio	1,327,407	10.4	26.8	32.8	6.3	63.2	2.3	$43,758	19.1	27.8
Dallas	1,197,816	8.8	26.5	31.6	24.6	42.4	2.8	$40,650	23.6	37.4
Austin	790,390	7.0	22.2	30.9	7.7	35.1	6.2	$47,434	20.8	27.6
Fort Worth	741,206	8.2	29.4	31.5	18.5	34.1	3.7	$48,224	17.9	24.5
El Paso	649,121	11.2	29.1	32.8	2.8	80.7	1.1	$37,278	21.6	29.6
Arlington	365,438	8.1	27.9	32.0	18.4	27.4	6.7	$48,752	15.0	20.1
Corpus Christi	305,215	11.9	25.8	34.2	3.9	59.7	1.8	$41,845	20.1	32.2
Plano	259,841	8.9	25.9	38.1	7.4	14.7	16.8	$79,234	7.9	10.6
Laredo	236,091	7.9	35.0	27.5	0.2	95.6	0.6	$35,997	31.4	41.7
State Totals	25,145,561	10.3	27.3	33.6	11.5	37.6	3.8	$48,615	17.9	25.5

SOURCE: U.S. Census Bureau, *American Community Survey, 2010.*

The Cities and the State

12.2 Compare and contrast the forms of government, election systems, sources of revenue, and issues facing Texas cities.

Since the nation's founding, Americans have expressed a strong belief in the right to local self-government.[6] In many areas of the young country, local governments existed long before there was a viable state or federal government. Early communities had to fend for themselves and had limited expectations of services or protections to be provided by state or federal governments.

This history of local self-help has led to the popular notion that local governments have fundamental rights based on the concept of local sovereignty, or ultimate power. Thomas Jefferson, for example, developed a theory of local government, designed in part to strengthen the powers of the states, in which local sovereignty was rooted in the sovereignty of the individual. Local governments, which he termed "wards," would have a wide range of responsibilities, including education, police, roads, caring for the poor, conducting elections, some minor judicial functions, and a semblance of a militia to maintain local defenses.[7]

In light of the expanded role of state and federal governments, we might find Jefferson's view outdated and naive. Nonetheless, the concept has permeated American attitudes toward government and continues to shape citizen responses to government initiatives. Some people suggest that this cultural legacy persists in grass-roots politics, the flight to suburbia, the creation of neighborhood organizations and gated communities, and the persistence of distrust of the national and state governments. Today, it is common to hear the argument that local government is closest to the people and best represents their interests and desires.[8]

The state has granted cities—unlike counties and special districts—a wide range of discretionary power over organizational structure and local public policy. Texas ranks high among the states in that regard, but cities still are strongly affected by state laws and policies. Cities, therefore, actively lobby the legislature and other state officials on numerous issues. Member cities support the Texas Municipal League (TML), which maintains a full-time staff in Austin to monitor the activities of the legislature and state agencies. Many of the larger cities also designate staff members to serve as legislative liaisons, or they retain professional lobbyists. The larger cities usually work with community leaders and civic organizations to establish legislative agendas. Houston, Dallas, and San Antonio have the potential for considerable impact on the state legislature when their legislative delegations share common interests or goals, but often sharp differences arise among local delegations. State legislators from numerous central city areas increasingly are collaborating on issues that affect all Texas municipalities.[9] Hundreds of pieces of legislation that could affect cities are introduced during each legislative session. TML's highest priority is to block "bad legislation" that it believes adversely affects the interests of Texas cities.[10]

Texas, like most other states, assigns the primary responsibility for public education to local school districts while retaining the primary responsibility for highways, public welfare, and public health at the state level. Police and fire protection, water and sanitation services, parks, recreation, and libraries are the primary responsibility of city governments. Public hospitals are a shared function of the state, counties, and special districts.[11] Texas counties share with the state a primary responsibility for the courts and criminal justice system.

General Law and Home Rule Cities

The prevailing constitutional theory on the relationship of local governments to the state is the unitary system, which holds that local governments are the creations of the state. The state government grants or delegates to local governments their

Dillon rule
A principle holding that local governments are creations of state government, and their powers and responsibilities are defined by the state.

general law cities
Texas cities with fewer than 5,000 residents. They are allowed to exercise only those powers specifically granted to them by the legislature. Most cities in Texas are classified as general law cities.

home rule cities
Texas cities with more than 5,000 residents. They can adopt any form of government residents choose, provided it does not conflict with the state constitution or statutes. Home rule powers are formalized through local voters' adoption of a city charter spelling out how the city is to be governed.

city charter
A document, defined or authorized by state law, under which a city operates. In Texas home rule cities, local voters may choose among several forms of city government.

powers, functions, and responsibilities, and no local government has sovereign powers. Numerous court cases have spelled out this principle, referred to as the **Dillon rule**, but the best summary is from an Iowa case in which a court held the following:

> The true view is this: Municipal corporations owe their origin to, and derive their powers and rights wholly from, the legislature. It breathes into them the breath of life, without which they cannot exist. As it creates, so it may destroy. If it may destroy, it may abridge and control. Unless there is some constitutional limitation on the right, the legislature might by a single act, if we can suppose it capable of so great a folly and so great a wrong, sweep from its existence all of the municipal corporations in the State, and the corporations could not prevent it. We know of no limitation on this right so far as the corporations are concerned. They are so to phrase it, the mere tenants at will of the legislature.[12]

The Dillon rule applies to local governments in Texas. Local governments are administrative subdivisions of the state and have no rights except those granted to them by the state. Moreover, as the state has grown, state and federal governments have ordered, or mandated, significant improvements in environmental, educational, health, and other services and have required cities, counties, and school districts to shoulder much of the cost. Local school districts, for example, are at the mercy of the legislature, which in recent years has ordered expensive educational programs and raised classroom standards without fully paying for them. Local governments have to shoulder much of the responsibility—and often take much of the public outrage—for policy decisions made in Austin and in Washington.

Although the Dillon rule subordinates local governments to the state, there are practical and political limitations on what the state can do with local governments.[13] More importantly, the state relies on local governments to carry out many of its responsibilities. The Texas Constitution provides for two general categories of cities: general law and home rule. **General law cities** have fewer than 5,000 residents and face restrictions in organizing their governments, setting taxes, and annexing territory. They are allowed only those powers specifically granted to them by the legislature. Most Texas cities—approximately 855—are general law cities.[14] Texas granted cities home rule authority in 1912. **Home rule cities**, which include all of the state's major and medium size cities, have considerable authority and discretion over their own local policies, but within limits set by state law.

A city with more than 5,000 inhabitants can adopt any form of government its residents choose, provided it does not conflict with the state constitution (Article 11, Sections 4, 5) or statutes. This option is called home rule and is formalized through the voters' adoption of a **city charter**, which is the fundamental document—something like a constitution—under which a city operates. A charter establishes a city's governing body; the organization of its administrative agencies and municipal courts; its taxing authority; and procedures for conducting elections, annexing additional territory, and revising the charter (see *Talking Texas: Is This Any Way to Change a City Charter?*). As of 2012, there were 357 home rule cities in Texas.[15]

Most Texas cities have functioned under more than one form of government. Changes in city charters often follow periods of crises, intense political conflict, or an inability of those in government to address long-term problems. Proposed changes in governmental structures and elections often threaten groups and interests that have a stake in the way business is currently being conducted, and charter revisions have a tendency to polarize a community.

☐ Forms of City Government

Many of the larger cities in Texas have gone through a succession of different forms of governments, and there are local histories behind these changes. However, citizens, elected officials, and those who study local governments continue to raise the question, "Does the form of city government make any difference in how a city is run, how

Talking ★ TEXAS Is This Any Way to Change a City Charter?

Boerne, Texas, which is just northwest of San Antonio, held a special election to amend its charter to bring it in line with a law enacted by the Texas legislature. The new law permitted local governments to purchase items valued at $25,000 or less without seeking bids. Prior to its enactment, the limit was $15,000, and Boerne's charter included this figure. To permit the city to follow the state law and to anticipate future increases in the cap, a charter amendment would have permitted the city council to change spending caps each year as allowed by state law.

In a cliffhanger election in which only 57 of 4,836 registered voters participated, the charter amendment was defeated, 29–28. The election occurred when there were no city or school board elections to draw voters to the polls. Few voters apparently were even aware the issue was on the ballot, and some just did not care or believe the issue was important to them.[a]

What happened in Boerne occurs throughout the state in charter elections. As is true for changes to the state constitution, all too often a small minority of a city's voters decides on changes in its fundamental law. Although we have no empirical evidence, it might be argued that most changes are well intentioned and necessary. It is evident, however, that a few individuals can use charter elections for their own self-interests.

CRITICAL THINKING QUESTIONS

1. **Why should a resident of the city of Boerne care if the limit on no-bid contracts is $15,000 or $25,000?**
2. **Should the legislature be involved in setting such limits for cities on no-bid contracts? Is that good government, or is the state micromanaging local government? Explain your answer.**

[a]Zeke MacCormack, "Boerne Rejects Charter Change," *San Antonio Express-News*, May 7, 2002, p. 5B.

responsive it is to its citizens, how able it is to address current issues and anticipate future issues, and how efficient and effective its government is?"

According to the Texas Municipal League, there were 1,209 municipal governments in Texas in 2007. More than 900 cities operated with some variation of the mayor-council form, approximately 280 used some form of council-manager or commission-manager government, and only a handful used the commission form of government.[16]

weak mayor
A form of city government in which the mayor shares authority with the city council and other elected officials but has little independent control over city policy or city administration.

strong mayor
A form of city government that gives the mayor considerable power, including budgetary control and appointment and removal authority over city department heads.

MAYOR-COUNCIL The mayor-council form, the most common type of municipal government in Texas, derived from the English model of city government. The legislative function of the city is vested in the city council, and the executive function is assigned to the mayor. This type of government is based on the separation of powers principle, which also characterizes the state and federal governments. In terms of power, however, the two distinguishable forms of mayor are the weak mayor and the strong mayor—and in most Texas cities, the mayor is weak.

The city charter determines a mayor's strength. The **weak mayor** has little control over policy initiatives or implementation. The mayor's power may be constrained by one or more of the following: limited or no appointment or removal power over city offices, limited budgetary authority, and the election of other city administrators independently of the mayor (see Figure 12–1). Under these circumstances, the mayor shares power with the city council over city administration and policy implementation and "is the chief executive in name only."[17] These restrictions limit both the political and administrative leadership of the mayor. Although it is possible for a mayor to use personal or political resources to influence the city council and other administrators and to provide energetic leadership, formidable obstacles need to be overcome.[18]

A **strong mayor** has real power and authority, including appointive and removal powers over city agency heads. Such appointments often require city council approval, but the appointees are responsible to the mayor and serve at mayoral discretion. The mayor has control over budget preparation and exercises some veto authority over city

city commission
A form of city government in which elected commissioners collectively serve as a city's policymaking body and individually serve as administrative heads of different city departments. Although once popular, this form of government is rarely used in Texas today.

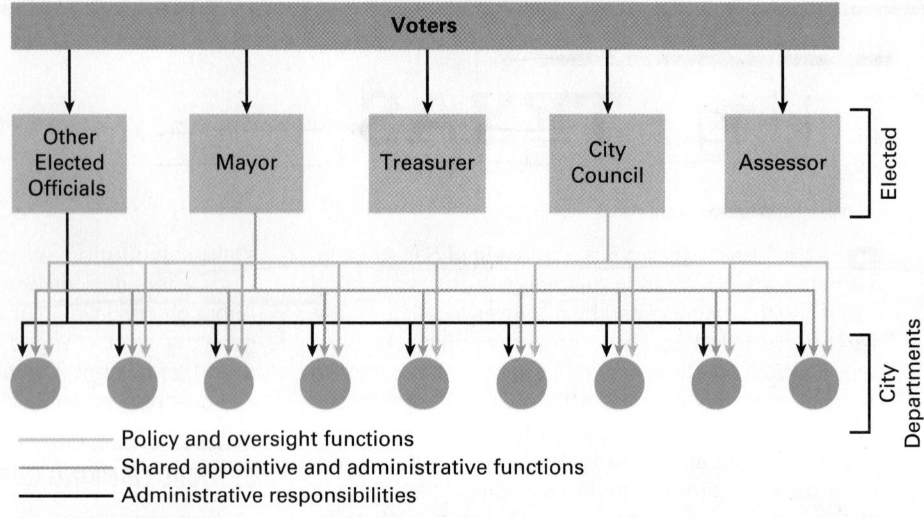

FIGURE 12–1 THE WEAK MAYOR FORM OF GOVERNMENT
Mayors have limited budget and administrative power under the weak mayor form of government.

council actions. This form of city government clearly distinguishes between executive and legislative functions.

The strong mayor form of government is found in many of the larger American cities, but it now is used by only one major city in Texas—Houston (see Figure 12–2). El Paso functioned under this form of government until 2004, when the city changed to the council-manager government. The strong mayor may be unpopular in the state because it often was associated with urban political machines, ward politics, and political corruption. Moreover, the fragmentation of authority and responsibility in local government parallels that found in state government and is another reminder of the deep distrust of government that Reconstruction produced in Texas. Finally, the state's individualistic and traditionalistic political subcultures reinforce hostile attitudes toward governmental institutions that are potentially more responsive to lower socioeconomic groups.

As might be expected, the salaries of the mayor and council members in a strong mayor city are generally higher than in cities with other forms of city government. In many cities, mayors and council members receive little or no pay or only modest reimbursements for services. But the mayor of Houston earned $209,138 in 2012, and each council member earned $55,770.[19]

CITY COMMISSION The commission and council-manager forms of government are products of the twentieth century. Both reflect, in part, efforts to reform city governments through administrative efficiency, the reduction of partisan conflict, and the adaptation of a businesslike approach to running city government.

The origin of the **city commission** usually is traced to the Texas island city of Galveston. After a hurricane and subsequent flooding devastated most of the city in 1900, the government then in office proved incompetent and incapable of responding. The crisis prompted a group of citizens to win the legislature's approval of a new form of government designed to be more responsive by combining the city's legislative and administrative functions in the offices of five city commissioners. City commissions soon were adopted by other major Texas cities, including Dallas, Houston, and San Antonio. With the subsequent development of council-manager government as an alternative, a marked decline in the city commission's popularity has occurred. All of the major cities have replaced the city commission with other forms of government, and only a few small cities in Texas still have this form of government.

Initially, the commission was supported as a businesslike approach to running city government. By eliminating partisan elections and combining the executive, administrative, and legislative functions, it was argued that cities could provide services

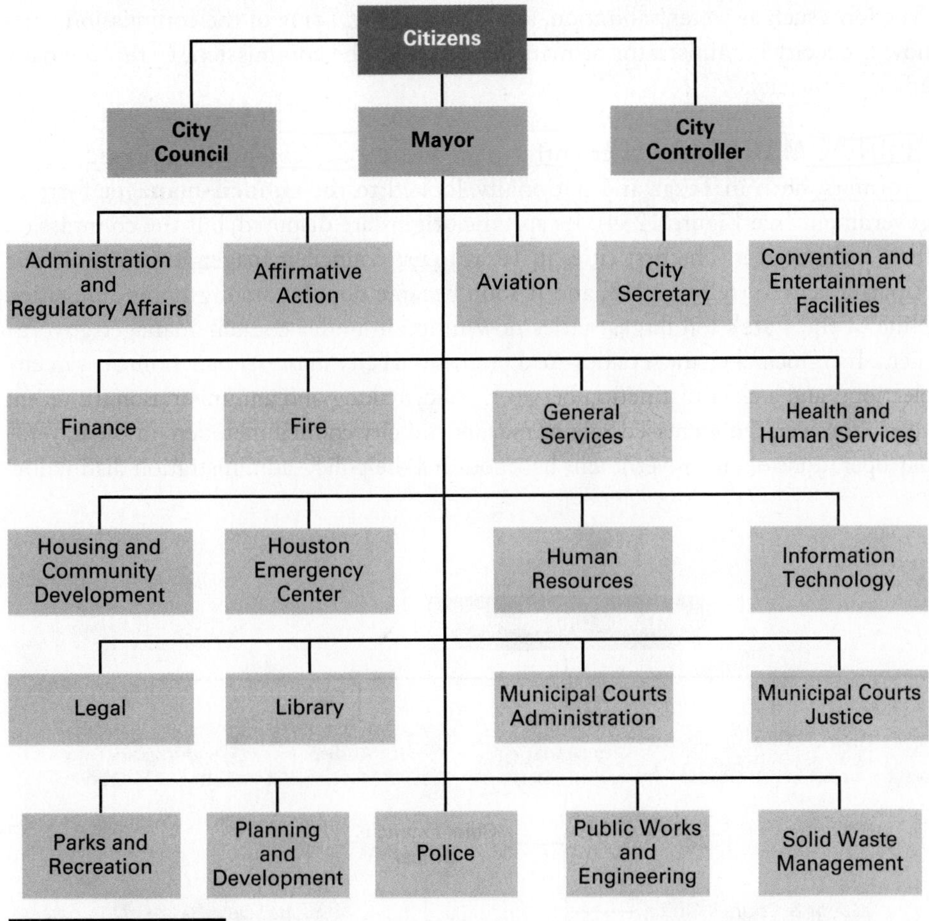

FIGURE 12–2 THE STRONG MAYOR FORM OF GOVERNMENT: ORGANIZATIONAL CHART OF THE CITY OF HOUSTON

Houston is the only large Texas city that uses the strong mayor form of government in which the mayor has major day-to-day administrative responsibilities.

Source: City of Houston, *Fiscal Year 2011 Budget.*

more efficiently. However, critics have identified several problems. The commission minimizes the potential for effective political leadership because no single individual can be identified as the person in charge. Moreover, oversight and review of policies and budgets is minimal. Commissioners are elected primarily as policymakers, not administrators, and there are downsides to electing amateurs to administer increasingly technical and complex city programs (see Figure 12–3).

The few cities in Texas that use the pure form of commission government now generally have three members—two commissioners and a mayor who is selected from among the commissioners—who are each assigned responsibilities for specific city

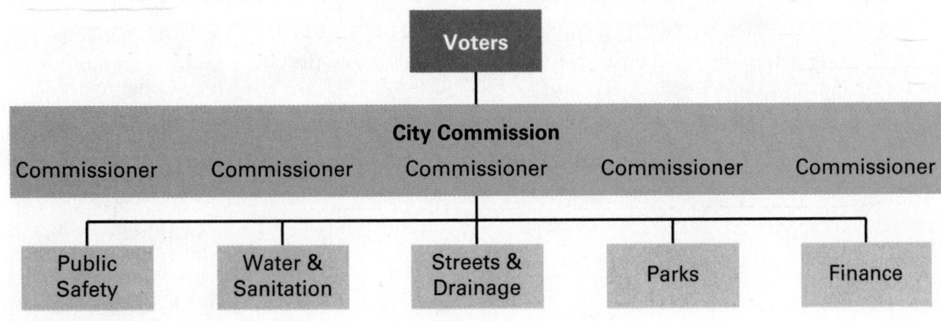

FIGURE 12–3 CITY COMMISSION FORM OF GOVERNMENT

Commissioners combine policy and administrative functions under the commission form of government, developed in Galveston after the 1900 hurricane. Few Texas cities use this form of government, and many that do have added a manager.

12.1
12.2
12.3
12.4
12.5
12.6

council-manager government
A form of city government in which policy is set by an elected city council, which hires a professional city manager to head the daily administration of city government.

functions, such as water, sanitation, and public safety. Some of the commission cities now use a city administrator or manager, hired by the commission, to run the daily affairs of the city.

COUNCIL-MANAGER After enthusiasm for the city commission waned, urban reformers, both in Texas and nationally, looked to the **council-manager** form of government (see Figure 12–4). Its specific origins are disputed, but the commission form influenced it. The first cities in Texas to use council-manager government were Amarillo and Terrell in 1913, and it soon became popular among home rule cities. Nine of the state's ten largest cities now function under council-manager government. Its principal characteristics are a professional city management, nonpartisan city elections, and a clear distinction between policymaking and administration. In recent years, however, the increased role of mayors and city council members in the day-to-day operations of city government has modified the policy-administration distinction.

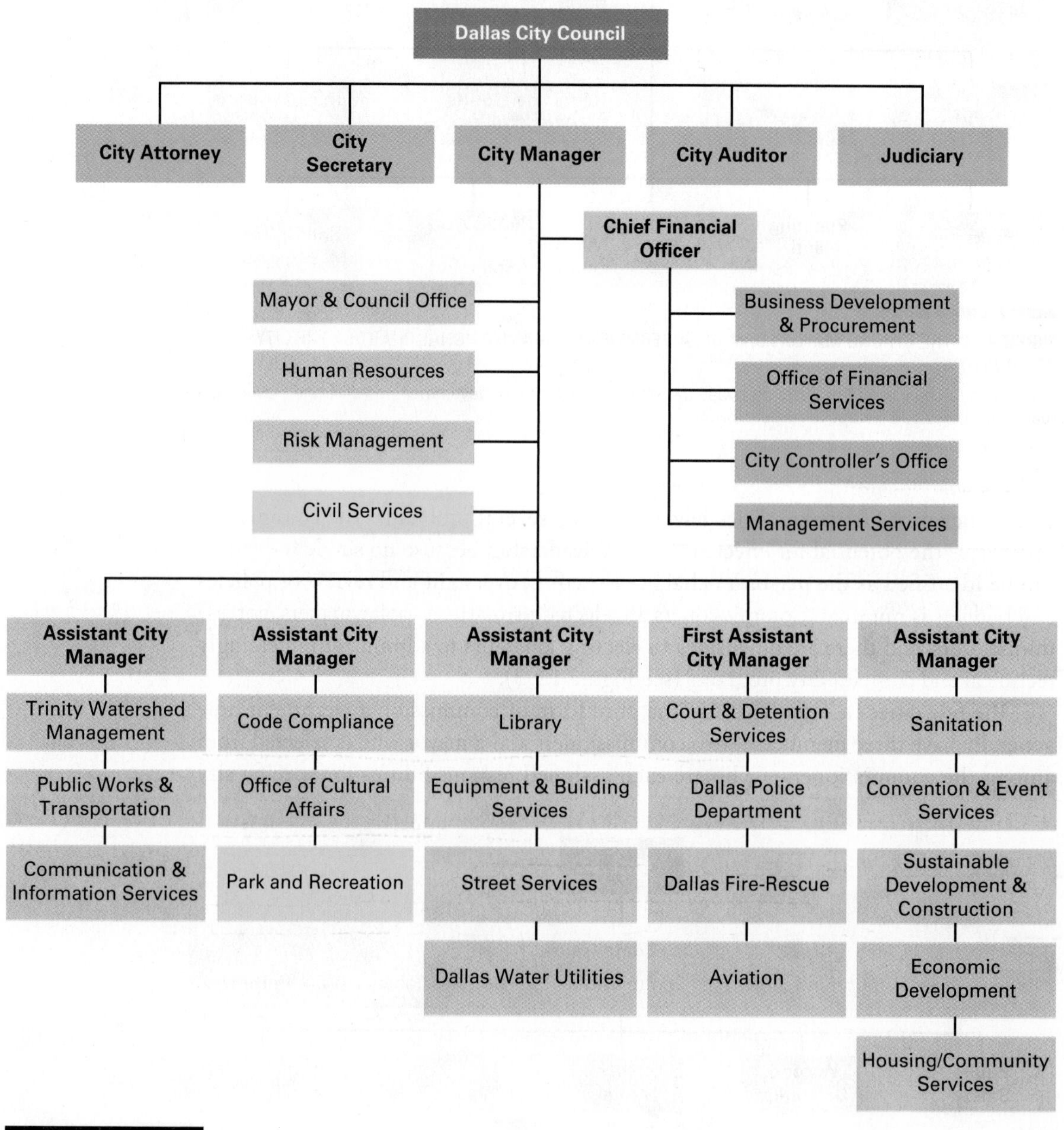

FIGURE 12–4 COUNCIL-MANAGER FORM OF GOVERNMENT: ORGANIZATIONAL CHART FOR THE CITY OF DALLAS

With the exception of Houston, all major Texas cities use the council-manager form of government in which the mayor and council set policy and the administrative responsibilities are assigned to a manager chosen by the council.

Source: City of Dallas, *FY 11–12 Budget.*

In some council-manager cities, the city council chooses the mayor from among its membership to preside over council meetings and fulfill a primarily symbolic role. In other cities, the mayor is elected citywide, an arrangement that enhances the political position of the office without necessarily giving it formal legal authority. The mayor is usually a voting member of city council but has few other institutional powers. The mayor does, however, have the opportunity to become a visible spokesperson for the city and has a forum from which to promote ideas and programs.

In the not too distant past, the salaries of mayors and council members serving in council-manager cities were very low, but a trend in recent years has increased salaries in response to the expanded workload. Annual salaries of the mayor and city council members in Austin were set in 2006 at $67,918 and $57,736, respectively, with provisions for annual cost-of-living adjustments. Until recently, the mayor and council members in Dallas received $50 per meeting, but voters approved a charter amendment in 2001 to raise the mayor's pay to $60,000 a year and council members to $37,500.[20] By contrast, San Antonio's council members and mayor currently earn $20 per meeting and the mayor an additional $3,000 per year.[21] Discussions about increasing their pay have occurred, but such changes would require an amendment to San Antonio's charter.

The city council is primarily responsible for developing public policy (see *Talking Texas: The Job of the City Council Member*). It creates, organizes, and restructures city departments; approves the city budget; establishes the tax rate; authorizes the issuance of bonds (subject to voter approval); enacts local laws (ordinances); and conducts inquiries and investigations into the operations and functions of city agencies.[22]

Talking ★ TEXAS The Job of a City Council Member

Regardless of the form of government, most city councils in Texas are small, with five to fifteen members elected for two-year terms. Most council seats are elected at-large, or citywide, and council elections are nonpartisan. Council members in most cities can serve for an unlimited number of terms. Referenda on term limitations, however, have been held recently in several Texas cities. San Antonio limits its council members and mayor to four 2-year terms, and Houston, three 2-year terms.

In most cities, a council office is a part-time position with little or no compensation. Although some large cities (e.g., Houston, Austin, and Dallas) recently have increased salaries significantly, many council members do not consider their pay to be commensurate with the time spent on the job. Council members in San Antonio still are paid $20 per meeting. Low salaries were part of the early urban reform tradition. The idea was that people would run for office out of a sense of civic duty rather than to advance themselves financially.

The frequency of council meetings varies. In many small towns, councils may meet for only a few hours each month; councils in large cities meet much more frequently, usually weekly, with meetings lasting several hours. Cities are dealing with a wider range of complex issues than ever before, and demands on a council member's time are great. In addition to their policymaking roles, council members in large cities face increased demands for constituent services. Many council members are finding that public service is extremely costly in terms of time lost from their families and the jobs or professions that provide their livelihoods.

Council members often complain that they had no idea how much time the public would demand of them and no idea of the personal costs of public service. Yet, public service has its rewards, and these rewards often come from a sense that one has made a significant contribution to the future well-being of his or her city.[a]

CRITICAL THINKING QUESTIONS

1. If council members are elected from a single-member district, how should they balance the interests or demands of their district with those interests and demands of the city as a whole?
2. Do you think most city council members seek election because they truly want to make their communities better places in which to live? Why or why not?

[a]Ernie Mosher, "Suggestions for Public Service," *Texas Town and City* 92 (June 2005): 14–16; and Nelson Wolff, "How I See It: Lessons for Leadership," in *Government and Politics in the Lone Star State: Theory and Practice*, 6th ed., edited by L. Tucker Gibson and Clay Robison (Upper Saddle River, NJ: Prentice Hall, 2008), pp. 397–98.

nonpartisan elections
Local elections in which candidates file for place, position, or district with no political party label attached to their names.

The council hires a full-time city manager, who is responsible for administering city government on a day-to-day basis. The manager hires and fires assistants and department heads, supervises their activities, and translates the policy directives of the city council into concrete action by city employees. The city manager also is responsible for developing a city budget for council approval and then supervising its implementation. Professionalism is one of the key attributes of the council-manager form of government. Initially, many city managers were engineers, but in recent years managers have tended to become generalists with expertise in public finance. City managers are fairly well paid. In 2012, the city manager of Dallas received $265,617. San Antonio's city manager was paid $355,000, and the city manager of Austin earned $249,288. Even city managers of small cities receive substantial compensation. The city manager of Seguin (population 25,000 in 2010) received $160,249.[23]

A delicate line exists between policymaking and administration, and a city manager is, in principle, supposed to be politically neutral. The overall effectiveness of city managers depends on three main factors: their relationships with their city councils, their ability to develop support for their recommendations within the council and the community at large without appearing to have gone beyond the scope of their authority, and the overall perception of their financial and managerial skills. In the real world of municipal government, city managers play a central role in setting policy as well as carrying it out. Managers' adroit use of their resources and their sensitivity to political factions and the personal agendas of elected officials are keys to determining their success.

☐ Municipal Election Systems

Unlike state and county officials, who are elected on partisan ballots, city officials in Texas are selected in nonpartisan elections. Cities differ, however, on whether their council members are elected citywide or in single-member districts. Much attention has been focused on that distinction in recent years because in some cities it can make a difference in who is elected to office and how well the interests of minority residents are represented.

NONPARTISAN CITY ELECTIONS Virtually every city in Texas elects its council members in **nonpartisan elections**. Claiming that there was "no Democratic or Republican way to pave a street," city reformers who were part of the nonpartisan movement (1920s to 1950s) expressed a strong aversion to political parties and particularly to the urban political machines. To enforce separation of city elections from party politics, most municipal elections are held at times other than the party primaries or the general election.

The nonpartisan ballot—combined with at-large, citywide elections—has historically benefited higher social and economic groups. Parties and party labels normally serve as cues for voters. When city elections eliminate these cues, voters are forced to find alternative sources of information about candidates. Many local newspapers, which endorsed candidates and decided how much coverage to give them, had ties to the dominant urban elites. Candidates from lower socioeconomic groups had few contacts with the influential civic and business organizations that recruited, supported, and endorsed candidates. Although no longer in existence, San Antonio's Good Government League and Dallas's Citizens Charter Association controlled the recruitment and election of candidates in those two cities for several decades. Both organizations drew members from the Democratic and the Republican Parties, but they reflected and pursued the interests of higher socioeconomic groups, often to the detriment of lower-income and minority populations.

Despite the nonpartisan characteristics of city election systems, partisanship and party affiliation can play a role in city elections. Although the ballot excludes party labels, some city council candidates are beginning to be identified by their party affiliations through news stories, endorsements by party organizations, and campaign advertisements. In the 2001 and 2003 city elections in Houston, for example, party affiliations of major candidates were widely known, and national party committees contributed money to some of the campaigns. Areas that are Republican in partisan orientation are likely to support individuals with Republican attributes, and, conversely, areas that vote Democratic in general elections are likely to support candidates with Democratic leanings. These developments clearly challenge the nonpartisan traditions of many cities throughout Texas.

AT-LARGE ELECTIONS Another notable feature of city politics in Texas is the general use of citywide or **at-large elections.** In 1992, the latest year for which comprehensive data were available from the U.S. Census Bureau, some 5,649 individuals, or 88 percent, were elected at-large in Texas.[24] In 2002, 86 percent of cities used at-large elections.[25]

In an at-large election, all of a city's voters participate in the selection of all the members of the city council. In a pure at-large system, every candidate runs against every other candidate. If there are eight candidates running for five positions on the city council, the candidates with the five highest vote totals are the winners.

A variation of the at-large system is the place system. Candidates file for a specific council seat and run citywide for places, or positions. Cities using the place system may require that the winning candidate receive a simple plurality of votes (more votes than any other candidate running for the same position) or an absolute majority of votes (more than half of the votes cast). If a city requires the latter and more than two persons are in a race, **runoff elections** between the two highest vote getters are often required.

SINGLE-MEMBER DISTRICTS An alternative to at-large elections is the **single-member district**, or ward. Under this system, a city is divided into separate geographic districts, each represented by a different council member. A candidate must live in and run for election from a specific district, and voters can cast a ballot only in the race for the council seat that represents their district. A person elected from a single-member district can, depending on the city's charter, be elected by a plurality or an absolute majority of votes.

LEGAL ATTACKS ON AT-LARGE ELECTIONS Election systems are not politically neutral. At-large systems have historically benefited the nonminority, high-income areas of a city, whereas single-member districts tend to be more inclusive of all groups and areas of a city.

Hispanics and African Americans, through various advocacy groups such as the National Association for the Advancement of Colored People, the Mexican American Legal Defense and Educational Fund, Texas Rural Legal Aid, the G.I. Forum, and the Southwest Voter Registration and Education Project, have challenged in federal courts the election systems used by numerous Texas cities. From the small East Texas town of Jefferson to El Paso, Houston, and Dallas, minority groups have, with considerable success, proved the inequities of at-large elections and forced city governments to adopt electoral plans with districts that give minorities a better chance of electing candidates to city councils. The ethnic and racial composition of city councils has changed dramatically since the mid-1970s, with a marked increase in Hispanics and African Americans elected to these governing bodies.

☐ City Revenues and Expenditures

Despite a growing number of expenses, Texas cities have limited financial options. Unlike counties and school districts, they receive no state appropriations. City governments are disproportionately dependent on **regressive taxes**, such as property taxes and a one-cent sales tax (see Figure 12–5). Other revenue sources include franchise

at-large election
A system under which city council members or other officeholders are elected by voters in the entire city, school district, or single-purpose district. Many of these election systems have been struck down by the federal courts or by the U.S. Justice Department under the Voting Rights Act as discriminatory against minorities.

runoff election
A second election if no candidate receives an absolute majority of the votes cast in a primary race or in many nonpartisan elections. The runoff is between the top two vote getters.

single-member districts
A system in which legislators, city council members, or other public officials are elected from specific geographic areas.

regressive tax
A tax that imposes a disproportionately heavier burden on low-income people than on the more affluent.

12.1

12.2

12.3

12.4

12.5

12.6

rollback election
An election in which local voters can nullify a property tax increase that exceeds 8 percent in a given year.

fees, court fines, hotel occupancy taxes, taxes on amusements, fees for various permits, and transfers from revenue generated by city-owned utilities.[26]

Texas cities have been given considerable discretion to determine what taxes they will impose, and to a large extent the state has not depended on the cities to fund state programs. Nevertheless, cities are continually threatened by legislative proposals to place caps or other restrictions on their taxing authority.[27] Through their associations and lobbyists, cities work hard to thwart such restrictions.

The state limits the property tax rate a city can impose and permits citizens to petition their city council for a **rollback election** to nullify any tax increase of more than 8 percent in a given year. Although there have been few rollback elections in recent years, the potential for such citizen initiatives serves to constrain policymakers. Proposals to lower the cap on annual increases in property appraisals, a key element in determining property tax bills, have been defeated in the legislature in recent years.

City revenues tend to track the state's economy. When the economy is robust and expanding, city revenues usually grow. Revenue from property taxes increases with the construction of new homes and businesses. Rising property values also result in higher tax appraisals and increased revenue. Sales tax revenue increases as retailers sell more products. When the economy weakens, however, cities are forced to raise property taxes, increase fees, lay off city workers, freeze the hiring of new employees, or reduce services.[28]

By early 2009, Texas had begun to experience recessionary conditions—higher unemployment and underemployment, decreases in manufacturing and sales, and declines in housing values. The state comptroller reported in July 2009 that sales tax allocations to local governments had decreased, and state sales tax revenues failed to show a rebound until the spring of 2010.[29] In a series of Texas Municipal League surveys from 2009 to 2011, cities across Texas reported that they anticipated lower revenues. Some cities increased property taxes, and a significant number of cities indicated that they had increased fees during these three years. As has frequently been the case since the late 1980s, capital improvements were put on hold and wage and hiring freezes imposed. Despite the drop in revenues, some "92 percent of the cities surveyed found ways to maintain current levels of services."[30] By late 2011, the Texas economy showed signs of improvement, and sales tax collections rebounded.

Although cities are required by law to balance their operating budgets, many municipal construction projects are financed by loans through the issuance of

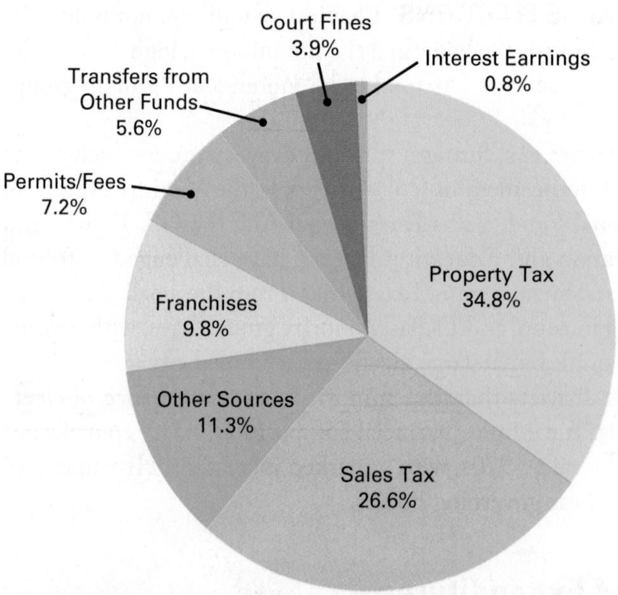

FIGURE 12–5 WHERE DO TEXAS CITIES GET THEIR MONEY?

Texas cities collect two-thirds of their local revenues from property and sales taxes, both of which are classified as regressive taxes. Other revenues come from franchise fees, court fines, hotel occupancy taxes, permit fees, and funds transferred from locally owned utilities.

Source: Texas Town and City, 98 (January 2011), p. 18.

general obligation bonds, which are subject to voter approval. These bonds are secured by the city's taxing power. The city pledges its full faith and credit to the lender and, over a number of years, repays the bonds with tax revenue. Cities also fund various projects through **revenue bonds** that are payable solely from the revenues derived from an income-producing facility, such as a city-owned parking garage, maintained by the city. With a significant pent-up demand for improving infrastructure (streets, waste disposal systems, libraries, and other facilities), cities entered an era beginning in the 1990s of bond financing radically altered by the performance of Wall Street and changes in state and federal tax laws.[31] It is more difficult to raise money during recessions, however, a prospect cities faced in 2009 and the years following.

Cities and towns share responsibilities for providing services with other local governments, but their primary functions are police and fire protection, streets and roads, solid waste management, sewer treatment and drainage, water supply, parks and recreation, public transportation, and libraries. Some Texas cities provide electricity and natural gas service, but private utilities provide those services in other communities. Cities often contract out services, such as garbage collection, to private companies, but the legal authority for such functions remains with the city. In some cases, special districts, which are independent of the cities, have been established within the boundaries of a city to provide specific services.

general obligation bonds
A method of borrowing money to pay for new construction projects, such as prisons or hospitals for the mentally ill. Interest on these bonds, which require voter approval in the form of constitutional amendments, is paid with tax revenue.

revenue bonds
Bonds sold by governments that are repaid from the revenues generated from income-producing facilities.

homestead exemption
Legal provision that permits a person who owns a home and is living in it to obtain a reduction in property taxes on the house.

□ Urban Problems

During the 1970s and through the early 1980s, Texas cities participated in the dramatic economic growth of the state. Many of the older cities of the country—particularly in the East and the Midwest—"looked at their Texas counterparts and envied their capacity to attract population and business."[32] Texas cities had low taxes, a pro-business tradition, few labor unions with significant economic clout, an abundant workforce, proximity to natural resources, and governing bodies that favored economic growth and development. At the beginning of the twenty-first century, however, many Texas cities confronted some of the problems associated with the older urban areas outside Texas.

GRAYING OF TEXAS CITIES The Texas population is aging, or graying, but at rates lower than other areas of the country. In fact, the average age of the state's population (33.6 years) was the second lowest in the nation, as a result in part of the large number of children born to the Hispanic population. Across the nation, Americans are living longer, and older age groups are among the fastest growing segments of the population. As a proportion of the total population in 2010, only 10 percent of Texans were age 65 years and older, but that translates into some 2.5 million people.

An aging population places additional pressures on city governments and the state for public services. The local property tax, a major source of revenue for city governments, is stretched almost to its limits. Moreover, in addition to the standard **homestead exemption**, many Texas cities have granted additional property tax exemptions for individuals older than age 65. Exemptions are special breaks that lower the amount of property taxes a person pays. As more and more people become old enough to claim these exemptions, younger taxpayers will be called upon to shoulder the burden through higher tax rates. It also is possible that older citizens on fixed incomes will be much more reluctant to support bond issues if they result in significant property tax increases.

"WHITE FLIGHT" The population characteristics of Texas cities have changed since the 1960s. Major metropolitan areas experienced a "white flight" to the suburbs, a dramatic increase in the growth rate of minority populations, and small growth rates among Anglos in the central cities.[33] Income levels for most minority Texans have always been lower than those of Anglos, and a larger proportion of the minority population falls below the poverty level. The increased concentration of lower-income people in the central cities increases pressure for more public services, while a declining proportion of affluent property owners weakens the local tax structures that pay for the services.

mandates

Federal laws or regulations that require state or local governments to take certain actions, often at costs that the federal government does not reimburse. The state government also imposes mandates on local governments.

DECLINING INFRASTRUCTURES There has been much concern across Texas and the United States about the declining infrastructures within local governments. In its 2008 "Report Card for American Infrastructure," the American Society of Civil Engineers gave Texas a mediocre score of C.[34] This survey mirrored a number of federal agency studies of the states' infrastructure problems. The message seems clear. Public facilities must be constantly maintained or expanded to support a growing population. Governments at all levels must plan for growth, allocate funds, and build facilities as this growth occurs. When they do not, infrastructure problems worsen, and the costs of improvements can begin to exceed the capacity of governments to pay for them. It has been projected that Texas will have to invest some $173 billion for water systems over the next fifty years. Many Texas cities already are out of compliance with federal standards for treating water and sewage and disposing of solid waste and are risking fines. Costs for these upgrades over the second decade of the 21st century alone are estimated at $25 billion.[35]

Some capital improvements are paid for out of current operating budgets, but a more common practice is for cities to borrow money to improve roads, streets, water systems, and the like. Property taxes are used to repay these bonds. When property values decline—as they did in the late 1980s—cities are restrained—by the constitution and statutes—in how much indebtedness they can incur to support needed improvements. A construction boom that began in the 1990s and continued through much of the first decade of the twenty-first century added a significant new tax base, but by 2011, the housing market had softened and evidence emerged that housing values had declined in many areas of the state.[36] Nevertheless, a growing population has increased the demand for roads, utilities, water and wastewater systems, and an array of other capital needs; cities are having trouble keeping up.

CRIME AND URBAN VIOLENCE Crime is a persistent problem facing Texas cities and counties, just as it is in many other parts of the country. Although crime rates in most offense categories in Texas declined in the 1990s and through the first decade of the twenty-first century, many Texans continued to believe that crime was on the rise.[37] Much of the problem was related to drug abuse, gang violence, and juvenile crime. These public perceptions also were shaped, in part, by anecdotal information, local news coverage focusing on "blood and guts," and political candidates who emphasized crime in their campaigns. Political candidates and elected officials often propose expansion of law enforcement, but many city and county budgets cannot absorb the costs.

STATE- AND FEDERAL-MANDATED PROGRAMS Both federal and state governments have increasingly used mandates in recent years to implement public policy. A **mandate** is a law or regulation enacted by a higher level of government that compels a lower level of government to carry out a specific action. In simpler terms, it is a form of "passing the buck." Federal mandates cover a wide range of governmental functions, including transportation, education for the disabled, water and air quality, and voter registration. States, meanwhile, have shifted much of the cost of public education to local governments.

Despite a decrease in federal funding for many programs to address urban problems since the 1980s, federal mandates on the states, counties, and the cities have increased, as have state mandates on local governments, often with no financial support. In some cases, the state simply passes the responsibility for—and the costs of—carrying out federal mandates to local governments. Congress enacted a law in 1995 to restrict unfunded mandates, but the law applied only to future, not existing, mandates. Such restrictions still can be circumvented if Congress chooses.

Although this practice may seem unfair and illogical, it is politically attractive to federal policymakers because they can "appease a large and vocal interest group that demands an extensive program without incurring the wrath of their constituents." They get the credit for such programs, but they do not get the blame for their costs.[38]

Cities and other local governments across Texas claim that these unfunded requirements are excessively expensive, force them to rearrange their priorities, and limit local initiatives dealing with their most pressing issues. If local governments do not comply with mandates, they can be subject to litigation and face the prospects of losing federal or state funds. If they comply with mandates, they then are likely to reduce other services or seek alternative sources of funding now denied them.

ENVIRONMENTAL ISSUES Texas is one of the most polluted states in the nation. Petrochemical industries generate a large amount of pollutants as by-products in processing fossil fuels or in manufacturing chemicals. The indiscriminate disposal of much of this waste in years past has produced toxic waste dumps in many cities, often in low-income, minority neighborhoods. Heavy automobile traffic and coal-burning power plants spew tons of pollutants into the air, and fertilizers and herbicides threaten local water supplies. Cities are frequently on "ozone alert" days, which could trigger additional federal and state requirements to contain the problems.

Some cities address these issues through "smart growth" programs and, more recently, "sustainability" and "green city" programs. After the administration of President George W. Bush made little effort to deal with the problem of global warming, many Texas cities joined other local governments with a wide array of environmental initiatives including efforts to reduce traffic congestion and air pollution, increase reliance on renewable energy, and reduce urban temperatures through extensive urban forestry, to name a few.

PUBLIC EMPLOYMENT As the baby boom generation retires, governmental agencies will face serious personnel issues. Since the late 1970s, bureaucrat bashing by political candidates, legislators, think tanks, and the media has helped increase public hostility toward government. This, in turn, has discouraged many highly skilled young people from seeking careers in public service. Retiring public employees also have accumulated expensive pensions, including health care benefits, which many cities may have trouble paying. Local governments often made commitments to provide retirement benefits without allocating sufficient funds to ensure that all benefits would be paid.

County Government in Texas

12.3 List the officials involved in and the consequences of the fragmented nature of county government.

Prior to Texas independence, local government was organized under both Spanish and Mexican law around the municipality. This unit consisted of large land areas with "presidios for military protection, missions established by the Catholic Church, and settlements established by various colonists and impresarios."[39] Twenty-three such municipalities existed at the time of independence, and they became the first twenty-three counties organized under the Texas Constitution of 1836.

Texas now has 254 counties, more than any other state. The state constitution gives the legislature the power to create, abolish, or alter counties. It also prescribes certain requirements for a new county, including its size and the proximity of its boundaries to the county seat of the county from which it is created. The last county created was Kenedy in 1921.[40]

Counties are administrative subunits of the state that were developed initially to serve a predominantly rural population and to administer state law. They possess powers delegated to them by the state, but they have relatively few implied powers.[41] Unlike home rule cities, counties lack the basic legislative power of enacting ordinances. They can carry out only those administrative functions granted them by the state. Counties administer and collect some state taxes and enforce a variety of state laws and regulations. They also build roads and bridges, administer local welfare programs, aid in fire protection, and perform other functions primarily local in nature.[42] All Texas counties function under the same constitutional restrictions and basic organizational structure, despite wide variations in population, local characteristics, and public needs.

☐ The Diversity of Counties

According to the 2010 census, Loving County, the state's least populous county, had only 82 residents, compared to 4.1 million in Harris County, the most populous (see Table 12–2). Rockwall County includes only 147 square miles; Brewster County covers 6,204 square miles. Some 58 percent of the state's population lives in the ten most populous counties.[43]

Motley County, with a population of about 1,210, had a 2010 budget of $798,735 and paid its county judge $16,226 a year and each of its commissioners $11,786. Dallas County had a $799 million budget and paid its county judge $153,853 and each commissioner $126,802 a year. Harris County's 2010 budget was $2.36 billion. Its county judge was paid $157,456, and each of its commissioners received $149,568.[44] Although there is an obvious relationship between the population of a county and salaries paid to its officials, the county's tax base also is a significant factor.

TABLE 12–2 TEN LARGEST AND TEN SMALLEST TEXAS COUNTIES, 1980–2010

	1980 Population	1990 Population	2000 Population	2010 Population
Ten Largest Texas Counties				
Harris County	2,409,547	2,818,199	3,400,578	4,092,459
Dallas County	1,556,390	1,852,810	2,218,899	2,368,139
Tarrant County	860,880	1,170,103	1,446,219	1,809,034
Bexar County	988,800	1,185,394	1,392,391	1,714,773
Travis County	419,573	576,407	812,280	1,024,426
El Paso County	479,899	591,610	679,622	800,647
Collin County	144,576	264,036	491,675	782,341
Hidalgo County	283,229	383,545	569,463	774,769
Denton County	143,126	273,525	432,976	662,614
Fort Bend County	130,846	225,421	354,452	585,375
Ten Smallest Texas Counties				
Motley County	1,950	1,532	1,426	1,210
Sterling County	1,206	1,438	1,393	1,143
Terrell County	1,595	1,410	1,081	984
Roberts County	1,187	1,025	887	929
Kent County	1,145	1,010	859	808
McMullen County	789	817	851	707
Borden County	859	799	729	641
Kenedy County	543	460	414	416
King County	425	354	356	286
Loving County	91	107	67	82

SOURCES: U.S Census Bureau, *U.S. Censuses, 1980, 1990, 2000, 2010.*

☐ The Structure of County Government

The organizational structure of county government is highly fragmented, reflecting the principles of Jacksonian democracy and the reaction of late-nineteenth-century Texans to Radical Reconstruction. The governing body of a county is the **commissioners court**, but it shares administrative functions with other independently elected officials (see Figure 12–6). Moreover, the name "commissioners court" is somewhat misleading because that body has no judicial functions.

commissioners court
The principal policymaking body for county government. It includes four commissioners and the county judge, all elected offices. It sets the county tax rate and supervises expenditures.

county judge
The presiding officer of a county commissioners court. This office also has some judicial authority, which is assumed by separate county courts-at-law in most urban counties.

COMMISSIONERS COURT AND COUNTY JUDGE The commissioners court includes a **county judge**, who is elected countywide, and four county commissioners, who are elected from a county's four commissioners precincts. Like other elected county officials, the judge and the commissioners serve four-year terms and are elected in partisan elections.

Until the 1960s, there were gross inequities in the population distributions among commissioners precincts in most counties. This issue of malapportionment came to a head in the 1968 case of *Avery* v. *Midland County*. Ninety-seven percent of the county's population, which lived in the city of Midland, elected only one commissioner, and the remaining 3 percent of the county's residents elected the other three. Similar inequities were prevalent all over the state, but the U.S. Supreme Court applied the "one person, one vote" principle to the counties and required that districts be equally apportioned.[45] Subsequently, Congress placed Texas under the Voting Rights Act in 1975,

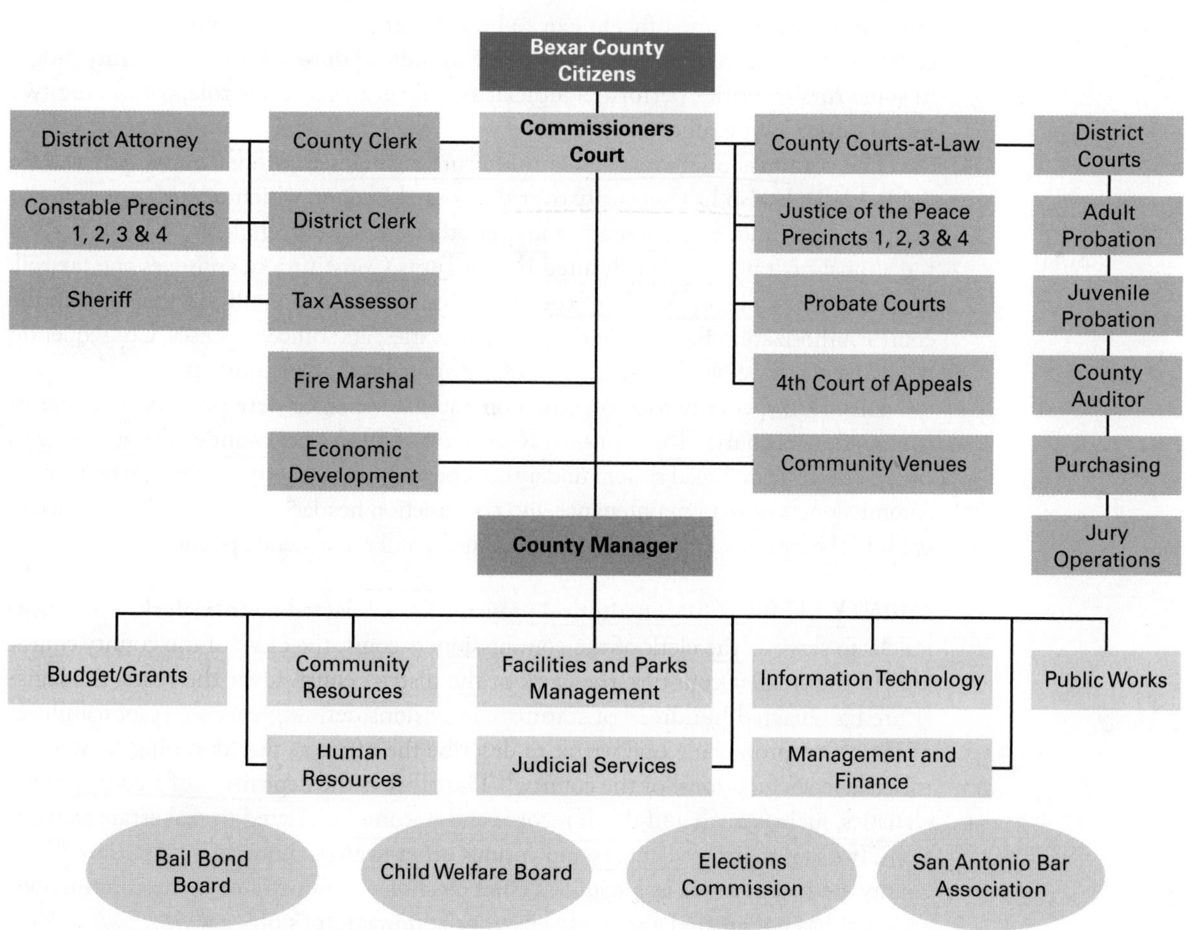

FIGURE 12–6 COUNTY GOVERNMENT: ORGANIZATIONAL CHART FOR BEXAR COUNTY

Whereas urban counties such as Bexar County function with many employees and provide a wide array of services, all counties in Texas function under a similar structure, which provides for the election of many officials and fragments authority among them.

Source: Bexar County, *Adopted Annual Budget, Fiscal Year 2011–2012.*

12.1

12.2

12.3

12.4

12.5

12.6

county clerk
The chief record-keeping officer of a county.

TABLE 12–3 MAJOR DUTIES OF THE COMMISSIONERS COURT

1. Set tax rate and adopt county budget.
2. Appoint county officials authorized under statutory law and hire personnel.
3. Fill county elective and appointive vacancies.
4. Administer elections, including the establishment of voting precincts, the appointment of an election administrator, the appointment of precinct judges, the calling of county bond elections, and the certification of election returns.
5. Award contracts and authorize payment of all county bills.
6. Build and maintain county roads and bridges.
7. Build, maintain, and improve county facilities, including jails.
8. Provide for libraries, hospitals, and medical care for the indigent.
9. Provide for emergency relief and civil disaster assistance.
10. Provide for fire protection and sanitation.

SOURCE: Texas Commission on Intergovernmental Relations, *An Introduction to County Government* (Austin, TX: Texas Commission on Intergovernmental Relations, 1985), p. 9.

and counties were required to consider the interests of minority populations in drawing the boundaries for commissioners precincts. African Americans and Hispanics across the state challenged county electoral systems and increased minority representation on county commissioners courts.

The county judge presides over the commissioners court, participates in the court's deliberations, and votes on issues before it. If there is a vacancy among the commissioners, the county judge appoints a replacement. If the county judge vacates his or her office, the commissioners choose a replacement.

The Texas Constitution also gives the county judge some judicial responsibilities but does not require the officeholder to be a lawyer. Most urban counties have county courts-at-law that relieve the county judge of judicial duties. However, county judges in some rural counties perform a judicial as well as an executive role, combining two sets of duties in one office.

The commissioners court fills midterm vacancies in other county offices (see Table 12–3). It also has authority over the county budget, which permits the court to exercise some influence, if not control, over other elected officeholders.[46] The court sets the annual tax rate, which is limited by the Texas Constitution, approves the tax roll, and supervises all expenditures of county money. Other county officials must obtain the court's authorization for personnel positions, salaries, and office expenses. Consequently, the budgetary process often sparks political disputes and other conflicts.

Historically, county road construction and maintenance were primary functions of commissioners courts. The Optional Road Law of 1947 gave counties the authority to create a consolidated road system under the supervision of a county engineer, who relieved commissioners of road maintenance and construction headaches. But the importance of roads to the commissioners and their constituents still can generate political disputes.

COUNTY CLERK The constitution provides for an elected **county clerk**, one officeholder to serve as the clerk of the commissioners court, the clerk of the county courts, and, in the smaller counties, the clerk of the district court. Over the years, the legislature has enacted hundreds of statutory provisions defining specific responsibilities of the office, prompting one writer to describe the office as the "dumping ground for miscellaneous functions" of the county.[47] The office is the depository of a county's vital statistics, such as birth and death records and documents related to real estate transactions. It issues marriage licenses and various other licenses required by state law.[48] The county clerk also serves as a county's chief elections administrator if the commissioners court has not created a separate elections administrator's office.[49]

DISTRICT CLERK The district clerk, also elected countywide, assists a county's district court or courts by maintaining custody of court documents and records.[50] In small counties, the county clerk is authorized to double as the district clerk, and sixty-two counties combined these two offices in 2010.[51]

COUNTY AND DISTRICT ATTORNEYS The state's legal interests in both civil and criminal matters are represented at the local level by one of three officers—the **county attorney**, the **district attorney**, or the criminal district attorney. The legislature has enacted numerous provisions for legal departments that vary from county to county. Some counties have no county attorney but have a criminal district attorney. Under state law, other counties are authorized to have both a county attorney and a district attorney. Inconsistencies exist in the specific functions and responsibilities of the offices from county to county.[52] District attorneys prosecute the more serious cases, usually felonies, in the district courts, whereas the county attorneys prosecute lesser offenses, primarily misdemeanors, in the county courts.[53]

These officers also can provide legal advice and opinions to other county officials and give legal counsel to public officials or employees who have been sued for acts committed in carrying out their official duties. Upon request of the commissioners court, the district attorney or county attorney may initiate lawsuits on behalf of the county. Various other laws charge these attorneys with protecting the public health, assisting the attorney general in cases involving deceptive trade practices, enforcing the state's election laws, collecting delinquent taxes, and even enforcing the Texas Communist Control Act of 1951.[54]

TAX ASSESSOR–COLLECTOR The property tax is the primary source of revenue for counties. Although the commissioners court sets property tax rates, the **county tax assessor–collector**, another elected officer, has the task of ascertaining who owns what property and how much tax is owed on that property and then collecting the tax. In counties with fewer than 10,000 people, these responsibilities are assigned to the sheriff, unless voters decide to create a separate tax assessor–collector office. Fourteen counties, mainly those with fewer than 5,000 in population, continue to let the sheriff handle the job.[55]

Prior to reforms enacted in the 1970s, the tax assessor–collector also was responsible for appraising property or determining its value. This process often was steeped in politics because the higher the value of a piece of property, the more taxes its owner has to pay. Lowering property values for selected friends or supporters gave those holding this office considerable power, which often was abused. In an effort to move toward greater consistency across the state and to enhance the professionalism of tax appraisals, the legislature now requires each county to create an **appraisal district** that is separate from the tax office.[56] The appraisal district, whose members represent other local governmental units, now determines the value of all property in the county. The district also certifies the tax rolls, and other governmental units are required by law to use its appraisals.[57]

COUNTY LAW ENFORCEMENT **Sheriffs** and **constables**, a county's law enforcement officers, are part of an old tradition under the Anglo-Saxon legal system. Each county has one sheriff with countywide jurisdiction, but the number of constables can vary. In counties with fewer than 18,000 residents, the commissioners court can designate the entire county as a single justice of the peace precinct or can create as many as four precincts, with each precinct assigned one constable. In the large counties, as many as eight justice of the peace precincts can be created with a constable assigned to each. Most larger counties have four constables.[58]

In a small rural county, the sheriff is the primary law enforcement officer for the entire county. In the urban counties, city police departments generally assume exclusive jurisdiction in the incorporated municipal areas, leaving the sheriff jurisdiction over the unincorporated areas. Most sheriffs have considerable discretion in the hiring, promotion, and firing of deputies and other employees, although some counties have adopted a merit employment system for the sheriff's office. The sheriff also serves as the administrative officer for the district and county courts.

Constables are authorized to patrol their precincts, make arrests, and conduct criminal investigations, but their primary function is to serve as administrative officers

county attorney
An elected official who is the chief legal officer of some counties. He or she also prosecutes lesser criminal offenses, primarily misdemeanors, in county courts.

district attorney
An elected official who prosecutes the more serious criminal offenses, usually felonies, in state district courts.

county tax assessor-collector
An elected official who determines how much property tax is owed on the different pieces of property within a county and then collects the tax. This officeholder acts on the basis of property values determined by the county appraisal district and a tax rate set by county commissioners court.

appraisal district
Countywide tax office that appraises the value of property and certifies the tax rolls used by every taxing authority in the county.

sheriff
An elected official who is the chief law enforcement officer of a county. In urban areas, his or her jurisdiction usually is limited to the unincorporated areas of a county, while local police departments have jurisdiction over incorporated cities.

constable
An elected law enforcement officer assigned as an administrative officer in a justice of the peace precinct. He or she is responsible primarily for executing court judgments, serving subpoenas, and delivering other legal documents. Constables also are authorized to patrol their precincts, make arrests, and conduct criminal investigations.

12.1

12.2

12.3

12.4

12.5

12.6

county auditor
An officer appointed by the district judges of the county. This person is primarily responsible for reviewing every bill and expenditure of a county to ensure that it is correct and legal. In counties with more than 225,000 people, the auditor also is the budget officer who prepares the county budget for consideration by commissioners court.

HOW WOULD YOU LIKE TO SPEND A FEW DAYS HERE?

Prior to federal court intervention, many local governments maintained aging jails that were small, crowded, and unsanitary. Most counties have replaced their aging jails, and until December 2011 when new facilities were completed, Blanco County utilized this jail that was constructed in 1893.

of the justice of the peace courts. They are responsible for serving subpoenas, executing judgments of the court, and delivering other legal documents.[59]

County governments are responsible for constructing and staffing county jails, which are managed in most counties by the sheriff and in some counties by a jail administrator. During the late 1980s and early 1990s, counties across the state pursued an aggressive policy of jail construction in response to court decisions, increased crime rates, and a shortage of state prison space. Jail construction was a "growth" industry during this period, but by the mid-1990s, some counties found that they had overextended their finances to construct these jails. They also were left with excess jail capacity after the state built new prisons. To compensate for these problems, several counties contracted with other states to house their prisoners in Texas jails.

All counties are authorized to create an office of the medical examiner. The commissioners court appoints this individual, who determines the cause of death of murder victims or others who die under suspicious or unusual circumstances. In counties that do not have a medical examiner, the justice of the peace must conduct an inquest to determine if there are conditions to merit an autopsy.

Counties, either individually or as part of multicounty judicial districts, must provide facilities for a criminal probation office. The state sets probation standards, and district judges choose the chief adult probation officer.

COUNTY AUDITOR All counties with 10,000 or more population are required to have a county auditor, and smaller counties may have one if the commissioners court chooses. Two counties with fewer than 25,000 residents may jointly agree to hire an auditor to serve both counties. The **county auditor** is appointed by the district judges of the county for a two-year term. He or she is primarily responsible for reviewing every bill and expenditure of a county to ensure its correctness and legality. Such oversight can, in effect, impose budgetary restrictions on commissioners courts and produce political conflict with other county officers.

The role of the auditor varies from county to county. In counties with more than 225,000 people, the auditor is the budget officer who prepares the county budget for submission to the commissioners court unless an alternative has been authorized by the legislature.[60] In smaller counties, the commissioners court prepares the budget, based on estimates provided by the auditor.

COUNTY TREASURER The **country treasurer** is responsible for receiving and disbursing county funds. Although it has existed since 1846, the primary functions of this office are now carried out by the county auditor, and constitutional amendments have eliminated this office in several counties.

county treasurer
An elected officer who is responsible for receiving and disbursing county funds. The office's primary functions are now carried out by the county auditor, and the office has been eliminated in a number of counties.

12.1 12.2 12.3 12.4 12.5 12.6

□ Criticisms of County Government

The structure of county government in Texas, designed for a rural state, has inhibited efforts of urban counties to respond to growing needs for public services. The state has experimented with county home rule, but the provisions were so poorly written, confusing, and contradictory that local home rule at the county level was never given a real chance. Efforts were made in the 1997 and 1999 sessions of the legislature to amend the constitution to once again allow counties to adopt home rule, but statewide support for this change was limited.

Even though the county functions primarily as an extension, or administrative subdivision, of state government, there is little supervision of the counties by the state and wide disparity in the way counties interpret and administer their functions. Some counties do a good job; others have a dismal record. The fragmentation represented by several independently elected officers always poses the potential for jurisdictional conflict, administrative inefficiency, and even government deadlock.

Like other local governments in Texas, counties rely heavily on the property tax for revenue but cannot exceed tax rate limits set by the state constitution. Those limits reflected a general apprehension about government when they were initially set in 1876. They now further restrict the counties' ability to provide services.

Historically, county courthouses were associated with political patronage and the **spoils system**. Victorious candidates claimed the right to appoint personal and political friends to work for them, and state courts held that elected county officials had wide discretion in the selection of their employees. Reformers advocated a **civil service system** for county employees based on merit and competitive examinations and offering job security from one election to the next. A 1971 law allows counties with more than 200,000 in population to create a civil service system, but it excludes several county offices, including the district attorney. An elected public official retains considerable control over the initial hiring of employees through a probationary period of six months.[61]

spoils system
Practice, usually identified with machine politics, of awarding public jobs to one's political friends or supporters with little regard to abilities or skills.

civil service system
A personnel system under which public employees are selected for government jobs through competitive examinations and the systematic evaluation of job performance.

special districts
Units of local government created by the state to perform a specific function or functions not met by cities or counties, including the provision of public services to unincorporated areas.

Special Districts in Texas

12.4 Explain the functions and problems associated with single-purpose districts.

Every day, Texans use the services of municipal utility districts (MUDs), water conservation and improvement districts (WCIDs), hospital districts, and a host of other local governments, which have been deemed by some as the "invisible governments" of the state.[62] Approximately 3,375 such governmental units across Texas have been classified as **special districts**, and every year additional ones are created. These include drainage districts, navigation districts, fresh water supply districts, river authorities, underground water districts, sanitation districts, housing authorities, and soil conservation districts. School districts also are considered a form of special district.

☐ Functions and Structures of Special Districts

Special districts are units of local government created by the state to perform specific functions. Wide variations in their functions, taxing and borrowing authority, governance, and performance limit generalizations about them. Most special districts are authorized to perform a single function and are designated single-purpose districts. Others are multipurpose districts (MUDs) because the laws creating them permit them to provide more than one service to constituents. For example, in addition to providing water to people in their service areas, MUDs may assume responsibility for drainage, solid waste collection, firefighting, parks, and other recreational facilities.[63] Some districts, such as hospital districts, normally cover an entire county. Others, such as MUDs, cover part of one county; still others, such as river authorities, cover a number of counties.

A board, either appointed by other governmental units or elected in nonpartisan elections, governs special districts. County commissioners courts appoint the board members of hospital districts, and mayors or city councils appoint city housing authority boards. Many of these districts have taxing and borrowing authority, but others have no taxing powers and are supported by user fees or funds dedicated to them by other governmental agencies. Many special districts are eligible for federal grants-in-aid.

Special districts exist for a variety of reasons. Independent school districts were created, in part, to depoliticize education and remove the responsibility for it from county and city governments. Reformers in the late nineteenth and early twentieth centuries argued that the governance of schools had to be autonomous and insulated from partisan politics. That goal could be accomplished only by the creation of districts that had their own governing bodies and tax bases. Similar arguments also have been made about other specialized governmental functions.[64]

In some cases, existing governments are unwilling or unable—because of state restrictions on their tax, debt, or jurisdictional authority—to provide essential services to developing communities. Counties are particularly limited by state law and the constitution and do not have the authority to provide many of the services now demanded by their citizens. Therefore, special districts were created to fill the gap. Because many districts can be created by statute, it has been far easier to create an additional layer of government than to change the authority or powers of existing governments by constitutional amendment.[65]

The cost of providing a particular governmental service is another reason for the growth of special districts. By creating a special district that includes a number of governmental units and a larger population and tax base, the costs can be spread over a wider area. Individuals, groups, or corporations often promote special districts for selfish gains (see *Talking Texas: The Ambitious Little Water District*). Builders, for example, sometimes develop plans for large tracts of land in the unincorporated areas of a county and then ask local governments or the legislature to create municipal utility or water districts to provide water and sewer services.[66]

Some special districts have been designed to serve specific geographical areas. River basins that extend for thousands of square miles and cover ten or twenty counties present a particular problem. Because no existing governments had jurisdiction over the use of water resources in these basins, the legislature created river authorities with multicounty jurisdictions.[67]

☐ Consequences of Single-Purpose Districts

From one perspective, special districts compensate for the fragmentation and limited authority of local governments that exist throughout Texas. But, ironically, these districts also contribute to further fragmentation and delay the more difficult development of comprehensive, multipurpose governmental units that could more efficiently provide public services.

Talking ★ TEXAS The Ambitious Little Water District

Most Texans have never heard of sparsely populated Roberts County, which sits over the Ogallala Aquifer in the Texas Panhandle. It also is highly unlikely that they have heard of Roberts County Water District #1, a "fresh water supply district" approved in 2007 by voters owning land in the eight square miles comprising the district. Yet, high-stakes politics over water supplies and private property rights played out in the district's organization.

Communities throughout the Southwest face severe water shortages that, if not cured, will limit their abilities to continue to grow and prosper. Quiet efforts by some wealthy individuals, including oilman T. Boone Pickens of Dallas, have been made to fill their needs and reap profits by purchasing water rights in sparsely populated areas that have access to underground water.

Roberts County Water District #1 sits over land to which Pickens has water rights and is the vehicle he has designed to pump water from the Ogallala through a pipeline to Dallas, some 300 miles away. Pickens initially tried to organize this water district in 2002 but was rebuffed by a group of Roberts County residents who initiated a plan for a countywide water district over which he would have little control. So Pickens pursued another strategy. During the 2006 election cycle, he gave $1.2 million to political candidates and political committees, including sixteen state senators and one-third of the members of the Texas House. Pickens also spent some $1 million on lobbyists working the Texas legislature in 2007.

During that session, the legislature enacted changes in state law to give Pickens virtual carte blanche to organize a special district with wide-ranging powers. The law pertaining to special districts was modified to permit people who owned property within the district but lived elsewhere to vote in the organization election. At the same time, lawmakers resisted efforts to make substantive changes in eminent domain laws, which give governments the power to take private property for public use. Consequently, the water district contemplated by Pickens would have eminent domain powers extending hundreds of miles beyond the small district's boundaries.

The outcome of the election on the district's creation in November 2007 was never in doubt. Only five voters owned land in the district, and all had business relationships with Pickens. The oilman had sold them small parcels of his huge holdings shortly after the end of the 2007 legislative session and before the November election. Two were residents of Roberts County, and three lived hundreds of miles away from the district.

As Pickens's plans for pumping water from the Ogallala unfold, it may become evident how individuals or corporations can use a special district to advance their own economic interests.

Pickens's water supply district will provide him with a wide range of legal powers to expedite the delivery of water to customers hundreds of miles away. Using the so-called "right of recapture" (access to water under one's own property), Pickens anticipates pumping 200,000 acre-feet of water out of the aquifer each year, which could place additional stress on the primary water source of West Texas. Using the power of eminent domain, he can force landowners to sell him access to their land for a pipeline. What is significant for the present are the actions of the legislature that weakened the public's control over the organization and governance of special districts. This opened the way for individuals or corporations to pursue actions that could be potentially harmful to a large number of Texans.[a]

CRITICAL THINKING QUESTIONS

1. **Should a property owner be allowed to pipe large quantities of water from under his or her property in an arid part of the state for resale hundreds of miles away? Why or why not?**
2. **Should there be a limit on how much an individual is allowed to contribute to members of the legislature? Why or why not?**

[a]Jim Landers, "T. Boone Pickens to Import Water, Wind Power to North Texas," *Dallas Morning News*, April 18, 2008, p. 3D; and Texans for Public Justice, "Watch Your Assets: T. Boone Pickens Land Grab," October 4, 2007.

A special district has been called a "halfway house between cityhood and noncityhood, between incorporation and nonincorporation."[68] Residents of a developing community or subdivision may not want to create a new city or become part of a nearby existing city, but they need certain basic services, such as water, electricity, and fire protection, some of which could be provided through the creation of special districts.

Many special districts are small operations with limited financial resources and few employees. Salaries often are low, and some districts have difficulty retaining the licensed technical people required to perform daily operations. In some cases, record keeping and management operations are shoddy and amateurish, and the costs of providing services by many of these operations may actually be higher than the costs of similar services in larger governmental systems. Special districts also may use outside

12.1

12.2

12.3

12.4

12.5

12.6

independent school district
A specific form of special district that administers the public schools in a designated area. It is governed by an elected board of trustees empowered to levy local property taxes, establish local school policies, and employ a school superintendent as its chief administrator.

legal and professional assistance, which can be very costly, and many districts lack the expertise to maximize their investments or borrowing potential.[69]

Some special districts expand their functions beyond the original purpose for which they were created. The metropolitan transit authority in San Antonio, for example, authorized under state law to impose a 1 percent sales tax for public transportation, became involved in building the Alamodome, a multipurpose convention and sports facility. As governments expand their functions, the potential for intergovernmental rivalry, conflict, deadlock, and duplication of costs increases.

Except for the 1,000-plus independent school districts and a small number of other highly visible districts, such as river authorities, most special districts operate in anonymity. The public has only limited knowledge of their jurisdiction, management, operations, or performance. Many taxpayers may not be aware that they pay taxes to some of these entities, nor do they have any concept of the districts' indebtedness. Their work gets little media coverage, few individuals attend their board meetings, and turnout for their elections is extremely low. In the case of the governing boards appointed by other governmental agencies, a small number of individuals or groups often dominate the appointment process and the activities of the special district.

Independent School Districts

12.5 Describe the governance structure and inequities of independent school districts.

The recurring controversy over educational quality and equity in Texas has roots in the early organization and governance of the public schools. Education was an issue in the Texas independence movement, but it was the Reconstruction period that set the stage for many of the long-term issues of school finance and governance. During Reconstruction, the Radical Republicans attempted to centralize the education system at the state level. With the end of Republican control prior to the Constitutional Convention of 1875, the centralized system was eliminated, and the control and financing of public education were transferred to the counties.

Instead of an orderly, comprehensive system that ensured public education to every child, community schools were created. They could be formed by any group of parents petitioning the county judge, who had considerable influence and control over the schools. County judges could appoint trustees nominated by the organizing parents and distribute money from the state's Available School Fund, based on mineral rights and other earnings from state lands, to the organized schools within their respective counties. This produced marked differences in the availability, funding, and quality of public education across the state. Community schools also were self-selective. People who initiated the creation of a school could decide which children attended. As a result, racial and economic segregation occurred, and the children of Texans with limited political clout were denied access to an adequate public education. These characteristics dominated public education in Texas at the end of the nineteenth century, and vestiges remained until 1909.

The **independent school district**, currently the basic organizational structure for public education in Texas, had its origins in the Constitution of 1876. Cities and towns were allowed to create independent school districts and to impose a tax to support them. Initially, the city government served as the school board, but in 1879, a school district was permitted to organize independently of the city or town, elect its own board of trustees, and impose its own school tax. However, residents of rural areas, where most nineteenth-century Texans lived, were denied these powers and had only the option of forming community schools. So, in effect, Texas operated under a dual school system, with the majority of students subject to the discretionary and often arbitrary powers of county governments.

Inequities in the Public Education System

From the very beginning, the inequities in such a school system were clear to many parents, elected officials, and educators, and early efforts were initiated to reform and modernize public schools. Most were linked to national education reform movements funded by northern philanthropists after the Civil War to promote public education in the South. George Peabody of Massachusetts created the Peabody Education Fund in 1867 to be followed by others, including John D. Rockefeller, who established the General Education Board. These organizations provided financial aid and technical support to leaders of state reform movements during the early part of the twentieth century.

Education reform efforts in Texas have been an ongoing saga. Early initiatives focused on the accessibility of schools to children in rural areas, compulsory school attendance, funding, recruitment of teachers, and teacher training. Schools were segregated, and school revenues were tied to local property taxes. Subsequent reforms were directed at the structure and governance of local school districts. The diverse and fragmented structure of Texas schools has been modified over the years through consolidation, greater uniformity in the organization of school districts, the extension of the independent school district to virtually every community in the state, and the expansion of the authority of the Texas Education Agency.

Texas now has almost 5 million children in public schools and a host of new issues, including bilingual and special education, graduation rates, student performance, and mandated testing for progress and accountability.

Differences among School Districts

Although regulation and coordination are provided on a statewide level through the State Board of Education (SBOE) and the Texas Education Agency (TEA), public education now is administered through approximately 1,050 local school districts, which include some 7,972 schools. In the 2009–2010 school year, some of the smallest, rural school districts had fewer than 75 students. The largest, the Houston Independent School District, had 200,904 students. The 17 largest districts—with more than 50,000 students each—enrolled approximately 1.37 million or 28 percent of the 4.8 million students attending prekindergarten through grade 12. By contrast, 463 rural districts, serving fewer than 500 students each, enrolled 116,309 students. Students from minority ethnic or racial groups constituted 67 percent of the public school population in Texas in 2009–2010, and their numbers are projected to increase.[70] As might be expected, school districts also vary in financial resources, facilities, graduation rates, and other performance measures.

Local School Governance

School boards, ranging in size from three to nine members, govern school districts; most boards have seven members. Trustees are elected in nonpartisan elections for terms that vary from two to six years, with most serving three-year terms. By 2012, more than 160 of the 1,000-plus school districts elected their boards from single-member districts.[71] School districts with significant minority populations have shifted from at-large elections to single-member districting, primarily as a consequence of lawsuits or the threats of lawsuits by minority plaintiffs under the Voting Rights Act.

Most school board elections are held on the first Saturday in May, the same day most cities hold their elections. School board election turnouts are low, usually less than 10 percent of registered voters. But turnout increases when there are highly visible issues, such as the firing of a superintendent or a dramatic increase in taxes. One unanticipated consequence of single-member districts has been a general decline in voter turnout for school board elections. Without a district-wide race for multiple

school boards
Governing bodies of public school districts.

12.1
12.2
12.3
12.4
12.5
12.6

school superintendent
Chief administrator of a school district who is hired by the school board.

privatization
Government contracting with private companies to provide some public services.

offices, fewer voters seem inclined to vote. Moreover, single-member districts limit the pool of candidates to residents living within each election district rather than from throughout the entire school district, potentially reducing the number of competitive races.

Recruiting qualified candidates for school boards often is difficult, and many elections are uncontested. The superintendent, other members of the board, or key community leaders often ask individuals to run, because it is difficult to find people who are willing to give the required time and energy. Individuals often have little knowledge of what school board members do, and because many trustees serve for only one term, some boards have high turnover rates. Moreover, a potential trustee cannot anticipate the amount of time it will take for briefings by the superintendent and staff, preparing for and participating in board meetings, and taking phone calls from parents and taxpayers. A board member also must deal with the political aspect of the job, including attendance at community functions and major school programs and meetings with teachers and taxpayer groups. Board members receive no salaries but are reimbursed for travel related to board business.

The most important decision that a school board makes is the hiring of a **school superintendent**. In organization and management structure, the school district is similar to the council-manager form of government used by many cities. The board hires a superintendent, who is in charge of the district's day-to-day operations. Although the board has the primary policymaking responsibility for a district, the superintendent and the superintendent's staff often dominate part-time board members. School trustees and superintendents tend to talk about "keeping politics out of education," and superintendents often attempt to convey the impression that they serve simply to carry out the will of their boards. In most instances, however, the superintendent establishes a school board's agenda, and the board members depend on the superintendent and other professional staff members for information and policy recommendations. Very few board members have much time to give to the district, and most have only limited knowledge of the many laws affecting education. State law, in fact, restricts the intrusion of board members into the daily management and administration of a district. An excessively politicized school board that becomes involved in day-to-day administration can be called to task by the Texas Education Agency. In an extreme case, the TEA can even take over the management of a school district.

Solutions to the Problems of Local Government

12.6 Assess the various proposed solutions to the problems of local government.

Finding solutions to their various challenges and problems is a never-ending task for many local governments, and what works for one city or county may not work for another. What follows are some solutions that governments have tried, with varying degrees of success.

☐ Privatization of Functions

As local governments have juggled their financial problems with increased demands for public services, they have resorted to contracting out some services to private companies. Many governments believe **privatization** can reduce costs through businesslike efficiency, and they consider it an attractive alternative in the face of voter hostility toward higher taxes. Cities, for example, contract for garbage pickup, waste disposal, towing, food services, security, and a variety of other services. Privatization also provides a way for local governments that have reached their limit on bonded indebtedness to make new capital improvements by leasing a facility from a private contractor. A civic center or a school facility can be constructed by a private contractor and leased back to the government for an extended period.

annexation
The authority of cities to add territory, subject to restrictions set by state law.

extraterritorial jurisdiction
The power of an incorporated city to control development within nearby unincorporated areas.

□ Annexation and Extraterritorial Jurisdiction

Population growth in the areas surrounding most large Texas cities has forced municipalities and counties to wrestle with urban sprawl. El Paso, for example, included 26 square miles in 1950 but had expanded to 255 square miles by 2010. Houston grew from 160 square miles in 1950 to 600 square miles in 2010, with its extraterritorial jurisdiction encompassing more than 1,300 square miles, excluding the cities that lie within this area.[72]

The cities' ability to expand their boundaries beyond suburban development derives from their **annexation** powers and their **extraterritorial jurisdiction** over neighboring areas. Faced with the prospect that areas surrounding them will eventually be annexed, cities do not want to be saddled with new communities when there has been limited or no planning and substandard buildings, roads, and infrastructure. With the Municipal Annexation Act of 1963, the legislature granted cities considerable discretionary authority over nearby unincorporated areas. Specific annexation powers and extraterritorial jurisdiction vary with the size of a city and the charter under which it functions. Generally, cities have extraterritorial jurisdiction over unincorporated areas within one-half mile to five miles of the city limits, making development in those areas subject to the city's building codes, zoning and land-use restrictions, utility easement requirements, and road and street specifications. This authority restricts the use of unincorporated land and requires those building outside the city to build according to at least minimal standards. Later, when the city annexes those areas, they are less likely to quickly degenerate into suburban slums that will require a high infusion of city dollars for basic services.

Residents and businesses outside of a city's corporate limits also benefit from access to public and private facilities and services in the city. City residents argue that those living or doing business outside the city should "share the tax burden associated with constructing and maintaining those facilities and services."[73]

Cities can annex areas equivalent to 10 percent of their existing territory in a given year, and if this authority is not exercised in one year, it can be carried over to subsequent years. Annexation usually does not require a vote of those people who are to be incorporated into the city. However, within two and a half years, a city is required to provide annexed areas with services comparable to those provided in its older neighborhoods. Otherwise, individuals living in these newly annexed areas can exercise an option to be de-annexed, a situation that rarely occurs.

Cities even have annexed thin strips of land, miles from urban development, along major roads and arteries leading into them. Because a city's extraterritorial jurisdiction extends as far as five miles on either side of the strip that is annexed, this practice enables a city to control future development in a large area. In San Antonio, these annexation policies often have been referred to as "spoke annexation," and it has taken more than thirty years for much of the territory brought under the city's jurisdiction to be developed and annexed by the city.[74]

The aggressive use of annexation has permitted most large cities in Texas to expand geographically with population growth. Texas cities have been able to share in the benefits of growth in the areas surrounding them and limit the development of small suburban towns that would potentially halt future expansion.[75]

For more than thirty years after the enactment of the Municipal Annexation Act, the state legislature did little to restrict the annexation powers of cities, but in recent legislative sessions, many lawmakers have demonstrated, along with their constituents,

tax abatements
Device used by governments to attract new businesses through the reduction or elimination of property taxes for a specific period of time.

12.1

12.2

12.3

12.4

12.5

12.6

an anticity sentiment with proposals that would have eroded municipal authority, reduced municipal revenues, and imposed costly new mandates. Of particular concern to cities were attacks on annexation powers. The Seventy-fifth Legislature in 1999 enacted a major overhaul of annexation authority, including a provision that requires cities to outline their annexation plans three years in advance. But city officials believed that they were able to obtain, through their lobbying efforts, a relatively "well-balanced" law.[76] The legislature in 2001 continued to reflect growing suburban-rural hostility toward the central cities. It enacted a law that modified the extraterritorial jurisdiction of cities by requiring city-county agreements on the regulation of subdivisions. In effect, this law placed more limits on the powers of Texas cities.[77]

☐ Modernization of County Government

City governments provide most basic public services in urban areas, and as cities expand to county boundaries and beyond, overlapping jurisdictions of county and city governments increase along with a reduction of county services in the annexed areas. Counties, nevertheless, still play an important role in Texas. Rural Texans, in particular, continue to rely on counties to provide a number of services, and demands on counties will increase. Recommendations to modernize county government include another attempt at county home rule; granting counties some legislative or ordinance-making authority; modernizing county information and communications systems; and creating an office of county administrator, appointed by a commissioners court, to run the departments now assigned to commissioners. Another recommendation is to extend the civil service system to smaller counties and to all county employees.[78]

☐ Economic Development

Historically, cities have collaborated with the private sector to stimulate local economies. Private sector initiatives have come from chambers of commerce or economic development foundations, corporations, other groups, or individuals, and city governments have participated. Cities also are using a variety of new financing techniques to assist in economic development, including development impact taxes and fees, user charges, creation of special district assessments, tax increment financing, and privatization of governmental functions.[79] A state law, enacted in 1989, permits cities, with the approval of local voters, to impose a 0.5 percent sales tax for local economic development.[80] Voters in several hundred cities have approved this tax option.

Texas cities, as well as some counties, aggressively court American and foreign companies to relocate or develop new plants or operations in their communities. Cities and local chambers of commerce sponsor public relations campaigns touting local benefits and attractions. Local governments offer **tax abatements**—exemptions from property taxes on a business for a specified period—to encourage a company to locate or expand in particular Texas cities. Other financial incentives to companies being courted include lowered utility bills and assistance in obtaining housing for employees. Many cities have established relationships with "sister cities" in foreign countries, and state government has assisted cities by establishing trade and commerce offices in a few key foreign cities. The city of San Antonio aggressively wooed Toyota to locate a new manufacturing plant in South Texas, and the coordinated efforts of the city, the state, and the private sector resulted in a decision in 2003 to bring the new plant to the city. State and local officials predicted the facility would be a major economic generator and help transform the city's economy. Toyota invested more than $2 billion in the facility, which now employs more than 2,200 workers and produces full-size and compact pickups.

The legislature permits counties to form industrial development corporations or enterprise zones and to relax state regulatory policies to encourage the redevelopment of depressed areas. Portions of a county may be designated as reinvestment zones, in which tax abatements can be offered to attract new businesses. Counties also can create county boards of development, civic centers, foreign trade zones, and research and development authorities.[81]

A wide range of federal programs for local economic development also are available. Most depend on local initiatives in the planning and application processes and require a political commitment by elected officials and a demonstrated rationale for the receipt of federal dollars.

☐ Interlocal Contracting

Because many small governments have limited tax bases and staffs, they enter into contracts with larger governments for various public services. In 1971, the legislature, following a constitutional amendment, enacted the Interlocal Cooperation Act, which gave cities, counties, and other political subdivisions rather broad authority for such contracts.[82] The law has been amended several times to expand the scope of these agreements, and local governments now contract with one another for services in at least twenty-five functional areas, ranging from aviation to water and wastewater management.[83] Contracting is not an alternative to consolidation of local governments, but it does hold out some promise for improving the quality of local services and reducing their costs.

☐ Metro Government and Consolidation

In the metropolitan areas of the state's ten largest counties, more than 1,100 cities, school districts, and special districts provide public services. Harris County (Houston) alone has 487 separate governmental units (see Table 12–4). Legislators, scholars, and

TABLE 12–4 LOCAL GOVERNMENTS IN THE TEN LARGEST AND TEN SMALLEST TEXAS COUNTIES, 2010

	Population (2010)	Total	County	Municipal	School Districts	Special Districts
			Ten Largest Texas Counties			
Harris	4,092,459	487	1	28	24	434
Dallas	2,368,139	63	1	25	16	21
Tarrant	1,809,034	67	1	34	18	14
Bexar	1,714,773	51	1	22	16	12
Travis	1,024,266	79	1	15	8	55
El Paso	800,647	36	1	6	10	19
Collin	782,341	51	1	24	15	11
Hidalgo	774,769	77	1	22	16	38
Denton	662,614	69	1	33	11	24
Fort Bend	585,375	138	1	16	5	116
			Ten Smallest Texas Counties			
Motley	1,210	7	1	2	1	3
Sterling	1,143	5	1	1	1	2
Terrell	984	4	1	0	1	2
Roberts	929	4	1	1	1	1
Kent	808	5	1	1	1	2
McMullen	707	5	1	0	1	3
Borden	641	2	1	0	1	0
Kenedy	416	2	1	0	1	0
King	286	3	1	0	1	1
Loving	82	2	1	0	0	1

SOURCE: U.S. Census Bureau, *Census of Governments, 2007, Government Organization;* and U.S. Census Bureau, *2010 Census.*

12.1

12.2

12.3

12.4

12.5

12.6

metro government
Consolidation of city and county governments to avoid duplication of public services. This approach has been tried in several other parts of the country but so far has attracted little interest in Texas.

public improvement district
Specific area of a city in which property owners pay special taxes in return for improvements to streets and other public facilities in their neighborhood.

reform groups have studied the duplication and other problems produced by such proliferation and fragmentation extensively and have made numerous recommendations over the years. A variety of proposals have been designed to eliminate duplication and overlap, including city-county consolidation and various forms of **metro government**. However, efforts in the late 1990s by counties to obtain constitutional authority to propose city-county consolidation to voters in the counties failed. Without such authority, county-city collaboration is more likely to take the form of increased intergovernmental contracting and the informal cooperation that local governments develop out of necessity and mutual self-interest.[84]

☐ Public Improvement Districts

Under one state law, property owners in a specific area of a city or its extraterritorial jurisdiction can petition the city to create a special **public improvement district (PID)**. These districts can undertake a wide range of improvements—landscaping, lighting, signs, sidewalks, streets, pedestrian malls, libraries, parking, water, wastewater, and drainage facilities. Public improvement districts do not have the same autonomy as other special districts. They are created solely through the discretionary powers of the city and are funded by assessments on property within their boundaries.[85] Although their budgets and assessments must be approved by the city, they can be operated and managed by private management companies or by the citizens themselves. Fort Worth created a public improvement district for its downtown area in 1986 and now has six additional functioning districts. Other cities including Dallas, Houston, and San Antonio also have created PIDs.

Review the Chapter

Listen to Chapter 12

Urban Texas

12.1 Trace Texas's transition from an agrarian state to an urban one, p. 354.

From Texas's formative period, local governments, which are created by and subordinate to the state, have played a central role in the state's development. What was once an overwhelmingly rural state has been transformed into a highly urbanized one with 88 percent of the population now living in urban areas. Of the ten largest cities in the nation, three—Houston, San Antonio, and Dallas—are located in Texas. Eight of the state's ten largest cities have more than 50 percent minority populations, contributing to a long-standing controversy over urban electoral systems.

The Cities and the State

12.2 Compare and contrast the forms of government, election systems, sources of revenue, and issues facing Texas cities, p. 357.

Texans use four forms of city government—the strong mayor-council, the weak mayor-council, the city commission, and the council-manager. For cities with populations of fewer than 5,000, the state limits the forms of government that can be used. But for cities with more than 5,000 residents, the legislature permits home rule, which allows a city to choose the form of government it wishes, provided that it does not conflict with the state constitution or state law. The form of government a city chooses reflects complex political dynamics; as social, economic, and political environments change, cities often change their form of government.

A notable feature of city politics in Texas is the widespread use of nonpartisan, at-large elections. In homogeneous communities, these election systems appear to work quite well. In communities with highly diverse racial, economic, and social groups—in which voting is polarized—at-large elections adversely affect key segments of the population. Prompted by legal attacks on at-large elections under the Voting Rights Act, many cities, as well as special purpose districts, have adopted single-member districts, thus increasing minority representation on local governing bodies.

Cities receive no state appropriations; have limited financial options; and are disproportionately dependent on regressive taxes, fees, or transfer of funds from locally owned utilities, if they have them.

County Government in Texas

12.3 List the officials involved in and the consequences of the fragmented nature of county government, p. 369.

County governments, initially created to serve a rural population, function primarily as the administrative subdivisions of the state. Much like state government, county government is highly fragmented, with administrative powers shared by a variety of elected officials—the county judge, the four commissioners, the district and county clerks, the tax assessor-collector, the sheriff, and constables. Although budgetary and policy factors often prompt cooperation among these officials, the fragmentation also creates the potential for personal or partisan conflicts over policy.

Special Districts in Texas

12.4 Explain the functions and problems associated with single-purpose districts, p. 375.

Thousands of special-purpose districts have been created across the state to provide public services that county and city governments cannot or do not provide. Some were created to serve a geographical area extending over many counties or to provide a single public service at a reduced cost. The services and facilities they provide include water service, solid waste management, firefighting, parks, public housing, and recreational facilities. Some districts cover multiple counties; others, a single county; and still others, a very small part of a county. Special districts have their own governing bodies, which can be elected or appointed. These special districts have added to the fragmentation of governments. Most people know little about them or their taxing authority, and few people participate in their board elections.

Independent School Districts

12.5 Describe the governance structure and inequities of independent school districts, p. 378.

Texas has approximately 1,050 independent school districts, ranging in size from the largest, the Houston Independent School District, with more than 200,000 students, to rural districts with only a few dozen students each. School boards elected in nonpartisan elections govern all districts. The board hires a superintendent to perform the daily administration of the district.

School districts are funded by a combination of state revenue and local property taxes. Districts with low levels of property wealth suffer from funding inequities, which have prompted districts to file a series of lawsuits over school funding against the state. Some funding improvements have been made over the years, but significant funding disparities—and educational opportunities—still exist among districts.

Solutions to the Problems of Local Government

12.6 Assess the various proposed solutions to the problems of local government, p. 380.

Increased population, urban sprawl, white flight, an increase in low-income residents, mandated programs from the state and federal government, limited revenue options, and inadequate and declining infrastructures are among a number of problems confronting local governments in Texas.

Local governments use a variety of strategies to deal with their problems. Cities have used their annexation powers and extraterritorial jurisdiction to expand their tax bases and exercise limited controls over development in adjacent areas. Cities also use public improvement districts to permit targeted areas to impose additional taxes for needed services. Both counties and cities privatize some governmental functions to decrease costs and increase efficiency. Interlocal contracting permits governments to provide services to one another on a contractual basis, and many counties and cities engage in aggressive economic development programs. Some people advocate consolidation of local governments, but support is limited for this alternative in Texas.

Learn the Terms

Study and **Review** the Flashcards

population density, p. 355
Dillon rule, p. 358
general law cities, p. 358
home rule cities, p. 358
city charter, p. 358
weak mayor, p. 359
strong mayor, p. 359
city commission, p. 360
council-manager government, p. 362
nonpartisan elections, p. 364
at-large election, p. 365
runoff election, p. 365
single-member districts, p. 365
regressive tax, p. 365
rollback election, p. 366
general obligation bonds, p. 367
revenue bonds, p. 367
homestead exemption, p. 367
mandates, p. 368
commissioners court, p. 371
county judge, p. 371
county clerk, p. 372
county attorney, p. 373
district attorney, p. 373
county tax assessor–collector, p. 373
appraisal district, p. 373
sheriff, p. 373
constable, p. 373
county auditor, p. 374
country treasurer, p. 375
spoils system, p. 375
civil service system, p. 375
special districts, p. 375
independent school district, p. 378
school boards, p. 379
school superintendent, p. 380
privatization, p. 380
annexation, p. 381
extraterritorial jurisdiction, p. 381
tax abatements, p. 382
metro government, p. 384
public improvement district, p. 384

Test Yourself

Study and **Review** the Practice Test

1. What does the Dillon rule state?

a. Local governments derive their authority from the consent of the governed.

b. State and local governments have equal and concurrent sovereign powers.

c. County governments have higher sovereign authority than city governments.

d. Local school districts are administrative subdivisions of the city.

e. Local governments are creations of the state and have no sovereign powers.

2. Texas became an urban state in

a. 1930.

b. 1940.

c. 1950.

d. 1960.

e. 1970.

3. Home rule cities

a. are allowed only those powers granted by the legislature.

b. are allowed only those powers granted by the county.

c. make up a majority of cities in Texas.

d. can adopt any form of government their residents choose, as long as it does not conflict with the state constitution.

e. are limited to cities that have fewer than 5,000 residents.

4. Which of the following is the most common form of city government in Texas?

a. council-manager form

b. mayor-council form

c. commission-manager form

d. commission form

e. strong mayor form

5. Most of the state's largest cities function under the

a. council-manager form of government.

b. mayor-council form of government.

c. commission-manager form of government.

d. commission form of government.

e. strong mayor form of government.

6. In the council-manager form of government,

a. the city council serves at the discretion of the mayor.

b. the city council sets policy, and the city manager handles administration.

c. the mayor shares administrative power with the city council.

d. no single individual can be identified as the person in charge.

e. the mayor appoints both a city council and a city manager.

7. At-large elections

a. require candidates to run without partisan labels.

b. tend to favor minority candidates.

c. are the most common form of election system in Texas cities.

d. have been opposed by high-income areas of cities.

e. require candidates to run in separate geographic districts.

8. Which of the following is one of the urban finance problems faced by Texas cities?

a. expanded homestead exemptions for older homeowners, which lower the amount of property taxes available to fund city operations

b. "white flight" from the suburbs to the city, putting greater pressure on city services

c. lower sales tax revenues as a result of the migration of businesses out of the state

d. declining federal mandates to provide certain services

e. increased sales tax collections as a result of a strengthening economy

9. The top official in county government is the

a. county clerk.

b. district attorney.

c. county tax assessor-collector.

d. county auditor.

e. county judge.

10. The primary function of a constable is to

a. review bills and expenditures of the county.

b. serve as the primary law enforcement officer over unincorporated areas.

c. enforce the Texas Communist Control Act of 1951.

d. serve as the administrative officer of a justice of the peace court.

e. collect property taxes.

11. The primary function of a sheriff is to

a. serve as the supervising authority over city police departments.

b. serve as the supervisor of the county attorney's office.

c. serve as the primary law enforcement officer in small rural counties and non-incorporated areas of metropolitan counties.

d. provide legal advice to the county commissioners.

e. appraise property values in small rural counties.

12. All of the following are criticisms of single-purpose districts EXCEPT that

a. the public has little knowledge of their operations.

b. public pressure inhibits neutral administration.

c. there is little media coverage of their work.

d. the appointment process is dominated by a small number of individuals.

e. the level of professionalism is low.

13. The governance of most Texas independent school districts can best be described as

a. school boards dependent on superintendents for the board's agenda.

b. school boards dictating policy to the superintendent.

c. school boards serving as the administrative arm of the school superintendent.

d. county commissioners setting policy for school boards and superintendents to administer.

e. high public participation as a result of the use of single-member districts.

14. Extraterritorial jurisdiction and annexation powers refer to the

a. contracting of city services to private companies.

b. ability of cities to annex smaller towns into their jurisdiction.

c. power of residents of unincorporated areas to remain free of city codes and regulations.

d. ability of cities to annex or control unincorporated territory near city limits.

e. authority of cities to absorb the functions of county governments.

15. Tax abatements are

a. programs that assist businesses in obtaining housing for employees.

b. programs used by cities to encourage unincorporated residents to consent to annexation.

c. increased sales taxes used to encourage economic development.

d. trade and commerce agreements with "sister cities" in foreign countries.

e. exemptions from property taxes on businesses for a specified period.

Explore Further

Bridges, Amy, *Morning Glories: Municipal Reform in the Southwest*. Princeton, NJ: Princeton University Press, 1997. Traces the development and successes of urban reformers in the Southwest.

Brooks, David B., *Texas Practice: County and Special District Law*, vols. 35 and 36. St. Paul, MN: West, 1989. Provides the definitive legal analysis of county and other local governments in Texas.

Burns, Nancy, *The Formation of American Local Governments*. New York: Oxford University Press, 1994. Analyzes the political and economic reasons citizens create local governments.

Domhoff, G. William, *Who Really Rules? New Haven and Community Power Reexamined*. Santa Monica, CA: Goodyear Publishing Company, 1978. Revisits the arguments of pluralists in the community power debates and argues that mistakes were made in the use of data demonstrating pluralism.

Hawley, Willis D., *Nonpartisan Elections and the Case for Party Politics*. New York: John Wiley & Sons, 1973. Analyzes nonpartisan elections, focusing on their sociopolitical biases and arguing for partisan elections in local governments.

Miller, Char, and Heywood T. Sanders, eds., *Urban Texas.* College Station: Texas A&M University Press, 1990. Provides multiple perspectives, through essays, on the development of urban Texas.

Perrenod, Virginia Marion, *Special Districts, Special Purposes: Fringe Governments and Urban Problems in the Houston Area.* College Station: Texas A&M University Press, 1984. Analyzes the explosion of special districts in Houston in the post–World War II era.

Polsby, Nelson, *Community Power and Political Theory,* 2nd ed. New Haven, CT: Yale University Press, 1980. Provides a theoretical perspective on community power focusing on research issues in identifying those who exercise influence and control in cities.

Stone, Clarence N., *Regime Politics: Governing Atlanta.* Lawrence: University Press of Kansas, 1989. Provides an alternative to elite and pluralist assessments of community power through a focus on regimes in which collective action of various community factions is required for a city's development.

Wolff, Nelson W., *Mayor: An Inside View of San Antonio Politics, 1981–1995.* San Antonio, TX: *San Antonio Express-News,* 1997. Focuses on the role of leadership in the transformation of a city's economy and political system; written by a former mayor of San Antonio who went on to serve as judge of Bexar County.

Listen on MyPoliSciLab

13 Contemporary Public Policy Issues in Texas

It's as big as the House and Senate want to make it, and it's as big as the needs of Texas are. I mean, goodness gracious, how long is a piece of string? How do we rank [in spending]? How do we look, compared to other states throughout the country?

—**Lieutenant Governor Bob Bullock, 1991**

For years, Texas leaders have struggled with how to manage the state's finite water resources to ensure an adequate future supply for a growing population. Developing policies that balance the concerns of environmentalists and conservationists with the demands and rights of property owners has not been easy. Water became particularly critical in 2011, when Texas suffered through the worst one-year drought on record. Water supplies for some small towns ran dangerously low, and at least one tiny rural community, Spicewood Beach, located on Lake Travis near Austin, saw its only water well dry up as the lake's shoreline receded.

Then, to complicate matters even more, the Texas Supreme Court in early 2012 issued a decision that threatened to dismantle the state's fragile system of regulating use of limited groundwater supplies. Ruling in a case brought by two ranchers challenging pumping restrictions imposed by the Edwards Aquifer Authority, the court held unanimously that property owners own the water beneath their land. Regulations limiting how much water they could pump on their own land could amount to an unconstitutional taking of their property, the court said. Property rights advocates hailed the ruling as a major victory. But environmentalists and water managers expressed serious concerns.

13.1 List the stages of the policymaking process and place them in the framework of issue networks, p. 392.

13.2 Outline recent budget developments in Texas and identify constraints on those responsible for the state's budget, p. 396.

13.3 Describe the different types of taxes in Texas and explain in what ways the tax system as a whole is regressive, p. 398.

13.4 Identify the factors affecting education policy in Texas and relate them to questions of equity and quality, p. 402.

13.5 Explain the implications of court-ordered prison reform, the continued high numbers of prisoners, and the state's high rate of executions, p. 409.

13.6 Evaluate the patterns of state support for health and human services, p. 412.

13.7 Assess the state's response to environmental issues, p. 414.

MORE WATER ON THE WAY
Workers flush water from a newly drilled well belonging to the Colorado River Municipal Water District in Ward County in 2012. The district provides water to Midland, Odessa, Big Spring, Snyder, Abilene, San Angelo and several smaller communities.

Under the regulatory system then in place, Texas's ninety-six groundwater districts gave landowners permission to pump only limited quantities of water. The purpose was to try to balance the landowners' needs with the needs of other people for water from the same aquifers—and to protect the aquifers' environmental soundness. The Edwards Aquifer, which was involved in the Texas Supreme Court decision, meanders for miles below much of Central Texas and is the major source of water for the city of San Antonio. "A couple of million Central Texans rely on the Edwards Aquifer. Where do an individual's property rights end and those 2 million others' rights begin?" the *Austin American-Statesman* asked in an editorial. The ruling, experts believed, was sure to prompt other water rights lawsuits and perhaps intimidate regulators who were fearful of being sued.[1] The decision also was sure to prompt renewed legislative debate and deliberations on a difficult policy issue. Whether or not the decision will make that issue any easier to resolve remains to be seen.

Water management is just one of many major policy issues facing Texas today. Education, health care, poverty, pollution, a clogged transportation system, and an outdated tax structure are a few of the others. These challenges are similar to those faced by other states. In Texas, as elsewhere, identifying a policy problem is often easier than forging a political solution.

With much difficulty, Texas survived the collapse of its traditional oil-based economy and then the collapse of its real estate industry in the 1980s. As the economy diversified, state government also spent billions of taxpayer dollars on major improvements in prisons and mental health facilities and a more equitable distribution of public education dollars. However, the work of addressing public needs is never completed, and the political controversy involved in setting policy is never stilled, as our discussion of selected, major issues in this chapter will show. These issues represent enduring problems, and the policy decisions made in recent years are part of a long sequence of actions and inactions by state officials.

The Policy Process

13.1 List the stages of the policymaking process and place them in the framework of issue networks.

Political scientists and policy analysts spend a lot of time defining public policy and all of its critical elements. We will use the definition developed by Thomas Dye, who defined public policy as "whatever governments choose to do or not to do."[2] Except for an occasional federal judge, individuals acting alone have not forced many changes in public policy. The political power necessary to shape policy is exercised through groups, and, as we have pointed out throughout this book, some groups or interests have been more influential than others. Before we discuss specific policy changes, we will attempt to outline the concepts involved in the process.

The Elements of Public Policy

Setting public policy usually involves the determination of costs and benefits. The ultimate political questions to resolve are who will benefit from specific policy decisions and who will pay the bill.[3] Certain groups, businesses, or individuals receive direct benefits from governmental decisions—benefits that are paid for by other individuals through taxes. In this process, in effect, money is transferred from one segment of the population to another. Critical decisions must be made on the allocation of the tax burden, which will inevitably produce intense political conflict.

Public policies also provide indirect benefits. Although low-income Texans may receive the direct benefits of welfare assistance, job training programs, and subsidized housing and health care, the entire population eventually stands to gain if the poverty cycle is interrupted. Similar arguments can be made for funding equity between poor and rich school districts. The state's economic growth and future prosperity will be adversely affected and its crime rate will rise if serious problems of illiteracy and school dropouts are not successfully addressed now.

Public policy also includes regulation of the private sector. Indiscriminate use of land, water, and other natural resources has been curtailed by environmental policies seeking to protect the best interests of the state as a whole. But those policies often conflict with property rights and spark angry responses from some businesses and other private property owners, who threaten political retaliation against public officeholders—or, as discussed at the beginning of this chapter, file lawsuits against government regulators.

Additionally, public policy affects the governmental process itself. Decisions on political redistricting, revisions in election laws, and changes in the structure and organization of state and local governments ultimately address the issue of how power is distributed. They help determine how many people will be able to achieve their personal and collective objectives and improve their lives.

Another dimension of public policy is rooted in the notion of the general good of the community. Related to the concept of indirect benefits, it reflects the values upon which a political culture is based. Whether defined in terms of "it's the right thing to do" or a more systematic theory of the bonds that create the political community, elements of public policy reflect the common needs or interests of those who live in the state.

☐ The Stages of the Policy Process

Many activities in the private sector have an effect on public policy, such as a decision by a large corporation to close its operations in a city. But the following discussion focuses on the governmental institutions that make binding and enforceable decisions affecting all those who live in the state.[4] A number of scholars have approached policymaking as a sequential process (Table 13–1). Although this approach may suggest artificial start and stop points, the process is dynamic and continuous.

People have to identify a problem before they can expect the government's help in resolving it.[5] Subsequent steps in the policymaking process include gaining access to public officials, getting a solution drawn up and adopted, seeing it carried out, and evaluating its effectiveness.

People in a particular neighborhood, for example, may experience an increase in respiratory problems. Right away, they suspect a nearby chemical plant, and their suspicions are reinforced every time winds blow across the neighborhood from the direction of the plant. After complaints to the plant manager bring no satisfaction—or relief—the unhappy neighbors turn to government. To make sure they are heard, they

TABLE 13–1 STAGES OF THE POLICY PROCESS

Stages of the Process	Actions Taken
Identification and Formation of an Issue	Defining a common problem and building coalitions to force the issue on the public agenda
Access and Representation	Gaining access to elected or administrative officials and getting them to see the problem
Formulation	Convincing those in government to initiate action on the problem by sifting through alternative solutions
Adoption or Legitimation	The government's specific solution to the problem, including the authorization of programs and allocation of funds
Implementation	The application of the government's policy to the problem
Evaluation	Assessing the effects of the policy and determining if its objectives were achieved

SOURCE: Charles O. Jones, *An Introduction to the Study of Public Policy*, 2nd ed. (North Scituate, MA: Duxbury, 1977); and James E. Anderson, David W. Brady, Charles S. Bullock III, and Joseph Stewart Jr., *Public Policy and Politics in America*, 2nd ed. (Monterey, CA: Brooks/Cole, 1984).

identify others affected by the same problem and join forces in a citizens' group. Such groups are central to the policymaking process. By banding together, people increase their financial resources, leadership capabilities, and political strength.

Their next step is to find the governmental body or agency that can address the problem and then convince it to do so. They may first approach the city council, only to learn that state laws and regulations govern emissions from the plant. They may then turn to the Texas Commission on Environmental Quality, which may determine that the plant is violating its state permit and may impose an administrative fine or seek legal action by the attorney general. Or the commission may find its hands tied by a loophole in the state's antipollution laws. In that case, the concerned citizens need help from the legislature, where they have to convince their elected representatives to translate their concerns into a change in policy.

Simply identifying a problem and convincing a large number of other people to share your concerns are not a solution. Solutions must be developed and enacted through specific laws, regulations, or other policy changes. Philosophically, there is little disagreement that every child in Texas should have access to a quality education. But what does that mean in practical political terms? Proposed solutions have been extremely diverse. Legislative staffs, blue ribbon committees, independent research organizations, academicians, and consultants from various points on the political spectrum have all contributed studies and opinions. The resolution of their differences is essentially a political process. In the final analysis, "successful policy formulations must deal with the question of selecting courses of action that can actually be adopted."[6]

The legislature is primarily responsible for sifting through proposed alternatives and setting policy at the state level. But the separation of powers doctrine under which our government operates gives the judiciary important scrutiny over legislative action—or inaction. In recent years, several major federal and state court decisions have forced the legislature to make far-reaching changes in education, criminal justice, and mental health and mental retardation programs. Those court orders have prompted some lawmakers and other critics to complain that the judiciary overstepped its authority and was attempting to preempt the legislature. Others believe, however, that the legislature had neglected its responsibilities and needed some prodding.

Virtually every public policy has a cost. It is not enough for the legislature to create a program. Programs have to be funded, or they are meaningless. Sometimes, the legislature requires local governments to pick up the tab, but most programs have to compete with hundreds of other programs for a limited number of state tax dollars. Thus, the state's complex budgetary process is at the heart of policymaking and is closely monitored by individuals and organizations interested in policy development. Conflicts over the budgetary process can be intense.

Once legislation has been enacted and funded, its specific provisions must be implemented, or carried out. Much of this activity is the responsibility of state and local agencies that have been created to carry "a program to the problem."[7] Earlier political scientists referred to this stage of the policy process as public administration, and much of it falls within the domain of administrative agencies and departments. But government bureaucrats are not the only ones involved in carrying out policy; so are legislators, judges, interest groups, and nonprofit organizations. The activities in this implementation phase include the following:

- **Interpretation**—the translation of program language into acceptable and feasible directives
- **Organization**—the establishment of organizational units and standard operating procedures for putting a program into effect
- **Application**—the routine provision of services, payments, or other agreed-upon program objectives or instruments.[8]

Governments spend a lot of time evaluating the effects of public policy. In Texas, this is called performance review. An enormous amount of information is gathered to determine if programs have met stated goals and, if not, what changes or adjustments are required. Legislative committees, in their oversight function, demand information from agencies to help determine whether to continue to fund programs, expand them, or change them. With an eye on future funding, agencies also spend considerable resources assessing the impact of their own activities and performance. Program evaluation also is part of the broader issue of accountability of public officials and their responsiveness to the needs, demands, and expectations of their constituents. Interest groups, think tanks, scholars, and the news media also actively participate in this phase of the policy process.

Program assessment and evaluation become the basis for future policy and funding decisions. We have found some comprehensive solutions to a limited number of problems, including some diseases, but most governmental policy produces only limited or partial solutions. Problems and issues are ongoing, and policymakers often have to adjust or redirect their efforts at problem solving. A solution enacted today can produce additional problems requiring further attention tomorrow. As we will discuss later in this chapter, for example, recent changes in public education policies and funding are part of a long history of efforts to improve the quality of education in Texas.

issue networks
Term coined by Hugh Heclo to describe the complex institutional and political relationships in the policymaking process.

☐ Iron Triangles and Issue Networks

Thousands of players interact in the policy arenas of state and local governments, including bureaucrats, the courts, interest groups, businesses, the news media, and policy specialists. Although some of these have a broad perspective on state policy and a wide range of policy interests, most have narrow and highly specialized interests. One way to think about the relationships among policy participants is to "identify the clusters of individuals that effectively make most of the routine decisions in a given substantive area of policy."[9]

At the state level, these clusters—sometimes referred to as iron triangles of government—include members of the House and the Senate and their staffs, high-level bureaucrats, and representatives of interest groups. Both houses of the legislature are divided into standing committees, which have jurisdiction over specific policy areas, and key committee members usually form one leg of each triangle. Hundreds of these subsystems exist in state government, although the use of this concept to explain policy development does not always identify all of the critical players or explain the complexity of the process.

Political scientist Hugh Heclo argues that "the iron triangle concept is not so much wrong as it is disastrously incomplete," and he offers a more complex model—**issue networks**—for mapping out the relationships inherent in the policy process.[10] This concept acknowledges the key roles of the iron triangle players but also takes into account other factors, including the increased interdependence between state and local governments and the federal government. Specialists from all three levels of government frequently are involved in developing specific policies. Groups such as the National Governors' Association, the Council of State Governments, and the U.S. Conference of Mayors actively seek to influence federal policies that affect state and local governments.

The policy process also is increasingly dominated by specialists who may be identified with interest groups, corporations, legislative committees, or administrative agencies. These experts, or "technopols," understand the technical nature of a problem and, more importantly, the institutional, political, and personal relationships of those involved in trying to solve it.[11]

The number of actual participants in policy development will vary, of course, from issue to issue. Sometimes, only a few individuals are involved in shaping a specific policy. On other occasions, when changes are being considered in tax law, health care, or public education, for example, a "kaleidoscopic interaction of changing issue networks" takes place.[12] In the discussions of contemporary state policies that follow, you will see some practical applications of these concepts.

deficit financing
Borrowing money to meet operating expenses. It is prohibited by the Texas Constitution, which provides that the state government operates on a pay-as-you-go basis.

The State Budget

13.2 Outline recent budget developments in Texas and identify constraints on those responsible for the state's budget.

Balancing a new state budget in the face of a $27 billion revenue shortfall dominated the regular legislative session in 2011. Governor Rick Perry, reelected the previous year with the support of conservative tea party voters, and courting their continued support as he eyed a race for the Republican presidential nomination, insisted that the budget gap be closed with spending cuts alone and without raising taxes. Schoolteachers, health care advocates, and other Texans rallied against the cuts. But, with a 101–49 Republican supermajority in the Texas House and a Republican majority in the state Senate, the governor got his way, and lawmakers cut billions of dollars from important state services over the next two years, including $5.4 billion from the public schools alone. At Perry's insistence, the legislature also left more than $7 billion unspent in the state's emergency Rainy Day Fund to please conservative Republican activists intent on shrinking state government.

The two-year 2012–2013 state budget totaled $173.5 billion, which was about $14 billion, or 7.5 percent, smaller than the previous budget, and the spending reductions would cost thousands of school teachers and other state workers their jobs and reduce health care benefits for thousands of low-income Texans. In 2003, the year Republicans first took over the Texas House, smaller spending reductions were imposed to bridge a $10 billion revenue shortfall, also without raising state taxes.

The Republican approach to these budgetary emergencies differed markedly from how the legislature had resolved a budgetary crisis in 1991, when Democrats still held the governor's office and a majority of both legislative houses. The legislature balanced the 1991 budget with some cuts and other cost-savings steps plus a $2.7 billion package of tax and fee increases. The legislature, with voter approval, also created the Texas lottery that year as a future revenue source. It obviously does make a difference who is in charge of setting policy in Austin; nevertheless, under Republicans and Democrats alike, Texas's budgetary and tax system has become increasingly strained in recent years, in part because of growing public needs and in part because of historic budgetary restrictions, including a two-year budgetary period.

Like most other states and unlike the federal government, Texas operates on a pay-as-you-go basis that prohibits **deficit financing**. The comptroller must certify that each budget can be paid for with anticipated revenue from taxes, fees, and other sources. Also like other states, Texas greatly increased its spending on state government programs in the 1970s, 1980s, and 1990s. Population growth and inflation were major factors, in addition to federal mandates and court orders for prison and education reforms.

The biggest share of state expenditures (including federal funds appropriated by the legislature) is for education, which—even after being reduced—accounted for approximately 42 percent of the 2012–2013 budget. Health and human services, which have seen a significant boost in recent years from increased Medicaid spending, but which suffered other cuts in the 2003 and 2011 sessions, were second at 32 percent. Business and economic development accounted for almost 14 percent (see Figure 13–1).

☐ Two-Year Budgets

The 2011 budgetary crisis came on the heels of a recession from which Texas was beginning to emerge. But even in more-normal times, the legislature's budget-writing problems are compounded by the length of the budget period and the structure of the budget itself. Since the Texas Constitution provides that the legislature meet in regular session only every other year, lawmakers must write two-year, or biennial, budgets

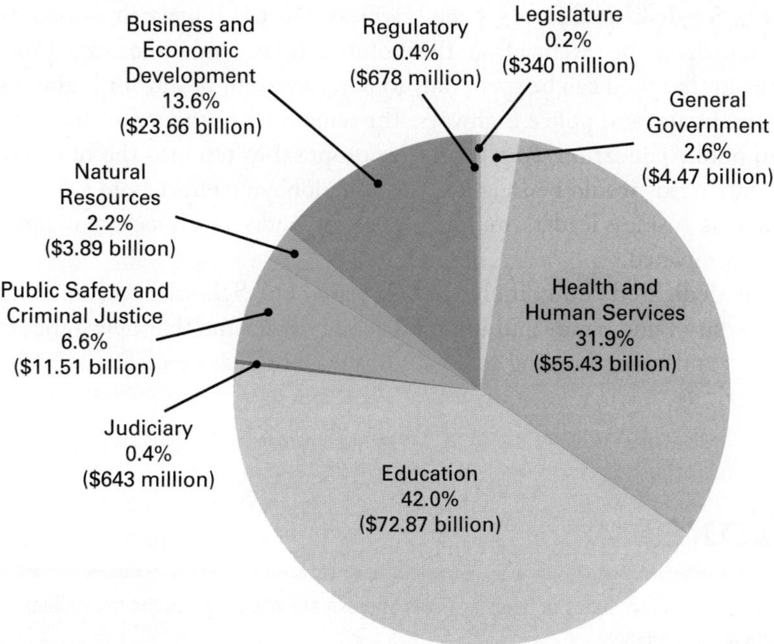

FIGURE 13–1 STATE APPROPRIATIONS FOR 2012–2013 BIENNIUM (ALL FUNDS)

Source: Legislative Budget Board, *Fiscal Size-Up: 2012–2013 Biennium,* January 2012.

for state government. That means state agencies, which begin preparing their budget requests several months before a session convenes, have to anticipate some of their spending needs three years in advance. Critics, including many legislators and agency directors, say two-year budgets require too much guesswork and cause inadequate funding of some programs and wasteful spending in other areas. They believe that Texas, which is the nation's second most populous state and has a wide diversity of needs in a changing economy, should have annual budgetary sessions of the legislature, a change that would require a constitutional amendment.

The governor and legislative leaders have the authority between legislative sessions to transfer appropriated funds between programs and agencies to meet some emergencies. The governor proposes transfers to the Legislative Budget Board (LBB), a ten-member panel that includes the lieutenant governor, the speaker, and eight key legislators. The LBB can accept, reject, or modify the governor's proposal and can propose budgetary changes to the governor.

Agencies submit their biennial appropriations, or spending, requests to the Legislative Budget Board. After its staff reviews the requests, the LBB normally recommends a budget that the full legislature uses as a starting point in its budgetary deliberations.

□ Dedicated Funds

The legislature's control over the budget-setting process is further restricted by legal requirements that dedicate or set aside a major portion of state revenue for specific purposes, leaving legislators with discretion over only about one-half of total appropriations. The remainder includes federal funds for programs, such as Medicaid or the Children's Health Insurance Program, earmarked for specific purposes by the federal government or monies dedicated to specific uses by the state constitution or state law. The state treasury has numerous separate funds, including many that are dedicated to highways, education, parks, teacher retirement, and dozens of other specific purposes. These restrictions hamper the legislature, particularly during lean periods. The dedicated funds are jealously guarded by the interest groups that benefit from them, and many funds have become "sacred cows" that most legislators dare not try to change.

13.1

13.2

13.3

13.4

13.5

13.6

13.7

dedicated funds
Constitutional or statutory requirements that restrict some state tax or fee revenues to spending on specific programs.

sales tax
A tax charged as a set percentage of most retail purchases and many services. It is the main source of tax revenue for state government and an important source of revenue for many cities and metropolitan transit authorities.

One of the major **dedicated funds** is the Highway Trust Fund, which automatically gets three-fourths of the revenue from the motor fuels tax. Under the Texas Constitution, revenue in that fund can be spent only to purchase right of way for highways or to construct, maintain, and police highways. The remainder of the motor fuels tax revenue goes to public education. Any legislative proposal to tap into the highway fund for other state needs would be fought by a strong lobbying effort from highway contractors as well as business leaders, mayors, and county judges with local road projects they wanted completed.

Other major dedicated funds include the Permanent School Fund and the Permanent University Fund, land- and mineral-rich endowments that help support the public schools and boost funding for the University of Texas and Texas A&M University systems.

State Taxes

13.3 Describe the different types of taxes in Texas and explain in what ways the tax system as a whole is regressive.

The legislature enacted a hybrid corporate income tax in 1991, but Texas entered the twenty-first century as one of only nine states without a personal income tax, and public and political opposition to that revenue source remained high.[13] Each budgetary crisis had seemingly stretched the existing tax structure to the breaking point, only to see the legislature come up with another patch. Critics compared the tax structure to an ugly patchwork quilt that had been stitched together over the years to accommodate various special interest groups and cover an assortment of emergencies.

The Regressive Tax System

A 2009 study by Citizens for Tax Justice and the Institute on Taxation and Economic Policy ranked Texas's tax system among the ten most regressive in the country. Texas's system is based largely on the sales tax, the local property tax, and fees that consume a larger portion of the incomes of the poor and the middle classes than the upper class. Based on this study's calculations, state and local governments in Texas taxed poor families at 12.2 percent of their incomes and middle-class families at 7.6 percent. By contrast, the wealthiest Texans (the richest 1 percent of the families) paid only 3.3 percent of their incomes in state and local taxes. Political leaders have long touted Texas as a low-tax state, but, according to this study, that is mainly from the perspective of wealthy Texans.[14]

SALES TAXES The legislature enacted the state's first **sales tax** in 1961, with an initial rate of 2 percent of the cost of purchased goods. The rate has since been increased several times, and now this tax is the single biggest generator of state revenue. At 6.25 percent, the statewide rate is among the highest sales tax rates in the country. An 8.25 percent rate is charged in most Texas metropolitan areas, where city and mass transportation authority taxes of 1 percent each are added to the state tax, a practice that many other states follow.[15] The sales tax generated $21.5 billion for state government in fiscal 2011. Sales tax collections had fallen by 6.6 percent in 2010, during the Great Recession, but the 2011 collections represented a 9.4 percent increase over 2010, as the Texas economy began to rebound.[16]

With each financial crisis, it becomes more difficult politically for the legislature to raise the sales tax rate. Even though groceries and medicine are tax exempt, critics charge that the sales tax is regressive because it affects low-income Texans disproportionately more than wealthier citizens. Moreover, the sales tax is heavily weighted toward products and leaves many services—including legal and medical fees and advertising—untaxed. Thus, sales tax revenue does not automatically grow with the state's economy because the Texas economy is becoming more and more service oriented.

BUSINESS TAXES The franchise tax, which was overhauled in 1991 and became a hybrid corporate income tax, was for many years the state's major business tax. It applied only to corporations, which were taxed on their income or assets, whichever was greater. The tax did not cover partnerships or sole proprietorships and was paid by fewer than 200,000 of the state's 2.5 million businesses. At the urging of Governor Rick Perry, the legislature in a special session in 2006 replaced the franchise tax with a broader-based business tax, also called a **margins tax**, which applied not only to corporations but also to professional partnerships, such as law firms, for the first time. The new tax was part of a "trade-off" for lower school property taxes. It was enacted in response to a Texas Supreme Court order for changes in the public school finance system. Although the smallest businesses were exempted from the tax, the new levy still raised taxes for many companies that had been paying little, if any, taxes under the franchise tax. The legislature tried to defuse opposition by raising the exemption in 2009 to exclude more businesses, but many members of the business community still were unhappy.

The legislature deliberately intended that the new business tax would raise less revenue than school districts had lost from the property tax reductions. This gave lawmakers and the governor the opportunity to say the new funding scheme had produced an overall tax cut. But the new tax performed even worse than expected during the subsequent recession, and its under-performance was a major part of the $27 billion shortfall the legislature confronted in 2011. The margins tax raised $8.7 billion in 2008–2009, short of the $12 billion that had been forecast. And it raised only $3.9 billion in 2011 due to the recession and additional businesses being exempted from paying the tax in 2009.[17]

margins tax
This is the state's main business tax. It was enacted in 2006 to replace the franchise tax and applies to corporations and professional partnerships, such as law firms. It imposes a one-percent levy on a company's annual revenue. Companies can deduct some of their costs, such as employees' salaries, from the tax base. Many of the smaller companies in the state do not have to pay the tax.

property or **ad valorem tax**
A tax on homes, businesses, and certain other forms of property that is the main source of revenue for local governments. The tax is based on the assessed value of the property.

sin tax
A common nickname for a tax on tobacco or alcoholic beverages.

PROPERTY TAXES The biggest source of taxpayer dissatisfaction and anger in Texas in recent years has been the local **property, or ad valorem, tax**, the major source of revenue for cities, counties, schools, and special districts. Total property tax levies increased by 246 percent between 1989 and 2008, from $11.3 billion to $39 billion, according to the state comptroller's office.[18] The greatest increases have been in local school taxes, which have been significantly raised to pay for state-mandated education programs and school finance requirements, including a law, to be discussed later in this chapter, ordering the transfer of millions of dollars from wealthy to poor school districts.

SEVERANCE TAXES Oil and gas severance or production taxes helped the legislature balance the budget with relative ease when oil prices were high in the 1970s, but energy-tax revenue slowed considerably after the energy industry crashed in the 1980s. Severance taxes accounted for 28 percent of state tax revenue in 1981, but less in recent years, mainly because of a more diversified economy.[19]

OTHER TAXES State government also has several volume-based taxes, such as taxes on cigarettes, alcoholic beverages, and motor fuels. They have set rates per pack or per gallon and do not take in more revenue when inflation raises the price of the product. These taxes, particularly the so-called **sin taxes** on cigarettes and alcohol, have been raised frequently over the years and produced $2.4 billion 2011.[20] The legislature raised the cigarette tax from 41 cents per pack to $1.41 per pack in 2006, as part of the trade-off for lower school property taxes.

☐ Gambling on New Revenue

For years, the Texas government maintained a strong moralistic opposition to gambling. Charitable bingo games were tolerated and eventually legalized. But the state constitution prohibited lotteries, and horse race betting was outlawed in the 1930s.

lottery
A form of gambling, conducted by many states, in which participants purchase tickets that offer an opportunity to cash in on a winning number or set of winning numbers. Voters legalized a state lottery in Texas in 1991.

GAMBLING ON NEW REVENUE
Texans approved a lottery in 1991, and by 2011, lottery sales produced $1.7 billion for public education.

After the oil bust in the 1980s, however, many legislators began to view gambling as a financial opportunity rather than a moral evil, and in key elections most Texas voters indicated they agreed.

In a special session in 1986, when spending was cut and taxes were raised to compensate for lost revenue from plummeting oil prices, the legislature legalized local option, pari-mutuel betting on horse and dog races. This is a form of betting in which bettors determine the size of the winning pool of money and the greater the number of people who vote for the winner in a race, the lower the payoff to each winning bettor. Voters approved the measure the next year. In 1991, under strong pressure from Governor Ann Richards, the legislature approved a constitutional amendment to legalize a state **lottery**, which voters also endorsed that year. Limited casino gambling on cruise ships operating off the Texas coast also has been legalized by the legislature. Gambling, however, has not cured the state's financial needs. Years after pari-mutuel betting had been approved, the horse and dog racing tracks still had not produced any significant revenue for the state.

Texas's lottery became the first in the United States to sell more than $4 billion worth of tickets in its first two years of operation, and it reached that milestone in twenty-two months. By late 1997, however, lottery sales had begun to lag behind projections, and even supporters of the game warned that the lottery could not necessarily be depended upon as a reliable, long-term revenue source. Lawmakers in 1997 dedicated lottery revenue to public education but also ordered that shortfalls in school funding from the lottery be made up with tax dollars.[21] The lottery generated almost $1.7 billion for public education in 2011.[22]

Despite its popularity in many other states, full-blown casino gambling remains a contentious issue in Texas. There are no commercial casinos in the state, and the efforts of the state's three Native American tribes to run casinos on their reservations have been challenged by state officials.

☐ Bonds: Build Now, Pay More Later

Although the Texas Constitution has a general prohibition against state government going into debt, the state had about $34.1 billion in state bonds outstanding at the end of fiscal 2009.[23] Taxpayer-supported debt ballooned when the legislature, prompted by federal court orders, used **general obligation bonds**, which are backed by state taxes, to finance the construction of prisons and facilities for those with mental health issues and those who are intellectually challenged. These expenses were submitted to the voters for approval in the form of constitutional amendments.

Some legislators have become increasingly uneasy about loading up the extra tax liability on future taxpayers. Interest on bonds can double the cost of a construction project, experts say. But bond issues traditionally have been widely supported by Democrats and Republicans alike. Debt service paid from taxes totaled more than $3.3 billion in the 2010–2011 budget period, or biennium, a 37 percent increase over the previous budget period. Much of this increase was debt service on bonds to pay for highway construction.[24] The legislature started turning to bond financing for highways, along with toll roads, when the motor fuels tax, the traditional source of highway funding, could no longer keep up with the mobility demands of a fast-growing, automobile-happy state.

Over the years, the state also has issued billions of dollars in bonds for such self-supporting programs as water development and veterans' assistance. These programs use the state's credit to borrow money at favorable interest rates. The state lends that money to a local government to help construct a water treatment plant or to a veteran to help purchase a house, and the loan recipients, not the state's taxpayers, repay the debt.

general obligation bonds
A method of borrowing money to pay for new construction projects, such as prisons or hospitals for the mentally ill. Interest on these bonds, which require voter approval in the form of constitutional amendments, is paid with tax revenue.

income tax
A tax based on a corporation's or an individual's income. Texas has a hybrid corporate income tax but is one of only a few states without a personal income tax.

The Income Tax: An Alternative to a Regressive Tax System?

Various liberal legislators and groups seeking more funding for state services have long advocated a state **income tax**. But until the late 1980s, no major officeholder or serious candidate for a major office dared even hint at support for such a politically taboo alternative. Finally, in late 1989, then–Lieutenant Governor Bill Hobby broke the ice for serious discussion of the issue in a speech to the Texas Association of Taxpayers, whose members included executives of many of the major businesses in Texas. Hobby, who already had announced that he would not seek reelection in 1990, proposed that a personal and corporate income tax be enacted, coupled with abolition of the corporate franchise tax and reductions in property and sales taxes. Hobby also told his audience that it would take the business community to convince the legislature to pass an income tax.

Lieutenant Governor Bob Bullock then shocked much of the political establishment by announcing in March 1991, less than two months after succeeding Hobby, that he would actively campaign for a state income tax. Bullock, a former state comptroller, said it was the only way to meet the state's present and future needs fairly and adequately while also providing relief from existing unpopular taxes. Bullock proposed making local school property taxes deductible from the income tax, and he recommended the repeal of the franchise tax. "I personally dislike—and I imagine most Texans do—any type of new taxes. But I also know deep down in my heart, deep down in my heart, that it's the right thing to do for Texas," he said.[25]

But opposition to an income tax still was widespread in Texas, and Bullock did not receive much support from lobbying groups. The Texas House, which initiates legislative action on tax bills, also remained strongly opposed to an income tax, as did the governor, Democrat Ann Richards. Eventually, the legislature that year changed the corporate franchise tax to include the hybrid corporate income tax described earlier in this chapter, while holding the line against a personal income tax.

During the 1993 legislative session, Bullock pulled another surprise and proposed a constitutional amendment, which won easy legislative approval, to ban a personal income tax unless the voters approved one. Bullock probably had more than one reason for his apparent about-face. One obvious factor was that his 1994 reelection date was approaching, and he needed to defuse any political problems caused by his endorsement of an income tax two years earlier. Moreover, Governor Richards and most legislators still strongly opposed an income tax. Some observers also believed that Bullock viewed his new proposal as a way to eventually win Texans' approval of the tax. His constitutional amendment provided that an income tax would have to help fund public education and be accompanied by a reduction in unpopular school property taxes, provisions similar to his 1991 income tax plan. Whatever Bullock's motivations, the amendment was overwhelmingly approved by Texas voters in November 1993, leaving many people convinced that a major revenue option had been removed from the state's budget picture for years to come.

Texas is one of only a handful of states without a personal income tax. If and when the legislature decides to try to sell one to voters, support from the business community will be crucial. The sales tax was first adopted after the business lobby got behind it, and business interests remain influential today. State government's ability to provide quality education, highways, and other public support systems is essential to the business community's long-term success. A personal income tax also would offer businesses the opportunity to transfer more of their tax load to consumers. That, ironically, could produce a conflict with some of the more liberal, longtime supporters of an income tax. A likely solution would be the enactment of generous tax exemptions for low-income Texans.

Educational Policies and Politics

13.4 Identify the factors affecting education policy in Texas and relate them to questions of equity and quality.

Texas spends more tax dollars on education than any other governmental program. In 1949, the legislature enacted the Gilmer-Aikin law, which made major improvements in the administration of public education and significantly increased school funding, but it soon became outdated. By the 1970s, it was obvious that quality and equity were lacking in many classrooms. Thousands of functional illiterates graduated from high school each year, and substandard facilities and educational aids shortchanged thousands of children in poor school districts.

Public Education: A Struggle for Equity and Quality

Public elementary and secondary education in Texas is financed by a combination of state and local revenue, a system that produced wide disparities in education spending among the state's approximately 1,050 school districts. The only local source of operating revenue for school districts is the property tax, and the money it raises is determined by the value of the property that is taxed and the tax rate that is imposed on that property. Districts with an abundance of oil production or expensive commercial property have high tax bases that enable them to raise large amounts of money with relatively low tax rates. Poor districts with low tax bases, on the other hand, have to impose higher tax rates to raise only a fraction of the money that the wealthy districts can spend on education.

Before the state began addressing this issue, many poor districts struggled to maintain minimal educational programs, whereas rich districts could attract the best teachers with higher pay; build more classrooms; purchase more books and computers; and, in some cases, have enough money left over to put AstroTurf in their football stadiums and construct indoor swimming pools. The glaring inequities did not exist only between different counties or regions of the state. In many cases, educational resources varied greatly between districts within the same county. Many of the poorest districts, though, were, and still are, in heavily Hispanic South Texas. Ethnicity became a significant factor in a protracted struggle between the haves and the have-nots. Hispanic leaders played major roles in the fight to improve their children's educational opportunities, and, over the years, they have had some success, thanks to a series of lawsuits. But inequities still persist.

The first major lawsuit (*Rodriguez* v. *San Antonio Independent School District*) was filed in 1968, when a group of parents led by Demetrio P. Rodriquez, a San Antonio sheet metal worker and high school dropout, went to federal court to challenge the school finance system. The plaintiffs had children in the Edgewood Independent School District, one of the state's poorest. A three-judge federal panel agreed with the parents and ruled in 1971 that the school finance system was unconstitutional. But the state appealed, and the U.S. Supreme Court in 1973 reversed the lower court decision. The high court said that the Texas system of financing public education was unfair but held that it did not violate the U.S. Constitution. Its consciousness raised, the legislature started pumping hundreds of millions of dollars in so-called "equalization" aid into the poorer school districts. But lawmakers did not change the system, and the inequities persisted and worsened.

By the early 1980s, Texas leaders expressed a growing concern over not just the financing of public education but also the quality of that education. In 1983, newly elected Governor Mark White joined Lieutenant Governor Bill Hobby and House Speaker Gib Lewis in appointing the Select Committee on Public Education. Computer magnate Ross Perot of Dallas—who several years later would be an independent candidate for president—was selected to chair it. In an exhaustive study, the panel found that high schools were graduating many students who could barely read and write and concluded that major reforms were necessary if the state's young people were to be able to compete for jobs in a changing and highly competitive state and international economy.

With Perot spending some of his own personal wealth on a strong lobbying campaign, the legislature in a special session in 1984 enacted many educational changes in a landmark piece of legislation known as **House Bill 72** and raised taxes to boost education spending. The bill raised teacher pay, limited class sizes, required prekindergarten classes for disadvantaged four-year-olds, required students to pass a basic skills test before graduating from high school, and required school districts to provide tutorials for failing students. It also replaced the elected State Board of Education, viewed as antireform by state leaders, with a new panel appointed by the governor. The new board became an elected body four years later, after the appointed panel had time to oversee the initial implementation of the new law.

The two most controversial provisions in the 1984 education reform law, however, were a literacy test for teachers and the so-called **no pass, no play rule**, both of which were to contribute to White's reelection defeat in 1986. Most teachers easily passed the one-time literacy—or competency—test, a requirement for keeping their jobs, but many resented it as an insult to their abilities and professionalism. The no pass, no play rule, which prohibited students who failed any course from participating in athletics and other extracurricular activities for six weeks, infuriated many coaches, students, parents, and school administrators, particularly in the hundreds of small Texas towns where Friday night football was a major social activity and an important source of community pride. Education reformers, however, viewed the restriction as an important statement that the first emphasis of education should be on the classroom, not on the football field or the band hall.

The 1984 law, however, did not change the basic, inequitable finance system, and the state was soon back in court. This lawsuit, ***Edgewood* v. *Kirby***, was filed in state district court in Austin, and it contended the inequities violated the Texas Constitution. It was initially filed in 1984, shortly before the enactment of House Bill 72, by the Edgewood Independent School District, twelve other low-income districts, and a number of families represented by the Mexican American Legal Defense and Educational Fund (MALDEF). Dozens of other districts and individuals joined the case as

House Bill 72

A landmark school reform law enacted in 1984. Among other provisions, it reduced class sizes; required teachers to pass a literacy test to keep their jobs; and imposed the no pass, no play rule.

no pass, no play rule

States that a student failing a course is restricted from participating in extracurricular activities.

Edgewood* v. *Kirby

A lawsuit in which the Texas Supreme Court in 1989 declared the Texas school finance system unconstitutional because of wide disparities in property wealth and educational opportunities between school districts.

plaintiff-intervenors, and, in 1987, state District Judge Harley Clark of Austin ruled the school finance system violated the state constitution.

The ruling was appealed, but the Texas Supreme Court, in a unanimous, landmark decision in October 1989, struck down the finance system and ordered lawmakers to replace it by May 1, 1990, with a new law that gave public school children an equal opportunity at a quality education. The bipartisan opinion, written by Democratic Justice Oscar Mauzy, a former chairman of the Senate Education Committee, did not outline a specific solution. But the court said the existing finance system violated a state constitutional requirement for an efficient system of public education. It warned the legislature that merely increasing the amount of state education aid was not enough. The decision concluded that "a Band-Aid will not suffice; the system itself must be changed."[26]

□ Persistence of Funding Problems

The issue was so divisive it took three more school finance plans and more than three years before the legislature enacted a school funding plan that met the Supreme Court's approval. It was a 1993 law, signed by Governor Ann Richards, that gave wealthy school districts several options for sharing property tax revenue with poor districts. The "Robin Hood" law, as it was soon dubbed, was upheld by the high court in 1995. Robin Hood remains in effect, although another lawsuit prompted additional school finance changes a few years later.

A number of school districts went to court again because more and more of the burden of school funding, approaching 60 percent, was being borne by local school taxes, whereas the state's share was decreasing. Consequently, many school districts were having to increase their local property taxes. The districts noted that many of them had been forced to raise their property tax rates to or near the limit allowed by the state for school maintenance and operations, $1.50 per $100 valuation. The districts argued that the situation amounted to, in effect, a state property tax, which was prohibited by the Texas Constitution. The districts also sought more state aid.

Ruling in the new lawsuit in 2005, the Texas Supreme Court held that the heavy reliance on property taxes for school funding amounted to an unconstitutional statewide property tax and gave the state until June 1, 2006, to correct the problem. Governor Rick Perry called the legislature into special session and won approval of a proposal to cut school tax rates by one-third over the next two years. To replace the lost revenue, legislators enacted the new, broad-based business tax described earlier in this chapter and raised the state cigarette tax by $1 per pack. The legislature, however, did not increase state funding for the public schools, and the local tax savings soon were eroded by rising property values. As property values increased, tax bills increased without any change in the tax rate.

The 2006 law also put strict limits on how much school districts could raise their local property tax rates in the future. These restrictions soon created budgetary problems for many districts. Moreover, the new business tax, as noted earlier in this chapter, failed to generate enough state revenue to make up for the local revenue lost to the 2006 property tax cuts. The result, according to an analysis by the Legislative Budget Board, had produced an annual "structural deficit" of $5 billion in the school finance budget by the time the legislature convened in 2011. That accounted for a big chunk of the $27 billion revenue shortfall that lawmakers faced that year. The legislature responded with $5.4 billion in school budget cuts, spread over two years. Some official budget documents underreport the depth of the cuts because those documents do not take into account the impact of enrollment growth (about 80,000 new students a year, statewide) on school district budgets. In reality, the new state budget imposed a $4 billion reduction in state formula funding—which is based on attendance and certain other factors—on school districts over the following two school years. It marked the first time in more than sixty years that the legislature had failed to meet its statutory funding obligations to schools. The legislature also cut another $1.4 billion from public education grants.

The National Education Association (NEA) estimated that the cuts reduced average per-student funding by $538 a year, from $9,446 to $8,908, which put Texas about $2,500 below the national average. Budget experts at the Center for Public Policy Priorities, an Austin-based think tank that advocates for low- and middle-income Texans, estimated that as many as 49,000 school jobs would be lost in Texas by the time the last of the spending reductions were carried out for the 2012–2013 school year.[27] In addition, the Texas Education Agency allowed school districts, because of financial hardship, to increase more than 8,400 elementary school classes above the limit (22 students per class) allowed by state law. Some districts considered school closures, and at least one district in North Texas started charging parents for their children to ride the school bus.

Within a few months after the new budget was adopted, several hundred school districts were back in court, suing the state yet again over the school finance system. A group of mostly property poor districts said the finance system was still inequitable because wealthier districts could still spend significantly more than poorer districts. Another group of plaintiffs, including some of the larger and wealthier districts, contended that state spending on public education was inadequate.

☐ Other Issues Affecting the Public Schools

The legislature also confronts a number of other issues affecting public schools, including teacher morale and student testing. Some new proposals, such as charter schools, have been adopted; others, including private school vouchers, have been rejected but may be revived in the future.

TEACHER PAY, WORKING CONDITIONS, AND MORALE According to a survey of its members commissioned by the Texas State Teachers Association in 2010, before the 2011 school budget cuts and layoffs, 40.8 percent of the respondents said they took extra jobs during the school year to make ends meet, and 56 percent said they took extra jobs during the summer. Almost 70 percent of the moonlighting teachers believed the quality of their teaching would improve if they did not have extra jobs but said they could not afford to lose the extra income.

Almost half of the respondents (46.7 percent) said they were seriously considering leaving the profession. But that prospect was difficult for many because most were their families' major breadwinners. Their average classroom experience was 17.7 years, and their average age was 49. Some 79 percent were women, and 43.8 percent had master's degrees. They spent an average of 15 hours a week outside of class on school-related work, and they reported spending, on average, $564 a year from their own pockets on school supplies.[28] The average teacher pay in Texas during the 2009–2010 school year was $48,261, according to the National Education Association. Texas ranked thirty-first among the states and $6,941 below the national average.

STUDENT TESTING AND "ACCOUNTABILITY" For years now, students in the public schools have been required to take standardized tests to be promoted to higher grades, graduate from high school, and help measure a school's effectiveness. But the tests and the so-called school "accountability" system to which the test results contribute have been controversial. There have been accusations that teachers were pressured to concentrate on teaching students how to pass the test in order to attain a favorable rating for their schools rather than present a more enriching educational curriculum. The testing and accountability systems have been revised several times, as legislators and educators struggled to balance political and educational concerns.

The most recent version—the State of Texas Assessments of Academic Readiness (STAAR)—debuted in the 2011–2012 school year. The new system, including end-of-course exams in core subject areas for high school students, was designed to be more difficult than the standardized tests it replaced, the Texas Assessment of Knowledge and Skills (TAKS). Some school officials questioned whether they would have enough

Permanent University Fund (PUF)

A land- and mineral-rich endowment that benefits the University of Texas and Texas A&M University systems, particularly the flagship universities in Austin and College Station.

money to adequately prepare students for the more difficult tests, following the deep budget cuts made by the legislature in 2011. Lawmakers insisted, nevertheless, that students be held accountable, even though the same lawmakers had enacted the stingiest public education budget in many years. State Education Commissioner Robert Scott, with the support of key legislators, did waive for one year a requirement that the end-of-course exams be counted toward a high school student's grades in those courses.

CHARTER SCHOOLS Upon taking office in 1995, Governor George W. Bush advocated more innovation for local schools and less red tape for teachers and administrators. The legislature responded with a major rewrite of the education law to allow school districts and other groups to create charter schools that would be free of some state regulations. The charter school movement got off to a mixed start. Several had financial problems or were mismanaged and had to shut down after brief periods of operation. Others flourished, strongly supported by parents and students who believed their innovative techniques enhanced the learning experience. By 2010, a total of 463 charter schools with approximately 119,000 students were operating in Texas.[29]

PRIVATE SCHOOL VOUCHERS For several years, a number of legislators, primarily Republicans, have advocated a voucher program that would allow some public school children to attend private schools at state expense. The idea, supporters say, is to allow disadvantaged children from failing schools to have a chance at a quality education. Opponents, including public education groups, say such a program would unfairly divert money from the public schools at a time when public classrooms need more funding. Voucher bills have failed during several recent legislative sessions.

HOME SCHOOLS In 1994, the Texas Supreme Court upheld the right of parents to educate their own children at home, ending a ten-year legal battle over the home school issue in Texas. The court said a home school was legitimate if parents met "basic education goals" and used a curriculum based on books, workbooks, or other written materials. It was reported at the time that nearly 1 million American families, including 100,000 in Texas, educated their children at home.[30] The U.S. Department of Education reported 1.5 million home-schooled students in the United States in 2007.[31]

Higher Education: The Continuing Quest for Excellence and Equity

Texas has more than 100 state-supported universities; medical, dental, law, and other professional schools; and community (or junior) college districts serving more than 1 million students. They are governed by numerous policy-setting boards appointed by the governor or, in the case of community colleges, elected by local voters. The Texas Higher Education Coordinating Board, which is appointed by the governor, oversees university construction and degree programs.

The University of Texas at Austin and Texas A&M University at College Station are the state's largest universities; have higher entrance requirements than other schools; fulfill important research functions; and, thanks to a constitutional endowment, have some of the state's best educational facilities. They receive revenue generated by the land- and mineral-rich **Permanent University Fund (PUF)**. These are the only state-supported Tier One, or research, universities in Texas. Texas voters in 2009 approved a constitutional amendment establishing a procedure under which other large universities in the state, including Texas Tech University, the University of Houston, and other branches of the University of Texas System, could compete for Tier One status, but none had achieved that goal by 2012.

Responding to a federal desegregation lawsuit, the state in the 1980s made a commitment to improve higher education opportunities for minority students and employment opportunities for minority faculty members. More funding was provided for predominantly African American Texas Southern University in Houston and Prairie View A&M University in nearby Waller County. Texas agreed to a five-year desegregation plan with the U.S. Department of Education in 1983 and subsequently created the Texas Educational Opportunity Plan, under which traditionally Anglo schools, including the University of Texas at Austin and Texas A&M, increased minority recruitment efforts.

Residents of heavily Hispanic South Texas, however, challenged the state's distribution of higher education dollars. In a lawsuit filed in state district court in Brownsville in 1987, several Hispanic groups and individuals represented by the Mexican American Legal Defense and Educational Fund contended the state's higher education system discriminated against Mexican American students by spending less on universities in the border area.

After the lawsuit was filed, several colleges in South Texas were made part of either the University of Texas or the Texas A&M system. But efforts to negotiate a settlement of the suit failed, and it went to trial in late 1991 as a class action on behalf of all Mexican Americans who allegedly suffered or stood to suffer discrimination in higher education in the Mexican border area of Texas. In January 1992, state District Judge Benjamin Euresti, Jr., of Brownsville ruled the higher education funding system unconstitutional because it discriminated against South Texas, but his ruling later was overturned by the Texas Supreme Court.[32]

In a related policy decision in 2001, the legislature overwhelmingly approved, and Governor Rick Perry signed, a law allowing some children of illegal immigrants to qualify for lower, in-state tuition rates at Texas colleges and universities. Fellow conservatives heavily criticized Perry for that law during his unsuccessful campaign for the 2012 Republican presidential nomination. Supporters of the law said it was important to encourage young, longtime residents of Texas, even immigrants, to obtain college educations and better prepare for productive futures.

□ Opposition to Affirmative Action in Higher Education

Texas's efforts to increase minority enrollments in its universities suffered a setback in 1996 when the Fifth U.S. Circuit Court of Appeals in New Orleans ruled that a race-based admissions policy previously used by the University of Texas School of Law was unconstitutional. The U.S. Supreme Court refused to grant the state's appeal and let the appellate court's decision stand. The so-called "Hopwood case" was named after lead plaintiff Cheryl Hopwood, one of four white students who sued after not being admitted into the law school.[33]

Then–Texas Attorney General Dan Morales held in 1997 that the Hopwood ruling went beyond the law school and prohibited all universities in Texas from using race or ethnicity as a preferential factor in admissions, scholarships, and other student programs. Morales's opinion was attacked as overly broad by many civil rights leaders and minority legislators, but it had the force of law.[34] The Texas legislature, meeting in 1997, attempted to soften the blow to affirmative action by enacting a new law that guaranteed automatic admissions to state universities for high school graduates who finished in the top 10 percent of their classes, regardless of their scores on college entrance examinations. The law was designed to give the best students from poor and predominantly minority school districts an equal footing in university admissions with better prepared graduates of wealthier school districts. The new law also allowed university officials to consider other admissions criteria, including a student's family income and parents' education level.

Little changed in minority enrollments at many Texas universities after the Hopwood decision because many universities had not used race as a factor in admissions anyway. But the two largest—the University of Texas at Austin and Texas A&M University—did. The drop-off in minority enrollment was particularly troubling at the UT Law School the first year after the Hopwood restrictions went into effect. The first-year law class of almost 500 students in the fall of 1997 included only four African Americans and twenty-five Hispanics. Thirty-one African Americans and forty-two Hispanics had entered the previous year. The more flexible admissions standards set by the legislature applied only to entering undergraduate students, not to those seeking admission to law school and other professional schools.[35]

In 2003, the U.S. Supreme Court, ruling in *Grutter* v. *Bollinger*, from the University of Michigan, effectively repealed Hopwood by holding that universities can use affirmative action programs to give minority students help in admissions, provided that racial quotas were not used. The University of Texas, among other institutions, then began steps to develop new, race-based admissions criteria.

Even so, the fight over affirmative action still was not won. In 2008, two Anglo students, Abigail Fisher and Rachel Michalewicz, who were denied admission as undergraduates to the University of Texas at Austin, filed another lawsuit challenging UT's consideration of race and ethnicity in admissions. They lost in federal district court in Austin and before the Fifth U.S. Circuit Court of Appeals in New Orleans. But Fisher appealed to the U.S. Supreme Court, which agreed in February 2012 to review her case. By then, the high court had undergone significant changes since its 5–4 decision in *Grutter*. Justice Sandra Day O'Connor, who wrote the majority decision in *Grutter*, had retired and been replaced by the more conservative Justice Samuel Alito, who in an earlier case had joined an opinion limiting the ability of school districts to use race in assigning students to schools. Justice Elena Kagan, the newest member of the court and an appointee of President Barack Obama, recused herself from participating in the latest case. She apparently wanted to avoid the appearance of a conflict because she had been solicitor general when the U.S. Justice Department sided with the University of Texas against the lawsuit in the lower courts. The changes on the court left many observers wondering if *Grutter* would be reversed or modified.[36]

Meanwhile, the Texas legislature in 2009 had put some limits on the top 10 percent law as it applied to admissions at the University of Texas at Austin. University officials sought the change because the law had been consuming a large share of each year's incoming class and limiting the school's options for admitting other students.

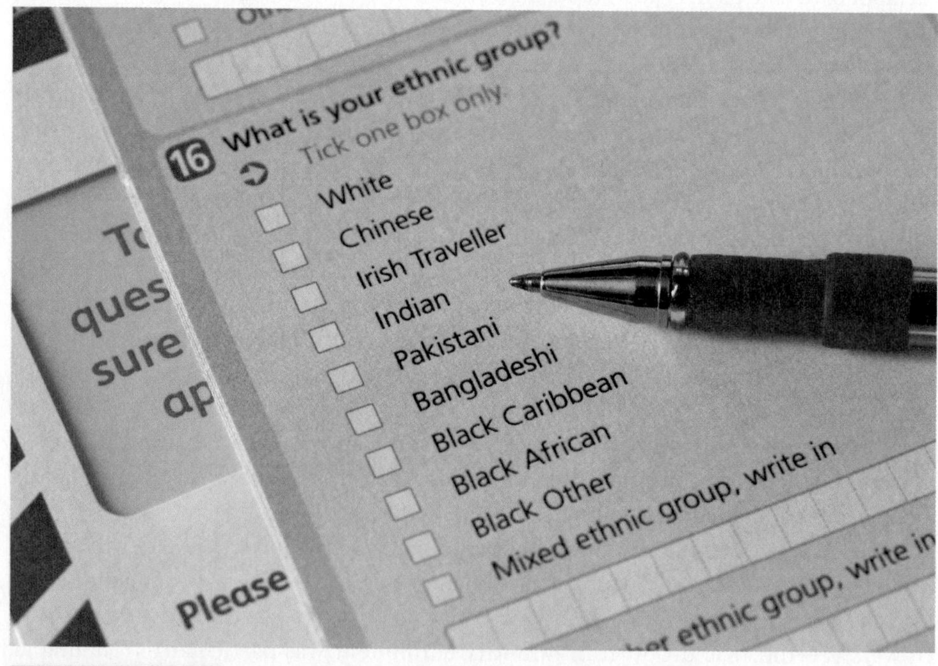

ADMISSIONS POLICY

The legal fight over whether race or ethnicity should be a factor in college admissions continues in Texas and in the courts.

For the first time in the history of UT-Austin, fewer than half (47.6%) of entering freshman in the fall of 2010 identified themselves as "white." The total UT-Austin enrollment that fall, including those who enrolled in undergraduate school, graduate schools, and the law school, was 52.1 percent white. Some 17 percent were Hispanic; 4.5 percent were African Americans; 15.2 percent were Asian Americans; and 0.4 percent were Native Americans. The remainder were foreign-born students or those who declined to report their race or ethnicity.[37]

☐ Tuition Deregulation

With tax dollars becoming increasingly tight, University of Texas officials successfully lobbied the legislature in 2003 for a new law that, for the first time, gave individual university governing boards the freedom to set tuition rates independently of legislative action. By the fall of 2009, tuition and fees at state-supported universities had increased an average 72 percent, whereas state appropriations for student financial aid increased by a much lower rate.[38] The Legislative Study Group, a caucus of progressive lawmakers, issued a report just prior to the 2009 session criticizing the legislative majority for shirking "its responsibility for funding colleges by shifting more of the burden onto the shoulders of parents and students in the form of tuition costs."[39] The legislature, facing increasing budgetary problems and cutting back on higher education appropriations during a recession, refused to change the law, and universities continued to raise tuition. The legislature compounded the problem for students in 2011 when it reduced funding for major student financial aid programs by 15 percent.

☐ A Political Interest in University Research

The Texas Public Policy Foundation (TPPF), an Austin-based conservative think tank with close ties to Governor Rick Perry, became increasingly influential over state policy as the Republican hold on state government tightened under Perry. TPPF found itself in a huge controversy when some individuals associated with it, including one of its former senior fellows, Rick O'Donnell, publicly argued in 2011 that much academic research at universities such as the University of Texas at Austin was pointless, a waste of tax dollars, and harmful to good teaching. O'Donnell's remarks were particularly attention getting because he also was a special adviser to the University of Texas System.

The remarks angered thousands of University of Texas alumni, who waged an email campaign urging UT regents—all Perry appointees—to avoid politics and keep their focus on both research and teaching. UT fired O'Donnell, and regents reaffirmed their support of Chancellor Francisco Cigarroa, who made it clear that research would remain a priority at the university.[40] A few months later, Marc Musick, a UT-Austin sociology professor, produced a study concluding that the vast majority of senior faculty at the Austin campus were extremely productive, as measured by teaching loads, and collectively attracted twice as much money in research grants and state funding as they cost taxpayers in salaries.[41]

Criminal Justice

13.5 Explain the implications of court-ordered prison reform, the continued high numbers of prisoners, and the state's high rate of executions.

Texas did away with public hangings on the courthouse square years ago but retained a frontier attitude toward crime and criminals, an attitude that produced a criminal justice system based more on revenge than rehabilitation. Candidates were elected to the legislature on tough, anticrime

13.1

13.2

13.3

13.4

13.5

13.6

13.7

Ruiz* v. *Estelle
A landmark federal court order (1980) that declared the state prison system unconstitutional and resulted in significant changes in state lockups.

promises to "lock 'em up and throw away the key." Once in office, they passed laws providing long sentences for more and more offenses and built more prisons. Eventually, the system was overwhelmed by sheer numbers, and crime, for a while, became a bigger problem than ever.

State policymakers ignored deteriorating prison conditions until U.S. District Judge William Wayne Justice of Tyler declared the prison system unconstitutional in 1980 in a landmark lawsuit brought by inmates (***Ruiz* v. *Estelle***). He cited numerous problems, including overcrowded conditions, poor staffing levels, inadequate medical and psychiatric care for prisoners, and the use of so-called "building tenders"—inmates who were given positions of authority over other prisoners, whom they frequently abused. Justice ordered extensive reforms with which the state agreed to comply, and he appointed a monitor to help him supervise what was then known as the Texas Department of Corrections and now is the institutional division of the Texas Department of Criminal Justice.[42]

One of Justice's key orders limited the population of prison units to 95 percent of capacity. This was instituted to guard against a recurrence of overcrowding and to allow for the housing of inmates according to their classifications, which separated youthful, first-time offenders from more hardened criminals and those with special needs from the general prison population.

☐ Reforms Prompted by Crowded Prisons

The prison population limit and an increase in violent crimes in the 1980s helped produce a criminal justice crisis that lasted for several years. By the time the *Ruiz* lawsuit was settled in 1992 and the state given more flexibility over its prison operations, Texas had spent hundreds of millions of dollars building new prisons but still could not accommodate all the offenders flooding the system. Thousands of convicted felons were backlogged in overcrowded county jails because of a lack of enough room in the prisons. Hundreds of dangerous criminals were paroled early to endanger and outrage law-abiding Texans.

Many of the convicts overloading the system were nonviolent, repeat offenders—among them alcoholics and drug addicts who continued to get in trouble because they were unable to function in the free world. Experts believed that alcoholism, drug addiction, or drug-related crimes were responsible for about 85 percent of the prison population.[43] At the urging of Governor Ann Richards in 1991, the legislature created a new alcoholism and drug abuse treatment program within the prison system, with the goal of reducing that recidivism.

In settling the *Ruiz* lawsuit in 1992, the state agreed to maintain safe prisons, and the federal court's active supervision of the prison system ended. Then, in 1993, the legislature enacted a major package of criminal justice reforms, including the first overhaul of the penal code in twenty years. The plan doubled the minimum time that violent felons would have to serve in prison—from one-fourth to one-half of their sentences—before becoming eligible for parole. To reserve more prison space for the most dangerous criminals, however, the legislature lowered the penalties for most property crimes and drug offenses. These nonviolent offenders were diverted to community corrections programs or a new system of state-run jails, to which they could be sentenced for a maximum of two years.

The legislature authorized doubling the size of the prison system during the 1994–1995 budget period, and a construction boom soon was underway. Although prisons had traditionally been located in East Texas, new prisons were built throughout the state. Small cities and rural counties, seeking to recover from the recession of the 1980s and eager for the new jobs that prisons would provide, offered the state free land and other considerations in an intense lobbying frenzy.

TABLE 13–2 COMPARISON OF STATE PRISON POPULATIONS, 2009

State	Male Inmates	Female Inmates	Total Inmates	2009 Population Estimates	Incarceration Rate*
Texas	156,760	13,399	170,159	24,782,302	649
California	158,793	11,233	170,026	36,961,664	460
Florida	96,074	7,349	103,423	18,537,969	558
New York	57,177	2,601	59,778	19,541,453	304
Georgia	50,690	3,762	54,452	9,829,211	533
Ohio	47,853	3,958	51,811	11,542,645	449
Pennsylvania	47,756	2,775	50,531	12,604,767	400
Michigan	45,384	1,800	47,184	9,969,727	473
Illinois	42,933	2,612	45,545	12,910,409	353
North Carolina	37,635	2,909	40,544	9,380,884	372
All 50 States	**1,502,499**	**114,979**	**1,617,478**	**307,006,550**	**504**

*Prisoners per 100,000 persons; includes federal and state prisoners.

SOURCE: U.S. Department of Justice, Bureau of Justice Statistics, "Prison Inmates at Midyear 2009," June 2010; U.S. Census Bureau, *Statistical Abstract*, 2012.

Private contractors also lobbied the Board of Criminal Justice, which chose the sites and granted the contracts.

By the late 1990s, Texas had room for more than 150,000 inmates in its prisons, state jails, and substance abuse facilities, eliminating the backlog of convicted felons in county jails. The prison population had increased to more than 170,000 in 2009, but it declined enough by 2011 for the legislature, seeking relief from a huge revenue shortfall, to order the closure of a state prison for the first time in Texas history (see Table 13–2). The Central Unit, built in what was an agricultural area in 1932 but in recent years had been increasingly surrounded by the suburban growth of Sugar Land, southwest of Houston, was shut down that summer, and its remaining inmates transferred to other prisons. The state expected to save about $12.5 million a year from the closure and anticipated collecting $4.6 million a year in sales tax revenue from a business park that the city of Sugar Land planned to develop on the site.[44]

☐ Continuing Popularity of the Death Penalty in Texas

Texas continues to lead the nation in executions. More than 470 persons, including three women, have been put to death in Texas since executions resumed in 1982. Although opponents are vocal, most Texans support the death penalty. Some 53 percent of respondents to a University of Texas/*Texas Tribune* poll in 2010 said they strongly supported the death penalty, and another 25 percent said they supported it "somewhat."[45] A *Houston Chronicle* survey in 2002 found that 69 percent of respondents supported the death penalty, even though 55 percent believed that innocent people probably had been executed.[46]

Twelve people have been released from death row in Texas after post-conviction evidence, mainly the result of DNA testing, proved them innocent. As forensic and DNA testing have become more sophisticated, challenges to murder convictions are more commonplace. In a nationally watched case, a state commission has considered the possibility that at least one executed inmate, Cameron Todd Willingham, was innocent of the crime for which he was put to death in 2004 (see *Talking Texas: Did Texas Execute an Innocent Man?*).

13.1

13.2

13.3

13.4

13.5

13.6

13.7

Talking ★ TEXAS Did Texas Execute an Innocent Man?

Cameron Todd Willingham always insisted he did not set the house fire in which his three young daughters died in 1991 in Corsicana, but prosecutors and a jury did not believe him. He was convicted and executed in 2004. Shortly before the execution, an internationally known arson scientist retained by Willingham's defense attorneys reviewed the evidence used to determine arson and concluded that it was flawed. The Texas Board of Pardons and Paroles and Governor Rick Perry refused to stay the execution.

The Texas Forensic Science Commission, which did not exist when Willingham was executed, decided in 2008 to review his case, at the request of the New York–based Innocence Project. The commission hired another arson expert, who also concluded that the arson science used to convict Willingham was seriously flawed. In 2009, as the commission prepared to meet to hear the expert's report, Perry abruptly replaced four of the nine commissioners, including the chairman. The scheduled meeting was canceled, and the panel's investigation was put on hold. Attorney General Greg Abbott eventually ended the investigation by ruling in 2011 that the panel could not consider evidence in cases that predated 2005, the year in which the legislature created the commission. The commission issued a report agreeing that the arson science used to secure Willingham's conviction was faulty, but it did not say whether it believed the executed convict was innocent or guilty. "There were other issues," said Dr. Nizam Peerwani, the commission's new chairman, "There were eyewitness accounts; there were hospital and doctor testimony given and investigative findings." The commission planned a review of other old arson cases to determine whether faulty science may have contributed to convictions in those cases.[a]

CRITICAL THINKING QUESTIONS

1. **Should Texas stay all pending executions in other arson-related capital cases until the Texas Forensic Science Commission completes its review? Why or why not?**
2. **Do you think Texas has executed innocent people? If so, does this affect your view of the death penalty? Why or why not?**

[a]Brandi Grissom, "New Head of Forensic Science Panel Takes on Arson Case," *The Texas Tribune*, July 22, 2011.

Health and Human Services

13.6 Evaluate the patterns of state support for health and human services.

Health and human services are areas in which the state government weighs compassion against the cold realities of its budget, and Texas has historically been stingy. Texas has traditionally spent less money per capita on health and welfare programs than most states. Even in the 1970s, when the oil industry was still pumping a healthy amount of tax revenue into the state treasury, Texas was slapped with two federal court orders for providing inadequate care to the mentally ill and the intellectually challenged people in state institutions.

Perhaps the tight-fisted attitude springs from the legacy of frontier colonists standing on their own two feet to fight adversity and win a better life. Countless politicians claiming that Texans could prevail in hard times by pulling up their bootstraps and hanging tough have perpetuated this view, but this perception ignores the reality that many people in modern Texas cannot pull up their bootstraps because they do not have any boots. According to the *2010 American Community Survey*, approximately 4 million Texans—17.9 percent of the state's population—live in poverty. Particularly hard hit are children (more than one of every four) and minorities.[47] In 2011, the legislature weakened the already fragile social safety net by slashing $10 billion, about 15 percent, from health and human services agencies' budgets.

☐ The Struggle of Many Texans for Health Care

Along with its high incidence of poverty, Texas also has the highest percentage among the states of residents, 24.6 percent, without health insurance. Some 6.2 million Texans lacked health coverage in 2010. That was about 250,000 fewer uninsured people than in 2009 because of the increased number of Texas children covered under Medicaid or the Children's Health Insurance Program (CHIP). Medicaid is for low-income children, and CHIP is for the children of working parents who earn too much to qualify for Medicaid but do not have insurance through their jobs and cannot afford to purchase private insurance. Even with the growth in Medicaid and CHIP coverage, however, Texas still had the highest percentage of children (as well as total residents) without health insurance—16.8 percent or 1.2 million children in 2010.[48]

It was too early to learn how the spending reductions imposed by the legislature in 2011 would affect the uninsured numbers, but in all likelihood Texas will remain at or near the top of that census category. The legislature cut $2 billion from Medicaid and deferred $4.8 billion in Medicaid funding that would have to be made up during the 2013 session. Payments to hospitals serving Medicaid patients were cut by 8 percent, and it was estimated that about 12,000 elderly and disabled Texans would suffer cuts in services.[49] The legislature also significantly reduced spending on health care services for low-income women, in part because of a Republican campaign against programs suspected of offering abortions (see *Talking Texas: An Uproar over Women's Health Care*).

Many low-income people who do not receive preventative care through Medicaid or CHIP often end up in public hospital emergency rooms when they become sick.

Talking ★ TEXAS An Uproar over Women's Health Care

Governor Rick Perry and Republican legislators said they were fighting abortion and Planned Parenthood. But advocates for women's health care were outraged when Texas in 2012 approved a rule banning Planned Parenthood clinics and other "affiliates of abortion providers" from participating in the Women's Health Program. This program, part of Medicaid and largely federally funded, helps low-income women obtain birth control pills, family-planning help, and cancer screenings. The federal government contributed $9 to the program for every $1 that Texas put in. The Obama administration said it could not renew the program if Texas excluded Planned Parenthood because that organization was responsible for serving about 40 percent of the women who participated. Planned Parenthood did not provide abortions at the clinics participating in the program because clinics that provide abortions were prohibited from receiving money from the Women's Health Program. Even so, Perry and Republican legislative leaders did not want Planned Parenthood to perform cancer screenings or dispense birth control pills either.

Perry said the state was "committed" to the $40 million-per-year program and would find money to replace lost federal dollars, if the federal government withheld funding. The governor blamed the Obama administration for the dispute, which potentially jeopardized important health care services for 115,000 Texas women. "This is the administration using abortion as a political tool," Perry said.[a] Many women and their supporters blamed the governor, instead, and they were particularly angry because the fight over the Women's Health Program followed deep cuts the legislature had made to other women's health services the previous year. Hundreds of people rallied at the state Capitol to protest against Perry and Republican legislators. "I just got fed up," said musician Marcia Ball, a protest organizer, "I suspected there were many people like me, including Christians and people of all ages, who think it's a mistake to defund low-income women's basic health care."[b]

CRITICAL THINKING QUESTIONS

1. **Was the Republican strategy to prevent abortions effective? Or did it put women's health care in jeopardy? Why or why not?**
2. **In what ways might human needs sometimes get lost in political disputes?**

[a] Jay Root, "Perry Says Women's Health Program Won't Die," *The Texas Tribune*, March 8, 2012.

[b] Holly Heinrich, "Rally Targets Possible End of Women's Health Program," *The Texas Tribune*, March 7, 2012.

Emergency room care, paid for by taxpayers in the communities where the hospitals are located, is much more expensive than preventative care under Medicaid or CHIP.

☐ The Squeezing of Nursing Homes

Because of the ever-increasing costs of medical services and rising caseloads in nursing homes, the Texas Department of Aging and Disability Services (or DADS) asked the legislature in 2011 for an additional $96.2 million, about half of which was intended to cover increases in nursing home costs. Instead of appropriating the additional money, the legislature reduced state funding for nursing homes by $20.4 million, even as the industry was anticipating cuts in federal funds as well.

According to the Texas Health Care Association, which represents nursing homes, Texas is forty-ninth in the nation in Medicaid reimbursement rates to nursing facilities. Nationally, the average reimbursement rate was $173 per day. In Texas, it was $126. Most nursing home residents in Texas are poor or disabled, and they ultimately will suffer the consequences if nursing home operators cannot absorb the additional spending cuts without compromising care.[50]

☐ Reorganizing Health and Human Services

The legislature in 2003 ordered a major reorganization of the state's health and human services agencies. The goal of the most sweeping overhaul of social services in modern Texas history was to make state government smaller and save tax dollars through administrative changes and some privatization. Republican leaders who backed the changes predicted they would benefit both the needy recipients of state services and the taxpayers footing the bill, but advocates for the poor were skeptical. It would take several years to complete the consolidation of twelve agencies into five and assess the results, but the reorganization caught the immediate attention of the business community. Several dozen companies submitted bids for consulting contracts to help the state carry out the privatization effort, but it got off to a rough start.

Accenture, a Bermuda-based company, was given an $899 million state contract to operate call centers to determine applicants' eligibility for public benefits. The company's work soon was embroiled in controversy, with many applicants complaining of delays in processing claims and lost paperwork. At one point, some applicants even faxed confidential financial and health information to a warehouse in Seattle, Washington, because an incorrect phone number had been printed on an information sheet. In late 2006, state officials announced that Texas was cutting the contract by $356 million and ending it two years early.

Environmental Problems and Policies

13.7 Assess the state's response to environmental issues.

Texas is blessed with an abundance of fragile natural resources that can no longer be taken for granted. But efforts to impose environmental regulations are difficult for a number of reasons. For one, Texas still has a large share of the nation's oil refining and chemical manufacturing industries, despite the 1980s oil bust. Although efforts have been made to reduce environmental risks, state policymakers are influenced by economic considerations because those same industries employ thousands of people and pump billions of dollars into the economy and the state treasury. Compounding the problem is the desire to attract

ANOTHER OZONE ALERT DAY IN HOUSTON

Houston, pictured here, often suffers from smog, a product of Texas's large petrochemical industry and Texans' love of their autos, pick-ups, and SUVs.

new industries, a legacy that emphasizes individual property rights and Texans' love for their automobiles, pickups, and sport utility vehicles. Consequently, regulation of polluters in Texas traditionally has been weak.

Dirty Air

Texas received some national notoriety in 1999 when Houston beat out Los Angeles for the dubious distinction of being the U.S. city with the "dirtiest air." The Houston metropolitan area led the nation that year in the number of days (fifty-two) in which the city's air violated the national health standard for ozone, the main ingredient in smog. Los Angeles regained its first place standing in 2002, but the problems in Texas persist.[51]

Unlike large cities in some other states, Texas cities have been slow to develop local rail transportation systems. Dallas and Houston only recently built the state's first two, and Austin followed with a third limited rail system. None of these, though, is comparable to the more extensive rail systems in major cities along the East Coast. So automobiles have continued to clog streets and freeways in urban Texas, spewing tons of pollutants into the air. State officials responded with antipollution restrictions only after being forced to do so by the federal government. To meet federal Clean Air Act standards for smog reduction, the state now requires motorists in the Houston, Dallas–Fort Worth, and certain other metropolitan areas to have special emissions inspections of their cars. Speed limits on freeways and highways in metropolitan areas have been lowered to 55 miles per hour. In 2003, the legislature—to avoid losing millions of dollars in federal highway funding—also enacted a plan for raising state funds to pay for the emission reduction effort. The plan, among other provisions, increased the cost of auto title transfers and imposed surcharges on some large diesel equipment.

Many state political leaders, including recent governors, also have preferred to encourage industries to voluntarily reduce pollution, rather than impose strict cleanup requirements. In 2010, President Barack Obama's administration attempted to crack down on Texas's regulatory system as too lax. The federal Environmental Protection Agency attempted to take over the permitting process for some industrial facilities, preempting the business-friendly Texas Commission on Environmental Quality and sparking a political battle.

In a related matter, President Obama in 2011, on the eve of his 2012 reelection campaign, rejected a proposed Environmental Protection Agency rule that would have significantly reduced emissions of smog-causing chemicals. The president said the rule, which had been strongly opposed by industry, would have imposed too severe a burden on industry while the country was trying to recover from the Great Recession. But the federal government remained ready to carry out a different federal rule aimed at reducing smog emissions from power plants in Texas and twenty-six other states. The operator of Texas's electric grid warned that the rule, which targeted nitrogen oxides and sulfur dioxide, would curtail the operations of some coal plants so severely that it could lead to rolling power blackouts.[52]

□ Global Warming

By 2007, Texas not only led the fifty states but also was responsible for more carbon dioxide emissions than the number two and three states—California and Pennsylvania—combined. Commenting in 2009 on a challenge filed by environmentalists against the expansion of coal-fired power plants in Texas, Bryan Shaw, chairman of the Texas Commission on Environmental Quality, said that the verdict on the dangers of global warming was not yet in.[53] Contradicting Shaw's assessment, however, scientists at Texas A&M University issued a report the same year emphasizing that not only was global warming real but also that, in the not-too-distant future, it would pose a potentially devastating threat to the Texas coast. The scientists predicted that global warming would cause sea levels to rise, spawn more intense hurricanes, and increase coastal flooding. Damage to coastal communities from hurricanes would more than triple by the 2080s, they said.[54] Governor Rick Perry may or may not have read the report, but during his campaign for the 2012 Republican presidential nomination, he made national headlines, and raised many eyebrows, by publicly disputing the science on global warming.

□ An Endangered Water Supply

Population growth has led to an increasing concern about the adequacy of Texas's water supply. As noted at the beginning of this chapter, that concern was heightened in 2011, when Texas was struck by the worst one-year drought on record, and again in 2012, when a Texas Supreme Court decision threatened to dismantle the state's regulatory plan for conserving groundwater. Also in 2011, the Texas Water Development Board published a draft report, warning that in serious drought conditions, "Texas does not and will not have enough water to meet the needs of its people, and its businesses, and its agricultural enterprises." As the Texas population increases from the current 25 million to an anticipated 46 million by 2060, the report said, existing water supplies would decrease by 10 percent as the Ogallala (in West Texas) and other aquifers are depleted.[55]

Despite water conservation concerns, the Texas Commission on Environmental Quality in 2011 approved a permit for a well through which to inject oil and gas industry waste into the ground in suburban Montgomery County, near Houston, which local officials feared would pollute an aquifer that provided the county with its drinking water. Every state and local official that represented Montgomery County objected to the permit, and an administrative law judge who heard evidence in the case recommended that the commission deny the permit. But the commission, all appointees of Governor Rick Perry, approved the permit, 2–1. Some people suspected the governor had influenced the commission because top investors in the company that would operate the well, TexCom, Inc., of Houston, included two men with close ties to Perry. The governor's office denied any involvement.[56]

Review the Chapter

Listen to Chapter 13

The Policy Process

13.1 List the stages of the policymaking process and place them in the framework of issue networks, p. 392.

In the broadest sense, public policy is what governments do or choose not to do. Policymaking can be broken down into a series of stages: identification of a problem, enactment of a solution into law, implementing—or carrying out—the solution, and evaluating the solution's effectiveness. This process plays out within a framework of issue networks that involves interactions among participants with interest in a specific policy. These participants include legislators, issue specialists, special interest lobbyists, and the courts.

The State Budget

13.2 Outline recent budget developments in Texas and identify constraints on those responsible for the state's budget, p. 396.

The Texas Constitution prohibits deficit financing by state government, which means the legislature must pass a balanced budget that can be financed from anticipated revenue. Since the legislature meets in regular session only every other year, state government in Texas operates under two-year budgets. This means agencies and legislators must anticipate spending needs months in advance, a prospect that can be difficult during recessions and other periods of economic uncertainty. The legislature's budget-setting prerogatives are constrained further by provisions in the state constitution and laws dedicating, or restricting, some sources of revenue to specific programs or purposes. Strong population growth and a healthy economy resulted in regular increases in state budgets until the recession that began in 2008. The legislature, meeting in 2011, reduced state spending to bridge a $27 billion revenue shortfall without raising state taxes.

State Taxes

13.3 Describe the different types of taxes in Texas and explain in what ways the tax system as a whole is regressive, p. 398.

Governments in Texas rely on a large number of taxes and fees. Unlike most other states, Texas has no personal income tax but relies on regressive taxes that include the sales tax and the property tax. A regressive tax places a disproportionate tax burden on lower income people. The sales tax is the primary revenue raiser for state government. Other state taxes include a business tax, motor fuels taxes, severance taxes on oil and natural gas production, and taxes on alcoholic beverages and tobacco products. Property taxes and sales taxes are the main revenue sources for local governments. Proponents of an income tax argue that it would be fairer and a more dependable revenue source, but historically there has been strong political opposition to an income tax in Texas.

Educational Policies and Politics

13.4 Identify the factors affecting education policy in Texas and relate them to questions of equity and quality, p. 402.

Despite years of debate and lawsuits, Texas's system of funding public schools is inequitable and, in many respects, inadequate. Texas's 1,000-plus school districts are funded by a combination of state aid and local revenue raised through property taxes. Districts with wealthier property tax bases, including those with mineral wealth or expensive commercial property, are able to raise more money for their schools than districts with less wealth. Prodded by a series of court orders, the legislature in recent years has taken steps to try to reduce disparities, including a law requiring rich districts to share some of their tax revenue with poor districts. But the struggle continues, with many school officials contending that the legislature also should increase state aid to the schools.

The state has established an accountability system for public schools, which is based largely on students' scores on standardized tests. Students have to pass these tests to be promoted and graduate from high school. The quality of Texas's public schools is a source of much political debate, with some critics proposing more charter schools and/or state-paid vouchers to help students from low-performing public schools transfer to private schools. Voucher proposals, opposed by teachers and other education groups, have been defeated in recent legislative sessions.

Texas's state-supported universities and junior colleges struggle with tightened budgets amid growing enrollments. In recent years, more and more of the cost of a college education has been transferred to students and their families in the form of higher tuition. In 2003, for the first time, the legislature deregulated university tuition, allowing appointed university governing boards to raise tuition without legislative approval. Universities also continue to deal with issues related to affirmative action at a time when the Hispanic population, in particular, is rapidly increasing in Texas.

Criminal Justice

13.5 Explain the implications of court-ordered prison reform, the continued high numbers of prisoners, and the state's high rate of executions, p. 409.

Texas spent millions of dollars expanding and improving its prison system, following a landmark federal court order for prison reform in 1980. The ruling stemmed from a lawsuit brought by an inmate over crowded and inhumane prison conditions. Texas has one of the largest prison systems in the world, and the state's criminal justice policies reflect a strong law-and-order tradition. Texas leads the nation in executions, and state law provides for long prison sentences for other violent offenders.

Many convicts have problems with drugs and alcohol, and some state leaders recognize that prisons alone will not solve the crime problem. More crucial in the long run will be the state's efforts to improve public schools and prepare young people for well-paying jobs.

Health and Human Services

13.6 Evaluate the patterns of state support for health and human services, p. 412.

Texas has a high incidence of poverty, and it leads the country in the percentage of people without health insurance. Texas also has ranked historically near the bottom of the states in per capita spending on health and human services programs for the poor and the elderly. One reason, some believe, is the state's conservative political culture, which is based on individualism and self-help. Others argue that many Texans, including business leaders, do not want to pay higher taxes, especially for social services. The state's regressive tax structure, it also is argued, cannot support an adequate expansion of health care and social services.

Environmental Problems and Policies

13.7 Assess the state's response to environmental issues, p. 414.

Texas has some of the highest pollution levels in the country, from both petrochemical and other industrial plants and heavy traffic on streets and highways. But the petrochemical plants provide thousands of jobs, and Texans love their automobiles, pickup trucks, and SUVs. Because of those factors and a conservative political climate, Texas has a lax environmental regulatory climate. Much of the regulation that Texas imposes is required by the federal government, which state officials have challenged on occasion. Governor Rick Perry also has been widely quoted as doubting the scientific reality of global warming, and many Texans share his view. But other Texans have no doubt that global warming is real and would support tougher state environmental enforcement. The recent extended droughts in the state have focused statewide attention on the availability of water for future generations.

Learn the Terms

Study and **Review** the Flashcards

issue networks, p. 395
deficit financing, p. 396
dedicated funds, p. 398
sales tax, p. 398
margins tax, p. 399
property or ad valorem tax, p. 399
sin tax, p. 399
lottery, p. 400
general obligation bonds, p. 401
income tax, p. 401
House Bill 72, p. 403
no pass, no play rule, p. 403
Edgewood v. *Kirby*, p. 403
Permanent University Fund (PUF), p. 406
Ruiz v. *Estelle*, p. 410

Test Yourself

Study and **Review** the Practice Tests

1. What happens in the performance review stage of the policy process?

a. People evaluate a problem and identify the responsible party.

b. Interest groups assess the effectiveness of their lobbying efforts.

c. Legislators review the various options to address a public policy problem.

d. Governmental agencies assess the impact of their activities.

e. Government bureaucrats determine the best way to implement a given policy.

2. Which of the following is an example of an iron triangle?

a. Texas Supreme Court—Texas Senate—governor
b. House Agriculture Committee—Senate Agriculture Committee—agriculture commissioner
c. Republican Party—Texas Department of Transportation—highway contractors
d. City mayors—Texas Department of Transportation—governor
e. Texas Department of Transportation—House and Senate Transportation Committees—highway contractors

3. Which of the following is the policymaking model that recognizes the importance of multiple levels of government activity and a range of participants in the policy process?

a. iron triangles
b. issue networks
c. federalism
d. policy articulation
e. separation of powers

4. The biggest share of state budget expenditures is for

a. health and human services.
b. economic development.
c. education.
d. road construction and maintenance.
e. prisons and criminal justice.

5. The Texas budgetary process

a. operates on a two-year cycle.
b. allows for limited levels of deficit financing.
c. uses lottery funds to reduce the deficit.
d. allows the Highway Trust Fund to be used for education during economic recessions.
e. bans the use of federal funds for state programs.

6. Which of the following is the single biggest generator of state revenue?

a. state income tax
b. Texas lottery
c. gasoline tax
d. property taxes
e. sales tax

7. Which of the following describes why the tax system in Texas is seen as regressive?

a. Wealthy families pay no property tax.
b. State and local governments' taxes take a larger share of the income of poor families than of wealthy families.
c. Wealthy families pay the same share of their income in taxes as poor families.
d. The franchise tax was expanded to include law firms.
e. Casino gambling revenues come from poor and middle-class families more than from wealthy families.

8. Which of the following is the only local source of operating revenue for school districts?

a. state sales tax
b. business franchise tax
c. cigarette taxes
d. property tax
e. motor fuels tax

9. Which of the following best describes the status of a state income tax in Texas?

a. Two successive governors endorsed it.
b. Democratic governors support it, and Republican governors oppose it.
c. The constitution bans a personal income tax without voter approval.
d. The constitution allows for a state income tax during times of severe recession.
e. The constitution allows for a personal income tax if two-thirds of the legislature votes for it.

10. What did the landmark court case *Edgewood* v. *Kirby* argue?

a. Inequities in school finance violated the Texas Constitution.
b. Large class sizes violated the Texas Constitution.
c. Students should pass a basic skills test before graduating from high school.
d. Teachers should be required to pass a literacy test to keep their jobs.
e. Students should pass all courses if they are to participate in any extracurricular activities.

11. All of the following were reforms enacted by the landmark House Bill 72, passed in 1984, EXCEPT that

a. teacher pay was raised.
b. class sizes were limited.
c. prekindergarten classes for disadvantaged four-year-olds were implemented.
d. students had to pass all courses to participate in extracurricular activities.
e. end-of-course exams had to be counted toward high school students' grades.

12. The *Hopwood* case led the state to

a. enact annual end-of-course exams in core subject areas for high school students.
b. provide vouchers that allowed children to attend private schools at state expense.
c. enact a law guaranteeing automatic admission to state universities for high school graduates who finished in the top 10 percent of their classes.
d. allow universities to set tuition rates independently of legislative action.
e. enact a law permitting parents to home school their children.

13. All of the following are prison reforms prompted by the landmark *Ruiz* lawsuit EXCEPT that the state

a. greatly expanded its prison capacity to alleviate overcrowding.
b. reduced the number of convicted murderers subject to capital punishment.
c. doubled the minimum time violent felons would have to serve in prison.
d. lowered penalties for property crimes and drug offenses.
e. diverted nonviolent offenders to community corrections programs.

14. Which of the following statements is TRUE about the delivery of health care in Texas?

a. Texas has the highest percentage of children covered by health insurance.
b. Texas has the highest reimbursement rate to nursing facilities.
c. Texas has the highest percentage of residents without health insurance.
d. Texas has the highest rate of minorities covered by health insurance.
e. Texas has expanded its spending on health care programs by an amount larger than any other state.

15. One reason for the increasing problem of dirty air in Texas is

a. the large number of automobiles.
b. the increasing use of rail transportation.
c. federal regulations that force emissions inspections on cars.
d. global warming.
e. severe drought.

Explore Further

Camarota, Steven A., and Ashley Monique Webster, *Who Benefited from Job Growth in Texas: A Look at Employment Gains for Immigrants and the Native-Born, 2007–2011.* Washington, DC: Center for Immigration Studies, 2011. Uses data from the *Current Population Survey* to challenge conclusions made by Texas officials, including Governor Rick Perry, regarding recent job growth in Texas. Job growth occurred, but immigrants, not native-born populations, filled new jobs disproportionately.

Cochran, Clarke E., Lawrence C. Mayer, T. R. Carr, N. Joseph Cayer, Mark J. McKenzie, and Laura R. Peck, *American Public Policy: An Introduction*, 10th ed. Belmont, CA: Thomson Wadsworth, 2011. Introduces the concepts or models employed in policy analysis and applies these concepts to specific policy issues including the national economy, taxes, budgeting, energy, and social welfare.

Crouch, Ben M., and James R. Marquart, *An Appeal to Justice: Litigated Reform of Texas Prisons*. Austin: University of Texas Press, 2010. Provides an account of the extensive litigation directed against Texas's prison system that resulted in wide-ranging reforms.

Dye, Thomas R., *Understanding Public Policy*, 14th ed. New York: Longman, 2012. Covers a number of conceptual models with applications to contemporary public policy issues; one of the classic introductory textbooks dealing with public policy.

Griffin, Roland C., ed., *Water Policy In Texas: Responding to the Rise in Scarcity*. Washington, DC: Resources for the Future Press, 2010. Provides perspectives on Texas water law, the development of water management policies in the state, and water marketing.

Heclo, Hugh, "Issue Networks and the Executive Establishment," in *The New American Political System*, edited by Anthony King. Washington, DC: American Enterprise Institute, 1978. Introduces the theoretical perspective of issue networks.

Hubner, John, *Last Chance in Texas: The Redemption of Criminal Youth.* New York: Random House, 2005. Provides a journalist's account of a successful treatment/rehabilitations program for violent offenders implemented at the Giddings State School in Texas.

Norwine, Jim, John R. Giardino, and Susha Krishnamurthy, eds., *Water for Texas*. College Station: Texas A&M University Press, 2005. Includes edited articles that came out of a 2000 water conference at Texas A&M University focused on historical perspectives on water issues in Texas, regional water agreements, the climate and water issues, and water issues in specific communities or areas of the state.

Preuss, Gene. B., *To Get a Better School System: One Hundred Years of Education Reform in Texas.* College Station: Texas A&M University Press, 2009. Discusses education reform in Texas. With increased population growth and urbanization, the Texas Legislature responded with a major overhaul of state education laws in the Gilmer-Aiken Act of 1949 that initiated major education reforms including increases in teachers' salaries and sweeping changes in the state's funding of local school districts.

Texas Education Agency, *Snapshot 2010: School District Profiles.* Austin: Texas Education Agency, 2011. Details information on Texas school districts; annual compendium.

Glossary

Absentee (or early) voting A period before the regularly scheduled election date during which voters are allowed to cast ballots. With recent changes in election law, a person does not have to offer a reason for voting absentee.

Activists A small segment of the population that is engaged in various political activities.

Agenda building The process of groups or individuals identifying problems or issues that affect them and keeping pressure on policymakers to develop and implement public policy solutions.

Agenda setting A theory that the media's choice of which news events and issues to cover helps define what is important for the public to know and what issues to think about.

Annexation The authority of cities to add territory, subject to restrictions set by state law.

Appellate jurisdiction The authority of a court to review the decisions of lower courts to determine if the law was correctly interpreted and legal procedures were correctly followed.

Appraisal district Countywide tax office that appraises the value of property and certifies the tax rolls used by every taxing authority in the county.

Appropriations bill A legislative action authorizing the expenditure of money for a public program or purpose. A general appropriations bill approved by the legislature every two years is the state budget.

At-large election A system under which city council members or other officeholders are elected by voters in the entire city, school district, or single-purpose district. Many of these election systems have been struck down by the federal courts or by the U.S. Justice Department under the Voting Rights Act as discriminatory against minorities.

Attorney general The state's chief legal officer. He or she represents the state in lawsuits; is responsible for enforcing the state's antitrust, consumer protection, and other civil laws; and issues advisory opinions on legal questions to state and local officeholders. This elected official has little responsibility for criminal law enforcement.

Bicameral legislature A lawmaking body, such as the Texas legislature, that includes two chambers.

Bifactionalism The presence of two dominant factions organized around regional, economic, or ideological differences within a single political party. For much of the twentieth century, Texas functioned as a one-party system with two dominant factions.

Bifurcated court system Existence of two courts at the highest level of the state judiciary. The Texas Supreme Court is the court of last resort in civil cases, and the Court of Criminal Appeals has the final authority to review criminal cases. Texas and Oklahoma are the only two states that use this system.

Block grants Federal grants of money to states and local governments for broad programs or services rather than narrowly defined programs. These grants give state and local governments more discretion over the use of the funds.

Bureaucracies The agencies of government and their employees responsible for carrying out policies and providing public services approved by elected officials.

Calendars Agendas or the lists of bills to be considered by the House or the Senate on a given day.

Calendars Committee A special procedural committee in the Texas House of Representatives that schedules bills that already have been approved by other committees for floor debate.

Campaign consultant A professional expert who helps political candidates plan, organize, and run their campaigns.

Capital murder Murder committed under certain circumstances for which the death penalty or life in prison must be imposed.

Capitol press corps Representatives of Texas newspapers, television and radio stations, and wire services who are assigned to Austin full time to report on state government and politics.

Categorical grants-in-aid Grants of federal money that can be spent only for specific programs or purposes. This is the source of most federal assistance to state and local governments.

Caucuses Groups of legislators who band together for common political or partisan goals or along ethnic or geographic lines.

City charter A document, defined or authorized by state law, under which a city operates. In Texas home rule cities, local voters may choose among several forms of city government.

City commission A form of city government in which elected commissioners collectively serve as a city's policymaking body and individually serve as administrative heads of different city departments. Although once popular, this form of government is rarely used in Texas today.

Civil lawsuits Noncriminal legal disputes between two or more individuals, businesses, governments, or other entities.

Civil service system A personnel system under which public employees are selected for government jobs through competitive examinations and the systematic evaluation of job performance.

Co-optation Influence over state regulatory boards by the industries they are supposed to regulate, often to the detriment of the general public.

commissioner of agriculture An elected state official responsible for administering laws and programs that benefit agriculture.

commissioner of the General Land Office An elected official who manages the state's public lands and administers the Veterans Land Program, which provides low-interest loans to veterans for the purchase of land and houses.

Commissioners court The principal policymaking body for county government. It includes four commissioners and the county judge, all elected offices. It sets the county tax rate and supervises expenditures.

comptroller of public accounts The state's primary tax administrator and revenue estimator. This is an elective position.

Concurrent powers Powers shared by both the national and state governments.

Confederacy A view of the constitution taken by eleven southern states, including Texas, that a state could withdraw, or secede, from the Union. Upon secession that began in 1860, the Confederate States of America was formed, leading to the Civil War.

Confederation A system in which each member government is considered sovereign, and the national government is limited to powers delegated to it by its member governments.

Conference committee A panel of House members and senators appointed to work out a compromise on a bill if the House and the Senate passed different versions of the legislation.

Constable An elected law enforcement officer assigned as an administrative officer in a justice of the peace precinct. He or she is responsible primarily for executing court judgments, serving subpoenas, and delivering other legal documents. Constables also are authorized to patrol their precincts, make arrests, and conduct criminal investigations.

Constitution A document that provides for the legal and institutional structure of a political system. It establishes government bodies and defines their powers.

Constitutional Convention of 1974 The last major attempt to write a new Texas constitution. Members of the legislature served as delegates and failed to overcome political differences and the influence of special interests.

Constitutional county court The Texas Constitution provides for 254 courts with limited jurisdiction. The county judge, who is also the presiding officer of a county's commissioners court, which is a policy-making body, performs some limited judicial functions in some counties.

Controlled media Paid advertising in the media whose content and presentation are determined by a political candidate or campaign.

Cooperative federalism Policies emphasizing cooperative efforts among the federal, state, and local governments to address common problems and provide public services to citizens.

Council-manager government A form of city government in which policy is set by an elected city council, which hires a professional city manager to head the daily administration of city government.

County attorney An elected official who is the chief legal officer of some counties. He or she also prosecutes lesser criminal offenses, primarily misdemeanors, in county courts.

County auditor An officer appointed by the district judges of the county. This person is primarily responsible for reviewing every bill and expenditure of a county to ensure that it is correct and legal. In counties with more than 225,000 people, the auditor also is the budget officer who prepares the county budget for consideration by commissioners court.

County chair The presiding officer of a political party's county executive committee. Voters in the party primary elect him or her in a countywide election.

County clerk The chief record-keeping officer of a county.

County executive committee A panel responsible on the local level for the organization and management of a political party's primary election. It includes the party's county chair and each precinct chair.

County judge The presiding officer of a county commissioners court. This office also has some judicial authority, which is assumed by separate county courts-at-law in most urban counties.

County tax assessor-collector An elected official who determines how much property tax is owed on the different pieces of property within a county and then collects the tax. This officeholder acts on the basis of property values determined by the county appraisal district and a tax rate set by county commissioners court.

County treasurer An elected officer who is responsible for receiving and disbursing county funds. The office's primary functions are now carried out by the county auditor, and the office has been eliminated in a number of counties.

Courts of appeals Intermediate-level courts that reviews civil and criminal cases from the district courts.

Dealignment A view that the party system is breaking up and the electoral influence of political parties is being replaced by interest groups, the media, and well-financed candidates who use their own media campaigns to dominate the nomination and election process.

Dedicated funds Constitutional or statutory requirements that restrict some state tax or fee revenues to spending on specific programs.

Deficit financing Borrowing money to meet operating expenses. It is prohibited by the Texas Constitution, which provides that the state government operates on a pay-as-you-go basis.

Delegated powers Powers specifically assigned to the national, or federal, government by the U.S. Constitution, including powers to tax, borrow and coin money, declare war, and regulate interstate and foreign commerce.

Denied powers Powers that are denied to both the states and national government. The best-known restrictions are listed in the Bill of Rights.

Devolution Return of powers assumed by the federal government to the states.

Dillon rule A principle holding that local governments are creations of state government and their powers and responsibilities are defined by the state.

Direct lobbying The communication of information and policy preferences directly to policymakers or their staffs.

District attorney An elected official who prosecutes the more serious criminal offenses, usually felonies, in state district courts.

District court Court with general jurisdiction over criminal felony cases and civil disputes.

Dual federalism Nineteenth century concept of federalism in which the powers or functions of the national and state governments were sharply differentiated with limited overlapping responsibilities.

Economic diversification The development of new and varied business activities. New businesses were encouraged to relocate to or expand in Texas after the oil and gas industry, which had been the base of the state's economy, suffered a major recession in the 1980s.

Edgewood* v. *Kirby A lawsuit in which the Texas Supreme Court in 1989 declared the Texas school finance system unconstitutional because of wide disparities in property wealth and educational opportunities between school districts.

Editorial autonomy The freedom of a local newspaper or television station to set its own news policies independently of absentee owners who may run a chain of media outlets throughout the country.

Edmund J. Davis Republican governor (1870–1874) whose highly unpopular policies contributed to the decisions of the Constitutional Convention of 1875 to limit and fragment the powers of the governor.

Elitism The view that political power is primarily held by a few individuals who derive power from leadership positions in large business, civic, or governmental institutions.

Extradition A process by which a person in one state can be returned to another state to face criminal charges.

Extraterritorial jurisdiction The power of an incorporated city to control development within nearby unincorporated areas.

Fat cat An individual who contributes a large amount of money to political candidates.

Federalism A system that balances the power and sovereignty of state governments with those of the national government. Both the states and the national government derive their authority directly from the people, and the states have considerable autonomy within their areas of responsibility.

Felony A criminal offense that can be punished by imprisonment and/or a fine. This is a more serious offense than a misdemeanor.

Filibuster A procedure that allows a senator to speak against a bill for as long as he or she can stand and talk. It can become a formidable obstacle or threat against controversial bills near the end of a legislative session.

Formula grant A federal grant based on specific criteria, such as income levels or population.

Full faith and credit clause A provision in the U.S. Constitution (Article 4, Section 1) that requires states to recognize civil judgments and official documents rendered by the courts of other states.

General election An election for state, federal, and county offices held in November of even-numbered years. The ballot includes nominees of the two major political parties plus other candidates who meet certain legal requirements.

General law cities Texas cities with fewer than 5,000 residents that are allowed to exercise only those powers specifically granted to them by the legislature. Most cities in Texas are classified as general law cities.

General obligation bonds A method of borrowing money to pay for new construction projects, such as prisons or mental hospitals. Interest on these bonds, which require voter approval in the form of constitutional amendments, is paid with tax revenue.

Gerrymandering Drawing of political district lines in such a way that they favor a particular political party or racial group.

Globalization of the economy Increased interdependence in trade, manufacturing, and commerce between the United States and other countries.

Governor The state's top executive officeholder.

Grand jury Panel that reviews evidence submitted by prosecutors to determine whether to indict, or charge, an individual with a criminal offense. A grand jury can hear witnesses; all its meetings are held behind closed doors.

Grange An organization formed in the late nineteenth century to improve the lot of farmers. Its influence in Texas after Reconstruction was felt in constitutional provisions limiting taxes and government spending and restricting banks, railroads, and other big businesses.

Grass roots A term used to describe a wide range of political activities designed to organize and mobilize the electorate at the local level. Modern campaigns are increasingly dominated by campaign consultants, but such support can prove crucial for political candidates, particularly for those with limited financial resources.

Home rule cities Texas cities with more than 5,000 residents. They can adopt any form of government residents choose, provided it does not conflict with the state constitution or statutes. Home rule powers are formalized through local voters' adoption of a city charter spelling out how the city is to be governed.

Homestead exemption Legal provision that permits a person who owns a home and is living in it to obtain a reduction in property taxes on the house.

House Bill 72 A landmark school reform law enacted in 1984. Among other items, it reduced class sizes; required teachers to pass a literacy test to keep their jobs; and imposed the no pass, no play rule, which restricts failing students from participating in extracurricular activities.

Hyperpluralism The rapid expansion of interest groups that serves to disrupt and potentially deadlock the policymaking process.

Implied powers Although not specifically defined by the U.S. Constitution, these are powers assumed by the national government as necessary in carrying out its responsibilities.

Income tax A tax based on a corporation's or an individual's income. Texas is one of only a few states without a personal income tax.

Independent school district A specific form of special district that administers the public schools in a designated area. It is governed by an elected board of trustees empowered to levy local property taxes, establish local school policies, and employ a school superintendent as its chief administrator.

Indictment A written statement issued by a grand jury charging a person or persons with a crime or crimes.

Indirect lobbying Activities designed to mobilize public support for a policy position and bring pressure to bear on public officials through electoral activities, public relations campaigns, and sometimes protests or marches.

Individualism An attitude, rooted in classical liberal theory and reinforced by the frontier tradition, that citizens are capable of taking care of themselves with minimal governmental assistance.

Individualistic subculture A view that government should interfere as little as possible in the private activities of its citizens while assuring that adequate public facilities and a favorable business climate are available to permit individuals to pursue their self-interests.

Information A document formally charging an individual with a misdemeanor.

Initiative A petition and election process whereby voters propose laws or constitutional amendments for adoption by a popular vote.

Institutionalization The complex process of institutional change and adaptation in the organization and operations of the legislature.

Interest group A group of people with common goals who are organized to seek political or policy objectives they are unable to achieve by themselves.

Interstate compacts Formal, long-term cooperative agreements among the states dealing with common problems or issues and subject to approval of the U.S. Congress.

Iron rule of oligarchy A theory developed by Robert Michels, a European sociologist, that all organizations inevitably are dominated by a few individuals.

Iron triangles of government Relationships among the interest groups, the administrative agencies, and the legislative committees involved in drafting the laws and regulations affecting a particular area of the economy or a specific segment of the population.

Issue networks Term coined by Hugh Heclo to describe the complex institutional and political relationships in the policymaking process.

Issue-attention cycle A pattern in which public interest in an issue or problem is heightened by intensive media coverage. Media attention and public interest will wane after government takes steps to address their concerns, but most issues or problems are never permanently resolved. Another crisis, perhaps years later, will restart the cycle.

Jim Crow laws Legislation enacted by many states after the Civil War to limit the rights and power of African Americans.

Justice of the peace court A low-ranking court with jurisdiction over minor civil disputes and criminal cases.

Licensing A key regulatory function of government that seeks to ensure that individuals and companies providing critical professional services to the public are properly trained or qualified.

Lieutenant governor The presiding officer of the Senate. This officeholder also becomes governor if the governor dies, resigns, becomes incapacitated, or is removed from office.

Limited government The constitutional principle restricting governmental authority and spelling out personal rights.

Line-item veto The power of the governor to reject certain parts of an appropriation, or spending, bill without killing the entire measure.

Lobbying An effort, usually organized and using a variety of strategies and techniques, to influence the making of laws or public policy.

Local election An election for a city council, school board, or other local offices. Most of these are nonpartisan.

Lottery A form of gambling, conducted by many states, in which participants purchase tickets that offer an opportunity to cash in on a winning number or set of winning numbers. Voters legalized a state lottery in Texas in 1991.

Mandates Federal laws or regulations that require state or local governments to take certain actions, often at costs that the federal government does not reimburse. The state government also imposes mandates on local governments.

Maquiladora program Economic program initiated by Mexico to increase manufacturing and the assembly of goods.

Margins tax This is the state's main business tax. It was enacted in 2006 to replace the franchise tax and applies to corporations and professional partnerships, such as law firms. It imposes a one-percent levy on a company's annual revenue. Companies can deduct some of their costs, such as employees' salaries, from the tax base. Many of the smaller companies in the state do not have to pay the tax.

Matching funds Money that states or local governments have to provide to qualify for certain federal grants.

Media bias A perception—sometimes real, sometimes imagined—that reporters and news organizations slant their news coverage to favor one side or the other in particular issues or disputes.

Media event An event staged by an officeholder or political candidate that is designed to attract media—especially television coverage.

Merit employment system A personnel system under which public employees are selected for government jobs through competitive examinations and the systematic evaluation of job performance.

Merit selection A proposal under which the governor would appoint state judges from lists of potential nominees recommended by committees of experts. Appointed judges would have to run later in retention elections in which voters would simply decide whether a judge should remain in office or be replaced by another gubernatorial appointee.

Metro government Consolidation of city and county governments to avoid duplication of public services. This approach has been tried in several other parts of the country but so far has attracted little interest in Texas.

Miranda ruling A far-reaching decision of the U.S. Supreme Court that requires law enforcement officers to warn a criminal suspect of his or her right to remain silent and have an attorney present during questioning.

Mischief of factions Term coined by James Madison to describe the complex relationships among groups and interests within the American political system and the institutional arrangements that potentially balance the power of groups.

Misdemeanor A minor criminal offense punishable by a fine or a short sentence in the county jail.

Moralistic subculture A view that government's primary responsibility is to promote the public welfare and should actively use its authority and power to improve the social and economic well-being of its citizens.

Motor voter registration Term referring to federal and state laws that allow people to register to vote at offices where they receive their drivers' licenses.

Municipal courts Courts of limited jurisdiction that hear cases involving city ordinances and primarily handles traffic tickets.

Negative television ads Television commercials in which political candidates attack their opponents, sometimes over a legitimate issue, but more often over an alleged flaw in their opponent's character or ability to hold office. Many such ads are deliberately misleading or outright false.

New federalism A term used to describe recent changes in federal-state relationships. Used primarily by conservative presidents, it suggests a devolution or return of power to the states and a decreased role of the federal government in domestic policy.

No pass, no play rule Provides that a student failing a course is restricted from participating in extracurricular activities.

Nolo contendere A plea of no contest to a criminal charge

Nonpartisan elections Local elections in which candidates file for place, position, or district with no political party label attached to their names.

Norms Unwritten rules of institutional behavior that are critical to the stability and effectiveness of the institution.

North American Free Trade Agreement (NAFTA) Treaty signed in 1993 to lower trade barriers among the United States, Mexico, and Canada and to create a common economic market. It is widely referred to as NAFTA.

One-party politics The domination of elections and governmental processes by a single party, which may be split into different ideological, economic, or regional factions. In Texas, the phrase is used to describe the period from the late 1870s to the late 1970s, when the Democratic Party claimed virtually all elected, partisan offices.

Open Meetings and Public Information Acts Laws that require state and local governmental bodies to conduct most of their actions in public and maintain records for public inspection.

Original jurisdiction The authority of a court to try to resolve a civil lawsuit or a criminal prosecution being heard for the first time.

Parole The early release of an inmate from prison, subject to certain conditions.

Party activist Member of a political party involved in organizational and electoral activities.

Pay-as-you-go A constitutional prohibition against state government borrowing money for its operating budget.

Penal Code A body of law that defines most criminal offenses and sets a range of punishments that can be assessed.

Permanent University Fund (PUF) A land- and mineral-rich endowment that benefits the University of Texas and Texas A&M University systems, particularly the flagship universities in Austin and College Station.

Petit jury A panel of citizens that hears evidence in a civil lawsuit or a criminal prosecution and decides the outcome by issuing a verdict.

Petition for discretionary review Petition to the Texas Court of Criminal Appeals claiming that legal or procedural mistakes were made in the lower court, thus meriting a hearing before the court.

Petition for review Petition to the Texas Supreme Court claiming that legal or procedural mistakes were made in the lower court, thus meriting a hearing before the court.

Platform A set of principles or positions on various issues adopted by a political party at its state or national convention.

Plea bargain A procedure that allows a person charged with a crime to negotiate a guilty plea with prosecutors in exchange for a lighter sentence than he or she would expect to receive if convicted in a trial.

Plural executive A fragmented system of authority under which most statewide, executive officeholders are elected independently of the governor. This arrangement, which is used in Texas, places severe limitations on the governor's power.

Pluralism Theory holding that diverse groups and people are instrumental in the policymaking process and no one group is able to dominate the decisions of government.

Political action committee (PAC) Often referred to as a PAC, this is a committee representing a specific interest group or including employees of a specific company, which raises money from its members for distribution to selected officeholders and political candidates.

Political culture A widely shared set of views, attitudes, beliefs, and customs of a people as to how their government should be organized and run.

Political myths Generally held views rooted in the political culture that are used to explain common historical and cultural experiences.

Political party A group that seeks to elect public officeholders under its own name.

Political patronage The hiring of government employees on the basis of personal friendships or favors rather than ability or merit.

Political socialization The process that begins in early childhood whereby a person assimilates the beliefs, attitudes, and behaviors of society and acquires views toward the political system and government.

Poll tax A tax that Texas and some other states used to require people to pay before allowing them to vote. The purpose was to discourage minorities and poor whites from participating in the political process. The tax was declared unconstitutional in the 1960s.

Popular sovereignty The constitutional principle of self-government; the belief that the people control their government and governments are subject to limitations and constraints.

Population density Number of persons residing within a square mile.

Precinct A specific, local voting area created by county commissioners court. The state election code outlines detailed requirements for drawing up these election units.

Precinct chair A local officer in a political party who presides over the precinct convention and serves on the party's county executive committee. Voters in each precinct elect a chair in the party's primary election.

Preemptions Federal laws that limit the authority or powers of state and local governments.

Primary election An election in which the Democratic or Republican Party chooses its nominees for public offices. In presidential election years, the primary also plays a key role in selecting Texas delegates to the parties' national nominating conventions.

Privatization Government contracting with private companies to provide some public services.

Privileges and immunities The right of a resident of one state to be protected by the laws and afforded the legal opportunities in any other state he or she visits. Certain exceptions, however, have been allowed by the courts, including the right of states to charge nonresidents higher college tuition or higher hunting and fishing license fees.

Probation A procedure under which a convicted criminal is not sent to prison if he or she meets certain conditions, such as restrictions on travel and with whom he or she associates.

Project grant A federal grant for a defined project.

Property or ad valorem tax A tax on homes, businesses, and certain other forms of property that is the main source of revenue for local governments. The tax is based on the assessed value of the property.

Prosecution The conduct of legal proceedings against an individual charged with a crime.

Public improvement district Specific area of a city in which property owners pay special taxes in return for improvements to streets and other public facilities in their neighborhood.

Public interest groups Groups that are primarily concerned with consumer or environmental protection, the promotion of strong ethical standards for public officials, or increased funding for health and human services programs. Since they often are poorly funded, grassroots, volunteer efforts are crucial to their success.

Public opinion polling The scientific compiling of people's attitudes toward business products, public issues, public officeholders, or political candidates. It has become a key ingredient of statewide political campaigns and is usually conducted by telephone, using a representative sample of voters.

Radical Reconstructionists The group of Republicans who took control of Congress in 1866 and imposed hated military governments on the former Confederate states after the Civil War.

Reading Bills are required to go through three readings in both houses of the legislature. The first reading occurs with the introduction of a bill in the House or the Senate and its referral to a committee by the presiding officer. The second reading is the initial debate by the full House or Senate on a bill that has been approved by a committee. The third occurs with the final presentation of a bill before the full House or Senate.

Realignment A major shift in political party support or identification, which usually occurs around a critical election. In Texas, this was a gradual transformation from a one-party system dominated by Democrats to a two-party system in which Republicans became the dominant party statewide.

Record votes Votes taken in the House or the Senate for which a permanent record is kept, listing how individual legislators voted. By contrast, with voice votes, legislators simply voice ayes or nays on an issue without being permanently recorded.

Redistricting The process of redrawing legislative and other political district boundaries to reflect changing population patterns. Districts for the Texas House, state Senate, the State Board of Education, and U.S. Congress are redrawn every ten years by the legislature.

Referendum An election, usually initiated by a petition of voters, whereby an action of a legislative body is submitted for approval or rejection by the voters.

Regressive tax A tax that imposes a disproportionately heavier burden on low-income people than on the more affluent.

Regular legislative session The 140-day period in odd-numbered years in which the legislature meets and can consider laws on any issue or subject.

Religious Right An ultraconservative political faction that draws considerable support from fundamentalist religious groups and economic conservatives.

Republic A political system in which sovereign power resides in the citizenry and is exercised by representatives elected by and responsible to them.

Reserved powers Powers given to state governments by the Tenth Amendment. These are powers not delegated to the national government nor otherwise prohibited to the states by the Constitution.

Retention elections Elections in which judges run on their own records rather than against other candidates. Voters cast their ballots on the question of whether the incumbent judge should stay in office.

Revenue bonds Bonds sold by governments that are repaid from the revenues generated from income-producing facilities.

Revenue sharing A program begun under President Nixon and later repealed in which state and local governments received federal aid that could be used for virtually any purpose the recipient government wanted.

Revolving door The practice of former members of state boards and commissions or key employees of agencies leaving state government for more lucrative jobs with the industries they used to regulate. It raises questions of undue industry influence over regulatory agencies.

Right-to-work law Law prohibiting the requirement of union membership in order to get or hold a job.

Rollback election An election in which local voters can nullify a property tax increase that exceeds 8 percent in a given year.

Ruiz* v. *Estelle A landmark federal court order (1980) that declared the state prison system unconstitutional and resulted in significant changes in state lockups.

Runoff election A required election if no candidate receives an absolute majority of the votes cast in a primary race or in many nonpartisan elections. The runoff is between the top two vote getters.

Sales tax A tax charged as a set percentage of most retail purchases and many services. It is the main source of tax revenue for state government and an important source of revenue for many cities and metropolitan transit authorities.

School boards Governing bodies of public school districts.

School superintendent Chief administrator of a school district who is hired by the school board.

Secretary of state Administers state election laws, grants charters to corporations, and processes the extradition of prisoners to other states. The governor appoints this officeholder.

Select committee A special committee—usually appointed by the governor, the lieutenant governor, and the speaker—that studies a specific issue and makes recommendations to the legislature. This panel usually includes private citizens as well as legislators.

Senatorial courtesy An unwritten policy that permits a senator to block the confirmation of a gubernatorial appointee who lives in the senator's district.

Separation of powers The division of authority among three distinct branches of government—the legislative, the executive, and the judicial—which serve as checks and balances on one another's power.

Sharpstown stock fraud scandal After rocking state government in 1971 and 1972, the scandal helped produce some far-reaching legislative and political changes. It involved the passage of banking legislation sought by Houston financier Frank Sharp and quick profits that some state officials made on stock purchased in an insurance company owned by Sharp with unsecured loans from Sharp's Sharpstown State Bank.

Sheriff An elected official who is the chief law enforcement officer of a county. In urban areas, his or her jurisdiction usually is limited to the unincorporated areas of a county, while local police departments have jurisdiction over incorporated cities.

Sin tax A common nickname for a tax on tobacco or alcoholic beverages.

Single-issue groups Single-purpose or highly ideological groups that promote a single issue or cause with only limited regard for the views or interests of other groups. Such groups often are reluctant to compromise.

Single-member districts A system in which a legislator, city council member, or other public official is elected from a specific geographic area.

Social contract The view that governments originated from the general agreement among and consent of members of the public to address common interests and needs.

Sound bite A short, quotable phrase by a public official or political candidate that may sound good on television or radio but lacks depth and often is meaningless.

Speaker The presiding officer of the House of Representatives.

Special districts Units of local government created by the state to perform a specific function or functions not met by cities or counties, including the provision of public services to unincorporated areas.

Special elections An election set by the legislature or called by the governor for a specific purpose, such as voting on constitutional amendments or filling a vacancy in a legislative office. Local governments also can call special elections.

Special sessions Legislative sessions that can be called by the governor at any time other than the regular legislative session. They are limited to thirty days and can consider only subjects or issues designated by the governor.

Spin The presentation of information in the best possible light for a public official or political candidate. It usually is provided by a press secretary, campaign consultant, or another individual representing the officeholder or candidate.

Spoils system Practice, usually identified with machine politics, of awarding public jobs to one's political friends or supporters with little regard to abilities or skills.

Staggered terms A requirement that members of state boards and commissions appointed by the governor serve terms that begin on different dates. This is to assure that a board maintains a level of experience by guarding against situations in which all board members leave office at the same time.

Standing committees Legislative committees that specialize in bills by subject matter. A bill has to win committee approval before the full House or Senate can consider it.

State Board of Education A fifteen-member body, whose members are elected by districts; has responsibility over textbook selection, curriculum standards for public schools, and Permanent School Fund investments.

State chair and **vice chair** The two top state leaders of a political party, one of whom must be a woman. Delegates to the party's state convention select them every two years.

State executive committee The statewide governing board of a political party. It includes a man and a woman elected by party members from each of the thirty-one state senatorial districts and the state chair and vice chair.

Statutory county court A court created by the legislature that exercises limited jurisdiction over criminal and/or civil cases. The jurisdiction of these courts varies from county to county.

Statutory law A law enacted by a legislative body. Unlike constitutional law, it doesn't require voter approval.

Strong mayor A form of city government that gives the mayor considerable power, including budgetary control and appointment and removal authority over city department heads.

Suffrage The right to vote.

Sunset review The process under which most state agencies have to be periodically reviewed and re-created by the legislature or eliminated.

Supremacy clause A provision of the U.S. Constitution that says federal law prevails in conflicts between the powers of the states and the national government.

Tags A rule that allows an individual senator to postpone a committee hearing on any bill for at least forty-eight hours, a delay that can be fatal to a bill during the closing days of a legislative session.

Tax abatements Device used by governments to attract new businesses through the reduction or elimination of property taxes for a specific period of time.

Texas Court of Criminal Appeals A Texas nine-member court with final appellate jurisdiction over criminal cases.

Texas Railroad Commission A three-member, elected body that regulates oil and natural gas production and lignite mining in Texas.

Texas Supreme Court A nine-member court with final appellate jurisdiction over civil lawsuits.

The Establishment In the days of one-party Democratic politics in Texas, it was a loosely knit coalition of Anglo businessmen, oilmen, bankers, and lawyers who controlled state policymaking through the dominant, conservative wing of the Democratic Party.

Third party A minor political party. There have been many in Texas over the years, but none has had significant success on a statewide level.

Ticket splitting The decisions of voters to divide their votes among candidates of more than one political party in the same election.

Tort reform Changes in state law to put limits on personal injury lawsuits and damage judgments entered by the courts.

Traditionalistic subculture A view that political power should be concentrated in the hands of a few elite citizens who belong to established families or influential social groups. Public policy basically serves the interests of this small group.

Transnational regionalism The expanding economic and social interdependence of South Texas and Mexico.

Two-party system A political system in which each of the two dominant parties has the possibility of winning national, statewide, or county elections.

Two-thirds rule A rule under which the Texas Senate has traditionally operated that requires approval of at least two-thirds of senators before a bill can be debated on the Senate floor. It allows a minority of senators to block controversial legislation.

Unicameral A single-body legislature.

Unitary system A system in which ultimate power is vested in a central or national government and local governments have only those powers granted to them by the central government. This principle describes the relationship between the state and local governments in Texas.

Urbanization The process by which a predominantly rural society or area becomes urban.

Veniremen Persons who have been called for a jury panel.

Veto The power of the governor to reject, or kill, a bill passed by the legislature.

Voting Rights Act A federal law designed to protect the voting rights of minorities by requiring the Justice Department's approval of changes in political districts and certain other electoral procedures. The act, as amended, has eliminated most of the more restrictive state laws that limited minority political participation.

Ward politics Term, often with negative connotations, that refers to partisan politics linked to political favoritism.

Weak mayor A form of city government in which the mayor shares authority with the city council and other elected officials but has little independent control over city policy or city administration.

Whistle-blower A government employee who publicly reports wrongdoing or unethical conduct within a government agency.

White primary A series of state laws and party rules that denied African Americans the right to vote in the Democratic primary in Texas in the first half of the twentieth century.

Writs of mandamus Court orders directing a lower court or a public official to take a certain action.

Endnotes

Chapter 1

1. Harold Lasswell, *Who Gets What, When, and How* (New York: Meridian, 1958).
2. Texas Comptroller of Public Accounts, *Fiscal Notes,* June 1998, p. 6; Texas Comptroller of Public Accounts, *Texas—Where We Stand,* February 2006; and Institute on Taxation and Economic Policy, "Texas Taxes Hit Poor and Middle Class Far Harder Than the Wealthy," January 7, 2003.
3. David Easton, *A Framework for Political Analysis* (Englewood Cliffs, NJ: Prentice Hall, 1965), Chapter 5.
4. Louise Cowan, "Myth in the Modern World," in *Texas Myths,* edited by Robert F. O'Conner (College Station: Texas A&M University Press, 1986), p. 4.
5. Joseph Campbell, *Thou Art That* (Novato, CA: New World Library, 2001), pp. 1–9.
6. Christopher G. Flood, *Political Myth* (New York: Garland, 1996), Chapter 2. The author also links political myths to political ideology.
7. Cowan, "Myth in the Modern World," p. 14. For an excellent analysis of the concept of the "myth of origin" as integrated into the American mythology, see Robert N. Bellah, *The Broken Covenant: American Civil Religion in Time of Trial* (New York: Seabury, 1975).
8. T. R. Fehrenbach, "Texas Mythology: Now and Forever," in *Texas Myths,* pp. 210–17.
9. Robin Doughty, "From Wilderness to Garden: Conquering the Texas Landscape," in *Texas Myths,* p. 105.
10. See James E. Crisp, *Sleuthing the Alamo* (New York: Oxford University Press, 2005), and William C. Davis, *Three Roads to the Alamo: The Lives and Fortunes of David Crockett, James Bowie, and William Barret Travis* (New York: HarperCollins, 1998).
11. Lucian W. Pye, "Political Culture," in *International Encyclopedia of the Social Sciences,* Vol. 12 (New York: Crowell, Collier and Macmillan, 1968), p. 218.
12. Ellen M. Dran, Robert B. Albritton, and Mikel Wyckoff, "Surrogate Versus Direct Measures of Political Culture: Explaining Participation and Policy Attitudes in Illinois," 21 *Publius: The Journal of Federalism* (Spring 1991), p. 17.
13. Daniel Elazar, *American Federalism: A View from the States* (New York: Thomas Y. Crowell, 1966), p. 86. Elazar's three subcultures closely parallel observations made in 1835 by Alexis de Tocqueville in *Democracy in America*, with an introduction by Joseph Epstein (New York: Bantam Dell, 2004).
14. Ibid., p. 86.
15. Ibid., pp. 86–89.
16. Ibid., p. 90.
17. Ibid., p. 90.
18. Ibid., p. 91.
19. Ibid., p. 92.
20. Ibid., pp. 92–94.
21. Ibid., pp. 97, 102, 108.
22. Kim Quaile Hill, *Democracy in the Fifty States* (Lincoln: University of Nebraska Press, 1994), Chapter 5.
23. Ellen N. Murray, "Sorrow Whispers in the Winds," *Texas Journal* 14 (Spring-Summer 1992), p. 16.
24. Terry G. Jordan, with John L. Bean Jr. and William M. Holmes, *Texas: A Geography* (Boulder, CO: Westview, 1984), pp. 79–86.
25. David Montejano, *Anglos and Mexicans in the Making of Texas, 1836–1986* (Austin: University of Texas Press, 1987), p. 38.
26. U.S. Census Bureau, *2010 American Community Survey.* Hispanics can be of any race.
27. Texas State Data Center, *Population Estimates and Projections Program, 2008.* This conclusion is based on Scenario 1.0 and Scenario 2000–2007.
28. National Association of Latino Elected Officials, *2011 National Roster of Hispanic Elected Officials.*(Los Angeles, CA: NALEO, 2012).
29. Jordan et al., *Texas: A Geography,* p. 71.
30. Ibid., pp. 71–77.
31. V. O. Key, *Southern Politics in State and Nation* (New York: Vintage, 1949), p. 261.
32. For an excellent analysis of Key's projections for political change in Texas, see Chandler Davidson, *Race and Class in Texas Politics* (Princeton, NJ: Princeton University Press, 1990).
33. U.S. Census Bureau, *2010 American Community Survey,* "Selected Social Characteristics in the U.S.," Five Year Estimates.
34. Ibid.
35. Office of the Governor, Texas 2000 Commission, *Texas Trends*, pp. 5–6; Office of the Governor, Texas 2000 Commission, *Texas Past and Future: A Survey,* p. 6.

36. U.S. Census Bureau, *2010 American Community Survey.*
37. Ibid.
38. Ibid.
39. Texas Transportation Institute, Texas A&M University, *2011 Urban Mobility Study,* September 2011.
40. Texas Transportation Institute, Texas A&M University, *2007 Urban Mobility Study,* September 2007.
41. U.S. Census Bureau, *2010 Census.*
42. Texas State Data Center, *2008 Population Projections.* Based on scenario 0.5 in which the 2040 estimated population is 35.7 million and the population 65-plus, 6.49 million.
43. U.S. Department of Agriculture, Economic Research Service, *State Fact Sheets: Texas,* data updated January 17, 2012.
44. U.S. Census Bureau, *Population Estimates,* July 2008.
45. U.S. Census Bureau, *2010 Census,* http://quickfacts.census.gov/qfd/states/48/48201.html.
46. U.S. Census Bureau, *2010 American Community Survey.*
47. U.S. Census Bureau, *2008 American Community Survey.*
48. U.S. Census Bureau, "Povery 2009 and 2010," *American Community Survey Briefs,* October 2011.
49. U.S. Census Bureau, *2010 American Community Survey.*
50. *Forbes,* "The Forbes Four Hundred: The Richest People in America," September 9, 2011, http://www.forbes.com/richest/.
51. Steve H. Murdock, Md. Nazrul Hoque, Martha Michael, Steve White, and Beverly Pecotte, *The Texas Challenge: Population Change and the Future of Texas* (College Station: Texas A&M University Press, 1997), pp. 64–65.
52. U.S. Census Bureau, *2000 Census of the Population*; U.S. Census Bureau, *2010 American Community Survey.*
53. Rupert N. Richardson, Ernest Wallace, and Adrian Anderson, *Texas: The Lone Star State,* 5th ed. (Englewood Cliffs, NJ: Prentice Hall, 1988), p. 2; U.S. Census Bureau, *2010 Quick Facts.*
54. Key, *Southern Politics in State and Nation,* p. 260.
55. Jordan et al., *Texas: A Geography,* p. 7.
56. Ibid., pp. 18–21.
57. For an expanded analysis of the Texas economy and the dominant role played by corporations, see James W. Lamare, *Texas Politics: Economics, Power and Policy,* 7th ed. (St. Paul, MN: West, 2001), Chapter 2.
58. Texas Comptroller of Public Accounts, "Texas Economic Outlook," *Texas Economic Quarterly* (December 1996), p. 2; Mine K. Yucel and Jackson Theis, "Oil and Gas Rises Again in a Diversified Texas," *Federal Reserve Bank of Dallas, Southwestern Economy,* First Quarter 2011.
59. "Boom, Bust and Back Again: Bullock Tenure Covers Tumultuous Years," *Fiscal Notes* (December 1990), pp. 6–7.
60. "Road to Recovery Long and Bumpy, but Positive Signs Begin to Appear," *Fiscal Notes* (March 1989), p. 4.
61. "Boom, Bust and Back Again," p. 7.
62. Mine Yucel, "Texas in the Most Recent Recession and Recovery," in Federal Reserve Bank of Dallas, *The Face of Texas: Jobs, People, Business, Change,* October 2005.
63. Ali Anari and Mark G. Dotzour, "Monthly Review of the Texas Economy—May 2009," Real Estate Center at Texas A&M University, Technical Report 1862.
64. U.S. Bureau of Economic Analysis, "Economic Recovery Widespread Across States in 2010," Tables 1 and 3, June 7, 2011.
65. Ibid.; Central Intelligence Agency, *The World Factbook,* "Find the Data," http://cia-world-factbook.findthedata.org/.
66. Harry Hurt, "Birth of a New Frontier," *Texas Monthly* (April 1984), pp. 130–35.
67. Laila Assanie and Mine Yucel, "Industry Clusters in Texas," in Federal Reserve Bank of Dallas, *The Face of Texas: Jobs, People, Business, Change,* October 2005.
68. U.S. Department of Commerce, International Trade Administration, "Texas: Exports, Jobs, and Foreign Investment," March 2012.
69. U.S. Census Bureau, *Foreign Trade,* "State Trade Data 2011."
70. The following discussion of the twelve economic regions is based on a series of reports produced by the Texas Comptroller of Public Accounts. The reports are part of a series entitled *Texas in Focus* that commenced with a statewide summary published in 2008. Reports for seven of the regions were available by June 2012.
71. Texas Comptroller of Public Accounts, *Texas in Focus: The High Plains,* April 2008.
72. Texas Comptroller of Public Accounts, *Texas in Focus: South Texas,* August 2008.
73. Texas Comptroller of Public Accounts, *Texas in Focus: Upper East Texas,* October 2008.

Chapter 2

1. G. Allan Tarr, *Understanding State Constitutions* (Princeton, NJ: Princeton University Press, 1998), p. 3.
2. Daniel Elazar, "The Principles and Traditions Underlying American State Constitutions," *Publius: The Journal of Federalism* 12 (Winter 1982), p. 23.
3. Tarr, *Understanding State Constitutions,* pp. 4–5.
4. Donald S. Lutz, "The Purposes of American State Constitutions," *Publius: The Journalism of Federalism* 12 (Winter 1982), pp. 31–36.
5. David Saffell, *State Politics* (Reading, MA: Addison-Wesley, 1984), pp. 23–24.
6. Tarr, *Understanding State Constitutions,* pp. 6–11.
7. Elazar, "Principles and Traditions," pp. 20–21.
8. T. R. Fehrenbach, *Lone Star: A History of Texas and Texans* (New York: Macmillan, 1968), pp. 152–73.
9. Richard Gambitta, Robert A. Milne, and Carol R. Davis, "The Politics of Unequal Educational Opportunity," in The *Politics of San Antonio,* edited by David R. Johnson, John A. Booth, and Richard J. Harris (Lincoln: University of Nebraska Press, 1983), p. 135.
10. Joe B. Frantz, *Texas: A Bicentennial History* (New York: W.W. Norton, 1976), p. 73.
11. Ibid., p. 76.
12. Fehrenbach, *Lone Star,* p. 265.
13. Frantz, *Texas,* p. 92.
14. Fehrenbach, *Lone Star,* p. 396.
15. Ibid., pp. 398–99.
16. Ibid., p. 401.
17. Ibid., p. 429.
18. J. E. Ericson, "The Delegates to the Convention of 1875: A Reappraisal," *Southwestern Historical Quarterly* 67 (July 1963), p. 22.
19. Ibid., p. 23.
20. Ibid.
21. Ibid., pp. 25–26.
22. Fehrenbach, *Lone Star,* pp. 374, 431, 434.
23. Ericson, "The Delegates to the Convention of 1875," pp. 24–25.
24. Fehrenbach, *Lone Star,* p. 435.
25. *Texas Constitution,* Art. I, Sec. 2 and 3.
26. See James Madison, "Federalist 10," in *The Federalist Papers,* by Alexander Hamilton, James Madison, and John Jay with an introduction by Clinton Rossiter (New York: New American Library, 1962), p. 77.
27. Janice May, "Constitutional Revision in Texas," in *The Texas Constitution: Problems and Prospects for Revision* (Arlington, TX: Texas Urban Development Commission, 1971), p. 82.
28. Ibid.
29. David Berman, *State and Local Politics,* 6th ed. (Dubuque, IA: Wm. C. Brown, 1991), p. 61.
30. May, "Constitutional Revision in Texas," p. 76.
31. John E. Bebout, "The Problem of the Texas Constitution," in *The Texas Constitution,* p. 9.
32. Ibid., p. 11.
33. *Houston Chronicle,* January 8, 1974.
34. Nelson Wolff, *Challenge of Change* (San Antonio, TX: Naylor, 1975), pp. 45–46.
35. Bebout, "The Problem of the Texas Constitution," pp. 45–46.
36. *Houston Chronicle,* October 15, 1975.
37. Lewis A. Froman Jr., "Some Effects of Interest Group Strength in State Politics," *American Political Science Review* 60 (December 1966), pp. 952–63.
38. Kate Galbraith, "Texas Supreme Court Rules for Landowners in Water Case," *The Texas Tribune*, February 24, 2012.
39. See Tarr, *Understanding State Constitutions* for an extensive discussion of the distinctive features of state constitutions, state constitutions within the federal context, and an analysis of state constitutional development.

Chapter 3

1. Joe Holley, "Patrick's 'Intrusive Touching' Bill Junked," *Houston Chronicle,* May 25, 2011, http://blog.chron.com/texaspolitics/2011/05/patricks-intrusive-touching-bill-junked/.
2. See Alexis de Tocqueville's highly informative assessment of the American experience with centralized authority. Alexis de Tocqueville, *Democracy in America,* with an introduction by Joseph Epstein (New York: Bantam Dell, 2004).
3. David C. Nice, "The Intergovernmental Setting of State-Local Relations," in *Governing Partners: State-Local Relations in the United States,* edited by Russell L. Hanson (Boulder, CO: Westview, 1998), p. 17.

4. For a discussion of the Dillon rule, see Anwar Syed, *The Political Theory of American Local Government* (New York: Random House, 1966), Chapter 3.
5. Thomas J. Anton, *American Federalism and Public Policy* (New York: Random House, 1989), p. 3.
6. See William H. Stewart, "Metaphors, Models, and the Development of Federal Theory," *Publius: The Journal of Federalism* 12 (Winter 1982), pp. 5–24; and William H. Stewart, *Concepts of Federalism* (Lanham, MD: Center for the Study of Federalism and University Press of America, 1984).
7. William T. Gormley Jr., "Money and Mandates: The Politics of Intergovernmental Conflict," *Publius: The Journal of Federalism* 36 (May 2006), pp. 523–540. This is an excellent article that provides a method for disaggregating broad trends in federal–state relationships.
8. Anton, *American Federalism and Public Policy*, p. 19.
9. U.S. Constitution, Article 1, Section 8, Paragraph 18.
10. U.S. Constitution, Article 6.
11. For an excellent summary of the guarantees to and limitations on state governments defined by the U.S. Constitution, see Thomas Dye, *American Federalism* (Lexington, KY: D. C. Heath, 1990), pp. 9–11.
12. U.S. Constitution, Article 4, Section 1.
13. Carol J. Williams, "Defense of Marriage Act Unconstitutional, Federal Judges Rules in California Case," *Los Angeles Times*, February 22, 2012.
14. Adam Nagourney, "Court Strikes Down Ban on Gay Marriage in California," *The New York Times*, February 7, 2012.
15. *Commonwealth of Kentucky* v. *Denison, Governor*, 65 U.S. (24 How.) 66 (1861).
16. *Puerto Rico* v. *Branstad,* 483 U.S. 219 (1987).
17. Kenyon Bunch and Richard J. Hardy, "Continuity or Change in Interstate Extradition? Assessing *Puerto Rico* v. *Branstad*," *Publius: The Journal of Federalism* 21 (Winter 1991), p. 59.
18. U.S. Constitution, Article 3, Section 2.
19. Morton Grodzins and Daniel Elazar, "Centralization and Decentralization in the American Federal System," in *A Nation of States,* 2nd ed., edited by Robert A. Goldwin (Chicago: Rand McNally, 1974), p. 4.
20. Deil S. Wright, *Understanding Intergovernmental Relations,* 2nd ed. (Monterey, CA: Brooks/Cole, 1982), pp. 60–68.
21. Ibid., p. 46.
22. *McCulloch* v. *Maryland,* 4 Wheaton 316 (1819).
23. Thomas R. Dye, *Politics in States and Communities,* 8th ed. (Englewood Cliffs, NJ: Prentice Hall, 1994), p. 67.
24. Timothy Conlan, with an introduction by Samuel H. Beer, *New Federalism* (Washington, DC: The Brookings Institution, 1988), p. 5.
25. V. O. Key, *The Responsible Electorate* (Cambridge, MA: Harvard University Press, 1966), p. 31.
26. Daniel J. Elazar, *American Federalism: A View from the States,* 2nd ed. (New York: Harper & Row Publishers, 1972), p. 47.
27. Thomas R. Dye with L. Tucker Gibson Jr. and Clay Robison, *Politics in America: Texas Edition,* 6th ed. (Upper Saddle River, NJ: Pearson/Prentice Hall, 2005), p. 122.
28. Office of Management and Budget, *Analytical Perspectives: Budget of the U.S. Government, Fiscal Year 2013*, http://www.whitehouse.gov/sites/default/files/omb/budget/fy2013/assets/spec.pdf
29. Conlan, *New Federalism,* p. 6.
30. Dye, *Politics in States and Communities*, p. 83.
31. Conlan, *New Federalism,* p. 3.
32. Ibid., pp. 3, 19–30, 77–81.
33. Ibid., p. 90.
34. Richard P. Nathan, Thomas L. Gais, and James W. Fossett, "Bush Federalism: Is There One, What is It, and How Does It Differ?" Paper presented at the Annual Research Conference Association for Public Policy Analysis and Management, November 7, 2003, Washington, DC, p. 5.
35. Ibid., p. 6.
36. Joseph F. Zimmerman, "Federal Preemption under Reagan's New Federalism," *Publius: The Journal of Federalism* 21 (Winter 1991), p. 11.
37. Ibid., p. 26.
38. Ibid.
39. Ibid., p. 27.
40. Timothy J. Conlan, "And the Beat Goes On: Intergovernmental Mandates and Preemption in an Era of Deregulation," *Publius: The Journal of Federalism* 21 (Summer 1991), p. 52.
41. Joseph F. Zimmerman, "Preemption in the U.S. Federal System," *Publius: The Journal of Federalism* 23 (Fall 1993), p. 9.
42. Timothy J. Conlan and David R. Beam, "Federal Mandates: The Record of Reform and Future Prospects," *Intergovernmental Perspective* 18 (Fall 1992), p. 9.
43. State of Texas, Legislative Budget Board, *Analysis of Federal Initiatives and State Expenditures,* June 15, 1994.

44. Michael A.Pagano, Ann O'M. Bowman, and John Kincaid, "The State of American Federalism, 1990–1991," *Publius: The Journal of Federalism* 21 (Summer 1991), p. 1.
45. Conlan, "And the Beat Goes On," pp. 44–46.
46. G. Ross Stephens and Nelson Wikstrom, *American Intergovernmental Relations: A Fragmented Federal Polity* (New York: Oxford University Press, 2007), pp. 40–41.
47. Paul L. Posner, "Unfunded Mandates Reform Act: 1996 and Beyond," *Publius: The Journal of Federalism* 27 (Spring 1997), p. 53.
48. Sanford F. Schram and Carol S. Weissert, "The State of American Federalism, 1996–1997," *Publius: The Journal of Federalism* 27 (Spring 1997), pp. 5–8.
49. Alan K. Ota, "Highway Law Benefits Those Who Held Purse Strings," *Congressional Quarterly Weekly* 56 (June 13, 1998), pp. 1595–96.
50. Schram and Weissert, "The State of American Federalism, 1996–1997," p. 8.
51. Ibid., p. 1.
52. John Kincaid, "The Devolution Tortoise and the Centralization Hare," *New England Economic Review* (May–June 1998), pp. 36, 38.
53. Richard L. Cole, Rodney V. Hissong, and Enid Arvidson, "Devolution: Where's the Revolution?" *Publius: The Journal of Federalism* 29 (Fall 1999), pp. 99–112.
54. George W. Bush, "Memorandum on the Interagency Working Group on Federalism," February 26, 2001; and Joseph Francis Zimmerman, *Contemporary American Federalism,* 2nd ed. (Albany: State University of New York Press, 2008), p. 127.
55. Daniel Henniger, "Homeland Security Will Reshape the Homeland," *Wall Street Journal,* November 22, 2002, p. 16.
56. Jonathan Osborne, "Criticism of Patriot Measure Endorsed—City's Resolution Also Opposes Passage of USA Patriot Act II," *Austin American-Statesman,* September 26, 2003, p. B1.
57. John Dinan, "The State of American Federalism 2007–2008: Resurgent State Influence in the National Policy Process and Continued State Policy Innovation," *Publius: The Journal of Federalism* 38 (May 2008), p. 383.
58. Ibid.
59. Deil S. Wright, "Federalism and Intergovernmental Relations: Traumas, Tensions, and Trends," *The Book of the States, 2003* (Lexington, KY: The Council of State Governments, 2003), p. 23.
60. Sidney M. Milkis and Jesse H. Rhodes, "George W. Bush, the Party System, and American Federalism," *Publius: The Journal of Federalism* 37 (May 2007), p. 483.
61. Gene Healy and Timothy Lynch, *Power Surge: The Constitutional Record of George W. Bush* (Washington, DC: Cato Institute, 2006).
62. Tim Conlan and John Dinan, "Federalism, the Bush Administration, and the Transformation of American Conservatism," *Publius: The Journal of Federalism* 37 (April 2007), pp. 283–88.
63. Milkis and Rhodes, "George W. Bush, the Party System, and American Federalism," p. 478.
64. John Dinan, "The State of American Federalism 2007–2008," p. 381.
65. Ibid., pp. 382–401.
66. "Economic Stimulus—Jobs Bills," *New York Times,* updated March 15, 2012.
67. U.S. General Accounting Office, "Recovery Act: As Initial Implementation Unfolds in States and Localities, Continued Attention to Accountability Issues Is Essential," GAO-09-580, April 23, 2009; and "Texas Comptroller of Public Accounts, "American Recovery and Reinvestment Act: A Texas Eye on the Dollars," *Window on State Government,* http://window.state.tx.us/recovery/.
68. Kate Nocera, "Perry's Texas Awash in Federal Money," *Politico,* December 25, 2011.
69. Barack Obama, "Memorandum for the Heads of Executive Departments and Agencies," May 20, 2009.
70. Gillian E. Metzger, "Federalism Under Obama" *William and Mary Law Review,* 53 (November 2011) pp. 567–69.
71. Ibid., p. 567.
72. *Garcia* v. *San Antonio Metropolitan Transit Authority,* 105 S. Ct. 1005 (1985).
73. Anton, *American Federalism and Public Policy,* pp. 14–16.
74. Dye, *American Federalism,* pp. 8–12.
75. *U.S.* v. *Lopez,* 115 S. Ct. 1624 (1995); and Schram and Weissert, "The State of American Federalism, 1996–1997," p. 10.
76. *Bush* v. *Vera,* 116 S. Ct. 1941 (1996); *Easley* v. *Cromartie,* 121 S. Ct. 2239 (2001); and *New York Times,* April 19, 2001, p. 1.
77. Weissert and Schram, "The State of American Federalism, 1995–1996," p. 12; and *Medtronic, Inc.* v. *Lohr et vir.,* 116 S. Ct. 2240 (1996).
78. *City of Boerne, Texas* v. *Flores,* 117 S.Ct. 2157 (1997).
79. Schram and Weissert, "The State of American Federalism, 1996–1997," p. 26.
80. *Printz* v. *U.S.,* 117 S.Ct. 2365 (1997).
81. Weissert and Schram, "The State of American Federalism, 1995–1996," p. 13.

82. Ibid., p. 10; *Romer et al.* v. *Evans et al.,* 116 S. Ct. 1620 (1996); and *U.S.* v. *Virginia et al.,* 116 S. Ct. 2264 (1996).
83. Ibid.; and *Seminole Tribe* v. *Florida,* 116 S. Ct. 1941 (1996).
84. Shama Gamkhar and J. Mitchell Pickerill, "The State of American Federalism 2010–2011: The Economy, Healthcare Reform, and Midterm Elections Shape the Intergovernmental Agenda," *Publius: The Journal of Federalism,* 41 (Summer 2011), p. 379.
85. Ibid.
86. Ibid., p. 380.
87. Ibid., pp. 382–84.
88. Internal Revenue Service, *Internal Revenue Service Data Book 2010,* Table 5; and U.S. Census Bureau, *Consolidated Federal Funds Report for Fiscal Year 2010: Detailed Federal Expenditure Data.*
89. U.S. Census Bureau, *Federal Aid to States for Fiscal Year 2010,* Table 1 and Figure 5.
90. Legislative Budget Board, *Fiscal Size-Up, 2012–2013* (Austin, TX: Legislative Budget Board, 2012), Figure 14.
91. Office of the Governor, State Grants Team, http://www.governor.state.tx.us/divisions/stategrants
92. Robert B. Hawkins, "Pre-emption: The Dramatic Rise of Federal Supremacy," *The Journal of State Government* 63 (January-March 1990), p. 12.
93. M. Delal Baer, "North American Free Trade," *Foreign Affairs* 70 (Fall 1991), p. 138.
94. Joan B. Anderson, "Maquiladoras and Border Industrialization: Impact on Economic Development in Mexico," *Journal of Borderland Studies* 5 (Spring 1990), p. 5.
95. Michael Patrick, "Maquiladoras and South Texas Border Economic Development," *Journal of Borderland Studies,* 4 (Spring 1989), p. 90.
96. Martin E. Rosenfeldt, "Mexico's In Bond Export Industries and U.S. Legislation: Conflictive Issues," *Journal of Borderland Studies* 5 (Spring 1990), p. 57.
97. Patrick, "Maquiladoras and South Texas Border Economic Development," p. 90.
98. M. Angeles Villarreal, "U.S.-Mexico Relations: Trends, Issues, and Implications," *Congressional Research Service,* January 25, 2012, p. 9. (After 2007, statistics for maquiladora plants were merged by the Mexican government with those of other manufacturing facilities).
99. Baer, "North American Free Trade," pp. 132–49.
100. Central Intelligence Agency, *The World Factbook—2012,* https://www.cia.gov/library/publications/the-world-factbook/
101. Ibid.
102. Binyamin Appelbaum, "U.S. and Mexico Sign Trucking Deal," *The New York Times,* July 6, 2011.
103. Ted Robbins, "Mexican Trucks in U.S. Still Face Political Long Haul," *National Public Radio,* October 29, 2011.
104. International Trade Administration, *TradeStats Express.* http://tse.export.gov/TSE/TSEhome.aspx
105. Texas Center for Border Economic and Enterprise Development, Texas A&M International University, *Border Crossings.* http://texascenter.tamiu.edu/texcen_ services/border_crossings.asp
106. This discussion of the history of immigration laws is based on Clarke E. Cochran, Lawrence C. Mayer, T. R. Carr, and N. Joseph Cayer, *American Public Policy,* 9th ed. (Boston: Wadsworth, 2009), pp. 400–406; Federation for American Immigration Reform, "History of U.S. Immigration Laws," January 2008; and Cornell University Law School, "Immigration Law: An Overview," http://www.law.cornell.edu/wex/Immigration
107. Robert W. Gardner and Leon F. Bouvier, "The United States," in *Handbook on International Migration,* edited by William J. Serow, Charles B. Nam, David F. Sly, and Robert H. Weller (New York: Greenwood Press, 1990), p. 342.
108. James F. Pearce and Jeffery W. Gunther, "Illegal Immigration from Mexico: Effects on the Texas Economy," *Federal Reserve Bank of Dallas Economic Review* (September 1985), p. 4.
109. "Congress Clears Overhaul of Immigration Law," *Congressional Quarterly Almanac,* 1986 (Washington, DC: Congressional Quarterly Press, 1987), pp. 61–67.
110. Dan Carney, "Law Restricts Illegal Immigration," *Congressional Quarterly Weekly Report* 54 (November 16, 1996), p. 3287.
111. Steven A. Camarota, "Immigrants in the United States, 2007: A Profile of America's Foreign-Born Population," Center for Immigration Studies, November 2007.
112. Jeffrey L. Katz, "Welfare Overhaul Law," *Congressional Quarterly Weekly Report* 54 (September 21, 1996), pp. 2696–2705; and Stephen A. Camarota, "Back Where We Started: An Examination of Trends in Immigrant Welfare Use Since Welfare Reform," Center for Immigration Studies, March 2003.
113. U.S. Customs and Border Protection, Secure Border Initiative, "Pedestrian Fence 225," November 2008.
114. Josh Gerstein and Jonathan Allen, "Barack Obama Orders Guard to Mexican Border," *Politico,* May 25, 2010.

115. Scott Wong and Shira Toeplitz, "DREAM Act Dies in Senate," *Politico,* December 20, 2010.
116. Brian Bennett, "Obama Administration Reports Record of Deportations," *Los Angeles Times,* October 18, 2011.
117. "Number of Illegal Immigrants in U.S. Is Stable: DHS," *Reuters,* March 24, 2012.
118. National Conference of State Legislators, Immigration Policy Project, "2009 Immigration-Related Bills and Resolutions in the States," April 2009.
119. Adam Liptak, "Court to Weigh Arizona Statute on Immigration," *The New York Times,* December 12, 2011.
120. Bill Mears, "Part of Alabama Immigration Law Blocked by Federal Appeals Court," *CNN,* October 14, 2011.
121. Tim Eaton, "ID Measure Passed Quietly, While Sanctuary Cities Bill Died Noisily," *Austin American-Statesman,* June 29, 2011.
122. Joan Anderson and Martin de la Rosa, "Economic Survival Strategies of Poor Families on the Mexican Border," *Journal of Borderland Studies* 6 (Spring 1991), p. 51.
123. Howard G. Applegate, C. Richard Bath, and Jeffery T. Trannon, "Binational Emissions Trading in an International Air Shed: The Case of El Paso, Texas and Ciudad Juarez," *Journal of Borderland Studies* 4 (Fall 1989), pp. 1–25.

Chapter 4

1. Jim Vertuno, "Texas Legislature Appears Set to Allow Guns on College Campuses," *Fort Worth Star-Telegram,* February 21, 2011.
2. See Robert S. Erikson, Norman R. Luttbeg, and Kent L. Tedin, *American Public Opinion,* 3rd ed. (New York: Macmillan Publishing Company, 1988), p. 118; Robert L. Lineberry, George C. Edwards III, and Martin P. Wattenberg, *Government in America,* 5th ed. (New York: HarperCollins Publishers, 1991), p. 341; Pew Research Center, "Distrust, Discontent, Anger, and Partisan Rancor," April 18, 2010.
3. Anna M. Tinsley, "Texas Poll: Texans Trust Local Government More Than State, Feds," Harte Hanks Communication, September 30, 1996; UT-Austin, *Texas Politics Poll,* July 2008.
4. Belle Zeller, *American State Legislatures* (New York: Thomas Y. Crowell, 1954), and Clive S. Thomas and Ronald J. Hrebenar, "Interest Groups in the States," in *Politics in the American States,* 6th ed., edited by Virginia Gray and Herbert Jacob (Washington, DC: Congressional Quarterly Press, 1996), p. 152.
5. Harmon L. Zeigler and Hendrik van Dalen, "Interest Groups in State Politics," in *Politics in the American States,* 3rd ed., edited by Herbert Jacob and Kenneth N. Vines (Boston: Little, Brown, 1976).
6. Dennis S. Ippolito and Thomas G. Walker, *Political Parties, Interest Groups, and Public Policy* (Englewood Cliffs, NJ: Prentice Hall, 1990), p. 271.
7. Ibid., pp. 270–71.
8. Gale (Cengage Learning), *Encyclopedia of Association: National Organizations of the U.S.* (Published/Released, March 2011), "Fact Sheet." http://www.gale.cengage.com/servlet/ItemDetailServlet?region=9&imprint=000&cf=p&titleCode=EA1&type=3&dc=null&dewey=null&id=250918
9. Kay Lehman Schlozman and John T. Tierney, *Organized Interests and American Democracy* (New York: Harper & Row, 1986), p. 75.
10. See E. E. Schattschneider, *The Semi-Sovereign People* (Hinsdale, IL: Dryden Press, 1975), and Ronald J. Hrebenar and Ruth K. Scott, *Interest Group Politics in America,* 2nd ed. (Englewood Cliffs, NJ: Prentice Hall, 1990), p. 29.
11. James Allan Davis and Tom W. Smith, *General Social Surveys, 1972–2006* [machine-readable data file] /Principal Investigator, James A. Davis; Director and Co-Principal Investigator, Tom W. Smith; Co-Principal Investigator, Peter V. Marsden; Sponsored by National Science Foundation.—NORC ed.—Chicago: National Opinion Research Center [producer]; Storrs, CT: The Roper Center for Public Opinion Research, University of Connecticut [distributor], 2007. Courtesy of Dr. Michael Kearl, Department of Sociology and Anthropology, Trinity University, San Antonio, Texas.
12. Schlozman and Tierney, *Organized Interests and American Democracy,* pp. 73–74.
13. Hrebenar and Scott, *Interest Group Politics in America,* p. 29.
14. Ippolito and Walker, *Political Parties, Interest Groups, and Public Policy,* p. 278.
15. For an extended discussion of these incentives, see Jeffrey M. Berry and Clyde Wilcox, *The Interest Group Society,* 5th ed. (New York: Pearson Longman, 2009), pp. 36–46. See also Robert H. Salisbury, "An Exchange Theory of Interest Groups," *Midwest Journal of Political Science* 13 (February 1969), pp. 1–32.
16. Greenwald, *Group Power,* pp. 32–35.
17. Ippolito and Walker, *Political Parties, Interest Groups, and Public Policy,* pp. 279–80.
18. Berry and Wilcox, *The Interest Group Society,* p. 42.
19. Lawrence J. R. Herson, *The Politics of Ideas* (Prospect Heights, IL: Waveland, 1990), p. 68.
20. David B. Truman, *The Governmental Process,* 2nd ed. (New York: Alfred A. Knopf, 1971).

21. For a succinct summary of the elitist-pluralist debate, see Thomas R. Dye and Harmon Zeigler, *The Irony of Democracy,* 7th ed. (Monterey, CA: Brooks/Cole, 1987), Chapter 1.
22. Truman, *The Governmental Process,* Chapter 4.
23. Ippolito and Walker, *Political Parties, Interest Groups, and Public Policy*, pp. 275–76.
24. Thomas R. Dye, *Who's Running America: The Bush Era,* 5th ed. (Englewood Cliffs, NJ: Prentice Hall, 1990), p. 4.
25. Robert Michels, *Political Parties: A Sociological Study of the Oligarchical Tendencies of Modern Democracy,* translated by Eden Paul (1915, reprint, New York: Free Press, 1962), p. 70.
26. C. Wright Mills, *The Power Elite* (New York: Oxford University Press, 1956).
27. See Dye and Zeigler, *The Irony of Democracy,* Chapter 1.
28. George Norris Green, *The Establishment in Texas Politics: 1938–1957* (Westport, CT: Greenwood, 1979), p. 1.
29. Ibid., p. 17.
30. Ibid., p. 1.
31. Ibid., p. 10.
32. Chandler Davidson, *Race and Class in Texas Politics* (Princeton, NJ: Princeton University Press, 1990), p. 54.
33. Ibid., Chapters 4 and 5.
34. Ibid., p. 83.
35. Ibid., p. 108.
36. Lineberry et al., *Government in America,* p. 342.
37. See Theodore J. Lowi, *The End of Liberalism,* 2nd ed. (New York: W. W. Norton, 1979).
38. Schlozman and Tierney, *Organized Interests and American Democracy*, p. 103.
39. See Green, *The Establishment in Texas Politics*, Chap. 1.
40. Cindy Rugeley, "Working to Adapt—Disabled Take Battle for Rights to the Streets," *Houston Chronicle,* September 15, 1991.
41. Armando Villafranca, "Perry Sighs Ethics Bill Expanding Disclosure," *Houston Chronicle,* June 20, 2003, p. 29A.
42. See Green, *The Establishment in Texas Politics,* for an excellent analysis of the labor-bashing techniques used by Texas business in the 1940s and 1950s.
43. U.S. Department of Labor, Bureau of Labor Statistics, "Economic News Release," January 27, 2012.
44. Texans for Public Justice, "Austin's Oldest Profession: Texas' Top Lobby Clients & Those Who Service Them," February 15, 2012.
45. Green, *The Establishment in Texas Politics*, Chapter 5.
46. See Davidson, *Race and Class in Texas Politics*, Chapter 10.
47. Texas Freedom Network, "About Us," TFN.org. http://www.tfn.org/site/PageServer?pagename=about_mission .
48. Texans for Public Justice, "Austin's Oldest Profession."
49. Hrebenar and Scott, *Interest Group Politics in America*, p. 83.
50. U.S. Constitution, First Amendment; Texas Constitution, Article 1, Section 27.
51. Alan Rosenthal, *Third House: Lobbyists and Lobbying in the States* (Washington, DC: Congressional Quarterly Press, 1993), p. 1.
52. Greenwald, *Group Power,* pp. 61–62.
53. Federal Election Commission, *Citizens Guide,* February 2011.
54. *Citizens United* v. *Federal Election Commission,* 130 S.Ct. 876 (2010).
55. Ippolito and Walker, *Political Parties, Interest Groups, and Public Policy*, p. 323.
56. Hrebenar and Scott, *Interest Group Politics in America,* pp. 114–15.
57. Ippolito and Walker, *Political Parties, Interest Groups, and Public Policy*, pp. 364–65.
58. This and the following sections draw from the research of Scholzman and Tierney, *Organized Interests and American Democracy,* Chapter 7.
59. Hrebenar and Scott, *Interest Group Politics in America,* pp. 148–53.

Chapter 5

1. Jay Root, "*Fort Worth Star-Telegram* Austin Bureau RIP," *The Texas Tribune*, March 2, 2012.
2. Maxwell E. McCombs and Donald L. Shaw, "The Agenda-Setting Function of the Press," in *Media Power in Politics,* 2nd ed., edited by Doris A. Graber (Washington, DC: Congressional Quarterly Press, 1990), p. 75.
3. Doris A. Graber, *Mass Media and American Politics,* 2nd ed. (Washington, DC: Congressional Quarterly Press, 1984), pp. 78–79.
4. Ibid., pp. 268–69.
5. Gladys Engel Lang and Kurt Lang, *The Battle for Public Opinion: The President, the Press, and the Polls during Watergate* (New York: Columbia University Press, 1983), p. 58.
6. Larry N. Gerston, *Making Public Policy: From Conflict to Resolution* (Glenview, IL: Scott, Foresman and Company, 1983), pp. 55–56.

7. The following discussion of the attention cycle is drawn from Anthony Downs, "Up and Down with Ecology—The Issue Attention Cycle," *Public Interest* 32 (Summer 1972), pp. 38–50.
8. See Marjorie Randon Hershey, *Party Politics in America,* 12th ed. (New York: Pearson Longman, 2007), Chapter 8.
9. Harte-Hanks Communications, *The Texas Poll,* April 1994. The questions were phrased, "How often do you watch television news? How often would you say your read a newspaper? How much trust do you place in facts you hear on televised newscasts? How must trust do you place in facts you read in the newspaper?
10. Walter Cronkite and Paul Taylor, "To Lift Politics Out of TV Swamp," *Houston Chronicle,* March 10, 1996, p. 1E.
11. In the early part of President Obama's campaign, he relied on contributions of $1,000 or more. By election day, he raised some $750 million with approximately one-half coming from persons contributing $200 or less.
12. "Alliance for Better Campaigns," *Political Standard* 3, no. 5 (July 2000), p. 1.
13. Ibid.
14. Evan Smith, "*The Dallas Morning News* Endorses White," *The Texas Tribune*, October 17, 2010.
15. John Williams, R. G. Ratcliffe, and Rachael Graves, "Poll Puts Perry in Double-digit Lead; Cornyn Maintains Slim Advantage over Kirk for Senate," *Houston Chronicle,* November 3, 2002, p. 1A.
16. Bob Sablatura, "Williams' Bank Suspect in Car Loans," *Houston Chronicle,* September 12, 1990, p. 1A.
17. Gibson, D. "Gib" Lewis, "Media Rushed to Judgment," *Houston Chronicle,* January 6, 1991, Outlook, p. 3.
18. Sam Attlesey, George Kuempel, and staff writers of *The Dallas Morning News,* "DA Reveals Evidence Against Hutchison—Loyalists' Public Opinion Campaign Dividends, Party Leaders Say," *Dallas Morning News,* February 13, 1994, p. 1A.
19. Pew Research Center for the People & the Press, "Press Accuracy Rating Hits Two Decade Low," September 13, 2009.
20. William Schneider and I. A. Lewis, "Views on the News," *Public Opinion* (August–September 1985), p. 7; Pew Research Center for the People & the Press, "Press Widely Criticized, but Trusted More than Other Information Sources," September 22, 2011.
21. Edward Jay Epstein, *News from Nowhere* (New York: Random House), pp. 13–14.
22. Graber, *Mass Media and American Politics*, pp. 71–74.
23. Michael Parenti, *Democracy for the Few,* 5th ed. (New York: St. Martin's Press, 1988), p. 170.
24. Paul Starr, "Goodbye to the Age of Newspapers (Hello to a New Era of Corruption)," *New Republic,* March 4, 2009, http://www.tnr.com/article/goodbye-the-the-age-newspapers-hello-new-era-corruption-o.
25. Archie P. McDonald, "Anglo-American Arrival in Texas," in *The Texas Heritage,* 2nd ed., edited by Ben Proctor and Archie McDonald (Arlington Heights, IL: Harlan Davidson, 1992), p. 28.
26. T. R. Fehrenbach, *Lone Star: A History of Texas and the Texans* (New York: Macmillan, 1968), p. 302.
27. Ibid., p. 303.
28. George Norris Green, *The Establishment in Texas Politics, 1938–1957* (Westport, CT: Greenwood, 1979), p. 10.
29. Ibid., p. 162.
30. Greg Hassell, "*San Antonio Light* Folds after 112 Years of Service," *Houston Chronicle,* January 28, 1993, p. 1A.
31. Vittorio Zucconi, "America's Media Empires," *World Press Review* (May 1986), p. 21. Excerpted from *La Republica* (Rome).
32. Erin Mulvaney, 'Capitol Press Corps Adapts to Technology's Impact on Journalism," *Daily Texan,* March 2, 2009.
33. Pew Research Center for the People & the Press, "Americans Spending More Time Following the News," *Pew Research Biennial News Consumption Survey,* September 12, 2010.
34. Pew Research Center, *Project for Excellence in Journalism,* "How People Learn About Their Local Community," September 26, 2011.
35. Pew Research Center, *Project for Excellence in Journalism,* "How Blogs and Social Media Agendas Relate and Differ from the Traditional Press," May 23, 2010.
36. Felicity Barringer, "Does Deal Signal Lessening of Media Independence?" *New York Times,* January 11, 2000, p. C12.
37. The three online newsletters—the *Quorum Report, Texas Weekly,* and *Capitol Weekly*—are available by subscription.
38. Starr, "Goodbye to the Age of Newspapers (Hello to a New Era of Corruption)."

39. See Jeffrey M. Berry and Clyde Wilcox, *The Interest Group Society,* 5th ed. (New York: Pearson Longman, 2009); Allan J. Cigler and Burdett A. Loomis, eds., *Interest Group Politics,* 8th ed. (Washington: CQ Press, 2012).
40. Pew Research Center for the People & the Press, "Americans Spending More Time Following the News."
41. Sara Lipka, "Freshmen Increasingly Discuss Politics, Worry About Money, Survey Finds," *Chronicle of Higher Education,* January 19, 2007, p. 21.

Chapter 6

1. Brandi Grissom, "For Tea Party, a Successful Legislative Session," *The Texas Tribune*, May 23, 2011. 1 Brandi Grissom, "For Tea Party, a Successful Legislative Session," *The Texas Tribune*, May 23, 2011.
2. William McKenzie, "Tea Party Has Taken over the Texas Senate," *The Dallas Morning News*, May 4, 2011.
3. Dennis S. Ippolito and Thomas G. Walker, *Political Parties, Interest Groups, and Public Policy: Group Influence in American Politics* (Englewood Cliffs, NJ: Prentice Hall, 1980), p. 2.
4. John F. Bibby, *Politics, Parties and Elections in America* (Chicago: Nelson-Hall, 1987), pp. 3–4.
5. Leon Epstein, *Political Parties in Western Democracies* (New York: Praeger, 1967), p. 9.
6. Bibby, *Politics, Parties, and Elections in America*, p. 15.
7. Sarah McCally Morehouse, *State Politics, Parties and Policy* (New York: Holt, Rinehart and Winston, 1981), p. 118.
8. Ibid., pp. 118–19.
9. Ibid., p. 117.
10. John Crittenden, *Parties and Elections in the United States* (Englewood Cliffs, NJ: Prentice Hall, 1982), p. 11.
11. Robert J. Huckshorn, *Political Parties in America,* 2nd ed. (Monterey, CA: Brooks/Cole Publishing Company, 1981), p. 11.
12. Daniel Mazmanian, *Third Parties in Presidential Elections* (Washington, D.C.: Brookings Institution Press, 1974), p. 5.
13. George Rivera, "Building a Chicano Party in South Texas," *New South*, 26 (Spring 1971), pp. 75–78.
14. Ibid.
15. Juan Gomez Quinones, *Chicano Politics* (Albuquerque, NM: University of New Mexico Press, 1990), pp. 128–31.
16. Samuel Huntington, *Political Order in Changing Societies* (New Haven, CT: Yale University Press, 1980), p. 91.
17. Huckshorn, *Political Parties in America* p. 23.
18. Bibby, *Politics, Parties and Elections in America*, p. 12.
19. V. O. Key, *Southern Politics* (New York: Vintage, 1949), p. 225.
20. Chandler Davidson, *Race and Class in Texas Politics* (Princeton, NJ: Princeton University Press, 1990), p. 21.
21. Ibid., p. 6.
22. Alexander P. Lamis, *The Two-Party South,* exp. ed. (New York: Oxford University Press, 1988), p. 23.
23. Ibid., p. 194.
24. George Norris Green, *The Establishment in Texas Politics, 1938–1957* (Westport, CT: Greenwood, 1979), p. 57
25. Ibid., pp. 121–34.
26. Key, *Southern Politics,* pp. 302–10.
27. Green, *The Establishment in Texas Politics*, pp. 142–48.
28. Key, *Southern Politics,* pp. 294–97.
29. Green, *The Establishment in Texas Politics*, p. 148.
30. Lamis, *The Two-Party South,* p. 195.
31. Ibid., p. 195; Davidson, *Race and Class in Texas Politics,* p. 201.
32. John R. Knaggs, *Two-Party Texas: The John Tower Era, 1961–1984* (Austin, TX: Eakin, 1986), p. 15.
33. Davidson, *Race and Class in Texas Politics*, p. 199.
34. Lamis, *The Two-Party South,* p. 194.
35. Ibid., pp. 196–97.
36. For an excellent summary of realignment theory and conditions under which realignment is likely to take place, see James L. Sundquist, *Dynamics of the Party System,* rev. ed. (Washington, DC: Brookings Institution Press, 1983).
37. James A. Dyer, Arnold Vedlitz, and David B. Hill, "New Voters, Switchers, and Political Party Realignment in Texas," *Western Political Quarterly,* 41 (March 1988), p. 164.

38. See Kevin P. Phillips, *The Emerging Republican Majority* (New Rochelle, NY: Arlington House, 1969), and Richard M. Scammon and Ben J. Wattenberg, *The Real Majority* (New York: Coward-McCann, 1970).
39. Green, *The Establishment in Texas Politics*, p. 208.
40. Dyer and Vedlitz, "New Voters, Switchers, and Political Party Realignment in Texas," p. 156.
41. University of Texas/*The Texas Tribune* Survey, February 2012, http://texaspolitics.laits.utexas.edu.
42. See surveys conducted by the University of Texas and *The Texas Tribune* from 2008 through 2012 for questions pertaining to party identification and voting for specific candidates. http://texaspolitics.laits.utexas.edu.
43. *Dallas Morning News,* November 9, 1994.
44. See surveys conducted by the University of Texas and *The Texas Tribune* in which positions on public policy issues are assessed by different age groups. http://texaspolitics.laits.utexas.edu.
45. Dyer and Vedlitz, "New Voters, Switchers, and Political Party Realignment in Texas," pp. 165–66; Scripps Howard, *Texas Poll,* Summer 2003, Fall 2003, Winter 2004, and Spring 2004; and *Rassmusen Reports,* "Election 2008: Texas Presidential Election," October 23, 2008.
46. Key, *Southern Politics,* p. 255.
47. Davidson, *Race and Class in Texas Politics*, p. 238.
48. Walter Dean Burnham, *Critical Elections and the Mainsprings of American Politics* (New York: W. W. Norton, 1970), Chapter 5; and Walter Dean Burnham, *The Current Crisis in American Politics* (Oxford: Oxford University Press, 1982).
49. See Huckshorn, *Political Parties in America,* pp. 358–60.
50. John F. Bibby, "State Party Organizations: Coping and Adapting to Candidate-Centered Politics and Nationalization," in *The Parties Respond: Changes in American Parties and Campaigns,* 3rd ed., edited by L. Sandy Maisel (Boulder, CO: Westview, 1998), pp. 23–49.
51. V. O. Key Jr., *Parties, Politics and Pressure Groups,* 4th ed. (New York: Thomas Y. Crowell Company, 1958), p. 347.
52. Bibby, *Politics, Parties and Elections in America*, p. 82.
53. This discussion of party activists draws from Marjorie Randon Hershey and Paul Allen Beck, *Party Politics in America,* 10th ed. (New York: Longman, 2003), Chapter 5; and Samuel J. Eldersveld and Hanes Walton Jr., *Political Parties in American Society,* 2nd ed. (Boston: Bedford/St. Martin's, 2000), Chapter 8.
54. Hershey and Beck, *Party Politics in America,* p. 97.
55. Ibid.
56. David Broder, *The Party's Over: The Failure of Politics in America* (New York: Harper & Row, 1971), p. xvi.
57. Eldersveld and Walton, *Political Parties in American Society,* pp. 166–68.

Chapter 7

1. Tim Eaton, "Neil Ends Fight Over Contested House Seat," *Austin American-Statesman*, March 18, 2011.
2. L. Sandy Maisel, *Parties and Elections in America* (New York: Random House, 1987), p. 1.
3. Gerald Pomper, *Elections in America* (New York: Dodd, Mead and Company, 1968), p. 12.
4. Herman Finer, *The Theory and Practice of Modern Government* (New York: Holt, 1949), p. 219.
5. Murray Edelman, *The Symbolic Uses of Politics* (Urbana: University of Illinois Press, 1964), p. 17.
6. V. O. Key Jr. with the assistance of Milton C. Cummings Jr., *The Responsible Electorate* (Cambridge, MA: Harvard University Press, 1965), p. 7.
7. Maisel, *Parties and Elections in America*, p. 1.
8. Ibid., p. 3.
9. See Caroline J. Tolbert, John A. Grummel, and Daniel A. Smith, "The Effects of Ballot Initiatives on Voter Turnout in the American States, *American Politics Research*, 29 (November 2001), pp. 625–648 for a bibliography on turnout rates in elections.
10. V. O. Key, Jr., *Southern Politics* (New York: Vintage Books, 1949), Chapter 12 and James E. Anderson, Richard W. Murray, and Edward L. Farley, *Texas Politics: An Introduction,* 4th ed (New York: Harper & Row, 1984), pp. 40–42, 65–67.
11. Frank J. Sorauf, *Party Politics in America*, 5th ed. (Boston: Little, Brown, 1984), p. 213; and George Norris Green, *The Establishment in Texas Politics* (Westport, CT: Greenwood, 1979), p. 164.
12. Douglas O. Weeks, "The Texas Direct Primary System," *Southwestern Social Science Quarterly,* 13 (September 1932), p. 99.
13. Chandler Davidson, *Race and Class in Texas Politics* (Princeton, NJ: Princeton University Press, 1990), p. 24.
14. *Carter* v. *Dies*, 321 F. Supp. 1358, 1970.
15. Office of the Secretary of State, Elections Division, telephone conversation, July 30, 2009.

16. Majorie Randon Hershey, *Party Politics in America,* 12th ed. (New York: Pearson Longman, 2007), pp. 158–59.
17. Sorauf, *Party Politics in America*, p. 220.
18. Davidson, *Race and Class in Texas Politics*, p. 24.
19. Janet Jacobs, "Cities, School Districts Cancel Elections," *Corsicana Daily Sun,* April 2, 2012.
20. National Association of Secretaries of State, "Engaging the Energized Electorate: NASS Survey on State Preparations for the 2008 Presidential Election," September 2008, Appendix D.
21. Robert S. Lorch, *State and Local Politics*, 3rd ed. (Upper Saddle River, NJ: Prentice Hall, 1989), p. 63; and Bexar County Elections Administration, phone conversation, November 26, 2003.
22. Office of the Secretary of State, "1992-Current Election History," http://elections.sos.state.tx.us/elchist.exe.
23. Office of the Secretary of State, Elections Division, telephone conversation on July 30, 2009.
24. Charlie Savage, "Justice Dept. Blocks Texas on Photo ID for Voting," *New York Times*, March 12, 2012.
25. Rupert Richardson, Ernest Wallace, and Adrian Anderson, *Texas: The Lone Star State*, 5th ed. (Englewood Cliffs, NJ: Prentice Hall, 1988), p. 231.
26. See Merline Pitre, *Through Many Dangers, Toils and Snares: Black Leadership in Texas, 1868–1890* (Austin, TX: Eakin, 1985).
27. Richardson, et al., *Texas*, p. 312.
28. Wilbourn E. Benton, *Texas Politics: Constraints and Opportunities*, 5th ed. (Chicago: Nelson Hall, 1984), pp. 72–73.
29. *Harper* v. *Virgina State Board of Elections*, 86 S. Ct. 1079 (1966).
30. Benton, *Texas Politics*, pp. 67–72.
31. *Nixon v. Herndon, et al.*, 273 U.S. 536 (1927).
32. *Nixon* v. *Condon*, 286 U.S. 73 (1932).
33. *Grovey* v. *Townsend*, 295 U.S. 45 (1935).
34. *Smith* v. *Allwright*, 321 U.S. 649 (1944).
35. *John Terry, et al., Petitioners* v. *A. J. Adams, et al.*, 345 U.S. 461; and National Voting Rights Institute, "'Wealth Primary'—Legal Theory," NVRI.org, http://www.nvri.org/about/wealth1.shtml
36. Beryl E. Pettus and Randall W. Bland, *Texas Government Today: Structures, Functions, Political Processes*, 3rd ed. (Homewood, IL: Dorsey, 1984), pp. 85–86.
37. *Beare, et al.* v. *Preston Smith, Governor of Texas*, 321 F. Supp. 1100 (1971).
38. Benton, *Texas Politics*, p. 65.
39. *Congressional Quarterly Weekly Report* 51 (September 1993), p. 2318.
40. U.S. Election Assistance Commission, "The Impact of the National Voter Registration Act of 1993 on the Administration of Elections for Federal Office, 2007–2008," June 30, 2009, Table 2a.
41. U.S. Census Bureau, "Voting and Registration in the Election of November 2004," *Current Population Reports*, P20–556, March 2006.
42. U.S. Census Bureau, "Voting and Registration in the Election of November 2008," *Current Population Reports*, Supplement, April 6, 2009, Table 4b.
43. Telephone conversation with Robert R. Brischetto, Southwest Voter Research Institute, Inc., November 1, 1991.
44. See William H. Flanigan and Nancy H. Zingale, *Political Behavior of the American Electorate* (Boston: Allyn and Bacon, 1987), p. 18; Steven J. Rosenstone and John Mark Hanson, *Mobilization, Participation, and Democracy in America* (New York: Macmillan, 1993); and Warren E. Miller and J. Merrill Shanks, *The New American Voter* (Cambridge, MA: Harvard University Press, 1996).
45. *Texas Poll*, Spring 2003, Summer 2003, Fall 2003, Winter 2004 (Austin, TX: Scripps Howard, 2004).
46. Telephone conversation with Robert Brischetto, November 1, 1991; and Robert R. Brischetto, *The Political Empowerment of Texas Mexicans, 1974–1988* (San Antonio, TX: Southwest Voter Research Institute, Latino Electorate Series, 1988), p. 5.
47. Pew Hispanic Center, "The Hispanic Vote in the 2008 Election," November 7, 2008, p. 11.
48. William C. Valasquez Institute, news release, March 13, 2002.
49. Texas Municipal League, *Texas Municipal League Directory of City Officials*, 2006 (Austin, TX: Author, 2006).
50. Data courtesy of Richard O. Avery, director of the V. G. Young Institute of County Government, Texas A&M University. Survey completed in 2006.
51. Texas Association of School Boards, data provided by the courtesy of the association.
52. For an excellent analysis of the early development of campaign professionals, see Larry J. Sabato, *The Rise of the Political Consultants* (New York: Basic Books, 1981).
53. Norris, *The Establishment in Texas Politics*, pp. 24–25.

54. For a general introduction to polls and polling techniques, see Herbert Asher, *Polling and the Public: What Every Citizen Should Know,* 7th ed. (Washington, DC: Congressional Quarterly Press, 2007).
55. W. Lance Bennett, *The Governing Crisis: Media, Money and Marketing in American Elections* (New York: St. Martin's Press, 1992), p. 32.
56. See Edwin Diamond and Stephen Bates, *The Spot: The Rise of Political Advertising on Television*, rev. ed. (Cambridge, MA: MIT Press, 1988).
57. *Texas Observer*, September 28, 1990, p. 8.
58. Bennett, *The Governing Crisis*, pp. 33–34.
59. Sabato, *The Rise of the Political Consultants*, p. 220.
60. S. J. Guzzeta, *The Campaign Manual: A Definitive Study of the Modern Political Campaign Process*, 6th ed. (Flat Rock, NC: AmeriCan GOTV Enterprises, 2002), Chapter 9.
61. Moveon.org—Democracy in Action and the campaign of President Obama are two cases that merit further attention for their fund-raising strategies.
62. Alan Bernstein, "Election '97—The Race for City Hall—Record Spent on Mayoral Election Despite Limits," *Houston Chronicle*, December 2, 1997, p. 1A.
63. John Williams, Salatheia Bryant, and Rachel Graves, "Election 2003—It's White in a Rout—Parker Wins Controller Post," *Houston Chronicle*, December 7, 2003, p. 1A.
64. Texans for Public Justice, "Money in PoliTex: A Guide to Money in the 2010 Texas Elections," December 19, 2011.
65. Texans for Public Justice, "Money in PoliTex: A Guide to Money in the 2002 Texas Elections," November 2003.
66. Frank J. Sorauf, *Money in American Elections* (Glenview, IL: Scott, Foresman, 1988), pp. 298–307.
67. Larry Sabato, *PAC Power* (New York: W. W. Norton, 1985), pp. 126–28.
68. Sorauf, *Money in American Elections*, pp. 306–17.
69. Texans for Public Justice, "Texas PACs: 2010 Cycle Spending," August 10, 2011.
70. Samuel H. Barnes and Max Kaase, *Political Action* (Beverly Hills, CA: Sage, 1979), Chapter 2.
71. Lance T. LeLoup, *Politics in America,* 2nd ed. (St. Paul, MN: West Publishing Co., 1989), p. 156.
72. Sidney Verba and Norman H. Nie, *Participation in America* (New York: Harper & Row, 1972) pp. 79–80, 118–19. Seven percent of the sample was not classified.
73. See Lester Milbrath, *Political Participation: How and Why Do People Get Involved in Politics?* (Chicago: Rand McNally, 1965).
74. Verba and Nie, *Participation in America* pp. 79–80, 118–19.
75. Jeff Manza and Clem Brooks, "The Gender Gap in U.S. Presidential Elections: When? Why? Implications?" *American Journal of Sociology,* 103 (March 1998), pp. 1235–66.
76. This term is the title of a book by Mancur Olson, *The Logic of Collective Action: Public Goods and the Theory of Groups* (Cambridge MA: Harvard University Press, 1965).

Chapter 8

1. Dave Montgomery, "Straus cruises to re-election as speaker of the Texas House," *Fort Worth Star-Telegram,* January 12, 2011, p. B1.
2. On the general concept of legislative institutionalization, see Nelson W. Polsby, "The Institutionalization of the U.S. House of Representatives," *American Political Science Review* 62 (March 1968), pp. 144–68. For a discussion of the emergence of the modern Congress, see Randall B. Ripley, *Congress: Process and Policy,* 4th ed. (New York: W. W. Norton, 1988), pp. 48–67.
3. Thomas R. Dye and Susan MacManus, *Politics in States and Communities,* 12th ed. (Upper Saddle River: NJ: Pearson Prentice Hall, 2007), pp. 209–12.
4. For an extended discussion of legislative functions, see William J. Keefe and Morris S. Ogul, *The American Legislative Process,* 10th ed. (Upper Saddle River, NJ: Prentice Hall, 2001), pp. 21–44.
5. Council of State Governments, *Book of the States, 2007 Edition,* vol. 39 (Lexington, KY: Council of State Governments, 2007), Table 3.4.
6. See Article 3 of the Texas Constitution for the constitutional provisions pertaining to the structure, membership, and selection of the Texas Legislature.
7. Council of State Governments, *Book of the States, 2011 Edition,* vol. 43 (Lexington, KY: Council of State Governments, 2011), Tables 3.8 and 3.9.
8. Dave McNeely, "Legislators' Recent Actions Fuel Public's Lack of Trust," *Austin American-Statesman,* June 11, 1991, p. A17.
9. For a comprehensive analysis of the literature on legislative recruitment and careers, see Donald R. Matthews, "Legislative Recruitment and Legislative Careers," *Legislative Studies Quarterly 9* (November 1984), pp. 547–85.

10. Gary F. Moncrief, Richard G. Niemi, and Lynda W. Powell, "Time, Term Limits, and Turnover: Trends in Membership Stability in U.S. State Legislatures," *Legislative Studies Quarterly* 29 (August 2004), p. 364.
11. Calculations for the tenure of house members is based on Texas House of Representatives, "Biographical Data, 82nd Legislature," http://www.house.state.tx.us/resources/. Data for the members of the Senate taken from Texas State Senate, "Facts About the Senate of the 82nd Legislature," http://www.senate.state.tx.us/75r/Senate/Facts.htm.
12. Paul T. David and Ralph Eisenberg, *Devaluation of the Urban and Suburban Vote* (Charlottesville: Bureau of Public Administration, University of Virginia, 1961).
13. Stephen Ansolabehere and James M. Snyder Jr., *The End of Inequality: One Person, One Vote and the Transformation of American Politics* (New York: W. W. Norton, 2008), pp. 50–51.
14. *Baker* v. *Carr,* 369 U.S. 186 (1962); *Reynolds v. Sims,* 337 U.S. 533 (1964); and *Kilgarlin v. Martin,* 252 F. Supp 404 (S.D. Tex 1966).
15. Ross Ramsey, "Court Delivers Election Maps for Texas House, Congress," *The Texas Tribune,* February 28, 2012.
16. Robert T. Garrett, "Hands-off Speaker Gets Mixed Reviews—Straus Ends First Session with Republicans Split on His Style," *Dallas Morning News,* June 1, 2009, p. 1A.
17. Ibid.
18. Fred Gantt, *The Chief Executive in Texas: A Study of Gubernatorial Leadership* (Austin: University of Texas Press, 1964), p. 238.
19. Ross Ramsey and Cindy Rugeley, "Leaders of the Pack—Bullock, Laney Carry a Big Stick in State Legislature," *Houston Chronicle,* June 6, 1993, state, p. 1A.
20. State Senator Bill Ratliff, quoted in Kathy Walt, "Texas Legislature—Jobs Well Done—Senators Give Perry High Marks After Starting with Low Expectations," *Houston Chronicle,* June 6, 1999, p. 1E.
21. Clay Robison and R. G. Ratcliffe, "A Reversal of Course for Ratliff—Lieutenant Governor Drops Plans to Run," *Houston Chronicle,* June 6, 2001, p. 1A.
22. For a summary of the earlier scholarly work on legislative committees, see Heinz Eulau and Vera McCluggage, "Standing Committees in Legislatures: Three Decades of Research," *Legislative Studies Quarterly 9* (May 1984), pp. 195–270.
23. For a general discussion of staff in state legislatures, see Alan Rosenthal, *Engines of Democracy: Politics and Policymaking in State Legislatures* (Washington, DC: Congressional Quarterly Press, 2007), pp. 185–89.
24. See Malcolm E. Jewell and Samuel C. Patterson, *The Legislative Process in the United States* (New York: Random House, 1966), Chapter 11, for a summary of the function of legislative rules and procedures. See Barbara Sinclair's *Unorthodox Lawmaking,* 3rd ed. (Washington, DC: Congressional Quarterly Press, 2007) for an expanded discussion of rule changes in the U.S. Congress and their impact on policy formulation.
25. There have been a number of studies of these informal norms within the legislative process. One is Donald R. Matthews's, *U.S. Senators and Their World* (New York: Vintage, 1960). For the adaptation of this concept to state legislatures, see Alan Rosenthal, *Legislative Life: People, Process, and Performance of the States* (New York: Harper & Row, 1981).
26. For a brief overview of the representative problem, see Neal Riemer, ed., *The Representative: Trustee? Delegate? Partisan? Politico?* (Boston: D. C. Heath, 1967). For a more comprehensive treatment of the subject, see Hanna F. Pitkin, *The Concept of Representation* (Berkeley: University of California Press, 1967).
27. For an excellent treatment of the relationship of U.S. legislators to their districts and constituencies, see Richard F. Fenno Jr., *Home Style: House Members in Their Districts* (Boston: Little Brown, 1978).
28. The general concepts for this discussion are based on John W. Kingdon, *Congressmen's Voting Decisions,* 2nd ed. (New York: Harper & Row, 1981).
29. These legislative styles are similar to those developed by James David Barber, *The Lawmakers* (New Haven, CT: Yale University Press, 1965), Chapters 2–5.
30. Richard Morehead, *50 Years in Texas Politics* (Burnet, TX: Eakin, 1982), pp. 236–37.
31. *Fort Worth Star-Telegram,* Dec. 4, 1990.
32. Bob Sablatura and Robert Cullick, "Lewis' Luxury Vacation at Mexico Resort Probed," *Houston Chronicle,* Dec. 12, 1990, p. 1A.
33. R. G. Ratcliffe, "Speaker Turns Himself in to Sheriff—Lewis Rips Indictment, Press," *Houston Chronicle,* Jan. 1, 1991, p. 1A.

Chapter 9

1. Ross Ramsey, "UT/TT Poll: Texans Split on Another Term for Perry," *The Texas Tribune,* February 22, 2012.
2. Fred Gantt Jr., *The Chief Executive in Texas* (Austin: University of Texas Press, 1964), p. 24.
3. Ibid., pp. 24–25.
4. Ibid., p. 27.

5. Ibid., pp. 27–32.
6. Ibid., pp. 32–36.
7. Ibid., p. 37.
8. Charles F. Cnudde and Robert E. Crew, *Constitutional Democracy in Texas* (St. Paul, MN: West, 1989), p. 90.
9. Texas Constitution, Art. 4, Sec. 4.
10. Gantt, *The Chief Executive in Texas,* p. 116.
11. Texas Constitution, Art. 1, Sec. 4.
12. Ray Long and Rick Pearson, "Impeached Illinois Gov. Rod Blagojevich Has Been Removed from Office," *Chicago Tribune,* January 20, 2009.
13. For an excellent treatment of the American governor through the Great Depression years, see Leslie Lipson, *The American Governor from Figurehead to Leader* (Chicago: University of Chicago Press, 1939).
14. Joseph A. Schlesinger, "The Politics of the Executive" in *Politics in the American States,* 2nd ed., edited by Herbert Jacob and Kenneth N. Vines (Boston: Little, Brown, 1971), Chapter 6; and Thad L. Beyle "The Governors, 1988–89," in *The Book of the States, 1990–1991* (Lexington, KY: Council of State Governments, 1990), p. 54.
15. Wayne Slater, "Clements Puts Stamp on Panels, Minorities, Women Neglected, Critics Say," *Dallas Morning News,* April 27, 1987, p. 1A.
16. Texans for Public Justice, "Governor Perry's Patronage," September 2010, http://info.tpj.org/reports/pdf/Perry%20Patronage2010.pdf, p. 1.
17. Kelly Shannon, "Perry Lags in Appointing Women, Analysis Shows," *Abilene Reporter-News,* September 24, 2011; U.S. Census Bureau, *2010 Census,* "State and County Quickfacts, Texas," http://quickfacts.census.gov/qfd/states/48000.html.
18. Texas Constitution, Art. 4, Sec. 11.
19. Wilbourn E. Benton, *Texas Politics: Constraints and Opportunities,* 5th ed. (Chicago: Nelson-Hall, 1984), pp. 164–66.
20. Ibid., pp. 166–67.
21. Texas Constitution, Art. 4, Sec. 7.
22. Gantt, *The Chief Executive in Texas,* pp. 90–107.
23. Robert S. Lorch, *State and Local Politics,* 3rd ed. (Englewood Cliffs, NJ: Prentice Hall, 1989), pp. 115–16.
24. Ibid., pp. 116–19.
25. See James E. Anderson, Richard W. Murray, and Edward L. Farley, *Texas Politics,* 6th ed. (New York: HarperCollins, 1991) for an excellent analysis of the leadership styles of Governors Shivers, Daniel, Connally, Smith, and Briscoe.
26. *Fort Worth Star-Telegram,* January 1, 1980.
27. *Houston Post,* June 17, 1979. (not available to us)
28. *Austin American–Statesman,* June 16, 1979. (not available to us)
29. Clay Robison, "The Clements Years," *Houston Chronicle,* December 2, 1990, p. 6.
30. *Texas Government Newsletter,* 19 (February 25, 1991), p. 1.
31. Clay Robison, "Richard's Caution Saves Precious Political Capital," *Houston Chronicle,* June 2, 1993, p. 1A.
32. R. G. Ratcliffe, "Away from the Spotlight, Governor Makes His Mark," *Houston Chronicle,* April 15, 1995, p. 1A.
33. R. G. Ratcliffe, "Legislature Fulfills Most Bush Promises," *Houston Chronicle,* May 31, 1995, p. 1A.
34. Jay Root, "Perry Leaning Toward a Run for Reelection," *The Texas Tribune,* February 21, 2012.
35. Daniel Elazar, "The Principles and Traditions Underlying State Constitutions," *Publius: The Journal of Federalism* 12 (Winter 1982), p. 17.
36. Texas Comptroller of Public Accounts, *Fiscal Notes* (December 1990), p. 9.
37. Kelley Shannon, "Texas Comptroller Susan Combs Apologizes for Data Breach, Offers Credit Monitoring to Millions Affected," *The Dallas Morning News,* April 28, 2011.
38. Gary Scharrer, "Gift of Christmas Mountains to Texas State Earns Praise," *Houston Chronicle,* September 15, 2011.
39. James C. McKinley Jr., "Texas Conservatives Win Curriculum Change," NYT, March 12, 2010. http://www.nytimes.com/2010/03/13/education/13texas.html

Chapter 10

1. Kate Alexander, "Texas, IBM Data Center Contract to End," *Austin American-Statesman,* March 12, 2012.
2. U.S. Office of Personnel Management, "*Historical Federal Workforce Tables: Executive Branch Civilian Employment Since 1940,*" http://www.opm.gov/feddata/HistoricalTables/Executive-BranchSince1940.asp: and "Rep. Gerry Connolly Says Federal Workforce Hasn't Grown Since 1990," *Richmond Times-Dispatch,* 12-21-2010.

3. U.S. Census Bureau, *2010 Annual Survey of Public Employment and Payroll,* http://www.census.gov/govs/apes/.
4. Ryan Murphy and Morgan Smith, "25,000 Fewer School Employees," *The Texas Tribune,* March 8, 2012; and Christy Hoppe, "Texas Cuts 7,000 Workers Over Past Year, *Dallas Morning News",* 5-3-2012, http://trailblazersblog.dallasnews.com/archives/2012/05/texas-cuts-7000-workers-over-p.html.
5. R. Sam Garrett, James A. Thurber, A. Lee Fritschler, and David H. Rosenbloom, "Assessing the Impact of Bureaucracy Bashing by Electoral Campaigns," *Public Administration Review* 66 (March/April 2006), pp. 228–40; and Marissa Martino Golden, *What Motivates Bureaucrats? Politics and Administration During the Reagan Years* (New York: Columbia University Press, 2000).
6. Donald F. Kettl and James W. Fesler, *The Politics of the Administrative Process,* 3rd ed. (Washington, DC: Congressional Quarterly Press, 2005), pp. 127–28.
7. See Max Weber, "Bureaucracy," in *Max Weber Essays in Sociology,* edited by H. H. Gerth and C. Wright Mills (New York: Oxford University Press, 1971), pp. 196–244.
8. Jeffrey D. Straussman, *Public Administration* (New York: Longman, 1990), p. 65.
9. The following discussion is based on Dennis Palumbo and Steven Maynard-Moody, *Contemporary Public Administration* (New York: Longman, 1991), pp. 26–31; and Straussman, *Public Administration,* pp. 63–64.
10. Melvin J. Dubnick and Barbara S. Romzek, *American Public Administration* (New York: Macmillan, 1991), p. 248.
11. Ibid, pp. 248–49.
12. The U.S. Census Bureau conducts a census of all U.S. governments every five years. In compiling employment data, part-time and full-time employees are counted. Using payroll data from the states, this total is recalculated as "full-time equivalent" employees.
13. U.S. Bureau of Labor Statistics, "State Government Employees per 10,000 Population, 2008," *Governing: State and Local Sourcebook,* http://sourcebook.governing.com/subtopicresults.jsp?ind=681. [This was the original source but the site "The State and Local Sourcebook is on hiatus." Please check link; did not open]
14. Kaiser Foundation, "Total State Expenditures per Capita, SFY 2010," *State Health Facts,* http://www.statehealthfacts.org/comparebar.jsp?ind=32&cat=1&sub=10&yr=256&typ=4&sort=a&o=a&print=1.
15. Murphy and Smith, "25,000 Fewer School Employees."
16. Theodore J. Lowi, *The End of Liberalism,* 2nd ed. (New York: W.W. Norton, 1979), p. 274.
17. Larry N. Gerston, *Making Public Policy* (Glenview, IL: Scott, Foresman, 1983), p. 95.
18. Palumbo and Maynard-Moody, *Contemporary Public Administration,* p. 304.
19. Straussman, *Public Administration,* p. 246.
20. Lee Hancock, "Nursing Homes Under Fire—Ex Official Defends His Facilities," *Dallas Morning News,* October 24, 1991, p. 1A.
21. Colorado was the first state to adopt sunset legislation in 1976. See Straussman, *Public Administration,* p. 39.
22. Texas Sunset Advisory Commission, *Texas Sunset Advisory Commission Report,* October 1991, http://www.lib.utexas.edu/taro/tslac/40063/tsl-40063.html.
23. Jim Mustian, "Kermit Nurse Not Guilty," *Odessa American Online,* March 27, 2010.
24. Texas Nursing Association, "Winkler County Nurses Update," *Advocacy,* March 27, 2010.
25. Jim Mustian, "Winkler Approves Nurses Settlement," *Odessa American Online,* January 6, 2012.
26. Clay Robison, "Long Wait for Justice Pays Off/$13.8 Million Goes to Whistle Blower," *Houston Chronicle,* November 16, 1995, p. 1A.
27. Straussman, *Public Administration,* p. 286.
28. William Lilley III and James C. Miller III, "The New Social Regulation," *Public Interest,* 47 (Spring 1977), p. 53.
29. Council of State Governments, *The Book of the States,* 1990–1991, vol. 28 (Lexington, KY: Council of State Governments, 1990), p. 346.
30. For a summary of the merit system movement, see Palumbo and Maynard-Moody, *Contemporary Public Administration,* pp. 165–74.
31. Office of the Governor, Division of Planning Coordination, *Quality Texas Government,* 1972. Much of this discussion is based on this report.

Chapter 11

1. *Smith* v. *Allwright,* 321 U.S. 649 (1944).
2. *Miranda* v. *Arizona,* 384 U.S. 436 (1966).
3. American Bar Association, "State and Federal Courts," in *ABA Family Legal Guide,* http://public.findlaw.com/abaflg/flg-2-2a-4.html.
4. Texas Research League, *The Texas Judiciary: A Structural-Functional Overview,* Report 1 (Austin, TX: Texas Research League, 1990).

5. Texas Research League, *Texas Courts: A Proposal for Structural-Functional Reform,* Report 2 (Austin: Texas Research League, May 1991), pp. 1–15.
6. The number of courts will change from year to year as a result of legislative action or actions of local governments.
7. Allen E. Smith, *The Impact of the Texas Constitution on the Judiciary* (Houston: University of Houston, Institute for Urban Studies, 1973), p. 45.
8. Office of Court Administration, "Constitutional County Courts: Activity Detail," *Annual Statistical Report for the Texas Judiciary,* 2011; Office of Court Administration, "Statutory County Courts: Activity Detail," *Annual Statistical Report for the Texas Judiciary,* 2011.
9. Office of Court Administration, "District Courts: Activity Detail," *Annual Statistical Report for the Texas Judiciary,* 2011.
10. Office of Court Administration, "Courts of Appeal: Activity Detail," *Annual Statistical Report for the Texas Judiciary,* 2011.
11. Smith, *The Impact of the Texas Constitution on the Judiciary,* p. 28.
12. Ibid., p. 31.
13. Clay Robison, "Bush Names Gonzales for High Court," *Houston Chronicle,* November 13, 1998, p. 1A.
14. Office of Court Administration, "Profile of Appellate and Trial Judges as of March 1, 2011, "*Annual Statistical Report for the Texas Judiciary*" 2011.
15. *Houston Post,* May 18, 1986.
16. Anthony Champagne, "Campaign Contributions in Texas Supreme Court Races," *Crime, Law and Social Change 17* (1992), pp. 91–106.
17. *Houston Post,* November 10, 1988.
18. Bruce Hight, "Texas Supreme Court Sides with Business," *Austin American-Statesman,* December 9, 1993. p. E1.
19. Clay Robison, "Texas' Chief Justice Resigning—Longtime Foe of State's System of Electing Judges to Teach Law," *Houston Chronicle,* April 30, 2004, p. 1A.
20. Jefferson, "The State of the Judiciary in Texas." Presented to the 81st Legislature, February 11, 2009, Austin, Texas.
21. Texas Watch, *The Food Chain: Winners and Losers in the Texas Supreme Court,* 1995–1999 (Austin: Texas Watch Foundation, 1999).
22. Texas Watch press release, May 3, 1999.
23. Texas Watch Foundation, *Court Watch,* "Thumbs on the Scale: A Retrospective of the Texas Supreme Court, 2000-2010," January 26, 2012.
24. Samuel Issacharoff, *The Texas Judiciary and the Voting Rights Act: Background and Options* (Austin: Texas Policy Research Forum), pp. 2, 13.
25. Jim Simon, "Judicial Election Plan Brings Quick Jockeying," *Houston Chronicle,* December 24, 1989, p. 1B.
26. *Texas Lawyer,* September 18, 1989.
27. *League of United Latin American Citizens* v. *Clements,* 999 F2d 831 (1993).
28. Office of Court Administration, "Profile of Appellate and Trial Judges as of March 1, 2012," *Annual Statistical Report for the Texas Judiciary,* 2011.
29. American Judicature Society at Drake University, "Judicial Selection Methods in the States: Appellate and General Jurisdiction Courts," update 2010, http://www.judicialselection.us/uploads/documents/Judicial_Selection_Charts_1196376173077.pdf.
30. *Texas Lawyer,* November 11, 1991.
31. *Paulson* v. *State,* Texas Court of Criminal Appeals, October 4, 2000.
32. *Texas Lawyer,* June 3, 1991.
33. Paul Burka, "Trial by Technicality," *Texas Monthly* (April 1982), pp. 126–31, 210–18, 241.
34. Rick Casey, "Tulia 35 Escape High Court Horror," *Houston Chronicle,* August 27, 2003, p. 23A.
35. *Edgewood* v. Meno, 893 S.W.2d 450 (1995).
36. *Richards* v. *LULAC,* 868 S.W.2d 306 (1993); and Wendy Benjaminson, "Home Schools Win Court Fight," *Houston Chronicle,* June 16, 1994, p. 1A.
37. *Texas Education Agency v. Leeper,* 893 S.W.2d 432 (1994).
38. Kate Galbraith, "Texas Supreme Court Rules for Landowners in Water Case," *The Texas Tribune,* February 24, 2012.
39. *Operation Rescue—National* v. *Planned Parenthood of Houston and Southeast Texas, Inc.,* 975 S.W.2d 546 (1998). See also Clay Robison, "Anti-abortion Protesters Lose '92 Case Ruling," *Houston Chronicle,* July 4, 1998, p. 1A.
40. *Madsen* v. *Women's Health Clinic, Inc.,* 512 U.S. (1994).
41. *Charles E. Bell* v. *Low Income Women of Texas,* 95 S.W.3d 253 (2002).

Chapter 12

1. Sarah Coppola, "Austin Passes Bag Ban," *Austin American-Statesman,* March 2, 2012.
2. For an excellent overview of urban development in Texas, see Char Miller and David R. Johnson, "The Rise of Urban Texas," in *Urban Texas: Politics and Development,* edited by Char Miller and Heywood T. Sander. (College Station: Texas A&M University Press, 1990).

3. U.S. Department of Agriculture, Economic Research Service, *State Fact Sheets: Texas,* data updated January 17, 2012.
4. U.S. Census Bureau, *2010 Census.*
5. See Richard L. Cole, Ann Crowley Smith, and Delbert A. Taebel, with a foreword by Marlan Blissett, *Urban Life in Texas: A Statistical Profile and Assessment of the Largest Cities* (Austin: University of Texas Press, 1986), for an example of rankings of larger Texas cities on various dimensions measuring aspects of urban quality of life.
6. Anwar Hussain Syed, *The Political Theory of American Local Government* (New York: Random House, 1966), p. 27.
7. Ibid., pp. 38–52. Syed presents a summary of Jefferson's theory of local government.
8. Roscoe C. Martin, *Grass Roots* (Tuscaloosa: University of Alabama Press, 1957), p. 5; and Robert C. Wood, *Suburbia* (Boston: Houghton Mifflin, 1958), p. 18.
9. Randy Cain, "TML and Large Cities Approach Legislature Together," *Texas Town and City,* 79 (January 1991), pp. 18–19.
10. "Seventy-fifth Texas Legislature Adjourns," *Texas Town and City,* 84 (June 1997), p. 10; and "Texas Legislature Adjourns," *Texas Town and City,* 88 (June 1999), p. LV1.
11. Advisory Commission on Intergovernmental Relations, *State and Local Roles in the Federal System* (Washington, DC: ACIR, 1982), pp. 32–33.
12. *City of Clinton* v. *The Cedar Rapids and Missouri River Railroad Co.,* 24 Iowa 455 (1868).
13. Roscoe C. Martin, *The Cities in the Federal System* (New York: Atherton, 1965), pp. 28–35.
14. Texas Municipal League, "Online Directory," March 15, 2012.
15. Ibid.
16. Ibid.; and Texas Municipal League research staff, telephone conversation, June 2004.
17. Murray S. Stedman, *Urban Politics,* 2nd ed. (Cambridge, MA: Winthrop, 1975), p. 51.
18. Beryl E. Pettus and Randall W. Bland, *Texas Government Today,* 3rd ed. (Homewood, IL: Dorsey, 1984), p. 347.
19. Telephone conversation with Office of Human Resources, Salary Administration, City of Houston, March 15, 2012.
20. City of Austin, Ordinance No. 20061116-081, November 16, 2006; *Dallas City Charter,* Chapter 3, Section 4.
21. See the city charter of San Antonio, Article 2, Sections 6 and 9.
22. Wilbourn E. Benton, *Texas Politics,* 5th ed. (Chicago: Nelson-Hall, 1984), p. 260.
23. Josh Baugh, "Extension Looms for Sculley," *San Antonio Express-News,* December 8, 2011, p. 1B; Director of Human Resources, City of Seguin, March 15, 2012.
24. Bureau of the Census, 1992 *Census of Government,* Table 11.
25. Texas Municipal League research staff, telephone conversation, May 2002.
26. "Where Do Texas Cities Get Their Money?" *Texas Town and City* 98 (January 2011), pp. 18–19.
27. Ibid.; Frank Sturzl, "The Courses of Municipal Revenue," *Texas Town and City* 93 (June 2006), pp. 14–16.
28. "Municipal Fiscal Conditions Are Improving," *Texas Town and City* 92 (March 2005), pp. 10–13.
29. Texas Comptroller of Public Accounts, "Comptroller Susan Combs Distributes Monthly Sales Tax Revenue to Local Governments," Press Release, July 10, 2009; and Texas Comptroller of Public Accounts, *Window on State Government,* "April 2010 State Sales Tax Collections to General Revenue."
30. "Fiscal Conditions Survey Shows Cities Struggle to Maintain Services," *Texas Town and City* 98 (March 2011), pp. 18–19, 26.
31. Lawrence E. Jordan, "Municipal Bond Issuance in Texas: The New Realities," T*exas Town and City,* 79 (December 1991), pp. 12, 25.
32. Miller and Sanders, *Urban Texas: Politics and Development,* p. xiv.
33. *Texas Almanac,* 1992–1993 (Dallas, TX: A.H. Belo, 1991), pp. 137–38; and U.S. Census, 2000.
34. American Society of Civil Engineers, "Report Card for American Infrastructure: Texas," September 2008.
35. Jennifer Stowe, "The Emerging Need for Water and Wastewater Affordability Programs," *Texas Town and City* 96 (May 2009), pp. 10–11.
36. Housing Predictor, "Real Estate News and Forecast in the Public Interest: Texas."
37. Texas Department of Public Safety," The Texas Crime Report for 2010," Chapter 2, http://www.dps.texas.gov/crimereports/10/citCh2.pdf.
38. Frank Sturzl, "The Tyranny of Environmental Mandates," *Texas Town and City* 79 (September 1991), pp. 14–15, 32, 65–66.
39. Brooks, *Texas Practice: County and Special District Law,* vol. 35, p. 2.
40. Ibid., p. 14.
41. For a sample of Texas court decisions that affirm the general principle of the Dillon rule, that the county can perform only those functions allocated to it by law, see Robert E. Norwood

and Sabrina Strawn, *Texas County Government: Let the People Choose,* 2nd ed. (Austin: Texas Research League, 1984), pp. 11–12.

42. Ibid., p. 9.
43. U.S. Census Bureau, *2010 Census*, "Texas Quick Facts."
44. Texas Association of Counties, *2010 Salary Survey* (Austin: Texas Association of Counties, 2010).
45. *Avery v. Midland County,* 88 S. Ct. 1114 (1968).
46. Norwood and Strawn, *Texas County Government,* p. 22.
47. Brooks, *Texas Practice: County and Special District Law,* vol. 35, p. 331.
48. Texas Commission on Intergovernmental Relations, *An Introduction to Texas County Government* (Austin, TX: Author, 1980), p. 10.
49. Brooks, *Texas Practice: County and Special District Law,* vol. 35, pp. 392–93.
50. Ibid., vol. 36, pp. 104–105.
51. Texas Association of Counties, *2010 Salary Survey.*
52. Brooks, *Texas Practice: County and Special District Law,* vol. 36, pp. 4–8.
53. Ibid., pp. 49–50.
54. Ibid., pp. 18–49.
55. Texas Association of Counties, *2010 Salary Survey.*
56. Norwood and Strawn, *Texas County Government,* p. 24.
57. Brooks, *Texas Practice: County and Special District Law,* vol. 35, p. 495.
58. Ibid., vol. 36, pp. 122–23.
59. Texas Commission on Intergovernmental Relations, *An Introduction to County Government,* p. 22.
60. Norwood and Strawn, *Texas County Government,* p. 27.
61. Brooks, *Texas Practice: County and Special District Law,* vol. 35, pp. 273–74.
62. Virginia Marion Perrenod, *Special Districts, Special Purposes: Fringe Governments and Urban Problems in the Houston Area* (College Station: Texas A&M University Press, 1984), p. 4.
63. Ibid.
64. Woodworth G. Thrombley, *Special Districts and Authorities in Texas* (Austin: Institute of Public Affairs, University of Texas, 1959), pp. 17–18.
65. Benton, *Texas Politics: Constraints and Opportunities,* p. 282.
66. Perrenod, *Special Districts, Special Purposes,* p. 18.
67. Thrombley, *Special Districts and Authorities in Texas,* p. 13.
68. Robert S. Lorch, *State and Local Politics,* 3rd ed. (Englewood Cliffs, NJ: Prentice Hall, 1989), p. 246.
69. Ibid., p. 247.
70. Texas Education Agency, *Snapshot 2009–2010: School District Profiles.*
71. Texas Association of School Boards, Membership Services, telephone conversation, April 22, 2008; summary documents of board electoral systems provided by the TASB.
72. "Houston: City/Community Information," http://www.texasbest.com/houston/houston.html; U.S. Census, *Census 2010*, "Texas Quick Facts."
73. City of San Marcos, Texas, "Annexation Policies," http://www.ci.san-marcos.tx.us/departments/planning/Annexation-Policies.htm.
74. For a more detailed discussion of annexation authority, see Benton, *Texas Politics,* pp. 264–66.
75. Scott N. Houston, "Municipal Annexation in Texas," Texas APA-Southmost Section, McAllen, Texas, November 2004, p. 10.
76. "Texas Legislature Adjourns," *Texas Town and City,* 86 (July 1999), p. 10.
77. "Texas Legislature Adjourns," *Texas Town and City,* 89 (July 2001), p. 11.
78. Norwood and Strawn, *Texas County Government,* pp. 75–81.
79. Joel B. Goldsteen and Russell Fricano, *Municipal Finance Practices and Preferences for New Development: Survey of Texas Cities* (Arlington: Institute of Urban Studies, University of Texas at Arlington, 1988), pp. 3–11.
80. Bill R. Shelton, Bob Bolen, and Ray Perryman, "Passing a Sales Tax Referendum for Economic Development," *Texas Town and City* 79 (September 1991), 10.
81. Brooks, *Texas Practice: County and Special District Law,* vol. 36, pp. 229–42.
82. Tom Adams, "Introduction and Recent Experience with the Interlocal Contract," in *Interlocal Contract in Texas,* edited by Richard W. Tees, Richard L. Cole, and Jay G. Stanford (Arlington: Institute of Urban Studies, University of Texas at Arlington, 1990), p. 1.
83. Tees et al., *Interlocal Contract in Texas,* pp. B1–B7.
84. Vincent Ostrom, *The Meaning of American Federalism* (San Francisco: Institute for Contemporary Studies, 1991), p. 161. Ostrom suggests that advocates of metropolitan government often overlook the "rich and intricate framework for negotiating, adjudicating, and deciding questions" that are now in place in many urbanized areas with multiple governmental units.
85. Ann Long Diveley and Dwight A. Shupe, "Public Improvement Districts: An Alternative for Financing Public Improvements and Services," *Texas Town and City* 79 (September 1991).

Chapter 13

1. Editorial Board, "Groundwater Ruling Potentially Unleashes Geyser of Future Cases," *Austin American-Statesman,* February 27, 2012.
2. Thomas R. Dye, *Understanding Public Policy,* 12th ed. (Upper Saddle River, NJ: Prentice Hall, 2008), p. 1.
3. This section draws primarily from L. L. Wade and R. L. Curry Jr., *A Logic of Public Policy: Aspects of Political Economy* (Belmont, CA: Wadsworth, 1970), Chapter 1.
4. Ibid. This same chapter is an excellent introduction to the definitional issues and approaches to public policy analysis.
5. The following discussion is organized around the general stages presented by James E. Anderson, David W. Brady, Charles S. Bullock III, and Joseph Stewart Jr., *Public Policy and Politics in America,* 2nd ed. (Monterey, CA: Brooks/Cole, 1984); and Charles O. Jones, *An Introduction to the Study of Public Policy,* 2nd ed. (North Scituate, MA: Duxbury Press, 1977).
6. Anderson et al., *Public Policy and Politics in America,* p. 8.
7. Jones, *An Introduction to the Study of Public Policy,* pp. 138–39.
8. Ibid., p. 139.
9. Randall B. Ripley and Grace A. Franklin, *Congress, the Bureaucracy, and Public Policy,* 3rd ed. (Homewood, IL: Dorsey, 1984), p. 10.
10. Hugh Heclo, "Issue Networks and the Executive Establishment," in *The New American Political System,* edited by Anthony King (Washington, DC: American Enterprise Institute, 1978), p. 88. Much of this section is based on this article.
11. Ibid., p. 107.
12. Ibid., p. 104.
13. Federation of Tax Administrators, "State Individual Income Taxes, 2008." New Hampshire and Tennessee tax income from dividends and interest but not salaries or wages.
14. Michael P. Ettlinger, Robert S. McIntyre, Elizabeth A. Fray, John F. O'Hare, Julie King, and Neil Miransky, *Who Pays? A Distributional Analysis of the Tax Systems* in *All 50 States*, 3rd ed. (Washington, DC: Citizens for Tax Justice and the Institute on Taxation and Economic Policy, 2009).
15. Federation of Tax Administrators, "*State* Sales Taxes," January 2008.
16. Comptroller of Public Accounts, *State of Texas Annual Cash Report 2011*, http://www.window.state.tx.us/finances/pubs/cashrpt/11/texas_annual_cash_report_2011.pdf, p. 33.
17. Comptroller of Public Accounts, *State of Texas Annual Cash Report* 2011, http://www.window.state.tx.us/finances/pubs/cashrpt/11/texas_annual_cash_report_2011.pdf , p. 33.
18. Texas Comptroller, *Window on State Government,* "Revenue by Source for Fiscal 2011," http://www.window.state.tx.us/taxbud/revenue.html.
19. Texas Comptroller, "Revenue by Source for Fiscal 2011."
20. Comptroller of Public Accounts, State of Texas Annual Cash Report 2011, http://www.window.state.tx.us/finances/pubs/cashrpt/11/texas_annual_cash_report_2011.pdf, p. 33.
21. R. G. Ratcliffe, "Lottery Names Latest Director—$248 Million Expected Shortfall to Schools Seen," *Houston Chronicle,* December 17, 1997, p. 37A.
22. Texas Comptroller of Public Accounts, "Revenue by Source for Fiscal Year 2011."
23. Texas Bond Review Board, *Debt Affordability Study, February 2010,* 3, www.brb.state.tx.us/pub/bfo/DAS2010.pdf.
24. Legislative Budget Board, "Fiscal Size-Up, 2010–11," p. 17.
25. Clay Robison, "Bullock Backs State Income Tax—Richards, Lewis Dubious," *Houston Chronicle,* March 7, 1991, p. 1A.
26. *Edgewood Independent School District, et al.* v. *William Kirby, et al.,* 777 S.W. 2d 391 (1989).
27. Center for Public Priorities, "How is your County Affected by the State Budget: As Adopted by the Senate," http://www.cppp.org/research.php?aid=1051.
28. "Texas Teachers, Moonlighting and Morale," survey conducted for the Texas State Teachers Association by faculty at Sam Houston State University, July 2010.
29. Texas Education Agency, "Snapshot 2010 Summary Tables," *Snapshot 2009–2010, http://ritter.tea.state.tx.us/perfreport/snapshot/2010/commtype.html.*
30. Wendy Benjaminson, "Home Schools Win Court Fight/Ruling Backs Right to Teach Their Own Children," *Houston Chronicle,* June 16, 1994, p. 1A.
31. U.S. Department of Education, National Center for Education Statistics, "1.5 Million Home-schooled Students in the United States in 2007," *Issue Brief,* December 2008.
32. *Ann Richards, et al.* v. *League of United Latin American Citizens, et al.,* S.W. 2d 306 (1993).
33. *Hopwood, et al.,* v. State of Texas, et al., 78 F.3d 932 (1996).
34. Lydia Lum, "UH Won't Award Scholarship Pending Review of AG Ruling," *Houston Chronicle,* February 7, 1997, p. 20A.
35. Lydia Lum, "The Hopwood Effect/Minorities Heading Out of State for Professional Schools," *Houston Chronicle,* August 25, 1997, p. 1A.
36. Ralph K. M. Haurwitz, "U.S. Supreme Court to Review UT Admissions," *Austin American-Statesman,* February 21, 2012.

37. UT-Austin News Release, "Class of First-time Freshman Not a White Majority This Fall Semester at the University of Texas at Austin," September 14, 2010.

38. Texas Higher Education Coordinating Board, "Overview: Tuition Deregulation," www.thecb.state.tx.us/Reports/PDF/1527.PDF?CFID=4796841&CFTOKEN=5900171; and Clay Robison, "Since Deregulation, College Tuition Costs 39% More than 3 Years Ago—Appropriations for Financial Aid Have Not Kept Pace," *Houston Chronicle,* September 24, 2006, p. A1.

39. Legislative Study Group, "LSG Analysis and Recommendations on State of Higher Education in Texas—Part 1," www.texas/sg.org/LSG_Higher_ED.pdf.

40. The Associated Press, "UT System Regents Vote to Support Chancellor," *Austin American-Statesman,* May 12, 2011.

41. Eric Dexheimer, "New UT Study Finds Its Professors Very Productive," *Austin American-Statesman,* November 14, 2011.

42. *Ruiz v. Estelle,* 503 F.Sup. 1265 (1980).

43. Clay Robison, Julie Mason, and Jim Zook, "Building of Prisons under Gun—2 Legislators Say It's up to County," *Houston Chronicle,* September 8, 1991, p. 25A.

44. Brandi Grissom, "Sugar Land's Prison a Casualty of Budget Cuts," *The Texas Tribune,* August 19, 2011.

45. Brandi Grissom, "Executions Probably Not an Issue—for Now," *Texas Weekly,* August 11, 2011.

46. *Houston Chronicle,* December 31, 2002. Poll was conducted by the University of Houston's Center for Public Policy Survey Research Institute which conducted random telephone interviews with 1,773 adults over age 18 from November 29 to December 21, 2002. http://www.deathpenaltyinfo.org/harrissupportdp.pdf

47. Center for Public Policy Priorities, "How Texas Measures Up in the 2010 American Community Survey," September 22, 2011.

48. Center for Public Policy Priorities, "New Census Data Show Texas' Uninsured Rate Tops Nation," September 13, 2011.

49. Kelley Shannon, "Texas Braces for Medicaid Cuts," *San Angelo Standard-Times,* October 7, 2011.

50. Thanh Tan, "Texas Nursing Homes Brace for Higher Costs, Sicker Patients," *The Texas Tribune,* August 31, 2011.

51. Dina Cappiello, "Houston Avoids Title of Smoggiest U.S. City," *Houston Chronicle,* September 24, 2003, p. 23A.

52. Kate Galbraith and Ari Auber, "Controversial Pollution Rule Still on Track for Texas," *The Texas Tribune,* September 5, 2011.

53. Chris Rizo, "Public Citizen Sues to Force Texas to Regulate Greenhouse Gases," *Southeast Texas Record,* November 7, 2009; and Associated Press, "Blame Coal: Texas Leads Carbon Emissions," MSNBC, June 2, 2007, www.msnbc.msn.com/id/19000614/.

54. Matthew Tresaugue, "Global Warming: Warning for Texas Coastal Damage Could Triple by 2080s," *Houston Chronicle,* June 2, 2009, p. 3B.

55. Kate Galbraith, "Draft Water Plan Says Texas 'Will Not Have Enough,'" *The Texas Tribune,* September 27, 2011.

56. R. G. Ratcliffe, "Project with Ties to Perry OK'd Despite Objections," *Austin American-Statesman,* November 14, 2011.

Photo Credits

Chapter 1 Page 3: David Gilder/Shutterstock; 8: RANDY ELI GROTHE KRT/Newscom; 22: REUTERS/Jessica Rinaldi

Chapter 2 Page 33: StockFusion/Alamy; 38: Published with permission of the Tarlton Law Library, Jamail Center for Legal Research, University of Texas School of Law; 41: Courtesy of Texas State Library and Archives Commission; 50: Texas Senate Media Services

Chapter 3 Page 59: U.S. Air Force photo/Tech. Sgt. Matthew McGovern; 65: Carlos Sanchez/Reuters; 81: Borderlands/Alamy; 84: US Immigration and Customs Enforcement (I.C.E.) July 2009

Chapter 4 Page 93: Bob Daemmrich/Alamy; 102: AP Photo/Harry Cabluck; 110: Jack Gullahorn; 115: Tucker Gibson

Chapter 5 Page 121: Matt Nager/Bloomberg via Getty Images; 139: Scott J. Ferrell/Congressional Quarterly/Getty Images; 140: Tucker Gibson; 142: AP Photo/Harry Cabluck

Chapter 6 Page 151: Pat Sullivan/AP Photo; 162: AP Photos; 174: AP Photo/Houston Chronicle, Eric Kayne; 176: Tucker Gibson

Chapter 7 Page 183: Tucker Gibson; 192: David R. Frazier Photolibrary, Inc./Alamy Limited; 194: Lee, Russell, 1903–1986/U.S. Farm Security Administration/Library of Congress Prints and Photographs Division[LC-USF3301-011961-M2]; 204: AP Photo/Wichita Falls Times Record New, Jason Palmer

Chapter 8 Page 219: David Sucsy/Getty Images; 227: Texas Legislative Council/AP Photos; 233: Courtesy of the Office of the Speaker, Texas House Media Services; 237: AP Photo/Harry Cabluck

Chapter 9 Page 261: ZUMA Wire Service/Alamy Limited; 268: Tucker Gibson; 277: AP Photo/Rick McFarland; 285: AP Photo/Jack Plunkett

Chapter 10 Page 295: Tucker Gibson; 303: AP Photo/LM Otero; 307: ZUMA Press/Newscom; 308: AP Photo/Merissa Ferguson

Chapter 11 Page 317: Tucker Gibson; 324: Bob Daemmrich/Alamy; 325: Texas Criminal Court of Appeals; 341: Tucker Gibson

Chapter 12 Page 353: Dorling Kindersley; 355: Samuel D. Barricklow/Workbook Stock/Getty Images; 374: Tucker Gibson

Chapter 13 Page 391: Mark Sterkel/AP Photos; 400: Tucker Gibson; 408: JoeFox/Alamy; 415: Rui Saraiva/Alamy

Index

U

V

W

Y

Answer Key

Chapter 1

1. b	**2.** e	**3.** d	**4.** c	**5.** a
6. a	**7.** d	**8.** b	**9.** c	**10.** e
11. c	**12.** e	**13.** b	**14.** a	**15.** d

Chapter 2

1. b	**2.** d	**3.** a	**4.** c	**5.** e
6. a	**7.** d	**8.** b	**9.** e	**10.** c
11. c	**12.** d	**13.** a	**14.** b	**15.** e

Chapter 3

1. d	**2.** a	**3.** c	**4.** e	**5.** b
6. b	**7.** c	**8.** b	**9.** d	**10.** e
11. b	**12.** d	**13.** c	**14.** a	**15.** b

Chapter 4

1. b	**2.** c	**3.** e	**4.** a	**5.** d
6. a	**7.** d	**8.** c	**9.** b	**10.** d
11. b	**12.** c	**13.** a	**14.** e	**15.** d

Chapter 5

1. c	**2.** d	**3.** b	**4.** a	**5.** e
6. a	**7.** c	**8.** b	**9.** e	**10.** d
11. d	**12.** b	**13.** a	**14.** e	**15.** c

Chapter 6

1. b	**2.** b	**3.** a	**4.** e	**5.** c
6. b	**7.** c	**8.** a	**9.** e	**10.** d
11. a	**12.** e	**13.** b	**14.** c	**15.** d

Chapter 7

1. a	**2.** d	**3.** c	**4.** e	**5.** b
6. b	**7.** d	**8.** a	**9.** c	**10.** e
11. c	**12.** e	**13.** d	**14.** a	**15.** b

Chapter 8

1. d	**2.** b	**3.** e	**4.** a	**5.** c
6. b	**7.** e	**8.** c	**9.** a	**10.** d
11. b	**12.** a	**13.** d	**14.** e	**15.** c

Chapter 9

1. e	**2.** a	**3.** c	**4.** b	**5.** d
6. c	**7.** e	**8.** b	**9.** a	**10.** d
11. d	**12.** a	**13.** b	**14.** c	**15.** e

Chapter 10

1. c	**2.** e	**3.** a	**4.** b	**5.** d
6. d	**7.** c	**8.** b	**9.** e	**10.** a
11. c	**12.** b	**13.** e	**14.** a	**15.** d

Chapter 11

1. a	**2.** b	**3.** d	**4.** e	**5.** c
6. c	**7.** d	**8.** a	**9.** b	**10.** e
11. d	**12.** a	**13.** e	**14.** c	**15.** b

Chapter 12

1. e	**2.** c	**3.** d	**4.** b	**5.** a
6. b	**7.** c	**8.** a	**9.** e	**10.** d
11. c	**12.** b	**13.** a	**14.** d	**15.** e

Chapter 13

1. d	**2.** e	**3.** b	**4.** c	**5.** a
6. e	**7.** b	**8.** d	**9.** c	**10.** a
11. e	**12.** c	**13.** b	**14.** c	**15.** a